U0941125

2015宁波统计年鉴

NINGBO Statistical YearBook

宁波市统计局
NINGBO MUNICIPAL STATISTICS BUREAU
国家统计局宁波调查队
NBS Survey Office in Ningbo
编

中国统计出版社
China Statistics Press

图书在版编目（C I P）数据

宁波统计年鉴. 2015 / 宁波市统计局, 国家统计局宁波调查队编. -- 北京 : 中国统计出版社, 2015.8

ISBN 978-7-5037-7537-6

Ⅰ. ①宁… Ⅱ. ①宁… ②国… Ⅲ. ①统计资料－宁波市－2015－年鉴 Ⅳ. ①C832.553-54

中国版本图书馆 CIP 数据核字(2015)第 192811 号

宁波统计年鉴-2015

作　　者/ 宁波市统计局　国家统计局宁波调查队

责任编辑/ 陈越月　李　丽　朱　惠

封面设计/ 赵　阳

出版发行/ 中国统计出版社

地　　址/ 北京市丰台区西三环南路甲 6 号

邮政编码/ 100073

电　　话/ 邮购(010)63376909　书店(010)68783171

E - mail / yearbook@gj.stats.cn

网　　址/ http://csp.stats.gov.cn

印　　刷/ 宁波银行印刷厂

经　　销/ 新华书店

开　　本/ 890mm×1240mm　1/16

字　　数/ 1135 千字

印　　张/ 28.5

版　　别/ 2015 年 8 月第 1 版

版　　次/ 2015 年 8 月第 1 次印刷

定　　价/ 368 元

本书附同版本 CD-ROM 一张，光盘内容以书面文字为准。

如有印装差错，由本社发行部调换。

编者说明

一、《宁波统计年鉴—2015》以大量统计数据，全面、系统地反映了2014年宁波经济、科技、社会各方面的发展情况，是一本信息密集的资料性年刊和工具书。本年鉴采用中英文排版方式。

二、《宁波统计年鉴—2015》在内容编排顺序上做了调整，本年鉴内容包括：

1.2014年宁波市国民经济和社会发展概况；2.综合；3.人口与劳动力；4.国民经济核算；5.财政、金融、保险、证券；6.物价指数、人民生活；7.农业；8.工业、能源消费和电力；9.固定资产投资和建筑业；10.港口、交通运输、邮电业；11.国内贸易、餐饮业；12.对外经济、旅游；13.文化、教育、卫生、体育、科学；14. 市政、环保、民政、政法及其他等十四个部分。为方便读者使用，各篇章前设有《主要统计指标》，篇末附有《主要统计指标解释》。

三、《宁波统计年鉴—2015》辑入的统计数据，以2014年年报为主，考虑到读者使用，年鉴中还列示了1978年改革开放以来历年的主要统计数据，这些统计数据已重新予以核实，凡以往发表过的统计数据与本年鉴有出入的，均以本年鉴为准。

四、《宁波统计年鉴—2015》在编辑中作如下规定，以使读者在使用时明了：

1、凡有注解均注在第一张表的下方。

2、凡在表内显示“空格”的，表示有数据但不足计量单位中的最小数，或表示该项统计数据不详或无该项统计数据；显示“#”表示其中的主要项。

五、《宁波统计年鉴—2015》辑入的统计数据，对来自非政府统计部门的，注明数据来源。

六、《宁波统计年鉴》出版以来，受到社会各界的关心、支持，不少读者对于年鉴的内容和编辑工作提出了许多宝贵的意见，对此，我们深表感谢。并欢迎读者一如既往地对年鉴的不足之处给予批评指正，以进一步提高编辑水平。

I. Ningbo Statistical Yearbook 2015 is an annual publication which provides comprehensive and systematic data covering the economic, technological and social development in Ningbo Municipality in 2014. This yearbook uses the Chinese and English mix typesetting the way.

II. This yearbook has made the adjustment in the content arrangement order. This yearbook is comprised of 14 parts including: 1.Brief Introduction of 2014 Ningbo National Economy and Social Development; 2.General Survey; 3.Population and labour force; 4.National Economic Accounting; 5.Finance, Banking, Insurance and Securities; 6.Price Index and People's Livelihood; 7. Agriculture; 8.Industry, Energy Consumption and Electricity; 9.Investment in Fixed Assets and Construction; 10.Port, Transportation, Post and Telecommunication; 11.Domestic Trade and Catering Trade; 12.Foreign Trade and Tourism; 13.Education, Culture, Public Health and Sports, Science and Technology; 14.Civil Facilities, Environmental Protection, Civil Affairs, Judicature and Others. Major statistical indicators at the beginning of each chapter, Explanatory Notes on Main Statistical Indicators are provided at the end of each chapter.

III. The content of this yearbook are comprised of mainly the statistic of 2014 and statistical data of those key years after reform and opening to the outside world. The data in this yearbook have been already checked. If ever the readers find inconsistency of data here as compared with those in previous year books, please refer to this yearbook as accurate and final.

IV. This yearbook makes following stipulation in the edition, causes the reader to use is clear about. The footnotes are placed at the first page. Explanations on symbols used in this yearbook: "space" indicates that the data are not large enough to be rounded into the minimal unit, or unknown or indicates the data not available; "#" indicates major item in a category.

V. In this yearbook, to come from the non- statistical department's statistical data, dedicates the data origin.

VI. Here we'd like to express our sincere thanks to the readers who have provided us so many invaluable suggestions on content selection and compilation of the yearbook. Our thanks also go to those friends in all circles of society who have shown their support and care to the publication of the yearbook. We welcome any suggestions and comments from readers at large so as to help us to further improve our work of compilation.

目 录
CONTENTS

第一篇 综 合 CHAPTER 1 GENERAL SURVEY

第二篇 人口与劳动力 CHAPTER 2 POPULATION AND LABOR FORCE

第三篇 国民经济核算 CHAPTER 3 NATIONAL ECONOMIC ACCOUNTING

第四篇 财政、金融、保险、证券 CHAPTER 4 FINANCE,BANKING,INSURANCE AND SECURITIES

第五篇 物价指数和人民生活 CHAPTER 5 PRICES INDEX AND PEOPLE'S LIVELIHOOD

第六篇 农 业 CHAPTER 6 AGRICULTURE

第七篇 工业、能源消费和电力 CHAPTER 7 INDUSTRY, ENERGY CONSUMPTION AND ELECTRICITY

第八篇 固定资产投资和建筑业 CHAPTER 8 INVESTMENT IN FIXED ASSETS AND CONSTRUCTION

第九篇 港口、交通、运输、邮电 CHAPTER 9 PORT,TRANSPORTATION,POST AND TELECOMMUNICATION SERVICE

第十篇 国内贸易、餐饮业 CHAPTER 10 DOMESTIC TRADE AND CATERING TRADE

第十一篇 对外经济、旅游 CHAPTER 11 FOREIGN TRADE AND TOURISM

第十二篇 文化、教育、卫生、体育、科学技术 CHAPTER 12 CULTURE,EDUCATION,PUBLIC HEALTH AND SPORTS, SCIENCE & TECHNOLOGY

第十三篇 市政、环保、民政、政法及其他 CHAPTER 13 CIVIL FACILITIES,ENVIRONMENT, CIVIL AFFAIRS,JUDICATURE AND OTHERS

2014年宁波市国民经济和社会发展统计公报

宁波市统计局　国家统计局宁波调查队

2015年1月30日

2014年，面对复杂多变的外部环境和艰巨繁重的改革发展任务，全市上下紧紧围绕市委“双驱动四治理”决策部署，全面实施经济社会转型发展三年行动计划，着力稳增长、促改革、调结构、防风险、惠民生，经济运行呈现“低开、稳走、缓升”的发展态势，产业发展稳中趋好，创新转型取得进展，质量效益逐步提升，民生福祉持续改善，为实现“两个基本”、建设“四好示范区”奠定了坚实基础。

一、综　合

地区生产总值。2014年全市实现地区生产总值7602.51亿元，按可比价格计算，比上年增长7.6%。其中，第一产业实现增加值275.18亿元，增长1.9%；第二产业实现增加值3935.57亿元，增长7.9%；第三产业实现增加值3391.76亿元，增长7.6%。三次产业之比为3.6 ∶ 51.8 ∶ 44.6。按常住人口计算，全市人均地区生产总值为98972元（按年平均汇率折合16112美元）。

图1：2013-2014年宁波市地区生产总值增速变化情况

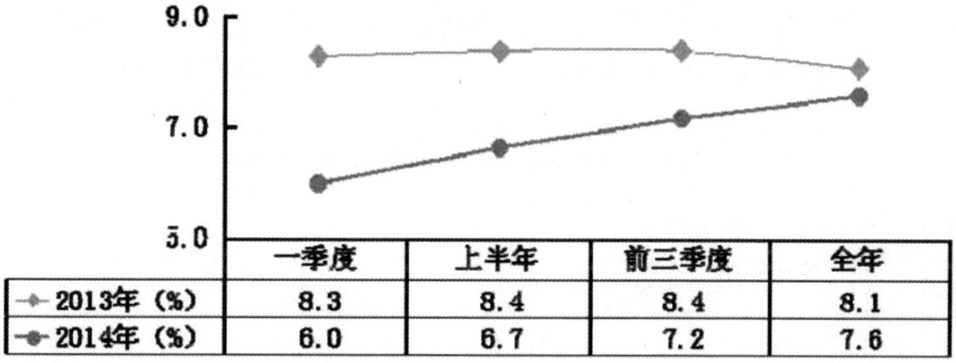

	一季度	上半年	前三季度	全年
2013年（%）	8.3	8.4	8.4	8.1
2014年（%）	6.0	6.7	7.2	7.6

图2：2008-2014年全市人均生产总值（按常住人口计算）

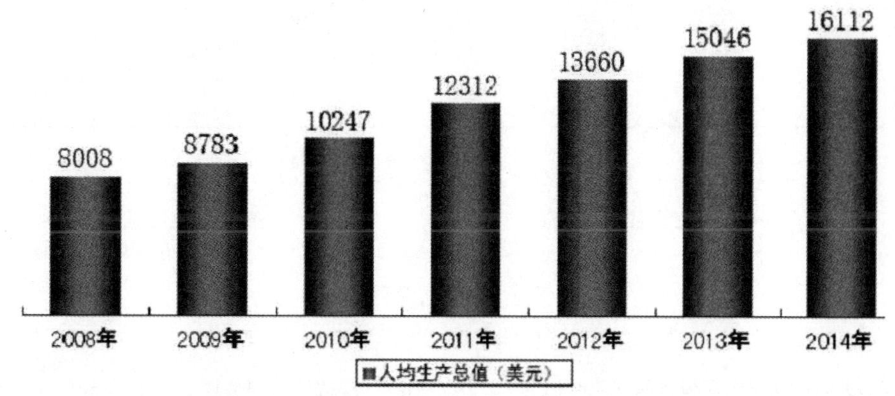

财政收支。2014年全市一般公共预算收入860.6亿元，比上年增长8.6%。一般公共预算支出1000.9亿元，增长6.5%，其中教育、医疗卫生与计划生育、节能环保、城乡社区支出分别增长7.5%、10.5%、28.8%和22.2%。

就业和再就业。2014年全市城镇新增就业岗位17.46万个，7.25万名失业人员实现再就业，其中困难人员1.84万人。年末城镇登记失业率为1.95%，为历年最低。创业带动就业工作成效显著，镇海大学生创业园被评为国家级创业孵化示范基地，新增市级大学生创业园3家，全年共发放小额担保贷款5.34亿元，新增创业实体11.01万家，创业带动就业53.54万人，高校毕业生就业率保持在95%以上。为全市703家“小升规”企业减征社保费1510.08万元；为4.6万家中小微工业企业临时性下浮社保缴费比例，共减负15.72亿元。全市各级人力资源市场服务企业10.7万家次，提供岗位176.43万个。

市场价格。2014年宁波市区居民消费价格上涨1.9%，涨幅比全国、全省城市平均水平分别低0.2和0.1个百分点。在全国36个大中城市中列第27位；在全省11个城市中列第9位。八大类商品和服务项目价格同比涨跌呈“五升三降”格局：食品类上涨2.7%，衣着类上涨2.7%，医疗保健和个人用品类上涨2.3%，娱乐教育文化用品及服务类上涨2.0%，居住类上涨2.4%；烟酒类下降0.2%，家庭设备用品及维修服务类下降0.1%，交通和通信类下降0.5%。全年工业生产者出厂价格下降2.19%，工业生产者购进价格下降2.49%。12月宁波新建住宅销售价格环比下降0.4%，同比下降5.3%，同比涨幅在全国70个大中城市中排第54位。

图3：2014年宁波居民消费价格分月变化情况

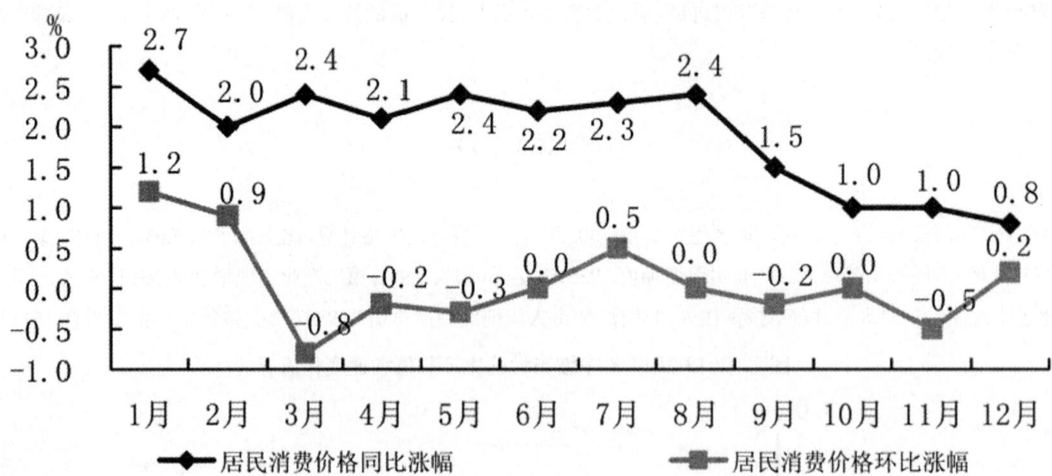

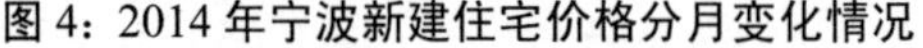
图4：2014年宁波新建住宅价格分月变化情况

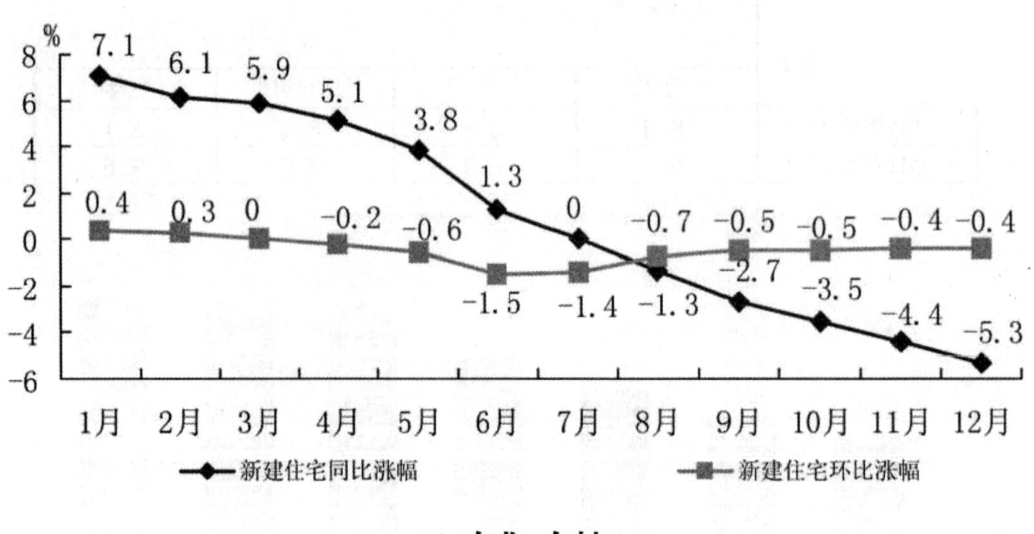

二、农业、农村

农业生产。2014年全市实现农林牧渔业总产值为431.6亿元，按可比价格计算，比上年增长1.6%。其中，完成农业产值209.1亿元，增长4.1%；林业产值12.6亿元，增长3.8%；牧业产值53.2亿元，减少8.4%；渔业产值150.2亿元，增长1.7%；农林牧渔服务业产值6.5亿元，增长6.3%。据粮食生产统计监测数据显示，全年粮食作物播种面积191.8万亩，增长2.0%，粮食总产量76.0万吨，增长7.1%。生猪和家禽生产形势依然严峻，生猪存栏、出栏同比分别减少13.6%和7.1%；家禽存栏、出栏同比分别减少20.4%和26.3%。全年新增市级农业龙头企业17家，累计286家，其中产值（销售额）上亿元的达95家。

新农村建设。2014年创建全面小康村43个、中心村24个、特色村31个、精品线8条，累计创建小康村568个、中心村101个、特色村79个、精品线23条。加快推进农村生活垃圾和生活污水集中处理，全市污水治理行政村覆盖率提高到55%以上，农村垃圾集中处理率达到100%。农房“两改”稳步推进，全年共投入148.5亿元，开工建设农村住房11.5万户，完成

4.66 万户，完成改建面积 664 万平方米，四年来累计完成农房建设投资 533.4 亿元，完成农房改建面积 3092 万平方米。村庄整治建设实现全覆盖，年内新确定 50 个村实施村庄整治建设提升行动，投入资金 1.7 亿元。农家乐休闲旅游业快速发展，全年农家乐休闲旅游业接待游客 2596 万人次，直接营业收入 27.94 亿元，比上年分别增长 19.3%和 28.0%。

三、工业、建筑业

工业经济。2014 年全市实现工业增加值 3490.1 亿元，按可比价计算，比上年增长 7.6%。其中规模以上工业企业实现增加值 2540.2 亿元，增长 7.4%。分行业看，在规模以上工业 35 个行业大类中，26 个行业增加值同比增长；有 9 个行业增加值超过 100 亿元，其中汽车制造业实现增加值 232.9 亿元，总量跃升至第三，增加值增长 31.9%，增速居九大行业之首，对全市规模以上工业增加值增长的贡献率达 30.8%。分企业类型看，规模以上工业大、中、小型企业工业增加值分别增长 6.2%、6.1%和 10.9%。分经济类型看，有限责任公司、国有企业增长较快，增加值分别增长 17.6%和 12.1%；港澳台投资企业、外商投资企业分别增长 4.3%和 3.5%。全年规模以上工业企业实现销售产值 13387.4 亿元，增长 6.6%。其中，内销为 10366.3 亿元，增长 8.5%；出口交货值为 3021.1 亿元，增长 5.5%。全年规模以上工业企业实现利润 648.1 亿元，下降 2.9%，实现利税总额 1280.6 亿元，增长 1.2%。

工业创新转型。装备制造业增速加快，2014 年全市规模以上装备制造业实现增加值 1054.7 亿元，比上年增长 11.1%，增速比全部规模以上工业高出 3.7 个百分点。高能耗行业占比降低，八大高耗能行业实现增加值 852.4 亿元，增长 2.7%，占整个规模以上工业的 33.6%，比重比上年下降 1.8 个百分点。全年规模以上工业单位增加值能耗同比下降 8.1%。创新驱动成效显现，全年规模以上工业新产品产值为 3606.6 亿元，增长 25.0%，新产品产值率由上年的 22.2%提高到 26.2%，再创历史新高。全年规模以上工业企业劳动生产率为 17.8 万元/人，增长 9.9%。

建筑业。2014 年全市完成建筑业产值 3714.1 亿元，比上年增长 18.5%。房屋建筑施工面积 27367.2 万平方米，增长 9.3%。全年建筑业从业人员平均人数 115.2 万人，比上年增加 14.3 万人。

四、固定资产投资、城市建设

固定资产投资。2014 年全市完成固定资产投资 3989.5 亿元，比上年增长 16.6%，其中民间投资 1955.0 亿元，增长 12.6%，占固定资产投资的比重为 49.0%。分产业看，第一产业完成投资 45.2 亿元，增长 113.3%；第二产业完成投资 1264.7 亿元，增长 18.6%；第三产业完成投资 2679.6 亿元，增长 14.7%。三次产业投资额之比为 1.1 ∶ 31.7 ∶ 67.2。全年完成工业投资 1263.2 亿元，增长 19.0%，其中工业技改投资 940.7 亿元，增长 23.9%，工业设备购置 542 亿元，增长 35.3%。全年完成房地产开发投资 1328.1 亿元，增长 18.3%，商品房销售面积 726.4 万平方米，下降 0.5%，其中住宅销售面积 595.2 万平方米，增长 2.3%。

图 5：2014 年全市固定资产投资主要构成

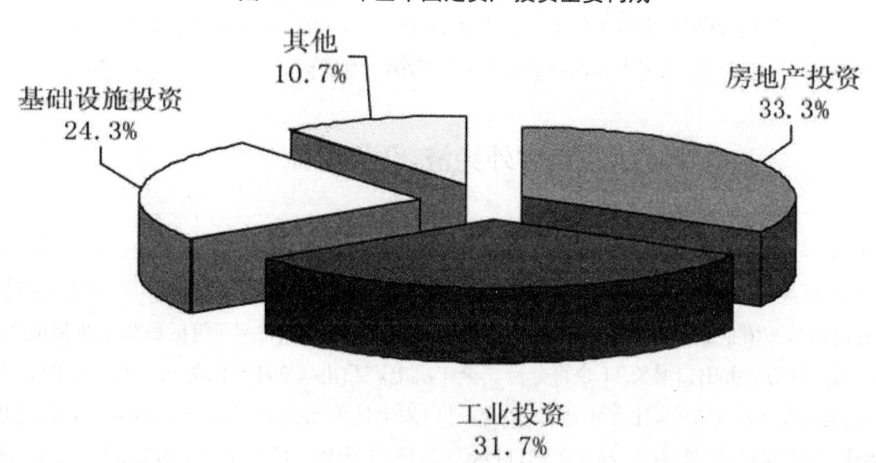

现代都市建设。深入实施现代都市战略“50100 工程”，“一核两翼、两带三湾”网络型现代都市格局进一步形成。“三江六岸”品质提升取得阶段性成果，奉化江两岸正式建成开放，姚江东岸开工建设，沿江 16 万平方米绿地焕然一新。快速路网建设扎实推进，基本建成南北环快速路。实施新一轮打通“断头路”行动，年内打通 11 条断头路。完成江东北路（中山路-民安路）、兴宁路（世纪大道-福庆路）综合整治。继续实施背街小巷综合整治，全年完成整治 90 条。推进园林绿化工程，中心城区新增公共绿地面积 170 公顷。道路清爽行动持续开展，中心城区道路保洁数量达 1223 条，清扫面积 3560 万平方米，机扫率维持在 75%以上。智慧城管二期建设全面启动，网格覆盖面积增至 321.4 平方公里，全年智慧城管共上报问题 92.6 万余件，主动发现率达 96.43%，解决率 99.97%。“三改一拆”保持强劲势头，累计完成“三改”建筑面积 2041.6 万平方米，拆除违法建筑面积 1644.1 万平方米。

五、贸易、旅游、会展

贸易业。2014 年全市商品销售总额 1.44 万亿元，比上年增长 18.1%。全年完成社会消费品零售总额 2992.0 亿元，增长 13.5%。分城乡看，城镇消费品市场实现零售额 2469.0 亿元，增长 13.1%，农村消费品市场实现零售额 523.0 亿元，增长 15.7%。在限额以上企业销售的商品类值中，汽车类增长 7.6%，石油及制品类增长 14.9%，食品、饮料、烟酒类增长 8.1%，服装、鞋帽、针纺织品类增长 22.5%。年末全市限额以上贸易企业达 2884 家，全年实现营业收入 9530.7 亿元，实现利润总额 108.5 亿元。

单位：亿元

图 6：2008-2014 年社会消费品零售总额

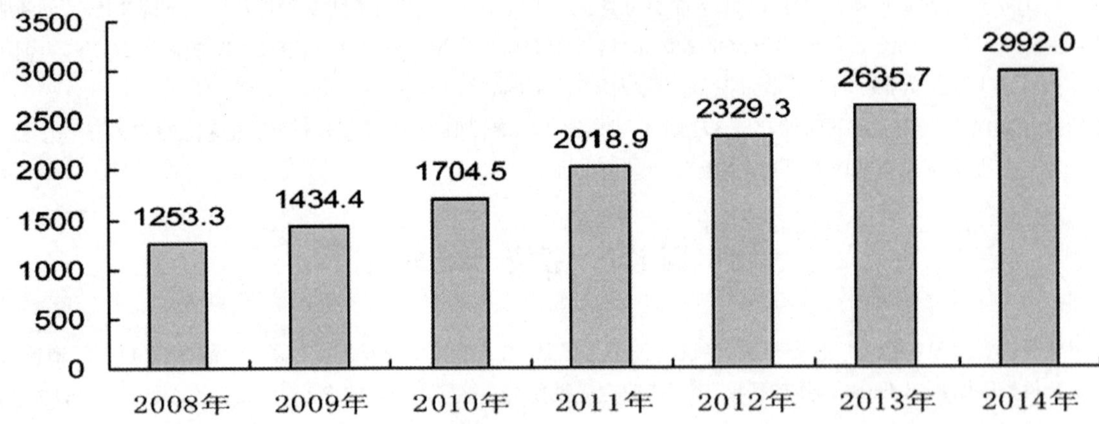

旅游业。2014 年全市实现旅游总收入 1068.1 亿元，比上年增长 12.0%。接待国内游客 6874.6 万人次，增长 10.4%；实现国内旅游收入 1020.3 亿元，增长 12.8%。接待入境游客 139.7 万人次，增长 9.7%。年末全市共有星级酒店 148 家，其中五星级 22 家；4A 以上风景区 30 处，其中 5A 级 1 处。

会展业。2014 年全市举办各类会展活动 295 个，比上年增长 6%。其中，举办展会 175 个，增长 9%，展览总面积达 196 万平方米，增长 5%；展览面积 2 万平方米以上的大型展会达 29 个。县级以上举办商务会议（论坛）79 个，增长 16%；特色节庆活动 41 个，减少 20%。年度荣获“中国十佳品牌会展城市”、“2014 中国十大影响力会展城市”等奖项。

六、对外经济、合作交流

对外贸易。2014 年全市口岸进出口总额 2186.1 亿美元，比上年增长 3.1%。外贸自营进出口总额 1047.0 亿美元，增长 4.4%，其中出口 731.1 亿美元，增长 11.3%；进口 315.9 亿美元，下降 8.7%。全年新增对外贸易经营备案登记企业 3757 家，累计达 26147 家。有进出口实绩企业 14810 家，比上年增加 922 家。其中，民营企业（包括私营企业和集体企业）出口额占全市出口总额的 63.1%，拉动全市出口增长 11 个百分点。全年机电产品出口 391.5 亿美元，增长 9.4%，占全市出口总额的 53.6%。出口额上亿美元的产品 157 个，比上年增加 22 个；进口额上亿美元的产品 47 个。2014 年直接与我市开展贸易往来的国家和地区 218 个，其中欧盟、美国、东盟、拉丁美洲、日本、大洋洲、非洲贸易额占比分别为 21.4%、16.3%、8.3%、7.5%、6.3%、5.1%和 4.5%。

利用外资。2014 年全市合同利用外资 70.2 亿美元，比上年增长 20.6%，实际利用外资首次突破 40 亿美元，达 40.3 亿美

图 7：2008-2014 年宁波自营进出口总额及增长速度

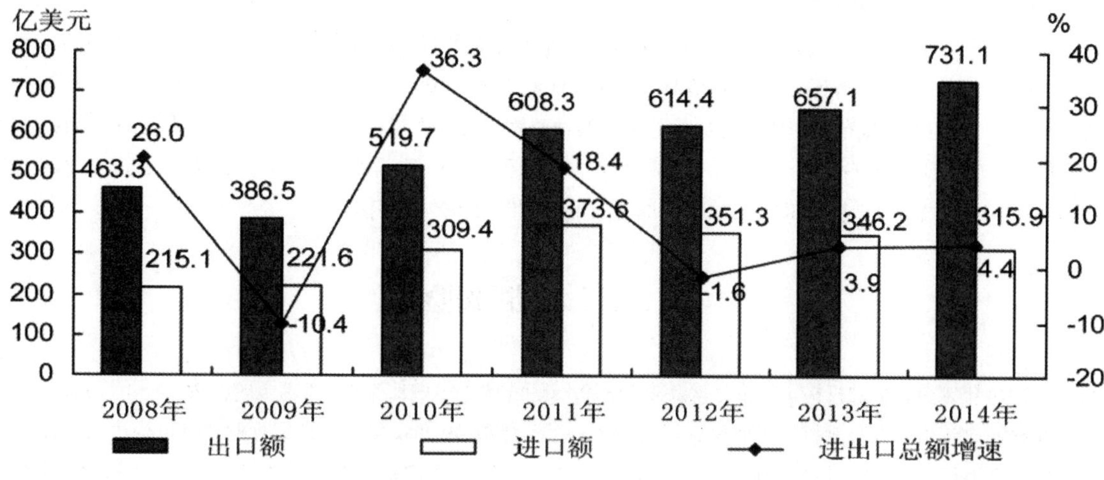

元，增长 22.9%。第三产业新批项目 321 个，增长 17.2%，合同利用外资 33.3 亿美元，增长 3.1%，其中批发和零售业合同利用外资 13.7 亿美元，增长 47.7%；金融业合同利用外资 5.1 亿美元，增长 321.7%。第三产业实际利用外资 21.4 亿美元，增长 16.6%，其中房地产业实际利用外资 11.1 亿美元，增长 18.1%；批发和零售业实际利用外资 7.1 亿美元，增长 122.3%。

对外合作。2014 年全市新批境外投资企业和机构 208 家；核准中方投资额 18.4 亿美元，比上年增长 16.9%，实际中方投资额 8.4 亿美元，增长 24.3%。完成境外承包工程劳务合作营业额 16.9 亿美元，增长 12.4%。

服务外包。2014 年全市承接服务外包执行额 140.6 亿元，比上年增长 30.1%；承接国际服务外包执行额 9.1 亿美元，增长 50.8%。年末服务外包企业达 1065 家，从业人员 4.14 万人。

国内合作。积极开展“宁波周”、“宁波行”、“出宁波”活动，努力推进招商转型，2014 年全市国内招商引资实到资金 745.4 亿元，比上年增长 13.2%，其中深圳“宁波周”达成的 31 个合作项目均为引进项目，协议总金额 265.8 亿元，创历届“宁波周”活动引进资金之最。全年达成浙商回归项目 889 个，实到资金 657.9 亿元，增长 30%。加大援助力度，帮扶黔西南州项目 69 个，资金 6149 万元；支援万州三峡库区 800 万元。推进山海协作工程，全年实施山海协作产业合作项目 78 个，实际到位资金 30.7 亿元。

七、港口、交通

港口生产。2014 年宁波港口货物吞吐量 5.26 亿吨，比上年增长 6.2%。完成外贸货物吞吐量 2.97 亿吨，增长 7.6%。大宗散货三大主要货种呈现“两增一减”的态势，其中完成铁矿石吞吐量 1.02 亿吨，增长 15.2%，完成原油吞吐量 6152.7 万吨，增长 0.5%，完成煤炭吞吐量 7412.8 万吨，减少 6.5%。全年宁波港集装箱吞吐量 1870.0 万标箱，增长 11.5%，吞吐量超过釜山港，排名跃至世界第 5 位，全国第 3 位。调整优化航线数量和航班密度，积极开发东盟、南亚、西亚等经济板块的“21 世纪海上丝绸之路”新航线，全年新开航线 11 条，现共拥有航线 228 条，其中远洋干线 113 条，近洋支线 62 条，内支线 21 条，内贸线 32 条。海铁联运业务进展快速，全年共完成海铁联运 13.5 万标箱，增长 28.4%，增幅列全国 6 个示范通道首位。

交通基础设施。2014 年全市完成交通基础设施投资 183 亿元。年末全市公路总里程 11045.4 公里，公路网密度 112.5 公里/百平方公里，达到中等发达国家水平。年末等级公路 10506.9 公里，其中高速公路 495.8 公里，一级公路 1125.9 公里，二级公路 777.2 公里，三级公路 1575.8 公里，四级公路 6532.2 公里。年内建成 3 个万吨级码头，万吨级码头总数达 102 个。铁路宁波北站搬迁及其配套工程完工，12 月洪塘至宝幢段货运铁路正式开通运营，宁波铁路“南客北货、客货分流”的环形枢纽最终形成。机场三期工程加快推进，完成投资 21.4 亿元。

综合运输。2014 年完成全社会货运量 4.04 亿吨，比上年增长 7.7%，货物周转量 2061.5 亿吨公里，增长 3.4%。其中，水路货运量 1.61 亿吨，货物周转量 1726 亿吨公里，分别增长 3.7%和 2.3%；公路货运量 2.19 亿吨，货物周转量 335.6 亿吨公里，分别增长 15%和 10%；铁路货物运输量 2364.1 万吨，减少 18.6%；机场货邮吞吐量 8.2 万吨，增长 23.4%。全社会客运量 1.65 亿人次，下降 2.6%。其中，公路客运量 1.21 亿人次，下降 10%；水路客运量 171.2 万人次，下降 24.2%；铁路客运量 3556.4 万人次，增长 32.2%；民航客运量 635.9 万人次，增长 16.5%。

公共交通体系。公交运能稳步增长，年内新辟公交线路 20 条，优化调整 48 条；年末公交标准运营车辆数 7445.8 标台，运营线路 698 条，新增公交专用道 40 公里以上，全年共完成公交客运总量 6.9 亿人次，比上年增长 7.5%。5 月 30 日轨道交通 1 号线一期工程开通试运营，日均开行 243 列次，电客车累计运营里程 112.04 万列公里，全线总计进站客流为 1387.51 万人次，平均 64237 人次/天，单日客流量最大为 15.14 万人次，列车兑现率 100%、正点率 99.94%；2 号线一期工程全线基本实现"轨通"，1 号线二期工程年底车站主体结构全部完成，3 号线一期工程开工建设。年末全市共有出租车 6370 辆，完成客运量 2.08 亿人次。年内新增公共自行车网点 200 个，新投放公共自行车 6000 辆，至年末，全市共建成公共自行车网点 992 个，投放公共自行车 21035 辆，办理租赁 IC 卡 32 万余张，累计租车量达 2899.7 万辆次。

八、银行、证券、保险

银行业。2014 年末全市金融机构本外币存款余额 13890.1 亿元，比上年增长 5.5%；年末金融机构本外币贷款余额 14569.8 亿元，增长 9.4%。全年银行业金融机构实现税后利润 148.5 亿元，下降 39.2%。年末全市银行业金融机构达 63 家，其中政策性银行 3 家，大型银行 5 家，股份制商业银行 11 家，城市商业银行 12 家，邮储银行 1 家，外资银行 5 家，农村合作金融机构 9 家，新型农村金融机构 14 家，非银行金融机构 3 家。

证券业。2014 年全市证券成交总额 3.17 万亿元，比上年增长 46.6%。其中股票和基金成交 2.07 万亿元，增长 50.7%，证券客户交易结算资金余额 144 亿元，增长 117.6%。期货代理交易量 5535.7 万手，增长 4.5%，代理交易额 5.31 万亿元，下降 0.7%。年末证券投资者开户 104.5 万户，增长 6.2%。年内新增证券公司分支机构 24 家，期货营业部 3 家，年末全市共有 98 家证券公司分支机构，1 家证券投资咨询公司，1 家期货公司和 38 家期货营业部。年内新增境内上市公司 3 家，累计实现首发和再融资额 73.9 亿元；境内上市公司总数达 45 家。

保险业。2014 年全市实现保费收入 207.0 亿元，比上年增长 11.6%。其中，财产险保费收入 111.6 亿元，增长 15.7%；人身险保费收入 95.4 亿元，增长 7.6%。赔款和给付 94.7 亿元，下降 8.9%。其中，财产险赔付支出 74 亿元，下降 17.4%；人身险赔付支出 20.7 亿元，增长 44%。

九、科技、教育、人才

科技创新。2014 年全市有 11 项农业和社会发展领域科技创新获得"863"计划、科技支撑计划等国家科技项目支持，荣获省级科学技术奖 26 项，其中一、二等奖 12 项，三等奖 14 项。全年专利申请量 58530 件，其中发明专利 12957 件，比上年增长 32.1%；专利授权量 43286 件，其中发明专利授权 2832 件，增长 26.1%。年末全市共有企业研究院 56 家、省级高新技术企业研究开发中心 284 家，市级以上企业工程（技术）中心 972 家（其中国家认定企业技术中心 8 家）；国家级创新型试点和创新型企业 15 家，省级创新型示范和试点企业 56 家，市级创新型试点企业 220 家；国家火炬计划重点高新技术企业 60 家，市科技型企业 950 家。培育创新型初创型企业 5134 家，产业技术创新联盟 14 家，科技部国际科技合作基地 8 家。

教育事业。2014 年末全市共有各级各类学校 2082 所，在校学生总数 132.07 万人。其中，普通高校 14 所，在校学生 15.09 万人；普通高中 83 所，在校学生 9.03 万人；中职学校 52 所，在校学生 7.28 万人；初中 209 所，在校学生 18.98 万人；小学 457 所，在校学生 48.26 万人；幼儿园 1254 所，在园学生 27.84 万人。年内全市投入建成学校共 106 所，投资 50.13 亿元。完善普惠性幼儿园扶持和规范政策，认定普惠性民办幼儿园 300 所，普惠性幼儿园招生覆盖率达 63%。年末全市共有全日制民办中小学（幼儿园）1089 所，在校（园）生 102.47 万人，占全市全日制中小学（幼儿园）在校（园）生数的 29.2%。27.58 万名随迁子女就学问题得到妥善解决。

人才开发。2014 年全市新增各类人才 19.5 万人，年末全市人才总量达 167.8 万人，比上年增长 13.1%。其中，新增博士、博士后 442 人，总量达 4069 人；新增省"千人计划"专家 23 人；新评审出市"3315 计划"人才 23 人、高端创业创新团队 27 个。引进海外人才 1404 人，总量达 5804 人。新建院士工作站 10 家，累计 77 家；新建技能大师工作室 16 家，累计 38 家；新建高技能人才公共实训基地 3 个，新增高技能人才 2.9 万人，总量达 26.3 万人。新引进人力资源服务机构 25 家，累计 407 家。4 个团队入选首批"浙江省领军型创新创业团队"。

十、文化、卫生、体育

文化建设。文化精品创作取得丰硕成果，歌剧《红帮裁缝》等3个作品获得全国“五个一工程”奖。文化惠民工程成效明显，全年实施“天然舞台”等文化惠民演出活动6000余场。深化农村电影放映工程改革，推进“电影惠农331工程”，创建室内固定放映点204个，公益电影放映基地58家，乡镇多厅数字影院54个厅。全年为农家书屋补充、更新、流转图书36.7万册。完成1401个行政村农村应急广播体系终端安装任务。申遗工作取得实效，6月22日中国大运河成功列入世界文化遗产。文物保护工作稳步推进，新公布宁波市第二批历史文化名村17座，县(市)区级文物保护单位(点)80余处。“前童元宵行会”、“董氏儿科”两个项目列入第四批国家级非物质文化遗产名录，非遗国宝数达23个，居计划单列市首位。文化走出去广受欢迎，市演艺集团舞剧《十里红妆·女儿梦》登上美国纽约林肯艺术中心舞台。宁波博物馆与香港历史博物馆签署五年合作意向书。文化产业和文化市场实现新发展，2家企业、1个园区被授予省文化产业示范基地、示范园区；9家企业、2个项目被授予2013-2014国家文化出口重点企业、重点项目；11个项目入围国家文化产业重点项目库。

卫生事业。2014年末全市实有病床3.0万张，拥有专业卫生人员6.4万人，卫生技术人员5.4万人，其中执业医师(含助理)2.1万人，注册护士2.1万人。按户籍人口统计，每千人床位数、卫技人员数、执业医师(含助理)数和注册护士数分别达到5.2张、9.2人、3.5人和3.5人。全市适龄儿童免疫规划疫苗接种率95.3%，免疫预防服务质量保持全省先进水平。加强妇幼保健服务与管理，全年常住人口孕产妇死亡率为7.2/10万，婴儿死亡率3.26‰，5岁以下儿童死亡率2.42‰，均稳定在较低水平。

体育事业。2014年全市共举办48项全国性以上赛事和活动，组队参加省第十五届运动会，共获得782.75枚奖牌，其中金牌数为414.25枚，总分7181.6分，均居全省第二。体育公共服务体系日趋完善，开通全民健身路径报修、维修平台，将海曙、江东、江北三区的健身路径管理纳入81890妇女儿童服务专线，自开通以来，实现零投诉，更好更便捷地服务了社会。建成各类球场173个，行政村体育健身路径拥有率达99%。积极推进大型体育场馆免费低收费向社会开放工作，有效提升体育系统直属体育场馆开放服务能力，年内新增5家大型场馆向社会开放，90%的城区公办中小学校体育设施向市民开放。全年体育彩票销售额达15.2亿元。

十一、人口、居民生活、社会保障

人口规模。2014年全市出生56398人，在出生人口中，男性29411人，女性26987人，男女性别比为109∶100。人口出生率、死亡率分别为9.69‰和6.10‰，自然增长率为3.59‰，比上年上升1.2个千分点，连续17年低于5‰。年末全市拥有户籍人口583.8万人，其中市区229.6万人。

居民收支。2014年宁波市全体居民人均可支配收入38074元，比上年增长9.9%。其中，城镇居民人均可支配收入44155元，增长9.2%；农村居民人均可支配收入24283元，增长11.0%。从收入构成看，城镇居民人均工资性收入27023元，增长9.9%；农村居民人均工资性收入15777元，增长8.7%。按一体化城乡住户调查新口径统计，城乡居民收入差距由2013年的1.85:1缩小为2014年的1.82∶1。2014年宁波市全体居民人均生活消费支出24324元，增长11.9%。其中，城镇居民人均生活消费支出27893元，增长11.5%，增幅较快的三类支出是医疗保健、食品烟酒和居住，人均分别支出1217元、8396元和7022元，分别增长15.9%、12.6%和10.9%；农村居民人均生活消费支出16228元，增长12.4%，增幅较快的三类支出是医疗保健、居住和交通通信，人均分别支出1105元、3230元和2592元，分别增长25.4%、18.8%和15.6%。

社会保险。社保覆盖面不断扩大，年末企业基本养老保险、职工基本医疗保险、失业保险、工伤保险、生育保险参保人数分别达542.23万人、368.54万人、243.39万人、291.09万人和252.25万人，比上年末分别净增33.29万人、22.26万人、11.65万人、7.71万人和6.71万人。全市城乡居民社会养老保险、被征地人员养老保障参保人数分别为124.76万和44.83万，16周岁以上应参保户籍人口养老保险参保率达91.5%。社保待遇持续提高，全市59.03万企业退休人员人均增发养老金243元/月，市区被征地人员养老保障按每人每月50元标准调整，城乡居民保险基础养老金按每人每月20元调整，惠及群体135万人。同时全市工伤保险、生育保险享受人数分别为3.95万人和3.68万人，待遇支出分别为6.94亿元和3.99亿元。政策范围内，职工医保和居民医保住院大病基金支付比例分别为86.8%和72.3%，新农合统筹地区住院医疗基金支付比例在75%以上。

民生保障。2014年市区居民最低生活保障标准从月人均588元提高到660元，年末全市共有最低生活保障对象5.13万人，低保资金实际支出2.4亿元。年末全市农村五保对象集中供养4245人，集中供养率为98.3%，城镇“三无”对象集中供养1220人，集中供养率为99.6%。各类收养性单位239个，床位数41996张，收养人员22701人。加大重度残疾人托(安)养工程的投入力度，一级残疾人集中托养补助从每人每年13200元调整到16200元，较省定标准高出1200元，年末全市累计托(安)养重度残疾人13003名。

保障性安居工程。2014年全市新开工各类保障性安居工程456万平方米、39960套，竣工213万平方米、24757套，解决9515户中低收入家庭住房困难问题。棚改项目融资进展顺利，我市已累计有3批、44个、总投资约966亿元的棚改项目向国开行申请棚改专项贷款，获批729亿元，放款总额64亿元。年末11个县(市)区已确定13个试点项目，计划改造住宅8491户、面积64万平方米，非住宅面积11万平方米。

慈善事业。2014年市县两级慈善机构募集善款6.13亿元，比上年增长11.1%。全年救助支出5.05亿元，受助的困难群众达43.2万人次。年末全市慈善机构累计募集已达46.03亿元，累计救助支出32.68亿元，受助257.4万人次。全年共开展各种志愿服务活动1800余次，参加服务的义工2万余人次，服务时间近4万小时。

十二、生态建设、社会安全

生态建设。加强环境专项治理，组织清理垃圾河174条，治理黑臭河613公里，实现全市1929条河道“河长制”的全覆盖；累计淘汰改造高污染燃料使用设备1398台，“禁燃区”面积扩大到1053平方公里；扩大黄标车限行区域，淘汰黄标车6.5万辆，发放补贴资金3.5亿元。实现新建项目排污权交易机制全覆盖，累计征收排污权有偿使用费1.94亿元。继续加强环境执法监管，累计出动执法人员63872人次，检查企业35622家次，立案查处1549件，处罚金额达7706.7万元。推进现代化环境监测监控体系建设，累计建成污染源自动监控设施438台套，基本实现重点污染源全天候实时监控。继续开展生态县(市)区创建工作，镇海区获国家级生态区命名，宁海、象山通过国家级生态县现场验收，北仑通过国家级生态区技术评估，全市累计9个县(市)区创建成省级生态县(市)区。

“平安宁波”建设。2014年全市共发生各类生产安全事故2599起、死亡690人、受伤2480人，分别比上年下降9.3%、7.4%和12.5%，连续第十年实现同比下降。发生较大事故4起，死亡14人，减少20人。全年共立案查处食品安全各类违法案件6794件，其中大要案1443件，罚没款6162.1万元，移送公安机关涉嫌犯罪案件37件。协助公安机关查获“3.13制售假药案”，涉案金额达上亿元，刑事拘留27人，为宁波食品药品监管史上最大案件。全年人民调解组织共调处各类民事纠纷11.59万件，调解成功11.45万件，成功率达98.7%，防止民间纠纷引起的自杀37件、37人次；防止民间纠纷转化为刑事案件188件、592人次。全年共受理群众信访7265件(人)次，下降31.3%，接待群众集体上访231批2877人次，分别下降18.4%和31.2%。

注：(1)本公报所列各项数据均为初步统计数。

(2)全市地区生产总值、各产业增加值绝对数按当年价格计算，增长速度按可比价格计算。

(3)规模以上工业企业指年主营业务收入2000万元及以上企业。

限额以上批发、零售、住宿、餐饮企业指：

批发业：年主营业务收入2000万元及以上；

零售业：年主营业务收入500万元及以上；

住宿业：年主营业务收入200万元及以上；

餐饮业：年主营业务收入200万元及以上。

(4)根据新修改的《预算法》，对财政收入的指标表述进行了规范，原“地方财政收入”改名为“一般公共预算收入”，具体统计口径保持不变。

(5)2014年7月开始出租车客运量纳入城市客运统计范围，故全社会客运量数据与上年同期不可比。

(6)城镇和农村居民收入均指常住居民收入

2014 Statistic Bulletin of National Economy and Social Development of Ningbo

Ningbo Municipal Statistics Bureau
State Statistical Bureau Ningbo Investigation Team

January 30, 2015

In the face of complex and various exterior environment and arduous tasks in reform and development in 2014, the whole city is tightly around the decisions and arrangements of "Dual Drive and Four Governance" and fully implements Three-year Action Plan on the development to social and economic transformation, focusing on stabilizing growth, promoting reform, adjusting economic structure, preventing risk and benefiting livelihood. With such actions taken, the economy has shown a trend of "low start, stable running and slowly increasing", the industry has better developed in steadiness, innovation and transformation had made progress, quality and benefit has gradually promoted and people's livelihood has continuously improving, thus laying a solid foundation for the achievement of "two basic points" and the construction of "four demonstration zones".

I. Overview

Regional GDP: The GDP in Ningbo in 2014 amounted to ￥760.251 billion, up by 7.6% compared with that of last year if calculated by comparable price, among which, the added value of primary industry was ￥27.518 billion, up by 1.9%; the added value of secondary industry was￥393.557 billion, up by 7.9%; and the added value of tertiary industry was ￥339.176 billion, up by 7.6%. The ration of the increase of the three industries was 3.6 ： 51.8 ： 44.6. The GDP per capita was ￥98,972 if calculated by permanent resident population (converted to USD 16,112 according to annual average exchange rate).

Graph 1: Regional GDP growth variation conditions of Ningbo in 2013-2014

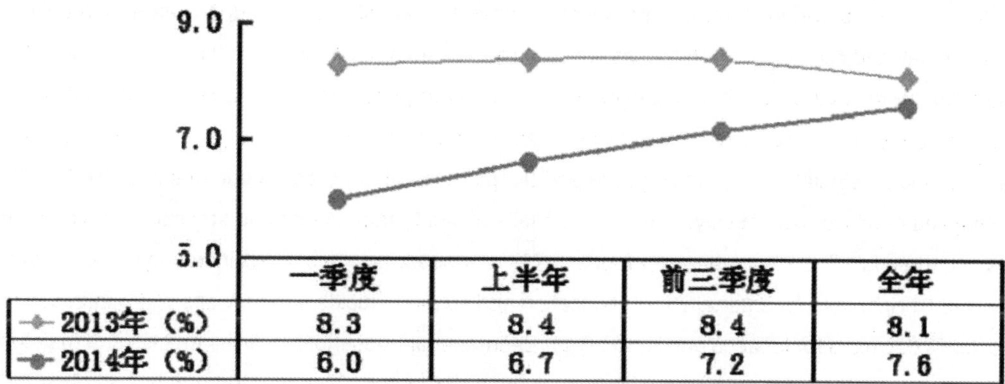

	一季度	上半年	前三季度	全年
2013年 (%)	8.3	8.4	8.4	8.1
2014年 (%)	6.0	6.7	7.2	7.6

	1st Quarter	1st Half	First 3 Quarters	Full Year
2013	8.3	8.4	8.4	8.1
2014	6.0	6.7	7.2	7.6

Graph 2: Per capital GDP of Ningbo in 2008-2014 (calculated by permanent resident population)

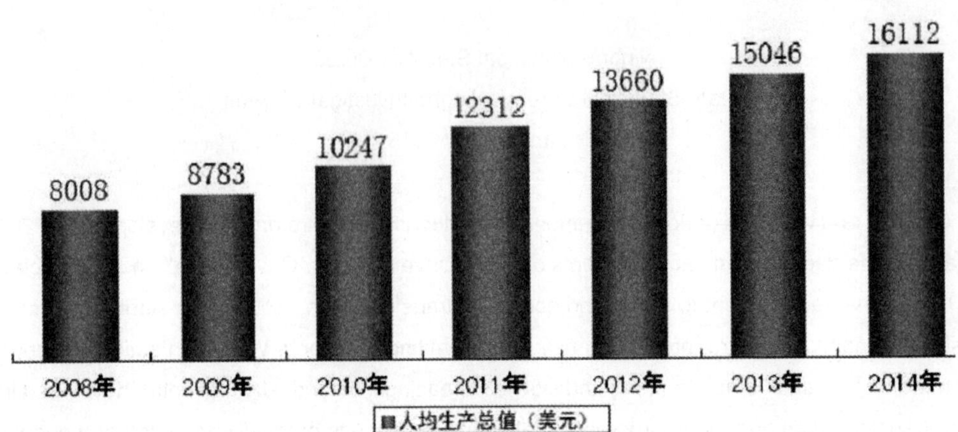

Fiscal revenue and expenditure: the general public fiscal budget revenue in Ningbo in 2014 was ￥86.06 billion, up by 8.6% compared with that of last year; the general public fiscal budget expenditure was ￥100.09 billion, up by 6.5%, among which, budget expenditures on education, medical care and family planning, energy conservation and environment protection as well as urban and rural communities were increased by 7.5%,10.5%,28.8% and 22.2% respectively.

Employment and re-employment: Employees newly created in urban areas and towns in Ningbo were 174,600 in 2014, and 72,500 laid-off workers were re-employed, 18,400 of which were the workers in trouble. The registered unemployment rate of city and towns is at an historical low level of 1.95% at the end of the year. The work of business startup driving the employment has achieved outstanding effects and College Students Pioneer Park of Zhenhai was awarded as national business incubator demonstration base, along with 3 college students innovation parks at the municipal level added. Total ￥534 million were issued as small-sum guaranteed loan in full year. 110,100 business entities were newly established, creating employment for 535,400 people and maintaining graduates' employment rate at over 95%. The reduction by the amount of ￥15,100,800 was made on social security charges to 703 small and micro enterprises which will be transformed and upgraded to scale enterprises; payment ration of social security was temporarily lowered for 46,000 medium small and micro-sized enterprises with total alleviated amount of ￥1.572 billion. Human resources markets of all different levels of the city offered service for 107,000 enterprises-times, providing 1.7643 million jobs.

Market price: The consumer price rose 1.9% in urban area of Ningbo in 2014, 0.2% and 0.1% respectively lower than those of national and provincial levels, ranking 27th and 9th place in 36 large and medium-sized cities in China and in 11 cities in Zhejiang province respectively. The rises and falls of eight major goods and services items present a pattern of "five rises and three falls": 2.7% increase for foods, 2.7% increase for clothes, 2.3% increase for health care and personal products, 2.0% increase for entertainment, education and cultural articles and services, 2.4% increase for residential products, 0.2% decrease for tobacco and liquor, 0.1% decrease for household facilities articles and maintenance service, and 0.5% decrease for transportation and communication. Ex-factory price and the purchasing price for manufacturers were declined by 2.19% and 2.49% respectively in 2014. The sales price of new commercial housing was down by 0.4% in December month on month and 5.3% year on year, with the increase ranking the 54th place among 70 large and medium-sized cities in China.

Graph 3: Monthly Fluctuation to consumer prices of household of Ningbo in 2014

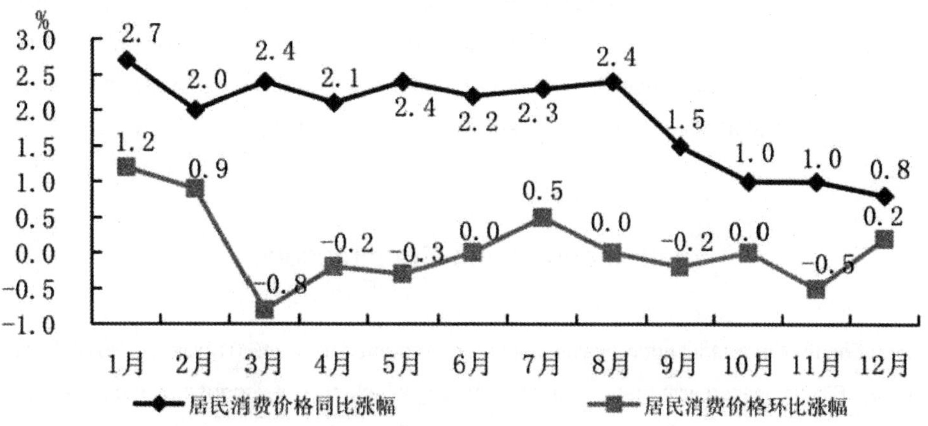

Graph 4: Monthly Fluctuation to newly built housing price of Ningbo in 2014

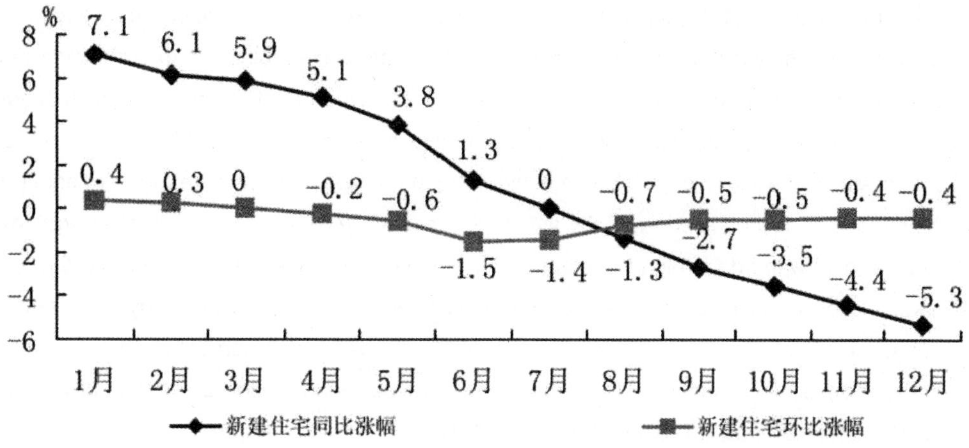

II. Agriculture and Rural Area

Agricultural production: The gross output value of farming, forestry, husbandry and fishing in Ningbo has reached ￥43.16 billion in 2014, up by 1.6% than that of last year if calculated by comparable price. Among the gross value, the farming was ￥20.91 billion, up by 4.1%; the forestry ￥1.26 billion, up by 3.8%; the husbandry ￥5.32 billion, down by 8.4%; the fishing ￥15.02 billion, up by 1.7%; and the service of farming forestry, husbandry and fishing ￥0.65 billion, up by 6.3%. According to statistical monitoring data of food production, the sowing area of food crops reached 1.018 million mu, up by 2.0%. The total output of grains reached 760,000 tons, up by 7.1%. The situation of pig and poultry production is still grim, with pig stock and slaughter were decreased by 13.6% and 7.1% respectively when compared with that of last year, as well as decreased by 20.4% and 26.3% in the case of poultry production. 17 new agricultural leading enterprises of the city were established in 2014, with a total 286 enterprises in accumulation and 95 of them reaching hundred million Yuan in production value (sales).

New countryside construction: 43 all-round well-off villages, 24 central villages, 31 featured villages and 8 top-quality tourist routes were built in 2014, with accumulative total of 568 all-round well-off villages, 101 central villages, 79 featured villages and 23 top-quality tourist routes. Centralized treatment of rural household garbage and domestic sewage is accelerated, along with sewage treatment coverage of administrative village in the city is raised to above 55% and centralized treatment rate of rural garbage in Ningbo reached to 100%. The policy of "two reconstructions" for countryside houses was steadily promoted with a total amount of ￥14.85 billion invested. The construction of 115,000 houses was started and 46,600 of them were completed, with 6.64 million square meters of rebuilt area in completion. The investment in rural housing construction totaled ￥53.34 billion and 30.92 million square meters of rebuilt areas were finished. With the realization of full coverage to village renovation, 50 villages were newly determined to implement the improvement action and ￥0.17 billion was invested to this renovation. As developing rapidly, rural leisure tourism has received up to 25.96 million tourism arrivals and created direct operation revenue of ￥2.794 billion, up by 19.3% and 28.0% respectively over the previous year.

III. Industry and Construction

Industrial economy: The total industrial added value in Ningbo amounted to ￥349.01 billion in 2014 if calculated by comparable price, up by 7.6% compared with that of last year. Among which, the total industrial added value for industrial enterprise above designated size was ￥254.02 billion, up by 7.4%. From the perspective of industries, in the 35 industries, the total industrial added value of 26 of which was on year-on-year growth; 9 of which have created industrial added value above ￥10 billion; of which automobile industry has realized added value of ￥23.29 billion, jumping to the third in gross and up by 31.9%, topping all nine industries in growth with 30.8% of rate of contribution to total industrial added value of enterprises above designated size in Ningbo. From the perspective of type of enterprise, the industrial added value of big, medium and small-size enterprises within above-scale industry were increased by 6.2%, 6.1% and 10.9% respectively. From the perspective of economic type, Limited Liabilities Companies (LLC) and state-owned enterprises are growing fast with their added value increased by 17.6% and 12.1% respectively; the added value of enterprises invested by Hong Kong, Macao and Taiwan and foreign-invested enterprises were increased by 4.3% and 3.5% respectively. The sales value for industrial enterprises above designated size in 2014 was ￥1338.74 billon, up by 6.6%; among which, the sales value in domestic market was ￥1036.63 billion, up by 8.5%; the value of export delivery was ￥302.11 billion, up by 5.5%. The profits achieved by the industrial enterprises above the designated size was ￥64.81 billion, down by 2.9%; and taxation of profits achieved was ￥128.06 billion, up by 1.2%.

Industrial transformation and innovation: equipment manufacturing industry is growing fast, with added value of manufacturing enterprises above designated size reaching ￥105.47 billion in 2014, up by 11.1% than that of last year, 3.7% higher compared with all industries above designated size. With low percentage of value, eight high energy-consuming industries realized added value of ￥85.24 billion, up by 2.7%, making up 33.6% of all industries above designated size and down by 1.8% in terms of proportion. Innovation-driven enterprises are showing effects with new production value of ￥360.66 billion achieved by those of above designated size in 2014, up by 25.0%; the output ration of new products risen to new record highs from 22.2% of last year to 26.2% in 2014; the labor productivity reached ￥178,000/person, up by 9.9%.

Construction industry: the output value of construction industry in Ningbo totaled ￥371.41 billion in 2014, up by 18.5% compared with that of last year. The construction area of house in 2014 was 273.672 million m2, up by 9.3%. The average construction employees in 2014 are 1.152 million people, an increase of 143,000 people over last year.

IV. Investment in Fixed Asset and Urban Construction

Investment in fixed asset: Investment in fixed asset in Ningbo was ￥398.95 billion in 2014, up by 16.6% compared with that of last year, of which, the private investment in 2014 reached ￥195.50 billion, up by 12.6%, and the ratio of private investment to fixed assets investment was 49.0%. In perspective of industries, investment in primary industry was ￥4.52 billion, up by 113.3%; investment in secondary industry was ￥126.47 billion, up by 18.6%; investment in tertiary industry was ￥267.96 billion, up by 14.7%; the investment ratio of the three industries was 1.1 ∶ 31.7 ∶ 67.2. The total industrial investment in 2014 reached ￥126.32 billion, up by 19.0%; Among which the investment in industrial technical transformation reached ￥94.07 billion, up by 23.9%; the purchasing of industrial equipments amounted to ￥54.2 billion, up to 35.3%. The total investment in real estate development in 2014 was ￥132.81 billion, up by 18.3%; The sales area of commercial residential building was 7.264 million m2, down by 0.5% and of which, the sales area of residential housing was 5.952 million m2, up by 2.3%.

Graph 5: Main Structure of Fixed-assets Investment in Ningbo in 2014

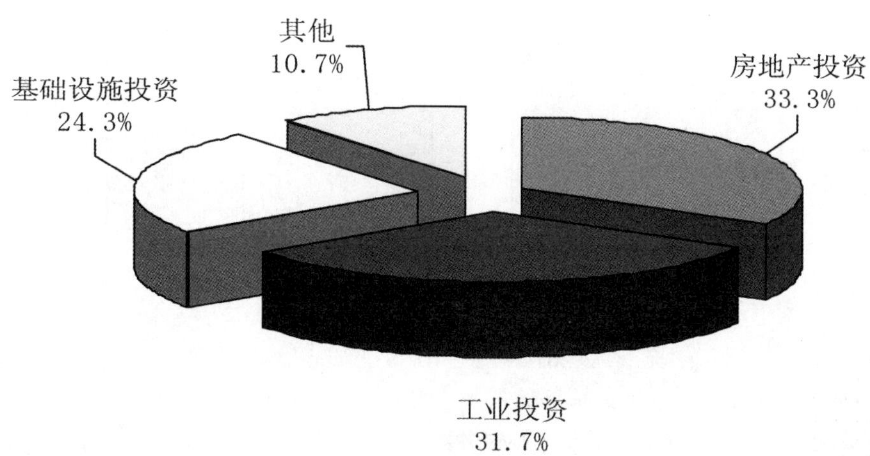

Modern urban construction: Modern metropolis strategy of "50100 project" is under thorough development and the network modern metropolis pattern of "one core, two wings and two zones and three bays" is further established. The project quality of "three rivers and six banks" obtained partial results, the construction on both sides of Fenghua River was officially opened, and the construction on east bank of Yaojiang River was came into operation, taking on a new look of 160,000 square meters greenbelt along the river. The construction of express road network was made solid progress with express ring road from north and south basically built. The action of new round of "unconnected roads" was put into implementation and 11 those of them were got connected. Jiangdong North Road (Zhogshan Road-Minan Road) and Xingning Road (Shiji Avenue-Fuqing Road) were comprehensively improved. Integrated improvement of alleys at back street was continuing and 90 of them were fully renovated. As promoting landscaping, the public green area of 170 hectare was newly increased in central urban area. With the continuous development on road refreshing, 1223 roads in central urban area are cleaned, covering sweep-out area of 35.6 million square meters, and the machine cleaning rate of roads was maintained at 75%. The second phase of Wisdom City Management was entirely started and grid cover area was increased to 321.4 square meters. Of total 926,000 issues about the project of Wisdom City Management in 2014, 96.43% of them were actively found and 99.97% of these issues were solved. The construction of "three transformations and one demolition" is strongly continued with the cumulative building area as "three transformations" of 20,416,000 square meters was rebuilt and illegal construction area of 16,441,000 square meters was dismantled.

V. Trade, Tourism and Exhibition

Trade: The total sales volume of goods in Ningbo reached ￥1.44 trillion in 2014, up by 18.1% compared with that of last year. The total retail sales of consumer goods reached ￥299.2 billion, up by 13.5%. If viewed by countryside and town respectively, the total volume of consumer retail sales in towns was ￥246.9 billion, up by 13.1%, and total volume of consumer retail sales in countryside was ￥52.3 billion, up by 15.7%. In goods sales volume enterprises above designated size, automobile sales have been up by 7.6%; petroleum and related products 14.9%; foods, beverage, tobacco and liquor 8.1%; clothing, shoes and hats, and needle textile 22.5%. The number of trade companies above designated size in Ningbo has reached 2,884 at the end of 2014. The total operation revenue was ￥953.07 billion and profits of ￥10.85 billion.

Graph 6: Total Retail Sales of Consumer Goods from 2008-2014

Unit: ￥100 million

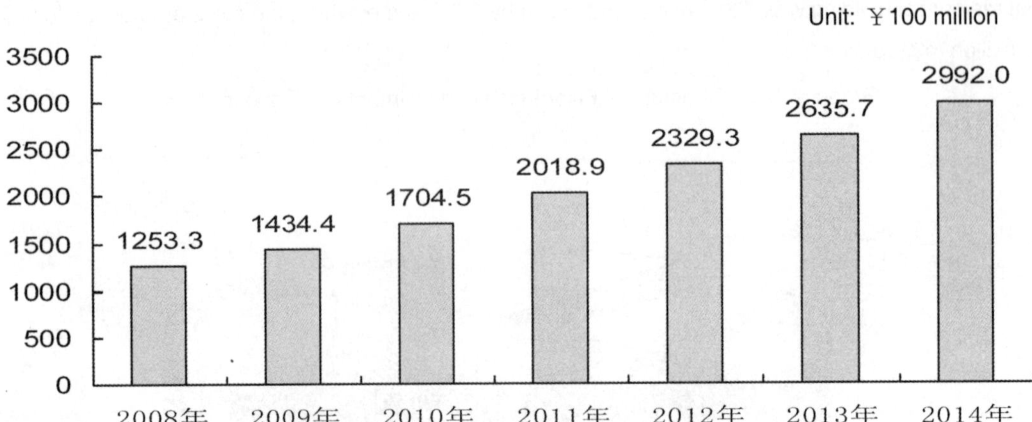

Tourism: Total revenue of tourism in Ningbo in 2014 was ￥106.81 billion, up by 12.0% compared with that of last year. The domestic tourists in 2014 were 68.746 million, up by 10.4%; revenue from domestic tourists was ￥102.03 billion, up by 12.8%. The inbound tourists hit 1.397 million, up by 9.7%. There were 148 star-rated hotels in Ningbo in 2014, where 22 were five-star hotels. There were 30 4A-class tourist attractions and 1 5A-class tourist attraction.

Exhibition: in 2014, 295 exhibition activities of various kinds were held in Ningbo, up by 6% compared with that of last year; of which 175 were exhibitions, up by 9%, with a total exhibition area of 1.96 million m2, up by 5%. A total number of 29 large-scale exhibitions with more than 20,000 m2 of exhibition area were held. In 2014, 79 business conferences (forums) and 41 festival activities above county level were held, which witnesses increase of 16% and decrease of 20% respectively. Ningbo had the honor to get the annual award of “Chinese Top Ten Exhibition City” and “2014 The Most Influential Exhibition City” etc.

VI. Foreign Economy and Cooperation & Exchange

Foreign trade: The total volume of export and import in Ningbo reached USD 218.61 billion in 2014, up by 3.1% compared to that of last year. The total volume of self-support export was USD 104.7 billion in 2014, up by 4.4%; of which the volume of export reached USD 73.11 billion, up by 11.3% and that of import reached USD 31.59 billion, down by 8.7%. The newly-increased enterprises for foreign trade registered in 2014 were 3757, totaling 26,147 by far, and the enterprises with actual export and import businesses were 14,810, an increase of 922 to that of last year. Among which, the export amount of individually-run enterprises (including private enterprises and collectively-owned enterprises) accounted for 63.1% of the total export volume in Ningbo, driving export growth of 11% in the city. The export volume of mechanical and electrical products in 2014 was USD 39.15 billion, up by 9.4% and making up 53.6% of the total export volume of the city. The number of product types generated both export volume and import volume reaching billions of dollars were 157 and 47 respectively, with an increase of 22 such product types exported. 218 nations and regions established direct trade relations with Ningbo in 2014, among which, the trade volume in EU, the United States, ASEAN, Latin America, Japan, Oceania and Africa accounted for 21.4%、16.3%、8.3%、7.5%、6.3%、5.1% and 4.5% respectively.

Graph 7: Self-support Import & Export Volume and Growth in Ningbo

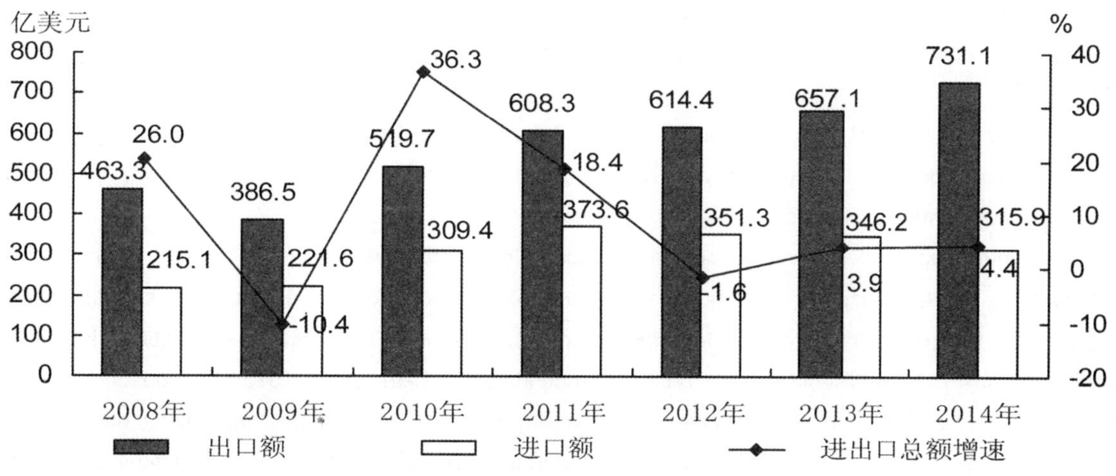

Foreign capital utilization: In 2014, foreign capital utilization by contract was USD 7.02 billion, up by 20.6 compared to that of last year; and actual utilization of foreign capital exceeded USD 4 billion for the first time and reached USD 4.03 billion, up by 22.9%. The total number of newly-approved projects in the tertiary industry reached 321, up by 17.2%. Foreign capital utilization by contract was USD 3.33 billion, up by 3.1%; among which the foreign capital utilization by contract of wholesale and retail industry was USD 1.37 billion, up by 47.7%; foreign capital utilization by contract of financial industry was USD 510 million, up by 321.7%. Actual utilization of foreign capital in tertiary industry reached USD 2.14 billion, up by 16.6%. Among the above, the actual utilization of foreign capital in real estate industry was USD 1.11 billion, up by 18.1%; the actual utilization of foreign capital in wholesale and retail industry was USD710 million, up by 122.3%.

Foreign cooperation: 208 overseas investment enterprises and organizations were approved in Ningbo in 2014, with Chinese investment approved up to USD 1.84 billion, up by 16.9% compared to that of last year, and the actual Chinese investment up to USD 840 million, up by 24.3%. The turnover of labor cooperation for overseas contracting projects was USD 1.69 billion, up by 12.4%.

Outsourcing service: the executed volume of undertaking service outsourcing in 2014 was ￥14.06 billion, up by 30.1 compared to that of last year; the executed volume of undertaking outsourcing of international service was ￥910 million, up by 50.8%. The enterprises specialized in outsourced services at the end of 2014 amounted to 1065, with total employees of 41,400.

Domestic cooperation: actively implement activities of "Ningbo Week", "a visit to Ningbo" and "go out of Ningbo", strive to advance investment promotion transformation; the attraction of domestic capital reached ￥74.54 billion, up by 13.2%; among which 31 cooperative projects reached in "Ningbo Week" are introduced projects with total agreement value of ￥26.58 billion, the largest canalization of funds of all previous "Ningbo Week". 889 Zhejiang merchants projects were reached in 2014 with actual paid in fund of ￥65.79 billion, up to 30%. Extended an offer of help and assisted 69 project for Qianxinan, with assisted capital of ￥61.49 million; assisted three Gorges Reservoir Region in Wanzhou District with a fund of ￥8 million. Advanced Shanhai cooperation project and implemented 78 cooperative projects in 2014 with actual paid-in fund of ￥3.07 billion.

VII. Port and Transportation

Port production: The cargo handling capacity of Ningbo in 2014 was 526 million tons, up by 6.2% compared with that of last year; the handling capacity of foreign trade goods completed was 297 million tons, up by 7.6%. The three major cargoes of major bulks were presented as "two increases and one decrease":102 million tons for iron ore, up by 15.2%; 61.527 million tons for crude oil, up by 0.5%; 74.128 million tons for coal, down by 6.5%. The container throughput in

2014 has exceeded 18.7 million TEU, up by 11.5% and exceeded that of Port of Busan, ranking the fifth among the worldwide ports and third among ports in China mainland. Made adjustment and optimization to air line number and flight frequency, actively develop new air lines of "21 century Maritime Silk Road" in economical plates of ASEAN, South Asia and West Asia etc. Of total 228 air lines at currently, 11 of them were newly developed in 2014, 113 are ocean main lines, 62 are offshore branch lines, 21 are inner branch lines and 32 are domestic trade lines. Combined transport of sea and rail was rapidly developed with 135,000 TEU were delivered in 2014, up by 28.4%, and the growing rate ranking the first place among 6 demonstration channels in the country.

Transportation infrastructure: The investment in the transportation infrastructure in Ningbo was ￥18.3 billion in 2014. At the end of 2014, the total mileage of roads has reached 11,045.4 km, and the highway density was 112.5 km per 100 km2, equaling the level of that in moderately developed countries. Of all classified highways with 10,506.9 km, the length of expressway was 495.8 km, first-class road 1125.9 km, secondary 777.2 km, tertiary 1575.8 km and forth-class 6532.2 km. 3 dwt ports were completed in 2014 and the total ports with dwt are 102 at present. The removal project of Ningbo north rail station and its auxiliary project were completed; the freight railway from Hongtang to Baozhuang were officially went into operation in December of 2014 and the circular junction terminal of Ningbo railway as "South station for passengers and North station for freight, distributary of passengers and freight" was finally formed. The third phase of airport construction was rapidly advanced with ￥2.14 billion of investment achieved.

Integrated transportation: The social cargo transportation volume in 2014 was 404 million tons, up by 7.7% compared with that of last year, with turnover volume of 206.15 billion tons, up by 3.4%. Among which, the water cargo transportation volume was 161 million tons and turnover volume was 17.26 billion tons, up by 3.7% and 2.3% respectively; road cargo transportation volume was 219 million tons with turnover volume of 33.56 billion tons, increased respectively by 15% and 10%; railway transportation volume was 23.641 million tons, down by 18.6%; airport cargo transportation volume was 82,000 tons, up by 23.4%; railway passenger transportation volume was 35.564 million person-time, up by 32.2%; and the passenger transportation volume by civil aviation was 6.359 million person-time, up by 16.5%.

Public transit system: Public transportation capacity was steadily expanded with 20 bus routes were newly built in 2014 and 48 routes were optimized and adjusted; at the end of 2014, the number of standard public operating vehicles was 7445.8, operating routes reached 698 and over 40 km public transportation lanes were newly added, with total bus passenger transport hit 690 million person-times, up by 7.5% compared with that of last year. On May 30, the first-stage of rail transit was put into trial operation with average of 243 times per day; the accumulative operation mileage of electric bus was 1.1204 km; the total passenger flow-in of the whole line was 13.8751 million person-times with average 64,237 people/day; the maximum passenger flow volume of per day was 151,400 person-times; the train-taking demand rate was 100% and the on-schedule rate was 99.94%; the first-stage of line 2 was basically linked; the major structure of the second stage of line 1 was completed at the end of 2014 and the first-stage of line 3 was started on construction. At the end of 2014, total 6370 taxis were on road with passenger capacity of 208 million person-times. 200 public bike sites were added in 2014 with 6000 new public bikes were put on use. Till the end of 2014, total 992 bike sites were built with capacity of 21035 bikes; over 320,000 IC lease cards were issued and accumulative car rental number was up to 28.997 million rent-times.

VIII. Banking, Securities and Insurance

Banking: The deposit of domestic and foreign currency in the financial institutions in Ningbo has reached ￥1.38901 trillion at the end of 2014, up by 5.5%; the loan balance of domestic and foreign currency in financial institutional at the end of 2014 was ￥1.45698 trillion, up by 9.4%. The net profits of financial institutions in 2014 were ￥14.85 billion, down by 39.2%. The number of financial institutions at the end of 2014 has totaled 63, including 3 policy banks, 5 large-scale banks, 11 joint-stock commercial banks, 12 city commercial banks, 1 postal saving bank, 5 foreign banks, 9 rural cooperative financial institutions, 14 new-type rural financial institutions and 3 non-bank financial institutions.

Securities: The total transaction volume of securities in Ningbo in 2014 has reached ￥3.17 trillion, up by 46.6%, where, the transaction volume of share and funds was ￥2.07 trillion, up by 50.7%. The settlement amount of securities transaction was ￥14.4 billion, up by 117.6%. The transaction volume of futures agent was 55.357 million, up by 4.5%; the agent transaction amount of ￥5.31 trillion, down by 0.7%. The new clients of securities at the end of 2014 were 1.045 million, up by 6.2%. The new securities company branches and futures operation offices were 24 and 3 respectively within 2014. By the end of 2014, there were 98 securities operation offices, 1 Securities Investment and Consultation Company, 1 Futures Company and 38 futures operation offices. 3 listed companies were newly increased with ￥7.39 billion accumulative total first financing and refinancing fund, totaling 45 public companies by far.

Insurance: The premium income of insurance industry in Ningbo in 2014 was ￥20.7 billion, up by 11.6% compared with that of last year. Among the above, ￥11.16 billion was for property insurance, up by 15.7%; ￥9.54 billion was for life insurance, up by 7.6%. The accumulative compensation and payment in insurance industry was ￥9.47 billion, down by 8.9%. Among the above, ￥7.4 billion was for property insurance, down by 17.4%; and ￥2.07 billion was for life insurance, up by 44%.

IX. Science & Technology, Education and Talents

Scientific and technical innovation: Total 11 science and technology innovations on agriculture and social development won the national support of "863" plan and science and technology support program etc in 2014, 26 science and technology awards were granted at provincial level. Among which, 12 was or first prizes and second prizes, and 14 was for third prizes. The number of patents applications was 58530 in 2014, of which 12957 were patents for innovation, up by 32.1%; 43286 were patents application granted with 2832 innovation patents licensing, up by 26.1%. By the end of 2914, there were 56 enterprise research institutions in Ningbo, 284 R&D centers of provincial high-tech technical enterprises, 972 engineering (technical) centers of municipal enterprises (8 of them were national enterprise technology centers), 15 national innovation units and innovation enterprises, 56 provincial innovation-type demonstration and pilot enterprises, 220 municipal innovation-type pilot enterprises; there were 60 key new high-tech enterprises of Torch Plan and 950 municipal scientific and technological enterprises. There also were 5134 newly established enterprises of cultivated-type, 14 industrial technology innovation associations and 8 international scientific and technological cooperation bases from Ministry of Science and Technology (MOST).

Education: There were 2,082 schools at different levels and varieties in Ningbo at the end of 2014, with students enrolled of 1.3207 million, among which there were 14 colleges and universities, with students enrolled of 150,900; 83 ordinary high schools, with students enrolled of 90,300; 52 secondary vocational schools, with students enrolled of 72,800; 209 middle schools, with students enrolled of 189,800; 457 primary schools, with students enrolled of 482,600; 1,254 kindergartens, with students enrolled of 278,400. With the improvement of supporting and standard policy for inclusive kindergarten, 300 civilian-run kindergartens were approved as inclusive ones with 63% coverage rate of recruit of kindergarten students. By the end of 2014, there were 1089 full-time civilian-run middle and primary schools (kindergartens), with 1.0247 million students in schools and covering 29.2% of students at full-time middle and primary schools (kindergartens) in Ningbo. The issue of entering school for 275,800 children of migrant workers was properly solved.

Talent cultivation: The number of talents of different industries was up by 195,000 in 2014, and the total talents in Ningbo at the end of 2014 amounted to 1.678 million, up by 13.1% compared with that of last year. Of which 442 were new PHDs and post doctoral students, with total number of 4069; there were 23 new experts from national "Program of Overseas Talent Introduction", 23 talents newly evaluated from "3315 plan", 27 high-end entrepreneurial innovation teams, 1404 overseas talents, with the total number of 5804. There were 10 new academician research stations, totaling 77 stations; there were 16 national postdoctoral research workstations, totaling 38 workstations; there were 3 public practical training bases for high-skilled talents, with 29,000 of high-skilled talents, totaling 263,000 talents. There were 25 human resource service agencies newly introduced with totaling 407 agencies. 4 teams were selected to the first group of "Zhejiang Leading Innovation Entrepreneur Team".

X. Culture, Health and Sports

Cultural construction: The creation of quality culture products made achievement and opera Hongbang Tailor and other 3 works won the award of "Five-One Project". The cultural people-benefit project also achieved remarkable effects and over 6000 performances were held on "natural stage". With the deepening reform to rural motion picture projection and the advancing "movie benefit-farmer 331 project", there were 204 inner fixed showing sites, 58 public motion picture projection bases and 54 digital cinema halls were created. Total 367,000 books were supplemented, updated and circulated for peasant bookstore. 1401 terminal installation tasks of emergency broadcast system in administrative villages were completed. With the success application, the Chinese Grand Canal was listed in world cultural heritage on June 22. As the steadily advancing of cultural relic protection, 17 famous historical and cultural villages of the second group in Ningbo, and over 80 cultural relic protection sites at county (municipality) and district level were newly published. Two projects of "Qiantong children sweet dumplings guild" and "the Dongs Pediatrics" were enrolled into the forth group of national intangible cultural heritage, with 23 non-heritage national treasures and ranking the first place among municipalities with independent planning status. The "Culture Going Out" was widely well-received, the dance drama Ten Li Dowry • Girl' s Dream were performed on Lincoln Art Center Stage at New York in America. Ningbo Museum and Hong Kong Historical Museum signed cooperation letter of intent for five years. With the new development on cultural industry and market, 2 enterprises and 1 garden were honored with provincial industrial demonstration bases and garden; 9 enterprises and 2 projects was awarded as 2013-2014 key enterprises and projects of national culture; 11 projects were entered into project library of national cultural industry.

Medical and health services: At the end of 2014, Ningbo owned 30,000 hospital beds, 54,000 health workers, including 21,000 medical practitioners (assistants included) and 21,000 registered nurses. According to the statistics of registered population, the number of hospital beds, health workers, medical practitioners (assistants included) and registered nurses per thousand people reached 5.2, 9.2, 3.5 and 3.5 respectively. The vaccine inoculation rate of children at school age was 95.3%. The immunoprophylaxis service quality stood out around the whole province. As enhancing the management on maternal and child health services, the maternal mortality rate of permanent resident population annual was 7.2/per 100 thousand people, infant mortality rate was 3.26‰ and that of children under 5 years old was 2.42‰, both kept at lower level.

Sports: Total 48 national competitions and activities were held in Ningbo in 2014, and total 782.75 medals were won by team, among which 414.25 was gold medals with total point of 7181.6, ranking as the second in the whole province. With increasing improvement to public sports service, the national fitness workout path and maintaining platform were opened, bringing workout paths from Haishu, Jiangdong and Jiangbei districts into 81890 women and children service line. Since the opening up, there is zero complaint with better serving society. 173 of all kinds of ball parks were built with 99% of owning rate in administrative village. Actively advance large stadium and open to the public with free charge or lower charge, thus effectively improving the open service ability of gyms directly under physical education system. 5 new large gyms were opened to the public in 2014 and 90% of sports facilities of state-run middle and primary schools were opened to citizens. The sales of sports lotteries in 2014 reached to ￥ 1.52 billion.

XI. Population, Livelihood, Social Insurance

Population size: There were 56,398 people born in Ningbo in 2014 and among them, 29411 are male and 26987 are female, with sex ration as 109：100. The birth rate and mortality rate were 9.69‰ and 6.10‰ respectively; the natural rate of growth was 3.59‰, up by 1.2‰ compared with that of last year and 17 years in succession lower 5‰. At the end of 2014, the registered population was 5.838 million and 2.296 of them were living in urban area.

Resident income & expenditure: The disposable income per urban resident was ￥38,047 in 2014, up by 9.9%; Among which, urban per capita disposable income was ￥44,155, up by 9.2%; rural per capita disposable income was ￥24,283, up by 11.0%. From the view of income structure, urban per capita income from wage and salary was ￥27,023, up by 9.9%; rural per capita income from wage and salary was ￥15,777, up by 8.7%. According to new statistics of urban and rural residency survey, the income gap between urban and rural residents were reduced from 1.85:1 in 2013 to 1.82：1 in 2014. In 2014, the per capita consumption expenditure of whole population in Ningbo was ￥24,324, up by11.5% compared with that of last year; Among which, the per capita consumption expenditure of urban residents was ￥27,893, up by 11.9%, and the three kinds of expenditures with fast growth were health care, residential housing and transportation communication, with expenditures of ￥1105，￥3230 and ￥2592 respectively, and up by 25.4%, 18.8% and 15.6% respectively.

Social insurance: As continuously extending social insurance coverage, at the end of 2014, the number of people purchasing basic retirement insurance in enterprises, basic medical insurance of employees, unemployment insurance, work-related injury insurance and maternity insurance was 5.4223 million, 3.6854 million, 2.4339 million, 2.9109 million and 2.5225 million respectively, with a net increase of 332,900 people, 222,600 people, 116,500 people, 77,100 people and 67,100 people respectively compared with that of last year. The number of people purchasing urban and rural resident endowment insurance and of people with land expropriated were 1.2476 million and 448,300, the rate of joining insurance for registered population with age of 16 and above reached 91.5%. The social security benefits were gradually improved and the per capita pension of590,300 enterprise retirees was increased by ￥243/month; urban and rural resident endowment insurance of people with land expropriated were adjusted based on the standard of ￥50 per month, and the basic retirement insurance of urban and rural residents were adjusted based on the standard of ￥20 per month, benefiting group of 1.35 million people. Meanwhile, the number of people benefiting from work-related injury insurance and maternity insurance was 395,00 and 368,00 people respectively, with expenditures of ￥0.694 billion and ￥0.399 billion respectively. The reimbursement proportion of hospital fund of serious illness within the policy area of urban employees and residents were 86.8% and 72.3% respectively; the reimbursement proportion of hospital medical funds in coordinating district of new rural cooperative medical system (NCMS) were over 75%.

People's livelihood security: In 2014, the minimum living standard of urban and rural residents in Ningbo was increased from ￥588/month to ￥660/month. At the end of 2014, the total number of people receiving basic cost of living allowances was 51,300 and the actual cost of minimum living allowances reached ￥240 million. At the end of 2014, the number of rural households enjoying the five guarantees was 4245 with concentrated proportion of 98.3%; the number of "three non-personnel" in urban area enjoying the supporting was 1220 with concentrated proportion of 99.6%. 239 shelter units were established with 41,996 beds, adopting 22701 people. Increase investment to the project of caring the handicapped people, and the caring subsidy of per head per year for level one disabled people was adjusted from ￥132,00 to ￥162,00, with ￥1200 higher than that of provincial standard; The accumulative number of the serious disabled received caring in Ningbo at the end of 2014 was 13,003.

Government-subsidized housing project: In 2014, the area and number of government-subsidized housing projects newly constructed in the city was 4.56 million m2 and 39,960 sets. The number of completed government-subsidized housing projects was 2.13 million m2 and 24,757 sets. The issue of housing difficulty to 9515 families with low and middle income was solved. The settlements project financing was running smooth and 44 these projects from 3 batches with total investment of ￥96.6 billion have applied from special purpose loans, with ￥72.9 billion approved and ￥0.64 billion issued. At the end of 2014, 13 pilot projects covering 11 counties (cities) and districts were determined, 8491 households with 640,000 square meters were planned to reconstruct and 110,000 square meters of non-residential housing were planned to reconstruct.

Charity: In 2014, city and county level charitable organizations have raised a donation of ￥613 million, up by 11.1% compared with that of last year and paid ￥505 million for aid work. The number of people in straitened circumstances and receiving help from such charitable organizations was 432,000. By the end of 2014, the accumulated funds raised by charitable organizations in the city have reached ￥4.603 billion and accumulated funds paid for aid work have been ￥3.268 billion. The number of people in straitened circumstances and receiving help from such charitable organizations was 2.574 million. Over 1,800 various voluntary service activities have been conducted and more than 20,000 volunteers have participated in providing the service all the year around. The accumulated service time was 40,000 hours.

XII. Ecological Construction and Social Safety

Ecological construction: Strength special management on environment, clean the rubbish in 174 rivers and control black and odorous rivers with 613 km in length, thus realizing the full cover of "river length control" of 1929 rivers in Ningbo. Accumulated 1398 sets of obsolete equipment with high-polluted fuel was eliminated and transformed, the area of "no burning zone" was expanded to 1053 sq.km; expand area to limit yellow label car and 65,000 of these cars were eliminated, with subsidies of ￥350 million issued. The emission trading scheme of new project was realized with full coverage and accumulated ￥194 million of emission rights compensated charge was collected. Environmental law enforcement and supervision were strengthened continuously and nearly 63,872 law enforcement officers were deployed to inspect more than 35,622 companies. A total number of 1549 illegal cases were filed, with the amount of ￥77.067 million penalties reached. Carry forward the construction of modern environmental monitoring and control system, accumulated 438 sets of automatic monitoring facilities for pollution sources were completed, basically realized all-weather real time monitoring key pollution sources. The establishment of ecological counties (cities) and districts were carried out continuously; Zhenhai district won the name of national ecological zone, Ninghai County and Xiangshan County passed national ecological county acceptance respectively, Beilun District passed technology assessment at national level, and accumulated 9 counties (cities) and districts were established as provincial ecological area.

"Peaceful Ningbo" construction: In 2014, there were 2,599 work safety accidents occurred in Ningbo, which resulted in 690 deaths, 2,480 injuries, such figures have dropped by 9.3%, 7.4%, 12.5% respectively when compared with those of last year. The three indicators of safety production have been lowered in the 10th consecutive year when compared with that of last year. Total 4 serious accidents occurred with 14 deaths, 20 people reduced. 6794 cases with all kinds of food safety violation were put on record and investigated in 2014, among which 1443 were major and serious criminal cases, ￥61.621 million were fined and 37 cases were transferred to public security organization as committing crimes. Work with public security organization to track down "3.13 fake medicine case", which has the amount of hundred million RMB related in case, 27 people were put into criminal detention. It is the largest case about food and drug administration in Ningbo. People's compromise organizations have mediated 115,900 civil disputes of all kinds during the whole year. Among these disputes, 114,500 disputes have been successfully settled through mediation with success rate of 98.7%. The 37 suicides committed by 37 people because of civil disputes have been prevented; 188 civil disputes involving 592 people have been prevented from developing into criminal cases. Total 7265 petition letters and visits were accepted during the whole year with down by 31.3%; 231 groups and 2877 people in collective petition were accepted, with down by 18.4% and 31.2%.

Note: (1) All figures in this Bulletin are preliminary statistics.

(2) Figures in value terms on gross municipal product and value-added quoted in this Bulletin are at current prices, whereas growth rates are calculated at comparable prices.

(3) Industrial enterprises above designated size refer to those enterprises with annual main business income equal to more than ￥20 million.

Wholesale, retail, accommodation and catering enterprises above the limit refer to:

Wholesale industry: wholesale enterprises with annual main business income equal to or more than ￥20 million;

Retail industry: retail enterprises with annual main business income equal to or more than ￥5 million;

Accommodation industry: enterprises with annual main business income equal to or more than ￥2 million;

Catering industry: catering enterprises with annual main business income equal to or more than ￥2 million.

(4) According to newly modified Budget Law, the expression of fiscal revenue was regulated as the original "local financial revenue" was changed to "general public budget revenue", with the specific statistical caliber unchanged.

(5) From July 2014, the passenger capacity of taxi was brought into scope of statistics of passenger transportation, so the data of whole passenger capacity in Ningbo cannot be compared with that of last year.

(6) Urban and rural resident's income refers to inhabitants' income.

NINGBO 2015 Statistical YearBook

CHAPTER 1

第一篇

综合

GENERAL SURVEY

综合
General Survey

宁波的经济发展
Economic Development of Ningbo

		2014	比上年增长(%) Increase Over Last Year
国内生产总值(亿元)	Gross Domestic Product(100 million yuan)	7610.28	7.6
第一产业	Primary Industry	275.70	2.0
第二产业	Secondary Industry	3980.41	8.1
第三产业	Tertiary Industry	3354.17	7.3
规模以上工业总产值	Gross Output Value of Above Designated Sized Industry	14028.05	7.8
固定资产投资	Investemnt in Fixed Assets	3989.46	16.6
社会消费品零售总额	Total Retail Sales of Consumer Goods	2992.03	13.5
财政总收入	Total Financal Revenue	1790.89	8.5
港口货物吞吐量(万吨)	Ports Cargo Handling Capacity(10000 tons)	52646	6.2
集装箱吞吐量(万标箱)	Container Handled at Ports(10000 TEU)	1870	11.5
自营进出口额(亿美元)	Directive Import and Export(USD 100 million)	1047.04	4.4
出口额(亿美元)	Export(USD 100 million)	731.09	11.3
实际利用外资	Amount of Foreign Capital Actually Used	40.25	22.9

宁波的一天
One Day in Ningbo

国内生产总值	Gross Domestic Product	208501	万元	10000 yuan
农业增加值	Value - added of Agriculture	7553	万元	10000 yuan
工业增加值	Value - added of Industry	96813	万元	10000 yuan
第三产业增加值	Value - added of Tertiary Industry	91895	万元	10000 yuan
固定资产投资	Investment in Fixed Assets	109300	万元	10000 yuan
社会消费品零售额	Retail of Consumer Goods	81973	万元	10000 yuan
财政总收入	Total Financal Revenue	49065	万元	10000 yuan
港口货物吞吐量	Ports Cargo Handling Capacity	144.24	万吨	10000 tons
集装箱吞吐量	Container Handled at Ports	51233	标箱	TEU
自营出口额	Directive Export	20030	万美元	USD 10000
全社会用电量	Electricity Consumption	15802	万千瓦时	10000 kwh

表1-1 行政区划和陆域面积(2014) Administrative Division and Land Area

单位:个(unit)

地区	Region	镇 Town	乡 Township	街道办事处 Subdistrict Offices	居民委员会 Neighborhood Committee	村民委员会 Villages Committee	陆域面积(平方公里) Land Area (sq. km)
全市	**Whole Municipality**	**76**	**10**	**66**	**680**	**2543**	**9816**
市区	**Urban Area**	**21**	**1**	**43**	**423**	**775**	**2462**
海曙	Haishu			8	76		29
江东	Jiangdong			8	81		34
江北	Jiangbei	1		7	68	87	208
北仑	Beilun	1		9	54	204	599
镇海	Zhenhai	2		4	33	60	246
鄞州	Yinzhou	17	1	7	111	424	1346
县级市	**County**	**55**	**9**	**23**	**257**	**1770**	**7354**
余姚	Yuyao	14	1	6	56	265	1501
慈溪	Cixi	14		5	78	297	1361
奉化	Fenghua	6		5	39	353	1268
象山	Xiangshan	10	5	3	45	490	1382
宁海	Ninghai	11	3	4	39	363	1843

表1-2 各月主要气象指标(2014) Main Climate Indicators

时间 Item	平均气温(℃) Average Temperature (℃)	降水量(毫米) Precipitation (millimeters)	相对湿度(%) Relative Humidity (%)	日照时数(小时) Sunshine Hours (hours)
1月 Jan.	7.3	26.9	71.0	195.7
2月 Feb.	7.0	132.4	82.0	68.9
3月 Mar.	12.5	77.3	72.0	154.4
4月 Apr.	16.4	85.9	76.0	120.3
5月 May	21.7	146.0	72.0	139.1
6月 June	23.9	186.1	82.0	90.2
7月 July	28.5	149.9	79.0	195.3
8月 Aug.	27.1	459.7	83.0	111.3
9月 Sept.	24.8	198.7	84.0	87.5
10月 Oct.	20.4	4.6	71.0	185.0
11月 Nov.	15.1	49.1	77.0	103.4
12月 Dec.	6.3	15.5	62.0	149.5

注:本表数据来自宁波市气象局。

Note: Data in this table are obtained from Ningbo Meteorological Bureau.

表1－3 部分年份国民经济主要指标
Main Indicators of National Economy in Partial Years

指标	单位	Indicators	Unit
人口		**Population**	
年末总人口	万人	Year－end Population	10000 persons
#非农业人口	万人	Non－Agriculture Population	10000 persons
地区生产总值	**亿元**	**Gross Domestic Product**	**100 million yuan**
第一产业增加值	亿元	Added Value of Primary Industry	100 million yuan
第二产业增加值	亿元	Added Value of Secondary Industry	100 million yuan
第三产业增加值	亿元	Added Value of Tertiary Industry	100 million yuan
人均生产总值(户籍人口)	**元**	**Per Capital GDP(by Registered Population)**	**yuan**
人均生产总值(常住人口)	**元**	**Per Capital GDP(by Permanent Population)**	**yuan**
农业		**Agriculture**	
农村实有劳动力	万人	Rural Labor force	10000 persons
粮食产量	万吨	Yield of Grain Crops	10000 tons
工业		**Industry**	
全部工业增加值	亿元	Added Value of Industry	100 million yuan
运输、邮电和通信		**Transportation. Post and Telecommunications Services**	
港口货物吞吐量	万吨	Cargo Handled at Ports	10000 tons
集装箱吞吐量	万标箱	Container Handled at Ports	10000 TEU
旅客运输量	万人	Passenger Traffic	10000 persons
货物运输量	万吨	Freight Traffic	10000 tons
固定电话用户	万户	Number of Local Telephone Subscribers	10000 subscribers
移动电话用户	万户	Number of Subscribers of Mobile Telephone	10000 subscribers
全社会用电量	**亿千瓦时**	**Total Consumption of Electricity**	**100 million kwh**
#工业用电	亿千瓦时	Electricity Consumption for Industry Use	100 million kwh
生活用电	亿千瓦时	Electricity Consumption for Urban and Rural Residents	100 million kwh
固定资产投资	**亿元**	**Investment in Fixed Assets**	**100 million yuan**
#房地产开发投资	亿元	Real Estate Development	100 million yuan

注:(1)本表价值量指标按当年价格计算,发展速度按可比价格计算;

(2)2014年为城乡住户一体化新口径,2013年(含)之前城镇均为市区口径,2013年(含)之前农村居民可支配收入指人均纯收入口径。

Note:Figures in value terms are calculated at current prices,While the indices and growth rates are calculated at comparable prices.

1978	2000	2010	2011	2012	2013	2014	指数(2014为以下各年%) Index(2014As Percentage of the Following Years) 1978	2000	2010	年平均增长(%) Average Annual Growth Rate(%) 1978-2014	2000-2014
457.70	540.94	574.08	576.40	577.71	580.15	583.78	127.5	107.9	101.7	0.7	0.5
63.42	142.03	205.23	208.18	211.45	214.35	217.73	343.3	153.3	106.1	3.5	3.1
20.17	**1144.57**	**5181.00**	**6074.94**	**6601.21**	**7164.51**	**7610.28**	**9960.9**	**462.9**	**137.9**	**13.6**	**11.6**
6.52	94.24	219.13	255.23	268.51	272.06	275.70	466.1	157.5	105.4	4.4	3.3
9.69	635.83	2856.74	3315.76	3475.08	3680.97	3980.41	17274.4	463.7	135.6	15.4	11.6
3.96	414.50	2105.13	2503.95	2857.62	3211.48	3354.17	12587.3	530.8	144.1	14.4	12.7
437	**21208**	**90490**	**105606**	**114394**	**123754**	**130769**	**7244.9**	**421.9**	**135.8**	**12.6**	**10.8**
		69610	**79730**	**86477**	**93641**	**98362**			**141.3**		
195.42	257.44	306.32	306.36	293.79	312.07	304.88	156.0	118.4	99.5	1.2	1.2
180.51	132.51	87.13	90.14	86.57	81.25	74.15	41.1	56.0	85.1	-2.4	-4.1
8.62	578.30	2559.64	2963.12	3097.25	3282.48	3533.68	22278.6	473.4	136.0	16.2	11.7
214	11547	41217	43339	45303	49592	52646	24601.1	455.9	127.7	16.5	11.4
	90.20	1300.35	1451.24	1567.14	1677.37	1870.00		2073.2	143.8		24.2
2966	22736	33911	28745	28053	24793	16508	556.6	72.6	48.7	4.9	-2.3
1385	10819	30553	31228	32616	35409	40407	2917.4	373.5	132.3	9.8	9.9
1.07	130.15	317.39	312.45	308	298	270	25233.6	207.5	85.1	16.6	5.4
	117.92	845.50	1029.46	1088	1228	1267		1074.5	149.9		18.5
7.09	**113.48**	**459.04**	**505.30**	**514.09**	**559.39**	**576.78**	**8135.1**	**508.3**	**125.6**	**13.0**	**12.3**
4.37	84.01	354.27	388.62	384.59	414.98	435.25	9960.0	518.1	122.9	13.6	12.5
0.43	15.13	49.83	53.59	59.31	66.13	60.83	14146.5	402.0	122.1	14.7	10.4
5.02	**360.75**	**2193.28**	**2385.50**	**2901.43**	**3422.95**	**3989.46**	**79471.3**	**1105.9**	**181.9**	**20.4**	**18.7**
	59.71	557.27	754.94	884.35	1123.14	1328.14		2224.3	238.3		24.8

表 1－3 续表 Continued

指标	单位	Indicators	Unit
财政金融		**Finance and Banking**	
财政总收入	亿元	Financial Budgetary Revenue	100 million yuan
#一般公共预算收入	亿元	General Public Budget Revenue	100 million yuan
一般公共预算支出	亿元	General Public Fiscal Budget Expenditure	100 million yuan
年末金融机构存款余额	亿元	Balance of Deposits of Financial Institutions	100 million yuan
#城乡居民储蓄存款	亿元	Saving Deposits of Urban and Rural Residents	100 million yuan
年末金融机构贷款余额	亿元	Balance of Loans of Financial Institutions	100 million yuan
社会消费品零售总额	**亿元**	**Total Retail Sales of Consumer Goods**	**100 million yuan**
对外经济		**Foreign Trade**	
进出口总额	亿美元	Total Exports and Imports Value	USD 100 million
#出口总额	亿美元	Total Exports Value	USD 100 million
进口总额	亿美元	Total Imports Value	USD 100 million
合同利用外资	亿美元	Foreign Investment Contracted	USD 100 million
实际利用外资	亿美元	Foreign Investments Actually Use	USD 100 million
城乡居民生活		**Living Standard**	
城镇居民人均可支配收入	元	Per Capital Disposable Income of Urban Households	yuan
城镇居民人均生活消费支出	元	Per Capital Annual Expenditure for Consumption of Urban Households	yuan
农村居民人均可支配收入	元	Per Capital Annual Disposable Income of Rural Housholds	yuan
农村居民人均生活消费支出	元	Per Capita Annual Living Expenditure of Rural Residents	yuan
教育		**Education**	
高等学校在校学生数	万人	Students Enrollment in Institutions of Higher Education	10000 persons
中等专业学校在校学生数	万人	Students Enrollment in Specializad Secondary Schools	10000 persons
中学在校学生数	万人	Students Enrollment in Secondary Schools	10000 persons
小学在校学生数	万人	Students Enrollment in Primary Schools	10000 persons
专任教师数	万人	Number of Full－times Teachers	10000 persons
卫生事业		**Health Care**	
卫生技术人员数	万人	Number of Medical Technical Personnel	10000 persons
#医生	万人	Doctor	10000 persons
卫生机构床位数	张	Number of Beds in Health Institutions	bed

1978	2000	2010	2011	2012	2013	2014	指数(2014为以下各年%) Index(2014As Percentage of the Following Years) 1978	2000	2010	年平均增长(%) Average Annual Growth Rate(%) 1978－2014	2000－2014
4.97	143.15	1171.75	1431.76	1536.51	1651.18	1790.89	36034.0	1251.1	152.8	17.8	19.8
	64.35	530.93	657.55	725.50	792.81	860.61		1337.4	162.1		20.4
	83.91	600.75	750.72	828.44	939.89	1000.86		1192.8	166.6		19.4
4.84	1172.94	9552.03	10435.92	11602.32	12740.52	13307.41	274946.5	1134.5	139.3	24.6	18.9
1.52	586.06	3282.26	3666.23	4175.96	4562.36	4780.31	314494.1	815.7	145.6	25.1	16.2
6.50	883.12	9000.62	10209.99	11300.32	12493.28	13610.61	209394.0	1541.2	151.2	23.7	21.6
7.07	**389.29**	**1704.51**	**2018.86**	**2329.26**	**2635.71**	**2992.03**	**42320.1**	**768.6**	**175.5**	**18.3**	**15.7**
	75.41	829.04	981.87	965.73	1003.29	1047.04		1388.5	126.3		20.7
	51.68	519.67	608.32	614.45	657.10	731.09		1414.6	140.7		20.8
	23.73	309.37	373.55	351.27	346.19	315.95		1331.4	102.1		20.3
	9.52	40.46	50.15	53.13	58.20	70.21		737.5	173.5		15.3
	6.22	23.23	28.09	28.53	32.75	40.25		647.1	173.2		14.3
306	10921	30166	34058	37902	41729	44155	14429.7	404.3	146.4	14.8	10.5
299	7997	19420	21779	23288	24685	27893	9328.8	348.8	143.6	13.4	9.3
	5069	14261	16518	18475	20534	24283		479.0	170.3		11.8
	3929	9794	11253	12699	13915	16228		413.0	165.7		10.7
0.10	2.59	14.08	14.44	14.54	14.90	15.09	15090.0	582.6	107.2	15.0	13.4
0.29	2.51	8.07	8.28	8.03	7.83	6.93	2389.7	276.1	85.8	9.2	7.5
27.16	27.98	32.54	30.86	29.52	28.59	28.01	103.1	100.1	86.1	0.1	0.0
59.11	42.40	46.19	47.61	47.88	48.70	48.26	81.6	113.8	104.5	-0.6	0.9
3.55	5.17	7.29	7.70	7.63	7.82	7.96	224.2	154.0	109.2	2.3	3.1
0.93	1.92	4.31	4.67	4.92	5.15	5.41	581.7	281.8	125.5	5.0	7.7
0.36	0.95	1.72	1.84	1.91	1.99	2.10	583.3	221.1	122.1	5.0	5.8
5989	14535	26097	27127	28290	29356	30852	515.1	212.3	118.2	4.7	5.5

表1-4 各县(市)社会经济基本情况(2014)
Main Indicators of Society and Economy by Region

指标	单位	Indicators	Unit
人口、劳动力及土地面积		**Population, Employment and Land Areas**	
年末总人口	万人	Year - end Population	10000 persons
年平均人口	万人	Annual Average Population	10000 persons
常住人口	万人	Permanent Population	10000 persons
年末总户数	万户	Total Households of Year - end	10000 households
全社会从业人员	万人	Total Employment Personnel	10000 persons
第一产业	万人	Primary Industry	10000 persons
第二产业	万人	Secondary Industry	10000 persons
第三产业	万人	Tertiary Industry	10000 persons
年末城镇集体以上从业人员数	万人	Employed Personnel in Urban Collective - owned Units and Above Level	10000 persons
第一产业	万人	Primary Industry	10000 persons
第二产业	万人	Secondary Industry	10000 persons
第三产业	万人	Tertiary Industry	10000 persons
城镇私营和个体从业人员	人	Employed Persons Individuals and Private Enterprises in Urban Areas	person
年末城镇登记失业人员数	人	Unemployed Persons in Urban Areas at Year - end	person
行政区域土地面积	平方公里	Land Area of Districts	sq. km
#建成区面积	平方公里	Developed Areas	sq. km
综合经济		**General Economy**	
生产总值(当年价格)	万元	Gross Domestic Product(at Current Price)	10000 yuan
第一产业增加值	万元	Value - added of Primary Industry	10000 yuan
第二产业增加值	万元	Value - added of Secondary Industry	10000 yuan
#工业增加值	万元	Value - added of Industry	10000 yuan
第三产业增加值	万元	Value - added of Tertiary Industry	10000 yuan
人均生产总值(常住)	元	Per Capital GDP(by Permanent Population)	yuan
人均生产总值(户籍)	元	Per Capital GDP(by Registered Population)	yuan
生产总值增长率	%	Increase Rate of GDP Ovcr 2012	%
地方财政收入	万元	Local Financial Revenue	10000 yuan
公共财政预算支出	万元	Public Fiscal Budget Revenue	10000 yuan
#一般性公共服务支出	万元	Expenditure for General Public Services	10000 yuan
科学技术支出	万元	Expenditure for Science and Technology Promotion	10000 yuan
教育支出	万元	Expenditure for Education	10000 yuan
文化体育与传媒支出	万元	Expenditure for Culture, Sports & Media Services	10000 yuan
医疗卫生支出	万元	Expenditure for Medical and Health	10000 yuan
节能保护支出	万元	Expenditure for Energy Saving and Environmental Protection	10000 yuan
城乡社区事务支出	万元	Expenditure for Urban and Rural Community Services	10000 yuan
交通运输支出	万元	Expenditure for Transportation	10000 yuan
社会保障和就业支出	万元	Expenditure for Social Security & Employment	10000 yuan
住房保障支出	万元	Expenditure for Housing Security	10000 yuan

注:本表非年报数据。
Note: Data in this table was not reported data.

全市 Total	市区 Urban District	#鄞州 Yinzhou	余姚 Yuyao	慈溪 Cixi	奉化 Fenghua	象山 Xiangshan	宁海 Ninghai
583.78	229.64	85.20	83.67	104.59	48.37	54.86	62.64
581.96	228.62	84.61	83.59	104.48	48.37	54.62	62.29
781.1	360.2	138.15	102.93	148.91	50.02	51.82	67.22
224.07	91.35	34.21	30.78	42.17	18.21	18.35	23.21
511.5	242.00	99.77	65.90	83.80	35.82	36.34	48.10
19.39		5.53	6.48	10.20	6.35	8.07	8.00
273.16	132.00	57.75	33.02	49.70	18.53	17.11	22.60
218.95	129.00	36.49	26.40	23.90	10.94	11.16	17.50
171.70	94.59	24.52	15.11	14.44	6.03	30.27	7.09
0.05	0.02						0.01
110.57	53.77	16.92	10.77	9.46	3.62	27.37	3.79
61.08	40.80	7.61	4.33	4.93	2.40	2.89	3.29
1869300	1294800	489500	188700	67000	107500	83300	128000
67187	55411	11462	2338	2749	2265	3296	1128
9816.23	2462.00	1345.54	1500.80	1360.63	1267.60	1382.18	1843.26
484.75	308.56		49.24	44.50	18.75	28.61	35.09
76102816	45893046	12966399	8043565	11094102	3089895	3880832	4101376
2756982	601232	393393	413400	484849	285034	579451	393016
39804092	23403124	7618244	4677313	6379252	1405983	1806461	2131959
35336797	20884457	7103263	4223413	5879517	1184305	1296603	1868502
33541742	21888690	4954762	2952852	4230001	1398878	1494920	1576401
98362	128863	94257	78650	74947	62083	75495	62057
130769	200743	153254	96227	106186	63877	71052	65847
7.6	7.4	8.5	8.5	8.4	6.4	7.0	6.5
8606109	5975334	1662205	648070	1000151	290233	331678	360643
10008563	6611346	1682225	804673	1078856	476853	527444	509391
1001565	659614	142765	83367	107408	51344	48108	51724
428212	295616	90626	30487	55720	18267	14067	14055
1596238	936153	260028	154466	220641	91463	90098	103417
169089	124713	24031	13090	11512	5023	7298	7453
746057	407246	129044	98722	101773	36569	42480	59267
190750	135423	68788	11166	18106	10162	7742	8151
1090941	963106	130995	30431	42962	23134	19826	11482
585244	436280	80214	40338	25291	17197	24215	41923
946512	603999	150665	96247	103230	41340	38864	62832
289635	229939	92887	9367	18874	7692	12408	11355

表 1 -4 续 1 Continued

指标	单位	Indicators	Unit
农林水事务支出	万元	Expenditure for Farming, Forestry and Fishery Service	10000 yuan
年末金融机构存款余额	万元	Balance of Deposits of Financial Institutions	10000 yuan
#城乡居民储蓄年末余额	万元	Saving Deposits of Urban and Rural Residents	10000 yuan
年末金融机构各项贷款余额	万元	Balance of Loans of Financial Institutions	10000 yuan
保险		**Insurance**	
保费收入	万元	Insurance Income	10000 yuan
#财产险	万元	Property Insurance	10000 yuan
人身险	万元	Life Insurance	10000 yuan
赔款、给付	万元	Insurance Paid	10000 yuan
规模以上工业企业		**Industry Enterprises Above Designated Size**	
工业企业数	个	Number of Industrial Enterprises	unit
从业人员年平均人数	万人	Annual Average Employees	10000 persons
工业总产值(当年价)	万元	Gross Output Value of Indutry (at current price)	10000 yuan
主营业务收入	万元	Prime Operating Revenue	10000 yuan
本年应交增值税	万元	Value - added Taxes Payable in This Year	10000 yuan
利润总额	万元	Total Profits	10000 yuan
交通运输、邮电通信、能源电力		**Transport, Post & Telecommunications, Energy and Electricity**	
铁路客运量	万人	Railway Passenger Traffic	10000 persons
铁路货运量	万吨	Railway Freight Traffic	10000 tons
公路客运量	万人	Highways Passenger Traffic	10000 persons
公路货运量	万吨	Highways Freight Traffic	10000 tons
水运客运量	万人	Waterways Passenger Traffic	10000 persons
水运货运量	万吨	Waterways Freight Traffic	10000 tons
民用航空客运量	万人	Civil Aviation Passenger Traffic	10000 persons
民用航空货邮运量	万吨	Civil Aviation Freight Traffic	10000 ton
民用汽车拥有量	辆	Number of Civil Motor Vehicles	unit
#私人汽车拥有量	辆	Number of Private Car	unit
公路里程	公里	Length of Highways	km
邮政业务收入	万元	Business Value of Post	10000 yuan
电信业务收入	万元	Business Value of Telecommunications	10000 yuan
本地电话用户数	万户	Number of Subscribers of Local Telephone	10000 subscribers
年末移动电话用户数	万户	Number of Mobile Telephone Subscribers at Year - end	10000 subscribers
#3G 移动电话用户	万户	User of 3G Mobile Phone	10000 subscribers
国际互联网用户数	万户	User of International Computer Network	10000 subscribers
能源消费量	万吨标准煤	Total Volume of Energy Consumptions	10000 tons SCE
全年用电量	万千瓦时	Electricity Consumption	10000 kwh
国内贸易、对外经济		Domestic Trade, Foreign Trade	

全市 Total	市区 Urban District	#鄞州 Yinzhou	余姚 Yuyao	慈溪 Cixi	奉化 Fenghua	象山 Xiangshan	宁海 Ninghai
819579	250694	106351	132577	104961	114980	147261	69106
133074057.36	91311400.29	16967727.54	11818683.34	16786956.76	4411759.79	4239794.55	4505462.62
47803125.97	26554803.27	7669925.06	6102543.29	8799375.56	2441900.84	1862886.16	2041616.85
136106068.68	89379873.60	15166859.81	12190861.17	17578427.52	5196727.77	6038970.10	5721208.52
2069615.68							
1115660.87							
953954.82							
946689.21							
7383	3461	1763	1193	1323	445	464	497
151.84	77.02	33.84	20.56	28.46	9.02	7.21	9.58
140280500	91816608	23619286	13354244	19831411	3763341	5396165	6118732
132546456	86797915	22885792	12779379	18743213	3584924	4938831	5702195
3533825	2162975	532230	324550	543433	102148	154892	245828
6882464	4497107	1448237	606148	824292	107142	339367	508409
3771.30	2816.05		713.21		49.87		192.17
2364.15	2200.57	27.37	95.86	67.71			
12144.00	4309.48	1095.57	324.37	1380.23	2048.82	2108.40	1972.70
21918.43	15853.00	4385.00	1595.43	1570.00	1220.00	820.00	860.00
171.17	32.65	15.06	0.51			88.90	49.11
16112.89	12098.38	839.54	15.03	13.50	395.00	2676.99	913.99
635.91	635.91	635.91					
113803.6	113803.6	113803.6					
1597218	874986	286672	202880	252620	90338	86611	89783
1237026	656077	217076	161329	204715	70886	72637	71382
11045.41	3343.73	1941.68	1937.04	1571.89	1303.15	1317.94	1571.66
82629	41071		10685	17321	5438	3209	4905
1204763	738663	181183	126373	210879	58511		70338
270.00	147.76	55.40	33.92	41.63	15.42	16.84	14.43
1267.00	598.60	229.17	161.56	285.73	64.17	76.90	80.04
507.5							
281.00		43.65	33.83	40.89	14.25	17.19	16.48
3741.3	2198.3	515.7	449.0	572.1	125.2	222.5	174.2
5767786.6	3181606.2	770919.3	733023.4	1116872.5	278990.8	195245.2	262048.5

表 1－4 续 2 Continued

指标	单位	Indicators	Unit
社会消费品零售额	万元	Total Retail Sales of Consumer Goods	10000 yuan
当年新签合同项目数	个	New Signed Constract	unit
当年实际使用外资金额	万美元	Amount of Foreign Capital Actually Used	USD 10000
进口额	万美元	Total Import	USD 10000
出口额	万美元	Total Export	USD 10000
固定资产投资		**Investemnt in Fixed Assets**	
固定资产投资	万元	Investment in Fixed Assets	10000 yuan
#房地产开发投资完成额	万元	Real Estate Development	10000 yuan
#住宅	万元	Residential Buildings	10000 yuan
全年新增固定资产	万元	Newly Increase Fixed Assets in This Year	10000 yuan
商品房屋销售面积	万平方米	Floor Space of Building Sold	10000 sq. m
#住宅	万平方米	Residential Buildings	10000 sq. m
商品房屋销售额	万元	Total Actually Sales of Commercial Buildings	10000 yuan
#住宅	万元	Residential Buildings	10000 yuan
待售面积	万平方米	Floor Space of Sale Building	10000 sq. m
文教、卫生、科技		**Culture, Education, Public Health, Science**	
全日制学校数	所	Number of Full－time Schools	unit
各类学校专任教师数	人	Teachers	person
各类学校在校学生数	人	Students in School	person
专利申请受理量	项	Number of Patent Appliactions	piece
专利申请授权量	项	Number of Patent Certified	piece
#发明专利	项	Inventions	piece
体育场馆数	个	Number of Public Stadiums and Gymnasiums	unit
剧场、影剧院数	个	Number of Cinemas and Theatres	unit
公共图书馆图书藏量	千册、件	Collection of Public Libraries	1000 copies
医院、卫生院数	个	Number of Health Institutions	unit
卫生机构床位数	张	Number of Beds in Health Institutions	bed
医生数	人	Number of Doctors	person
注册护士	人	Number of Register Nurses	person
人民生活		**People's Livelihood**	
在岗职工平均人数	万人	Number of Full Employed Staff and Workers	10000 persons
在岗职工工资总额	万元	Total Wage of Full Employed Staff and Workers	10000 yuan
城镇居民人均可支配收入	元	Per Capital Annual Disposable Income of Urban Residents	yuan
城镇居民人均消费支出	元	Per Capital Annual Expenditure for Consumption of Urban Residents	yuan
农村居民人均纯收入	元	Per Capital Annual Net Income of Rural Residents	yuan
农村居民人均消费性支出	元	Per Capital Annual Expenditure for Consumption of Rural Residents	yuan
居民消费价格指数(上年＝100)	%	Consumer Price Index (Preceding Year＝100)	%

全市 Total	市区 Urban District	#鄞州 Yinzhou	余姚 Yuyao	慈溪 Cixi	奉化 Fenghua	象山 Xiangshan	宁海 Ninghai
29920296.5	16197617.5	4049648.0	3880757.5	4848567.0	1446516.4	1883153.9	1663684.2
468	311	91	66	32	13	29	17
402514	286706	58874	39133	43717	11745	10013	11200
3159502	2668298.00	257363.00	208899.00	198352.00	41704.00	18234.00	24015.00
7310904	4953985	1207326	708408	937140	253201	235448	222722
39894626	22452497	5933325	5156152	6360715	1821652	1852034	2251576
13281390	8485334	2503754	1403302	1781399	546751	528123	536481
7732540	4685346	1552799	775534	1234033	376104	380440	281083
27485651	14750141	3162524	4387679	4668089	891292	1239680	1548770
726.44	458.56	185.62	81.27	83.51	27.02	32.81	43.26
595.20	373.24	164.32	64.20	69.49	22.30	31.90	34.06
7805375	5446111	2241854	680931	716486	263792	344254	353801
6481530	4550787	2010850	528069	583997	220339	335372	262966
677.24	385.20	73.90	97.31	83.56	30.08	27.64	53.44
2080		303	306	409	156	148	225
79578		8860	7256	10513	3880	4139	4906
1317239		185655	148835	200746	74076	83273	109529
58530	32262	17224	8645	9879	1885	2623	3236
43286	22342	12081	7093	7867	1335	1939	2710
2832	1884	697	259	385	96	88	120
128	72	24	11	29	8	3	5
90	60	25	5	7	9	4	5
7218.0	4956.0	1316.5	578.4	666.2	219.5	421.6	376.3
233	94	29	22	33	31	25	28
29652	17905	3472	2676	3361	2196	1879	1635
20984	11733	3021	2124	3126	1315	1211	1475
20864	12135	2639	2214	2925	1134	1137	1319
146.15	81.93	22.50	13.61	13.48	5.57	21.65	6.24
10263767.80	6248840.00	1574073.60	838338.80	875305.30	356151.10	1236564.30	409580.80
44155	47190	46324	41921	43526	38755	40189	40664
27893	30674	30307	27109	27714	28522	18587	25363
24283	25815	26682	24312	25041	22033	22146	22209
16228	16363	18697	17977	18118	13492	12666	14935
101.9	101.9		101.9	101.7	102.1	101.7	101.6

表 1－4 续 3 Continued

指标	单位	Indicators	Unit
基本养老保险参保人数	人	Number of Personnel Engaged Basic Endowment Insurance	person
基本医疗保险参保人数	人	Number of Personnel Engaged Basic Medical Insurance	person
失业保险参保人数	人	Number of Personnel Engaged Unemployment Insurance	person
社会福利院床位数	张	Number of Beds in Social Welfare Institutions	bed
社区服务设施数	个	Volunm of Service Establishment in Community	unit
城镇居民最低生活保障人数	人	Number Personnel Below Minimum Standard of Living	person
社会治安		**Social Security**	
交通事故死亡人数	人	Death of Traffic Accidents	person
交通事故损失额	万元	Losses Converted into Cash of Traffic Accidents	10000 yuan
刑事案件立案数	件	Number of Criminal Cases Registered	case
犯罪人数	人	Number of People of the Crime	person
市政公用事业		**Civil Facilities, Environment Protection**	
城市维护建设资金支出	万元	Expenditure on Urban Construction and Maintenance	10000 yuan
年末实有城市道路面积	万平方米	Area of City Roads(Year－end)	10000 sq. m
排水管道总长度	公里	Length of Sewage Pipes	km
供水综合生产能力(含自备水源)	万吨/日	General Productive Capacity of Tap Water Supply	10000 tons/day
全年售水总量	万吨	Annuall Volume of Tap Water Sale	10000 tons
#居民家庭用水量	万吨	Water Consumption for Residents Use	10000 tons
用水人口	万人	Population with Access Tap Water	10000 persons
液化石油气供气总量	吨	Total Volume of Liquefied Petroleum Gas	ton
#家庭用量	吨	For Residents Use	ton
用液化气人口	万人	Population with Access Liquefied Petroleum Gas	10000 persons
年末实有公共汽(电)车营运车辆数	辆	Number of Public Transportations Vehicles under Operation	unit
全年公共汽(电)车客运总量	万人次	Number of Passengers Carried with Public Transportations Vehicles	10000 person－times
年末实有出租汽车数	辆	Operating Taxes at	Year－end
绿地面积	公顷	Green Areas	hectare
#公园绿地面积	公顷	Public Green Areas	hectare
建成区绿化覆盖面积	公顷	Coverage Area of Green Area in Developed Area	hectare
环境保护		**Environment Protect**	
工业废水排放量	万吨	Valume of Industrial Waste Water Discharged	10000 tons
工业二氧化硫产生量	吨	Volume of Industrial sulfur dioxide production	ton
工业二氧化硫排放量	吨	Volume of Industrial Sulphur Dioxide Emission	ton
工业烟(粉)尘排放量	吨	Volume of Industrial Soot Emission	ton
一般工业固体废物综合利用率	%	Rate of General Industrial Solid Waste Treated and Utilized	%
污水处理厂集中处理率	%	Rate of Disposal Living Waste Water in Sewage Treatment Plant	%
生活垃圾无害化处理率	%	Rate of Living Garbage Harmless Treatment	%

全市 Total	市区 Urban District	#鄞州 Yinzhou	余姚 Yuyao	慈溪 Cixi	奉化 Fenghua	象山 Xiangshan	宁海 Ninghai
5422266	3232930	914737	634136	789502	252297	239107	274294
4786997	3106863	794148	577522	422141	259395	199616	221460
2433876	1663595	451148	205990	248479	99179	107021	109612
41996	20589	9313	5609	4178	2863	5225	3532
2523	1008	92	582	374	33	500	26
7712	5303	567	698	491	575	407	238
605	230	93	105	110	46	33	50
710.29	285.49	85.13	76.95	59.32	119.79	72.44	61.91
13299	6043	1681	1946	2052	1244	1081	933
17893	8286	2323	2662	2858	1544	1222	1323
1301041	762250		53227	266974	11314	185060	22216
7423.94	2950.83		1071.97	1716.50	434.65	741.29	508.70
8099.21	4669.97		771.21	1299.00	206.60	564.63	587.80
366.8	225.0		32.5	44.0	20.8	21.5	23.0
64372.17	42721.66		4527.22	8921	2651	2999.39	2551.9
27568.59	18520.81		2141.29	2976	1317	1194.79	1418.7
355.46	186.32		44.9	51.79	33.28	20.59	18.58
162309.16	98346		4932	29910	6483	13976	8663
99944.04	47006		3629	27980	5318	9470	6541
1565900	300000		270000	400000	250000	205900	140000
6570	4516	1549	631	709	227	270	217
68955.0	49468.6	13114.9	6356.5	5754.6	2014.8	2553.5	2807.0
6370	4627	1603	450	605	200	210	278
18682.56	11390.00		2103.96	1911.97	975.68	977.95	1323.00
4068.8	1983.0		481.1	673.3	401.0	285.4	245.0
18685.42	11811.00		2086.94	1745.29	764.20	863.99	1414.00
16545.63	10678.03	1202.08	1381.34	1588.65	899.42	1373.73	624.47
523570.78	375318.26	10335.10	5786.74	9966.92	2761.44	52544.15	77193.27
118101.6	79723.24	3213.34	3894.63	8174.76	2352.77	9064.46	14891.73
30577.38	20066.29	622.53	2904.25	2021.61	384.46	2884.35	2316.42
90.76	82.00	86.44	89.33	47.12	65.64	91.17	98.56
81.11	78.97		86.30	86.00	85.18	79.94	88.15
100.00	100.00		100.00	100.00	100.00	100.00	100.00

表 1－5　部分年份经济社会结构指标
Structural Indicators of Society and Economy in Partial Years

单位:%

指标	Indicators	2010	2011	2012	2013	2014
生产总值产业结构	**Industrial Structure of GDP**					
第一产业	Primary Industry	4.2	4.2	4.1	3.8	3.6
第二产业	Secondary Industry	55.1	54.6	52.6	51.4	52.3
第三产业	Tertiary Industry	40.6	41.2	43.3	44.8	44.1
农林牧渔业产值结构	**Structure of Agricultural Gross Output Value**					
农业	Farming	49.3	48.2	47.9	47.2	48.4
林业	Forestry	2.9	2.7	2.7	2.7	2.9
牧业	Animal Husbandry	15.2	15.7	15.4	14.1	12.3
渔业	Fishery	31.1	32.1	32.6	34.6	34.8
农林牧渔服务业	Services	1.4	1.3	1.4	1.4	1.5
规模以上工业总产值比例	**Structure of Gross Industrial Output Value**					
轻工业	Light Industry	31.4	28.8	28.0	28.0	27.6
重工业	Heavy Industry	75.4	71.2	72.0	72.0	72.4
全社会固定资产投资产业结构	**Industrial Structure of Fixed Assets Investment**					
第一产业	Primary Industry	0.5	0.8	0.9	0.6	1.1
第二产业	Secondary Industry	31.8	28.0	28.3	31.2	31.7
第三产业	Tertiary Industry	67.7	71.2	70.8	68.2	67.2
自营进出口结构	**Structure of Directive Import and Export**					
出口	Exports	62.7	62.0	63.6	65.5	69.8
进口	Imports	37.3	38.0	36.4	34.5	30.2
社会消费品零售额结构	**Structure of Retail Sales of Consumer Goods**					
批发和零售贸易业	Wholesale and Retail Sale Trades	90.7	90.9	90.8	91.2	91.2
餐饮业	Catering Trade	9.3	9.1	9.2	8.8	8.8
其他	Others					
农业人口与非农业人口比例	**Structure of Population by Agriculture and Non－argiculture**					
农业人口	Agriculture	64.3	63.9	63.4	63.1	62.7
非农业人口	Non－Agriculture	35.7	36.1	36.6	36.9	37.3

表1-6 部分年份平均每天主要社会经济活动
Indicators on Average Daily Social and Economic Activities in Partial Years

指标	单位	Indicators	unit	2000	2010	2011	2013	2014
平均每天创造财富		**Daily Production**						
生产总值	万元	Gross Domestic Product	10000 yuan	31358	141945	166437	196288	208501
第一产业	万元	Primary Industry	10000 yuan	2582	6004	6993	7454	7553
第二产业	万元	Secondary Industry	10000 yuan	17420	78267	90843	100848	109052
#工业增加值	万元	Added - value of Industry	10000 yuan	15844	70127	81181	89931	96813
第三产业	万元	Tertiary Industry	10000 yuan	11356	57675	68601	87986	91895
财政总收入	万元	Financial Revenue	10000 yuan	3922	32103	39226	45238	49065
一般公共预算收入	万元	General Public Budget Revenue	10000 yuan	1763	14546	18015	21721	23578
每天其他经济活动		**Other Daily Economic Activities**						
固定资产投资额	万元	Invesment in Fixed Assets	10000 yuan	9884	60452	65356	93780	109300
社会消费品零售总额	万元	Total Retail Sales of Consumer Goods	10000 yuan	10666	46699	55311	72211	81973
港口货物吞吐量	万吨	Cargo Throughput	10000 tons	31.64	112.92	118.74	135.87	144.24
集装箱吞吐量	标箱	Container Throughput	TEU	2471	35627	39760	45955	51233
全社会用电量	万千瓦时	Total Electricity Consumption	10000 kwh	3109	12577	13844	15326	15802
#工业用电量	万千瓦时	Industrial Electricity Consumption	10000 kwh	2302	9706	10647	11369	11925
客运量	万人	Passenger Traffic	10000 persons	62.29	92.91	78.75	67.93	45.23
货运量	万吨	Freight Traffic	10000 tons	29.64	83.71	85.56	97.01	110.70
进出口总额	万美元	Total Imports and Exports	USD 10000	2066	22713	26900	27487	28686
#出口	万美元	Exports	USD 10000	1416	14238	16666	18003	20030
实际利用外资	万美元	Foreign Capital Actually Used	USD 10000	170	637	770	897	1103
人口变动和婚姻		**Population Changes and Marriages**						
出生	人	Births	person	137	134	126	135	155
死亡	人	Deaths	person	92	97	95	97	97
结婚	对	Marriages	couple	111	146	136	147	158
离婚	对	Divorces	couple	10	38	38	45	41

注:本表价值量指标按当年价格计算。

Note:The data in value terms in the table are calculated at current prices.

表1-7 部分年份国民经济主要指标人均水平
Main Per Capita Indicators of National Economy in Partial Years

单位:元(yuan)

指标	Indicators	2000	2010	2011	2013	2014
经济活动	**Economical Indicators**					
生产总值(户籍)	Gross Domestic Products(by Registered Population)	21208	90490	105606	123754	130769
农业总产值	Gross Agritural Output Value	2749	5931	6918	7405	7431
固定资产投资额	Investment in Fixed Assets	6685	38307	41470	59125	68552
社会消费品零售总额	Total Retail Sales of Consumer Goods	7213	29769	35096	45527	51413
自营进出口额(美元)	Directive Exports and Imports(USD)	1397	14480	17069	17330	17991
#出口(美元)	Export(USD)	958	9076	10575	11350	12562
实际利用外资(美元)	Foreign Capital Actually Used(USD)	115	406	488	566	692
财政总收入	Financial Revenue	2653	20465	24890	28521	30773
一般公共预算收入	General Public Budget Revenue	1192	9273	11431	13694	14788
公共财政预算支出	Public Fiscal Budget Expenditure	1653	10492	13051	16235	22822
人民生活	**People's Livelihood**					
城镇集体以上在岗职工工资	Avergae Wage of Working Staff and Workers in Urban Collective - owned Units and Above	14823	43476	49755	63152	70226
城镇居民人均可支配收入	Annual Disposable Income of Urban Residents	9193	30166	34058	41729	44155
城镇居民人均消费性支出	Annual Living Expenditures of Urban Residents	7912	19420	21779	24685	27893
农村居民人均可支配收入	Annual Net Income of Rural Residents	4697	14261	16518	20534	24283
农村居民生活消费支出	Annual Living Expenditure of Rural Residents	3929	9794	11253	13915	16228
城乡居民储蓄存款余额	Balance of Saving Deposits of Urban and Rural Households	10859	57850	63734	78807	82141
人均生活用电量(千瓦时)	Residential Electricity Consumption(kwh)	280	870	932	1142	1045
社会事业	**Society Indicators**					
人均拥有道路面积(平方米)	Per Capita Area of Roads (sq. m)	13.85	19.65	20.44	20.54	20.89
人均公园绿地面积(平方米)	Per Capita Public Green Area (sq. m)	7.32	10.62	10.80	11.25	11.45

表1-8 部分年份社会经济发展相对指标
Relative Indicators on Social and Economic Development in Partial Yeats

指标	Indicators	2000	2010	2011	2013	2014
人口与劳动力	**Population and Labor**					
出生率(‰)	Birth Rate(‰)	9.3	8.5	8.0	8.5	9.7
死亡率(‰)	Death Rate(‰)	6.2	6.2	6.1	6.1	6.1
自然增长率(‰)	Natural Growth Rate(‰)	3.1	2.3	2.0	2.4	3.6
人口净迁移率(‰)	Migration Rate(‰)	2.3	3.4	2.4	2.0	3.1
全社会从业人员结构（%）	Structure of Total Employment Personnel（%）					
第一产业比重	Perentage of Primary Industry	31.0	6.8	6.6	5.7	3.8
第二产业比重	Perentage of Secondary Industry	43.1	55.9	55.4	54.4	53.4
第三产业比重	Perentage of Tertiary Industry	25.9	37.3	38.0	39.8	42.8
国民经济	**Domestic Economic**					
第三产业占GDP比重（%）	Perentage of Tertiary Industry as GDP（%）	36.2	40.6	41.2	44.8	44.1
固定资产投资占GDP比重(%)	Perentage of Investment in Fixed Assets as GDP（%）	31.5	39.3	39.3	47.8	52.4
社会消费品零售额占GDP比重(%)	Perentage of Total Retail Sales of Cunsumer Goods as GDP（%）	34.0	32.9	33.2	36.8	39.3
财政总收入占GDP比重(%)	Total Fiscal Revenue as Percentage of GDP（%）	12.9	22.6	23.6	23.0	23.5
进出口总额占GDP比重(%)	Total Value of Imports and Exports as Perentage of GDP（%）	54.6	109.3	101.8	86.7	84.5
出口总额占GDP比重(%)	Total Value of Exports as Perentage of GDP（%）	37.4	68.5	63.1	56.8	59.0
研究与实验发展经费占GDP比重（%）	R&D Expenditure as Percentage of GDP（%）		1.66	1.89	2.20	2.31
外资项目平均利用合同外资（万美元）	Contractual Foreign Investment on Per Project（USD 10000）	173.0	817.4	1220.1	1316.8	1500.2
金融机构贷款占存款比重（%）	Loans as Percentage of Deposits in Financial Institutions（%）	75.3	96.5	100.2	98.1	102.3

注:在进出口、出口总额占GDP比重中,美元汇率按当年平均汇率计算。

Note:Total Value of Imports and Exports as Perentage of GDP, Exchange rate of USD are calculated according to in those years.

表 1 - 8 续表 Continued

指标	Indicators	2000	2010	2011	2013	2014
每公顷播种面积农产品产量(公斤)	Output of Farm Crops Per Hectare of Sowning Area (kg)					
粮食	Grain	5369	5765	5972	5469	5800
油料	Oil Plants	2023	2438	2512	2518	2509
蔬菜	Vegetables	29662	31790	32764	31079	31532
城乡居民收入比例	Ratio of Annual Disposable Income of Urban Resident to Rural's	2.15	2.12	2.06	2.03	1.82
社会发展	Social Development					
日均接待境外旅游者人数(人)	Number of Oversea Tourists Average Daily (person)	339	2608	2943	3489	3827
日均旅客周转量(万人公里)	Turnover Volume of Passengers Average Daily (10000 persons - km)	2192	3732	3789	3405	2138
日均货物周转量(万吨公里)	Turnover Volume of Freight Traffic Average Daily (10000 tons - km)	6486	43160	57270	61115	56480
每万人拥有在校大学生数(人)	Students Enrollment of Higher Education Per 10000 Persons(person)	48.0	245.3	245.7	257.3	259.3
初中毕业生升学率(%)	Enrollment Rate of Junior Middle School Graduates (%)	82.4	99.0	99.1	99.0	99.1
每万人拥有移动电话数	Subscribers of Mobile Telephone Per 10000 Persons (subscriber)	2185	14728	17860	21212	21771
每万人拥有医生数(人)	Number of Doctors Per 10000 Persons (Person)	17.0	30.0	31.8	34.4	35.9
每万人拥有病床数(张)	Total Beds of Per 10000 Persons(bed)	26.93	45.46	47.06	50.60	52.80
每万人拥有公共图书馆藏书量(册)	Number of Publice Libraries Collection Book Per 10000 persons(volume)	3280	12786	12712	11535	12403
每万人拥有公共交通车辆(辆)	Number of Buses Per 10000 Persons (vehicle)		6.5	7.0	12.3	11.3
每十万人拥有律师数(人)	Number of Lawyer Per 100,000 Persons (persons)	9.9	21.4	24.1	29.9	29.8
建成区绿化覆盖率(%)	Coverage Rate of Green Area in Developed Area (%)	28.44	37.52	37.82	38.23	38.55
污水处理率(%)	Percentage of Sewage Disposed (%)	35.92	82.81	84.16	88.42	89.95
计划生育率(%)	Rate of Famili Planning	99.22	95.50	96.15	95.92	95.95

表1-9 "六五"以来各计划时期社会经济主要指标 Major Social and Economic Indicators of Each Period since "Sixth Five - Year Plan" Period

单位:亿元(100 million yuan)

时期	Period	生产总值 Gross Domestic Product	其中 of Which 第一产业 Primary Industyr	第二产业 Secondary Industyr	第三产业 Tertiary Industry	工业增加值 Value - added of Industry
"六五"时期	"Sixth Five - Year Plan" Period	234.77	61.74	128.16	44.87	118.28
"七五"时期	"Seventh Five - Year Plan" Period	573.48	128.31	322.89	122.28	292.77
"八五"时期	"Eighth Five - Year Plan" Period	1760.34	258.75	1016.17	485.42	893.52
"九五"时期	"Ninth Five - Year Plan" Period	4777.61	450.59	2671.33	1655.69	2412.79
"十五"时期	"Tenth Five - Year Plan" Period	9038.13	564.69	4047.17	3526.27	4399.42
"十一五"时期	"11th Five - Year Plan" Period	19754.84	859.74	10879.04	8016.06	9733.05
"十二五"时期	"12th Five - Year Plan" Period	27450.94	1071.50	14452.22	11927.22	12876.53
2014	2014	7610.28	275.70	3980.41	3354.17	3533.68

表1-9续1 Continued

单位:单位:亿元(100 million yuan)

时期	Period	固定资产投资 Investment in Fixed Assets	社会消费品零售总额 Retail Sale of Consumer Goods	自营出口总额(亿美元) Value of Direct Exports (100 million USD)	财政总收入 Financial Revenue	一般公共预算支出 General Public Fiscal Budget Expenditure
"六五"时期	"Sixth Five - Year Plan" Period	51.68	86.81	0.04	40.23	
"七五"时期	"Seventh Five - Year Plan" Period	159.35	222.77	5.88	66.07	
"八五"时期	"Eighth Five - Year Plan" Period	705.73	651.23	63.86	161.00	
"九五"时期	"Ninth Five - Year Plan" Period	1600.03	1596.17	168.72	475.78	
"十五"时期	"Tenth Five - Year Plan" Period	4347.56	2825.19	654.04	1641.17	922.53
"十一五"时期	"11th Five - Year Plan" Period	9026.05	6325.15	2039.70	4233.99	2209.97
"十二五"时期	"12th Five - Year Plan" Period	12699.34	9975.86	2610.96	6410.34	3519.92
2014	2014	3989.46	2992.03	731.09	1790.89	1000.86

表1-9续表2 Continued

时期	Period	港口货物吞吐量(万吨) Cargo of Ports Throughput (10000 tons)	集装箱吞吐量(万标箱) Container Throughput (10000 TEU)	全社会用电量(亿千瓦时) Total Electricity Consumption (100 million Kwh)	粮食产量(万吨) Yield of Grain (10000 tons)	人口自然增长(人) Population NaturalIncrease (person)
"六五"时期	"Sixth Five - Year Plan" Period	2840		74.52	913.51	191824
"七五"时期	"Seventh Five - Year Plan" Period	10502	2.2	135.67	936.76	203889
"八五"时期	"Eighth Five - Year Plan" Period	25781	45.3	244.06	907.96	128862
"九五"时期	"Ninth Five - Year Plan" Period	45772	231.5	423.77	850.60	102695
"十五"时期	"Tenth Five - Year Plan" Period	96260	1505.7	955.17	446.52	49734
"十一五"时期	"11th Five - Year Plan" Period	181275	5069.1	1924.91	417.94	60064
"十二五"时期	"12th Five - Year Plan" Period	190880	6565.8	2155.57	332.11	58055
2014	2014	52646	1870.0	576.78	74.15	20870

注:2006年粮食产量根据农普数据调整。
Note: Yield of grain crops of the year 2006 has been amended according to the last census of agriculture.

表1-10 “六五”以来各计划时期社会经济主要指标平均增长率 Growth Rate of Major Social and Economic Indicators of Each Period since "Sixth Five-Year Plan" Period

单位:%

时期	Period	生产总值 Gross Domestic Product	其中 of Which 第一产业 Primary Industyr	第二产业 Secondary Industyr	第三产业 Tertiary Industry	工业增加值 Value-added of Industry
“六五”时期	"Sixth Five-Year Plan" Period	17.2	8.5	21.0	17.4	21.7
“七五”时期	"Seventh Five-Year Plan" Period	8.8	0.9	10.9	8.5	11.0
“八五”时期	"Eighth Five-Year Plan" Period	21.0	7.7	23.4	23.9	27.2
“九五”时期	"Ninth Five-Year Plan" Period	13.0	3.6	13.9	14.2	14.7
“十五”时期	"Tenth Five-Year Plan" Period	13.7	3.9	14.4	14.5	14.1
“十一五”时期	"11th Five-Year Plan" Period	12.0	4.3	11.7	13.3	12.5
“十二五”时期	"12th Five-Year Plan" Period	8.4	1.3	7.9	9.6	8.0
2014	2014	7.6	2.0	8.1	7.3	7.7

表1-10续1 Continued

单位:%

时期	Period	固定资产投资 Investment in Fixed Assets	社会消费品零售总额 Retail Sale of Consumer Goods	自营出口总额 Value of Direct Exports	财政总收入 Financial Revenue	一般公共预算支出 General Public Fiscal Budget Expenditure
“六五”时期	"Sixth Five-Year Plan" Period	15.9	17.8		10.1	
“七五”时期	"Seventh Five-Year Plan" Period	19.5	16.8	135.1	11.7	
“八五”时期	"Eighth Five-Year Plan" Period	46.2	32.8	52.0	27.3	
“九五”时期	"Ninth Five-Year Plan" Period	6.5	11.4	17.9	21.9	
“十五”时期	"Tenth Five-Year Plan" Period	30.9	11.8	33.9	26.7	25.8
“十一五”时期	"11th Five-Year Plan" Period	10.4	17.5	18.5	20.2	17.8
“十二五”时期	"12th Five-Year Plan" Period	18.4	15.1	8.8	11.1	13.6
2014	2014	16.6	13.5	11.3	8.5	6.5

表1-10续表2 Continued

单位:%

时期	Period	港口货物吞吐量 Cargo of Ports Throughput	集装箱吞吐量 Container Throughput	全社会用电量 Total Electricity Consumption	粮食产量 Yield of Grain	人口自然增率(‰) Natural Growth Rate
“六五”时期	"Sixth Five-Year Plan" Period	26.1		11.7	1.9	8.0
“七五”时期	"Seventh Five-Year Plan" Period	19.7		11.2	0.1	8.2
“八五”时期	"Eighth Five-Year Plan" Period	21.8	48.7	14.5	-1.8	5.1
“九五”时期	"Ninth Five-Year Plan" Period	11.0	41.3	12.9	-5.2	3.9
“十五”时期	"Tenth Five-Year Plan" Period	18.4	42.0	18.8	-9.6	1.8
“十一五”时期	"11th Five-Year Plan" Period	8.9	20.1	11.3	1.7	3.0
“十二五”时期	"12th Five-Year Plan" Period	6.3	9.5	5.6	-1.2	2.4
2014	2014	6.2	11.5	3.1	2.0	3.6

表1-11 国民经济主要指标比上年增长(1978-2014)
Growth Rate of Major National Economic Indicators Increase Precding Year

单位:%

年份 Year	生产总值 Gross Domestic Product	#第二产业 Secondary Industry	第三产业 Tertiary Industry	工业增加值 Value-added of Industry	固定资产投资 Investment in Fixed Assets	社会消费品零售总额 Retail Sales of Consumer Goods	财政总收入 Financial Revenue
1978	22.5	33.2	6.7		54.9	15.1	22.7
1979	13.4	16.4	19.2	14.1	15.3	24.0	-1.7
1980	17.7	28.4	4.9	38.7	12.3	27.6	15.2
1981	9.3	16.4	11.4	20.3	-1.7	16.4	16.2
1982	13.7	5.5	16.1	4.0	34.1	7.4	9.3
1983	17.7	24.8	15.0	21.3	-10.3	12.2	12.9
1984	18.0	19.5	19.1	25.0	42.4	19.7	15.5
1985	28.1	41.4	25.7	40.7	65.1	34.8	-2.2
1986	9.0	8.0	16.9	7.4	21.7	20.2	12.1
1987	14.1	18.2	11.1	18.6	33.8	16.5	10.8
1988	11.1	16.2	6.8	19.2	21.6	38.3	17.7
1989	4.5	8.8	-4.6	7.2	-8.4	7.7	14.5
1990	5.7	4.0	13.6	3.7	19.8	4.1	4.0
1991	24.9	18.2	52.0	24.0	30.9	15.3	11.9
1992	17.9	26.2	15.6	29.4	48.3	25.3	11.5
1993	20.8	26.4	14.8	37.4	69.5	48.9	42.4
1994	21.1	22.6	25.1	21.4	42.8	38.2	48.8
1995	20.5	24.0	15.5	24.4	43.1	38.8	26.4
1996	17.2	18.5	17.9	18.3	17.3	14.3	24.2
1997	13.7	16.4	15.4	19.4	-3.0	11.3	13.8
1998	11.1	11.5	12.1	12.0	3.1	8.6	16.8
1999	11.0	10.7	12.7	11.2	2.9	10.3	18.7
2000	12.0	12.6	13.2	12.7	13.1	12.6	37.6
2001	12.1	13.0	12.4	12.9	30.4	6.4	32.9
2002	13.2	15.0	12.4	15.0	27.9	11.8	35.8
2003	15.6	16.9	15.9	15.7	39.0	12.7	25.8
2004	15.5	16.6	15.7	16.0	32.1	14.2	-11.3
2005	12.3	10.8	16.3	10.9	21.1	14.0	16.4
2006	13.6	12.6	16.2	13.9	12.5	16.1	20.3
2007	14.7	15.1	15.2	16.4	6.3	17.3	29.0
2008	10.3	9.7	11.7	9.9	8.2	19.6	12.0
2009	8.7	8.4	9.7	8.6	16.0	15.9	19.2
2010	13.0	13.1	13.7	13.7	9.4	19.2	21.3
2011	10.3	9.8	11.8	10.3	17.6	18.4	22.2
2012	7.5	5.7	10.5	5.4	21.6	15.4	7.3
2013	8.1	8.1	9.0	8.5	18.0	13.2	7.5
2014	7.6	8.1	7.3	7.7	16.6	13.5	8.5

表 1-11 续表 Continued

单位:%

年份 Year	自营进出口总额 Value of Direct Exports and Imports	#出口 Export	实际利用外资 Foreign Capital Actually Used	港口货物吞吐量 Cargo at Throughput Ports	集装箱吞吐量 Container Throughput	城镇居民人均可支配收入 Per Capital Annual Disposable Income of Urban Residents
1978						
1979				10.3		11.1
1980				38.1		26.2
1981				7.1		12.1
1982				6.3		5.8
1983				30.2		4.1
1984				23.6		21.3
1985			1609.5	74.2		38.3
1986	102.0	38.8	39.3	72.8		24.9
1987	-0.9	46.5	-14.2	8.0		7.4
1988	616.4	1348.5	60.6	3.2		27.3
1989	49.2	57.1	155.2	10.3		14.8
1990	35.5	55.3	25.0	15.6		12.7
1991	92.2	70.0	22.0	32.7	63.6	11.2
1992	72.8	64.9	329.0	28.8	47.2	22.5
1993	71.0	41.4	199.7	21.8	49.1	49.0
1994	48.4	57.9	3.9	9.9	58.2	50.8
1995	53.2	29.6	11.4	17.1	28.0	21.1
1996	8.6	2.7	25.7	11.5	26.3	14.8
1997	10.1	25.9	10.5	7.6	27.2	8.6
1998	-8.6	1.0	-9.2	5.9	37.4	1.4
1999	18.9	17.3	3.4	10.9	70.3	3.3
2000	50.5	48.6	19.5	19.5	50.1	15.1
2001	17.9	20.8	40.6	11.3	34.5	9.8
2002	38.0	30.7	42.6	19.8	53.3	8.2
2003	53.3	47.9	38.5	20.4	49.1	10.1
2004	38.8	38.2	21.8	21.8	44.5	11.2
2005	28.5	33.2	9.9	19.0	30.0	9.6
2006	26.0	29.4	5.2	15.2	35.7	13.0
2007	33.8	33.0	3.1	11.5	32.3	13.4
2008	20.1	21.1	1.3	4.8	16.0	13.4
2009	-10.4	-16.6	-13.1	6.1	-3.9	9.2
2010	36.3	34.5	5.3	7.4	24.8	10.2
2011	18.4	17.1	20.9	5.1	11.6	12.9
2012	-1.6	1.0	1.5	4.5	8.0	11.3
2013	3.9	7.0	14.8	9.5	7.0	10.1
2014	4.4	11.3	22.9	6.2	11.5	9.2

主要统计指标解释

【行政区划】 指国家对行政区域的划分。根据宪法规定,我国的行政区域划分如下:(1)全国分为省、自治区、直辖市;(2)省、自治区分为自治州、县、自治县、市;(3)自治州分为县、自治县、市;(4)县、自治县分为乡、民族乡、镇;(5)直辖市和较大的市分为区、县;(6)国家在必要时设立的特别行政区。

【气温】 指空气的温度,我国一般以摄氏度(℃)为单位表示。气象观测的温度表是放在离地面约 1.5 米处通风良好的百叶箱里测量的,因此,通常说的气温指的是离地面 1.5 米处百叶箱中的温度。其统计计算方法为:

月平均气温是将全月各日的平均气温相加,除以该月的天数而得。

年平均气温是将 12 个月的月平均气温累加后除以 12 而得。

【相对湿度】 指空气中实际水气压与当时气温下的饱合水气压之比。其统计方法与气温相同。

【降水量】 指从天空降落到地面的液态或固态(经融化后)水,未经蒸发、渗透、流失而在地面上积聚的深度。其统计计算方法为:

月降水量是将全月各日的降水量累加而得。

年降水量是将 12 个月的月降水量累加而得。

【日照时数】 指太阳实际照射地面的时间。其统计方法与降水量相同。

【可比价格】 指计算各种总量指标所采用的扣除了价格变动因素的价格,可进行不同时期总量指标的对比。按可比价格计算总量指标有两种方法:一种是直接用产品产量乘某一年的不变价格计算;另一种是用价格指数进行缩减。

【不变价格】 指以同类产品某年的平均价格作为固定价格,用于计算各年的产品价值。按不变价格计算的产品价值消除了价格变动因素,不同时期对比可以反映生产的发展速度。新中国成立后,随着工农业产品价格水平的变化,国家统计局先后五次制定了全国统一的工业产品不变价格和农业产品不变价格。从 1952 年到 1957 年使用 1952 年工(农)业产品不变价格,从 1957 年到 1970 年使用 1957 年不变价格,从 1971 年到 1980 年使用 1970 年不变价格,从 1981 年到 1990 年使用 1980 年不变价格,从 1991 年开始使用 1990 年不变价格。

【平均增长速度】 我国计算平均增长速度有两种方法:一种是习惯上经常使用的"水平法",又称几何平均法,是以间隔期最后一年的水平同基期水平对比来计算平均每年增长(或下降)速度;另一种是"累计法",又称代数平均法或方程法,是以间隔期内各年水平的总和同基期水平对比来计算平均每年增长(或下降)速度。在一般正常情况下,两种方法计算的平均每年增长速度比较接近;但在经济发展不平衡、出现大起大落时,两种方法计算的结果差别较大。

本《年鉴》内所列的平均增长速度,除固定资产投资用"累计法"计算外,其余均用"水平法"计算。从某年到某年平均增长速度的年份,均不包括基期年在内。

Explanatory Notes on Main Statistical Indicators

[Administrative Division] refers to the division of administrative areas by the state. The Constitution of the People's Republic of China stipulates that the administrative areas in China are divided as: 1) The whole country is divided into provinces, autonomous regions and municipalities directly under the central government; 2) Provinces and autonomous regions are divided into autonomous prefectures, counties, autonomous counties and cities; 3) Autonomous prefectures are divided into counties, autonomous counties and cities; 4) Counties and autonomous counties are divided into townships, nationality townships and towns; 5) Municipalities and large cities are divided into districts and counties, 6) The state shall, when necessary, establish special administrative regions.

[Temperature] refers to the air temperature. China uses centigrade as the unit. The thermometry used for weather observation is put in a breezy shutter, which is 1.5 meters high from the ground. Therefore, the commonly used temperature refers to the temperature in the breezy shutter 1.5 meters away from the ground. The calculation method is as follows:

Monthly average temperature is the summation of average daily temperature of one month divided by the actual days of that particular month.

Annual average temperature is the summation of monthly average of a year divided by 12 months.

[Relative Humidity] refers to the ratio of actual water vapor pressure to the saturation water vapor density under the current temperature. The statistical method is the same as that of temperature.

[Volume of Precipitation] refers to the deepness of liquid state or solid state (thawed) water falling from the sky to the ground that has not been evaporated, infiltrated or run off. The calculation method is as follows:

Monthly precipitation is the summation of daily precipitation of a month.

Annual precipitation is the summation of 12 months precipitation of a year.

[Sunshine Hours] refer to the actual hours of sun irradiating the earth. The calculation method is the same as that of the precipitation.

[Comparable Prices] refer to prices that are used to remove the factors of price change in calculating economic aggregates, so as to facilitate comparison of aggregates over time. Two methods are used for calculating economic aggregates at comparable prices: 1. Multiplying the output of products by their constant prices of certain year; 2. Deflation of data at current prices by relevant price index.

[Constant Price] refers to the average price of a given product in certain year, which is used for comparison of output value over time. As the output value at constant prices removes the factor of price changes, it reflects the trend of production development over time. Since 1949, with the changes in general price level, National Bureau of Statistics has issued nationally unified constant prices five times: the 1952 constant prices for 1949 - 1957; the 1957 constant prices for 1957 - 1971; the 1970 constant prices for 1971 - 1981; the 1980 constant prices for 1981 - 1990; and the 1990 constant prices have been used since 1991.

[Average Annual Growth Rate] Two methods for calculating average annual growth rate are applied in China, one is often called "level approach", or the method of calculating geometric average, which is derived by comparing the level of the last year of the interval with that of the beginning year; the other is called "accumulative approach" or algebraic average or equation method, which is derived by the summation of the actual figure of each year in the interval divided by the figure in the base year.

Usually the results calculated by the two methods are fairly close, but they differed sharply when uneven economic development occurred with striking fluctuations in growth.

The average annual growth rates listed in this statistical yearbook are calculated by "level approach" except for the growth rate of investment in fixed assets. The base years are not listed when the years are listed for average annual growth rates.

NINGBO 2015 Statistical YearBook

2 CHAPTER

第二篇

人口与劳动力

POPULATION AND LABOR FORCE

人口和劳动力
Population and Labour Force

主要统计指标
Major Statistics Indicators

2014 年末户籍人口数	2013 Year - end Registred Populations	583.78	万人	10000 persons
其中:非农业人口	Non - agriculture	217.73	万人	10000 persons
其中:市区	Urban Districts	229.64	万人	10000 persons
2014 年出生人口	Birth Population	56398	人	persons
2014 年死亡人口	Death Population	35528	人	persons
2014 年人口自然增长率	Natural Growth Rate	3.59	‰	
2014 年人口净迁移率	Migration Rate	3.14	‰	
2014 年末人口密度	Density of Population	595	人/平方公里	person/sq. km
2014 年计划生育率	Rate of Family Planning	95.95	%	
2014 年末全社会从业人员数	Total Employmed Personnel at The Year - end	511.5	万人	10000 persons
2014 年城镇从业人员数	Number of Employed Personnel at The Year - end Above Town Level	171.33	万人	10000 persons
2014 年城镇在岗职工数	Number of Staff and Workers at Work Above Town Level	148.9	万人	10000 persons
2014 年城镇集体以上在岗职工平均工资	Average Wage of Staff and Workers at Work Above Town Level	68672	元	yuan
2014 城镇集体以上在岗职工大专以上人数	Number of Junior College and Above at Worker at Work Above Toen Level	60.71	万人	10000 persons
2014 年末城镇登记失业人员数	Number of Registered Urban Unemployment at the Year - end	67187	人	persons
2014 年末城镇登记失业率	Registered Urban Unemployed Rate	1.95	%	

表2-1 历年总户数和总人口 Households and Population Over the Years

单位:万户,万人(10000 households,10000 persons)

年份 Year	总户数 Total Households	总人口 Total Population	其中 of Which			
			按性别分 By Sex		按农业和非农业分 By Agriculture &Non - agriculture	
			男性 Male	女性 Female	农业人口 Agriculture	非农业人口 Non - agriculture
1978	123.30	457.70	234.18	223.52	394.28	63.42
1979	124.48	462.07	235.78	226.29	394.31	67.76
1980	128.57	465.99	237.98	228.01	393.13	72.86
1981	136.86	471.76	240.95	230.81	394.39	70.37
1982	140.56	478.33	244.20	234.13	396.40	81.93
1983	143.27	481.46	245.79	235.67	397.68	83.78
1984	147.57	484.18	247.26	236.92	398.64	85.54
1985	153.57	487.74	249.24	238.50	394.50	93.24
1986	158.53	491.89	251.56	240.33	394.69	97.20
1987	164.78	498.15	254.80	243.35	399.48	98.67
1988	170.92	503.06	257.19	245.89	402.81	100.25
1989	175.12	507.64	259.75	247.89	406.08	101.56
1990	176.06	510.76	260.99	249.77	407.78	102.98
1991	179.22	514.16	262.68	251.48	409.61	104.55
1992	180.89	516.72	264.09	252.63	409.90	106.82
1993	182.80	519.85	265.72	254.26	410.17	109.81
1994	184.38	522.85	267.24	255.61	410.17	112.68
1995	186.26	526.20	268.72	257.48	410.94	115.29
1996	186.82	530.08	270.30	259.78	410.57	119.51
1997	188.83	533.31	271.89	261.42	409.81	123.50
1998	190.39	535.27	272.40	262.87	404.79	130.48
1999	192.52	538.41	273.65	264.76	401.29	137.12
2000	193.99	540.94	274.50	266.44	398.91	142.03
2001	196.10	543.34	275.50	267.84	392.48	150.86
2002	198.94	546.19	276.60	269.60	383.76	162.43
2003	203.47	549.07	277.64	271.44	380.26	168.81
2004	207.01	552.69	278.84	273.85	376.50	176.19
2005	211.17	556.70	280.35	276.35	374.09	182.61
2006	215.03	560.45	281.71	278.74	371.47	188.98
2007	218.77	564.56	283.42	281.14	370.35	194.21
2008	221.48	568.09	284.84	283.25	369.60	198.49
2009	222.46	571.02	285.96	285.05	368.98	202.04
2010	222.98	574.08	287.15	286.93	368.86	205.23
2011	223.79	576.40	287.90	288.50	368.23	208.18
2012	223.46	577.71	288.30	289.41	366.26	211.45
2013	223.56	580.15	289.15	290.99	365.80	214.35
2014	224.07	583.78	290.52	293.26	366.05	217.73

表2-2 历年人口自然变动情况
Population Natural Changes Over the Years

单位：人，‰（persons，‰）

年份 Year	出生 Birth		死亡 Death		自然增长 Natural Growth	
	人数 Population	出生率 Birth Rate	人数 Population	死亡率 Death Rate	人数 Population	自然增长率 Natural Growth Rate
1978	75180	15.06	26150	5.74	49030	9.32
1979	71642	15.58	27393	5.96	44249	9.62
1980	57417	12.37	27989	6.03	29428	6.34
1981	78132	16.66	28557	6.09	49575	10.57
1982	84905	17.87	28258	5.95	56647	11.92
1983	69668	14.52	30875	6.43	38793	8.09
1984	51040	10.57	28114	5.82	22926	4.75
1985	53366	10.98	29483	6.07	23883	4.91
1986	62535	12.77	28738	5.87	33797	6.90
1987	83541	16.88	30239	6.11	53302	10.77
1988	69248	13.83	30171	6.03	39077	7.80
1989	71283	14.11	30364	6.01	40919	8.10
1990	67464	13.25	30670	6.02	36794	7.23
1991	60140	11.74	29329	5.75	30811	6.01
1992	50700	10.22	30573	5.93	20127	4.29
1993	55242	10.66	29169	5.63	26073	5.03
1994	54990	10.55	30050	5.76	24940	4.78
1995	59600	11.36	32689	6.23	26911	5.13
1996	58282	11.04	30652	5.80	27630	5.24
1997	55231	10.39	31417	5.91	23814	4.48
1998	47116	8.82	32902	6.16	14214	2.66
1999	51544	9.57	31237	5.80	20307	3.77
2000	50168	9.30	33438	6.20	16730	3.10
2001	39867	7.35	30632	5.65	9235	1.70
2002	41404	7.60	32361	5.94	9043	1.66
2003	42445	7.80	35173	6.40	7272	1.30
2004	49192	8.93	36558	6.64	12634	2.29
2005	45185	8.15	33635	6.06	11550	2.08
2006	41749	7.47	31380	5.62	10369	1.86
2007	46830	8.33	33737	6.00	13093	2.33
2008	46155	8.15	33804	5.97	12351	2.18
2009	45114	7.92	34277	6.02	10837	1.90
2010	48837	8.53	35423	6.19	13414	2.34
2011	46103	8.01	34816	6.05	11287	1.96
2012	49998	8.66	37907	6.57	12091	2.10
2013	49321	8.53	35514	6.15	13807	2.38
2014	56398	9.69	35528	6.10	20870	3.59

表 2－3 历年人口迁移情况 Bacis Statistics on Migration Over the Years

单位：人，‰(person，‰)

年份 Year	迁入 inflows	其中 of Which 省内迁入 From Zhejiang	省外迁入 Form Other Province	迁出 Outflows	其中 of Which 迁往省内 Outflow to Zhejiang	迁往省外 Outflow to Other Province	净迁移率 Migration Rate
1990	43055	34763	8292	43996	35646	8350	-0.18
1991	35526	27628	7898	32260	25142	7118	0.64
1992	54895	46773	8122	49969	43721	6248	0.96
1993	51257	41921	9336	43716	36697	7019	1.45
1994	55877	46390	9487	49826	42731	7095	1.16
1995	61832	50483	11349	52873	45598	7275	1.71
1996	66392	53141	13251	55103	47097	8006	2.14
1997	64083	51097	12986	53669	45306	8363	1.96
1998	73735	59605	14130	67191	58068	9123	1.22
1999	99809	82531	17278	89491	79170	10321	1.92
2000	85277	66946	18331	73024	60774	12250	2.27
2001	112559	91837	20722	95907	82261	13646	3.07
2002	105609	77127	28482	85498	71518	13980	3.69
2003	105057	76140	28917	80102	65019	15083	4.56
2004	104523	72455	32068	74307	59665	14642	5.49
2005	93433	64157	29276	62900	48874	14026	5.50
2006	90684	60320	30364	59694	46742	12952	5.55
2007	85199	55378	29821	54649	44955	9694	5.43
2008	77022	46195	30827	52036	40749	11287	4.41
2009	69949	40163	29786	48037	37595	10442	3.85
2010	67588	40093	27495	47814	37584	10230	3.45
2011	56088	31626	24462	42543	31859	10684	2.35
2012	47704	25619	22085	39715	28056	11659	1.38
2013	46493	24467	22026	34645	22518	12127	2.05
2014	67125	41165	25960	48879	36593	12286	3.14

表 2－4 部分年份各县(市)人口密度 Density of Population by Region in Partial Years

单位：人/平方公里(person/sq. km)

地区	Region	2008	2009	2010	2011	2012	2013	2014
全市	**Total**	**579**	**582**	**585**	**587**	**588**	**590**	**595**
市区	Urban Districts	894	901	907	913	916	922	933
#鄞州	Yinzhou	592	597	604	611	614	621	633
余姚	Yuyao	553	554	556	556	556	556	558
慈溪	Cixi	758	761	764	765	766	766	769
奉化	Fenghua	380	380	381	382	382	382	382
象山	Xiangshan	387	389	391	392	391	392	397
宁海	Ninghai	326	328	331	334	334	335	340

表2-5 各县(市)、区人口、户口情况(2014年底)
Basic Statistics on Population and Households by Region(End of 2014)

指标	单位	Indiators	Unit	全市 Total	市区 Urban District	海曙 Haishu
总户数	户	**Total Households**	**household**	**2240741**	**913528**	**113272**
总人口	人	**Total Population**	**person**	**5837767**	**2296382**	**298486**
男性	人	Male	person	2905164	1131316	146157
女性	人	Female	person	2932603	1165066	152329
非农业人口	人	Non - agriculture Population	person	2177284	1460405	298480
未落常住户口的	人	Non - registered Residence	person	898	17	1
平均人口	人	Average Population	person	5819616	2286162	298577
出生人数	人	**Birth Population**	**person**	**56398**	**21227**	**2638**
男性	人	Male	person	29411	10905	1342
女性	人	Female	person	26987	10322	1296
出生率	‰	Birth Rate	‰	9.69	9.28	8.84
死亡人数	人	**Death Population**	**person**	**35528**	**12310**	**1471**
男性	人	Male	person	19972	6792	801
女性	人	Female	person	15556	5518	670
死亡率	‰	Death Rate	‰	6.10	5.38	4.93
本年自然增加人数	人	**Natural Growth Population**	**person**	**20870**	**8917**	**1167**
人口自然增长率	‰	Natural Growth Rate	‰	3.59	3.90	3.91
迁入人数	人	**Number of the Persons Moved in**	**person**	**67125**	**25041**	**2747**
省内迁入	人	From Zhejiang Province	person	41165	9747	1390
省外迁入	人	From Other Province	person	25960	15294	1357
迁出人数	人	**Number of the Persons Moved Out**	**person**	**48879**	**12632**	**1777**
迁往省内	人	To Zhejiang Province	person	36593	5719	984
迁往省外	人	To Other Province	person	12286	6913	793

注:本表数据来自宁波市公安局。

Note: Data in this table are obtained from Bureau of Public Security of Ningbo Municipality.

各区 by Districts									
江东 Jiangdong	江北 Jiangbei	北仑 Beilun	镇海 Zhenhai	鄞州 Yinzhou	余姚 Yuyao	慈溪 Cixi	奉化 Fenghua	象山 Xiangshan	宁海 Ninghai
107750	**101669**	**155485**	**93222**	**342130**	**307795**	**421729**	**182070**	**183516**	**232103**
281316	**242710**	**390182**	**231656**	**852032**	**836717**	**1045942**	**483728**	**548572**	**626426**
138234	119051	192455	116114	419305	413629	514579	243650	278394	323596
143082	123659	197727	115542	432727	423088	531363	240078	270178	302830
281316	161931	227751	173430	317497	191507	196699	110660	115793	102220
		1		15	29	852			
280819	242256	388083	230358	846070	835893	1044776	483726	546199	622862
2825	**2416**	**3476**	**1601**	**8271**	**7215**	**8329**	**3754**	**7441**	**8432**
1432	1258	1799	863	4211	3849	4383	1935	3847	4492
1393	1158	1677	738	4060	3366	3946	1819	3594	3940
10.06	9.97	8.96	6.95	9.78	8.63	7.97	7.76	13.62	13.54
1233	**1349**	**2190**	**1110**	**4957**	**6170**	**6813**	**3297**	**3386**	**3552**
704	781	1194	614	2698	3407	3787	1895	2011	2080
529	568	996	496	2259	2763	3026	1402	1375	1472
4.39	5.57	5.64	4.82	5.86	7.38	6.52	6.82	6.20	5.70
1592	**1067**	**1286**	**491**	**3314**	**1045**	**1516**	**457**	**4055**	**4880**
5.67	4.40	3.31	2.13	3.92	1.25	1.45	0.94	7.42	7.83
2913	**2655**	**5359**	**3110**	**8257**	**12191**	**8009**	**4131**	**3467**	**14286**
1322	989	1152	1003	3891	9791	5443	2955	1709	11520
1591	1666	4207	2107	4366	2400	2566	1176	1758	2766
1718	**2240**	**1826**	**1103**	**3968**	**11316**	**6403**	**4471**	**2463**	**11594**
887	981	645	390	1832	9837	5239	3553	1465	10780
831	1259	1181	713	2136	1479	1164	918	998	814

表2-6 部分年份各县(市)、区总户数与总人口
Householes and Population by Region in Partial Years

单位:人(person)

指标	Indicators	2010	2011	2012	2013	2014
总户数(户)	**Total Households(Household)**	**2229770**	**2237911**	**2234602**	**2235581**	**2240741**
海曙区	Haishu	112893	112571	112502	112937	113272
江东区	Jiangdong	105321	105832	106262	106858	107750
江北区	Jiangbei	99171	99999	100458	101013	101669
北仑区	Beilun	153297	153468	153703	154327	155485
镇海区	Zhenhai	91962	91916	92107	92404	93222
鄞州区	Yinzhou	329992	334318	335535	338187	342130
余姚市	Yuyao	311793	311331	310127	308894	307795
慈溪市	Cixi	425462	427423	425201	422646	421729
奉化市	Fenghua	183049	182987	182404	182013	182070
象山县	Xiangshan	190604	189901	188281	186169	183516
宁海县	Ninghai	226226	228165	228022	230133	232103
总人口	**Total Population**	**5740836**	**5764042**	**5777125**	**5801464**	**5837767**
海曙区	Haishu	302384	300047	298843	298667	298486
江东区	Jiangdong	277701	278472	279291	280322	281316
江北区	Jiangbei	238867	240498	241105	241802	242710
北仑区	Beilun	377206	380081	383034	385983	390182
镇海区	Zhenhai	225227	226140	227611	229059	231656
鄞州区	Yinzhou	812068	822140	831232	840108	852032
余姚市	Yuyao	833837	834611	834493	835068	836717
慈溪市	Cixi	1038847	1041503	1041904	1043609	1045942
奉化市	Fenghua	483455	483937	483548	483723	483728
象山县	Xiangshan	540330	541688	540322	543825	548572
宁海县	Ninghai	610914	614925	615742	619298	626426
男性人数	**Number of Male**	**2871526**	**2878994**	**2882985**	**2891546**	**2905164**
海曙区	Haishu	149091	147710	146903	146532	146157
江东区	Jiangdong	137400	137566	137711	138046	138234
江北区	Jiangbei	117948	118508	118564	118739	119051
北仑区	Beilun	187357	188416	189500	190688	192455
镇海区	Zhenhai	113711	113959	114615	115028	116114

表2－6 续表 Continued 单位:人(person)

指标	Indicators	2010	2011	2012	2013	2014
鄞州区	Yinzhou	400771	405477	409748	413768	419305
余姚市	Yuyao	414593	414333	413670	413428	413629
慈溪市	Cixi	513088	513813	513540	513762	514579
奉化市	Fenghua	244773	244708	244207	243953	243650
象山县	Xiangshan	275805	275688	275230	276757	278394
宁海县	Ninghai	316989	318816	319297	320845	323596
女性人数	**Number of Female**	**2869310**	**2885048**	**2894140**	**2909918**	**2932603**
海曙区	Haishu	153293	152337	151940	152135	152329
江东区	Jiangdong	140301	140906	141580	142276	143082
江北区	Jiangbei	120919	121990	122541	123063	123659
北仑区	Beilun	189849	191665	193534	195295	197727
镇海区	Zhenhai	111516	112181	112996	114031	115542
鄞州区	Yinzhou	411297	416663	421484	426340	432727
余姚市	Yuyao	419244	420278	420823	421640	423088
慈溪市	Cixi	525759	527690	528364	529847	531363
奉化市	Fenghua	238682	239229	239341	239770	240078
象山县	Xiangshan	264525	266000	265092	267068	270178
宁海县	Ninghai	293925	296109	296445	298453	302830
非农业人口	**Number of Non－agriculture**	**2052283**	**2081751**	**2114509**	**2143489**	**2177284**
海曙区	Haishu	302362	300036	298834	298658	298480
江东区	Jiangdong	277701	278472	279291	280322	281316
江北区	Jiangbei	153572	155843	158246	159523	161931
北仑区	Beilun	199283	206123	214948	221079	227751
镇海区	Zhenhai	162701	164720	167357	169533	173430
鄞州区	Yinzhou	269344	281656	294546	305024	317497
余姚市	Yuyao	184515	186617	188594	190017	191507
慈溪市	Cixi	186892	189741	192089	194232	196699
奉化市	Fenghua	107531	108168	108814	109534	110660
象山县	Xiangshan	111861	112558	113391	115245	115793
宁海县	Ninghai	96521	97817	98399	100322	102220

表2－7 部分年份各县(市)、区人口自然变动情况
Natural Changes of Population by Region in Partial Years

单位:人(person)

指标	Indicators	2010	2011	2012	2013	2014
出生人口	**Birth**	**48837**	**46103**	**49998**	**49321**	**56398**
海曙区	Haishu	2397	2390	2622	2348	2638
江东区	Jiangdong	2688	2465	2780	2417	2825
江北区	Jiangbei	2035	2228	2431	2160	2416
北仑区	Beilun	3248	3125	3516	3113	3476
镇海区	Zhenhai	1105	1229	1428	1366	1601
鄞州区	Yinzhou	6306	6766	7485	7034	8271
余姚市	Yuyao	5624	5396	6035	6503	7215
慈溪市	Cixi	7797	7349	7723	8338	8329
奉化市	Fenghua	4013	3285	3490	3416	3754
象山县	Xiangshan	5497	5031	5741	6171	7441
宁海县	Ninghai	8127	6839	6747	6455	8432
死亡人口	**Death**	**35423**	**34816**	**37907**	**35514**	**35528**
海曙区	Haishu	1404	1432	1487	1391	1471
江东区	Jiangdong	1165	1123	1430	1161	1233
江北区	Jiangbei	1250	1187	1442	1257	1349
北仑区	Beilun	2098	2192	2188	2232	2190
镇海区	Zhenhai	1159	1169	1248	1145	1110
鄞州区	Yinzhou	4995	4719	5025	5061	4957
余姚市	Yuyao	6023	6233	6421	6333	6170
慈溪市	Cixi	7011	6803	7386	6986	6813
奉化市	Fenghua	3293	3129	3440	3097	3297
象山县	Xiangshan	3352	3265	3497	3331	3386
宁海县	Ninghai	3673	3564	4343	3520	3552

表 2 - 7 续表 Continued　　　　单位：人(person)

指标	Indicators	2010	2011	2012	2013	2014
自然增长	**Natural Growth**	**13414**	**11287**	**12091**	**13807**	**20870**
海曙区	Haishu	993	958	1135	957	1167
江东区	Jiangdong	1523	1342	1350	1256	1592
江北区	Jiangbei	785	1041	989	903	1067
北仑区	Beilun	1150	933	1328	881	1286
镇海区	Zhenhai	-54	60	180	221	491
鄞州区	Yinzhou	1311	2047	2460	2243	3314
余姚市	Yuyao	-399	-837	-386	170	1045
慈溪市	Cixi	786	546	337	1352	1516
奉化市	Fenghua	720	156	50	319	457
象山县	Xiangshan	2145	1766	2244	2840	4055
宁海县	Ninghai	4454	3275	2404	2935	4880
自然增长率(‰)	**Natural Growth Rate(‰)**	**2.34**	**1.96**	**2.10**	**2.38**	**3.59**
海曙区	Haishu	3.27	3.18	3.79	3.20	3.91
江东区	Jiangdong	5.50	4.83	4.84	4.49	5.67
江北区	Jiangbei	3.30	4.34	4.11	3.74	4.40
北仑区	Beilun	3.07	2.46	3.48	2.30	3.31
镇海区	Zhenhai	-0.24	0.27	0.79	0.97	2.13
鄞州区	Yinzhou	1.62	2.51	2.98	2.36	3.92
余姚市	Yuyao	-0.48	-1.00	-0.46	0.20	1.25
慈溪市	Cixi	0.76	0.52	0.32	1.30	1.45
奉化市	Fenghua	1.49	0.32	0.10	0.66	0.94
象山县	Xiangshan	3.98	3.26	4.15	5.24	7.42
宁海县	Ninghai	7.33	5.34	3.91	4.75	7.83

表2－8　部分年份各县(市)、区人口迁移情况
Migration of Population by Region in Partial Years

单位:人(person)

指标	Indicators	2010	2011	2012	2013	2014
迁入人口	**Population Inflows**	**67588**	**56088**	**47704**	**46493**	**67125**
海曙区	Haishu	3203	2815	2759	2980	2747
江东区	Jiangdong	3384	2995	2854	2882	2913
江北区	Jiangbei	4477	3758	3171	2927	2655
北仑区	Beilun	5099	4355	4061	4323	5359
镇海区	Zhenhai	2723	2413	2461	2206	3110
鄞州区	Yinzhou	9934	8631	7263	7100	8257
余姚市	Yuyao	13589	9498	8289	6741	12191
慈溪市	Cixi	9728	7517	6735	6024	8009
奉化市	Fenghua	4222	3596	3336	3035	4131
象山县	Xiangshan	5176	5939	2575	3422	3467
宁海县	Ninghai	6053	4571	4200	4853	14286
其中:省内迁入	**of Which:From Zhejiang**	**40093**	**31626**	**25619**	**24467**	**41165**
海曙区	Haishu	1482	1259	1231	1439	1390
江东区	Jiangdong	1577	1339	1384	1316	1322
江北区	Jiangbei	1610	1267	1132	999	989
北仑区	Beilun	1188	1077	904	876	1152
镇海区	Zhenhai	866	732	722	677	1003
鄞州区	Yinzhou	4682	3763	3336	3217	3891
余姚市	Yuyao	10964	7134	6063	4939	9791
慈溪市	Cixi	6947	4961	4483	4029	5443
奉化市	Fenghua	2796	2352	2201	1961	2955
象山县	Xiangshan	3851	4703	1357	1443	1709
宁海县	Ninghai	4130	3039	2806	3571	11520

表 2－8 续表 Continued　　单位：人(person)

指标	Indicators	2010	2011	2012	2013	2014
迁出人口	**Population Outflows**	**47814**	**42543**	**39715**	**34645**	**48879**
海曙区	Haishu	2587	2478	2453	2144	1777
江东区	Jiangdong	1668	1620	1694	1641	1718
江北区	Jiangbei	3495	3166	2899	2514	2240
北仑区	Beilun	2019	2244	2154	1899	1826
镇海区	Zhenhai	1263	1200	1045	1077	1103
鄞州区	Yinzhou	6401	5403	4807	4096	3968
余姚市	Yuyao	11648	7823	7284	6202	11316
慈溪市	Cixi	6560	5353	5868	5274	6403
奉化市	Fenghua	3564	3195	3428	3079	4471
象山县	Xiangshan	4122	6358	4366	2574	2463
宁海县	Ninghai	4487	3703	3717	4145	11594
其中：迁往省内	**Of Which：To Zhejiang**	**37584**	**31859**	**28056**	**22518**	**36593**
海曙区	Haishu	1777	1571	1444	1172	984
江东区	Jiangdong	885	833	841	861	887
江北区	Jiangbei	2332	1840	1596	1230	981
北仑区	Beilun	933	891	787	709	645
镇海区	Zhenhai	702	572	468	438	390
鄞州区	Yinzhou	4782	3749	2987	2080	1832
余姚市	Yuyao	10522	6723	6108	5134	9837
慈溪市	Cixi	5473	4312	4659	3996	5239
奉化市	Fenghua	2825	2614	2538	2419	3553
象山县	Xiangshan	3587	5677	3531	1063	1465
宁海县	Ninghai	3766	3077	3097	3416	10780

表2-9 各县(市)计划生育情况(2014)
Basic Statistics on Family Planning by Region

指标	单位	Indicators	Unit
计划生育率	%	Rate of Family Planning	%
年内出生人数	人	Number of Birth in This Year	person
#女	人	Female	person
1. 一孩人数	人	One - Child	person
#计划内	人	Under Control	person
2. 两孩人数	人	Two - Child	person
#计划内	人	Under Control	person
3. 多孩人数	人	Over Two Child	person
#政策性	人	Policy	person
计划内出生人数	人	Number of Birth Under Control	person
计划外出生人数	人	Number of Birth Out of Control	person
1. 一孩人数	人	One - Child	person
2. 两孩人数	人	Two - Child	person
3. 多孩人数	人	Over Two Child	person
育龄妇女人数	万人	Number of Women at Child - Bearing Age	10000 persons
已婚育龄妇女人数	万人	Number of Marriged Women at Child - Bearing Age	10000 persons
#已有一孩	万人	1st Birth	10000 persons
#已领独生证	万人	With One - Child Certificate	10000 persons
#已婚育龄妇女一孩率	%	Rate of 1st Birth of Marriged Women at Child - Bearing Age	%
#已婚育龄妇女领独生证率	%	Rate of One - Child Certificate	%
初婚妇女人数	人	Number of First Marrige for Women	10000 persons
已婚育龄妇女节育率	%	Rate of Controlling - Birth for Marriged Women at Child - Bearing Age	%
采取节育措施人数	万人	Number of Controlling - Birth Method	10000 persons
年内节育手术例数	例	Number of Controlling - Birth Surgery in This Year	case
年内取环例数	例	Number of Remove Contraceptive	case
出生率	‰	Brith Rate	‰
死亡率	‰	Death Rate	‰

注:本表数据来自宁波市计划生育委员会。

Note: Data in this table are obtained from Ningbo Family Planning Committee.

全市 Total	市区 Urban District	#鄞州 Yinzhou	余姚 Yuyao	慈溪 Cixi	奉化 Fenghua	象山 Xiangshan	宁海 Ninghai
95.95	97.25	96.66	97.35	95.82	96.49	92.80	92.30
48667	20452	7924	6406	7730	3474	4803	5802
23413	9935	3854	3038	3708	1663	2304	2765
35941	16016	6000	4735	5624	2543	3209	3814
35824	15979	5979	4725	5603	2537	3196	3784
12423	4358	1888	1631	2057	915	1561	1901
10777	3876	1665	1494	1785	811	1257	1554
303	78	36	40	49	16	33	87
95	34	15	17	19	4	4	17
46696	19889	7659	6236	7407	3352	4457	5355
1971	563	265	170	323	122	346	447
117	37	21	10	21	6	13	30
1646	482	223	137	272	104	304	347
208	44	21	23	30	12	29	70
145.53	56.53	22.03	20.91	25.89	11.93	14.35	15.93
112.06	44.41	17.25	15.63	19.38	9.16	10.91	12.57
84.72	36.08	13.90	11.99	14.17	7.20	7.50	7.77
41.02	19.79	7.74	6.29	7.69	3.64	2.05	1.55
75.60	81.24	80.56	76.74	73.08	78.67	68.76	61.81
36.60	44.57	44.88	40.27	39.67	39.76	18.82	12.31
37085	13621	5294	6246	7189	2714	3486	3829
88.18	87.47	88.52	88.87	89.38	91.06	87.22	86.72
98.82	38.85	15.27	13.89	17.33	8.34	9.52	10.90
27857	6795	3723	1894	3858	2329	5504	7477
9402	3333	1762	945	1394	836	1284	1610
9.69	9.28	9.90	8.63	7.97	7.76	13.62	13.54
6.10	5.38	5.77	7.38	6.52	6.82	6.20	5.70

表2－10 各县(市)婚姻状况(2014)
Basic Statistics on Marrige by Region

指标	单位	Indicators	Unit	全市 Total
准予登记结婚数	**对**	**Registering Marrige Permitted**	**couple**	**57597**
#涉外婚姻	人	Chinese－Foreign Marrige	person	232
(1)国内公民	人	Demestic Citizen	person	114
#女性	人	Female	person	103
(2)港澳台同胞	人	Chinese of Hong Kong,Macao and Taiwan	person	30
(3)华侨	人	Overseas Chinese	person	6
(4)外国人	人	Foreigner	person	82
1. 初婚人数	人	First Marriage	person	91632
2. 再婚人数	人	Remarriage	person	23562
#再婚中恢复结婚	对	Resume Marriage	couple	4306
准予离婚数	**对**	**Divorce Approved**	**couple**	**15045**

注:本表数据由市民政局提供。

Note:Data in this table are obtained from Ningbo Municipal Bureau of Civil Affairs.

表2－11 主要年份婚姻状况
Marriage Statistics in Main Years

年份 Year	准予登记结婚(对) Marriage Registration Permitted (Couple)	初婚(人) First Marriage (person)	再婚(人) Remarriage (person)	再婚中恢复结婚(对) Resume Marriage (Couple)	准予离婚数(对) Divorce Approved (couple)
1990	51349	96680	3312		1378
1991	46429	88283	4373	85	1508
1992	47504	91636	3372	152	1543
1993	43522	83451	3593	224	1815
1994	48029	92611	3447	209	2201
1995	45950	88406	3494	160	2501
1996	47197	89369	5025	169	2870
1997	40432	75369	5495	228	3689
1998	44559	83403	5715	466	3623
1999	39616	72299	6531	269	3881
2000	40505	74415	6125	242	3781
2001	38813	70658	6326	288	4206
2002	46931	85892	7572	371	4444
2003	42075	75735	8097	394	5538
2004	48214	86584	9518	743	7570
2005	39445	68699	9835	525	8570
2006	51725	90762	12688	736	9687
2007	41954	73877	10031	840	10232
2008	51956	90228	13684	509	11376
2009	46181	77918	14444	961	12698
2010	52508	87780	17236	1333	13754
2011	49710	83624	15796	2291	13911
2012	53721	92191	15251	2787	14893
2013	53742	71166	14968	6998	16414
2014	57597	91632	23562	4306	15045

市区 Urban District	#鄞州 Yinzhou	余姚 Yuyao	慈溪 Cixi	奉化 Fenghua	象山 Xiangshan	宁海 Ninghai
23937	**8071**	**8010**	**9357**	**3901**	**5961**	**6431**
232						
114						
103						
30						
6						
82						
37855	13313	13413	16010	5874	8763	9717
10019	2829	2607	2704	1928	3159	3145
2226	663	308	381	309	589	493
6868	**2180**	**1611**	**1719**	**1220**	**1740**	**1887**

涉外婚姻 (对) Chinese – Foreign Marriage (couple)	其中:of Which				
	国内公民 (人) Chinese Citizens (person)	#女性 Female	港澳台同胞 (人) Cninese of HongKong, Macao, Taiwan(person)	华侨 (人) Overseas Chinese (person)	外国人 (人) Foreigner (person)
85	85	80	69	11	5
101	101	95	88	8	5
133	133	127	114	9	10
157	157	150	128	20	9
119	119	112	93	20	6
127	127	121	70	27	30
160	160	154	105	23	32
144	144	144	84	16	44
142	142	134	82	16	44
201	201	188	144	14	43
235	235	229	177	7	51
321	321	313	249	10	62
199	199	189	137	10	52
159	159	152	106	8	45
163	163	154	88	14	61
178	178	166	96	9	73
181	178	162	100	13	71
170	170	154	78	10	82
172	168	148	60	17	99
162	160	133	63	7	94
138	136	114	44	8	88
306	153	127	69	4	80
284	142	113	45	9	88
326	160	113	58	5	103
232	114	103	30	6	82

表2-12 城乡劳动力资源配置情况(2014年底)
Sources and Distribution of Urban and Rural Labor Force(End of 2014)

单位:万人(10000 persons)

项目	Item	城乡合计 Total	其中 of Which 城镇 Urban	乡村 Rural
年末人口数	**Total Population at The Year - end**	**781.10**	**475.10**	**306.00**
年末16岁以上全部人口数	Total Population Above 16 Ages at the Year - end	683.00	430.30	252.70
#不计入劳动力资源的人数	Non labor Force Resource	26.00	10.40	15.60
年末劳动力资源总数	**Total Labor Force Resource at The Year - end**	**657.00**	**419.90**	**237.10**
经济活动人口	**Economically Activity Population**	**518.20**	**364.96**	**153.24**
从业人员数	Number of Employmed Person	511.50	358.26	153.24
按就业身份分组	Group by Employment Identity			
城镇集体以上单位从业人员	Urban Collective - Owned Level and Above	171.33	171.33	
私营业主	Private Owner	39.87	26.18	13.69
个体户主	Self - employed Worker	40.11	19.28	20.83
私营企业和个体从业人员	Employed Persons in Private and Individual Units	245.19	141.47	103.72
乡镇企业从业人员	Employed Persons in Township Enterprises			
乡村农业劳动力	Rural Labor Force	15.00		15.00
其他	Others			
按登记注册类型分组	Group by Registered Type			
国有单位	State - Owned Units	29.06	29.06	
集体单位	Collective - Owned Units	17.58	2.58	15.00
股份合作单位	Share - holding Cooperative Units	1.26	1.26	
联营单位	Joint Ownership Units	0.08	0.08	
有限责任公司	Limited Liability Corporations	37.07	37.07	
股份有限公司	Share - holding Coporations Ltd.	36.23	36.23	
私营单位	Private Enterprises	238.03	145.23	92.80
其他	Others	1.95	1.95	
港、澳、台商投资单位	HongKong, Macao and Taiwan Funded	34.87	34.87	
外商投资单位	Foreign Funded Units	28.23	28.23	
个体	Self - employed Individual	87.14	41.70	45.44

表 2－12 续表 Continued　　单位:万人(10000 persons)

项目	Item	城乡合计 Total	其中 of Which 城镇 Urban	乡村 Rural
按国民经济行业分组	Group by Sector			
农、林、牧、渔业	Framing, Forestry, Animal Husbandry and Fishery	19.39	1.31	18.08
采矿业	Mining and Quarrying	0.14	0.04	0.10
制造业	Manufacuring	229.48	142.19	87.29
电力、燃气及水的生产和供应业	Electric Power, Gas and Water Production and Supply	1.92	1.82	0.10
建筑业	Construction	41.62	38.51	3.11
交通运输、仓储和邮政业	Transportation, Storage and Post	15.47	12.00	3.47
信息传输、计算机服务和软件业	Information Transmission, Computer Service and Software	6.04	5.22	0.82
批发和零售业	Wholesale and Retail Trade	95.79	69.74	25.96
住宿和餐饮业	Hotel and Catering Services	10.87	4.84	6.03
金融业	Financial Industries	7.70	7.40	0.30
房地产业	Real Estate Industries	5.87	4.84	1.03
租赁和商务服务业	Leasing and Business Service Industries	23.03	21.07	1.96
科学研究、技术服务和地质勘查业	Scientific Research, Technical Service and Geologic Prospecting	13.33	10.05	3.26
水利、环境和公共设施管理业	Water Conservancy, Environment and Public Facility Management	2.13	1.93	0.20
居民服务和其他服务业	Resident Service and Other Service Industries	10.51	9.70	0.92
教育	Education	9.08	9.04	0.04
卫生、社会保障和社会福利业	Health Care, Social Security and Social Welfare	6.28	6.21	0.07
文化、体育和娱乐业	Culture, Sports and Entertainment	3.76	3.26	0.50
公共管理和社会组织	Public Management and Social Organizations	9.09	9.09	
国际组织	International Organizations			
城镇登记失业人员数	**Number of Registered Unemployed Persons in Urban**	**6.70**	**6.70**	
非经济活动人口	**Non Economically Activity Population**	**138.80**	**54.94**	**83.86**
#16 岁以上在上在校学生	Student Enrollment Above 16 Ages	25.00	16.00	9.00
家务劳动者	House Work Labourer	73.00	8.00	65.00

表2－13 部分年份按就业者身份和经济类型分组的从业人员
Employees Grouped by Identity and Registered Type in Partail Years

单位：万人（10000 persons）

指标	Indicators	2012	2013	2014
从业人员数	**Number of Employmed Person**	**501.58**	**503.36**	**511.50**
按就业身份分组	**Group by Employment Identity**			
城镇集体以上单位从业人员	Urban Collective－Owned and Above	174.22	171.38	171.33
私营业主	Private Owner	30.91	34.32	39.87
个体户主	Self－employed Worker	35.99	36.98	40.11
私营企业和个体从业人员	Employed in Private and Individual Units	233.46	235.58	245.19
乡镇企业从业人员	Employed in Township Enterprises			
乡村农业劳动力	Rural Labor Force	27.00	25.00	15.00
按登记注册类型分组	**Group by Registered Type**			
国有单位	State－Owned Units	31.18	30.34	29.06
集体单位	Collective－Owned Units	30.23	27.90	17.58
股份合作单位	Share－holding Cooperative Units	1.63	1.24	1.26
联营单位	Joint Ownership Units	0.13	0.10	0.08
有限责任公司	Limited Liability Corporations	30.03	34.90	37.07
股份有限公司	Share－holding Coporations Ltd.	36.70	35.09	36.23
私营单位	Private Enterprises	198.80	224.39	238.03
其他	Others	1.71	1.88	1.95
港、澳、台商投资单位	HongKong, Macao and Taiwan Funded	38.20	36.05	34.87
外商投资单位	Foreign Funded Units	31.41	28.94	28.23
个体	Self－employed Individual	101.56	82.53	87.14

表2-14 部分年份按国民经济行业分组的从业人员数 Employees Grouped by Sectors in Partail Years

单位:万人(10000 persons)

指标	Indicators	2012	2013	2014
从业人员数	**Number of Employmed Person**	**501.58**	**503.36**	**511.50**
按国民经济行业分组	**Group by Sector**			
农、林、牧、渔业	Framing, Forestry, Animal Husbandry and Fishery	29.74	28.85	19.39
采矿业	Mining and Quarrying	0.12	0.16	0.14
制造业	Manufacuring	231.55	230.71	229.48
电力、燃气及水的生产和供应业	Electric Power, Gas and Water Production and Supply	2.03	2.03	1.92
建筑业	Construction	41.57	41.17	41.62
交通运输、仓储和邮政业	Transportation, Storage and Post	15.87	15.58	15.47
信息传输、计算机服务和软件业	Information Transmission, Computer Service and Software	4.80	4.59	6.04
批发和零售业	Wholesale and Retail Trade	89.48	89.62	95.79
住宿和餐饮业	Hotel and Catering Services	10.36	9.36	10.87
金融业	Financial Industries	7.06	7.64	7.70
房地产业	Real Estate Industries	5.14	5.77	5.87
租赁和商务服务业	Leasing and Business Service Industries	17.66	17.80	23.03
科学研究、技术服务和地质勘查业	Scientific Research, Technical Service and Geologic Prospecting	8.43	9.86	13.33
水利、环境和公共设施管理业	Water Conservancy, Environment and Public Facility Management	1.95	2.01	2.13
居民服务和其他服务业	Resident Service and Other Service Industries	10.46	10.96	10.51
教育	Education	8.54	9.04	9.08
卫生、社会保障和社会福利业	Health Care, Social Security and Social Welfare	5.72	6.09	6.28
文化、体育和娱乐业	Culture, Sports and Entertainment	2.39	3.06	3.76
公共管理和社会组织	Public Managemen and Social Organizations	8.71	9.06	9.09
国际组织	International Organizations			

表2－15　全市城镇集体以上从业人员和劳动报酬情况(2014)
Employed Personnel and Remuneration Payment in Urban Collective－owned Units and Above Level

指标	Indicators
总计	**Total**
按企、事业和机关分组	**Grouped by Enterprises, Institutions and Agencies**
企业	Enterprises
事业	Institutions
机关	Agencies
按国民经济行业分组	**Grouped by Sector**
农、林、牧、渔业	Framing, Forestry, Animal Husbandry and Fishery
采矿业	Mining and Quarrying
制造业	Manufacuring
电力、燃气及水的生产和供应业	Electric Power, Gas and Water Production and Supply
建筑业	Construction
交通运输、仓储和邮政业	Transport, Storage and Post
信息传输、计算机服务和软件业	Information Transmission, Computer Service and Software
批发与零售业	Wholesale and Retail Trade
住宿与餐饮业	Hotels and Catering Trade
金融业	Financial Industries
房地产业	Real Estate Trade
租赁与商务服务业	Leasing and Business Services
科学研究、技术服务与地质勘查业	Scientific Research, Technical Service and Geologic Prospecting
水利环境和公共设施管理业	Water Conservancy, Environment and Public Facility Management
居民服务和其他服务业	Resident Service and Other Service Industries
教育	Education
卫生、社会保障和社会福利业	Health Care, Sports and Social Welfare
文化、体育和娱乐业	Culture, Sports and Entertainment
公共管理与社会组织	Public Management and Social Organizations
按经济类型分	**Group by Type of Ownership**
国有单位	State－Owned Units
城镇集体单位	Collective Owned Units
其他单位	Others Units

单位从业人员年末人数(人) Number of Employees at the Year-end (person)	其中 of Which		职工平均工资(元) Average Wage of Staff and Workers (yuan)
	女性 Female	在岗职工合计 Working Staff and Workers	
1717100	**667277**	**1489475**	**68672**
1447826	533433	1253715	62175
184495	106817	164980	102755
73924	21233	60986	112681
495	127	481	69779
48	7	44	44933
765130	362206	715944	56561
17636	4030	13338	107614
322950	28938	235924	54729
62192	14826	53103	82360
13793	5643	10817	105494
70276	40462	62954	63390
17059	8690	15904	44585
71228	39801	50782	156413
25401	8900	23344	71649
60748	10806	52627	62596
19960	6207	17058	100633
16187	5706	15190	60341
4243	1434	3772	46167
89628	57294	78577	104095
59682	41018	54491	106593
9501	4213	8742	97740
90943	26969	76383	107825
293184	128460	250522	103356
25945	14636	23830	78705
1397971	524181	1215123	61125

表2-16 城镇集体以上从业人员文化程度情况(2014) Educational Level of Working Staff and Workers in Urban Collective-owned Units and Above Level

指标	Indicators	单位从业人员 Working Staff and Workers
总计	**Total**	**1713472**
按企、事业和机关分组	**Grouped by Enterprises, Institutions and Agencies**	
企业	Enterprises	1444251
事业	Institutions	183736
机关	Agencies	74334
按国民经济行业分组	**Grouped by Sector**	
农、林、牧、渔业	Framing, Forestry, Animal Husbandry and Fishery	581
采矿业	Mining and Quarrying	51
制造业	Manufacuring	787853
电力、燃气及水的生产和供应业	Electric Power, Gas and Water Production and Supply	19042
建筑业	Construction	313553
交通运输、仓储和邮政业	Transport, Storage and Post	58106
信息传输、计算机服务和软件业	Information Transmission, Computer Service and Software	11748
批发与零售业	Wholesale and Retail Trade	64120
住宿与餐饮业	Hotels and Catering Trade	18203
金融业	Financial Industries	71827
房地产业	Real Estate Trade	25006
租赁与商务服务业	Leasing and Business Services	56903
科学研究、技术服务与地质勘查业	Scientific Research, Technical Service and Geologic Prospecting	19406
水利环境和公共设施管理业	Water Conservancy, Environment and Public Facility Management	15656
居民服务和其他服务业	Resident Service and Other Service Industries	4987
教育	Education	89132
卫生、社会保障和社会福利业	Health Care, Sports and Social Welfare	57653
文化、体育和娱乐业	Culture, Sports and Entertainment	8979
公共管理与社会组织	Public Management and Social Organizations	90666
按经济类型分	**Group by Type of Ownership**	
国有单位	State-Owned Units	297262
城镇集体单位	Collective Owned Units	28687
其他单位	Others Units	1387523

单位:人(person)

单位从业人员按文化程度分 Group by Educational Background of Personnel				单位从业人员人才资源 Number of Trained Personnel Resources	单位从业人员专业技术人员 Specialized Technical Personnel
大学本科及以上 Regular Collage and Higher Level	大专 Junior College	中专及高中 Specialized Secondary Schools & Senior Secondary Schools	初中及以下 Junior Secondary Schools and Below Level		
330422	**276721**	**476656**	**633301**	**1122510**	**364144**
177607	221505	443692	605022	897978	231922
106659	106659	34593	21278	21965	121817
43161	18205	9386	3172	65721	6722
96	49	104	246	218	103
3	10	24	11	38	3
59210	105922	235226	364772	454372	81161
5859	4387	4087	3303	15769	4706
22693	37606	116963	145688	231716	65453
10448	14966	19263	17515	40424	8369
5904	4835	2473	581	9100	4694
13778	17204	20192	19102	22252	5658
915	3071	6602	6471	4042	941
40211	17145	12114	1758	57348	42280
5026	4805	5918	9652	11929	4335
6103	7589	16900	30156	37012	4937
11406	4099	2651	1804	16020	11404
1791	1816	2443	10137	7271	2194
286	516	1102	2339	1264	190
61741	12935	6847	8105	76145	66006
30544	15448	9561	4129	55130	48644
3858	2354	1901	1388	6624	3907
50550	21964	12285	6144	75836	9159
152984	60632	40966	38602	235490	127059
9324	5679	4974	5968	18974	14167
168114	210410	430716	588731	868046	222918

表2－17 部分年份按行业分组的城镇集体以上在岗职工平均工资 Avergae Wage of Working Staff and Workers in Urban Collective－owned Units and Above Grouped by Sectors in Partial Years

单位:元(yuan)

指标	Indicators	2012	2013	2014
总计	**Total**	**56257**	**63152**	**68672**
按企业、事业、机关分组	**Grouped by Enterprises, Institutions and Agencies**			
企业	Enterprises	50372	56718	62175
事业	Institutions	86337	94279	102755
机关	Agencies	99162	108444	112681
按国民经济行业分组	**Grouped by Sector**			
农、林、牧、渔业	Framing, Forestry, Animal Husbandry and Fishery	52338	60061	69779
采矿业	Mining and Quarrying	46143	48766	44933
制造业	Manufacuring	42850	47924	56561
电力、燃气及水的生产和供应业	Electric Power, Gas and Water Production and Supply	104106	114530	107614
建筑业	Construction	46214	53123	54729
交通运输、仓储和邮政业	Transport, Storage and Post	67595	75085	82360
信息传输、计算机服务和软件业	Information Transmission, Computer Service and Software	94701	102259	105494
批发与零售业	Wholesale and Retail Trade	52335	56078	63390
住宿与餐饮业	Hotel and Catering Services	35872	39706	44585
金融业	Financial Industries	152892	160763	156413
房地产业	Real Estate Industries	57260	66543	71649
租赁与商务服务业	Leasing and Business Service	55313	60618	62596
科学研究、技术服务与地质勘查业	Scientific Research, Technical Service and Geologic Prospecting	90803	97540	100633
水利环境和公共设施管理业	Water Conservancy, Environment and Public Facility Management	46023	54267	60341
居民服务和其他服务业	Resident Service and Other Service	40808	41888	46167
教育	Education	86924	94346	104095
卫生、社会保障和社会福利业	Health Care, Social Security and Social Welfare	90517	99262	106593
文化、体育和娱乐业	Culture, Sports and Entertainment	81832	89868	97740
公共管理与社会组织	Public Management and Social Organizations	94610	102931	107825
按经济类型分	**Group by Type of Ownership**			
国有单位	State－Owned Units	88219	98291	103356
城镇集体单位	Collective Owned Units	61678	70763	78705
其他单位	Others Units	48895	55413	61125

表2-18 部分年份城镇登记失业人数和城镇登记失业率 Number of Registered Urban Unemployed and Registered Urban Unemployed Rate in Partial Years

单位：人(person)

指标	Indicators	2010	2011	2012	2013	2014
新增失业人员	Newly Added Unemployment	64116	70550	14965	67404	55974
#女性	Female	32451	35591	7765	34997	29248
失业人员转就业人数	Unemployed to Reemployed	66657	62673	20331	80252	58017
#女性	Female	31226	31019	9115	39738	30534
城镇登记失业人员数	Registered Urban Unemployment	56642	64519	82078	69230	67187
#女性	Female	27175	30763	38891	34150	32864
#长期失业者	Long - term Unemployment	6880	6955	8577	762	18903
城镇登记失业率(%)	Registered Urban Unemployed Rate(%)	3.03	3.44	2.55	2.16	1.95

注：本表至2-21表数据来自宁波市劳动和社会保障局。

Note: Dara from Tables 2-18 to 2-21 are obtained from Ningbo Municipal Bureau of Labor and Social Security.

表2-19 部分年份社会保险基本情况 Basic Statistics on Social Insurance in Partial Years

单位：万人(10000 persons)

指标	Indicators	2010	2011	2012	2013	2014
企业养老保险参保人数	Number of Staff and Worker Participated in Basic Pension Insurance at the year - end	383.50	434.44	474.30	508.94	542.23
企业养老保险实际缴费人数	Number of Factial Pay Participated in Basic Pension Insurance at the year - end	241.27	261.22	277.02	291.95	304.77
基本医疗保险参保人数	Population Particaipated Medical Insurance at the year - end	281.28	304.98	326.56	346.28	368.54
失业保险参保人数	Population Particaipated Unemployment Insurance at the year - end	186.25	200.62	216.22	231.74	243.39
工伤保险参保人数	Population Particaipated Work Injury Insurance at the year - end	238.14	253.36	270.22	283.38	291.09
生育保险参保人数	Population Particaipated Maternity Insurance at the year - end	201.46	214.71	233.09	245.54	252.25
被征地人员养老保障参保人数	Number of Taken Over Land Farmers Participated in Rural Social Old - aged Security	56.78	56.61	55.85	51.20	44.83

表2－20　各县(市)城镇登记失业人员基本情况(2014)
Basic Statistics On Unemployed Persons in Urban Areas by Region

指标	Indicators	全市 Total
总计	**Total**	**67187**
按年龄和性别分	**Group by Age and Sex**	
16－25周岁	Between 15 to 25 Years Old	3103
#女性	Female	1558
26岁及以上	26 Years Old and Above	64084
#女性	Female	31306
按失业时间分	**Group by Unemployment Time**	
六个月以下	Below 6 Months	48284
#女性	Female	23618
六个月以上	6 Months and Above	18903
#女性	Female	9246
按文化程度分	**Group by Education Background**	
大专及以上	Junior College Degree and Above	8617
#女性	Female	4471
中专和高中	Special Secondary school and Senior Secondary Schools Degree	22843
#女性	Female	10862
初中及以下	Junior Secondary Schools Degree and Below	35727
#女性	Female	17531

注:失业时间以办理失业登记时间开始计算。

Note:Unemployment time begins to calculate with the time of applying for unemployment registration.

表2－21　各县(市)城镇就业和失业人员变化情况(2014年底)
Number of Being Employed and Being Unemployed by Region (End of 2014)

指标	Indicators	全市 Total
上期末结转的失业人数	**From the Previous Year**	**69230**
本期增加的失业人员	**Newly Added in this Year**	**55974**
#女性	Female	29248
由就业转失业	Reemployed to Unemployed	43125
本期失业人员就业人数	**Unemployed to Reemployed at This Year**	**58017**
#女性	Female	30534
期末实有登记失业人数	**Registered Unemployment at the Year－end**	**67187**
#女性	Female	32864
长期失业者	Long－term Unemployment	18903
城镇登记失业率(%)	**Registered Urban Unemployed Rate (%)**	**1.95**

单位:人(person)

市区 Urban District	#鄞州 Yinzhou	余姚 Yuyao	慈溪 Cixi	奉化 Fenghua	象山 Xiangshan	宁海 Ninghai
55411	**11462**	**2338**	**2749**	**2265**	**3296**	**1128**
1937	34	37	11	341	479	298
986	16	19	4	160	228	161
53474	11428	2301	2738	1924	2817	830
26360	5581	1094	1121	779	1489	463
40334	8214	1548	696	2230	3239	237
19770	3988	754	313	919	1681	181
15077	3248	790	2053	35	57	891
7576	1609	359	812	20	36	443
7289	1943	340	464	7	120	397
3907	1120	72	209	4	78	201
18349	3390	815	681	1184	1513	301
8697	1680	372	306	542	785	160
29773	6129	1183	1604	1074	1663	430
14742	2797	669	610	393	854	263

单位:人(person)

市区 Urban District	#鄞州 Yinzhou	余姚 Yuyao	慈溪 Cixi	奉化 Fenghua	象山 Xiangshan	宁海 Ninghai
56100	**13917**	**3544**	**3116**	**2259**	**3046**	**1165**
30360	**6172**	**2719**	**2142**	**4891**	**3969**	**11893**
15895	3024	1431	972	2502	2076	6372
23977	3643	2519	2142	2256	2621	9610
31049	**8627**	**3925**	**2509**	**4885**	**3719**	**11930**
16408	4307	2115	1248	2493	1941	6329
55411	**11462**	**2338**	**2749**	**2265**	**3296**	**1128**
27346	5597	1113	1125	939	1717	624
15077	3248	790	2053	35	57	891
1.93	**1.93**	**1.03**	**2.08**	**2.56**	**2.95**	**2.03**

主要统计指标解释

【出生率(又称粗出生率)】 指在一定时期内(通常为一年)平均每千人所出生的人数的比率,一般用千分率表示。计算公式为:

出生率=年出生人数/年平均人数×1000‰

式中:出生人数指活产婴儿,即胎儿脱离母体时(不管怀孕月数),有过呼吸或其他生命现象。年平均人数指年初、年底人口数的平均数,也可用年中人口数代替。

【死亡率(又称粗死亡率)】 指在一定时期内(通常为一年)一定地区的死亡人数与同期平均人数(或期中人数)之比,一般用千分率表示。计算公式为:

死亡率=年死亡人数/年平均人数×1000‰

【人口自然增长率】 指在一定时期内(通常为一年)人口自然增加数(出生人数减死亡人数)与该时期内平均人数(或期中人数)之比,一般用千分率表示。计算公式为:

人口自然增长率=(本年出生人数-本年死亡人数)/年平均人数×1000‰=人口出生率-人口死亡率

【经济活动人口】 指在16岁以上,有劳动能力,参加或要求参加社会经济活动的人口;包括从业人员和失业人员。

【单位从业人员】 各单位的从业人员是指在各级国家机关、政党机关、社会团体及企业、事业单位中工作,并取得劳动报酬的全部人员。包括:在岗职工、再就业的离退休人员、民办教师以及在各单位中工作的外方人员和港澳台方人员、兼职人员、聘用的外单位下岗人员、借用的外单位人员和第二职业者。不包括离开本单位仍保留劳动关系的职工。

【在岗职工】 指在本单位工作并由单位支付劳动报酬的职工。包括由单位派出学习、劳务及病伤产假且仍由单位支付劳动报酬的人员。

【职工平均工资】 指企业、事业、机关单位的职工在一定时期内平均每人所得的货币工资额。它表明一定时期职工工资收入的高低程度,是反映职工工资水平的主要指标。计算公式为:

职工平均工资=报告期实际支付的全部职工工资总额/报告期全部职工平均人数

【专业技术人员】 指从事专业技术和从事专业技术管理工作的人员。统计对象为事业、企业单位中已经聘任专业技术职务从事专业技术工作的人员,以及未聘任专业技术职务,现在专业技术岗位上工作的具有中专以上学历的人员。

【城镇登记失业人员】 指有非农业户口,在一定的劳动年龄内,有劳动能力,无业而要求就业,并在当地就业服务机构进行求职登记的人员。

【城镇登记失业率】 指城镇登记失业人数同城镇从业人数与城镇登记失业人数之和的比。计算公式为:

城镇登记失业率=城镇登记失业人数/(城镇从业人数+城镇登记失业人数)×100%

Explanatory Notes on Main Statistical Indicators

[Birth Rate or (Crude Birth Rate)] refers to the ratio of the number of births to the average population (or mid – period population) during a certain period of time (usually a year) which is often expressed in ‰. Birth rate in the chapter refers to annual birth rate. The following formula is used:

Birth Rate = Number of Births/Average Number of Population × 1000‰

Number of births refers to live births i. e. the births when babies had showed any vital phenomena regardless of the length of pregnancy. Annual Average Number of Population is the average of the number of population at the beginning of the year and that at the end of the year. Sometimes it is substituted for with the mid year population.

[Death Rate (or Crude Death Rate)] refers to the ratio of the number of deaths to the average population (or mid – period population) during a certain period of time (usually a year) which is often expressed in ‰. Death rate in the chapter refers to annual death rate. The following formula is used:

Death Rate = Number of Deaths/Annual Average Number of Population × 1000‰

[Natural Growth Rate of Population] refers to the ratio of natural increase in population (number of births minus number of deaths) in a certain period of time (usually a year) to the average population (or mid – period population) of the same period which is often expressed in ‰. The following formulas are applied:

Natural Growth of Population = (Number of Births – Number of Deaths)/Average Number of Population × 1000‰

Natural Growth Rate of Population = Birth Rate – Death Rate

[Economically Active Population] refers to the population aged 16 and over who are capable to work, are participating in or willing to participate in economic activities, including employed persons and unemployed persons.

[Employees of the Unit] refers to the personnel who work in the government offices, political parties, social communities, enterprises and public undertakings and get paid. Including: on – the – job employees, reemployed retirees, teachers in schools run by the local people, personnel from abroad or HK, Macao, TW who work in the unit, persons on part time, laid – off personnel from other units, hands borrow ed from other units and concurrent employees. Employees who had left their units but still retain labor contracts with them are excluded.

[Full Employed Staff and Workers] refers to the employees who work for the unit and get paid by it, including those who are leave because of illness, injuries and pregnancies.

[Average Wage of Staff and Workers] refers to the average wage in money terms per person during a certain period of time for staff and workers in enterprises, institutions, and government agencies, which reflects the general level of wage income during a certain period of time and is calculated as follows:

Average Wage of Staff and Workers = Total Wages of Staff and Workers in Reference Period/Average Number of Staff and Workers in Reference Period.

[Specialized Technical Personnel] refer to the professional technology and administrative personnel. Its statistical targets include personnel who had been employed and given professional posts by the enterprises and pubic under takings, and the personnel who work in the unit have degrees higher than polytechnic school, but not given professional posts.

[Registered Urban Unemployed Persons] The registered unemployed persons in urban areas refer to the persons who are registered as permanent residents in the urban areas engaged in non – agricultural activities, aged within the range of working age, capable to labor, unemployed but desirous to be employed and have been registered at the local employment service agencies to apply for a job.

[Registered Urban Unemployment Rate] Registered unemployment rate in urban areas refers to the ratio of the number of the registered unemployed persons to the sum of the number of employed persons and the registered unemployed persons . The formula is as follows:

Registered urban unemployment rate = number of registered urban unemployed persons ÷ (number of urban employed persons + number of registered urban unemployed persons) × 100%.

Explanatory Notes on Main Statistical Indicators

NINGBO

2015

Statistical YearBook

3

CHAPTER

第三篇

国民经济核算

NATIONAL ECONOMIC ACCOUNTING

国民经济核算
National Economic Accounting

主要统计指标
Major Statistics Indicators

		总量 Total	比上年增长(%) Increase Over Last Year
宁波市生产总值(亿元)	Gross Domestic Product (100 million yuan)	7610.28	7.6
第一产业	Primary Industry	275.70	2.0
第二产业	Secondary Industry	3980.41	8.1
工业增加值	Value - added of Industry	3533.68	7.7
第三产业	Tertiary Industry	3354.17	7.3
			比上年增减(百分点) Increase Over Last Year(percent)
产业结构(%)	Structure of Gross Domestic Product		
总计	Total		
第一产业	Primary Industry	3.62	-0.18
第二产业	Secondary Industry	52.30	0.92
第三产业	Tertiary Industry	44.08	-0.74
支出法生产总值构成(%)	Gross Domestic Product		
总计	Total		
最终消费	Final Consumption	41.20	0.58
居民消费	Resident Consumption	31.83	0.53
资本形成总额	Total Capital Formation	51.63	0.86
货物和服务净流出	Net Outflows of Goods and Services	7.17	-1.44

表3-1 历年生产总值
Gross Domestic Product Over the Years

单位:亿元、元(100 million yuan、yuan)

年份 Year	生产总值 Gross Domestic Product	其中 of Which				人均生产总值(按户籍人口) Per Capita GDP (by Registered Population)	人均生产总值(按常住人口) Per Capita GDP (by Permanent Population)
		第一产业 Primary Industry	第二产业 Secondary Industry	#工业 Industry	第三产业 Tertiary Industry		
1978	20.17	6.52	9.69	8.62	3.96	437	
1979	24.15	7.99	11.43	10.11	4.73	522	
1980	29.53	8.69	15.54	14.21	5.30	634	
1981	31.99	7.85	18.11	16.82	6.03	680	
1982	36.88	11.20	18.79	17.26	6.89	776	
1983	41.68	10.91	22.63	21.22	8.14	864	
1984	53.17	14.93	28.23	26.02	10.01	1096	
1985	71.05	16.85	40.40	36.96	13.80	1455	
1986	80.22	18.61	44.47	40.59	17.14	1626	
1987	95.99	22.11	53.99	48.76	19.89	1928	
1988	118.62	27.11	66.43	60.28	25.08	2356	
1989	137.25	31.13	77.69	71.02	28.43	2702	
1990	141.40	29.35	80.31	72.12	31.74	2777	
1991	169.87	32.75	98.39	88.22	38.73	3315	
1992	213.05	35.32	128.70	116.20	49.03	4516	
1993	315.11	46.09	189.12	165.61	79.90	6079	
1994	459.66	63.48	260.97	227.59	135.21	8815	
1995	602.65	81.11	338.99	295.90	182.55	12024	
1996	784.07	92.21	442.64	390.74	249.22	14846	
1997	879.10	84.53	500.06	452.24	294.51	16534	
1998	952.79	87.76	528.73	478.67	336.30	17832	
1999	1017.08	91.85	564.07	512.84	361.16	18946	
2000	1144.57	94.24	635.83	578.30	414.50	21208	
2001	1278.75	98.53	690.81	624.92	489.41	23587	
2002	1453.34	103.60	793.01	715.24	556.73	26678	
2003	1749.27	109.77	954.04	847.79	685.46	31943	
2004	2109.45	120.54	1167.44	1027.26	821.47	38292	
2005	2447.32	132.25	1341.87	1184.21	973.20	44120	36824
2006	2874.42	139.31	1580.70	1412.87	1154.41	51459	42299
2007	3418.57	150.92	1894.14	1703.20	1373.51	60774	49142
2008	3946.52	166.85	2190.78	1957.42	1588.89	69687	55616
2009	4334.33	183.53	2356.68	2099.92	1794.12	76101	60070
2010	5181.00	219.13	2856.74	2559.64	2105.13	90490	69610
2011	6074.94	255.23	3315.76	2963.12	2503.95	105606	79730
2012	6601.21	268.51	3475.08	3097.25	2857.62	114394	86477
2013	7164.51	272.06	3680.97	3282.48	3211.48	123754	93641
2014	7610.28	275.70	3980.41	3533.68	3354.17	130769	98362

表3-2 历年生产总值指数(以1978年为100)
Index of Gross Domestic Product Over the Years(1978 = 100)

年份 Year	生产总值 Gross Domestic Product	其中 of Which 第一产业 Primary Industry	第二产业 Secondary Industry	#工业 Industry	第三产业 Tertiary Industry	人均生产总值(按户籍人口) Per Capita GDP (by Registered Population)
1978	100.0	100.0	100.0	100.0	100.0	100.0
1979	113.4	106.4	116.4	114.1	119.2	113.6
1980	133.5	108.8	156.0	158.3	125.0	132.7
1981	145.9	103.1	181.6	190.5	139.2	143.6
1982	165.9	134.7	191.5	198.2	161.6	161.1
1983	195.2	143.1	239.0	240.4	185.8	187.5
1984	230.4	162.8	285.7	300.5	221.3	219.9
1985	295.1	163.6	403.9	422.8	278.2	279.8
1986	321.7	171.5	436.2	454.0	325.2	302.4
1987	367.0	177.3	515.6	538.5	361.3	341.4
1988	407.8	170.2	599.2	641.9	385.9	374.9
1989	426.1	163.6	651.9	688.1	368.1	388.0
1990	450.4	171.1	678.0	713.5	418.2	407.0
1991	562.5	188.7	801.3	884.8	635.6	479.9
1992	663.2	184.0	1011.3	1144.9	734.8	566.8
1993	801.2	203.0	1278.3	1573.1	843.5	664.9
1994	970.2	217.2	1567.2	1909.8	1055.2	803.1
1995	1169.1	247.6	1943.3	2373.8	1218.8	960.5
1996	1370.2	269.1	2302.8	2808.3	1436.9	1118.0
1997	1558.0	252.2	2680.5	3353.1	1658.2	1261.1
1998	1730.9	265.0	2988.7	3755.4	1858.9	1394.8
1999	1921.3	286.5	3308.5	4176.0	2094.9	1541.3
2000	2151.9	296.0	3725.4	4706.4	2371.5	1717.0
2001	2412.3	310.8	4209.7	5313.5	2665.5	1916.2
2002	2730.7	322.6	4841.2	6110.5	2996.1	2161.5
2003	3156.7	334.2	5659.4	7069.8	3472.4	2485.7
2004	3646.0	350.9	6598.9	8201.0	4017.6	2853.6
2005	4094.5	357.6	7311.6	9094.9	4672.5	3121.4
2006	4651.3	374.8	8230.6	10362.1	5429.9	3521.3
2007	5332.8	395.0	9474.3	12059.2	6254.1	4009.1
2008	5880.5	411.0	10394.0	13259.0	6986.9	4391.0
2009	6394.5	426.7	11265.5	14403.9	7666.2	4747.7
2010	7223.1	442.3	12742.1	16382.3	8715.1	5334.8
2011	7968.3	459.3	13984.9	18077.1	9739.6	5857.7
2012	8566.9	464.1	14786.3	19054.6	10763.7	6277.9
2013	9261.6	457.1	15983.9	20678.3	11727.6	6771.5
2014	9960.9	466.1	17274.4	22278.6	12587.3	7244.9

表3-3 历年生产总值比上年增长
Growth Rate of Gross Domestic Product Raised Preceding Year Over the Years

单位:%

年份 Year	生产总值 Gross Domestic Product	其中 of Which				人均生产总值（按户籍人口） Per Capita GDP (by Registered Population)	人均生产总值（按常住人口） Per Capita GDP (by Permanent Population)
		第一产业 Primary Industry	第二产业 Secondary Industry	#工业 Industry	第三产业 Tertiary Industry		
1978	22.5	19.8	33.2		6.7	21.4	
1979	13.4	6.4	16.4	14.1	19.2	13.6	
1980	17.7	2.3	34.0	38.7	4.9	16.8	
1981	9.3	-5.2	16.4	20.3	11.4	8.2	
1982	13.7	30.6	5.5	4.0	16.1	12.2	
1983	17.7	6.2	24.8	21.3	15.0	16.4	
1984	18.0	13.8	19.5	25.0	19.1	17.3	
1985	28.1	0.5	41.4	40.7	25.7	27.2	
1986	9.0	4.8	8.0	7.4	16.9	8.1	
1987	14.1	3.4	18.2	18.6	11.1	12.9	
1988	11.1	-4.0	16.2	19.2	6.8	9.8	
1989	4.5	-3.9	8.8	7.2	-4.6	3.5	
1990	5.7	4.6	4.0	3.7	13.6	4.9	
1991	24.9	10.3	18.2	24.0	52.0	17.9	
1992	17.9	-2.5	26.2	29.4	15.6	18.1	
1993	20.8	10.3	26.4	37.4	14.8	17.3	
1994	21.1	7.0	22.6	21.4	25.1	20.8	
1995	20.5	14.0	24.0	24.4	15.5	19.6	
1996	17.2	8.7	18.5	18.3	17.9	16.4	
1997	13.7	-6.3	16.4	19.4	15.4	12.8	
1998	11.1	5.1	11.5	12.0	12.1	10.6	
1999	11.0	8.1	10.7	11.2	12.7	10.5	
2000	12.0	3.3	12.6	12.7	13.2	11.4	
2001	12.1	5.0	13.0	12.9	12.4	11.6	
2002	13.2	3.8	15.0	15.0	12.4	12.8	
2003	15.6	3.6	16.9	15.7	15.9	15.0	
2004	15.5	5.0	16.6	16.0	15.7	14.8	
2005	12.3	1.9	10.8	10.9	16.3	9.4	
2006	13.6	4.8	12.6	13.9	16.2	12.8	11.1
2007	14.7	5.4	15.1	16.4	15.2	13.9	12.0
2008	10.3	4.1	9.7	9.9	11.7	9.5	8.1
2009	8.7	3.8	8.4	8.6	9.7	8.1	6.9
2010	13.0	3.7	13.1	13.7	13.7	12.4	9.5
2011	10.3	3.8	9.8	10.3	11.8	9.8	7.8
2012	7.5	1.0	5.7	5.4	10.5	7.2	7.3
2013	8.1	-1.5	8.1	8.5	9.0	7.8	7.9
2014	7.6	2.0	8.1	7.7	7.3	7.0	6.4

表3－4 历年生产总值构成
Strucure of Gross Domestic Productoin Over the Years

单位:%

年份 Year	生产总值 Gross Domestic Product	其中 of Which 第一产业 Primary Industry	第二产业 Secondary Industry	#工业 Industry	第三产业 Tertiary Industry
1978	100.00	32.33	48.04	42.74	19.63
1979	100.00	33.08	47.33	41.86	19.59
1980	100.00	29.43	52.62	48.12	17.95
1981	100.00	24.54	56.61	52.58	18.85
1982	100.00	30.37	50.95	46.80	18.68
1983	100.00	26.18	54.29	50.91	19.53
1984	100.00	28.08	53.09	48.94	18.83
1985	100.00	23.72	56.86	52.02	19.42
1986	100.00	23.20	55.43	50.60	21.37
1987	100.00	23.03	56.25	50.80	20.72
1988	100.00	22.85	56.00	50.82	21.15
1989	100.00	22.68	56.60	51.74	20.71
1990	100.00	20.76	56.80	51.00	22.45
1991	100.00	19.28	57.92	51.93	22.80
1992	100.00	16.58	60.41	54.54	23.01
1993	100.00	14.63	60.02	52.56	25.35
1994	100.00	13.81	56.77	49.51	29.42
1995	100.00	13.46	56.25	49.10	30.29
1996	100.00	11.76	56.45	49.83	31.79
1997	100.00	9.62	56.88	51.44	33.50
1998	100.00	9.21	55.49	50.24	35.30
1999	100.00	9.03	55.46	50.42	35.51
2000	100.00	8.23	55.55	50.53	36.22
2001	100.00	7.71	54.02	48.87	38.27
2002	100.00	7.13	54.56	49.21	38.31
2003	100.00	6.28	54.54	48.47	39.18
2004	100.00	5.71	55.34	48.70	38.95
2005	100.00	5.40	54.83	48.39	39.77
2006	100.00	4.85	54.99	49.15	40.16
2007	100.00	4.41	55.41	49.82	40.18
2008	100.00	4.23	55.51	49.60	40.26
2009	100.00	4.24	54.37	48.45	41.39
2010	100.00	4.23	55.14	49.40	40.63
2011	100.00	4.20	54.58	48.78	41.22
2012	100.00	4.07	52.64	46.92	43.29
2013	100.00	3.80	51.38	45.82	44.82
2014	100.00	3.62	52.30	46.43	44.08

表3-5 按产业划分的生产总值(2013-2014)
Gross Domestic Product Classified by Industries

单位:万元(10000 yuan)

指标	Indicators	2013	2014	发展速度(%) Growth Rate over 2013(%)
宁波市生产总值	**Gross Domestic Product**	**71645060**	**76102816**	**107.6**
第一产业	Primary Industry	2720551	2756982	102.0
第二产业	Secondary Industry	36809712	39804092	108.1
第三产业	Tertiary Industry	32114797	33541742	107.3
农林牧渔业	Agriculture, Forestry, Animal Husbandry and Fishery	2757136	2795578	102.0
工业	Industry	32824779	35336797	107.7
建筑业	Constructions	4051538	4525916	110.8
批发和零售业	Retail and Wholesale Industries	8388742	8900663	113.9
交通运输、仓储和邮政业	Transportation, Storage and Post	3146273	3444851	110.0
住宿和餐饮业	Hoteling and Catering	967592	1138285	114.1
信息传输、软件和信息技术服务业	Information Transmission, Software and Information Technology Service	1119121	1124273	110.2
金融业	Financial Industry	4915573	4408978	94.7
房地产业	Real Estate Industry	4266710	3825494	92.4
租赁和商务服务业	Leasehold and Business Service	2183604	2663853	117.2
科学研究和技术服务业	Scientific Research and Technology Service	829274	888541	104.0
水利、环境和公共设施管理业	Water Conservancy, Environment and Public Facility Management	243399	261553	103.9
居民服务、修理和其他服务业	Residential Service, Repairing & Maintenance and Other Service	683555	778236	113.5
教育	Education	1585357	1731866	106.0
卫生和社会工作	Health Care and Social Work	953208	1159436	118.0
文化、体育和娱乐业	Culture, Sports and Entertainment	501576	583218	115.4
公共管理、社会保障和社会组织	Public Management, Social Security and Social Organizations	2227623	2535278	111.5

表3-6 生产总值项目构成(1993-2014)
Structure of Gross Domestic Product

单位:万元(10000 yuan)

年份	增加值 Value-Added	其中 of Which 劳动者报酬 Compensation of Employees	生产税净额 Net Taxes on Production	固定资产折旧 Depreciation of Fixed Assets	营业盈余 Operating Surplus
总计					
Gross Domestic Product					
1993	3151137	1506857	499355	311430	833495
1994	4596645	2480140	699264	432964	984277
1995	6026524	3092917	953362	589020	1391225
1996	7840727	4197455	1297978	761269	1584025
1997	8791042	4760824	1466876	1000186	1563156
1998	9527859	4405743	1756795	1329018	2036303
1999	10170826	4858140	1765615	1485977	2061094
2000	11445653	5197257	1898185	1503767	2846444
2001	12787531	6129433	1872390	1619514	3166194
2002	14533421	6574217	2288833	1702915	3967456
2003	17492728	7522559	2888138	1983778	5098253
2004	21094461	8252916	3428099	2584132	6829314
2005	24473219	9538821	3773843	3121554	8039001
2006	28744210	11332844	4850566	3698732	8862068
2007	34185710	12843300	5480230	4593868	11268312
2008	39465245	16647075	6572526	5614314	10631330
2009	43343293	15945404	8618928	5210030	13568931
2010	51810011	.19727913	9971000	5580245	16530853
2011	60749371	24759130	12200952	6923405	16815884
2012	66012145	28798875	13312197	8269721	15631352
2013	71645060	32642277	13604005	8409135	16989643
2014	76102816	36087718	14306639	8876385	16832074
第一产业					
Primary Industry					
1993	460932	362995	6022	12583	79332
1994	634751	497816	11730	16599	108606
1995	811080	642492	17182	24416	126990
1996	922101	715773	17978	29039	159311
1997	845307	665351	21563	32441	125952
1998	877645	691633	15435	34769	135808
1999	918527	722231	15389	38032	142875
2000	942353	737186	14797	39345	151025
2001	985257	770231	15638	41004	158384
2002	1035968	812679	16182	43465	163642
2003	1097567	861928	10418	46163	179058
2004	1205371	1156158	10467	38746	
2005	1322475	1250993	14513	56969	
2006	1393123	1338826	-9413	63710	
2007	1509165	1473464	-33840	69541	
2008	1668464	1651964	-61244	77744	
2009	1835300	1785500	-42700	92500	
2010	2191327	2143132	-60191	108386	
2011	2552270	2498175	-70923	125018	
2012	2685159	2627034	-75549	133674	
2013	2720551	2663706	-81407	138252	
2014	2756982	2699883	-82200	139299	

表 3-6 续 Continued 单位:万元(10000 yuan)

年份	增加值 Value - Added	其中 of Which 劳动者报酬 Compensation of Employees	生产税净额 Net Taxes on Production	固定资产折旧 Depreciation of Fixed Assets	营业盈余 Operating Surplus
第二产业 Secondary Industry					
1993	1891201	822727	360007	189250	519217
1994	2609752	1307376	541991	254130	506255
1995	3389919	1499859	728377	342581	819102
1996	4426403	2279485	966565	422195	758158
1997	5000559	2709675	1035314	520105	735465
1998	5287306	2080907	1265643	708150	1232606
1999	5640654	2355823	1271128	809524	1204179
2000	6358306	2462503	1378338	794615	1722850
2001	6908111	2768675	1404624	806206	1928606
2002	7930119	3381081	1752335	730237	2066466
2003	9540385	4030508	1808864	912346	2788667
2004	11674425	4360196	2305394	1266901	3741934
2005	13418692	4952203	2504702	1602800	4358987
2006	15806994	6113649	3285801	2129942	4277602
2007	18941412	7005672	3824969	2450357	5660414
2008	21907835	9744814	3606886	3451214	5104921
2009	23566764	8128171	5177252	2888622	7372719
2010	28567355	10136715	5733699	2907755	9789186
2011	33157597	12862801	7063591	3797512	9433693
2012	34750779	14695471	7496727	4236528	8322053
2013	36809712	14718220	8159467	4203069	9728956
2014	39804092	16755847	8044183	4219734	10784328
第三产业 Tertiary Industry					
1993	799004	321135	133326	109597	234946
1994	1352142	674948	145543	162235	369416
1995	1825525	950566	207803	222023	445133
1996	2492223	1202197	313435	310035	666556
1997	2945176	1385798	409999	447640	701739
1998	3362908	1633203	475717	586099	667889
1999	3611645	1780086	479098	638421	714040
2000	4144994	1997568	505050	669807	972569
2001	4894163	2590527	452128	772304	1079204
2002	5567334	2380457	520316	929213	1737348
2003	6854776	2630123	1068856	1025269	2130528
2004	8214665	2736562	1112238	1278485	3087380
2005	9732052	3335625	1254628	1461785	3680014
2006	11544093	3880369	1574178	1505080	4584466
2007	13735133	4364164	1689101	2073970	5607898
2008	15888946	5250297	3026884	2085356	5526409
2009	17941229	6031733	3484376	2228908	6196212
2010	21051329	7448066	4297492	2564104	6741667
2011	25039504	9398154	5208284	3000875	7382191
2012	28576207	11476370	5891019	3899519	7309299
2013	32114797	15260351	5525945	4067814	7260687
2014	33541742	16631988	6344656	4517352	6047746

表3－7　部分年份按支出法计算的生产总值
Gross Domestic Product Calculated with Expenditure Approach in Partial Years

单位:亿元(100 million yuan)

指标	Indicators	2010	2011	2012	2013	2014
支出法生产总值	**Gross Domestic Product**	**5181.00**	**6074.94**	**6601.21**	**7164.51**	**7610.28**
最终消费	Final Consumption	2252.54	2553.59	2789.17	2910.52	3135.84
居民消费	Resident Consumption	1669.87	1963.75	2181.09	2242.34	2422.04
城镇居民	Urban Resident	1293.62	1550.82	1730.81	1756.14	1891.94
农村居民	Rural Resident	376.25	412.93	450.28	486.20	530.10
政府消费	Government Consumption	582.67	589.84	608.08	668.18	713.80
资本形成总额	Total Capital Formation	2451.91	2826.19	3133.00	3637.54	3928.95
固定资本形成总额	Fixed Capital Formation	1886.83	2502.22	2874.97	3213.73	3548.93
存货变动	Stock Change	565.08	323.97	258.03	423.81	380.02
货物和服务净流出	Net Outflows of Goods and Services	476.55	695.16	679.04	616.45	545.49

表3－8　部分年份按支出法计算的生产总值指数(以上年为100)
Index of Gross Domestic Product Calculated with Expenditure Approach in Partial Years(Preceding Year = 100)

指标	Indicators	2011	2012	2013	2014
支出法生产总值	**Gross Domestic Product**	**110.3**	**107.5**	**108.1**	**107.6**
最终消费	Final Consumption	107.1	107.6	102.4	107.3
居民消费	Resident Consumption	111.0	109.4	101.0	108.0
城镇居民	Urban Resident	113.3	110.1	99.6	107.5
农村居民	Rural Resident	102.8	106.8	106.4	109.7
政府消费	Government Consumption	96.1	101.4	107.6	104.7
资本形成总额	Total Capital Formation	104.9	111.1	116.6	109.3
固定资本形成总额	Fixed Capital Formation	120.1	115.0	112.1	111.8
存货变动	Stock Change	54.1	81.0	166.5	90.4
货物和服务净流出	Net Outflows of Goods and Services	153.3	92.7	92.3	98.7

表3-9 部分年份按行业划分的资本形成总额 Total Capital Formation by Sector in Partial Years

单位:亿元(100 million yuan)

指标	Indicators	2010	2011	2012	2013	2014
资本形成总额	**Total Capital Formation**	**2451.91**	**2826.19**	**3133.00**	**3637.54**	**3928.95**
固定资本形成总额	Fixed Capital Formation	1886.83	2502.22	2874.97	3213.73	3548.93
住宅	Residential Buildings	448.70	706.13	807.33	811.56	837.45
非住宅建筑物	Non - Residential Construction	902.62	1207.49	1390.56	1552.42	1627.58
机器和设备	Machinery and Equipment	338.72	330.37	373.68	480.85	651.00
土地改良支出	land Ameioration Expenditure	4.42	6.00	8.64	10.90	9.46
矿藏勘探费	Mineral Reserves Prospecting Cost	0.60	0.69	1.70	0.97	0.89
计算机软件	Computer Software	21.17	29.90	39.47	45.41	80.02
其他	Others	170.60	221.64	253.59	311.62	342.53
存货变动	Stock Change	565.08	323.97	258.03	423.81	380.02
农林牧渔业	Agriculture, Forestry, Animal Husbandry and Fishery	-0.26	1.22	-1.33	0.23	-1.61
工业	Industry	168.73	204.96	95.73	97.05	135.97
建筑业	Constructions	-18.62	44.15	22.22	72.11	52.91
交通运输、仓储和邮政业	Transportation, Storage and Post	-0.82	0.18	-0.76	4.10	0.10
批发和零售业	Retail and Wholesale Industries	77.77	42.88	-23.30	39.14	7.35
住宿和餐饮业	Hoteling and Catering	0.13	0.44	-0.07	-1.16	0.57
房地产业	Real Estate Industry	320.66	18.90	139.48	199.60	162.29
其他服务业	Other Service	17.49	11.24	26.06	12.74	22.44

表3-10 最终消费(2013-2014)
Final Consumption

单位:亿元(100 millon yuan)

指标	Indicators	2013	2014
最终消费支出	**Final Consumption**	**2910.52**	**3135.84**
一、居民消费支出	**Resident Consumption Expenditures**	**2242.34**	**2422.04**
(一)城镇居民	Urban Resident	1756.14	1891.94
1.食品烟酒	Food, Tobacco and Alcohol	501.35	455.06
2.衣着	Garments	103.70	113.98
3.居住(含自有住房服务)	Residence (Includes Self-Owned Housing Services)	229.39	299.49
4.生活用品及服务	Living Supplies and Services	73.04	69.32
5.交通和通信	Transportation and Communication	151.04	166.07
6.教育文化娱乐	Education, Culture and Entertainment	46.46	65.96
7.医疗保健	Medical and Health Care	316.99	328.38
8.银行中介服务	Banking Intermediary Services	223.05	252.85
9.保险服务	Insurance Services	64.59	95.41
10.其它商品和服务	Other Commodities and Services	46.53	45.42
(二)农村居民	Rural Resident	486.20	530.10
1.食品烟酒	Food, Tobacco and Alcohol	127.99	135.34
2.衣着	Garments	22.00	25.39
3.居住(含自有住房服务)	Residence (Includes Self-Owned Housing Services)	94.97	94.61
4.生活用品及服务	Living Supplies and Services	14.33	15.45
5.交通和通信	Transportation and Communication	53.85	60.06
6.教育文化娱乐	Education, Culture and Entertainment	24.56	32.04
7.医疗保健	Medical and Health Care	29.95	35.28
8.银行中介服务	Banking Intermediary Services	95.75	106.39
9.保险服务	Insurance Services	12.64	18.26
10.其它商品和服务	Other Commodities and Services	10.16	7.28
二、政府消费支出	**Government Consumption Expenditures**	**668.18**	**713.80**

表3-11 部分年份居民总消费水平
Resident Consumption Level in Partial Years

单位:元/人(yuan/person)

指标	Indicators	2010	2011	2012	2013	2014
当年价居民消费水平	**Resident Consumption Level at Current Price**	**22436**	**25773**	**28573**	**29315**	**31305**
城镇居民	Urban Resident	26255	29586	32766	32991	34907
农村居民	Rural Resident	14956	17368	19152	20904	22879
居民年平均人口(万人)	**Annual Average Population(10000person)**	**744.29**	**761.94**	**763.35**	**764.90**	**773.70**
城镇居民	Urban Resident	492.72	524.18	528.24	532.31	542.00
农村居民	Rural Resident	251.57	237.76	235.11	232.59	231.70

表3-12 部分年份居民消费指数(以上年为100)
Index of Resident Consumption in Partial Years(Preceding Year=100)

指标	Indicators	2011	2012	2013	2014
当年价居民消费水平	**Resident Consumption Level at Current Price**	**108.4**	**109.2**	**100.8**	**106.8**
城镇居民	Urban Resident	106.5	109.3	98.8	105.6
农村居民	Rural Resident	108.8	108.0	107.6	110.1
居民年平均人口	**Annual Average Population**	**102.4**	**100.2**	**100.2**	**101.2**
城镇居民	Urban Resident	106.4	100.8	100.8	101.8
农村居民	Rural Resident	94.5	98.9	98.9	99.6

表3－13 各县（市）按产业划分的生产总值（2014）
Gross Domestic Product Classified by Industries and by Region

指标	Indicators	全市 Total
地区生产总值	**Gross Domestic Product**	**76102816**
第一产业	Primary Industry	2756982
第二产业	Secondary Industry	39804092
第三产业	Tertiary Industry	33541742
农林牧渔业	Agriculture, Forestry, Animal Husbandry and Fishery	2795578
工业	Industry	35336797
建筑业	Constructions	4525916
批发和零售业	Retail and Wholesale Industries	8900663
交通运输、仓储和邮政业	Transportation, Storage and Post	3444851
住宿和餐饮业	Hoteling and Catering	1138285
信息传输、软件和信息技术服务业	Information Transmission, Software and Information Technology Service	1124273
金融业	Financial Industry	4408978
房地产业	Real Estate Industry	3825494
租赁和商务服务业	Leasehold and Business Service	2663853
科学研究和技术服务业	Scientific Research and Technology Service	888541
水利、环境和公共设施管理业	Water Conservancy, Environment and Public Facility Management	261553
居民服务、修理和其他服务业	Residential Service, Repairing & Maintenance and Other Service	778236
教育	Education	1731866
卫生和社会工作	Health Care and Social Work	1159436
文化、体育和娱乐业	Culture, Sports and Entertainment	583218
公共管理、社会保障和社会组织	Public Management, Social Security and Social Organizations	2535278

单位:万元(10000 yuan)

市区 Urban Districts	#鄞州 Yinzhou	余姚 Yuyao	慈溪 Cixi	奉化 Fenghua	象山 Xiangshan	宁海 Ninghai
45893046	**12966399**	**8043565**	**11094102**	**3089895**	**3880832**	**4101376**
601232	393393	413400	484849	285034	579451	393016
23403124	7618244	4677313	6379252	1405983	1806461	2131959
21888690	4954762	2952852	4230001	1398878	1494920	1576401
613719	401493	417000	496241	288200	585774	394644
20884457	7103263	4223413	5879517	1184305	1296603	1868502
2548658	520088	455000	503607	224992	524066	269593
5379799	1246853	894034	1466135	343248	376857	440590
2538902	216084	151600	331366	118969	131592	172422
597835	153133	140100	163628	69051	93832	73839
753522	147806	98943	129046	41306	53557	47899
3191607	843396	339864	404980	157960	153920	160647
2400259	1008237	392864	628801	114025	168225	121320
2235333	193949	94700	122080	36526	69393	105821
719118	146992	47700	53889	18086	27310	22438
167448	32055	15100	28537	14865	14261	21342
369279	97179	105939	150456	61685	48484	42393
1024087	378967	171082	236941	83399	107775	108582
738064	163796	110629	112812	78189	56888	62854
367628	41477	58560	61845	50697	25066	19422
1363331	271631	327037	324221	204392	147229	169068

表3－14 各县(市)生产总值结构及增长速度(2014)
Structure and Grawth Rate of Gross Domestic Product by Region

单位:%

地区	Region	生产总值 Gross Domestic Product	其中 of Which 第一产业 Primary Industry	第二产业 Secondary Industry	#工业 Industry	第三产业 Tertiary Industry
产业结构	**Structure**					
全市	Ningbo	100.0	3.6	52.3	46.4	44.1
市区	Urban Districts	100.0	1.3	51.0	45.5	47.7
#鄞州	Yinzhou	100.0	3.0	58.8	54.8	38.2
余姚	Yuyao	100.0	5.1	58.2	52.5	36.7
慈溪	Cixi	100.0	4.4	57.5	53.0	38.1
奉化	Fenghua	100.0	9.2	45.5	38.3	45.3
象山	Xiangshan	100.0	14.9	46.6	33.4	38.5
宁海	Ninghai	100.0	9.6	52.0	45.6	38.4
增长速度	**Growth Rate**					
全市	Ningbo	7.6	2.0	8.1	7.7	7.3
市区	Urban Districts	7.4	0.5	7.2	6.9	7.7
#鄞州	Yinzhou	8.5	1.2	8.5	8.5	9.1
余姚	Yuyao	8.5	5.3	8.8	8.4	8.4
慈溪	Cixi	8.4	1.4	11.4	11.5	4.3
奉化	Fenghua	6.4	1.9	6.1	5.3	7.5
象山	Xiangshan	7.0	1.6	10.3	10.0	4.7
宁海	Ninghai	6.5	1.2	4.9	3.7	10.2

主要统计指标解释

【国内生产总值(GDP)】 指一个国家(或地区)所有常住单位在一定时期内生产活动的最终成果。国内生产总值有三种表现形态,即价值形态、收入形态和产品形态。从价值形态看,它是所有常住单位在一定时期内生产的全部货物和服务价值超过同期中间投入的全部非固定资产货物和服务价值的差额,即所有常住单位的增加值之和;从收入形态看,它是所有常住单位在一定时期内创造并分配给常住单位和非常住单位的初次收入分配之和;从产品形态看,它是所有常住单位在一定时期内最终使用的货物和服务价值与货物和服务净出口价值之和。在实际核算中,国内生产总值有三种计算方法,即生产法、收入法和支出法。三种方法分别从不同的方面反映国内生产总值及其构成。

【三次产业】 根据社会生产活动历史发展的顺序对产业结构的划分,产品直接取自自然界的部门为第一产业;对初级产品进行再加工的部门称为第二产业;为生产和消费提供服务的部门称为第三产业。它是世界上通用的产业结构分类,但各国的划分不尽一致。我国的三次产业划分为:

第一产业:农业(包括种植业、林业、牧业、渔业、农林牧渔服务业)。

第二产业:工业(包括采掘业、制造业、电力、燃气及水的生产和供应业)和建筑业。

第三产业:除第一、第二产业以外的其他各业。

【劳动者报酬】 指劳动者因从事生产活动所获得的全部报酬。包括劳动者获得的各种形式的工资、奖金和津贴,既包括货币形式的,也包括实物形式的;还包括劳动者所享受的公费医疗和医药卫生费、上下班交通补贴和单位支付的社会保险费等。

【生产税净额】 指生产税减生产补贴后的余额。生产税指政府对生产单位生产、销售和从事经营活动以及因从事生产活动使用某些生产要素(如固定资产、土地、劳动力)所征收的各种税、附加费和规费。生产补贴与生产税相反,指政府对生产单位的单方面收入转移,因此视为负生产税,包括政策亏损补贴、粮食系统价格补贴、外贸企业出口退税收入等。

【固定资产折旧】 指一定时期内为弥补固定资产损耗按照核定的固定资产折旧率提取的固定资产折旧,或按国民经济核算统一规定的折旧率虚拟计算的固定资产折旧。它反映了固定资产在当期生产中的转移价值。各类企业和企业化管理的事业单位的固定资产折旧是指实际计提并计入成本费中的折旧费;不计提折旧的政府机关、非企业化管理的事业单位和居民住房的固定资产折旧是按照统一规定的折旧率和固定资产原值计算的虚拟折旧。原则上,固定资产折旧应按固定资产的重置价值计算,但是目前我国尚不具备对全社会固定资产进行重估价的基础,所以暂时只能采用上述办法。

【营业盈余】 指常住单位创造的增加值扣除劳动者报酬、生产税净额和固定资产折旧后的余额。它相当于企业的营业利润加上生产补贴,但要扣除从利润中开支的工资和福利等。

【支出法国内生产总值】 指一个国家(或地区)所有常住单位在一定时期内用于最终消费、资本形成总额,以及货物和服务的净出口总额,它反映本期生产的国内生产总值的使用及构成。

【最终消费】 指常住单位在一定时期内对于货物和服务的全部最终消费支出,也就是常住单位为满足物质、文化和精神生活的需要,从本国经济领土和国外购买的货物和服务的支出;不包括非常住单位在本国经济领土内的消费支出。最终消费分为居民消费和政府消费。

【资本形成总额】 指常住单位在一定时期内获得的减去处置的固定资产加存货的变动,包括固定资本形成总额和存货增加。

Explanatory Notes on Main Statistical Indicators

[Gross Domestic Product (GDP)] refers to the final products of all resident units in a country (or a region) during a certain period of time. Gross domestic product is expressed in three different forms, i. e. value, income, and products respectively. The form of value refers to the total value of all products and services produced by all resident units during a certain period of time ,minus total value of intimidate input of materials and services of the nature of non - fixed assets or the summation of the value - added of all resident units; the form of income includes all the income created by all resident units and distributed primarily to all resident and non - resident units; the form of products refers to the value of all final goods and services for final use by all resident units plus the value of net exports of goods and services during a given period of time. In the practice of national accounting, gross domestic product is calculated with three approaches, i. e. production approach, income approach, and expenditure approach, which reflect gross domestic product and its composition from different aspects.

[Three Industries Industry] structure has been classified according to the historical sequence of development. Primary industry refers to extraction of natural resources; secondary industry involves processing of primary products; and tertiary industry provides services of various kinds for production and consumption. The above classification is universal although it various to some extent from country to country. Industry in China comprises;

Primary Industry: agriculture (including farming, forestry, animal husbandry,fishery and services).

Secondary Industry: industry (including mining and quarrying, manufacturing, electric power,Gas and water production and supply) and construction.

Tertiary Industry: all other industries not included in primary or secondary industries.

[Laborers´Remuneration] refers to the whole payment of various forms earned by the laborers from the productive activities they are engaged in. It includes wages, bonuses and allowances the laborers earned in monetary form and in kind. It also includes the free medical services provided to the laborers and the medicine expenses, traffic subsidies and social insurance fee paid by the laborers´working units for them.

[Net Taxes on Production] refers to the residual of the taxes on production minus the subsidies on production. The taxes on production refers to the various taxes, extra charges and fees levied on the production units on their production, sale and business activities as well as on some factors of production, such as fixed assets, land and labor force, used in the production activities they are engaged in. In contrast to the taxes on production, the subsidies on production refer to the unilateral transfer of part of the government's revenue to the production units and is therefore regarded as negative taxes on production. They include subsidies on the loss due to implementation of government policies, price subsidies to the grain institutions, foreign trade corporations receipts from drawback, etc.

[Depreciation of Fixed Assets] refers to the depreciation of fixed assets of a given period, drawn in accordance with the stipulated depreciation rate for the purpose of compensating the wear loss of the fixed assets or the depreciation of fixed assets calculated in a fictitious way in accordance with the stipulated unified depreciation rate in the national economic accounting system. It reflects the value of transfer of the fixed assets in the production of the current period. The depreciation of fixed assets in various enterprises and institutions managed as enterprises refers to the depreciation expenses actually drawn and calculated as part of the cost. In government agencies and institutions not managed as enterprises which do not draw the depreciation expenses, as well as for the houses of residents, the depreciation of fixed assets is the imputed depreciation, which is calculated in accordance with the stipulated unified depreciation rate. In principle, the depreciation of fixed assets should be calculated on the basis of the re - purchased value of the fixed assets. However, there is no actual condition to re - evaluate all the fixed assets in China. Therefore, the above - mentioned methods are temporarily adopted at present.

[Operating Surplus] refers to the balance of the value added created by the resident units deducting the laborers´remuneration, net taxes on production and the depreciation of fixed assets. It is equivalent to the business profit of the enterprises plus subsidies on production, but the wages and welfare expenses paid from the profits should be deducted.

[GDP Calculated with Expenditure Approach] refers to total expenditure on final consumption, total capital formation and net export of goods and services by resident units of a country in a certain period of time. It reflects the composition of GDP by its use.

[Final Consumption] refers to the total expenditure of resident units on final consumption of goods and services in a certain period, namely the expenditure of the resident units for purchases of goods and services from domestic economic territory and abroad to meet the requirements of material, cultural and spiritual life. It excludes the expenditure of non – resident units on consumption in the economic territory of the country. The final consumption is classified into household consumption and government consumption.

【Total Capital Formation】 refers to the fixed assets acquired minus those disposed and the change in inventory, including the total fixed assets formation and the increase in inventory.

NINGBO

2015

Statistical YearBook

4

CHAPTER

第四篇

财政、金融、保险、证券

FINANCE, BANKING INSURANCE AND SECURITIES

财政、金融、保险、证券
Finance, Banking, Insurancen and Securities

主要统计指标
Major Statistics Indicators

2014 年全市财政总收入	Total Financial Revenue	1790.89	亿元	100 million yuan
比上年增长	Increase Over Last Year	8.5	%	
2014 年一般公共预算收入	General Public Budget Revenue	860.61	亿元	100 million yuan
比上年增长	Increase Over Last Year	8.6	%	
2014 年一般公共预算支出	General Public Financial Budget Expenditure	1000.86	亿元	100 million yuan
比上年增长	Increase Over Last Year	6.5	%	
2014 年金融机构本外币存款余额	Total Deposits in RMB and Foreign Currency	13890.12	亿元	100 million yuan
比上年增长	Increase Over Last Year	5.5	%	
2014 年储蓄存款	Household Savings Deposits in RMB and Foreign Currency	4819.68	亿元	100 million yuan
比上年增长	Increase Over Last Year	4.9	%	
2014 年金融机构本外币贷款余额	Total Loans in RMB and Foreign Currency	14569.78	亿元	100 million yuan
比上年增长	Increase Over Last Year	9.4	%	
2014 年保费收入	Premiums	206.97	亿元	100 million yuan
比上年增长	Increase Over Last Year	11.6	%	
2014 年赔付支出	Claim and Payment	94.67	亿元	100 million yuan
比上年增长	Increase Over Last Year	-8.9	%	
2014 年证券成交总额	Total Negotiable Securities Turnover	31669.98	亿元	100 million yuan
比上年增长	Increase Over Last Year	46.6	%	

表4-1　历年公共财政预算收入及支出情况
The Public Fiscal Budget Revenue and Expenditure Over Years

单位:万元(10000 yuan)

年份 Year	财政总收入 Financial Revenue	一般公共预算收入 General Public Budget Revenue	一般公共预算支出 General Public Fiscal Budget Expenditure
1978	49697		
1979	48860		
1980	56290		
1981	65432		
1982	71546		
1983	80801		
1984	93318		
1985	91237		
1986	102264		
1987	113351		
1988	133395		
1989	152751		
1990	158910		
1991	177875		
1992	198354		
1993	282429		
1994	420202		
1995	531135		
1996	659529		
1997	750412		
1998	876351		
1999	1039976		
2000	1431511	643518	839068
2001	1903064	991088	1162797
2002	2583984	1118368	1452639
2003	3250078	1394092	1802609
2004	4009592	1517489	2159498
2005	4664968	2123797	2647749
2006	5611702	2573799	2926969
2007	7239222	3291218	3710400
2008	8109020	3903874	4394083
2009	9662496	4327676	5060788
2010	11717470	5309278	6007447
2011	14317563	6575531	7507223
2012	15365101	7255003	8284437
2013	16511797	7928080	9398939
2014	17908862	8606120	10008563

注:本表至4-3表数据来自宁波市财政局。根据新修改的《预算法》,对财政收入的指标表述进行了规范,原"地方财政收入"改名为"一般公共预算收入",具体统计口径保持不变。

Note: Data from Tables 4-1 to 4-3 are obtained from Finance Bureau of Ningbo. " According to newly modified Budget Law, the expression of fiscal revenue was regulated as the original "local financial revenue" was changed to "general public budget revenue", with the specific statistical caliber unchanged.

表4－2 各县(市)财政收入情况(2014)
Basic Statistics on Financial Revenue by Region

指标	Indicators	全市 Total	市区 Urban District
一、财政总收入	Total Financial Revenue	17908862	12989350
(一)中央财政收入	Revenue of Central Government	9302742	7014005
#消费税	Consumption Tax	2275442	2183302
(二)一般公共预算收入	General Public Budget Revenue	8606120	5975345
1.税收收入小计	Total Tax Revenue	7957351	5554138
增值税	Value－added Tax	1759543	1220872
#成品油价税费改革增值税划出	Refined Oil Prices to Draw	－44404	－44403
改征增值税	VAT	332798	295261
营业税	Business Tax	1897182	1299268
企业所得税	Enterprises Income Tax	1374818	1046614
个人所得税	Individual Income Tax	431864	286663
城市维护建设税	Tax on Urban Construction and Maintenance	583103	432474
#成品油价税费改革城市维护建设税划出	Refined Oil Prices to Draw	－85757	－85756
耕地占用税	Tax on the Use of Cultivated Land	100167	42423
契税	Contract Tax	498241	325316
2.非税收收入小计	Total non－Tax Revenue	648769	421207
专项收入	Special Projects Income	294570	200436
#教育费附加	Additional Education Tax	271234	185559
#成品油价税费改革教育费附加收入划出	Refined Oil Prices to Draw	－36537	－36536
排污费	Sewage Tax	12787	9241
行政事业性收费收入	Administrative Fees and Charges Income	175732	96641
罚没收入	Penally and Confiscatory Income	153538	90416
国有资本经营收收入	State－owned Capital Management Income	－183101	－118942
#国有企业计划亏损补贴	Subsidies to Loss of State－owned Enterprises	－183640	－119240
二、政府性基金收入	Government Fund Revenue	6765586	4813497

单位:万元(10000 yuan)

海曙 Haishu	江东 Jiangdong	江北 Jiangbei	北仑 Beilun	镇海 Zhenhai	鄞州 Yinzhou	余姚 Yuyao	慈溪 Cixi	奉化 Fenghua	象山 Xiangshan	宁海 Ninghai
808973	721127	719206	3475969	891518	2794653	1194262	1969161	552828	547676	655585
240130	200505	258307	1945229	405815	1132448	546192	969010	262595	215998	294942
3030	372	270	226992	-3817	5053	1661	64087	24189	32	2171
568843	520622	460899	1530740	485703	1662205	648070	1000151	290233	331678	360643
544936	495898	446025	1415040	457407	1547233	627030	931554	259390	291316	293923
61554	47472	90172	432256	106959	279688	127673	224869	62208	50245	73676
			-8684	139	-1	-1				
30909	27436	41298	79180	15319	48046	9376	13686	3743	5471	5261
196607	211230	107209	242199	125047	392094	158625	210088	70273	83474	75454
60053	60508	49195	346461	68325	205781	84620	132367	28358	41740	41119
35994	31049	24561	75608	22806	83311	44618	52393	14568	14651	18971
24952	21709	24317	115256	33748	97831	36786	59010	19823	15877	19133
			-16908	266	-2	-1				
	735	7487	13769	5098	15334	10223	15283	7311	17676	7251
25711	59731	57724	44767	29730	107653	43160	71190	18955	22214	17406
23907	24724	14874	115700	28296	114972	21040	68597	30843	40362	66720
10339	9301	10614	55515	18626	45162	24736	33386	10441	10613	14958
10339	9301	10336	50450	14457	41504	22788	32809	9424	9142	11512
			-7047	116	-1	-1				
			3638	3997	1079	640	276	408	735	1487
5793	1706	8483	11434	3378	28922	6162	21832	8483	11743	30871
2314	2771	1592	11173	7297	30020	12169	14494	10769	14999	10691
		-13700	-16440	-10000	-19702	-23359	-40800			
		-13700	-16440	-10000	-20000	-23600	-40800			
20312	19077	495329	389197	362796	1178529	398558	491175	403808	356455	302093

表4-3　各县(市)财政支出情况(2014)
Basic Statistics on Financial Expenditure by Region

指标	Indicators	全市 Total	市区 Urban District
一般公共预算支出	**General Public Fiscal Budget Expenditure**	**10008563**	**6611346**
一般公共服务	General Public Service	1001565	659614
公共安全	Public Safety	640304	404755
教育	Education	1596238	936153
科学技术	Science and Technology	428212	295616
文化体育与传媒	Culture, Sports and Media	169089	124713
社会保障和就业	Social Security and Reemployment	946512	603999
医疗卫生	Health Care	746057	407246
节能环保	Energy Saving and Environmental Protection	190750	135423
城乡社区服务	Community Service in Urban and Rural Areas	1090941	963106
农林水事务	Affairs Such as Agriculture, Forestry, Water Conservancy, etc.	819579	250694
交通运输	Communications and Transportation	585244	436280
资源勘探电力信息等事务	Resource exploration and Power Information	597850	408215
商业服务业等事务	Business services and Other Services	374616	310346
基金支出	**Fund Expenditure**	**6200617**	**4035668**
政府性基金	Government Funds	6200617	4035668

单位:万元(10000 yuan)

海曙 Haishu	江东 Jiangdong	江北 Jiangbei	北仑 Beilun	镇海 Zhenhai	鄞州 Yinzhou	余姚 Yuyao	慈溪 Cixi	奉化 Fenghua	象山 Xiangshan	宁海 Ninghai
310694	**292354**	**383275**	**1464937**	**438615**	**1682225**	**804673**	**1078856**	**476853**	**527444**	**509391**
48530	39469	58241	125704	57783	142765	83367	107408	51344	48108	51724
33990	24054	28385	49185	30916	83940	55445	88597	29476	29783	32248
46757	46060	66221	167068	74365	260028	154466	220641	91463	90098	103417
14020	20184	16025	79850	23594	90626	30487	55720	18267	14067	14055
2050	3653	4348	12155	8583	24031	13090	11512	5023	7298	7453
38572	30508	18645	132976	44334	150665	96247	103230	41340	38864	62832
18661	20607	23142	61303	35537	129044	98722	101773	36569	42480	59267
1688	779	4187	34762	8245	68788	11166	18106	10162	7742	8151
50112	50008	33752	276884	67151	130995	30431	42962	23134	19826	11482
3958	964	24484	31750	18046	106351	132577	104961	114980	147261	69106
681	884	42422	79114	8891	80214	40338	25291	17197	24215	41923
19456	5006	26806	179281	31124	127748	19220	133639	8894	10306	17576
4378	23262	7153	163814	6510	67498	8878	35428	5324	6711	7929
133326	**189340**	**381988**	**352154**	**293569**	**1261851**	**467482**	**568746**	**396619**	**369887**	**362215**
133326	189340	381988	352154	293569	1261851	467482	568746	396619	369887	362215

表4－4 历年金融机构人民币存贷款与现金收支情况
Savings Deposits and Loans Balances of Financial Institutions & Cash Revenue and Expenditures Over the Years(RMB)

单位:万元(10000 yuan)

年份 Year	存款余额 Deposits Balance	#城乡居民储蓄 Urban and Rural Savings Deposits	贷款余额 Loans Balance	现金收入 Cash Income	现金支出 Cash Expenditure	货币投放(＋)回笼(－) Currency Issues (＋) or Cash Withdrawal(－)
1978	50194	14997	68843	92387	101326	8939
1979	64379	20612	78939	119923	130544	10621
1980	90536	28781	107339	159955	174339	14384
1981	107253	34418	114394	187306	198061	10755
1982	130697	46298	130617	216530	227547	11017
1983	154150	60536	146636	277321	288711	11390
1984	207363	81558	242546	356422	392814	36392
1985	266510	109853	304823	522442	562304	39862
1986	354390	149451	414921	640814	679516	38702
1987	445081	199524	522160	860563	926247	65684
1988	522116	215357	643234	1212594	1328827	116233
1989	639228	317572	765704	1344442	1415310	70868
1990	899295	461220	973946	1044032	1102545	58513
1991	1180588	605796	1227009	1321446	1401416	79970
1992	1605229	792466	1603689	1957225	2099612	142387
1993	2012813	979740	2116122	3295921	3441608	145687
1994	2972601	1468634	2671174	4949086	5199010	249924
1995	4546806	2094162	3892271	7121855	7452530	330675
1996	5981440	2846051	5240845	9312625	9789622	476997
1997	7172242	3644769	5747533	12202712	12646470	443758
1998	8552754	4596343	6700817	19733593	20136905	403312
1999	10080232	5296350	7734820	24090235	24591240	501005
2000	11729400	5860592	8831213	30467325	31088353	621028
2001	14445304	6994639	10515601	36286694	37062049	775355
2002	19062375	8623909	14794722	49240318	50379541	1139223
2003	26290346	10596339	21027772	68390220	69703625	1313405
2004	30917954	12089813	24836090	90446530	91895140	1448610
2005	37919362	14588012	29597759	100679426	102368573	1689147
2006	45734811	17520388	37274957	121414154	123296128	1881974
2007	51772379	18274856	47359146	153033733	155234259	2200526
2008	62164580	23670651	56727416	155387621	157911068	2523447
2009	80839363	28695587	74248698	143230611	145798647	2568037
2010	95520308	32822564	90006170	158421425	161613115	3191690
2011	104359176	36662324	102099855			
2012	116023188	41759634	113003187			
2013	127405215	45623634	124932759			
2014	133074057	47803126	136106069			

注:本表至4－8表数据来自中国人民银行宁波中心支行。2011年现金收支统计制度取消。

Note: Data from Tables 4－4 to 4－8 are obtained from Central Subbranch of Ningbo of The People's Bank of China. Cancel the cash income and expenditure statistics system in 2011.

表4-5 金融机构人民币信贷资金来源主要指标(2014)
Main Indicators of Credit Funds of Financial Institutions - Sources of Funds

(年末余额)单位:万元(year - end)(10000 yuan)

指标	Indicators	2014
资金来源总计	**Funds Sources**	**193081715**
一、各项存款	Total Deposits	133074057
1.单位存款	Unit Deposits	73333648
其中按产品	By Product	
活期存款	Demand Deposits	22625784
定期存款	Time Deposits	22892633
通知存款	Call Deposits	1450274
保证金存款	Margin Deposits	12461884
其中按交易对手	By Counterparty	
企业存款	Deposits by Enterprises	52295493
机关团体存款	Deposits by Government Departments & Organizations	11695811
社保基金存款	Social Security Fund Deposits	7586281
部队存款	Force Deposits	807186
住房公积金存款	Housing Provident Fund Deposits	894842
非居民存款	Nonresisdent Deposits	54035
2. 个人存款	Individual Deposits	50039854
储蓄存款	Household Savings Deposits	47803126
保证金存款	Margin Deposits	138418
结构性存款	Structured Deposits	2098309
3. 财政性存款	Fiscal Deposits	3005343
4. 临时性存款	Temporary Deposits	125935
5. 委托存款	Commissiom Deposits	566669
6. 其他存款	Other Deposits	6002609
二、金融债券	Financial Bond	1746866
三、中长期借款	Medium&Long - Term Deposits	
四、应付及暂收款	Account Payable and Collecting of Money for the Time Being	4618721
其中:应付利息	Interest Payable	2389978
五、同业往来(来源方)	Inter - bnak Credits	5186796
六、系统内资金往来(来源方)	Inter - system Credit	27884676
七、外汇买卖(来源方)	Foreign Exchange	27133475
其中:结售汇	Exchange Settlement and Sales	25521290
八、各项准备	Provisions	3548501
其中:贷款损失准备金	Loan Loss Provisions	3467637
九、所有者权益	Creditors Equity	7801277
其中:实收资本	Capital Obtained	2047533
十、其他	Others	-17912655

注:金融机构包括人民银行、政策性银行、国有商业银行、邮政储蓄银行、股份制商业银行、城市商业银行、农村合作银行、农村信用社、城市信用社、外资银行、村镇银行、信托投资公司、租赁公司、财务公司等。

Note: Financial institutions including the people's Bank of China, policy banks, state - owned commercial banks, postal savings banks, joint - stock commercial banks, city commercial banks, rural cooperative banks, rural credit cooperatives, city credit cooperatives, rural banks, foreign banks, Trust Investment Company, financial leasing companies etc.

表4－6 金融机构人民币信贷资金运用主要指标(2014)
Main Indicators of Credit Funds of Financial Institutions – Use of Funds (RMB)

(年末余额)单位:万元(year – end)(10000 yuan)

指标	Indicators	2014
资金运用总计	**Funds Uses**	**193081715**
一、各项贷款	Total Loans	136106069
(一)境内贷款	Domestic Loans	136096428
1.短期贷款	Short – term Loans	69811885
(1)个人贷款及透支	Individual Loans and Overdrafts	15163365
其中:个人消费贷款	Individual Consumption Loans	7320283
其中:住房贷款	Housing Mortgage	89143
(2)单位普通贷款及透支	Unit Loans and Overdrafts	52261671
其中:经营贷款	Business Loans	51752784
固定资产贷款	Fixed Asset Loans	486083
(3)普通并购贷款	Ordinary Aquasition Loans	
(4)银团贷款	Syndicated Loans	
(5)贸易融资	Trade Loans	2386848
(6)境外筹资转贷款	Overseas Financing Transiferred Loans	
2.中长期贷款	Medium&Long – Term Loans	60994618
(1)个人贷款	Individual Loans	16384537
其中:个人消费贷款	Individual Consumption Loans	14552090
其中:住房贷款	Housing Mortgage	12841117
(2)单位普通贷款	Unit Loans	37599252
其中:经营贷款	Business Loans	3878856
固定资产贷款	Fixed Asset Loans	33720396
(3)普通并购贷款	Ordinary Aquasition Loans	308435
(4)银团贷款	Syndicated Loans	6177556
(5)贸易融资	Trade Loans	524839
(6)境外筹资转贷款	Overseas Financing Transiferred Loans	
3. 融资租赁	Financial and Leasehold	528004
4. 票据融资	Bill Financing	4298131
其中:贴现	Discount	4298131
5. 各项垫款	Advances	463790
(二)境外贷款	Foreign Loans	9641
二、有价证券	Securities	8509845
三、股权及其他投资	Euqities and Other Investment	17736250
四、应收及预付款	Receivables and Prepayments	2105834
其中:应收利息	Interest Receivable	1194739
五、同业往来(运用方)	Inter – Bank Transactions/use	1075654
六、系统内资金往来(运用方)	Inter – systmen Trasacton/use	
七、金银占款	Gold and Silver	
八、外汇买卖(运用方)	Foreign Exchange	24962546
其中:结售汇	Exchange Settlement and Sales	19596698
九、固定资产	Fixed Asset	1714616
十、库存现金	Cashes	861107
十一、投资性房地产	Investment Real Estate	9794

表4-7 各县(市)金融机构人民币存贷款情况(2014)
Savings Deposits and Loans Balances of Financial Institutions by Region(RMB)

单位:万元(10000 yuan)

地区	Region	存款余额 Deposits	其中 of Which				贷款余额 Loans	其中 of Which	
			单位存款 Unit Deposits	企业存款 by Enterprise	个人存款 Individual Deposits	储蓄存款 Savings Deposits		短期贷款 Short-term Loans	中长期贷款 Medium and Long-term Loans
全市	**Total**	**133074057**	**73333648**	**52295493**	**50039854**	**47803126**	**136106069**	**69811885**	**60994618**
市区	Urban Districts	91311400	54224999	39171831	28240532	26554803	89379874	40570867	44604050
#鄞州	Yinzhou	16967728	8324610	6607131	8258002	7669925	15166860	9594477	4775383
余姚	Yuyao	11818683	5347708	3931677	6270058	6102543	12190861	7718547	4071064
慈溪	Cixi	16786957	7387138	5397184	9010158	8799376	17578428	11750625	5235434
奉化	Fenghua	4411760	1827141	947140	2512629	2441901	5196728	2999799	2187652
象山	Xiangshan	4239795	2193387	1549563	1908066	1862886	6038970	3758630	2251965
宁海	Ninghai	4505463	2353276	1298098	2098411	2041617	5721209	3013416	2644454

表4-8 部分年份金融机构本外币存贷款情况
Savings Deposits and Loans Balances of Financial Institutions in Partial Years(in RMB and Foreign Currency)

单位:万元(10000 yuan)

指标	Indicators	2011	2012	2013	2014
本外币存款余额	**Total Deposits in RMB and Foreign Currency**	**106592654**	**119804984**	**131646045**	**138901232**
#人民币	RMB	104359176	116023188	127405215	133074057
外币	Foreign Currency	2233478	3781795	4240830	5827175
#本外币储蓄存款	Household Savings Deposits in RMB and Foreign Currency	36962819	42088122	45964728	48196821
本外币贷款余额	**Total Loans in RMB and Foreign Currency**	**106768424**	**119610158**	**133140166**	**145697768**
#人民币	RMB	102099855	113003187	124932759	136106069
外币	Foreign Currency	4668569	6606972	8207408	9591699

表4-9　保险公司业务经济技术指标(2014)
Economic and Technical Indicators of Insurance Companies

单位:万元(10000 yuan)

指标	Indicators	保费收入 Premiums		赔付支出 Claim and Payment	
		绝对量 Total	同比增长(%) Growth Rate(%)	绝对量 Total	同比增长(%) Growth Rate(%)
合计	**Total**	**2069616**	**11.6**	**946689**	**-8.9**
财产险	Property Insurance	1115661	15.2	739728	-17.4
#机动车辆保险	Motor Vehicle Insurance	808696	14.8	507954	-13.6
人身险	Life Insurance	953955	7.6	206961	44.0
寿险	Life insurance	814451	4.3	162078	45.4
健康险	Health insurance	84343	43.3	35692	44.4
人身意外伤害险	Personal Accident Insurance	55160	18.3	9191	22.4
按公司类别分	**Of Which**				
财产保险公司	**Property Insurance Companies**	**1158734**	**15.7**	**757700**	**-16.5**
财产险	Property Insurance	1115661	15.2	739728	-17.4
#机动车辆保险	Motor Vehicle Insurance	808696	14.8	507954	-13.6
人身险	Life Insurance	43073	28.7	17972	45.6
寿险	Life insurance				
健康险	Health insurance	19756	64.2	13381	54.2
人身意外伤害险	Personal Accident Insurance	23317	8.8	4591	25.3
人寿保险公司	**Property Insurance Companies**	**911068**	**6.8**	**189041**	**43.9**
财产险	Property Insurance				
#机动车辆保险	Motor Vehicle Insurance				
人身险	Life Insurance	911068	6.8	189041	43.9
寿险	Life insurance	814451	4.3	162078	45.4
健康险	Health insurance	64771	38.2	22363	39.4
人身意外伤害险	Personal Accident Insurance	31846	26.5	4600	19.7

注:本表数据来自于中国保险监督管理委员会宁波监管局。

Note: Data in this table are obtained from China Insurance Regulatory Commission Ningbo Burean.

表4-10 部分年份保险业务情况 Conditions of Insurance Business in Partial Years

单位:亿元(100 million yuan)

指标	Indicators	2008	2009	2010	2011	2012	2013	2014
保费收入	**Premiums**	**87.11**	**107.44**	**144.06**	**148.60**	**164.71**	**185.50**	**206.97**
财产险	Property Insurance	40.34	51.08	66.20	77.29	86.23	96.84	111.57
人身险	Life Insurance	46.76	56.37	77.86	71.31	78.48	88.66	95.40
赔付支出	**Claim and Payment**	**37.90**	**36.29**	**38.14**	**48.19**	**64.27**	**103.91**	**94.67**
财产险	Property Insurance	24.54	25.44	27.45	37.47	51.91	89.54	73.97
人身险	Life Insurance	13.37	10.85	10.69	10.72	12.37	14.37	20.70

注:2011年起,保险业采用新会计准则二号解释的新口径进行计算。

Note: From 2011, the insurance industry in accordance with the new accounting standards new dianeter calculation.

表4-11 证券市场基本情况(2014) Basic Statistics on Securities Markets

指标	单位	Indicators	unit	绝对量 Total	比上年增长(%) Growth Rate(%)
上市公司总家数	家	Total Listed Companies (A Share and H Share)	Unit	59	
#A股上市公司	家	A Share	Unit	45	
A股上市公司总股本	亿股	Total Issued Capital of Listed Companies (A Share)	100 million shares	373.13	7.9
A股上市公司总市值	亿元	Total Market Capitalization of Listed Companies (A Share)	100 million yuan	3281.29	61.1
境内证券市场融资额	亿元	Total Financing on Securities Markets in Mainland	100 million yuan	73.93	15.2
证券成交总额	亿元	Total Negotiable Securities Turnover	100 million yuan	31669.98	46.6
#股票和基金	亿元	Stock and Fund	100 million yuan	20663.10	50.7
证券客户交易结算资金余额	亿元	Total Exchange and Settlement Capital of Securities Customer	100 million yuan	143.96	117.6
指定与托管证券市值	亿元	Securities Market Capitalization of Appointment and Trusteeship	100 million yuan	2433.52	88.9
证券投资者股票账户数	万户	Total Stock Investors	10000 accounts	104.53	6.2
证券公司分支机构利润总额	亿元	Total Branch Profits of Stock Exchange	100 million yuan	8.03	45.7
期货代理交易量	万手	Agency's Trading Volume of Futures	10000 pieces	5535.73	4.5
期货代理交易额	亿元	Agent's Turnover of Futures	100 million yuan	53108.44	-0.7
期货保证金余额	万元	Balance Cover Cost	10000 yuan	423890.45	33.5
期货投资者开户数	万户	Total Future Investors	10000 accounts	2.25	9.2

注:本表数据来自于中国证券监督管理委员会宁波监管局。

Note: Data in this table are obtained from China Securities Regulatory Commission Ningbo Burean.

表4-12 银行业分支机构及人员数(2014)
Branches and Personnel of the Banking Sector

单位:家,人(Unit,person)

行列名称		法人 corporation	分行(分公司) Branch	支行 Subbranch	分理处(储蓄所) Saving Branch	机构小计 Total	人员数 Employee
全市	**Total**	**29**	**38**	**1394**	**741**	**2202**	**45501**
政策性银行合计	**Policy Bank**		**3**	**8**		**11**	**414**
国家开发银行	China Development Bank		1			1	177
进出口银行	Export - Import Bank		1			1	58
农业发展银行	Agricultural Development Bank of China		1	8		9	179
大型银行合计	**State - owned Commercial Bank**		**9**	**634**	**78**	**721**	**16814**
工商银行	Industrial and Commercial Bank of China		1	175	5	181	4297
农业银行	Agricultural Bank of China		1	164	37	202	4346
中国银行	Bank of China		5	128		133	3435
建设银行	China Constuction Bank		1	127	36	164	3640
交通银行	Bank of Communications		1	40		41	1096
股份制商业银行合计	**Joint - stock Commercial Bank**		**11**	**157**		**168**	**7347**
中信银行	China CITIC Bank		1	23		24	916
光大银行	China Everbright Bank Co. , Ltd.		1	17		18	833
华夏银行	Huaxia Bank		1	8		9	429
广发银行	China Guangfa Bank		1	14		15	508
平安银行	Ping An Bank Co. ,Ltd		1	12		13	717
招商银行	China Merchants Bank		1	19		20	953
浦东发展	Shanghai Pudong Development Bank		1	21		22	1010
兴业银行	Industrial Bank Co. , Ltd.		1	12		13	648
民生银行	China Minsheng Banking Co. , Ltd.		1	23		24	803
浙商银行	China Zheshang Bank Co. , Ltd.		1	8		9	407
恒丰银行	EverGrowing Bank Co. ,Ltd		1			1	123
城市商业银行合计	**City Commercial Bank**	**3**	**9**	**248**		**260**	**8855**
宁波银行(宁波地区)	Bank of Ningbo (Ningbo Area)	1		169		170	4991

表 4 – 12 续表 单位:家,人(Unit, person)

行列名称		法人 corporation	分行 (分公司) Branch	支行 Subbranch	分理处 (储蓄所) Saving Branch	机构 小计 Total	人员数 Employee
宁波通商银行	**Ningbo Commerce Back Company Limited**	**1**		**4**		**5**	**440**
宁波东海银行	Ningbo Donhai Bank	1		10		11	427
上海银行	Shanghai Bank		1	8		9	408
包商银行	Baoshang Bank		1	9		10	242
温州银行	Wenzhou Bank		1	5		6	185
泰隆银行	Zhejiang Tailong Commercial Bank		1	15		16	555
临商银行	Linshang Bank		1	7		8	368
杭州银行	Bank of Wenzhou		1	8		9	364
民泰银行	Zhejiang Mintai Commercial Bank		1	7		8	424
稠州银行	Zhejiang Chouzhou Commercial Bank		1	3		4	216
台州银行	Taizhou Bank		1	3		4	235
邮储银行	**Postal Savings Bank of China**		**1**	**148**	**166**	**315**	**2765**
农村中小金融机构	Rural Small and Medium Financial Institutions	23		196	497	716	9010
农村合作金融机构	Rural Cooperative Financial Institutions	9		179	496	684	8309
新型农村金融机构	New – type Rural Financial Institutions	14		17	1	32	701
非银行金融机构合计	**Non – bank Financial Institutions**	**2**	**1**			**3**	**99**
信托投资公司	Trust and Investment Corporation	1				1	52
财务公司	Finance Company	1				1	28
租赁公司	Leasing Company		1			1	19
外资银行合计	**Foreign Bank**	**1**	**4**	**3**		**8**	**197**
协和银行	**Union Bank**	**1**				**1**	**13**
恒生银行(中国)	**Hang Seng Bank(China)**		**1**			**1**	**25**
汇丰银行(中国)	**HSBC Bank (China)**		**1**	**1**		**2**	**51**
渣打银行(中国)	**Standard Chartered Bank (China)**		**1**	**2**		**3**	**76**
东亚银行(中国)	**The Bank of East Asia Limited**		**1**			**1**	**32**

注:本表数据来自于中国银行业监督管理委员会宁波监管局。

Note: Data in this table are obtained from China Banking Regulatory Commission Ningbo Burean.

主要统计指标解释

【财政收入】 国家财政参与社会产品分配所取得收入,是实现国家职能的财力保证。财政收入包括的内容几经变化,目前主要包括:

(1)各项税收 包括增值税、营业税、消费税、土地增值税、城市维护建设税、资源税、城市土地使用税、印花税、固定资产投资方向调节税、个人所得税、企业所得税、关税、农牧业税和耕地占用税等。

(2)专项收入 包括征收排污费、征收城市水资源费收入,教育费附加收入等。

(3)其他收入 包括基本建设贷款归还收入、国家能源交通重点建设基金收入、国家预算调节基金等。

(4)国有企业计划亏损补贴 这项为负收入,冲减财政收入。

【财政支出】 国家财政将筹集起来的资金进行分配使用,以满足经济建设和各项事业的需要,主要包括(2007 年支出项目作过调整):

(1)基本建设支出

(2)企业挖潜改造资金

(3)地质勘探费用

(4)科技三项费用

(5)支援农村生产支出

(6)农林水利气象等部门的事业费用

(7)工业交通商业等部门的事业费

(8)文教科学卫生事业费

(9)抚恤和社会福利救济费

(10)国防支出

(11)行政管理费

(12)价格补贴支出

【存款】 企业、机关、团体或居民根据可以收回的原则,把货币资金存入银行或其他信用机构保管并取得一定利息的一种信用活动形式。根据存款对象的不同可划分为企业存款、财政存款、机关团体存款、基本建设存款、城镇储蓄存款、农村存款等科目。它是银行信贷资金的主要来源。

【贷款】 银行或其他信用机构根据必须归还的原则,按一定利率,为企业、个人等提供资金的一种信用活动形式。我国银行贷款分为流动资金贷款、固定资产贷款、城乡个体工商户贷款以农业贷款等科目。

【承保额】 又叫保险金额。它是保险人员对被保险人负提损失补偿或约定给付的金额。它是保险合同上的最高责任额,也是计算保费的依据。

【保费】 又叫保险费。是保险人根据保险合同的有关规定,为被保险人取得因约定危险事故发生所造成的经济损失补偿(或给付)权利,付给保险人的代价。包括财产险和人身险储金收入。

【赔款】 保险事故发生后,经查证确属保险责任范围以内的保险标的损失,保险人根据保险合同的规定履行赔偿义务,给与被保险人的款项叫做赔款。赔款可以分为已决赔款和未决赔款两种。

Explanatory Notes on Main Statistical Indicators

[Government Revenue] refers to the revenue of government finance by means of participating the distribution of the social products, which is the financial resources for ensuring the government to function. The contents of government revenue have been changed several times. Now it includes the following main items:

(1) Various tax revenue, including value added tax, business tax, consumption tax, land value added tax, tax on city maintenance and construction, resources tax, tax on the urban land, stamp tax, tax on the adjustment of orientation of investment in the fixed assets, personal income tax, tariff, tax on agriculture and animal husbandry and tax on occupation of cultivated land, etc.

(2) Special revenues, including revenue collected from imposing fee on sewage treatment, revenue collected from imposing fee on urban water resources, and extra – charges for educations, etc.

(3) Other revenues, including revenue from the re – payment of capital construction loan, the funds for the state key construction projects in energy industry and transportation, and the funds for state budget adjustment, etc.

(4) Planned subsidies for the losses of the state – = owned enterprises. This is an item of negative revenue, used to eat up part of the government revenue.

[Government Expenditure] refers to the distribution and use of the funds the government finance has raised, so as to meet the need s of economic construction and various causes. It included the following main items(The items has changed from the year of 2007):

(1) Expenditure for capital construction

(2) Innovation funds of the enterprises(3) Geological prospecting expenses

(4) Expenditures for science and technology promotion

(5) Expenditure for supporting rural production

(6) Operating Expenses of departments of farming, forestry, water conservancy and meteorology etc.

(7) Operating expenses of departments of industry, transport and commerce

(8) Operating expenses of departments of culture, education, science and public health

(9) Pension for the disabled or the families of the bereaved and relief funds for social welfare

(10) Expenditures for national defense

(11) Administrative expenses:

(12) Expenditure for price subsidies

[Deposit] is a form a of credit by which enterprises, institutions, organizations or residents can put money into banks and other credit institutions for safekeeping and interest earning under the principle of free withdrawal. According to different depositors, deposits are divided into enterprise deposits, deposits of government agencies and institutions, capital construction deposits, urban savings deposits, rural deposits and other deposits. Deposits are major sources of the credit funds of banks.

[Loan] is a form a of credit by which banks and other institutions provide funds at a certain interest rate to enterprise sand individuals in light of the principle of unconditional re – payment. Loans from Chinese banks include circulating capital loans, fixed assets loans, loans to urban and rural individuals engaged in industrial and commercial business and agricultural loans.

[Amount Insured] refers to the amount of compensation for loss or agreed sum of money to be paid by the insurer to the insurant. It is the maximum amount of liabilities written in the insurance contract and is also used as a basis to calculate the premium.

[Premium] is the fee paid by the insurant based on a proportion of the benefit he or she may get from the insurance plus the insurance value. It includes the income from the deposit of property insurance and personal insurance.

[Settled Claim] is the compensation paid by the insurer to the insurant in accordance with the insurance contract for the loss which has been checked and found to be in the range of liability of insurance after an accident has happened to the insured property or to a person who has insured for his life. It is further divided into settled and unsettled claim.

NINGBO 2015 Statistical YearBook

5 CHAPTER

第五篇

物价指数和人民生活

PRICES INDEX AND PEOPLE'S LIVELIHOOD

物价指数和人民生活
Price Index and People's Livelihood

主要统计指标
Major Statistics Indicators

以上年价格为 100	The Price of Preceding Year is Taken as 100			
2014 年市区居民消费价格总指数	General Consumer Price Index of Urban Residents	101.9		
2014 年市区商品零售价价格指数	General Retail Price Index of Commodities in Urban Area	100.3		
2014 年全部工业品出厂价格指数	Total Industrial Products Producer Price Index	97.81		
2014 年全部原材料购进价格指数	Purchase Price Indices of Raw Mater, Fuels and Power	97.51		
2014 年城镇居民人均可支配收入	Per Capital Disposable Income of Urban Resident	44155	元	yuan
2014 年城镇居民人均生活消费支出	Per Capita Living Expenditure of Urban Resident	27893	元	yuan
2014 年农村居民人均可支配收入	Per Capital Net Income of Rural Resident	24283	元	yuan
2014 年农村居民人均生活消费支出	Per Capita Living Expenditures of Rural Resident	16228	元	yuan

表5-1 市区居民消费价格指数及商品零售价格指数(以上年价格为100) Consumer Price Indices and Retail Price Indices in Urban Area(Preceding Year = 100)

年份 Year	各年以上年价格为100 (The Price of Preceding Year is Taken as 100)		
	居民消费价格总指数 General Consumer Price Index	#服务项目 Service	商品零售价格总指数 General Retail Price Index of Commodities
1978	100.0	104.4	99.3
1985	116.6	113.6	116.9
1986	106.4	106.0	106.4
1987	110.6	105.2	111.1
1988	124.2	123.9	124.2
1989	116.7	111.6	117.1
1990	104.0	113.7	103.2
1991	106.8	111.5	106.4
1992	112.2	119.5	111.4
1993	126.0	149.5	122.8
1994	123.5	129.8	118.0
1995	119.1	129.8	112.6
1996	110.4	122.0	106.3
1997	103.9	119.5	100.8
1998	99.8	108.4	97.6
1999	100.1	117.8	97.3
2000	100.3	114.0	98.3
2001	99.3	105.4	94.8
2002	99.2	100.6	98.6
2003	101.2	101.3	101.6
2004	102.7	101.9	102.0
2005	102.0	101.7	101.1
2006	101.9	101.2	101.8
2007	103.9	100.6	103.3
2008	105.0	98.2	107.1
2009	99.4	97.7	98.8
2010	103.7	102.0	103.9
2011	105.3	101.8	105.7
2012	101.7	99.5	101.8
2013	102.2	103.8	101.0
2014	101.9	103.6	100.3

表 5 - 2 市区居民消费价格指数及商品零售价格指数(以 1952 年为 100)
Residents Consumer Price Indices and Retail Price Indices in Urban Area(1952 = 100)

年份 Year	以 1952 年为 100 (1952 = 100) 居民消费价格总指数 General Consumer Price Index	#服务项目 Service	商品零售价格总指数 General Retail Price Index of Commodities
1953	106.8	100.0	106.1
1957	110.7	113.6	108.8
1965	117.2	114.2	116.4
1975	116.5	105.2	116.5
1978	116.3	109.8	115.4
1980	135.4	109.8	124.6
1985	171.6	137.4	158.2
1989	292.7	211.8	272.1
1990	304.4	240.9	280.8
1991	325.1	268.5	298.7
1992	364.7	320.9	332.8
1993	459.6	479.8	408.7
1994	567.6	622.7	482.2
1995	676.0	808.3	543.0
1996	746.3	986.1	577.2
1997	775.4	1178.4	581.8
1998	773.8	1277.4	567.8
1999	774.6	1504.8	552.5
2000	776.9	1715.5	543.1
2001	771.5	1808.1	514.9
2002	765.3	1819.0	507.7
2003	774.5	1842.6	515.8
2004	795.4	1877.6	526.1
2005	811.3	1909.6	531.9
2006	826.8	1932.5	541.5
2007	859.0	1944.1	559.3
2008	901.9	1909.1	599.1
2009	896.5	1865.2	591.9
2010	929.7	1902.5	614.9
2011	979.0	1936.7	650.0
2012	995.6	1927.0	661.7
2013	1017.5	2000.3	668.3
2014	1036.8	2072.3	670.3

表5-3 城市及农村居民消费价格分类指数(2014)
Residents Consumer Price Indices by Category and by Urban and Rural

(以上年价格为100 The Price of Preceding Year is Taken as 100)

指标	Indicators	城市 Urban	农村 Rural
居民消费价格总指数	**General Consumer Price Index**	**101.9**	**101.8**
服务项目价格指数	**Price Index for Service**	**103.6**	**102.4**
一、食品	Food	102.7	103.2
1.粮食	Grain	100.3	101.0
2.肉禽及其制品	Meat, Poultry and Related Products	99.7	99.5
3.蛋	Eggs	114.0	108.5
4.水产品	Aquatic Products	101.6	108.4
5.蔬菜	Vegetables	99.1	98.7
#鲜菜	Fresh Vegetables	98.3	97.3
6.在外用膳食品	Eating Outside	104.0	101.1
二、烟酒	Tobacco and Liquor	99.8	99.8
三、衣着	Garments	102.7	102.6
四、家庭设备用品及维修服务	Houshold Facilities Articles and Maintenance Services	99.9	100.1
#耐用消费品	Durable Consumer Goods	98.8	98.6
五、医疗保健和个人用品	Medicine, Medical Articles and Personal Goods	102.3	101.8
#医疗保健	Medicine and medical Articles	102.4	102.4
六、交通和通信	Transportation and Communication	99.5	99.5
1.交通	Transportation	99.3	99.5
2.通信	Communication	99.9	99.6
七、娱乐教育文化用品及服务	Recreation. Education. Culture Articles and Services	102.0	101.3
#文娱用耐用消费品及服务	Durable Consumer Goods for Recreational Use	99.1	99.2
教育	Education	102.4	102.2
八、居住	Residence	102.4	101.7

表5－4　市区商品零售价格分类指数(2014)
Urban Retail Price Index by Category of Commodities

(以上年同期价格为100 The Price of Preceding Years is Taken as 100)

指标	Indicators	城市 Urban
商品零售价格总指数	**General Retail Price Index**	**100.3**
一、食品	Food	102.8
1.粮食	Grain	100.3
2.油脂	Oil or Fat	91.7
3.肉禽及其制品	Meat,Poultry and Eggs	99.8
4.水产品	Aquatic Products	101.6
5.蔬菜	Vegetables	99.1
#鲜菜	Fresh Vegetables	98.3
6.在外用膳食品	Eating Outside	104.0
二、饮料、烟酒	Beverages,Tobacco and Liguor	99.8
三、服装、鞋帽	Garments,Shoes and Hats	102.6
四、纺织品	Textiles	101.5
五、家用电器及音像器材	Household Appliance and Audio－video Apparatus	98.3
六、文化办公用品	Stationery and Office Goods	100.3
七、日用品	Daily Use Articles	100.2
八、体育娱乐用品	Sports and Recreation Articles	100.2
九、交通、通信用品	Transportation and Communication Articles	98.4
十、家具	Furniture	100.7
十一、化妆品	Cosmetics	100.1
十二、金银珠宝	Gold,silvrt and Jewelry	90.5
十三、中西药品及医疗保健用品	Traditional Chinese and Western Medicines, Medical Treatment &Health Proterction Articles	96.7
十四、书报杂志及电子出版物	Book,Newspapers,Magazines and Electronic Publication	99.6
十五、燃料	Fuels	99.4
十六、建筑材料及五金电料	Building,Hardware and Electrical Equipment Materials	99.5

表5－5 部分年份工业生产者出厂价格指数
Industrial Producers Ex－factory Price Index in Partial Years

指标	Indicators	各年以上年价格为100 (The Price of Preceding Years is Taken as 100)				
		2010	2011	2012	2013	2014
总指数	**Combined Index**	**108.89**	**105.86**	**97.05**	**96.67**	**97.81**
轻工业	Light Industry	104.66	104.92	98.46	97.54	98.43
以农产品为原料	Using Farm Products as Raw Materials	106.04	106.93	98.39	97.29	98.62
以非农产品为原料	Using Non Farm Products as Raw Materials	103.98	103.11	98.52	97.76	98.26
重工业	Heavy Industry	113.13	106.36	96.31	96.21	97.48
采掘	Mining and Quarrying Industry	127.80	100.00	100.00	100.00	100.00
原料	Raw Material Industry	119.57	110.77	98.18	97.32	95.72
加工	Manufacturing Industry	108.00	104.19	95.41	95.64	98.35
生产资料	Production Goods	111.61	106.31	95.73	96.04	97.38
采掘	Mining and Quarrying Industry	127.80	100.00	100.00	100.00	100.00
原料	Raw Material Industry	119.94	110.08	97.36	96.96	95.36
加工	Manufacturing Industry	107.43	104.54	94.98	95.58	98.33
生活资料	Means of Subsistence	101.83	104.67	100.55	98.27	98.94
食品	Food	107.58	108.09	101.97	96.84	96.34
衣着	Garments	102.43	106.05	100.85	98.44	99.33
一般日用品	Articles for Daily Use	100.53	104.09	101.51	99.46	100.26
耐用消费品	Durable Consumer Goods	100.53	102.55	98.32	97.05	97.81

表5-6 部分年份工业生产者购进价格指数
Purchase Price Index of Industrial Producers in Partial Years

指标	Indicators	各年以上年价格为100 (The Price of Preceding Years is Taken as 100)				
		2010	2011	2012	2013	2014
总指数	**Combined Index**	**113.10**	**108.56**	**97.05**	**96.34**	**97.51**
燃料动力类	Fuels and Energy	124.81	113.15	100.53	93.94	96.64
黑色金属材料类	Ferrous Metals	110.95	108.10	91.46	94.18	95.64
有色金属材料及电线类	Nonferrous Metal and Electric Wire	137.74	112.68	90.48	95.37	96.26
化工原料类	Chemical Raw Materials	115.82	111.94	93.15	97.36	98.79
木材及纸浆类	Wood and Paper Pulps	122.53	101.35	95.02	96.31	96.59
建筑材料及非金属矿类	Building Materials and Nonmetal Minerals	106.97	118.75	93.65	98.35	100.39
其它工业原材料及半成品类	Other Industrial Raw and Processed Materials	101.39	102.33	98.52	97.85	97.74
农副产品类	Farm and Sideline Products	122.45	124.93	101.73	99.75	101.57
纺织原料类	Textile Raw Materials	112.08	110.02	92.57	97.49	99.01

表5-7 住宅销售价格指数(2014)
Residential Building Sales Price Index

(以上年同期价格为100 The Price of Preceding Years is Taken as 100)

月份	Mouth	新建住宅 New Residential Buildings	新建商品住房 New Commodity Housing	按套型分 By House Size			二手住宅 Second-hand Residential Buildings	按套型分 By House Size		
				90平方及以下 90 Sq. m and Below	90-144平方米 90-144 Sq. m	144平方米以上 More than 144 Sq. m		90平方及以下 90 Sq. m and Below	90-144平方米 90-144 Sq. m	144平方米以上 More than 144 Sq. m
一月份	January	107.1	107.5	107.0	107.6	107.6	104.7	105.0	103.7	105.5
二月份	February	106.1	106.4	105.4	106.3	106.9	103.5	103.5	103.1	104.5
三月份	March	105.9	106.3	104.8	105.8	107.1	103.2	103.3	102.6	103.9
四月份	April	105.1	105.4	104.1	105.3	105.9	102.7	102.8	102.4	102.9
五月份	May	103.8	104.0	102.6	104.0	104.4	101.7	101.6	101.5	102.0
六月份	June	101.3	101.4	99.4	101.5	102.0	100.5	100.6	100.5	100.3
七月份	July	100.0	100.0	96.8	100.0	101.1	99.5	99.3	99.9	99.2
八月份	August	98.7	98.6	96.2	98.7	99.3	98.4	98.2	99.1	98.0
九月份	September	97.3	97.2	94.8	97.1	98.0	97.5	97.2	98.2	97.3
十月份	October	96.5	96.3	94.4	96.0	97.2	96.1	95.9	96.5	95.8
十一月份	November	95.6	95.3	93.4	95.7	95.7	95.0	94.7	95.8	94.7
十二月份	December	94.7	94.4	93.1	95.0	94.4	94.1	93.8	94.7	94.0

注:1. 由于2011年房地产价格专业制度全方面改革,故指标分类有所变化。且只计算月度数据,没有季度和年度汇总数据。

2. 2014年起取消土地交易价格、住宅租赁和物业服务价格报表。

Note: Due to the reform of the professional system of 2011 real estate prices, so the index classification are subject to change. And only monthly data, there is no summary of quarterly and annual data.

Price report of land trunsaction, domestic tenancy property service canceled since 2014.

表5－8 历年城乡居民人均收支及住房情况
Per Capita Annual Income and Living Expenditures and Housing Conditions of Urban and Rural Residents Over the Years

单位:元,平方米(yuan,sq. m)

年份 Year	城镇居民人均可支配收入 Per Capita Disposable Income of Urban Residents	城镇居民人均生活消费支出 Per Capita Living Expenditure of Urban Residents	农村居民人均可支配收入 Per Capita Disposable Income of Rural Residents	农村居民人均生活消费支出 Per Capita Living Expenditure of Rural Residents	城镇居民人均自有现住房面积 Per Capita Private Housing Area of Urban Residents	农村居民人均自有现住房面积 Per Capita Private Housing Area of Rural Residents
1978	306	299				
1979	340	332				
1980	429	419	222	183		
1981	481	490	217	274		
1982	509	492	353	338		
1983	530	502	340	375	12.62	
1984	643	561	483	428	12.84	
1985	889	862	627	564	12.94	21.30
1986	1110	1057	735	673	12.92	22.80
1987	1192	1076	871	762	13.44	24.50
1988	1518	1469	1066	964	14.49	26.00
1989	1742	1543	1199	1051	15.32	27.30
1990	1963	1628	1254	1166	15.56	27.70
1991	2182	1854	1441	1221	15.93	29.90
1992	2674	2204	1624	1368	16.00	31.00
1993	3983	3139	2060	1599	16.08	30.20
1994	6008	4442	2685	2215	17.25	33.60
1995	7275	5566	3484	2432	17.41	31.30
1996	8354	6545	4267	3283	17.09	30.75
1997	9069	7189	4568	3483	17.42	39.95
1998	9193	7912	4697	3589	18.21	37.58
1999	9492	7493	4798	3591	19.40	39.78
2000	10921	7997	5069	3929	20.34	41.57
2001	11991	9463	5362	4383	21.53	43.14
2002	12970	9396	5764	4508	21.86	45.74
2003	14277	10463	6221	4194	23.22	46.86
2004	15882	11283	7018	6102	23.85	49.90
2005	17408	11758	7810	6623	24.92	50.44
2006	19674	12666	8847	7378	24.91	51.88
2007	22307	13921	10051	8062	26.09	53.24
2008	25304	16739	11450	9174	28.85	55.86
2009	27368	18203	12641	9789	29.72	55.88
2010	30166	19420	14261	9794	30.22	56.00
2011	34058	21779	16518	11253	32.88	57.22
2012	37902	23288	18475	12699	32.55	58.29
2013	41729	24685	20534	13915	33.58	58.87
2014	44155	27893	24283	16228	39.70	47.76

注:2014年为城乡住户一体化新口径,2013年(含)之前城镇均为市区口径,2013年(含)之前农村居民可支配收入指人均纯收入口径。

表5-9 分城乡居民收入与支出(2014)
Urban and rural residents income and expenditure

指标	Indicators	单位	Unit	城镇 Cities& Towns	农村 Rural
一、人口就业情况	**Population employment**				
1. 住户数	Household number	户	Households	1869	904
2. 期内住户常住成员数	Resident membership of the period	人	person	5007	2368
3. 劳动力人数	Labor force	人	person	3814	1824
4. 常住成员从业人数	Number of permanent members employed	人	person	3133	1596
二、可支配收入	**Disposable income**	**元**	**yuan**	**44155**	**24283**
(一)工资性收入	Wages Income	元	yuan	27023	15777
(二)经营净收入	Net operating income	元	yuan	8219	5600
1. 第一产业经营净收入	Net income of the first industry operation	元	yuan	419	1676
2. 第二产业经营净收入	Net income of the second industry operation	元	yuan	3613	2150
3. 第三产业经营净收入	Net income of the third industry operation	元	yuan	4187	1774
(三)财产和转移净收入	Net income of property and transfer	元	yuan	8913	2906
三、总支出	**Total expenditure**	**元**	**yuan**	**53828**	**31578**
1. 生产经营费用支出	Production and operating expenses	元	yuan	344	1670
2. 财产性支出	Prorerty Expenditure	元	yuan	352	35
3. 转移性支出	Transfer Expenditure	元	yuan	2773	1145
4. 部分商业保险支出	Part of commercial insurance expenses	元	yuan	62	10
5. 购置资产及非经常性转移支出	Acquisition of assets and non recurrent transfer expenses	元	yuan	4652	2726
6. 借贷性支出	Borrowing expenses	元	yuan	17753	9764
四、消费支出	**Consumption expenditure**	**元**	**yuan**	**27893**	**16228**
(一)食品烟酒	**Food alcohol and tobacco**	元	**yuan**	8396	5841
(二)衣着	**Garments**	元	**yuan**	2103	1096
(三)居住	**Residence**	元	**yuan**	7022	3230
(四)生活用品及服务	**Daily necessities and services**	元	**yuan**	1279	667
(五)交通通信	**Transportation and Communication**	元	**yuan**	3974	2592
1. 交通	**Transportation**	元	**yuan**	3092	1885
2. 通讯	**Communication**	元	**yuan**	882	707
(六)教育文化娱乐	**Recreation, Education and Cultural**	元	**yuan**	3064	1383
1 教育	**Education**	元	**yuan**	1615	983
2 文化娱乐	**Cultural recreation**	元	**yuan**	1449	400
(七)医疗保健	**Medicine and medical Articles**	元	**yuan**	1217	1105
(八)其他用品和服务	**Other supplies and services**	元	**yuan**	838	314

表5－10　各地城镇居民收入与支出(2014)
Urban residents income and expenditure

指标	Indicators	单位	Unit
可支配收入	**Disposable income**	元	yuan
(一)工资性收入	Wages Income	元	yuan
(二)经营净收入	Net operating income	元	yuan
(三)财产净收入	Net income of property	元	yuan
(四)转移净收入	Net income of transfer	元	yuan
消费支出	**Consumption expenditure**	元	**yuan**
(一)食品烟酒	Food alcohol and tobacco	元	yuan
(二)衣着	Garments	元	yuan
(三)居住	Residence	元	yuan
(四)生活用品及服务	Daily necessities and services	元	yuan
(五)交通通信	Transportation and Communication	元	yuan
(六)教育文化娱乐	Recreation, Education and Cultural	元	yuan
(七)医疗保健	Medicine and medical Articles	元	yuan
(八)其他用品和服务	Other supplies and services	元	yuan

单位:元(yuan)

全市 Total	市区 Urban District	鄞州 Yinzhou	象山 Xiangshan	宁海 Ninghai	余姚 Yuyao	慈溪 Cixi	奉化 Fenghua
44155	**47190**	**46324**	**40189**	**40664**	**41921**	**43526**	**38755**
27023	29328	28023	22215	22077	27126	23422	25319
8219	5954	7041	8528	11060	8248	11728	4651
5407	6289	8704	5592	4808	3977	4731	4284
3506	5620	2556	3854	2719	2570	3645	4501
27893	**30674**	**30307**	**18587**	**25363**	**27109**	**27714**	**28522**
8396	8919	8136	5817	5915	8366	7638	8552
2103	2335	2613	1490	1752	1918	2168	2055
7022	6779	6560	5070	9016	5704	6898	7243
1279	1544	1527	842	1411	1437	996	1122
3974	4969	4679	2334	3423	4949	5145	4663
3064	3492	3758	1971	2340	3046	2714	3526
1217	1542	1857	703	1039	994	1378	652
838	1094	1178	360	468	695	776	709

表5-11　各地农村居民收入与支出(2014)
Income and expenditure of rural residents

指标	Indicators	单位	Unit
可支配收入	**Disposable income**	元	**yuan**
(一)工资性收入	Wages Income	元	yuan
(二)经营净收入	Net operating income	元	yuan
(三)财产和转移净收入	Net income of property and transfer	元	yuan
消费支出	**Consumption expenditure**	元	**yuan**
(一)食品烟酒	Food alcohol and tobacco	元	yuan
(二)衣着	Garments	元	yuan
(三)居住	Residence	元	yuan
(四)生活用品及服务	Daily necessities and services	元	yuan
(五)交通通信	Transportation and Communication	元	yuan
(六)教育文化娱乐	Recreation, Education and Cultural	元	yuan
(七)医疗保健	Medicine and medical Articles	元	yuan
(八)其他用品和服务	Other supplies and services	元	yuan

单位:元(yuan)

全市 Total	市区 Urban District	鄞州 Yinzhou	象山 Xiangshan	宁海 Ninghai	余姚 Yuyao	慈溪 Cixi	奉化 Fenghua
24283	**25815**	**26682**	**22146**	**22209**	**24312**	**25041**	**22033**
15777	18425	17360	10500	11448	16161	14757	11823
5600	3891	5546	7740	7891	5134	7138	7789
2906	3499	3776	3906	2870	3017	3146	2421
16228	**16363**	**18697**	**12666**	**14935**	**17977**	**18118**	**13492**
5841	6196	6493	4033	5073	6230	5951	5770
1096	1248	1480	681	1058	920	1259	687
3230	2960	3453	3303	3063	3463	3315	3323
667	801	1063	581	744	794	414	393
2592	2252	2690	1752	1682	3701	3937	1339
1383	1364	1878	812	1592	1554	1844	856
1105	1164	1196	1337	1418	1035	1029	889
314	377	444	168	306	280	369	236

表5－12 分城乡居民耐用消费品拥有量(2014)
The amount of consumer durable goods of urban and rural areas

指标	Indicators	单位	Unit	城镇 Cities &Towns	农村 Rural
家用汽车拥有量	Homeuse Car Ownership	辆/百户	car/hundred families	45	20
洗衣机拥有量	Washing Machines Ownership	台/百户	set/hundred families	87	69
电冰箱(柜)拥有量	Refrigerators Ownership	台/百户	set/hundred families	95	93
彩色电视机拥有量	Color TV Sets Ownership	台/百户	set/hundred families	187	171
空调拥有量	Air－conditioners Ownership	台/百户	set/hundred families	179	116
固定电话拥有量	Fixed phone Ownership	线/百户	line/hundred families	70	70
移动电话拥有量	Mobile Phone Ownership	部/百户	set/hundred families	218	197
#其中:接入互联网	Which: access to the Internet	部/百户	set/hundred families	116	67
计算机拥有量	Computer Ownership	台/百户	set/hundred families	95	46
#其中:接入互联网	Which: access to the Internet	台/百户	set/hundred families	86	40

表5－13 按收入等级分的城乡居民人均可支配收入
Disposable income of urban and rural residents by income levels

指标 Indicators	年份 Year	按人均可支配收入等级分组 Grouped by Level of Disposable Income				
		低20%收入户 Lower Income Households (20%)	次低20%收入户 Low Income Households (20%)	中等20%收入户 Middle Income Households (20%)	次高20%收入户 High Income Households (20%)	高20%收入户 Higher Income Households (20%)
城镇 Town	2014年	18739	29376	38525	51258	99131
农村 Rural	2014年	9491	17652	23127	29473	43037
城镇 Town	2013年	17335	27531	35971	47593	88589
农村 Rural	2013年	8046	15288	20162	26592	43205

主要统计指标解释

【居民消费价格指数】 居民消费价格，是指城乡居民支付生活消费品和服务项目消费的价格，是社会产品和服务项目的最终价格。居民消费价格指数，就是反映一定时期内居民消费价格变动趋势和变动程度的相对数。利用居民消费价格指数，可以全面观察居民消费价格变动对居民生活的影响。居民消费价格指数还是反映通货膨胀程度的重要指标。

【商品零售价格指数】 商品的零售价格是商品在流通过程中的最后一个环节的价格，是工业、商业、餐饮业和其他零售企业向城乡居民、机关团体出售生活消费品和办公用品的价格。因此，商品零售价格指数是全面反映市场零售物价总水平变动趋势和程度的相对数。其目的在于掌握零售商品的价格变动状况，为国家制定经济政策、研究城乡市场流通和为国民经济核算提供科学依据。

【工业生产者出厂价格指数】 工业生产者出厂价格，是指工业企业向商业（物资）部门或商业企业、其他生产单位、个人出售的或调拨产品的价格，亦称工业生产者价格。它是工业品进入流通领域的最初价格。工业生产者出厂价格指数是指反映一定时期内工业品出厂价格水平变动趋势及变动程度的相对数，是国民经济核算和计算工业发展速度的一个重要参考指标。

【原材料、燃料和动力购进价格指数】 是反映工业企业作为生产投入，而从物资交易市场和能源、原材料生产企业购买原材料、燃料、动力产品时，所支付的价格水平变动趋势和程度的统计指标，是扣除工业企业物质消耗成本中价格变动影响的重要依据。

【房屋销售价格指数】 房屋销售价格是指房产所有权转移时买卖双方实际成交的价格。它包括商品房销售、旧房交易和公有住房出售三部分。房屋销售价格指数，就是反映一定时期内房屋销售价格变动趋势和变动程度的相对数。

【可支配收入】 指调查户在调查期内获得的、可用于最终消费支出和储蓄的总和，即调查户可以用来自由支配的收入。可支配收入既包括现金，也包括实物收入。按照收入的来源，可支配收入包含四项，分别为：工资性收入、经营净收入、财产净收入和转移净收入。

【生活消费支出】 是指住户用于满足家庭日常生活消费需要的全部支出，包括用于消费品的支出和用于服务性消费的支出。根据用途不同，消费支出可划分为食品烟酒、衣着、居住、生活用品及服务、交通通信、教育文化娱乐、医疗保健、其他用品及服务八大类。

Explanatory Notes on Main Statistical Indicators

【Consumer Price Index】 refers to the consumption price for living necessities and services by people in urban and rural areas. It is the ultimate price of consumer goods and services. Thus it reflects the relative change in prices of consumer goods and services purchased by urban and rural families and can be used to observe and analyse the impact of price changes in consumer goods and services on living expenditure and actual charge in urban and rural households. The index also serves as a key norm in inflation.

【Retail Price Index】 refers to the last price of goods in the circulation. It is the price that industry, commerce, catering trade and other retail enterprises sell consumer goods and appliances to urban and rural residents, institutions and social organizations. The index thus reflects the relative change of the price in retail markets and as a result the index provides basis for the government on the policy-making, studies of market circulation in urban and rural areas, and national economy accounting.

【Ex – factory Price Index of Industrial Products】 It means that the industrial enterprises sell, allocate and transfer the products price from the commercial (or goods and material) departments or commercial enterprises, other manufactures and individuals, it is also called as industrial producers price. It is the initial price that the industrial products enter into circulate domain. The industrial products Ex – factory price index means that it reflects the ex – factory price level alteration trend and the change degree comparative figure for the industrial products within a certain period of time. It is an important reference target for the national economy accounting and calculation industry development speed as well.

【Price Index of the Purchased Materials, Fuel and Power】 refers to the statistical index of the trend and extent of the price fluctuation which industrial enterprises paid in purchasing the raw materials, fuel and power from goods exchange markets and fuel, material manufacturing enterprises for their own production needs. It is an important basis for the industrial enterprises in deducting fluctuant affections of the price from the material consumption cost.

【Price Index of Houses Selling】 houses selling price refers to the actual price paid in the deal between buyer and seller when the proprietary of houses transfers. Include commodity houses sales, second – hand houses transactions and the public – owned houses sales. The price index of house selling reflects the relative figures which indicate the trend and extent of house price fluctuations within a certain period.

【Disposable Income】 indicates the sum of income the surveyed acquired during the survey period that can be used as final consumption expenditure and savings, i. e. the income can be freely disposed by the surveyed. Disposable income include money income as well as in – kind income. Disposable income is composed of four parts according to source of income, they are: salary income, net business income, net property income and net transfer income.

【Living Consumption Expenditure】 indicates the total expenditure to meet the consumption demand of inhabitant's daily life, including expenditure on consumer goods and expenditure on service consumption. Consumption Expenditure can be divided into eight main categories according to different purposes: food, liquor & tobacco, clothing, dwelling, articles & services for daily use, transportation & communication, education, culture & recreation, medical care, other articles & services.

NINGBO 2015

Statistical YearBook

6

CHAPTER

第六篇

农业

AGRICULTURE

农业
Agriculture

主要统计指标
Major Statistics Indicators

2014 年农村劳动力资源数	Rural Laborers in this Year	336.67	万人	10000 persons
比上年增长	Increase Over Last Year	-1.33	%	
2014 年农业总产值	Total Output Value of Agriculture	432.48	亿元	100 million yuan
比上年增长	Increase Over Last Year	0.88	%	
2014 年粮食总产量	Total Yield of Grain Grops	741491	吨	ton
比上年增长	Increase Over Last Year	2.0	%	
2014 年油料总产量	Yield of Oil - bearing Crops	31689	吨	ton
比上年增长	Increase Over Last Year	-1.28	%	
2014 年肉类产量	Output of Meat	173160	吨	ton
比上年增长	Increase Over Last Year	-11.22	%	
2014 年水产品总产量	Total Aquatic Products	1010556	吨	ton
比上年增长	Increase Over Last Year	1.87	%	
2014 农业机械总动力	Total Power of Agricultural Machinery	3127706	千瓦	kw
比上年增长	Increase Over Last Year	-3.38	%	

表6-1 部分年份农村基本情况
Basic Statistics on Rural Areas in Partial Years

项目	Item	2011	2012	2013	2014
农村基层组织	**Rural Grass Roots Units**				
乡镇政府(个)	Township and Town Governments(unit)	89	89	88	88
#镇政府(个)	Township Governments(unit)	78	78	77	77
乡政府(个)	Town Governments(unit)	11	11	11	11
村民委员会(个)	Villages Committees(unit)	2559	2558	2555	2539
农村人口与从业人员	**Rural Population & Employmed Person**				
农村户数(万户)	Rural Households (10000 households)	180.19	174.84	175.29	175.19
农村人口(万人)	Rural Population (10000 persons)	475.77	462.97	497.11	486.93
按性别分:	Grouped by Sex				
男	Male	244.36	237.93	254.99	249.33
女	Female	231.41	225.04	242.11	237.60
农村劳动力资源数(万人)	Total Rural Laborers (10000 persons)	330.75	320.31	341.21	336.67
按性别分:	Grouped by Sex				
男	Male	173.97	167.74	177.91	176.66
女	Female	156.78	152.57	163.30	160.01
农村从业人员数(万人)	Rural Employmed Person (10000 persons)	306.36	293.79	312.07	304.88
按性别分:	Grouped by Sex				
男	Male	161.88	154.43	163.02	161.36
#从事农业人员	Personnel engaged in agriculture				31.16
女	Female	144.48	139.36	149.05	143.52
#从事农业人员	Personnel engaged in agriculture				19.96
农村基础设施	**Social Basic Facilities in Rural Areas**				
通自来水受益村数(个)	Villages with Tap Water (unit)	2558	2557	2552	2538
通有线电视村数(个)	Villages with Cable TV(unit)	2559	2558	2553	2539
通宽带村数(个)	Villages with Broadband Access (unit)		2544	2547	2537

注:2012年起,年报填报通宽带村数,不再填报通电村数,以下表同。

Note:Since 2012,annuat report began to fill in the broadband village number,no longer fill electricity villiage number,the same as the following table.

表6-2 历年农村从业人员数 Composition of Rural Labor Force Over the Years

单位:万人(10000 persons)

年份 Year	乡村实有劳动力 Rural Laborers	按三次产业分 Group by Three Industries					
		第一产业 Primary Industry		第二产业 Secondary Industry		第三产业 Tertiary Industry	
		人数 Population	比重% Proportion	人数 Population	比重% Proportion	人数 Population	比重% Proportion
1978	195.42						
1979	196.47						
1980	197.16						
1981	197.91						
1982	201.95						
1983	211.75						
1984	225.96						
1985	234.79	131.71	56.10	80.37	34.23	22.71	9.67
1986	240.88	130.51	54.18	85.73	35.59	24.64	10.23
1987	246.55	131.22	53.22	90.79	36.82	24.54	9.96
1988	250.35	132.86	53.07	90.64	36.21	26.85	10.72
1989	252.37	138.57	54.91	85.19	33.76	28.61	11.33
1990	254.12	142.33	56.01	81.83	32.20	29.96	11.79
1991	256.36	141.80	55.31	83.49	32.57	31.07	12.12
1992	260.65	141.29	54.21	82.79	31.76	36.57	14.03
1993	261.89	132.39	50.55	87.99	33.60	41.51	15.85
1994	263.13	126.79	48.19	89.13	33.87	47.21	17.94
1995	260.40	116.99	44.93	91.08	34.98	52.33	20.09
1996	260.37	115.02	44.18	93.06	35.74	52.29	20.08
1997	259.99	110.34	42.44	93.18	35.84	56.47	21.72
1998	259.23	109.77	42.35	91.96	35.47	57.50	22.18
1999	257.77	105.86	41.07	93.36	36.22	58.55	22.71
2000	257.44	99.83	38.78	97.90	38.03	59.71	23.19
2001	266.14	95.70	35.96	107.68	40.46	62.76	23.58
2002	270.04	92.29	34.17	114.46	42.39	63.29	23.44
2003	290.30	87.04	29.98	135.08	46.53	68.18	23.49
2004	306.15	78.32	25.58	153.53	50.15	74.30	24.27
2005	324.92	75.27	23.17	167.12	51.43	82.53	25.40
2006	320.85	69.14	21.55	170.56	53.16	81.15	25.29
2007	317.16	65.44	20.63	180.86	57.03	70.86	22.34
2008	305.56	64.14	21.00	173.42	56.75	68.00	22.25
2009	304.12	62.29	20.48	173.83	57.16	68.00	22.36
2010	306.32	59.17	19.32	177.28	57.87	69.87	22.81
2011	306.36	58.25	19.01	181.24	59.16	66.87	21.83
2012	293.79	55.31	18.83	175.83	59.85	62.65	21.32
2013	312.07	53.28	17.08	194.60	62.36	64.19	20.57
2014	304.88	51.12	16.77				

表6-3 历年农林牧渔业总产值 Gross Output Value of Farming, Forestry, Animal Husbandry and Fishery Over the Years

单位:亿元(100 million yuan)

年份 Year	农林牧渔业总产值 Gross Output Value	其中 Of Which				
		农业 Farming	林业 Forestry	牧业 Animal Husbandry	渔业 Fishery	服务业 Services
1978	8.83					
1979	10.93					
1980	11.70					
1981	11.07					
1982	14.79					
1983	14.81					
1984	19.68					
1985	21.89	15.40	0.83	3.53	2.13	
1986	24.31	16.85	0.93	4.26	2.27	
1987	28.99	19.47	1.13	5.71	2.68	
1988	36.23	23.41	1.28	7.53	4.01	
1989	40.98	27.37	1.52	8.31	3.78	
1990	40.68	26.94	1.30	8.30	4.14	
1991	45.86	29.35	1.74	8.42	6.35	
1992	51.47	31.51	1.57	9.59	8.80	
1993	69.89	40.29	2.40	11.75	15.45	
1994	96.40	51.60	3.00	17.26	24.54	
1995	123.95	67.22	4.18	20.71	31.84	
1996	138.65	75.77	3.92	22.85	36.11	
1997	129.44	67.19	4.22	21.65	36.38	
1998	136.36	71.92	4.09	20.53	39.82	
1999	142.82	73.04	4.34	20.16	45.28	
2000	148.37	71.57	4.59	20.45	51.76	
2001	156.43	74.31	5.14	22.21	54.77	
2002	163.31	73.65	4.92	24.25	60.49	
2003	173.75	77.42	5.03	26.03	63.10	2.17
2004	193.13	86.94	5.01	29.61	69.18	2.39
2005	207.40	91.14	5.31	32.93	75.31	2.71
2006	207.93	97.14	6.01	32.20	68.97	3.60
2007	236.96	107.22	6.77	46.27	72.67	4.02
2008	262.44	119.31	7.32	48.29	83.27	4.25
2009	286.78	134.64	8.85	47.87	90.82	4.60
2010	339.59	167.51	9.83	51.74	105.62	4.89
2011	397.93	191.64	10.86	62.54	127.68	5.21
2012	419.81	201.19	11.43	64.70	136.73	5.76
2013	428.72	202.28	11.64	60.54	148.29	5.96
2014	432.48	209.51	12.51	53.33	150.71	6.42

注:本表按现行价格计算,2006及2007年数据已根据农普数据进行调整

Note:Note:Data in this table are calculated at current prices. Data of the year 2006 & 2007 has been amended according to the last census of agriculture

表6-4 历年主要农作物播种面积及产量
Sown Areas and Yield of Major Farm Crops Over the Years

单位:面积:千公顷 Sown:1000 hectares
产量:万吨 Yield:10000 tons

年份 Year	农作物播种面积 Sown Area	其中 of Which							
		粮食 Grain		棉花 Cotton		油料 Oil Plants		蔬菜 Vegetables	
		面积 Area	产量 Yield	面积 Area	产量 Yield	面积 Area	产量 Yield	面积 Area	产量 Yield
1978	638.43	422.61	180.51						
1979	638.61	420.13	196.36						
1980	625.37	413.95	171.60						
1981	622.19	396.91	153.88						
1982	626.41	402.19	191.11						
1983	624.95	410.17	166.30	51.88	4.79	40.21	5.97		
1984	616.76	410.39	213.70	51.36	6.98	32.96	5.99		
1985	612.90	380.39	188.52	48.13	3.91	44.45	7.99	34.57	143.97
1986	596.50	361.81	188.65	41.39	3.66	48.70	8.41	36.09	158.75
1987	595.54	372.05	185.23	34.27	2.95	45.09	7.77	42.89	166.61
1988	580.01	369.58	189.98	34.65	1.80	46.70	8.47	41.01	161.74
1989	579.97	360.69	183.84	31.30	2.07	49.44	7.55	47.79	151.00
1990	591.03	368.77	189.06	34.55	3.34	52.51	9.50	48.79	135.64
1991	587.53	372.02	205.63	33.84	3.84	52.08	9.19	44.58	135.36
1992	572.68	357.66	181.62	33.03	2.59	49.15	8.62	46.82	126.89
1993	522.02	317.08	175.44	27.37	2.36	32.28	6.13	52.73	152.20
1994	504.73	308.04	172.51	26.93	2.07	30.17	4.84	56.37	162.65
1995	512.08	316.57	172.76	27.59	2.48	40.29	7.34	50.04	144.62
1996	519.48	318.99	190.30	27.14	2.73	40.37	8.00	54.20	164.26
1997	502.21	316.44	173.73	24.19	1.53	35.27	6.81	51.86	158.10
1998	510.73	317.76	180.39	25.81	2.69	34.21	5.05	58.01	174.67
1999	504.82	308.98	173.67	14.75	1.59	36.16	7.37	69.73	207.62
2000	445.90	246.79	132.51	9.69	1.05	32.58	6.59	82.16	243.70
2001	406.64	200.16	112.17	10.20	1.18	27.28	5.59	99.25	299.22
2002	386.85	172.34	94.89	6.85	0.80	24.51	4.76	104.71	291.67
2003	348.64	136.73	75.61	6.55	0.76	19.98	4.21	98.86	275.04
2004	338.09	145.12	83.73	6.53	0.74	17.67	4.04	91.80	286.76
2005	332.53	145.27	80.12	6.77	0.72	17.71	4.01	93.36	274.86
2006	317.17	141.01	81.30	6.21	0.73	14.91	3.62	88.75	264.73
2007	314.67	134.98	74.77	6.11	0.69	14.47	3.52	94.03	266.00
2008	330.07	153.80	88.42	6.45	0.75	14.21	3.55	89.49	272.92
2009	321.72	148.14	86.32	6.53	0.75	17.52	4.33	86.76	274.42
2010	318.56	151.14	87.13	6.73	0.77	16.82	4.10	83.59	265.73
2011	314.28	150.95	90.14	6.48	0.82	15.05	3.78	82.13	269.09
2012	309.45	148.53	86.57	5.98	0.71	14.70	3.67	80.73	261.20
2013	307.91	148.57	81.25	5.32	0.61	14.22	3.58	80.05	248.79
2014	286.61	127.84	74.15	4.48	0.52	12.63	3.17	77.44	244.17

注:2008 年年报开始,马铃薯作为粮食,不算蔬菜。从 2014 年年报开始数据实行"下管一级",省级核定。

Note: Potato is classified as food, not vegetable from 2008. Starting from 2014 annual report data "down level", approved by the provincial

表6-5 部分年份农林牧渔业分项产值
Gross Output Value of Farming, Forestry, Animal Husbandry and Fishery by Branch in Partial Years

单位：万元 (10000 yuan)

指标	Indicators	2010	2011	2012	2013	2014
合计	**Gross Output Value**	**3395923**	**3979320**	**4198058**	**4287181**	**4324760**
农业产值	**Farming**	**1675123**	**1916397**	**2011924**	**2022774**	**2095141**
#副产品产值	By - products	7127	7968	7806	7448	6697
粮食作物	Grain	241746	280624	281189	280973	266118
谷物	Cereal	167853	197813	200171	191106	198654
豆类	Beans	31790	39763	36593	41051	33667
薯类	Tubers	42103	43048	44425	48816	33797
油料	Oil Plants	23455	24580	26516	26750	23340
棉花	Cotton	17832	17253	16410	13762	11950
麻类	Fiber Crops					
甘蔗	Sugarcane	9392	10113	7514	7940	7496
药材类	Crude Drugs	12356	24220	25897	29413	31510
蔬菜	Vegetables	547737	607582	631964	612131	620426
食用菌	Edible Mushroom	556	612	722	3265	6313
花卉园艺	Flower & Horticulture	239054	274437	297568	301148	322441
茶、桑、水果、坚果	Tea, Mulberry & Fruits	559431	643140	687225	709048	741734
其他	Others	23564	33836	36919	38344	63813
林业产值	**Forestry**	**98252**	**108564**	**114301**	**116442**	**125057**
人造林木生长	Artificial Forestry	8349	11441	11383	12194	17660
林产品	Forest Products	62801	69674	72556	71899	74056
竹木采运	Cut Lumbering	24660	24509	26069	26041	29905
采集野生作物	Wild Plant Collected	2442	2940	4293	6308	3436
牧业产值	**Animal Husbandry**	**517412**	**625444**	**646977**	**605389**	**533264**
牲畜	Livestock Raising	293829	385045	414026	390299	323190
家禽饲养	Poultry Raising	90666	104780	101292	83393	58878
活的畜禽产品	Livestock Products	94687	102513	96978	91433	106569
捕猎野兽野禽	Hunting Wild Beast and Wild Fowl	592	552	1151	3829	3538
其他动物饲养	Other Animals Raising	37638	32554	33530	36435	41089
渔业产值	**Fishery**	**1056250**	**1276779**	**1367257**	**1482936**	**1507117**
海水产品	Seawater Aquatic Products	901585	1095365	1179800	1282520	1305757
淡水产品	Freshwater Aquatic Products	154665	181414	187457	200416	201360
农林牧渔服务业	**Services**	**48886**	**52136**	**57599**	**59640**	**64181**

注：本表按当年价格计算整。

Note: Data in this table are calculated at current prices.

表6－6　各地农林牧渔业中间消耗(2014)
Intermediate Consumption of Farming, Forestry, Animal Husbandry and Fishery by Region

单位:万元(10000 yuan)

地区	Region	中间消耗 Intermediate Consumption	其中 of Which 农业 Farming	林业 Forestry	牧业 Animal Husbandry	渔业 Fishery	服务业 Services
全市	**Total**	**1529182**	**538096**	**43218**	**297219**	**625064**	**25585**
市区	Urban Area	278429	172626	5254	45327	46887	8335
海曙	Haishu						
江东	Jiangdong						
江北	Jiangbei	31972	13438	1560	9254	7198	522
北仑	Beilun	27070	17593	555	4274	3445	1203
镇海	Zhenhai	44381	31798	1590	8718	1065	1210
鄞州	Yinzhou	175006	109797	1549	23081	35179	5400
县市	Rural Area						
余姚	Yuyao	214522	104046	10198	82969	15039	2270
慈溪	Cixi	226311	121410	2285	47360	47688	7568
奉化	Fenghua	180163	42974	14666	35719	84693	2111
象山	Xiangshan	483766	52333	7079	39230	380909	4215
宁海	Ninghai	145991	44707	3736	46614	49848	1086

表 6－7　农林牧渔业增加值(2014)
Value Added of Farming, Forestry, Animal Husbandry and Fishery

单位:万元(10000 yuan)

指标	Indicators	总产值 Gross Output Value	其中 of Which 中间消耗 Depreciation	增加值 Value－added	增加值率(%) Value－adding Rate
总计	**Total**	**4324760**	**1529182**	**2795578**	**64.64**
农业	Farming	2095141	538096	9621557045	74.32
林业	Forestry	125057	43218	81839	65.44
牧业	Animal Husbandry	533264	297219	236045	44.26
渔业	Fishery	1507117	625064	882053	58.53
服务业	Services	64181	25585	38596	60.14

表 6－8　各县(市)农林牧渔业增加值(2014)
Value Added of Farming, Forestry, Animal Husbandry and Fishery by Region

单位:万元(10000 yuan)

地区	Region	增加值 Value－added	其中 of Which 农业 Farming	林业 Forestry	牧业 Animal Husbandry	渔业 Fishery	服务业 Services
全市	**Total**	**2795578**	**1557045**	**81839**	**236045**	**882053**	**38596**
市区	Urban Area	613749	474316	20742	56190	50001	12500
余姚	Yuyao	416970	322552	23090	30490	37251	3587
慈溪	Cixi	496241	334236	2165	45787	102661	11392
奉化	Fenghua	288200	152023	15937	43110	73964	3166
象山	Xiangshan	585774	148888	5540	33927	391096	6323
宁海	Ninghai	394644	125030	14365	26541	227080	1628

表6－9 各县(市)、区农村基本情况(2014)
Basic Statistics on Rural Areas by Region

指标	Indicators	全市 Total	市区 Urban District	海曙 Haishu
农村基层组织	**Rural Grass Roots Units**			
乡镇政府(个)	Township and Town Governments(unit)	88	24	
#镇政府(个)	Town Governments(unit)	77	22	
乡政府(个)	Township Governments(unit)	11	2	
村民委员会(个)	Villages Committees(unit)	2539	768	
农村人口与从业人员	**Rural Population & Employmed Person**			
农村户数(万户)	Rural Households (10000 households)	175.19	58.54	
农村人口(万人)	Rural Population (10000 persons)	486.93	149.06	
按性别分:	Grouped by Sex			
男	Male	249.33	76.69	
女	Female	237.60	72.37	
农村劳动力资源数(万人)	Total Rural Laborers	336.67	99.78	
按性别分:	Grouped by Sex			
男	Male	176.66	53.01	
女	Female	160.01	46.77	
农村从业人员数(万人)	Rural Employmed Person	304.88	90.37	
按性别分:	Grouped by Sex			
男	Male	161.36	48.46	
#从事农业人员	Personnel engaged in agriculture	31.16	6.00	
女	Female	143.52	41.91	
#从事农业人员	Personnel engaged in agriculture	19.96	3.65	
农村基础设施	**Social Basic Facilities in Rural Areas**			
通自来水受益村数(个)	Villages with Tap Water (unit)	2538	768	
通有线电视村数(个)	Villages with Cable TV(unit)	2539	768	
通宽带村数(个)	Villages with Broadband Access (unit)	2537	768	

各区 by Districts									
江东 Jiangdong	江北 Jiangbei	北仑 Beilun	镇海 Zhenhai	鄞州 Yinzhou	余姚 Yuyao	慈溪 Cixi	奉化 Fenghua	象山 Xiangshan	宁海 Ninghai
	1	3	2	18	15	14	6	15	14
	1	2	2	17	14	14	6	10	11
		1		1	1			5	3
	92	195	60	421	265	297	356	490	363
	4.99	12.31	10.20	31.04	26.88	45.40	14.87	12.84	16.66
	13.12	31.22	24.60	80.12	89.77	119.44	40.32	39.43	48.91
	6.75	15.51	13.23	41.20	45.54	60.39	20.59	20.40	25.72
	6.37	15.71	11.37	38.92	44.23	59.05	19.73	19.03	23.19
	8.13	22.09	17.16	52.40	58.24	85.96	30.27	27.67	34.75
	4.24	11.38	9.58	27.81	30.23	44.36	15.84	14.84	18.38
	3.89	10.71	7.58	24.59	28.01	41.60	14.43	12.83	16.37
	7.23	19.43	15.50	48.21	53.87	78.37	26.49	24.62	31.16
	3.76	10.21	8.83	25.66	28.24	40.72	13.90	13.34	16.70
	0.31	1.53	0.66	3.50	4.60	6.14	4.08	5.61	4.73
	3.47	9.22	6.67	22.55	25.63	37.65	12.59	11.28	14.46
	0.21	1.07	0.53	1.84	3.15	3.76	2.53	3.62	3.25
	92	195	60	421	265	297	355	490	363
	92	195	60	421	265	297	356	490	363
	92	195	60	421	265	297	356	488	363

表6-10 各县(市)、区农林牧渔业总产值(2014)
Gross Output Value of Farming, Forestry, Animal Husbandry and Fishery by Region

指标	Indicators	全市 Total	市区 Urban District	海曙 Haishu
合计	**Gross Output Value**	**4324760**	**892178**	
农业产值	**Farming**	**2095141**	**646942**	
#副产品产值	By-products	6697	1668	
粮食作物	Grain	266118	69453	
谷物	Cereal	198654	66224	
豆类	Beans	33667	1930	
薯类	Tubers	33797	1299	
油料	Oil Plants	23340	2018	
棉花	Cotton	11950	184	
麻类	Fiber Crops			
甘蔗	Sugarcane	7496	2095	
药材类	Crude Drugs	31510	22096	
蔬菜	Vegetables	620426	194508	
食用菌	Edible Mushroom	6313	1210	
花卉园艺	Flower & Horticulture	322441	117285	
茶、桑、水果、坚果	Tea, Mulberry & Fruits	741734	187287	
其他	Others	63813	50806	
林业产值	**Forestry**	**125057**	**25996**	
人造林木生长	Artificial Forestry	17660	2452	
林产品	Forest Products	74056	9028	
竹木采运	Cut Lumbering	29905	12524	
采集野生作物	Wild Plant Collected	3436	1992	
牧业产值	**Animal Husbandry**	**533264**	**101517**	
牲畜	Livestock Raising	323190	46792	
家禽饲养	Poultry Raising	58878	8932	
活的畜禽产品	Livestock Products	106569	37383	
捕猎野兽野禽	Hunting Wild Beast and Wild Fowl	3538	76	
其他动物饲养	Other Animals Raising	41089	8334	
渔业产值	**Fishery**	**1507117**	**96888**	
海水产品	Seawater Aquatic Products	1305757	54381	
淡水产品	Freshwater Aquatic Products	201360	42507	
农林牧渔服务业	**Services**	**64181**	**20835**	

注:本表按当年价格计算。

Note: Data in this table are calculated at current prices

单位:万元(10000 yuan)

各区 by Districts									
江东 Jiangdong	江北 Jiangbei	北仑 Beilun	镇海 Zhenhai	鄞州 Yinzhou	余姚 Yuyao	慈溪 Cixi	奉化 Fenghua	象山 Xiangshan	宁海 Ninghai
	94914	**109045**	**111720**	**576499**	**631492**	**722552**	**468363**	**1069540**	**540635**
	54609	**93476**	**87016**	**411841**	**426598**	**455646**	**194997**	**201221**	**169737**
	414	44	245	965	892	1788	562	674	1113
	6973	1268	4776	56436	58334	40052	21905	31987	44387
	6821	501	4334	54568	47101	18622	16212	27917	22578
	90	463	245	1132	6030	20155	1216	1547	2789
	62	304	197	736	5203	1275	4477	2523	19020
	99	191	71	1657	5895	10311	759	2132	2225
		86	3	95	1408	6696		79	3583
	49	7	189	1850	324	852	36	4003	186
		400	30	21666	2468	5480	185	581	700
	16413	16288	28480	133327	146969	184461	10182	56272	28034
		225	985		566	183	2354	1440	560
	4628	50101	32015	30541	61761	27860	87062	23623	4850
	22500	23535	13386	127866	147818	173424	71553	76540	85112
	3947	1375	7081	38403	1055	6327	961	4564	100
	3696	**1928**	**2600**	**17772**	**33288**	**4450**	**30603**	**12619**	**18101**
	353	1161	296	642	9963	254	1089	3408	494
	1146	512	357	7013	19628	2271	23468	7849	11812
	2197	255	569	9503	3607	1374	5811	1144	5445
			1378	614	90	551	235	218	350
	18767	**6242**	**17304**	**59204**	**113459**	**93147**	**78829**	**73157**	**73155**
	7991	4066	7096	27639	73267	60819	55644	43355	43313
	2530	495	1818	4089	21444	5641	4543	10294	8024
	8204	455	3586	25138	9128	11876	18126	12963	17093
				76	69	2	12	3359	20
	42	1226	4804	2262	9551	14809	504	3186	4705
	16538	**4393**	**1775**	**74182**	**52290**	**150349**	**158657**	**772005**	**276928**
	15564	3197	584	35036	7870	80324	154868	740699	267615
	974	1196	1191	39146	44420	70025	3789	31306	9313
	1304	**3006**	**3025**	**13500**	**5857**	**18960**	**5277**	**10538**	**2714**

表6－11　各县(市)、区农作物播种面积和产量(2014)
Total Sown Area and Yield of Major Farm Crops by Region

指标	Indicators	全市 Total	市区 Urban District	海曙 Haishu
农作物播种面积总计	**Sown Area of Farm Crops**	**286607**	**77236**	
粮食作物播种面积	**Sown Area of Grain**	**127837**	**32129**	
总产量	**Total Yield of Grain**	**741491**	**207528**	
谷物面积	Sown Area of Cereal	96615	29763	
总产量	Yield of Cereal	636412	198076	
稻谷面积	Sown Area of Rice	78877	26280	
总产量	Yield of Rice	558606	182128	
#早稻面积	Sown Area of Early Rice	11485	5162	
总产量	Yield of Early Rice	75929	33823	
晚稻及单季稻	Sown Area of Late Rice & Single Season Rice	67392	21118	
总产量	Yield of Late Rice & Single Season Rice	482677	148305	
小麦面积	Sown Area of Wheat	9155	2415	
总产量	Yield of Wheat	40264	11014	
大麦面积	Sown Area of Barley	1239	280	
总产量	Yield of Barley	4518	1015	
豆类面积	Sown Area of Beans	23648	1604	
总产量	Yield of Beans	67633	5076	
蕃薯面积	Sown Area of Tubers	2750	283	
总产量	Yield of Tubers	16272	1776	
油料播种面积	**Sown Area of Oil Plants**	**12630**	**1255**	
总产量	**Yield of Oil Plants**	**31689**	**3664**	
油菜籽面积	Sown Area of Rapeseeds	8374	662	
总产量	Yield of Rapeseeds	18596	1518	
花生面积	Sown Area of Peanuts	3552	551	
总产量	Yield of Peanuts	11763	2063	
芝麻面积	Sown Area of Sesame	704	42	

单位:公顷,吨(hectare ton)

各区 by Districts									
江东 Jiangdong	江北 Jiangbei	北仑 Beilun	镇海 Zhenhai	鄞州 Yinzhou	余姚 Yuyao	慈溪 Cixi	奉化 Fenghua	象山 Xiangshan	宁海 Ninghai
	7716	**6907**	**9436**	**53177**	**56327**	**75967**	**20763**	**29207**	**27107**
	3116	**811**	**2899**	**25303**	**29004**	**26120**	**10515**	**13363**	**16706**
	22214	**3436**	**19507**	**162371**	**179207**	**111085**	**62529**	**85612**	**95530**
	3011	360	2541	23851	24657	11082	8627	10165	12321
	21836	1956	18137	156147	162618	65484	56355	73785	80094
	2941	181	2345	20813	20179	6000	7691	9238	9489
	21518	1189	17182	142239	139133	44745	52682	70435	69483
	97	15	756	4294	4444	47	913	783	136
	659	100	5046	28018	29328	299	5900	5579	1000
	2844	166	1589	16519	15735	5953	6778	8455	9353
	20859	1089	12136	114221	109805	44446	46782	64856	68483
	18	2	71	2324	2458	1629	468	335	1850
	83	8	291	10632	12533	6326	2036	1307	7048
	27			253	22	334	54	213	336
	104			911	103	1136	219	799	1246
	73	366	227	938	3428	14408	818	1617	1773
	231	1010	665	3170	11647	41674	1779	3868	3589
	8	21	78	176	193	314	336	745	879
	34	135	450	1157	1058	2566	1617	4247	5008
	103	**126**	**90**	**936**	**2121**	**6251**	**355**	**1317**	**1331**
	204	**326**	**235**	**2899**	**5962**	**15092**	**761**	**3585**	**2625**
	101	80	67	414	1697	4323	97	823	772
	200	169	162	987	4134	10145	133	1358	1308
	1	41	20	489	371	1433	244	455	498
	3	148	66	1846	1698	3999	606	2158	1239
	1	5	3	33	53	495	14	39	61

表6－11续表 Continued

指标	Indicators	全市 Total	市区 Urban District	海曙 Haishu
总产量	Yield of Sesame	1330	83	
棉花(皮棉)播种面积	Sown Area of Cotton	4479	74	
棉花(皮棉)总产量	Yield of Cotton	5211	112	
麻类播种面积	Sown Area of Fiber Crops			
麻类总产量	Yield of Fiber Crops			
甘蔗播种面积	Sown Area of Sugarcane	576	210	
甘蔗总产量	Yield of Sugarcane	33423	13538	
药材类播种面积	Sown Area of Medicinal Material	1558	779	
药材类总产量	Yield of Medicinal Material	6191	3230	
蔬菜类播种面积	Sown Area of Vegetables	77437	18669	
蔬菜类总产量	Yield of Vegetables	2441707	554760	
食用菌产量	Edible Mushroom	7056	1195	
果用瓜播种面积	**Sown Area of Melon as Fruits**	**17079**	**3972**	
总产量	**Yield of Melon as Fruits**	**488569**	**135066**	
西瓜播种面积	Sown Area of Watermelon	12153	2946	
总产量	Yield of Watermelon	371174	109696	
草莓面积	Sown Area of Strawberry	1075	244	
总产量	Yield of Strawberry	21070	5451	
花卉苗木播种面积	**Sown Area of Flowers and Plants Nursery Stock**	**23534**	**9202**	
花卉面积	Sown Area of Flowers	4486	2369	
苗木面积	Sown Area of Plants Nursery Stock	18598	6751	
盆栽类园艺(万盆)	Potted Horticulture(10000 units)	184	144	
其他农作物播种面积	**Sown Area of Other Farm Crops**	**21477**	**10946**	
绿肥面积	Sown Area of Green Manure	3431	1830	
席草面积	Sown Area of Rush	3751	3216	
总产量	Yield of Rush	37474	33496	

单位:公顷,吨(hectare ton)

各区 by Districts									
江东 Jiangdong	江北 Jiangbei	北仑 Beilun	镇海 Zhenhai	鄞州 Yinzhou	余姚 Yuyao	慈溪 Cixi	奉化 Fenghua	象山 Xiangshan	宁海 Ninghai
	1	9	7	66	130	948	22	69	78
		27	4	43	415	2888		78	1024
		60	5	47	478	3290		58	1273
	5	1	14			107	10	162	30
	310	40	858	12330	4008	6440	296	8149	992
	8	4	1	766	128	568	20	31	32
	18	4	1	3207	489	2015	40	172	245
	2241	1400	3083	11945	16747	27398	2561	7687	4375
	54745	36939	81421	381655	759924	794691	44910	176263	111159
		265	930		694	167	2700	1800	500
	229	**398**	**811**	**2534**	**1327**	**6623**	**932**	**1979**	**2246**
	6816	**9170**	**20685**	**98395**	**49157**	**158441**	**22265**	**48105**	**75535**
	196	287	414	2049	979	4867	614	1326	1421
	6104	7082	12893	83617	37574	123277	16902	35046	48679
	14	29	120	81	108	234	260	125	104
	274	578	2658	1941	2171	4669	4538	2131	2110
	924	**3820**	**1547**	**2911**	**4423**	**2933**	**5190**	**1119**	**667**
	168	309	561	1331	180	711	798	370	58
	739	3508	951	1553	4178	2136	4178	749	606
	55	37	24	28	26	5	7	2	
	1090	**320**	**987**	**8549**	**2105**	**3079**	**1180**	**3471**	**696**
	99	5	66	1660	435	12	624	414	116
				3216	28		507		
				33496	321		3657		

表6-12 各县(市)、区农业机械拥有量(2014年末)
Possession of Agricultural Machinery by Region (End of 2014)

指标	单位	Indicators	Unit	全市 Total	市区 Urban District	海曙 Haishu
农业机械总动力	**千瓦**	**Total Power of AgriculturalMachinery**	**kw**	**3127706**	**637686**	**99**
耕作机械		Cultivation Machinery				
耕作机械动力合计	台	Mechanical Power of Cultivation	unit	24226	7841	4
	千瓦		kw	299548	88794	36
大中型拖拉机	台	Large and Medium Sized Tractors	unti	2678	587	
	千瓦		kw	103818	21069	
农用小型拖拉机	台	Mini – tractors for Agriculture	unit	13867	3320	2
	千瓦		kw	132226	33201	18
收获机械		Harvest Machinery				
收获机械动力合计	台	Mechanical Power of Harvesting	unit	3118	927	1
	千瓦		kw	103885	29619	15
联合收割机	台	Combine Harvesters	unit	2668	755	1
	千瓦		kw	90209	23412	15
谷物烘干机	台	Cereal Dryer	unit	913	273	
植保机械		Plant Protection Machinery				
植保机械动力合计	台	Mechanical Power of Plant Protection	unit	32925	2136	
	千瓦		kw	56932	4442	
机动喷雾(粉)器	架	Motorized Sprayer	unit	29519	1983	
	千瓦		kw	49341	3873	
排灌机械		Drainage &Irrigation Machinery				
排灌机械动力	台	Mechanical Power of Drainage and Irrigation	unit	76501	16092	2
	千瓦		kw	303607	71693	28
农用水泵	台	Water Pump for Agricultural Use	unit	61720	15595	2
农副产品加工机械		Processing Machinery of Agricultural Products				
农副产品加工机械动力合计	台	Mechanical Power of Farm Sideline Products Manufacturing	unit	15323	4136	1
	千瓦		kw	127081	24935	10
运输机械		Transport Machinery				
运输机械动力	台	Mechanical Power of Transportation	unit	33798	5172	
	千瓦		kw	651870	115935	
农用运输车	辆	Vehicles for Agricultural Use	unit	17020	2221	
	千瓦		kw	292308	62706	
运输型拖拉机	辆	Transport Tractors	unit	16422	2963	
	千瓦		kw	320089	51896	
其他农用机械		Other Mechanical				
其他农业机械动力合计	台	Other Mechanical Power	unit	33960	12422	10
	千瓦		kw	345538	115936	10

注:本表数据来自宁波市农业机械服务总站。

Note: Date in this table are obtained from Agricultural Machinery General Servise Station of Ningbo.

各区 by Districts									
江东 Jiangdong	江北 Jiangbei	北仑 Beilun	镇海 Zhenhai	鄞州 Yinzhou	余姚 Yuyao	慈溪 Cixi	奉化 Fenghua	象山 Xiangshan	宁海 Ninghai
220	**43383**	**169254**	**65800**	**358930**	**635356**	**437852**	**280922**	**825505**	**310385**
	625	2072	635	4505	3724	5847	3161	1801	1852
	7386	12441	7386	61545	61241	66383	34752	25940	22438
	164	46	54	323	759	604	237	311	180
	3889	1960	2232	12988	33003	21300	8703	11556	8187
	218	187	207	2706	2244	3727	2544	1027	1005
	1931	1852	2132	27268	22928	33959	24278	9677	8183
	180	10	43	693	764	240	475	460	252
	3375	313	2150	23766	30242	7592	8415	15417	12600
	180	10	43	521	722	234	332	389	236
	3375	313	2150	17559	28880	7347	7791	14290	8489
	24	13	47	189	248	112	80	100	100
	383	488	247	1018	2398	17975	432	4688	5296
	716	901	611	2214	5330	25758	1290	8465	11647
	381	488	247	867	847	17781	404	3211	5293
	714	901	611	1647	3385	24828	1216	5453	10586
	1256	5670	1636	7528	21109	9670	9179	11491	8960
	10851	20171	6987	33656	93079	44233	34532	28833	31237
	1059	5491	1409	7634	13475	6551	8277	10757	7065
	286	272	213	3364	4451	2277	1726	1262	1471
	3313	2130	1267	18215	41572	19952	15767	11000	13855
15	168	1634	371	2984	9091	7789	3112	3413	5221
220	3271	32352	6274	73818	155007	116044	85287	97500	82097
		965		1256	5734	5283	1349	140	2293
		21173		41533	85867	63637	47921	5624	26553
15	168	679	371	1730	3357	2548	1774	2870	2910
220	3271	11179	6274	30952	69140	47003	37246	71689	43115
	714	673	883	10142	6138	5910	3509	4625	1356
	1985	27800	3779	82362	94459	65064	21641	23640	24798

表6－13 各县(市)、区灌溉和水利情况(2014)
Irrigation and Water Conservancy Facilities of Farmland by Region

指标	单位	Indicators	Unit	全市 Total	市区 Urban District	海曙 Haishu
水库年末累计	座	Total Number of Reservoirs at the Year－end	set	419	98	
总库容量	万立方米	Total Capacity of Reservoirs at the Year－end	10000 cu. m	187496	55982	
#大型水库	座	Large－sized Reservoirs	set	6	2	
总库容	万立方米	Capacity	10000 cu. m	78527	23185	
中型水库	座	Medium－sized Reservoirs	set	26	7	
总库容	万立方米	Capacity	10000 cu. m	72165	21782	
小型水库	座	Small－sized Reservoirs	set	387	89	
总库容	万立方米	Capacity	10000 cu. m	36804	11015	
水电站数量	座	Hydropower Station	set	102	13	
泵站数量	处	Pumping Station	unit	7162	717	4
灌溉面积总计	千公顷	Total Irrigated Area	1000 hectares	201.39	56.45	
有效灌溉面积	千公顷	Effective Irrigated Area	1000 hectares	186.11	52.95	
有效实灌面积	千公顷	Effective Fact Irrigated Area	1000 hectares	143.40	50.53	
旱涝保收面积	千公顷	Farmland Area of Stable Yields Despite Drought or Excessive Rain	1000 hectares	110.41	31.71	
节水灌溉面积	千公顷	Water－saving Irrigation Area	1000 hectares	120.90	39.97	
除涝面积	千公顷	Drainage Area	1000 hectares	69.65	21.74	
水土流失综合治理面积	千公顷	Area of Soil Erosion under Control	1000 hectares	189.16	39.12	
水闸座数	座	Sluice	set	1903	427	8
堤防长度	公里	Total Length of Dikes	km	1927.46	711.06	9.57
全部供水工程总供水量	万立方米	Annually Water Supply of Water Conservancy	10000 cu. m	197560	49395	
#区域内农业供水	万立方米	Water Supply for Agriculture Within the Region	10000 cu. m	60252	11727	
区域内工业供水	万立方米	Water Supply for]Industry Within the Region	10000 cu. m	46394	25139	
区域内城镇生活用水	万立方米	Water Supply for Urban life Within the Region	10000 cu. m	23550	8159	

注：本表数据来自宁波市水利局。

Note: Data in this tables are obtained from Ningbo Municipal Bureau of Water Conservancy.

各区 by Districts									
江东 Jiangdong	江北 Jiangbei	北仑 Beilun	镇海 Zhenhai	鄞州 Yinzhou	余姚 Yuyao	慈溪 Cixi	奉化 Fenghua	象山 Xiangshan	宁海 Ninghai
	5	33	6	54	56	23	92	81	69
	2169	4383	4602	44828	26698	12632	31638	17719	42827
				2	1		2		1
				23185	12272		26230		16840
		1	1	5	3	4		6	6
		1474	2300	18008	9149	7334		11169	22731
	5	32	5	47	52	19	90	75	62
	2169	2909	2302	3635	5277	5298	5408	6550	3256
				13	76	3			10
10	419	244	14	26	4081	71	595	1086	612
	6.83	9.56	7.07	32.99	38.58	41.30	20.96	20.47	23.63
	6.20	8.36	6.42	31.97	36.73	40.29	20.40	16.58	19.16
	6.20	8.36	4.00	31.97	36.73		20.40	16.58	19.16
	3.15	4.01	1.50	23.05	30.41		22.00	15.42	10.87
	7.11	7.19	5.28	20.39	34.63	13.65	3.48	12.80	16.37
	3.50	9.61	6.42	2.21	8.10	5.94		18.22	15.65
	3.13	14.33	1.81	19.85	27.72	8.88	60.91	47.38	5.14
7	98	142	41	131	458	158	119	362	379
9.76	83.23	133.71	155.28	319.51	211.36	73.82	102.90	263.39	564.93
	15	1973	3656	43751	33012	30515	25606	17064	41968
		96	2210	9421	15465	7454	8042	8064	9500
	5	1525	950	22659	4772	6412	4095	2325	3650
				8159	5234	4081	2118	1987	1971

表6-14 各县(市)、区林业生产情况(2014)
Basic Statistics on Forestry by Region

指标	Indicators	全市 Total	海曙 Haishu	江北 Jiangbei
营林情况(公顷)	**Afforestation(hectare)**			
造林面积合计(公顷)	Total Afforestation Area(hectare)	3008		58
按方式分	By Way of Afforestation			
当年人工造林面积	Area of Afforest artificially in this Year	2357		58
按用途分	By Use of Afforestation			
经济林	Economic Forest	871		
防护林	Shelter Forest	2072		58
迹地更新面积	Area of Forest Updating	633		
封山育林面积	Area of Afforestation in Enclosed Mountain	179073		3640
零星(四旁)植树(万株)	Planting Trees Piecemeal(10000 trees)	160		2
育苗面积(公顷)	Area of Growing Seedings(hectare)	21336		407
未成林抚育作业面积	Unpaired Forest Tending Operations Area	1744		
成林抚育面积	Area of Grown Forest Cultivated			
其中:中、幼龄林抚育面积	In, Young Forest Tending Area	15969		300
低产林改造面积	Area of Transform Low Yield Forest	472		
抚育改造出材量(立方米)	Output of Transform and Foster (Cubic Meter)			
主要林产品产量(吨)	**Output of Major Forest Products(ton)**			
笋罐头	Bamboo Can			
板栗	Chestnut	1788		
竹笋干	Dried Bamboo Shoots	14446		331
竹壳	Shell of Bamboo	250		
白果	Gingko	200		

注:本表数据来自宁波市林业局。

Note: Data in this tables are obtained from Ningbo Municipal Bureau of Forestry.

各县(市)、区 by Region								
北 仑 Beilun	镇海 Zhenhai	大榭 Daxie	鄞州 Yinzhou	余姚 Yuyao	慈溪 Cixi	奉化 Fenghua	象山 Xiangshan	宁海 Ninghai
273	85	5	443	578	333	208	428	597
235	85	5	443	532	333	208	228	230
			67	203	205	143	98	155
273	85		316	375	128	65	330	442
33	1		310	33	1	100	19	136
667	1320	100	18569	17987	6664	44134	36800	49192
5	1		11	26	12	13	49	41
4009	191		2089	4178	2266	7243	866	87
		125		119			1500	
1335	533	65	2135	2067	667	2000	3534	3333
33		40	33	70		33	241	22
14				620		150	4	1000
187	35		1541	3400	663	4880	500	2909
							250	
						150		50

表6－15 各县(市)、区茶叶和水果生产情况(2014)
Basic Statistics on Tea and Fruits Production by Region

指标	Indicators	全市 Total	市区 Urban District	海曙 Haishu	江东 Jiangdong
茶叶生产	**Tea**				
茶园总面积(公顷)	**Tea Field Area(hectare)**	**13498**	**3984**		
本年新增	New－added in This Year	273	4		
本年采摘	Pluck in This Year	10589	2635		
茶叶总产量(吨)	**Output of Tea (ton)**	**15921**	**3527**		
春茶	Spring Tea	8532	1890		
夏茶	Summer Tea	4604	1048		
秋茶	Autumn Tea	2785	589		
水果生产	**Fruits**				
果园面积合计(公顷)	**Area of Orchards(hectare)**	**50715**	**6465**		
柑桔园	Citrus	10921	1554		
梨园	Pears	4791	677		
桃园	Peaches	4569	371		
李子园	Plums	109	16		
杨梅园	Red Bayberry	17687	1324		
枇杷园	Loquat	2243	76		
柿子园	Persimmon	263	61		
葡萄园	Grapery	6445	1815		
弥猴桃园	Kiwi Fruit	487	28		
其他果园	Others	3200	543		
水果总产量(吨)	**Output of Fruits (ton)**	**1205112**	**266390**		
柑桔	Citrus	250330	42306		
柑	Mandarin Orange	14998	5640		
桔	Mandarin	232406	35351		
橙	Orange	1324	283		
柚	Shaddock	1298	728		
梨	Pears	103372	19400		
桃子	Peaches	56325	5411		
李子	Plum	1222	241		
杨梅	Red Bayberry	113450	14341		
枇杷	Loquat	9746	430		
柿子	Persimmon	2796	888		
葡萄	Grapes	154418	43507		
弥猴桃	Kiwi Fruit	2907	127		
果用瓜	Melon Used as Fruits	488569	135066		
其他	Others	21977	4673		

各区 by Districts								
江北 Jiangbei	北仑 Beilun	镇海 Zhenhai	鄞州 Yinzhou	余姚 Yuyao	慈溪 Cixi	奉化 Fenghua	象山 Xiangshan	宁海 Ninghai
237	**800**	**80**	**2867**	**3944**	**254**	**897**	**1061**	**3358**
3		1		3		28	2	236
228	680	20	1707	3827	240	681	754	2452
90	**510**	**127**	**2800**	**4829**	**101**	**1436**	**1254**	**4774**
52	355	55	1428	3178	97	756	520	2091
33	115	32	868	1075		391	579	1511
5	40	40	504	576	4	289	155	1172
1337	**1148**	**988**	**2992**	**8209**	**11722**	**3997**	**11990**	**8332**
97	520	337	600	104	264	587	5961	2451
278	53	30	316	1455	1983	47	252	377
35	46	14	276	202	672	2100	307	917
1			15	34		20	26	13
262	270	80	712	4798	4932	646	3692	2295
5	5	8	58	45	35	13	1111	963
5	18	1	37	86	23	17	32	44
609	215	304	687	792	3189	155	393	101
10	5	4	9	77	33	49	53	247
35	16	210	282	616	591	363	163	924
32837	**34925**	**32568**	**166060**	**156271**	**324294**	**82959**	**200207**	**174991**
2522	14702	3645	21437	2572	6185	11814	117396	70057
222	1467	955	2996	321	3555	15	5126	341
2282	13104	1844	18121	1748	2623	11438	111613	69633
18	55		210		7	358	604	72
	71	646	11	503		3	53	11
8812	1273	1032	8283	35744	38478	762	4274	4714
422	809	201	3979	3946	9536	30589	2762	4081
3	12		226	209		549	69	154
1639	3388	165	9149	26771	40238	5491	12718	13891
11	53	40	326	407	256	353	6397	1903
73	351	39	425	1029	375	134	264	106
12267	5048	6026	20166	30575	67002	3912	7392	2030
35	35	20	37	156	309	656	108	1551
6816	9170	20685	98395	49157	158441	22265	48105	75535
237	84	715	3637	5705	3474	6434	722	969

表6-16 各县(市)、区畜牧业生产情况(2014)
Basic Statistics on Animal Husbandry By Region

指标	Indicators	全市 Total	市区 Urban District	海曙 Haishu
生猪(万只)	**Hogs (10000 heads)**			
年末存栏头数(含未断奶小猪)	Being Raised at Year - end	105.50	15.12	
#能繁殖的母猪	Reproducable	9.56	1.53	
年内肥猪出栏头数	Slaughtered Fattened Hogs	165.95	31.90	
全年饲养量	Number of Hogs Raised	271.45	47.02	
牛(头)	**Cattles & Buffaloes(head)**			
年末存栏头数	Being Raised at Year - end	17141	5977	
#良种及改良种乳牛	Milch Cows of Fine Breed and Improved Varieties	8042	4610	
年内出栏头数	Slaughtered Cattles & Buffaloes of the Year	7106	1806	
羊(万只)	**Sheep & Goat(10000 heads)**			
年末存栏只数	Being Raised at Year - end	11.17	0.91	
年内出栏只数	Slaughtered Sheep & Goat of the Year	10.72	0.94	
家禽(万只)	**Poultry(10000 heads)**			
年末存栏只数	Being Raised at Year - end	1006.25	164.16	
年内出栏只数	Slaughtered Poultry of the Year	1598.34	300.65	
兔(万只)	**Rabbits (10000 heads)**			
年末存栏只数	Being Raised at Year - end	43.00	7.23	
年内出栏只数	Slaughtered Rabbits	62.00	14.72	
养蜂年末箱数(箱)	**Number of Beehives(box)**	**83502**	**2416**	
畜禽产品产量(吨)	**Output of Livestock Production(ton)**			
肉类产量	Output of Meat	173160	31857	
猪肉	Pork	142119	25527	
牛肉	Beef	1177	298	
羊肉	Mutton	1824	187	
禽肉	Poultry Meat	26528	5440	
兔肉	Rabbits Meat	1226	399	
其他	Others	286	6	
禽蛋产量	Poultry Eggs	73232	15725	
蜂蜜产量	Honey	7220	96	
蜂皇浆产量(公斤)	Royal Jelly(kg)	284540	6410	
牛奶产量(吨)	Milk (ton)	25564	14782	
兔毛产量	Rabbit Wool	149	14	

各区 by Districts									
江东 Jiangdong	江北 Jiangbei	北仑 Beilun	镇海 Zhenhai	鄞州 Yinzhou	余姚 Yuyao	慈溪 Cixi	奉化 Fenghua	象山 Xiangshan	宁海 Ninghai
	2.99	0.90	1.13	10.10	22.70	22.63	18.39	11.48	15.18
	0.37	0.09	0.09	0.98	1.92	2.01	1.65	1.17	1.28
	4.77	1.99	2.95	22.19	34.05	35.32	24.39	18.12	22.17
	7.76	2.89	4.08	32.29	56.75	57.95	42.78	29.60	37.35
	3534	387	523	1533	2326	841	1822	636	5539
	3467		363	780	1565	455	435		977
	564	257	255	730	509	358	1215	362	2856
	0.06	0.18	0.13	0.54	2.44	3.49	1.27	1.98	1.08
	0.04	0.16	0.24	0.50	2.52	3.60	0.87	1.91	0.88
	54.77	10.19	36.28	62.92	247.45	160.40	154.96	132.74	146.54
	111.81	13.75	56.86	118.23	464.25	209.62	164.71	159.94	299.17
	2.10	0.30	4.57	0.26	12.72	22.36		0.59	0.10
	1.24	0.56	12.40	0.52	22.44	22.65	0.02	2.02	0.15
	260	**793**	**668**	**695**	**6990**	**46978**	**4031**	**5246**	**17841**
	5860	2031	4530	19436	38565	34030	24582	19722	24404
	3962	1679	2744	17142	27923	28923	21955	16845	20946
	95	46	42	115	104	60	183	53	479
	7	34	58	88	517	567	130	290	133
	1765	261	1340	2074	9484	4041	2314	2406	2843
	31	11	340	17	382	414		28	3
			6		155	25		100	
	4257	463	2925	8080	7529	9668	15425	12852	12033
	7	19	22	48	794	4192	199	87	1852
	1100	3147	1334	829	23273	204402	10975	5130	34350
	11605		681	2496	4506	1890	913		3473
			13	1	45	90			

表6－17 各县（市）、区水产品产量及养殖面积（2014）
Output and Area of Artificially Cultured of Aquatic Production by Region

指标	Indicators	全市 Total	市区		
			海曙 Haishu	江东 Jiangdong	江北 Jiangbei
水产品总产量	**Total Aquatic Products**	**1010556**			**20560**
海水产品产量	**Seawater Aquatic Products**	**891866**			**5750**
按生产性质分	**By Production Character**				
海洋捕捞	Catching in Ocean	609748			5750
鱼类	Fish	477870			5750
甲壳类	Shrimps. Prawns and Crabs	69331			
贝类	Shell－Fish	8339			
其他类	Others	10354			
海水养殖	Seawater Aquiculture	282118			
鱼类	Fish	11882			
甲壳类	Shrimps. Prawns and Crabs	40271			
贝类	Shell－Fish	220113			
其他类	Others	1672			
远洋渔业产品产量	**Pelagic Fishery**	**38096**			**13684**
淡水产品产量	**Freshwater Aquatic Products**	**80594**			**1126**
按生产性质分	By Production Character				
淡水捕捞	Catching in Freshwater	9603			620
淡水养殖	Freshwater Aquiculture	70991			506
按类别分	By Category				
鱼类	Fish	49064			437
甲壳类	Shrimps. Prawns and Crabs	19463			49
贝类	Shell－Fish	850			
其他类	Others	1614			20
海水养殖面积（公顷）	**Seawater Aquiculture Area(ha)**	**35918**			
淡水养殖面积（公顷）	**Freshwater Aquiculture Area(ha)**	**22178**			**486**

注：本表数据来自宁波市海洋渔业局。

Data in this tables are obtained from Ningbo Municipal Bureau of Ocean and Fishery.

单位:吨(ton)

Urban Districts			余姚 Yuyao	慈溪 Cixi	奉化 Fenghua	象山 Xiangshan	宁海 Ninghai
北仑 Beilun	镇海 Zhenhai	鄞州 Yinzhou					
1685	**810**	**19225**	**23763**	**52191**	**151212**	**584940**	**150816**
1131	**48**	**8042**	**2200**	**26003**	**148120**	**555038**	**145407**
939	48	3202	2148	3544	141863	443211	8916
673	36	937	903	779	121126	345718	1821
266	12	83	608	819	5789	58401	3353
			473	1780	803	2088	3195
		2077	72	166	7183	856	
192		4840	52	22459	6257	111827	136491
			20	3381	1191	5137	2153
103		2510	32	8180	1087	15861	12498
89		2220	0	10898	1864	83202	121840
					155	1517	
						19185	
554	**762**	**11183**	**21563**	**26188**	**3092**	**10717**	**5409**
373	93	3058	2253	2078	911		217
181	669	8125	19310	24110	2181	10717	5192
164	648	7092	14904	18939	1324	2755	2801
17	13	644	3036	4802	705	7806	2391
	8	133	425	126	98	60	
		256	945	243	54	96	
91		**1020**	**17**	**7229**	**1621**	**10748**	**15192**
334	**464**	**4065**	**3786**	**6709**	**1545**	**2703**	**2086**

表6-18 各县(市)、区农村能源和农业物资消耗情况(2014)
Consumption of Energy and Agriculture Materials in Rural Areas by Region

指标	Indicators	全市 Total	市区 Urban District	海曙 Haishu
农村用电量(万千瓦小时)	**Electricity Consumed for Rural (10000 kwh)**	**1832695**	**592472**	
农用化肥施用量(吨)	**Agricultural Consumption of Chemical Fertilizers (ton)**			
按实物量计算	Calculated by Fact Use	358188	108245	
氮肥	Nitrogenous Fertilizer	153007	39537	
磷肥	Phosphate Fertilizer	69924	26345	
钾肥	Potash Fertilizer	27449	14674	
复合肥	Compound Fertilizer	107808	27689	
按折纯法计算	Calculated by Pure Consumption	111447	28492	
氮肥	Nitrogenous Fertilizer	46477	8324	
磷肥	Phosphate Fertilizer	14736	4861	
钾肥	Potash Fertilizer	8144	3858	
复合肥	Compound Fertilizer	42090	11449	
农用塑料薄膜使用量(吨)	**Plastic Film Use for Agriculture(ton)**	**11261**	**2418**	
#地膜使用量	Use of Plastic Film	4352	889	
地膜覆盖面积(公顷)	Overcast Area of Plastic Film (hectate)	23559	8061	
农用柴油(吨)	**Consumption of Diesel Oil(ton)**	**335162**	**10295**	
农药使用量(吨)	**Consumption of Pesticide(ton)**	**7340**	**1483**	

单位:吨(ton)

各区 by Districts									
江东 Jiangdong	江北 Jiangbei	北仑 Beilun	镇海 Zhenhai	鄞州 Yinzhou	余姚 Yuyao	慈溪 Cixi	奉化 Fenghua	象山 Xiangshan	宁海 Ninghai
	17419	**39704**	**76410**	**458939**	**250151**	**702476**	**123108**	**58210**	**106278**
	22471	6984	3482	75308	43037	99233	55169	27983	24521
	8206	1488	1121	28722	20689	36979	27692	16560	11550
	4463	1657	874	19351	3026	23341	8846	4540	3826
	2549	455	735	10935	235	7129	3945	1150	316
	7253	3384	752	16300	19087	31784	14686	5733	8829
	4690	2992	1389	19421	14024	27051	20276	11688	9916
	1724	361	208	6031	4759	10354	11235	6955	4850
	804	396	178	3483	605	4668	1592	1635	1375
	638	234	251	2735	71	2495	987	575	158
	1524	2001	752	7172	8589	9534	6462	2523	3533
	334	**150**	**288**	**1646**	**239**	**5554**	**545**	**1410**	**1095**
	103	52	119	615	82	1964	276	873	268
	808	210	581	6462	532	7953	1889	2731	2393
	280	**4570**	**2290**	**3155**	**9093**	**9183**	**108442**	**193944**	**4205**
	128	**174**	**469**	**712**	**2196**	**1067**	**499**	**1145**	**950**

主要统计指标解释

【农林牧渔业总产值】 指以货币表现的农、林、牧、渔业全部产品的总量。它反映一定时期内农业生产总规模和总成果。

农林牧渔业的统计范围是:

(1) 农业 包括种植业和其他农业。

(2) 林业 包括林木的载培(不包括茶园、桑园和果园的栽培、管理和收获等活动)、林产品的采集和村及村以下合作经济和农户的竹木采伐。

(3) 牧业 包括除渔业养殖以外的一切动物饲养和放牧以及野生动物的捕猎和饲养。

(4) 渔业 包括水生动物和海藻类植物的养殖和捕捞。

农林牧渔业总产值的计算方法通常是按农林牧渔产品及其副产品的产量分别乘以各自单位产品价格求得,少数生产周期长,当年没有产品或产品产量不易统计,则采用间接方法匡算其产值,然后将四业产品产值相加即为农林牧渔业总产值。

1957 年以前的农业总产值包括了厩肥和农名自给性手工业(如农民自制衣服、鞋、袜,自己从事粮食加工等)。1958 年以后的农业总产值,林业中增加了村以及村以下的竹木采伐产值;牧业取消了厩肥产值;副业中取消了农民自给性手工业产值,增加了村以及村以下的工业产值;渔业中增加了海洋捕捞产品产值。1980 年及以后的农业总产值,在副业中增加了农民家庭兼营工业商品部分的产值。从 1984 年起村以及村以下半工业产值划归工业。从 1993 年起,取消副业,将野生动物的捕猎划入牧业。2010 年起野生植物采集从农业划入林业,坚果从林业划入农业。

【粮食产量】 指全社会的产量。包括国有经济经营的、集体统一经营的和农民家庭经营的粮食产量,还包括工矿企业办的农场和其他生产单位的产量。粮食除包括稻、小麦、玉米、高粱、谷子及其他杂粮外,还包括薯类和豆类。其产量计算方法,豆类按去豆荚后的干豆计算;薯类(番薯和马铃薯,不包括芋头和木薯) 1963 年以前按每 4 公斤鲜薯折 1 公斤粮食计算,从 1964 年开始及以后改为按 5 公斤鲜薯折 1 公斤粮食计算。其他粮食一律按脱粒后的原粮计算。2008 年起马铃薯从蔬菜中划出 5 折 1 后作为粮食统计。

【油料产量】 指全部油料作物的生产量。包括花生、油菜籽、芝麻、向日葵籽、胡麻籽(亚麻籽)和其他油料。不包括大豆,也不包括木本油料和野生油料。花生以带壳干花生计算。

【水产品产量】 指人工养殖的水产品和天然生长的水产品的捕捞量。包括海水的鱼类、虾蟹类、贝类和藻类以及内陆水域的鱼类、虾蟹类和贝类,不包括淡水生植物。

【猪、牛、羊肉产量】 指当年出栏并已屠宰后除去头蹄下水后带骨肉(即胴体重)的重量。

【农作物播种面积】 指实际播种或移植有农作物的面积。凡是实际种植有农作物的面积,不论种植在耕地上还是种植在非耕地上,均包括在农作物播种面积中,同时还包括因遭灾而重新改种和补种的农作物面积。

【农用化肥施用量】 指本年内实际用于农业生产的化肥数量。包括氮肥、磷肥、钾肥和复合肥。化肥施用量要求按折纯量计算数量。折纯法化肥施用量是把氮肥、磷肥和钾肥分别按含氮、含五氧化二磷、含氧化钾的百分之一百成份折算后的数量。复合肥按其所含主要成分折算。

【农业机械总动力】 指主要用于农、林、牧、渔业的各种动力机械的动力总和。包括耕作机械、排灌机械、收获机械、农产品加工机械、运输机械、植物保护机械、牧业机械、林业机械、渔业机械和其他农业机械[内燃机按引擎马力折成瓦(特)计算,电动机按功率折成瓦(特)计算]。不包括专门用于乡、镇、村、组办工业、基本建设、非农业运输、科学试验和教学等非农业生产方面用的动力机械与作业机械。

Explanatory Notes on Main Statistical Indicators

[Gross Output Value of Farming, Forestry, Animal Husbandry and Fishery] refers to the total volume of products of farming, forestry, animal husbandry and fishery in value terms, which reflects the total scale and total result of agricultural production during a given period of time.

The statistical coverage of farming, forestry, animal husbandry and fishery is as follows:

(1) Farming includes cultivation of farm crops and other agricultural activities.

(2) Forestry refers to planting trees of various kinds (excluding tea plantations, mulberry fields and orchards), gathering of the forest products, and cutting and felling of bamboo and trees by villages and other cooperative organizations under villages.

(3) Animal Husbandry refers to raising and grazing of all animals except fishery and aquaculture, and hunting and raising of wild animals.

(4) Fishery refers to cultivation and catching of fish and other aquatic animals and cultivation and collection of seaweed and other aquatic plants.

Gross output value of farming, forestry, animal husbandry and fishery is obtained by first multiplying the output of each product by its price, resulting in the output of each single item. For a small number of products, animal output of which is not available or difficult to get due to the long production/growing process involved, the output value is estimated through an indirect approach. The sum of output value of all products of farming, forestry, animal husbandry and fishery is then equal to their gross output value.

Prior to 1957, China's gross agricultural output value included barnyard manure and handicraft products for self - consumption (clothes, shoes, stockings, and initial grain processing undertaken by peasants). Since 1958, cutting and felling of bamboo and trees by villages and other cooperative organizations under villages have been included in forestry. ; value of barnyard manure has been excluded from animal husbandry; self - consumed handicrafts have been excluded from sideline occupations, while the output value of industries run by villages and cooperative organizations under village has been included in sideline occupations and the out put value of fish catches by motor fishing boats has been added to fishery. Since 1980, the value of handicraft products made for sale by individual in the households has been added to sideline occupations. Since 1984, industries run by villages and cooperatives organizations under villagers have been included in the sector of industry. Since 1993, the subdivision of sideline occupations has been canceled, and the hunting of wild animals has been classified into animal husbandry, Since 1993, the subdivision of sideline occupations has been canceled, and the hunting of wild animals has been classified into animal husbandry. Since 2010, collection of wild plants has been classified from agriculture into forestry, nuts from forestry into agriculture..

[Grain Yield] refers to the yield in the whole country including grains produced by state farms, collective units, industrial enterprises and mines. Grain includes rice, wheat, corn, sorghum, millet and other miscellaneous grains as well as tubers and beans. Output of beans refers to dry beans without pods. The output of tubers (potatoes, do not including taros and cassava) was converted into that of grain at the ratio 4:1,I. e. Four kilograms of fresh tubers was equivalent to one kilogram of grain up to 1963. Since 1964 the ratio for conversion has been 5:1. Output of all other grains refers to husked grain. Since 2008, potato has been classified from vegetables into food crops at the ratio 5:1.

[Yield of Oil - bearing Crops] refers to the total yield of oil bearing crops of various kinds, including peanuts, (dry, in shell) rapeseeds, sesame, sunflower seeds, flax seeds, and other oil bearing crops. Soybeans, oil bearing woody plants, and wild oil - bearing crops are not included.

[Output of Aquatic Products] refers to catches of both artificially cultured and naturally grown aquatic products, including fish, shrimps, crabs and shellfish in sea and inland water as well as seaweed. Freshwater plants are not included.

[Output of Pork, Beef, and Mutton] refers to the meat of slaughtered hogs, cattle, sheep and goats with head, feet, and offal taken away.

[Sown Area of Crops] refers to area of land sown or transplanted with crops regardless of being in cultivated area or non cultivated area. Area of land re sown due to natural disasters is also included, every sown hectare is calculated.

[Consumption of Chemical Fertilizers in Agriculture] refers to the quantity of chemical fertilizers applied in agriculture in the year, including nitrogenous fertilizer, phosphate fertilizer ,potash fertilizer and compound fertilizer. The consumption of chemical fertilizers is required in calculation to convert the gross weight into weight containing 100% effective component(e. g. 100% nitrogen content in nitrogenous fertilizer, 100% phosphorous pentoxide contents in phosphate fertilizer, 100% potassium oxide contents in potash fertilizer). Compound fertilizer is converted with its major component.

【Total Power of Farm Machinery】 refers to total mechanical power of machinery used in farming, forestry, animal husbandry, and fishery, including ploughing, irrigation and drainage, harvesting, transport, plant protection, stock breeding, forestry and fishery. The power of internal combustion engines is required to convert horsepower into watts and the power of electric motors is required to be converted into watts. Machinery employed for non agricultural purposes, such as the machines used in township run and village run industry, construction, non agricultural transport, scientific experiments and teaching, is excluded.

NINGBO 2015

Statistical YearBook

7

CHAPTER

第七篇

工业、能源消费和电力

INDUSTRY, ENERGY CONSUMPTION AND ELECTRICITY

工业、能源消费和电力
Industry, Energy Consumption and Electricity

主要统计指标
Major Statistics Indicators

2014年规模以上工业企业数	Number of Industrial Enterprises Above The Set Scale	7383	家	unit
比上年增长	Increase Over Last Year	3.0	%	
2014年规模以上工业总产值	Output Value of Industrial Enterprises Above The Set Scale	140280500	万元	10000 yuan
比上年增长	Increase Over Last Year	7.8	%	
2014年规模以上工业销售产值	Gross Industrial Products Sales of Industrial Enterprises Above The Set Scale	136189593	万元	10000 yuan
比上年增长	Increase Over Last Year	8.2	%	
2014年规模以上工业实现利税	Total Profits and Taxes of Industrial Enterprises Above The Set Scale	13474199	万元	10000 yuan
比上年增长	Increase Over Last Year	2.4	%	
2014年规模以上工业实现利润	Total Profits of Industrial Enterprises Above The Set Scale	6882464	万元	10000 yuan
比上年增长	Increase Over Last Year	-1.9	%	
2014年规模以上应交增值税	Value-added Taxes Payable of Industrial Enterprises Above The Set Scale	3533825	万元	10000 yuan
比上年增长	Increase Over Last Year	4.6	%	

表7－1 部分年份规模以上工业企业单位数
Number of Industrial Enterprises Designated Size in Partial Years

单位:个(unit)

指标	Indicators	2010	2011	2012	2013	2014
工业企业单位数	**Number of Industrial Enterprises**	**12492**	**6616**	**6804**	**7167**	**7383**
按轻重工业分	**By Light and Heavy Industry**					
轻工业	Light Industry	5392	2792	2801	2939	3005
重工业	Heavy Industry	7100	3824	4003	4228	4378
按注册登记类型分	**By Registered Type**					
国有企业	State – owned Enterprises	36	32	36	17	17
集体企业	Collective – owned Enterprises	80	26	23	15	11
股份合作企业	Share Cooperative Enterprises	59	18	25	21	24
联营企业	Joint – owned	6	2	1		
有限责任公司	Limited Liability Corporations	886	540	546	590	610
股份有限公司	Share – holding Corporations Ltd.	140	101	109	123	126
私营企业	Private Enterprises	8325	3715	3958	4401	4704
港、澳、台商投资公司	Hongkong, Macao and Taiwan Funded	1529	1163	1118	1066	1002
外商投资企业公司	Enterprises with Foreign Investment	1431	1019	983	930	885
在总计中:亏损企业	Of the Total: Loss Making Enterprises	1377	826	1034	1230	1157
在总计中:国有及国有控股	Of the Total: State – owned and State – holding	99	91	97	100	103
按规模分	By Enterprises Size					
大型企业	Large – Sized	35	108	107	109	115
中型企业	Medium – Sized	1014	1086	1005	998	965
小型企业	Small – Sized	11443	5352	5539	5893	6077

注:2011 年起,规模以上工业企业为年主营业务收入 2000 万元及以上的企业,下表同。

Note: From 2011, Industrial enterprises above designated size are those with annual revenue from principal business over 20 million yuan. The others table are the same.

表7-2 部分年份规模以上工业企业总产值
Gross Output Value of Industrial Enterprises Above Designated Size in Partial Years

单位:万元(10000 yuan)

指标	Indicators	2010	2011	2012	2013	2014
工业总产值	**Gross Industrial Output Value**	**108535474**	**120447699**	**121550760**	**130100892**	**140280500**
按轻重工业分	**By Light and Heavy Industry**					
轻工业	Light Industry	34112854	34683454	34049449	36404426	38647586
重工业	Heavy Industry	74422621	85764245	87501311	93696465	101632914
按注册登记类型分	**By Registered Type**					
国有企业	State - owned Enterprises	7193904	8013730	8547018	6304640	6618178
集体企业	Collective - owned Enterprises	193152	170815	111059	76561	82991
股份合作企业	Share Cooperative Enterprises	163059	106743	137049	91655	107251
联营企业	Joint - owned	20762	11779	9128		
有限责任公司	Limited Liability Corporations	11145328	12189111	12142989	17136831	21036324
股份有限公司	Share - holding Corporations Ltd.	13630949	17468406	17252477	19191004	20082463
私营企业	Private Enterprises	31749621	31028632	32872411	37126092	41499737
港、澳、台商投资公司	Hongkong, Macao and Taiwan Funded	24131396	29448789	28862744	29547796	30705908
外商投资企业公司	Enterprises with Foreign Investment	20307304	22009694	21553507	20604783	20122025
在总计中:亏损企业	Of the Total: Loss Making Enterprises	5055244	10908447	13314051	12879241	16283107
在总计中:国有及国有控股	Of the Total: State - owned and State - holding	24426588	31162756	30369003	32757503	33932611
按规模分	**By Enterprises Size**					
大型企业	Large - Sized	21449940	38131433	40247278	42694441	42200816
中型企业	Medium - Sized	40851033	39522112	36402444	39503925	41778329
小型企业	Small - Sized	46234502	42444047	43739373	46430882	49513741

注:工业总产值按现行价格计算。

Note: Gross industrial output value are calculated at current prices.

表7-3 部分年份规模以上工业企业销售产值
Sales Value of Industrial Enterprises Above Designated Size in Partial Years

单位:万元(10000 yuan)

指标	Indicators	2010	2011	2012	2013	2014
工业销售产值	**Gross Industrial Products Sales**	**105629245**	**117898629**	**117880641**	**125914244**	**136189593**
按轻重工业分	**By Light and Heavy Industry**					
轻工业	Light Industry	33032063	33639832	33104213	35404606	37470703
重工业	Heavy Industry	72597182	84258797	84776428	90509638	98718890
按注册登记类型分	**By Registered Type**					
国有企业	State - owned Enterprises	7189224	8017179	8536128	6292237	6579551
集体企业	Collective - owned Enterprises	187285	165908	111743	73095	81828
股份合作企业	Share Cooperative Enterprises	160539	102713	131655	88018	104814
联营企业	Joint - owned	20716	11688	9125		
有限责任公司	Limited Liability Corporations	10887393	11969274	11928565	16867818	20565673
股份有限公司	Share - holding Corporations Ltd.	13387235	17376222	16889319	18057626	19906883
私营企业	Private Enterprises	30779754	29950680	31394168	35742934	39974045
港、澳、台商投资公司	Hongkong, Macao and Taiwan Funded	23226285	28642232	28044561	28934977	29620191
外商投资企业公司	Enterprises with Foreign Investment	19790814	21662734	20772067	19836017	19331314
在总计中:亏损企业	Of the Total: Loss Making Enterprises	4896009	10657194	13013311	12605094	15900741
在总计中:国有及国有控股	Of the Total: State - owned and State - holding	24149681	31299012	30125079	31813141	33446733
按规模分	**By Enterprises Size**					
大型企业	Large - Sized	20807766	37600731	38897059	41044813	41332458
中型企业	Medium - Sized	39727953	38561314	35321924	38237444	40223577
小型企业	Small - Sized	45093526	41391137	42512942	45162152	47898223

注:工业销售产值按现行价格计算。

Note: Sales value of industrial products are calculated at current prices.

表7-4 规模以下工业企业及个体工业单位主要经济指标(2014) Main Economic Indicators of Industrial Enterprises Below Designated Size and Private and Individuals

指标	单位	Indicators	Unit	总计 Total
总计		**Total**		
企业(单位)数	个	Number of Enterprises(unit)	unit	115980
期末从业人员	人	Total Employees at Year - end	person	1448403
工业总产值	万元	Gross Industrial Output Value	10000 yuan	36235966
资产总计	万元	Total Asset	10000 yuan	29398050
企业主要经济指标		Main Economic Indicators of Enterprises		
企业数	个	Number of Enterprises(unit)	unit	39789
期末从业人员	人	Total Employees at Year - end	person	854193
工业总产值	万元	Gross Industrial Output Value	10000 yuan	21042452
主营业务收入	万元	Prime Operating Revenue	10000 yuan	20834111
#出口产品销售收入	万元	Export Sales Revenue	10000 yuan	3560625
主营业务成本	万元	Operating Costs	10000 yuan	16657872
税金总额	万元	Total Taxes	10000 yuan	1120626
#所得税	万元	Income Taxes	10000 yuan	175978
营业利润	万元	Business Profits	10000 yuan	987820
应付职工薪酬	万元	Employee Compensation Payable	10000 yuan	2970472
本年折旧	万元	Depreciation	10000 yuan	719520
资产总计	万元	Total Asset	10000 yuan	22279149
负债合计	万元	Total Liabilities	10000 yuan	12469837
固定资产原值	万元	Actual Value of Fixed Assets	10000 yuan	8723723
固定资产净值	万元	Net Fixed Assets	10000 yuan	5414549
应收帐款	万元	Accounts Receivable	10000 yuan	4592373
利息支出	万元	Interest Expense	10000 yuan	301277
#银行借款利息	万元	Interest on Bank Borrowings	10000 yuan	278102
民间借款利息	万元	Civil Borrowing Interest	10000 yuan	23175
期末剩余订单额	万元	Final Remaining Orders	10000 yuan	935143
生产能力(设备)利用率	%	Capacity Utilization	%	81.19
个体工业主要经济指标		Main Economic Indicators of Individuals		
单位数	个	The Number of Units	unit	76191
期末从业人员	人	Total Employees at Year - end	person	594210
营业收入	万元	Operating Revenue	10000 yuan	15043084
生产支出	万元	Production Expenditure	10000 yuan	11323543
应付职工薪酬	万元	Employee Compensation Payable	10000 yuan	2082184
资产总计	万元	Total Asset	10000 yuan	7118900

表7-5 历年工业企业主要经济指标 Main Economic Indicators of Industrial Enterprises Over the Years

单位:亿元 万人(100 million yuan, 10000 persons)

年份 Year	总产值(当年价) Gross Industrial Output Value (current prices)	固定资产原值 Original Value of Fixed Assets	固定资产净值 Net Value of Fixed Assets	主营业务收入 Prime Operating Revenue	利税总额 Total Profits and Taxes	利润总额 Total Profits	全部从业人员年平均人数 Annual Average Employees
1978	15.79	7.07			4.29	2.59	
1979	18.11	8.25	6.28	18.71	4.73	2.86	
1980	23.73	9.59	7.35	24.89	6.17	3.93	
1981	29.67	11.38	8.76	30.05	6.94	4.26	
1982	29.99	13.53	10.49	32.36	7.99	4.86	
1983	35.23	15.84	12.17	38.98	9.07	5.57	
1984	50.93	21.09	16.67	54.57	11.30	6.53	
1985	68.63	32.55	26.43	76.16	14.62	7.65	65.48
1986	81.96	38.43	30.49	86.67	15.86	7.94	68.69
1987	102.16	52.61	41.79	110.96	18.54	9.92	71.29
1988	132.17	62.81	48.85	147.85	23.24	12.00	72.06
1989	159.41	74.80	56.60	162.81	23.64	11.47	69.05
1990	200.00	89.31	64.39	167.35	20.99	8.21	67.71
1991	261.62	107.17	79.45	218.15	25.27	11.79	72.02
1992	341.42	128.57	95.03	282.90	31.65	14.82	73.15
1993	491.07	192.06	147.38	430.65	45.15	22.68	73.94
1994	642.18	276.98	225.18	480.46	53.56	26.06	71.53
1995	837.80	357.05	281.28	664.70	62.61	29.46	66.08
1996	843.48	407.73	312.70	722.15	66.57	28.63	64.60
1997	842.62	496.05	374.92	747.51	78.60	33.32	55.88
1998	940.59	567.09	423.50	835.24	88.00	37.52	50.78
1999	1062.29	668.71	490.07	985.32	118.65	61.21	52.38
2000	1427.70	829.69	601.93	1350.52	163.26	88.11	58.42
2001	1629.66	926.49	648.50	1538.70	213.72	115.95	66.90
2002	2000.16	1058.90	727.01	1945.02	267.09	152.34	77.22
2003	2630.29	1251.24	854.79	2604.90	322.01	189.30	91.96
2004	3815.04	1602.75	1113.37	3660.69	417.63	241.31	128.94
2005	4890.97	1926.51	1337.30	4698.16	446.13	262.36	140.82
2006	6187.91	2469.35	1755.66	5930.59	525.65	312.63	159.64
2007	7789.01	2886.87	2013.56	7456.24	639.83	387.31	174.24
2008	8746.36	3422.49	2363.23	8283.18	489.32	221.25	178.59
2009	8272.85	3908.81	2633.33	7824.88	867.35	462.11	168.67
2010	10853.55	4431.40	2920.36	10396.63	1160.55	657.77	181.09
2011	12044.77	4543.83		11803.24	1193.21	631.66	152.25
2012	12155.08	4792.65		11795.98	1112.86	553.21	147.06
2013	13010.09	5092.25		12594.24	1315.94	701.68	147.50
2014	14028.05	5595.92		13254.65	1347.42	688.25	151.84

注:1997年以前为乡及乡以上独立核算工业企业。1998年及以后为规模以上工业企业。

Note: Data in this table refer to all industrial enterprises with annual revenue from principal business over 5 million yuan, before 1997 to enterprises with independent accounting at townships and above level.

表7-6 全市及各县(市)、区规模以上工业企业总产值(现行价格、2014) Gross Output Value of Industrial Enterprises Above Designated Size by Region (at Current Price)

指标	Indicators	全市 Toal	市区 Urban District	海曙 Haishu
工业总产值	**Gross Industrial Output Value**	**140280500**	**91816608**	**3724926**
按轻重工业分	**Grouped by Light and Heavy Industry**			
轻工业	Light Industry	38647586	20920228	303703
重工业	Heavy Industry	101632914	70896380	3421223
按注册登记类型分	**Grouped by Registered Type**			
国有企业	State - owned Enterprises	6618178	5105570	3113223
集体企业	Collective - owned Enterpriese	82991	47457	
股份合作企业	Share Cooperative Enterprises	107251	63511	
有限责任公司	Limited Liability Corporations	21036324	13980208	476751
股份有限公司	Share - holding Corporations Ltd.	20082463	17419826	21186
私营企业	Private Enterprises	41499737	16764041	17321
港澳台商投资企业	Hong Kong. Macao & Taiwan Funded	30705908	23795387	94126
外商投资企业	Foreign Funded Enterprises	20122025	14614984	2319
在总计中:亏损企业	Of the Total:Loss Making Enterprises	16283107	12189898	20175
在总计中:国有及国有控股	Of the Total:State - owned and State - holding	33932611	30237237	3314580
按规模分	Grouped by Enterprises Size			
大型企业	Large - Sized	42200816	32034921	71365
中型企业	Medium - Sized	41778329	25523221	345423
小型企业	Small - Sized	49513741	28047251	221003
按工业行业分	Grouped by Sector			
非金属矿采选业	Non - metallic Mining Industry	37042	33022	
农副食品加工业	Farm and Sideline Products Processing	1621749	641642	
食品制造业	Food Manufacturing	876078	225319	26923
酒、饮料和精制茶制造业	Wine,Beverages and Refined Tea Manufacturing	302056	183565	4117
烟草制品业	Tobacco Manufacturing	1476678	1476678	
纺织业	Textile Industry	3769195	2427148	59982
纺织服装、服饰业	Clothing, Apparel Industry	6726465	5119030	96159
皮革、毛皮、羽毛及其制品和制鞋业	Leather, Fur, Feather and Its Products and Footwear Industry	134639	62180	

单位:万元(10000 yuan)

各区 by Districts					余姚 Yuyao	慈溪 Cixi	奉化 Fenghua	象山 Xiangshan	宁海 Ninghai
江东 Jiangdong	江北 Jiangbei	北仑 Beilun	镇海 Zhenhai	鄞州 Yinzhou					
1992754	**4891790**	**31187656**	**25141597**	**23619286**	**13354244**	**19831411**	**3763341**	**5396165**	**6118732**
1667128	775817	4607173	2060072	11131871	4438669	7731492	1312040	1843187	2401971
325625	4115972	26580484	23081525	12487416	8915575	12099919	2451301	3552978	3716761
1490429		16270		485649	454625	569901	162062	164570	161449
		7105	14588	25765	23249	5685			6599
	24267	5847	4301	22589	8945	5804		28992	
186865	1689737	6289952	2350673	2805722	1086363	3413902	198254	989833	1367763
13367	950173	408423	14133833	1709488	1198057	539163		539257	386160
134442	1134111	2110120	2877468	10307026	6233118	10611329	2030337	2499197	3361715
164765	531289	13589131	2950653	6232665	2529138	2526489	931644	491896	431354
2885	562213	8750030	2797423	2028196	1820748	2159138	441043	682419	403692
23044	1357155	6841777	2537982	1218324	737878	1854187	525941	422293	552910
1603000	129373	8862338	15639396	650251	759341	677863	187406	811782	1258983
112571	879143	11505050	14473759	4687504	1706610	5253935	723204	608148	1873998
201827	2233513	10836012	4401226	7171405	4729320	6759566	1042965	2033357	1689901
197216	1753481	8684621	5443986	11131581	6701333	7627593	1934663	2720320	2482582
	2650	15550		14822				4020	
	29651	391435		205608	339473	161648	76447	395936	6603
	45448	63634	36436	52878	455820	12694	33241	76077	72927
	2699	129493		47256	74526		24675		19291
1476678									
	157127	712272	616401	877336	413515	596324	68275	160467	103467
65909	99713	1422203	77956	3321134	45240	93626	448471	932627	87472
	3012	5995	16585	36587	15112	36267	10597		10483

表7-6 续表 Continued

指标	Indicators	全市 Toal	市区 Urban District	海曙 Haishu
木材加工及木、竹、藤、棕、草制品业	Timber Processing, Bamboo, Rattan, Cane Palm, and Straw Products	126836	74484	
家具制造业	Furniture Manufacturing	947148	551621	
造纸及纸制品业	Paper - making and Paper Products Manufacturing	1649424	1156107	
印刷和记录媒介复制业	Printing and Record Duplicating	815707	637921	1554
文教、工美、体育和娱乐用品制造业	Culture, Art, Sports and Recreation Supplies Manufacturing	3207034	1582703	
石油加工、炼焦和核燃料加工业	Petroleum Processing, Coking & Nuclear Fuel Processing	16702181	16686199	
化学原料和化学制品制造业	Raw Chemical Materials and Chemical Products	14380931	13179399	
医药制造业	Medicines Manufacturing	604026	443870	7652
化学纤维制造业	Chemical Fiber Manufacturing	1663084	280052	
橡胶和塑料制品业	Rubber and Plastic Products Industry	4054640	1930596	6087
非金属矿物制品业	Nonmetal Mineral Products	2336575	1277812	
黑色金属冶炼和压延加工业	Smelting and Pressing of Ferrous Metals	5244771	3824468	
有色金属冶炼和压延加工业	Smelting and Pressing of Nonferrous Metals	6417383	3530041	
金属制品业	Metal Products Manufacturing	4141277	2476217	3797
通用设备制造业	General Purpose Equipment Manufacturing	8037982	4412802	11568
专用设备制造业	Special Purpose Equipment Manufacturing	4181916	2666237	
汽车制造业	Automobile Manufacturing	11150545	5030969	40209
铁路、船舶、航空航天和其他运输设备制造业	Railroad, Marine, Aviation and Other Transport Equipment Manufacturing	1836694	604883	
电气机械和器材制造业	Electric Equipment and Machinery Manufacturing	15895591	5878947	80014
计算机、通信和其他电子设备制造业	Computer, Communications and Other Electronic Equipment Manufacturing	8727259	6712843	70066
仪器仪表制造业	Instrument Manufacturing	1852855	945503	8068
其他制造业	Other Manufacturing	464490	178398	
废弃资源综合利用业	Waste Comprehensive Utilization of Resources Industry	737239	722019	
金属制品、机械和设备修理业	Metal Products, Machinery and Equipment Repair Industry	62481	9003	
电力、热力的生产和供应业	Production and Supply Electric Power and Thermal Power	8743197	5661203	3107374
燃气生产和供应业	Production and Supply Gas	1100482	1054994	201357
水的生产和供应业	Production and Supply Tap Water	254851	138736	

单位:万元(10000 yuan)

各区 by Districts					余姚 Yuyao	慈溪 Cixi	奉化 Fenghua	象山 Xiangshan	宁海 Ninghai
江东 Jiangdong	江北 Jiangbei	北仑 Beilun	镇海 Zhenhai	鄞州 Yinzhou					
	5821			68664	24286	2484	25581		
2969	50916	79006	15518	388259	255273	99573	20508	14896	5278
	7468	635566	5483	507590	120159	245225	33107	4022	90804
	10075	62661	55302	508330	59478	56528	32275	21010	8495
6679	148987	383580	89531	944304	117814	491062	75183	17494	922779
		2733347	13939605	13246			9156	6826	
	130000	7699950	4438106	911343	491978	497385	84375	31233	96561
	20264	21934	110291	270923	24010	50996	52042	10995	22114
		77686	180555	21811	174258	1129473	8984	70317	
3558	123534	353223	210401	1221679	870378	631493	192257	96478	333439
	172276	288054	168367	619755	425961	177827	62949	210399	181627
9972	39512	2506251	439473	758958	671281	347877	215461	117531	68154
30096	1869009	226582	501799	843135	1101917	1399759	185413	16942	183312
38325	151349	875038	331423	1058574	541955	606259	221109	54399	241338
29099	294335	1000489	1233545	1734624	744505	1367146	555057	508099	450373
34196	151140	1422064	372717	679088	676518	261591	45312	228679	303579
12823	386440	2269373	147516	2072366	361328	4157709	153660	843458	603422
13751		336104	60085	149217	49727	504402	399868	254875	22940
5208	498169	1260049	460302	3173997	2886120	5198581	276827	625914	1029202
150920	199679	3868829	326035	1880924	1104733	599952	218682	15851	75198
	256932	56726	18712	547731	572987	268513	29362		36490
	23440	10056	34685	110217	57228	172476	33771		22617
		5586	707445	8987		12284		2936	
			9003					46345	7133
		1428588	524301	562641	636496	578789	164368	614679	1087662
		846334		7303	11998	29218			4272
112571	12144		14021		30172	44252	6330	13660	21701

表7-7 全市及各县(市)、区规模以上工业企业销售产值(2014)
Sales Value of Industrial Enterprises Above Designated Size by Region

指标	Indicators	全市 Toal	市区 Urban District	海曙 Haishu
工业销售产值	Gross Industrial Products Sales	**136189593**	**89667576**	**3750064**
按轻重工业分	Grouped by Light and Heavy Industry			
轻工业	Light Industry	37470703	20462946	330430
重工业	Heavy Industry	98718890	69204630	3419633
按注册登记类型分	Grouped by Registered Type			
国有企业	State - owned Enterprises	6579551	5066943	3113422
集体企业	Collective - owned Enterpriese	81828	47176	
股份合作企业	Share Cooperative Enterprises	104814	61949	
有限责任公司	Limited Liability Corporations	20565673	13674766	501496
股份有限公司	Share - holding Corporations Ltd.	19906883	17345575	21337
私营企业	Private Enterprises	39974045	16381015	17530
港澳台商投资企业	Hong Kong, Macao & Taiwan Funded	29620191	22880518	93935
外商投资企业	Foreign Funded Enterprises	19331314	14184339	2344
在总计中:亏损企业	Of the Total: Loss Making Enterprises	15900741	11978017	19543
在总计中:国有及国有控股	Of the Total: State - owned and State - holding	33446733	29794463	3314779
按规模分	Grouped by Enterprises Size			
大型企业	Large - Sized	41332458	31333697	68530
中型企业	Medium - Sized	40223577	24741898	374753
小型企业	Small - Sized	47898223	27414612	219445
按工业行业分	Grouped by Sector			
非金属矿采选业	Non - metallic Mining Industry	35779	32686	
农副食品加工业	Farm and Sideline Products Processing	1565484	647131	
食品制造业	Food Manufacturing	810501	216520	26923
酒、饮料和精制茶制造业	Wine, Beverages and Refined Tea Manufacturing	302292	184076	4095
烟草制品业	Tobacco Manufacturing	1440136	1440136	
纺织业	Textile Industry	3658877	2389981	89872
纺织服装、服饰业	Clothing, Apparel Industry	6516805	4971606	96319
皮革、毛皮、羽毛及其制品和制鞋业	Leather, Fur, Feather and Its Products and Footwear Industry	131289	59203	

单位:万元(10000 yuan)

各区 by Districts					余姚 Yuyao	慈溪 Cixi	奉化 Fenghua	象山 Xiangshan	宁海 Ninghai
江东 Jiangdong	江北 Jiangbei	北仑 Beilun	镇海 Zhenhai	鄞州 Yinzhou					
1933723	**4829582**	**30000838**	**24751294**	**23159933**	**12836199**	**19038879**	**3833302**	**4968964**	**5844673**
1629062	762304	4479806	1939881	10945840	4293237	7450546	1257814	1751380	2254781
304661	4067278	25521033	22811413	12214093	8542962	11588333	2575488	3217584	3589893
1452159		15910		485452	454625	569901	162062	164570	161449
		7105	14990	25081	22466	5685			6502
	24189	5369	3747	22200	8555	5661		28649	
185249	1661783	6126359	2239616	2784457	1043100	3354555	192346	962858	1338047
13161	945061	395220	14132184	1664242	1170272	514964		489059	387012
138194	1123668	2046175	2768172	10106329	5979567	10228813	1962895	2245335	3176420
142115	515962	12989860	2825375	6084469	2411106	2378818	1089457	458099	402193
2846	558921	8404063	2754879	1985516	1746507	1980481	426543	620393	373051
23710	1373014	6693423	2473167	1203630	709913	1785970	510171	405912	510758
1564730	103537	8463048	15663722	646347	759341	670924	186613	785223	1250170
112571	876359	10942587	14481460	4543618	1627422	5035602	892222	575017	1868498
179466	2195156	10438554	4143694	7078146	4541859	6520201	1007838	1837011	1574770
196402	1733211	8459608	5320186	10887899	6457561	7293671	1873630	2527540	2331209
	2650	15453		14583				3093	
	27458	403570		201002	326368	147970	67953	369443	6619
	44347	64326	30113	50811	444943	10339	29717	48652	60330
	2699	129478		47804	73907		24789		19519
1440136									
	152224	704819	587827	851180	388199	562386	65378	157465	95469
64394	92704	1400495	76262	3203925	43400	95044	436537	901770	68448
	2817	6131	15180	35075	15089	35909	10822		10266

表7－7 续表 Continued

指标	Indicators	全市 Toal	市区 Urban District	海曙 Haishu
木材加工及木、竹、藤、棕、草制品业	Timber Processing, Bamboo, Rattan, Cane Palm, and Straw Products	122602	73013	
家具制造业	Furniture Manufacturing	922433	540747	
造纸及纸制品业	Paper－making and Paper Products Manufacturing	1547798	1065194	
印刷和记录媒介复制业	Printing and Record Duplicating	805567	633263	1722
文教、工美、体育和娱乐用品制造业	Culture, Art, Sports and Recreation Supplies Manufacturing	3125494	1546947	
石油加工、炼焦和核燃料加工业	Petroleum Processing, Coking & Nuclear Fuel Processing	16427301	16411580	
化学原料和化学制品制造业	Raw Chemical Materials and Chemical Products	13988149	12831281	
医药制造业	Medicines Manufacturing	558282	418982	6779
化学纤维制造业	Chemical Fiber Manufacturing	1623968	266458	
橡胶和塑料制品业	Rubber and Plastic Products Industry	3916030	1887785	6930
非金属矿物制品业	Nonmetal Mineral Products	2291292	1257156	
黑色金属冶炼和压延加工业	Smelting and Pressing of Ferrous Metals	5126853	3757727	
有色金属冶炼和压延加工业	Smelting and Pressing of Nonferrous Metals	6295483	3525584	
金属制品业	Metal Products Manufacturing	3982035	2391130	3812
通用设备制造业	General Purpose Equipment Manufacturing	7619148	4234330	11620
专用设备制造业	Special Purpose Equipment Manufacturing	4049806	2607770	
汽车制造业	Automobile Manufacturing	10672995	4881418	38700
铁路、船舶、航空航天和其他运输设备制造业	Railroad, Marine, Aviation and Other Transport Equipment Manufacturing	1764538	454434	
电气机械和器材制造业	Electric Equipment and Machinery Manufacturing	15387777	5793267	77229
计算机、通信和其他电子设备制造业	Computer, Communications and Other Electronic Equipment Manufacturing	8410756	6492302	69741
仪器仪表制造业	Instrument Manufacturing	1755240	905537	7592
其他制造业	Other Manufacturing	451963	173662	
废弃资源综合利用业	Waste Comprehensive Utilization of Resources Industry	745739	732434	
金属制品、机械和设备修理业	Metal Products, Machinery and Equipment Repair Industry	62481	9003	
电力、热力的生产和供应业	Production and Supply Electric Power and Thermal Power	8719711	5641503	3107374
燃气生产和供应业	Production and Supply Gas	1100140	1054994	201357
水的生产和供应业	Production and Supply Tap Water	254851	138736	

单位:万元(10000 yuan)

各区 by Districts					余姚 Yuyao	慈溪 Cixi	奉化 Fenghua	象山 Xiangshan	宁海 Ninghai
江东 Jiangdong	江北 Jiangbei	北仑 Beilun	镇海 Zhenhai	鄞州 Yinzhou					
	5821			67192	22383	2366	24840		
2969	50520	75335	14069	383214	242483	98681	20844	14476	5203
	7072	554823	5388	497910	121742	238712	32834	3706	85610
	10030	63026	55606	502880	58760	53236	31630	20629	8049
6676	149410	375435	85996	919809	115320	475445	73334	17155	897293
		2426129	13972138	13313			9068	6652	
	129002	7567142	4233656	901481	461617	494540	82873	31646	86193
	19663	21331	92071	268320	22723	45921	45519	10044	15093
		72223	172389	21847	174793	1105551	8641	68525	
3475	123303	316972	209096	1215546	836199	596953	184624	95375	315094
	169701	287314	156801	617001	418822	176752	62140	202536	173887
11218	39841	2473581	431308	731478	648967	336734	206245	112699	64481
30086	1889605	225315	500177	821537	1050545	1350805	179904	16921	171724
37077	150424	827824	311872	1042796	513267	577665	216711	53296	229967
29941	277537	964825	1174307	1675218	694949	1292042	537456	432670	427702
34761	149581	1386279	362779	667508	651522	251546	43482	220757	274729
12662	382581	2175318	140449	2030265	342886	3967818	149953	748002	582918
12022		196083	59384	141218	48768	492111	578109	168279	22837
5161	497593	1213492	430044	3166121	2782339	4988892	268118	574709	980453
130574	172424	3730591	320364	1856531	1065693	559773	210260	15049	67679
	244691	52156	17725	527191	539750	249308	28170		32474
	23741	9584	30904	109434	54629	169115	32654		21904
		5586	718065	8782		11650		1656	
			9003					46345	7133
		1409871	524301	561658	633965	578492	164368	613756	1087626
		846334		7303	11998	28876			4272
112571	12144		14021		30172	44252	6330	13660	21701

表7-8 全市规模以上工业企业主要经济指标(2014)
Main Economic Indicators of Industrial Enterprises Above Designated Size

指标	Indicators	企业个数(个) Number of Enterprises (unit)	#亏损企业 Loss Making
总计	**Total**	**7383**	**1157**
按轻重工业分	**Grouped by Light and Heavy Industry**		
轻工业	Light Industry	3005	515
重工业	Heavy Industry	4378	642
按注册登记类型分	**Grouped by Registered Type**		
国有企业	State - owned Enterprises	17	
集体企业	Collective - owned Enterpriese	11	
股份合作企业	Share Cooperative Enterprises	24	2
有限责任公司	Limited Liability Corporations	610	91
股份有限公司	Share - holding Corporations Ltd.	126	17
私营企业	Private Enterprises	4704	619
港澳台商投资企业	Hong Kong,Macao & Taiwan Funded	1002	213
外商投资企业	Foreign Funded Enterprises	885	214
在总计中:亏损企业	Of the Total:Loss Making Enterprises	1157	1157
在总计中:国有及国有控股	Of the Total:State - owned and State - holding	103	17
按规模分	Grouped by Enterprises Size		
大型企业	Large - Sized	115	3
中型企业	Medium - Sized	965	133
小型企业	Small - Sized	6077	940
按工业行业分	Grouped by Sector		
非金属矿采选业	Non - metallic Mining Industry	5	
农副食品加工业	Farm and Sideline Products Processing	81	14
食品制造业	Food Manufacturing	48	14
酒、饮料和精制茶制造业	Wine, Beverages and Refined Tea Manufacturing	20	2
烟草制品业	Tobacco Manufacturing	1	
纺织业	Textile Industry	287	54
纺织服装、服饰业	Clothing, Apparel Industry	588	111
皮革、毛皮、羽毛及其制品和制鞋业	Leather, Fur, Feather and Its Products and Footwear Industry	29	5

单位:万元(10000 yuan)

工业总产值(现价) Gross Industrial Output Value (Current Prices)	工业销售产值 Value of Industrial Products Sales	#出口交货值 Value of Export Products	资产合计 Total Asset	流动资产小计 Current Assets	固定资产小计 Total Fixed Assets	固定资产原价 Original Value of Fixed Assets
140280500	**136189593**	**30423607**	**122049745**	**70776014**	**34694550**	**55959206**
38647586	37470703	14880415	39994629	25400532	8126640	13507825
101632914	98718890	15543192	82055116	45375481	26567910	42451380
6618178	6579551	24289	3626162	1339623	1827632	3549379
82991	81828	1145	97479	68221	26121	41050
107251	104814	24889	88771	66480	18840	40612
21036324	20565673	1896534	22545675	9975019	9704419	15258063
20082463	19906883	1013570	11813389	5971172	3702363	5522288
41499737	39974045	10374715	37129111	24324139	7633744	11553974
30705908	29620191	8340203	29628198	18151322	7043180	11710134
20122025	19331314	8748262	17093756	10858180	4734092	8274688
16283107	15900741	2297981	20022264	11001012	6369006	8727153
33932611	33446733	379527	20307701	7349278	11418079	19751260
42200816	41332458	9351285	32638981	17608210	10051435	15831295
41778329	40223577	9750712	36276662	20906012	9970613	15981021
49513741	47898223	10950724	47837414	29756789	12822500	20524205
37042	35779		67600	40453	10230	13785
1621749	1565484	445139	1487963	847605	369888	541171
876078	810501	414788	803144	466594	205842	266538
302056	302292	65810	402974	233243	126940	234195
1476678	1440136	24182	1396957	985483	159759	344701
3769195	3658877	906352	4556228	3088186	870947	1578256
6726465	6516805	3254509	6145899	4161585	956682	1578130
134639	131289	67671	125918	83739	27837	44582

表 7 - 8 续 1 Continued

指标	Indicators	企业个数(个) Number of Enterprises (unit)	#亏损企业 Loss Making
木材加工及木、竹、藤、棕、草制品业	Timber Processing, Bamboo, Rattan, Cane Palm, and Straw Products	25	2
家具制造业	Furniture Manufacturing	106	28
造纸及纸制品业	Paper - making and Paper Products Manufacturing	78	19
印刷和记录媒介复制业	Printing and Record Duplicating	90	12
文教、工美、体育和娱乐用品制造业	Culture, Art, Sports and Recreation Supplies Manufacturing	266	46
石油加工、炼焦和核燃料加工业	Petroleum Processing, Coking & Nuclear Fuel Processing	13	2
化学原料和化学制品制造业	Raw Chemical Materials and Chemical Products	228	55
医药制造业	Medicines Manufacturing	36	7
化学纤维制造业	Chemical Fiber Manufacturing	65	18
橡胶和塑料制品业	Rubber and Plastic Products Industry	477	68
非金属矿物制品业	Nonmetal Mineral Products	196	21
黑色金属冶炼和压延加工业	Smelting and Pressing of Ferrous Metals	215	32
有色金属冶炼和压延加工业	Smelting and Pressing of Nonferrous Metals	202	43
金属制品业	Metal Products Manufacturing	518	74
通用设备制造业	General Purpose Equipment Manufacturing	894	119
专用设备制造业	Special Purpose Equipment Manufacturing	394	55
汽车制造业	Automobile Manufacturing	486	54
铁路、船舶、航空航天和其他运输设备制造业	Railroad, Marine, Aviation and Other Transport Equipment Manufacturing	100	18
电气机械和器材制造业	Electric Equipment and Machinery Manufacturing	1220	155
计算机、通信和其他电子设备制造业	Computer, Communications and Other Electronic Equipment Manufacturing	366	53
仪器仪表制造业	Instrument Manufacturing	159	18
其他制造业	Other Manufacturing	65	9
废弃资源综合利用业	Waste Comprehensive Utilization of Resources Industry	53	40
金属制品、机械和设备修理业	Metal Products, Machinery and Equipment Repair Industry	4	
电力、热力的生产和供应业	Production and Supply Electric Power and Thermal Power	42	2
燃气生产和供应业	Production and Supply Gas	7	2
水的生产和供应业	Production and Supply Tap Water	19	5

单位:万元(10000 yuan)

工业总产值(现价) Gross Industrial Output Value (Current Prices)	工业销售产值 Value of Industrial Products Sales	#出口交货值 Value of Export Products	资产合计 Total Asset	流动资产小计 Current Assets	固定资产小计 Total Fixed Assets	固定资产原价 Original Value of Fixed Assets
126836	122602	68238	113453	73274	28322	51924
947148	922433	515148	1053354	721346	210228	292036
1649424	1547798	394572	3218069	1548531	713333	1490210
815707	805567	219522	988861	612801	211042	397126
3207034	3125494	1447652	2780633	1788047	530396	840645
16702181	16427301	15743	4419947	1836294	2378562	3679867
14380931	13988149	1022581	13065410	6218178	5317622	7321617
604026	558282	83600	596379	353595	160478	236401
1663084	1623968	182144	1651260	1114925	372200	645609
4054640	3916030	1322291	3527792	2167748	830097	1369070
2336575	2291292	108426	2382658	1642325	537409	882561
5244771	5126853	360768	4697669	2482397	1872830	3220030
6417383	6295483	258277	3248816	2174815	664999	1005811
4141277	3982035	1788942	3674943	2508732	755426	1210330
8037982	7619148	2262774	8060776	5227244	1894665	3103487
4181916	4049806	1135923	5027598	3145084	1034219	1665111
11150545	10672995	1247758	10703539	6127383	2443535	3290482
1836694	1764538	876838	1988002	1275724	496849	756993
15895591	15387777	6092192	15421843	10423119	2819045	4135004
8727259	8410756	5102995	7213331	4918951	1307167	2607200
1852855	1755240	487494	2599072	1627543	379492	578631
464490	451963	251173	417267	296630	76722	145165
737239	745739		253531	211489	11635	20008
62481	62481	107	123459	79735	39383	56410
8743197	8719711		6938276	1205656	5375692	10361969
1100482	1100140		1063903	344440	627073	636830
254851	254851		1833224	743124	878005	1357324

表7－8 续2 Continued

指标	Indicators	本年折旧 Depreciation in This Year	负债小计 Total Liabilities
总计	**Total**	**3309181**	**73376205**
按轻重工业分	**Grouped by Light and Heavy Industry**		
轻工业	Light Industry	807109	24743955
重工业	Heavy Industry	2502072	48632250
按注册登记类型分	**Grouped by Registered Type**		
国有企业	State－owned Enterprises	162062	1773527
集体企业	Collective－owned Enterpriese	2550	41138
股份合作企业	Share Cooperative Enterprises	2889	56768
有限责任公司	Limited Liability Corporations	878955	14240682
股份有限公司	Share－holding Corporations Ltd.	318357	5353329
私营企业	Private Enterprises	799847	26481578
港澳台商投资企业	Hong Kong, Macao & Taiwan Funded	648969	15906221
外商投资企业	Foreign Funded Enterprises	494979	9495763
在总计中：亏损企业	Of the Total: Loss Making Enterprises	488051	15484535
在总计中：国有及国有控股	Of the Total: State－owned and State－holding	1002676	10484902
按规模分	**Grouped by Enterprises Size**		
大型企业	Large－Sized	919827	17820037
中型企业	Medium－Sized	955576	21439214
小型企业	Small－Sized	1309351	30829087
按工业行业分	**Grouped by Sector**		
非金属矿采选业	Non－metallic Mining Industry	1345	48839
农副食品加工业	Farm and Sideline Products Processing	26424	866171
食品制造业	Food Manufacturing	15203	411192
酒、饮料和精制茶制造业	Wine, Beverages and Refined Tea Manufacturing	14736	271655
烟草制品业	Tobacco Manufacturing	20551	264158
纺织业	Textile Industry	93810	2476954
纺织服装、服饰业	Clothing, Apparel Industry	84668	3373948
皮革、毛皮、羽毛及其制品和制鞋业	Leather, Fur, Feather and Its Products and Footwear Industry	2546	96033

单位:万元(10000 yuan)

所有者权益 Creditors' Equity	实收资本 Paid - in Capital	主营业务收入 Prime Operating Revenue	主营业务成本 Operating Costs	主营业务税金及附加 Tax and Extra Charge	销售费用 Sales Expenses	管理费用 Administrative Expenses	财务费用 Finance Charge
48393142	**25218307**	**132546456**	**113392659**	**3021154**	**2713673**	**6169397**	**1767924**
14932084	6744978	37072584	30459610	1135689	1213799	2102108	635010
33461059	18473328	95473872	82933049	1885464	1499875	4067288	1132914
1852635	111424	6656857	5109781	973684	53688	97018	6106
56340	13701	83342	69586	415	305	8056	226
31979	9052	104860	87659	963	2362	8612	1383
8281857	4972635	20256673	17106929	178000	286143	835548	353552
6325195	3499235	17264298	14637827	1215536	187661	505240	124517
10679133	4407176	40048208	34332790	198776	1064657	2419011	751200
13669993	7059121	28746426	24895852	382532	665607	1335449	323769
7496005	5144776	19360478	17129559	71038	452986	958970	206670
4389566	4964731	15940282	15288592	52486	343818	725172	466883
9815143	6573181	30903707	25693171	2496778	140492	548190	192401
14805241	7552545	38148581	32269037	1385139	738403	1363546	274578
15001853	7339210	39775677	34429174	434050	864765	1922863	550282
16940668	9969687	47853416	41561392	226939	1048535	2734153	890924
18761	22085	35162	26283	760	44	3708	1406
621762	248665	1589741	1444305	4006	40930	52083	28128
273655	96287	816543	660057	3637	26624	37650	20640
131269	131175	303439	238328	13531	20199	16646	3425
1132799	35136	1506032	287023	958370	43329	63463	- 1225
1991490	818481	3711595	3214897	17909	67453	195956	48674
2733717	1053816	6392807	5327294	36088	276949	342590	68208
29746	24495	130930	112857	817	5002	8016	3662

表 7－8 续 3 Continued

指标	Indicators	本年折旧 Depreciation in this Year	负债小计 Total Liabilities
木材加工及木、竹、藤、棕、草制品业	Timber Processing, Bamboo, Rattan, Cane Palm, and Straw Products	2557	84262
家具制造业	Furniture Manufacturing	17746	760864
造纸及纸制品业	Paper－making and Paper Products Manufacturing	70478	1980250
印刷和记录媒介复制业	Printing and Record Duplicating	26330	557759
文教、工美、体育和娱乐用品制造业	Culture, Art, Sports and Recreation Supplies Manufacturing	50351	1750610
石油加工、炼焦和核燃料加工业	Petroleum Processing, Coking & Nuclear Fuel Processing	200512	1787160
化学原料和化学制品制造业	Raw Chemical Materials and Chemical Products	442777	8349543
医药制造业	Medicines Manufacturing	16696	268097
化学纤维制造业	Chemical Fiber Manufacturing	45172	1311618
橡胶和塑料制品业	Rubber and Plastic Products Industry	90307	2264469
非金属矿物制品业	Nonmetal Mineral Products	56566	1603495
黑色金属冶炼和压延加工业	Smelting and Pressing of Ferrous Metals	175219	3080355
有色金属冶炼和压延加工业	Smelting and Pressing of Nonferrous Metals	62052	2033932
金属制品业	Metal Products Manufacturing	83071	2425436
通用设备制造业	General Purpose Equipment Manufacturing	211998	4806819
专用设备制造业	Special Purpose Equipment Manufacturing	113932	2648046
汽车制造业	Automobile Manufacturing	276217	6405750
铁路、船舶、航空航天和其他运输设备制造业	Railroad, Marine, Aviation and Other Transport Equipment Manufacturing	34959	1431795
电气机械和器材制造业	Electric Equipment and Machinery Manufacturing	284237	10268039
计算机、通信和其他电子设备制造业	Computer, Communications and Other Electronic Equipment Manufacturing	161998	3970185
仪器仪表制造业	Instrument Manufacturing	37768	1200525
其他制造业	Other Manufacturing	9996	316905
废弃资源综合利用业	Waste Comprehensive Utilization of Resources Industry	1735	267015
金属制品、机械和设备修理业	Metal Products, Machinery and Equipment Repair Industry	2114	67705
电力、热力的生产和供应业	Production and Supply Electric Power and Thermal Power	477714	3917801
燃气生产和供应业	Production and Supply Gas	30702	704753
水的生产和供应业	Production and Supply Tap Water	66698	1304068

单位:万元(10000 yuan)

所有者权益 Creditors' Equity	实收资本 Paid - in Capital	主营业务收入 Prime Operating Revenue	主营业务成本 Operating Costs	主营业务税金及附加 Tax and Extra Charge	销售费用 Sales Expenses	管理费用 Administrative Expenses	财务费用 Finance Charge
28690	20614	123497	105153	956	3299	7616	3301
286991	214312	948380	805213	4340	41384	62829	22364
1237231	1016669	1289946	1105909	4178	39422	60836	54078
429097	102278	789838	679956	3556	13909	40124	16096
1006603	451521	3119771	2646773	14527	107174	181734	45156
2632787	2567132	13818380	11883842	1473547	25328	180120	-6762
4683011	3232047	13716703	12578737	30911	178931	364125	240635
328278	135060	563023	395677	3744	45859	58023	10448
339566	330845	1567160	1457384	3931	13642	42771	49566
1256441	542817	3913767	3306740	19180	119858	246456	67270
772506	386100	2284305	1955954	11913	65920	99960	41159
1617058	1741082	5098435	4719036	15842	32852	145220	78405
1210116	620312	6276851	5960631	11163	36422	146234	64154
1245256	580923	3957544	3390424	22079	93440	240710	67199
3235743	1312451	7524756	6103458	42042	244642	618406	121095
2374405	932215	4005301	3086599	23514	178785	376246	55745
4474601	1587430	10750891	8931634	144229	247952	691318	93746
564186	372811	1465064	1285763	6791	25120	98126	29735
5096376	2161619	15353773	12945427	66944	478600	1009105	288836
3213983	1623703	8374801	7440588	24301	118022	420303	69169
1395629	456220	1752996	1372919	9962	70682	169947	18572
100048	80985	453103	384720	2447	18381	29847	9001
-19085	50557	743085	739332	805	3266	15693	9802
55754	48900	68242	57510	466	1231	5751	-272
3014028	1518043	8753538	7493634	42506	10690	105215	110698
359150	325102	1100360	1076295	648	4371	11187	14751
521499	376419	246699	172309	1518	13966	21387	21061

表 7－8 续 4 Continued

指标	Indicators	营业利润 Business Profits	利润总额 Total Profits	#应交所得税 Income Tax Payable
总计	**Total**	**6259061**	**6882464**	**1319097**
按轻重工业分	**Grouped by Light and Heavy Industry**			
轻工业	Light Industry	1728426	1847197	368206
重工业	Heavy Industry	4530636	5035268	950891
按注册登记类型分	**Grouped by Registered Type**			
国有企业	State－owned Enterprises	399321	396268	32154
集体企业	Collective－owned Enterpriese	5498	5860	1583
股份合作企业	Share Cooperative Enterprises	4134	4534	557
有限责任公司	Limited Liability Corporations	1695188	1874347	371339
股份有限公司	Share－holding Corporations Ltd.	790698	847089	122481
私营企业	Private Enterprises	1451798	1605702	333616
港澳台商投资企业	Hong Kong, Macao & Taiwan Funded	1286002	1417838	274459
外商投资企业	Foreign Funded Enterprises	626097	730544	182690
在总计中：亏损企业	Of the Total: Loss Making Enterprises	－897255	－816102	－2671
在总计中：国有及国有控股	Of the Total: State－owned and State－holding	1959572	2129375	418185
按规模分	**Grouped by Enterprises Size**			
大型企业	Large－Sized	2381308	2679673	455955
中型企业	Medium－Sized	1859542	2004535	387109
小型企业	Small－Sized	1607207	1794424	439988
按工业行业分	**Grouped by Sector**			
非金属矿采选业	Non－metallic Mining Industry	2860	1799	396
农副食品加工业	Farm and Sideline Products Processing	29088	43713	8366
食品制造业	Food Manufacturing	68691	70235	9485
酒、饮料和精制茶制造业	Wine, Beverages and Refined Tea Manufacturing	13101	12366	1255
烟草制品业	Tobacco Manufacturing	139703	132563	28408
纺织业	Textile Industry	199040	226341	47452
纺织服装、服饰业	Clothing, Apparel Industry	429631	455608	97680
皮革、毛皮、羽毛及其制品和制鞋业	Leather, Fur, Feather and Its Products and Footwear Industry	545	458	498

单位:万元(10000 yuan)

亏损企业亏损总额 Total Loss	利税总额 Total Profits and Taxes	本年应付职工薪酬 Employee Compensation Payable the Year	本年应交增值税 Value - added Taxes Payable the Year	本年进项税额 Withholdings on VAT the Year	本年销项税额 Substituted Money on VAT the Year	全部从业人员年平均人数(人) Annual Average Employees (person)
816102	**13474199**	**7988806**	**3533825**	**15912984**	**16497061**	**1518374**
197403	4031266	3224803	1045671	4589586	4291618	703945
618699	9442933	4764003	2488154	11323397	12205443	814429
	1627102	163661	256351	442315	648919	9843
	9611	9930	3302	10298	13419	1218
765	9251	11646	3750	12229	14650	2609
101657	2735319	910150	676673	2326767	2564103	134890
8909	2514239	461676	451515	2429312	2711744	60031
210920	2861428	3344961	1029492	5285467	5238373	718418
204030	2583816	1719977	782084	3436717	3557834	344295
289283	1131835	1362628	329552	1966660	1743694	246069
816102	-544600	878865	194243	2334173	2167565	186435
31759	5860714	604347	1233247	3192851	4226516	42421
7489	5063470	1644952	969169	4576022	4763646	267145
165444	3576153	2675529	1135698	4896965	5093937	487159
590201	3213533	3520911	1187584	6005094	5993609	739997
	4171	2389	1513	282	1100	417
8776	71768	67501	23987	135968	127080	15246
4406	97535	47266	23663	83209	71126	12423
2187	37528	20016	11625	37776	35355	3189
	1278675	28398	187685	251246	436465	1063
21370	335269	307102	90085	459383	475826	63635
28137	674236	798109	182187	766296	742944	194842
1978	4406	18622	3097	16777	12563	4763

表 7－8 续 5 Continued

指标	Indicators	营业利润 Business Profits	利润总额 Total Profits	#应交所得税 Income Tax Payable
木材加工及木、竹、藤、棕、草制品业	Timber Processing, Bamboo, Rattan, Cane Palm, and Straw Products	4383	4958	769
家具制造业	FurnitureManufacturing	15542	20920	4671
造纸及纸制品业	Paper－making and Paper Products Manufacturing	33398	35972	7017
印刷和记录媒介复制业	Printing and Record Duplicating	40555	42959	8906
文教、工美、体育和娱乐用品制造业	Culture, Art, Sports and Recreation Supplies Manufacturing	134133	136447	20625
石油加工、炼焦和核燃料加工业	Petroleum Processing, Coking & Nuclear Fuel Processing	333786	387155	78137
化学原料和化学制品制造业	Raw Chemical Materials and Chemical Products	350544	390709	145623
医药制造业	Medicines Manufacturing	53228	57080	10360
化学纤维制造业	Chemical Fiber Manufacturing	－156	8131	7247
橡胶和塑料制品业	Rubber and Plastic Products Industry	160863	168012	34653
非金属矿物制品业	Nonmetal Mineral Products	118836	139034	27500
黑色金属冶炼和压延加工业	Smelting and Pressing of Ferrous Metals	127942	209455	23284
有色金属冶炼和压延加工业	Smelting and Pressing of Nonferrous Metals	63246	78718	17461
金属制品业	Metal Products Manufacturing	161545	163659	37538
通用设备制造业	General Purpose Equipment Manufacturing	436799	456398	89196
专用设备制造业	Special Purpose Equipment Manufacturing	331440	356575	58696
汽车制造业	Automobile Manufacturing	793996	940349	134085
铁路、船舶、航空航天和其他运输设备制造业	Railroad, Marine, Aviation and Other Transport Equipment Manufacturing	32575	36516	8291
电气机械和器材制造业	Electric Equipment and Machinery Manufacturing	641527	694668	122035
计算机、通信和其他电子设备制造业	Computer, Communications and Other Electronic Equipment Manufacturing	373878	398231	55885
仪器仪表制造业	Instrument Manufacturing	148885	156975	21292
其他制造业	Other Manufacturing	9684	10042	3130
废弃资源综合利用业	Waste Comprehensive Utilization of Resources Industry	－38970	－33976	－4599
金属制品、机械和设备修理业	Metal Products, Machinery and Equipment Repair Industry	3953	3898	762
电力、热力的生产和供应业	Production and Supply Electric Power and Thermal Power	1024631	1043042	198033
燃气生产和供应业	Production and Supply Gas	73	5654	8138
水的生产和供应业	Production and Supply Tap Water	20090	27805	6825

单位:万元(10000 yuan)

亏损企业 亏损总额 Total Loss	利税总额 Total Profits and Taxes	本年应付 职工薪酬 Employee Compensation Payable the Year	本年应交 增值税 Value - added Taxes Payable the Year	本年 进项税额 Withholdings on VAT the Year	本年 销项税额 Substituted Money on VAT the Year	全部从业人员 年平均人数(人) Annual Average Employees (person)
551	9099	13590	3161	13165	10687	3050
14141	43212	107774	17903	114844	84146	21454
6820	62113	79517	21963	205634	189505	14473
1711	65464	66609	18924	95975	105802	13866
14838	221992	292802	70809	370653	281313	63043
2826	2438565	147679	577863	1771068	2312682	7652
268990	630539	279905	208867	1864369	1878901	33318
3223	84663	45929	23828	53801	72436	6709
26905	35154	49062	23093	219944	230647	9767
32001	282558	336001	95093	506802	481292	73128
6700	241475	117059	90509	149642	206409	20963
30113	326436	210031	101070	744282	791578	33565
24928	149957	158754	60007	962889	988558	28620
14634	288640	389089	102325	451803	387557	77731
43248	724786	760791	225542	1011300	1005328	144940
22143	508813	379176	128178	470679	486604	65446
43374	1465494	701035	351163	1438102	1493266	112769
16870	74359	121081	30947	145017	138454	23172
71060	1141609	1295541	379122	1928125	1640300	270495
31143	524040	602636	101268	697626	626596	122164
4131	216314	187788	49206	246273	246707	36392
2939	22212	61692	9658	55949	46743	14538
37858	-28999	17130	4171	88760	93330	5122
	7234	14902	2871	1053	2828	1584
5644	1385304	227357	298626	526853	754397	13876
19569	10467	13482	4032	26976	30923	989
2888	39110	22988	9786	463	7614	3970

表7-9 各县(市)、区规模以上工业企业主要财务指标(2014)
Main Financial Indicators of Industrial Enterprises Above Designated Size by Region

指标	Indicators	全市 Toal	市区 Urban District	
				海曙 Haishu
企业单位数(个)	Number of Enterprises(unit)	7383	3461	27
#亏损企业	Deficits Enterprises	1157	615	4
工业总产值(现价)	Gross Industrial Output Value(Current Prices)	140280500	91816608	3724926
工业销售产值	Value of Industrial Products Sales	136189593	89667576	3750064
#出口交货值	Value of Export Products	30423607	17788254	169383
资产合计	Total Asset	122049745	73700887	2048502
流动资产小计	Current Assets	70776014	40925468	583299
固定资产小计	Total Fixed Assets	34694550	22457251	1126733
本年折旧	Depreciation in this year	3309181	2071822	62955
负债合计	Total Liabilities	73376205	40790468	1556621
流动负债小计	Current Liabilities	64286663	35207780	893689
所有者权益合计	Total Owner´Equity	48393142	32725630	491882
#实收资本	Paid - in Capital	25218307	18274271	240588
主营业务收入	Prime Operating Revenue	132546456	86797915	3782109
主营业务成本	Operating Costs	113392659	74627889	3421720
主营业务税金及附加	Tax and Extra Charge	3021154	2716797	11964
销售费用	Sales Expenses	2713673	1605809	34031
管理费用	Administrative Expenses	6169397	3449989	39122
#税金	Tax	232434	128577	1137
财务费用	Finance charge	1767924	854588	7154
#利息支出	Interest Exchange	1933763	954430	10476
营业利润	Business Profits	6259061	4044334	304579
利润总额	Total Profits	6882464	4497107	308538
应交所得税	Income Tax Payable	1319097	892154	13107
亏损企业亏损总额	Total Loss	816102	605943	903
利税总额	Total Profits and Taxes	13474199	9405295	340658
本年应付职工薪酬	Employee Compensation Payable in this Year	7988806	4441708	119496
本年应交增值税	Value - added Taxes Payable in this Year	3533825	2162975	19659
本年进项税额	Withholdings on VAT in this Year	15912984	10312551	85711
本年销项税额	Substituted Money on VAT in this Year	16497061	11138857	96455
全部从业人员年平均人数(人)	Annual Average Employees(person)	1518374	770160	11796

单位:万元(10000 yuan)

各区 by Districts					余姚 Yuyao	慈溪 Cixi	奉化 Fenghua	象山 Xiangshan	宁海 Ninghai
江东 Jiangdong	江北 Jiangbei	北仑 Beilun	镇海 Zhenhai	鄞州 Yinzhou					
37	301	688	576	1763	1193	1323	445	464	497
6	68	165	181	179	101	179	88	80	94
1992754	4891790	31187656	25141597	23619286	13354244	19831411	3763341	5396165	6118732
1933723	4829582	30000838	24751294	23159933	12836199	19038879	3833302	4968964	5844673
155355	813404	7914650	1824622	6496425	3691955	4682176	1525812	1299182	1436228
2619789	4503707	29487683	13528569	19762938	11940777	18784486	3924233	6627566	7071796
1464936	2810985	15682571	6865122	12478901	7807766	11839756	2503463	3870763	3828798
645003	987794	10054170	5519191	3745173	2867106	4246076	1022361	1807927	2293829
62201	94940	889035	518963	409694	288797	500818	104244	155201	188298
920201	2621249	15660736	7780301	11186193	8085592	13004431	2773071	4290756	4431888
672445	2370724	13274989	6696923	10372077	7483665	11360649	2591444	3825805	3817321
1700470	1877038	13804034	5745984	8432932	3697259	5692397	1138329	2322617	2816912
313390	911597	8879804	4345126	3222558	1705355	2552054	576778	1044447	1065401
2025230	4875099	29650361	22232158	22885792	12779379	18743213	3584924	4938831	5702195
740233	4236609	26376621	19399812	19359409	10903657	16158302	3036164	4147819	4518827
960702	18668	373534	1235734	109519	56797	163351	26385	23533	34291
59499	119034	492902	211161	645905	298430	451365	84862	115508	157699
96522	291802	988528	671137	1258595	750027	1077065	276160	245611	370544
4506	9302	50350	23485	36685	32218	42603	6925	8732	13381
8444	56696	280098	191618	274555	237577	312759	81243	124278	157479
12959	63455	324322	199546	311907	251763	356149	80813	128324	162283
182692	193359	1297225	615408	1380359	561913	722435	94152	330011	506217
183105	237626	1581413	653944	1448237	606148	824292	107142	339367	508409
33652	47443	360274	165904	251901	98602	135914	23192	59435	109799
2517	20758	317892	174891	62392	34747	101315	27543	17634	28920
1340561	344053	2759732	2416424	2092040	987859	1538150	236118	517977	788801
72591	346077	1456894	705153	1640534	913114	1379925	417090	365733	471235
196698	87364	779681	526465	532230	324550	543433	102148	154892	245828
313562	720721	3140283	3165291	2740365	1503120	2507951	404668	566340	618353
490712	732857	3359834	3468784	2835434	1400319	2277120	396567	608287	675912
9161	58680	232980	102776	338426	205581	284648	90159	72075	95751

表7－10 各县(市)、区国有控股工业企业主要财务指标(2014)
Main Financial Indicators of State Holding Shares Industrial Enterprises by Region

指标	Indicators	全市 Toal	市区 Urban District	海曙 Haishu
企业单位数(个)	Number of Enterprises(unit)	103	67	4
#亏损企业	Deficits Enterprises	17	10	
工业总产值(现价)	Gross Industrial Output Value(Current Prices)	33932611	30237237	3314580
工业销售产值	Value of Industrial Products Sales	33446733	29794463	3314779
#出口交货值	Value of Export Products	379527	350189	
资产合计	Total Asset	20307701	15705907	1466557
流动资产小计	Total Current Assets	7349278	5833248	176743
固定资产原价	Original Value of Fixed Assets	19751260	15214635	2148910
#累计折旧	Accumulative Depreciation	9395434	7569787	1091638
负债合计	Total Liabilities	10484902	7767589	1248733
流动负债小计	Current Liabilities	8008708	6107764	623694
所有者权益合计	Total Owners´Equity	9815143	7938319	217825
#实收资本	Paid－in Capital	6573181	5663661	165672
主营业务收入	Prime Operating Revenue	30903707	27216587	3312617
主营业务成本	Operating Costs	25693171	22637872	3036758
主营业务税金及附加	Tax and Extra Charge	2496778	2474893	9253
销售费用	Sales Expenses	140492	113423	5398
管理费用	Administrative Expenses	548190	447711	5843
财务费用	Finance Charge	192401	112515	－62
营业利润	Business Profits	1959572	1540422	264681
利润总额	Total Profits	2129375	1701188	266363
亏损企业亏损总额	Total Loss	31759	25429	
本年应付职工薪酬	Employee Compensation Payable in this Year	604347	475166	75054
本年应交增值税	Value－added Taxes Payable in this Year	1233247	1046415	4187
本年进项税额	Withholdings on VAT in this Year	3192851	2781627	26644
本年销项税额	Substituted Money on VAT in this Year	4226516	3669238	30344
全部从业人员年平均人数(人)	Annual Average Employees(person)	42421	30026	3557

单位:万元(10000 yuan)

各区 by Districts					余姚 Yuyao	慈溪 Cixi	奉化 Fenghua	象山 Xiangshan	宁海 Ninghai
江东 Jiangdong	江北 Jiangbei	北仑 Beilun	镇海 Zhenhai	鄞州 Yinzhou					
3	5	20	23	11	9	6	5	7	9
	1	2	5	1	1	1	1	2	2
1603000	129373	8862338	15639396	650251	759341	677863	187406	811782	1258983
1564730	103537	8463048	15663722	646347	759341	670924	186613	785223	1250170
24182	12997	272022	40971	17			2559	26779	
1997365	228432	6635747	5000775	338275	1001711	477595	189571	1141184	1791732
1038380	85297	2651683	1811054	62496	545899	155000	90303	327258	397570
1090862	155008	6530587	4888120	358847	633326	439806	207883	1292013	1963596
503344	40760	3227142	2554824	140191	277875	177026	115330	572729	682687
650196	166890	3500356	2053034	118027	660160	236000	93006	707928	1020218
463074	75280	2938422	1883473	99887	501974	179437	65435	539448	614650
1347168	61542	3135391	2947740	220250	341551	241595	96565	425599	771515
225233	64613	2360463	2771047	66635	144056	51588	35472	243500	434903
1623180	124017	8429742	13044205	645260	758191	672228	188140	828007	1240554
384136	89701	7248144	11208667	632563	699237	636711	170696	672140	876515
959052	534	302272	1201779	1801	3689	1884	1021	5385	9907
49102	4837	25930	26539	1617	5044	3925	2743	5739	9619
70750	17850	119626	225055	7944	16263	20189	9904	9304	44819
4816	5395	86598	12251	2307	11549	5428	1117	20696	41096
142622	6405	686341	441638	421	32272	3291	2820	111283	269484
140747	8942	829823	451360	5110	38513	4699	3158	111490	270327
	638	19567	1994	2072	1172	1074	963	923	2199
38771	12778	144968	186064	16276	23554	13435	11040	36241	44910
192421	4034	472090	356822	15171	32657	18527	9147	47426	79075
252431	15172	601228	1854263	27425	102199	109949	31492	67673	99910
441215	18893	955768	2187839	28937	131743	123098	25038	105145	172256
2879	1317	9598	11126	1459	2337	1705	886	3580	3887

表7-11 各县(市)、区规模以上私营工业企业主要财务指标(2014)
Main Financial Indicators of Private Industrial Enterprises Above Designated Size by Region

指标	Indicators	全市 Toal	市区 Urban District	海曙 Haishu
企业单位数(个)	Number of Enterprises(unit)	4704	1888	3
#亏损企业	Deficits Enterprises	619	271	
工业总产值(现价)	Gross Industrial Output Value(Current Prices)	41499737	16764041	17321
工业销售产值	Value of Industrial Products Sales	39974045	16381015	17530
#出口交货值	Value of Export Products	10374715	3773223	3115
资产合计	Total Asset	37129111	14046500	9145
流动资产小计	Total Current Assets	24324139	9258046	7471
固定资产原价	Original Value of Fixed Assets	11553974	4237837	2679
#累计折旧	Accumulative Depreciation	4460736	1686351	1161
负债合计	Total Liabilities	26481578	9717937	3412
流动负债小计	Current Liabilities	24802356	9054174	3412
所有者权益合计	Total Owners´Equity	10679133	4292876	5733
#实收资本	Paid - in Capital	4407176	1731915	350
主营业务收入	Prime Operating Revenue	40048208	16725678	17367
主营业务成本	Operating Costs	34332790	14435975	14380
主营业务税金及附加	Tax and Extra Charge	198776	89437	76
销售费用	Sales Expenses	1064657	424113	396
管理费用	Administrative Expenses	2419011	979818	1152
财务费用	Finance Charge	751200	258031	-6
营业利润	Business Profits	1451798	612073	1399
利润总额	Total Profits	1605702	715754	1433
亏损企业亏损总额	Total Loss	210920	97416	
本年应付职工薪酬	Employee Compensation Payable in this Year	3344961	1287153	2047
本年应交增值税	Value - added Taxes Payable in this Year	1029492	393120	507
本年进项税额	Withholdings on VAT in this Year	5285467	2359942	2268
本年销项税额	Substituted Money on VAT in this Year	5238373	2454287	2465
全部从业人员年平均人数(人)	Annual Average Employees(person)	718418	260213	407

单位:万元(10000 yuan)

各区 by Districts					余姚 Yuyao	慈溪 Cixi	奉化 Fenghua	象山 Xiangshan	宁海 Ninghai
江东 Jiangdong	江北 Jiangbei	北仑 Beilun	镇海 Zhenhai	鄞州 Yinzhou					
22	157	223	290	1176	796	983	334	337	366
4	34	42	93	96	51	115	63	57	62
134442	1134111	2110120	2877468	10307026	6233118	10611329	2030337	2499197	3361715
138194	1123668	2046175	2768172	10106329	5979567	10228813	1962895	2245335	3176420
32566	240198	349058	544450	2576046	1501875	3063039	500823	750831	784925
135483	1201584	2355614	2289167	7890019	4907566	10414789	2006155	2521698	3232404
121069	777733	1363645	1560371	5318512	3211339	6733245	1313769	1646973	2160767
23725	386608	694446	816322	2268378	1745686	3193673	694000	779827	902951
11711	152364	268370	329896	906435	629167	1254672	274420	254508	361618
102155	836440	1800909	1710760	5167555	3588658	7650847	1476806	1739290	2308041
95776	793222	1613285	1619387	4844027	3448123	7091977	1413990	1605633	2188459
33187	365114	552732	580831	2686498	1298626	2676706	514271	786721	1109933
14461	191328	285364	303594	900359	510047	1220618	268812	382247	293538
137669	1124218	2428528	2783489	10057017	5953465	10055575	1977725	2235944	3099822
119357	915767	2163490	2503894	8573313	5114411	8670090	1671189	1899735	2541390
566	6633	18633	12175	50578	27781	40990	12969	10232	17368
5695	44123	98693	50839	218283	143000	285079	56393	52620	103452
10043	92417	143443	151158	566439	342550	610213	150993	123229	212210
2664	20107	40727	54333	136995	103761	209975	53725	54985	70724
-63	51565	-5588	7227	549729	228552	300877	41399	97141	171756
1840	56478	45324	21607	579712	242454	326021	47117	101695	172661
1196	5620	20325	47325	22131	12652	54841	20069	10178	15763
14891	111836	182464	201606	758681	464311	866190	253642	181600	292065
1945	31623	52781	51809	249668	146108	260634	61635	59256	108740
20595	151510	489200	428661	1243491	694519	1377828	239856	260598	352724
19113	157686	503095	419835	1326689	658755	1231783	253311	267615	372623
2987	22902	35244	41042	154933	104901	191053	57787	40283	64181

表7－12　各县(市)、区规模以上大中型工业企业主要财务指标(2014)
Main Financial Indicators of Large and Medium Size Industrial Enterprises Above Designated Size by Region

指标	Indicators	全市 Toal	市区 Urban District	海曙 Haishu
企业单位数(个)	Number of Enterprises(unit)	1080	516	7
#亏损企业	Deficits Enterprises	136	71	
工业总产值(现价)	Gross Industrial Output Value(Current Prices)	83979144	57558142	416787
工业销售产值	Value of Industrial Products Sales	81556035	56075595	443283
#出口交货值	Value of Export Products	19101996	11925216	100755
资产合计	Total Asset	68915643	43476447	646644
流动资产小计	Total Current Assets	38514222	23592969	329658
固定资产原价	Original Value of Fixed Assets	31812316	21214964	214070
#累计折旧	Accumulative Depreciation	13562289	9507106	39651
负债合计	Total Liabilities	39259251	22814523	377209
流动负债小计	Current Liabilities	34580338	20094401	291937
所有者权益合计	Total Owners´Equity	29807093	20642776	269436
#实收资本	Paid－in Capital	14891755	11507970	187945
主营业务收入	Prime Operating Revenue	77924257	52981844	472876
主营业务成本	Operating Costs	66698211	45805738	407804
主营业务税金及附加	Tax and Extra Charge	1819189	1617790	1840
销售费用	Sales Expenses	1603168	998645	22383
管理费用	Administrative Expenses	3286409	1838329	18602
财务费用	Finance Charge	824860	394938	7247
营业利润	Business Profits	4240850	2706930	30906
利润总额	Total Profits	4684208	3023785	31501
亏损企业亏损总额	Total Loss	172933	120447	
本年应付职工薪酬	Employee Compensation Payable in this Year	4320481	2501152	32049
本年应交增值税	Value－added Taxes Payable in this Year	2104867	1302719	11042
本年进项税额	Withholdings on VAT in this Year	9472986	6419131	59483
本年销项税额	Substituted money on VAT in this Year	9857582	6989304	65877
全部从业人员年平均人数(人)	Annual Average Employees(person)	754304	396660	5812

单位:万元(10000 yuan)

各区 by Districts					余姚 Yuyao	慈溪 Cixi	奉化 Fenghua	象山 Xiangshan	宁海 Ninghai
江东 Jiangdong	江北 Jiangbei	北仑 Beilun	镇海 Zhenhai	鄞州 Yinzhou					
8	47	152	67	221	153	222	71	52	66
	10	26	15	19	12	28	11	7	7
314398	3112655	22341062	18874985	11858910	6435930	12013501	1766169	2641505	3563898
292038	3071515	21381141	18625154	11621765	6169281	11555803	1900060	2412028	3443268
99162	353731	6897738	898851	3270386	1854640	2912398	1021877	706884	680981
992341	2300410	20282344	8195860	10148488	5308960	10533330	1983240	3192616	4421049
281657	1425661	11114288	3991664	5930020	3388252	6395985	1210824	1788282	2137910
803041	746270	10421139	5451939	3251503	1872273	3722454	911413	1646214	2444998
344274	263667	4637742	2585766	1510868	743736	1332113	358622	739708	881005
477999	1195917	10866603	4051790	5298038	3470347	6932531	1394047	2064368	2583436
260437	1103750	9269175	3744988	4950373	3215697	5910554	1357876	1848782	2153029
514342	1100468	9415697	4144070	4835372	1825170	3591341	589126	1118648	2040032
253776	500851	5598057	3081518	1695419	789452	1263200	230721	493615	606798
317019	3060254	20993381	16050963	11378952	6157659	11359448	1648484	2383735	3393087
275925	2720596	18609379	13799818	9425872	5287394	9678815	1373354	1920511	2632399
1749	8497	341045	1211097	49954	22932	132164	13892	12483	19929
9912	63384	322124	117443	436510	127808	289884	33019	65600	88212
19232	141693	626424	372339	606711	348305	665921	131760	110159	191935
6413	21185	144440	77859	119289	103679	132030	38206	62723	93284
41259	136065	1056653	565284	831323	286347	567297	62606	217776	399895
46654	156424	1299539	582995	852384	313129	657380	69514	222521	397879
	6131	49621	35029	13324	6548	35863	5334	876	3864
28617	175492	1040675	366963	801718	400502	808763	194116	172581	243369
5831	41914	579125	404345	253892	139764	361764	42143	96359	162117
31805	505497	2091400	2319193	1343389	758677	1521552	169080	256471	348075
24950	512237	2319189	2612932	1379158	674719	1345348	156582	290515	401114
5161	27490	164304	44186	141312	88457	154562	40472	30247	43906

表7-13 各县(市)、区规模以上外商和港澳台投资工业企业主要财务指标(2014) Main Financial Indicators of Foreign Funded and Hongkong, Macao, Taiwan Funded Industrial Enterprises Above Designated Size by Region

指标	Indicators	全市 Toal	市区 Urban District	海曙 Haishu
企业单位数(个)	Number of Enterprises(unit)	1887	1130	7
#亏损企业	Deficits Enterprises	427	273	2
工业总产值(现价)	Gross Industrial Output Value(Current Prices)	50827933	38410371	96446
工业销售产值	Value of Industrial Products Sales	48951505	37064857	96280
#出口交货值	Value of Export Products	17088465	12458189	60267
资产合计	Total Asset	46721954	33631628	53085
流动资产小计	Total Current Assets	29009502	20008868	41881
固定资产原价	Original Value of Fixed Assets	19984822	15740179	17874
#累计折旧	Accumulative Depreciation	8838833	7054594	10487
负债合计	Total Liabilities	25401984	17146219	25028
流动负债小计	Current Liabilities	22732968	15122932	23165
所有者权益合计	Total Owners´Equity	21165998	16351882	28057
#实收资本	Paid - in Capital	12203897	9599717	11471
主营业务收入	Prime Operating Revenue	48106904	36635427	96621
主营业务成本	Operating Costs	42025411	32303159	77007
主营业务税金及附加	Tax and Extra Charge	453570	398896	758
销售费用	Sales Expenses	1118593	828659	1232
管理费用	Administrative Expenses	2294419	1516564	7968
财务费用	Finance Charge	530439	327667	509
营业利润	Business Profits	1912099	1420288	9319
利润总额	Total Profits	2148382	1580447	9547
亏损企业亏损总额	Total Loss	493313	416984	358
本年应付职工薪酬	Employee Compensation Payable in this Year	3082604	2117234	13710
本年应交增值税	Value - added Taxes Payable in this Year	1111635	811740	4941
本年进项税额	Withholdings on VAT in this Year	5403377	3998778	11710
本年销项税额	Substituted money on VAT in this Year	5301528	4073370	13869
全部从业人员年平均人数(人)	Annual Average Employees(person)	590364	387750	2742

单位:万元(10000 yuan)

各区 by Districts					余姚 Yuyao	慈溪 Cixi	奉化 Fenghua	象山 Xiangshan	宁海 Ninghai
江东 Jiangdong	江北 Jiangbei	北仑 Beilun	镇海 Zhenhai	鄞州 Yinzhou					
4	86	388	197	419	281	216	81	82	97
	19	109	71	66	45	49	20	15	25
167650	1093502	22339161	5748075	8260861	4349887	4685628	1372687	1174315	835046
144961	1074882	21393923	5580254	8069985	4157613	4359300	1516000	1078492	775244
67255	367566	7273930	1174665	3188389	1646161	1230374	956131	379823	417787
108412	1417384	19768805	4201520	6996410	4083635	5156966	1540186	1384157	925383
87745	911664	11272319	2509966	4570200	2853062	3536309	975706	994612	640945
21201	440403	10105720	2155517	2613646	1379184	1433405	735234	379588	317232
11429	160968	4430063	1002057	1284340	627139	555515	296716	170161	134708
75387	792582	9640991	2252676	3717743	2689276	3052065	1040668	869144	604612
61555	743801	8455798	1957565	3357554	2485173	2783162	952258	830510	558933
33025	619481	10108841	1944143	3185379	1386028	2108178	502474	505164	312271
13840	281719	6449459	1123691	1463516	856337	1006373	266986	287125	187360
174117	1102703	21055824	5538578	7877366	4126658	4321641	1248765	1041739	732674
159890	877392	19062108	4934347	6548371	3500311	3723046	1050033	852231	596630
515	6733	326601	19822	40557	16528	17054	11294	5275	4522
1859	40384	349851	101009	306677	100611	108660	20873	35004	24787
5226	89437	674202	234579	441076	277047	257178	101245	74914	67472
479	11961	137645	70555	83047	68038	69029	20690	24119	20896
8782	98006	589962	187038	495987	172112	187036	49464	59892	23308
8727	106120	708421	191687	515216	180078	242099	55883	63388	26488
	7191	264989	94489	29959	18444	38745	5479	6015	7646
8694	114670	1059975	249389	617499	324644	313418	127597	111277	88436
162	24596	517139	94610	161856	93142	125720	25900	29985	25148
28287	116053	2131860	720061	921843	507982	585078	110803	118762	81974
19476	106979	2246640	723321	892233	418270	544400	95307	106828	63354
1737	19979	174171	39696	140886	76691	60216	26034	20585	19088

表7-14 部分年份工业主要产品产量
Output of Major Industrial Products in Partial Years

主要工业产品	单位	Major Industrial Products	Unit	2011	2012	2013	2014
大米	万吨	Rice	10000 tons	8.36	8.19	6.87	18.49
配合饲料	万吨	Formulated Feed	10000 tons	25.41	25.51	28.91	32.36
食用植物油	万吨	Edible Vegetable Oil	10000 tons	25.78	16.88	12.64	13.24
水产加工品	万吨	Processed Aquatic Products	10000 tons	39.84	27.76	24.98	26.56
罐头	万吨	Canned Food	10000 tons	16.43	15.00	17.00	16.92
味精	万吨	Monosodium Glutamate	10000 tons				0.77
啤酒	千万升	Beer	ten million liters	48.39	48.82	48.59	40.95
软饮料	万吨	Soft Beverage	10000 tons	17.03	6.94	4.70	5.37
瓶(罐)装饮用水	万吨	Bottled Drinking Water	10000 tons				
精制茶	万吨	Refine Tea	10000 tons	5.14	2.64	6.19	3.12
卷烟	亿支	Cigarette	100 million	372.49	394.92	380.61	359.16
纱	万吨	Yarn	10000 tons	29.86	44.82	41.32	24.82
布	万米	Cloth	10000 m	38045	35380	33486	34929
印染布	万米	Printing and Dyeing Cloth	10000 m	90652	57673	50980	47613
帘子布	万吨	Curtain Cloth	10000 tons	3.37	2.67	4.06	3.38
绒线(毛线)	吨	Knitting Wool	ton	6488	5381	5905	6171
呢绒	万米	Wool Fabric	10000 m	2143	3284	1162	1455
服装	万件	Garment	10000 units	111977	113948	114648	126414
梭织服装	万件	Shuttle Woven Garment	10000 units	15792	15141	14252	15367
#西服及西服套装	万件	Western - style Clothes	10000 units	2291	1693	1524.71	1537.17
衬衫	万件	Shirt	10000 units	6029	6378	5881.44	6513.66
羽绒服装	万件	Eiderdown Garment	10000 units	622.74	26.76	36.50	31.26
针织服装	万件	Knitting Garment	10000 units	96185	98807	100397	111047
机制纸及纸板	万吨	Paper - making and Paperboard	10000 tons	208.23	221.81	224.77	242.36
纸制品	万吨	Paper Products	10000 tons	86.91	84.21	83.10	80.24
原油加工量	万吨	Crude Oil Processed	10000 tons	2717.43	2506.12	2688.75	2586.60
汽油	万吨	Gasoline	10000 tons	295.53	264.08	279.64	308.44
煤油	万吨	Kerosene	10000 tons	162.89	156.23	208.97	218.77
柴油	万吨	DieselOil	10000 tons	742.00	679.24	686.55	625.41
石油沥青	万吨	Asphalt	10000 tons	277.43	263.53	322.32	319.38
液化石油气	万吨	Liquefied Petroleum Gas	10000 tons	110.37	96.40	106.22	97.22
硫酸(折100%)	万吨	Sulphuric Acid(100%)	10000 tons	10.27	9.65	10.22	38.03
盐酸(含量31%以上)	万吨	Hydrochloric Acid (above31% percent)	10000 tons	16.90	8.98	15.81	19.50
烧碱(折100%)	万吨	CausticSoda(100%)	10000 tons	46.10	55.37	59.64	65.64
合成氨	万吨	SyntheticAmmonia	10000 tons	4.04	7.24	7.48	7.57
农用化肥(折纯)	万吨	ChemicalFertilizers	10000 tons	1.17	1.28	1.51	1.10

7-14 续表 Continued

主要工业产品	单位	Major Industrial Products	Unit	2011	2012	2013	2014
氮肥(折含N100%)	万吨	NitrogenousFertilizer(100%)	10000 tons	1.17	1.28	1.51	1.10
尿素	万吨	Urea	10000 tons				
化学农药	吨	ChemicalPesticide	ton	4912.54	2796.50	2364.15	2410.16
纯苯	万吨	PureBenzene	10000 tons	41.05	37.92	39.90	34.60
建筑涂料	吨	BuildingDope	ton				
染料	吨	Dye	ton				
塑料树脂及共聚物	万吨	Plastic Resinand Copolyment	10000 tons	369.13	315.56	372.43	475.47
化学原料药	吨	Chemical Raw Medicine	ton	2647.62	2104.77	1545.61	501.99
塑料制品	万吨	Plastic Products	10000 tons	88.77	92.00	76.89	91.08
水泥	万吨	Cement	10000 tons	1303.81	1289.44	1598.53	1693.00
粗钢	万吨	Rural Steel	10000 tons	471.37	456.77	486.09	467.26
成品钢材	万吨	Rolled-steel Final Products	10000 tons	762.50	830.16	882.20	803.16
铜	万吨	Copper	10000 tons	5.61	6.79	4.80	4.38
铜加工材	万吨	Copper Material	10000 tons	51.67	61.51	75.28	92.62
铝材	万吨	Aluminium	10000 tons	25.57	18.89	21.97	28.15
液压元件	万件	Hydraulic Pressure Elements	10000 units	6363.74	7000.93	6439.14	3931.44
气动元件	万件	Pneumatic Element	10000 units	7311.24	6857.91	7217.65	12873.83
粉末冶金制品	万吨	Powder Metallurgy Products	10000 tons	3.30	3.35	3.75	4.34
大中型拖拉机	台	Lager and Medium-sized Tractor	unit	45990	28262	39069	24532
汽车	辆	Motor Vechicle	unit	170754	128942	129125	96942
轿车	辆	Car	unit	170754	128942	129125	96942
摩托车	万辆	Motorcycles	10000 units	7.67	9.12	9.37	13.02
自行车	万辆	Bicycles	10000 units	403.39	371.76	384.23	265.86
民用钢质船舶	载重吨	Civil Steel Ship	DWT	1032565	650674	359228	924931
交流电动机	万千瓦	Alternating Current Motor	10000 kw	103.64	80.69	47.25	51.43
变压器	万千伏安	Transformer	10000 kev	1829.46	1797.18	1543.74	1963.04
电力电缆	万公里	Power Cable	10000 km	33.00	126.50	64.69	42.09
自动化仪表系统	万套	Instrument and Meter for Automation	10000 units				
原电池(折一号电池)	万只	Primary Cellsand Batterices	10000 units	459965	437644	440383	460224
家用洗衣机	万台	Household Washing Machine	10000 units	1337.46	1483.26	1397.18	1167.94
吸尘器	万台	Dust Catcher	10000 units	1282.17	1109.28	1249.51	1265.89
电风扇	万台	Electric Fan	10000 units	595.76	632.10	601.12	605.69
房间空气调节器	万台	Home Air Conditioner	10000 units	380.56	414.03	429.81	495.99
排油烟机	万台	Range Hoods	10000 units	62.81	145.98	191.48	202.40
移动电话机	万部	Mobile Phone	10000 units	233.14	253.12	586.44	445.25
光学仪器	万台	Optical Instrument	10000 units	280.48	336.85	368.17	509.16
发电量	亿千瓦小时	Generating Capacity	100 million kwh	952.48	887.22	948.17	866.50

表7-15 各县(市)、区规模以上工业企业主要经济效益指标(2014)
Main Indicators on Ecnomic Benefit of Industrial Enterprises Above Designated Size by Region

指标	单位	Indicators	Unit	全市 Toal	市区 Urban District
产销率	%	Proportion of Products Sold	%	97.08	97.66
资产负债率	%	Assets Liability Ratio	%	60.12	55.35
成本费用利润率	%	Ratio of Profits to Industrial Cost	%	5.55	5.58
每百元固定资产原值实现利税	元	Pre-tax Profits Per 100 Yuan Original Value of Fixed Assets	yuan	24.08	25.12
每百元主营业务收入实现利税	元	Pre-tax Profits Per 100 Yuan Main Business	yuan	10.17	10.84
流动比率	%	Ratio of Circulating Funds to Current Liabilities	%	1.10	1.16
速动比率	%	Ratio of Quickassets to Current Liabilities	%	0.84	0.87
企业亏损面	%	Ratio of Number of Deficit Enterprises to Total Enterprises Number	%	15.67	17.77
亏损率	%	Losing Rate	%	10.60	11.87
出口交货值占工业销售产值比重	%	Ratio of Exports Products Value to Industrial Sales Value	%	22.34	19.84
利润总额占利税比重	%	Ratio of Total Profits to Total Pre-tax	%	51.08	47.81
存货周转次数	次	Number of Times of Turnover of Inventories	times	6.87	7.35

各区 by Districts						余姚 Yuyao	慈溪 Cixi	奉化 Fenghua	象山 Xiangshan	宁海 Ninghai
海曙 Haishu	江东 Jiangdong	江北 Jiangbei	北仑 Beilun	镇海 Zhenhai	鄞州 Yinzhou					
100.67	97.04	98.73	96.19	98.45	98.06	96.12	96.00	101.86	92.08	95.52
75.99	35.13	58.20	53.11	57.51	56.60	67.71	69.23	70.67	64.74	62.67
8.81	20.24	5.05	5.62	3.19	6.72	4.97	4.58	3.08	7.32	9.77
15.33	113.55	22.93	16.21	27.87	33.21	22.80	24.05	14.00	19.15	23.21
9.01	66.19	7.06	9.31	10.87	9.14	7.73	8.21	6.59	10.49	13.83
0.65	2.18	1.19	1.18	1.03	1.20	1.04	1.04	0.97	1.01	1.00
0.55	0.91	0.88	0.94	0.69	0.94	0.84	0.81	0.76	0.79	0.79
14.81	16.22	22.59	23.98	31.42	10.15	8.47	13.53	19.78	17.24	18.91
0.29	1.36	8.03	16.74	21.10	4.13	5.42	10.95	20.45	4.94	5.38
4.52	8.03	16.84	26.38	7.37	28.05	28.76	24.59	39.80	26.15	24.57
90.57	13.66	69.07	57.30	27.06	69.23	61.36	53.59	45.38	65.52	64.45
37.49	0.87	5.93	8.06	8.72	7.05	7.24	6.08	5.76	4.94	5.49

表7－16　各县(市)、区规模以上工业企业综合能耗及产值能耗(2014)
Comprehensive Energy Consumption of Industrial Enterprises Above Designated Size by Region

指标	Indicators	全市 Toal	市区 Urban District
综合能耗(吨标准煤)	**Final Energy Consumption(Ton of SCE)**	**30706672**	**21651710**
黑色金属矿采选业	Ferrous Metals Mining and Dressing		
非金属矿采选业	Non－metallic Mining Industry	3721	3721
农副食品加工业	Farm and Sideline Products Processing	87370	44832
食品制造业	Food Manufacturing	85732	11738
酒、饮料和精制茶制造业	Wine, Beverages and Refined Tea Manufacturing	46048	33668
烟草制品业	Tobacco Manufacturing	9502	9502
纺织业	Textile Industry	644759	360655
纺织服装、服饰业	Clothing, Apparel Industry	101689	65159
皮革、毛皮、羽毛及其制品和制鞋业	Leather, Fur, Feather and Its Products and Footwear Industry	4209	1969
木材加工及木、竹、藤、棕、草制品业	Timber Processing,Bamboo,Rattan,Cane Palm,and Straw Products	5867	3419
家具制造业	Furniture Manufacturing	19883	9238
造纸及纸制品业	Paper－making and Paper Products Manufacturing	784545	706480
印刷和记录媒介复制业	Printing and Record Duplicating	31505	19054
文教、工美、体育和娱乐用品制造业	Culture, Art, Sports and Recreation Supplies Manufacturing	84037	31378
石油加工、炼焦和核燃料加工业	Petroleum Processing. Coking & Nuclear Fuel Processing	6073430	6072442
化学原料和化学制品制造业	Raw Chemical Materials and Chemical Products	2996779	2858394
医药制造业	Medicines Manufacturing	28539	18370
化学纤维制造业	Chemical Fiber Manufacturing	290478	144660
橡胶和塑料制品业	Rubber and Plastic Products Industry	194270	86498
非金属矿物制品业	Nonmetal Mineral Products	393590	165155
黑色金属冶炼和压延加工业	Smelting and Pressing of Ferrous Metals	2886113	2699602
有色金属冶炼和压延加工业	Smelting and Pressing of Nonferrous Metals	263301	137615
金属制品业	Metal Products Manufacturing	204054	117426
通用设备制造业	General Purpose Equipment Manufacturing	226325	121219
专用设备制造业	Special Purpose Equipment Manufacturing	104755	65781
汽车制造业	Automobile Manufacturing	316263	145518
铁路、船舶、航空航天和其他运输设备制造业	Railroad, Marine, Aviation and Other Transport Equipment Manufacturing	48901	24191
电气机械和器材制造业	Electric Equipment and Machinery Manufacturing	283119	84551
计算机、通信和其他电子设备制造业	Computer, Communications and Other Electronic Equipment Manufacturing	127291	99885
仪器仪表制造业	Instrument Manufacturing	29742	9535
其他制造业	Other Manufacturing	17012	5194
废弃资源综合利用业	Waste Comprehensive Utilization of Resources Industry	4499	3908
金属制品、机械和设备修理业	Metal Products, Machinery and Equipment Repair Industry	976	5
电力、热力的生产和供应业	Production and Supply Electric Power and Thermal Power	14288000	7477478
燃气生产和供应业	Production and Supply Gas	6034	5758
水的生产和供应业	Production and Supply Tap Water	14333	7712

各区 by Districts						余姚 Yuyao	慈溪 Cixi	奉化 Fenghua	象山 Xiangshan	宁海 Ninghai
海曙 Haishu	江东 Jiangdong	江北 Jiangbei	北仑 Beilun	镇海 Zhenhai	鄞州 Yinzhou					
96627	**21015**	**162295**	**11262529**	**8858946**	**1149429**	**1046493**	**961747**	**202173**	**2533758**	**4310792**
			974		2747					
	1082	884	37295		5527	6723	11368	5695	17643	1109
180		2358	3808	3291	2101	63118	1073	3505	3863	2435
590		2	26418		6658	850		7451	4	4076
	9502									
186		3981	231266	54910	68751	96962	88050	7223	84713	7155
1311	659	892	22214	863	38704	713	1152	15435	12858	6372
			149	666	1154	118	542	187		1393
			111		3308	680		1768		
	70	642	2404	193	5724	5903	3404	255	363	720
		1351	386953	2303	315507	8444	39975	5032	2265	22349
260	19	261	2338	5803	10373	3242	6031	996	1966	217
	73	3687	11881	1970	13715	3556	30561	909	664	16969
			164739	5906324	1378			936	52	
		6130	1723573	1098371	25165	52940	70290	5638	1357	8160
42		216	2307	11776	3689	839	4731	2312	969	1318
			36658	107377	625	16187	127101	619	1898	13
406	55	4464	39312	15991	26088	50607	29384	8348	3210	16223
		9447	35784	77172	42753	138335	13118	6023	28630	42329
	1179	6493	2522627	49150	114385	76799	52329	40926	9417	7039
172	271	62056	14889	27089	31365	35480	65517	9251	173	15266
173	106	7971	37572	35997	34991	32552	25981	14385	1581	12130
93	136	5941	22873	57350	33560	23833	48230	17970	3637	11436
141	399	2034	39141	7619	16117	20641	5481	523	4840	7489
592	151	24492	54452	3999	60484	9782	121171	4703	15896	19193
	376		20083	1475	1895	1025	8286	12182	2915	302
1204	63	8703	17453	7941	41969	53985	107170	10405	6100	20907
927	2478	4241	48629	5464	35475	10582	11708	2914	291	1912
33		3687	635	184	4235	15243	3164	1204		596
		1159		720	3261	2529	5768	3022		499
			1216	2509	183		584		7	
				5				103	867	1
89825			5749514	1370369	197492	313285	76069	12015	2326469	4082684
494			5262		2	21	171			83
	4395	1205		2066	46	1517	3339	238	1110	416

表7－16 续表 Continued

指标	Indicators	全市 Toal	市区 Urban District
产值能耗（吨标煤/万元）	**Energy Consumption of Output Value(Ton of SCE/10000 yuan)**	**0.2227**	**0.2387**
黑色金属矿采选业	Ferrous Metals Mining and Dressing		
非金属矿采选业	Non－metallic Mining Industry	0.1121	0.1121
农副食品加工业	Farm and Sideline Products Processing	0.0546	0.0693
食品制造业	Food Manufacturing	0.0992	0.0534
酒、饮料和精制茶制造业	Wine, Beverages and Refined Tea Manufacturing	0.1534	0.1877
烟草制品业	Tobacco Manufacturing	0.0064	0.0064
纺织业	Textile Industry	0.1753	0.1509
纺织服装、服饰业	Clothing, Apparel Industry	0.0157	0.0132
皮革、毛皮、羽毛及其制品和制鞋业	Leather, Fur, Feather and Its Products and Footwear Industry	0.0377	0.0334
木材加工及木、竹、藤、棕、草制品业	Timber Processing,Bamboo,Rattan,Cane Palm,and StrawProducts	0.0485	0.0481
家具制造业	Furniture Manufacturing	0.0211	0.0170
造纸及纸制品业	Paper－making and Paper Products Manufacturing	0.4785	0.6069
印刷和记录媒介复制业	Printing and Record Duplicating	0.0386	0.0301
文教、工美、体育和娱乐用品制造业	Culture, Art, Sports and Recreation Supplies Manufacturing	0.0267	0.0201
石油加工、炼焦和核燃料加工业	Petroleum Processing. Coking & Nuclear Fuel Processing	0.3636	0.3639
化学原料和化学制品制造业	Raw Chemical Materials and Chemical Products	0.2005	0.2096
医药制造业	Medicines Manufacturing	0.0479	0.0417
化学纤维制造业	Chemical Fiber Manufacturing	0.1862	0.4809
橡胶和塑料制品业	Rubber and Plastic Products Industry	0.0501	0.0479
非金属矿物制品业	Nonmetal Mineral Products	0.1743	0.1340
黑色金属冶炼和压延加工业	Smelting and Pressing of Ferrous Metals	0.5423	0.7068
有色金属冶炼和压延加工业	Smelting and Pressing of Nonferrous Metals	0.0417	0.0399
金属制品业	Metal Products Manufacturing	0.0510	0.0483
通用设备制造业	General Purpose Equipment Manufacturing	0.0298	0.0287
专用设备制造业	Special Purpose Equipment Manufacturing	0.0254	0.0248
汽车制造业	Automobile Manufacturing	0.0308	0.0330
铁路、船舶、航空航天和其他运输设备制造业	Railroad, Marine, Aviation and Other Transport Equipment Manufacturing	0.0269	0.0407
电气机械和器材制造业	Electric Equipment and Machinery Manufacturing	0.0181	0.0144
计算机、通信和其他电子设备制造业	Computer, Communications and Other Electronic Equipment Manufacturing	0.0151	0.0156
仪器仪表制造业	Instrument Manufacturing	0.0164	0.0104
其他制造业	Other Manufacturing	0.0380	0.0312
废弃资源综合利用业	Waste Comprehensive Utilization of Resources Industry	0.0062	0.0055
金属制品、机械和设备修理业	Metal Products, Machinery and Equipment Repair Industry	0.0146	0.0005
电力、热力的生产和供应业	Production and Supply Electric Power and Thermal Power	1.6098	1.2907
燃气生产和供应业	Production and Supply Gas	0.0055	0.0055
水的生产和供应业	Production and Supply Tap Water	0.0559	0.0532

各区 by Districts						余姚 Yuyao	慈溪 Cixi	奉化 Fenghua	象山 Xiangshan	宁海 Ninghai
海曙 Haishu	江东 Jiangdong	江北 Jiangbei	北仑 Beilun	镇海 Zhenhai	鄞州 Yinzhou					
0.0257	**0.0106**	**0.0342**	**0.3666**	**0.3536**	**0.0496**	**0.0790**	**0.0502**	**0.0553**	**0.4878**	**0.7267**
			0.0482		0.2116					
	0.2932	0.0328	0.0933		0.0274	0.0201	0.0702	0.0759	0.0480	0.0860
0.0067		0.0519	0.0625	0.0903	0.0420	0.1385	0.0760	0.1054	0.0525	0.0357
0.0964		0.0008	0.2142		0.1409	0.0114		0.2821	0.0067	0.2113
	0.0064									
0.0031		0.0242	0.3187	0.0931	0.0815	0.2341	0.1605	0.1058	0.5401	0.0713
0.0137	0.0100	0.0109	0.0160	0.0133	0.0120	0.0161	0.0122	0.0349	0.0152	0.0746
			0.0259	0.0401	0.0316	0.0128	0.0256	0.0155		0.1329
			0.0582		0.0478	0.0280		0.0691		
	0.0224	0.0112	0.0293	0.0124	0.0152	0.0220	0.0365	0.0159	0.0292	0.1053
		0.1859	0.6087	0.1538	0.6257	0.0924	0.1603	0.1413	0.5631	0.2353
0.0485	0.0185	0.0260	0.0335	0.1158	0.0209	0.0374	0.1168	0.0435	0.0936	0.1004
	0.0109	0.0256	0.0307	0.0242	0.0147	0.0260	0.0642	0.0205	0.0436	0.0187
			0.0602	0.4237	0.1040			0.1019	0.0076	
		0.0423	0.2127	0.2476	0.0277	0.1108	0.1133	0.0641	0.0580	0.0858
0.0054		0.0107	0.1065	0.1055	0.0138	0.0349	0.0928	0.0458	0.0906	0.0675
			0.4719	0.5269	0.0324	0.0951	0.1261	0.0689	0.0270	0.0080
0.0719	0.0156	0.0418	0.1151	0.0786	0.0228	0.0609	0.0469	0.0493	0.0379	0.0453
		0.0554	0.1243	0.4584	0.0705	0.3396	0.0763	0.0969	0.1376	0.2404
	0.1105	0.1643	1.0065	0.1124	0.1515	0.1109	0.1497	0.1939	0.0519	0.1033
0.0853	0.0090	0.0332	0.1207	0.0537	0.0378	0.0317	0.0475	0.0514	0.0121	0.0862
0.0455	0.0027	0.0559	0.0439	0.1120	0.0336	0.0620	0.0445	0.0695	0.0459	0.0555
0.0087	0.0050	0.0224	0.0252	0.0478	0.0196	0.0336	0.0380	0.0344	0.0085	0.0256
0.0179	0.0108	0.0136	0.0278	0.0207	0.0248	0.0291	0.0233	0.0148	0.0219	0.0279
0.0147	0.0219	0.0646	0.0323	0.0271	0.0303	0.0290	0.0306	0.0327	0.0187	0.0345
	0.0315		0.0612	0.0241	0.0129	0.0206	0.0166	0.0306	0.0114	0.0132
0.0150	0.0219	0.0182	0.0132	0.0174	0.0134	0.0189	0.0213	0.0341	0.0100	0.0220
0.0144	0.0170	0.0277	0.0129	0.0167	0.0193	0.0096	0.0209	0.0128	0.0165	0.0221
0.0041		0.0146	0.0111	0.0129	0.0078	0.0268	0.0121	0.0412		0.0163
		0.0552		0.0207	0.0309	0.0432	0.0344	0.0895		0.0242
			0.2176	0.0036	0.0204		0.0475		0.0023	
				0.0005				0.0237	0.0187	0.0002
0.0287			3.9761	2.6068	0.3026	0.4922	0.1314	0.0731	3.7813	3.7536
0.0025			0.0062		0.0003	0.0018	0.0058			0.0195
	0.0390	0.0992		0.1474	0.0073	0.0503	0.0806	0.0377	0.0954	0.0191

表7-17 各县(市)、区千吨以上工业综合能源消费量(2014)
Comprehensive Energy Consumption of Industrial Enterprises Above One Thousand Tons

指标	Indicators	全市 Toal	市区 Urban District
综合能源消费量总计(吨标准煤)	**Final energy comprehensive consumption per million (Tons of standard coal)**	**29244425**	**20995226**
黑色金属矿采选业	Ferrous Metals Mining and Dressing		
农副食品加工业	Farm and Sideline Products Processing	70468	37686
食品制造业	Food Manufacturing	71247	5560
酒、饮料和精制茶制造业	Wine, Beverages and Refined Tea Manufacturing	42214	32587
烟草制品业	Tobacco Manufacturing	9502	9502
纺织业	Textile Industry	559951	339599
纺织服装、服饰业	Clothing, Apparel Industry	47614	33071
皮革、毛皮、羽毛及其制品和制鞋业	Leather, Fur, Feather and Its Products and Footwear Industry	880	880
木材加工及木、竹、藤、棕、草制品业	Timber Processing, Bamboo, Rattan, Cane Palm, and Straw Products	1215	
家具制造业	Furniture Manufacturing	4352	2649
造纸及纸制品业	Paper - making and Paper Products Manufacturing	766220	703328
印刷和记录媒介复制业	Printing and Record Duplicating	18100	9949
文教、工美、体育和娱乐用品制造业	Culture, Art, Sports and Recreation Supplies Manufacturing	37912	11302
石油加工、炼焦和核燃料加工业	Petroleum Processing. Coking & Nuclear Fuel Processing	6071218	6070282
化学原料和化学制品制造业	Raw Chemical Materials and Chemical Products	2918059	2790267
医药制造业	Medicines Manufacturing	20623	13702
化学纤维制造业	Chemical Fiber Manufacturing	274088	144035
橡胶和塑料制品业	Rubber and Plastic Products Industry	85918	50980
非金属矿物制品业	Nonmetal Mineral Products	340439	135098
黑色金属冶炼和压延加工业	Smelting and Pressing of Ferrous Metals	2825950	2671744
有色金属冶炼和压延加工业	Smelting and Pressing of Nonferrous Metals	202047	110807
金属制品业	Metal Products Manufacturing	115409	75664
通用设备制造业	General Purpose Equipment Manufacturing	81818	46721
专用设备制造业	Special Purpose Equipment Manufacturing	41426	29611
汽车制造业	Automobile Manufacturing	145917	96843
铁路、船舶、航空航天和其他运输设备制造业	Railroad, Marine, Aviation and Other Transport Equipment Manufacturing	28486	16011
电气机械和器材制造业	Electric Equipment and Machinery Manufacturing	111616	36618
计算机、通信和其他电子设备制造业	Computer, Communications and Other Electronic Equipment Manufacturing	69317	62722
仪器仪表制造业	Instrument Manufacturing	5666	
其他制造业	Other Manufacturing	7384	3664
废弃资源综合利用业	Waste Comprehensive Utilization of Resources Industry	1216	1216
金属制品、机械和设备修理业	Metal Products, Machinery and Equipment Repair Industry	867	
电力、热力的生产和供应业	Production and Supply Electric Power and Thermal Power	14252386	7442378
燃气生产和供应业	Production and Supply Gas	5262	5262
水的生产和供应业	Production and Supply Tap Water	9638	5488

各区 by Districts						余姚 Yuyao	慈溪 Cixi	奉化 Fenghua	象山 Xiangshan	宁海 Ninghai
海曙 Haishu	江东 Jiangdong	江北 Jiangbei	北仑 Beilun	镇海 Zhenhai	鄞州 Yinzhou					
90865	**16957**	**111865**	**10981771**	**8832731**	**871919**	**848771**	**621213**	**108937**	**2458788**	**4211489**
	1082		36604			4787	11300	5026	11670	
		585	3444	1532		62978			2709	
			26398		6189			5699		3929
	9502									
		2058	227370	51600	57687	92575	66426	3312	53899	4139
			18454		14617			2607	5877	6059
					880					
								1215		
					2649	1703				
		1351	384997	1760	315220	6231	30501	3132	2265	20762
			1543	5472	2934	928	5378		1845	
		910	5862		4530		20837			5773
			164066	5906217				936		
		4688	1566717	1196511	17419	50800	66846	3569	1301	5275
			1265	10315	2121		4731	2190		
			36658	107377		15822	112721		1510	
		857	30144	8490	11490	18171	14059	1507	1201	
		4152	29078	75342	26526	132827	2788	2817	26415	40493
		6493	2519010	45728	94745	66733	46821	27677	8003	4972
		59396	10587	19904	19903	27697	50458	5642		7442
		3911	27459	27039	17256	17422	14239	6760		1324
			7894	32363	6464	8104	16328	6626		4038
			23944	1683	3984	7819			2632	1364
		21134	39574	428	35707	1661	23170	1560	10173	12510
			16011				1171	11305		
1068		2657	8617	1633	17367	7934	50369	3540	2347	10808
	1978	2515	40213	2778	14275	4393	2202			
						5666				
		1159			2505		1918	1802		
			1216							
									867	
89797			5749385	1335467	197451	313285	76035	12015	2326072	4082600
			5262							
	4395			1092.57		1237	2913			

表7－18 各县(市)、区千吨以上工业万元产值综合能耗(2014) Comprehensive Energy Consumption of Industrial Enterprises Above One Thousand Tons

指标	Indicators	全市 Toal	市区 Urban District
万元产值综合能耗总计(吨标准煤)	**Final energy comprehensive consumption per million (Tons of standard coal)**	**0.3535**	**0.3363**
黑色金属矿采选业	Ferrous Metals Mining and Dressing		
农副食品加工业	Farm and Sideline Products Processing	0.0753	0.0971
食品制造业	Food Manufacturing	0.1271	0.0775
酒、饮料和精制茶制造业	Wine, Beverages and Refined Tea Manufacturing	0.2279	0.2265
烟草制品业	Tobacco Manufacturing	0.0064	0.0064
纺织业	Textile Industry	0.2484	0.2208
纺织服装、服饰业	Clothing, Apparel Industry	0.0201	0.0153
皮革、毛皮、羽毛及其制品和制鞋业	Leather, Fur, Feather and Its Products and Footwear Industry	0.0679	0.0679
木材加工及木、竹、藤、棕、草制品业	Timber Processing, Bamboo, Rattan, Cane Palm, and Straw Products	0.1997	
家具制造业	Furniture Manufacturing	0.0216	0.0206
造纸及纸制品业	Paper－making and Paper Products Manufacturing	0.5597	0.6410
印刷和记录媒介复制业	Printing and Record Duplicating	0.0776	0.0548
文教、工美、体育和娱乐用品制造业	Culture, Art, Sports and Recreation Supplies Manufacturing	0.0386	0.0541
石油加工、炼焦和核燃料加工业	Petroleum Processing. Coking & Nuclear Fuel Processing	0.3661	0.3662
化学原料和化学制品制造业	Raw Chemical Materials and Chemical Products	0.2223	0.2303
医药制造业	Medicines Manufacturing	0.1085	0.1430
化学纤维制造业	Chemical Fiber Manufacturing	0.1992	0.5117
橡胶和塑料制品业	Rubber and Plastic Products Industry	0.0705	0.0655
非金属矿物制品业	Nonmetal Mineral Products	0.2819	0.2182
黑色金属冶炼和压延加工业	Smelting and Pressing of Ferrous Metals	0.6567	0.8072
有色金属冶炼和压延加工业	Smelting and Pressing of Nonferrous Metals	0.0434	0.0405
金属制品业	Metal Products Manufacturing	0.0839	0.0729
通用设备制造业	General Purpose Equipment Manufacturing	0.0590	0.0601
专用设备制造业	Special Purpose Equipment Manufacturing	0.0338	0.0333
汽车制造业	Automobile Manufacturing	0.0351	0.0437
铁路、船舶、航空航天和其他运输设备制造业	Railroad, Marine, Aviation and Other Transport Equipment Manufacturing	0.0425	0.0579
电气机械和器材制造业	Electric Equipment and Machinery Manufacturing	0.0202	0.0156
计算机、通信和其他电子设备制造业	Computer, Communications and Other Electronic Equipment Manufacturing	0.0137	0.0148
仪器仪表制造业	Instrument Manufacturing	0.0488	
其他制造业	Other Manufacturing	0.0461	0.0529
废弃资源综合利用业	Waste Comprehensive Utilization of Resources Industry	0.2176	0.2176
金属制品、机械和设备修理业	Metal Products, Machinery and Equipment Repair Industry	0.0187	
电力、热力的生产和供应业	Production and Supply Electric Power and Thermal Power	1.6286	1.3076
燃气生产和供应业	Production and Supply Gas	0.0062	0.0062
水的生产和供应业	Production and Supply Tap Water	0.0592	0.0469

各区 by Districts						余姚 Yuyao	慈溪 Cixi	奉化 Fenghua	象山 Xiangshan	宁海 Ninghai
海曙 Haishu	江东 Jiangdong	江北 Jiangbei	北仑 Beilun	镇海 Zhenhai	鄞州 Yinzhou					
0.0286	**0.0100**	**0.0458**	**0.4331**	**0.4150**	**0.1087**	**0.1443**	**0.0778**	**0.0858**	**1.1088**	**1.4316**
	0.2932		0.0952			0.0189	0.0971	0.1090	0.0887	
		0.0613	0.0680	0.1326		0.1448			0.0502	
			0.2301		0.2122			0.2310		0.2354
	0.0064									
		0.0241	0.3405	0.0987	0.2219	0.3192	0.2351	0.3863	0.5801	0.0979
			0.0147		0.0161			0.0228	0.3167	0.0885
					0.0679					
								0.1997		
					0.0206	0.0232				
		0.1859	0.6396	0.5924	0.6498	0.1311	0.2254	0.2727	0.5631	0.2836
			0.1921	0.1814	0.0205	0.0647	0.2104		0.1532	
		0.0424	0.0423		0.0927		0.0977			0.0103
			0.0620	0.4240				0.1019		
		0.1587	0.2074	0.2935	0.0418	0.1249	0.1311	0.0573	0.0771	0.3127
			0.2219	0.1393	0.1323		0.0928	0.0505		
			0.4719	0.5269		0.0946	0.1310		0.0227	
		0.0281	0.2028	0.1191	0.0217	0.1027	0.0662	0.0959	0.0340	
		0.0890	0.1482	0.5595	0.1098	0.4971	0.2465	0.3378	0.1489	0.3255
		0.1643	1.0900	0.1502	0.1620	0.1326	0.1759	0.2069	0.1224	0.1976
		0.0323	0.1549	0.0485	0.0534	0.0314	0.0549	0.0812		0.1647
		0.3048	0.0483	0.1670	0.0587	0.1568	0.0725	0.2666		0.2720
			0.0378	0.0667	0.0771	0.0642	0.0582	0.0715		0.0369
			0.0315	0.0225	0.0742	0.0316			0.0478	0.0414
		0.1124	0.0378	0.0530	0.0366	0.0772	0.0236	0.0279	0.0173	0.0429
			0.0579				0.0516	0.0305		
0.0150		0.0383	0.0163	0.0138	0.0133	0.0201	0.0242	1.0330	0.0096	0.0240
	0.0181	0.0585	0.0117	0.0148	0.0324	0.0063	0.0188			
						0.0488				
		0.0552			0.0518		0.0219	0.5544		
			0.2176							
									0.0187	
0.0289			4.0145	2.8357	0.3058	0.4922	0.1329	0.0731	3.8326	3.7805
			0.0062							
	0.0390			0.2510		0.1219	0.0814			

表7-19 按工业行业分组的主要能源消费量(2014)
Comprehensive Energy Consumption by Industrial Sector

指标	Indicators	能源合计 吨标准煤 Total Ton of SCE	原煤 Raw Coal	焦炭 Coke
按工业行业分	**Grouped by Sector**	**87243372**	**38678400**	**1636484**
非金属矿采选业	Non-metallic Mining Industry	3752		
农副食品加工业	Farm and Sideline Products Processing	90929	33460	
食品制造业	Food Manufacturing	86978	14500	
酒、饮料和精制茶制造业	Wine, Beverages and Refined Tea Manufacturing	46405	13925	
烟草制品业	Tobacco Manufacturing	9950		
纺织业	Textile Industry	663538	161590	
纺织服装、服饰业	Clothing, Apparel Industry	108813	30131	
皮革、毛皮、羽毛及其制品和制鞋业	Leather, Fur, Feather and Its Products and Footwear Industry	4545	2790	
木材加工及木、竹、藤、棕、草制品业	Timber Processing, Bamboo, Rattan, Cane Palm, and Straw Products	6151	3428	
家具制造业	Furniture Manufacturing	22406	2414	2
造纸及纸制品业	Paper-making and Paper Products Manufacturing	1006079	1070521	
印刷和记录媒介复制业	Printing and Record Duplicating	34695	15601	
文教、工美、体育和娱乐用品制造业	Culture, Art, Sports and Recreation Supplies Manufacturing	90833	9749	189
石油加工、炼焦和核燃料加工业	Petroleum Processing. Coking & Nuclear Fuel Processing	47519516	1965331	
化学原料和化学制品制造业	Raw Chemical Materials and Chemical Products	3161420	1078731	
医药制造业	Medicines Manufacturing	29761	3012	
化学纤维制造业	Chemical Fiber Manufacturing	292204	45316	
橡胶和塑料制品业	Rubber and Plastic Products Industry	202496	21941	
非金属矿物制品业	Nonmetal Mineral Products	420795	209785	980
黑色金属冶炼和压延加工业	Smelting and Pressing of Ferrous Metals	5514721	828645	1630131
有色金属冶炼和压延加工业	Smelting and Pressing of Nonferrous Metals	268384	32348	1222
金属制品业	Metal Products Manufacturing	214214	20131	73
通用设备制造业	General Purpose Equipment Manufacturing	241663	8010	1004
专用设备制造业	Special Purpose Equipment Manufacturing	113051	1369	168
汽车制造业	Automobile Manufacturing	329459	6193	
铁路、船舶、航空航天和其他运输设备制造业	Railroad, Marine, Aviation and Other Transport Equipment Manufacturing	60036	2105	
电气机械和器材制造业	Electric Equipment and Machinery Manufacturing	314426	15642	2715
计算机、通信和其他电子设备制造业	Computer, Communications and Other Electronic Equipment Manufacturing	140060	2560	
仪器仪表制造业	Instrument Manufacturing	33227	7	
其他制造业	Other Manufacturing	19267	979	
废弃资源综合利用业	Waste Comprehensive Utilization of Resources Industry	5025	77	
金属制品、机械和设备修理业	Metal Products, Machinery and Equipment Repair Industry	1431		
电力、热力的生产和供应业	Production and Supply Electric Power and Thermal Power	26166317	33078111	
燃气生产和供应业	Production and Supply Gas	6187		
水的生产和供应业	Production and Supply Tap Water	14640		

单位：吨（ton）

原油 Crude Oil	汽油 Gasoline	煤油 Kerosene	柴油 Diesel Oil	燃料油 Fuel Oil	液化石油气 LPG	其他油制品 Other Petroleum Products	热力 百万千焦 Heat million kilo－joule	电力 万千瓦时 Electricity 10000 kwh
25865981	**60759**	**7088**	**127498**	**367362**	**221892**	**2760546**	**48947559**	**3671061**
	1		1929					763
	698		1422	2253	60		886094	19969
	442		495		284		576635	21038
	158		168				704899	9231
	35		1812				106503	2348
	1856		1725	17	1154	1142	7528711	147506
	4421	20	3587		72	7	855642	33725
	118		79				9242	1585
	140	23	211					2346
	702		852		1	4	4956	10460
	701	3	3970	1815	37		1414614	165735
	1234	27	1150		30		52695	11500
	2069	115	2103		833	217	147696	39400
25865963	71		3744	318260	205269	2705575	1047101	273837
	2901	49	7804	28615	5141	44281	27133341	665406
	312		509		1		436207	8351
	237		414		2		3946599	79542
	3135	5	2754	61	976	385	457015	115747
	973	8	34919	7302	1377		311144	96330
	1145	19	3109	10	208	19	412834	356340
	979	134	3850	5164	376	234	86421	130543
	3383	335	5622	535	1288	463	869328	102519
3	8010	5629	8602	150	918	3675	20807	148268
	5204	53	5072	380	237	1289	29967	62078
	4686	75	4957	1422	97	659	1282200	154610
	791	181	6335	736	296	936	55879	29542
	9281	207	9926	118	1789	1205	122481	204768
15	3182	34	2401	1	357	419	231018	93313
	1312	159	1195	12	11	36		23349
	496		921		863		49566	9989
	169		1743		209			1433
	98		216					790
	1436	12	3777	510	3	2	167964	632436
	164		98					4654
	219		27		1			11612

表7-20 各县(市)、区规模以上工业企业等价综合能源消费量(2014)
Equivalent Comprehensive Energy Consumption of Industrial Enterprises Above Designated Size by Region

指标	Indicators	全市 Toal	市区 Urban District	海曙 Haishu
综合能源消费量总计(吨标准煤)	**Final energy comprehensive consumption per million (Tons of standard coal)**	**23673168**	**18543940**	**244093**
黑色金属矿采选业	Ferrous Metals Mining and Dressing			
非金属矿采选业	Non-metallic Mining Industry	5225	5225	
农副食品加工业	Farm and Sideline Products Processing	129489	61138	
食品制造业	Food Manufacturing	127602	18385	313
酒、饮料和精制茶制造业	Wine, Beverages and Refined Tea Manufacturing	64230	47623	698
烟草制品业	Tobacco Manufacturing	14484	14484	
纺织业	Textile Industry	935575	507347	404
纺织服装、服饰业	Clothing, Apparel Industry	173935	115940	2270
皮革、毛皮、羽毛及其制品和制鞋业	Leather, Fur, Feather and Its Products and Footwear Industry	7605	3419	
木材加工及木、竹、藤、棕、草制品业	Timber Processing, Bamboo, Rattan, Cane Palm, and Straw Products	10682	6397	
家具制造业	Furniture Manufacturing	42604	21101	
造纸及纸制品业	Paper-making and Paper Products Manufacturing	946641	842881	
印刷和记录媒介复制业	Printing and Record Duplicating	56901	36635	491
文教、工美、体育和娱乐用品制造业	Culture, Art, Sports and Recreation Supplies Manufacturing	166914	66871	
石油加工、炼焦和核燃料加工业	Petroleum Processing. Coking & Nuclear Fuel Processing	6063488	6062298	
化学原料和化学制品制造业	Raw Chemical Materials and Chemical Products	4295497	4080583	
医药制造业	Medicines Manufacturing	45887	28239	87
化学纤维制造业	Chemical Fiber Manufacturing	445799	167442	
橡胶和塑料制品业	Rubber and Plastic Products Industry	426004	179449	1050
非金属矿物制品业	Nonmetal Mineral Products	582472	234104	
黑色金属冶炼和压延加工业	Smelting and Pressing of Ferrous Metals	3394030	3029743	
有色金属冶炼和压延加工业	Smelting and Pressing of Nonferrous Metals	520462	277269	441
金属制品业	Metal Products Manufacturing	412179	237670	456
通用设备制造业	General Purpose Equipment Manufacturing	527968	281835	253
专用设备制造业	Special Purpose Equipment Manufacturing	232923	138243	311
汽车制造业	Automobile Manufacturing	628011	287781	1534
铁路、船舶、航空航天和其他运输设备制造业	Railroad, Marine, Aviation and Other Transport Equipment Manufacturing	117081	50902	
电气机械和器材制造业	Electric Equipment and MachineryManufacturing	709833	208121	3201
计算机、通信和其他电子设备制造业	Computer, Communications and Other Electronic Equipment Manufacturing	320248	246022	2317
仪器仪表制造业	Instrument Manufacturing	78314	25107	79
其他制造业	Other Manufacturing	38555	13093	
废弃资源综合利用业	Waste Comprehensive Utilization of Resources Industry	7791	6351	
金属制品、机械和设备修理业	Metal Products, Machinery and Equipment Repair Industry	2956	12	
电力、热力的生产和供应业	Production and Supply Electric Power and Thermal Power	2089546	1207718	228804
燃气生产和供应业	Production and Supply Gas	15175	14735	1385
水的生产和供应业	Production and Supply Tap Water	37063	19774	

各区 by Districts					余姚 Yuyao	慈溪 Cixi	奉化 Fenghua	象山 Xiangshan	宁海 Ninghai
江东 Jiangdong	江北 Jiangbei	北仑 Beilun	镇海 Zhenhai	鄞州 Yinzhou					
40374	**334310**	**7649891**	**8488826**	**1708679**	**1479051**	**1868522**	**400910**	**557669**	**823077**
		1255		3970					
1242	2124	47486		10143	11373	19001	9113	27344	1521
	3500	5452	5578	3543	94503	2002	4412	5065	3234
	6	37575		9344	1974		9503	10	5119
14484									
	9701	310297	81464	102925	138645	156860	12004	102617	18101
1242	2387	33492	2115	73009	1408	3024	22208	22973	8382
		396	1227	1796	305	1188	541		2152
		284		6113	1697		2589		
139	1902	5892	588	12184	12605	6418	692	896	892
	1806	501875	4236	334537	10962	53246	6670	3358	29526
86	745	4356	7886	23071	6357	8960	2076	2564	308
215	9131	24255	4666	28455	8665	48952	2444	1732	38250
		174104	5886653	1540			1127	63	
	13969	2434307	1576780	47700	82142	108435	8970	2651	12716
	636	3653	16380	6753	2161	7567	3958	1514	2448
		41634	124476	1331	31558	240259	1612	4884	43
143	9971	77865	32722	57212	120090	66469	19885	7456	32655
	14532	68974	90976	59621	180873	21505	9732	63025	73233
2579	11818	2682829	115689	201843	164591	95584	76745	15370	11996
408	121585	28748	48195	73817	68662	133031	19097	451	21950
296	16938	79951	64366	74125	63184	55475	30351	3314	22186
357	14109	53380	129719	80838	57224	114862	43419	7212	23416
817	5535	80330	15099	35450	47696	15845	1485	10663	18991
360	44978	105189	9686	122375	22165	224911	10949	37250	44955
762		42340	2665	4294	2092	22139	34478	7038	431
117	20547	42904	21748	101101	133851	279964	21089	15307	51501
6098	11259	123570	13419	82038	27357	33798	7847	743	4481
	10585	1271	513	10707	39047	9680	3209		1272
	3301		1489	8151	6428	13542	4525		967
		1498	4391	462		1423		17	
			12				277	2663	4
		621384	220768	130046	137403	115394	29165	208697	391169
		13344		6	80	251			109
11030	3243		5320	181	3954	8738	735	2791	1070

表7－21 全市规模以上工业企业能源购、消、存情况(2014) Purchases, Sales and Inventory of Energy of Industrial Enterprises Above the Set Scale

指标	单位	Indicators	Unit	年初库存 Stock (Year－head)	购进量 Purchases 实物量 Material Amount	购进量 Purchases 金额(千元) Value (1000 yuan)	消费量合计 Consumption
原煤	吨	Raw Coal	ton	1510939	38739186	22768589	38678400
洗精煤	吨	Clenedcoal	ton	128484	1466314	2101762	1473155
煤制品	吨	Coal Products	ton	4114	560503	360080	545990
焦炭	吨	Coke	ton	37160	567041	1155692	1636484
天然气(气态)	万立方米	Natural Gas(Gas)	10000 Cubic Meters	577	171722	5749308	171721
液化天然气(液态)	吨	Liquefied Natural Gas(Liquid)	ton	175	26480	162892	26602
原油	吨	fx Crude Oil	ton	862748	25955510	131042958	25865981
汽油	吨	Gasoline	ton	381	59056	512668	60759
煤油	吨	Kerosene	ton	972	7022	54091	7088
柴油	吨	Diesel Oil	ton	4548	124020	923123	127498
燃料油	吨	Fuel Oil	ton	9978	133596	471717	367362
液化石油气	吨	Liquefied Petroleum Gas	ton	244	17484	121944	221892
炼厂干气	吨	Refinery Dry Gas	ton	81	3450	19159	1121851
石油焦	吨	Petroleum Coke	ton	17554	42911	44640	660353
其他石油制品	吨	Other Petroleum Products	ton	10681	548138	2043508	2760546
热力	百万千焦	Heat	million kilo－joule		48708979	3108401	48947559
电力	万千瓦时	Electricity	10000 kwh		2762590	21004121	3671061
余热余压	百万千焦	Residual Heat and Pressure	million kilo－joule		14297	833	9695353
能源合计	吨标准煤	Total	Ton of SCE				87243372

工业生产消费 Consumptiop of Industrial Production	非工业生产消费 Consumptiop of Non – Industrial Production	年末库存 Stock (Year – end)	能源转出量 Energy Producing	能源投入 Energy Input	火力发电 Generation of Electric Power by Thermal Power	供热 Heat Supply	炼油投入 Input of Oil Refining
38628190	50210	1628969		34683177	31219170	3448379	
1473155		121644		1379702			
545869	121	18581					
1636159	325	29011	1061230				
171243	478	7		129255	126172	3083	
26551	51	50		106	101	5	
25865978	3	936323		25865963			25865963
20319	40440	185	3084420				
7055	33	803	2187671	12	12		
96655	30843	4899	6254081	398	398		
366124	1238	10816	802173	316272			316272
220124	1768	39	972246	199517			199517
1121851			1121034	178339		1998	176341
660353		12389	1099866	412204	317362	94842	
2760509	37	4930	8086461	284902			284902
48084967	862592		68005545				
3599720	71340		8588591				
9695353				3382524	3382524		
86976377	266995		54942130	69741165	24777711	2539003	41102571

表7-22 全市及各县(市)全社会用电量(2014)
Total Electricity Consumption by Region

指标	Indicators	全市 Total	为上年(%) The Preceding Year=100(%)
总计	**Total**	**5767787**	**3.11**
全行业用电量	**Electricity Consumption for Non-Living Electricity**	**5159482**	**4.60**
农林牧渔业	Farming, Forestry, Animal Husbandry, Fishery	33393	-0.09
#排灌	Irrigation and Drainage	8251	-10.68
①农业	Farming	8709	2.80
②林业	Forestry	332	-21.11
③畜牧业	Animal Husbandary	4825	-0.20
④渔业	Fishery	8254	15.54
⑤其他	Others	11273	-10.18
工业	Industry	4352456	4.88
轻工业	Light Industry	1322290	1.47
重工业	Heavy Industry	3030166	6.45
建筑业	Construction	81207	-0.75
交通运输、仓储和邮政业	Transportation, Storage and Post	99360	16.58
交通运输	Transportation	84603	17.72
仓储业	Warehousing Industry	12970	12.18
邮政	Post	1788	-0.70
信息传输、计算机服务和软件业	Information Transmission, Computer Service and Software	33640	12.74
商业、住宿和饮食业	Trade, Hotel and Catering Trade	231694	0.42
金融、房地产、商务及居民服务业	Financial, Real Estate, Business and Resident Service	142018	5.70
公共事业及管理组织	Public Service and Management Organizations	185713	-0.94
城乡居民生活用电量	**Electricity Consumption for Urban and Rural Residents**	**608304**	**-8.01**
城市	Urban Residents	310525	-7.27
乡村	Rural Residents	297779	-8.77

单位:万千瓦时(10000 kwh)

市区 Urban District	#鄞州 Yinzhou	余姚 Yuyao	慈溪 Cixi	奉化 Fenghua	象山 Xiangshan	宁海 Ninghai
3181606	**770919**	**733023**	**1116873**	**278991**	**195245**	**262049**
2884399	**663958**	**659464**	**1003616**	**240528**	**154883**	**216592**
10606	6707	4577	7546	2403	4914	3348
2248	1506	1965	724	690	2031	593
4490	2261	475	1439	855	787	664
145	75	29	35	54	28	42
774	389	1239	1373	462	495	482
1113	1028	697	3409	248	1394	1393
4084	2954	2137	1290	784	2211	766
2374295	542136	577211	896209	203297	115104	186342
552182	195582	218456	396791	45066	45369	64425
1822113	346554	358755	499418	158230	69734	121916
44881	16020	7628	17712	3175	4033	3777
77244	5087	11423	1818	7002	812	1062
64062	3917	11053	1207	6762	600	919
12047	733	192	399	187	99	45
1135	437	177	212	53	113	98
20037	5445	3519	4216	2063	1759	2046
141550	28980	25891	29324	10421	13842	10665
103948	29441	10056	18783	3596	3008	2627
111839	30141	19158	28007	8570	11413	6725
297208	**106962**	**73560**	**113256**	**38463**	**40362**	**45456**
206470	54146	21924	29733	15522	19813	17063
90738	52816	51635	83523	22940	20549	28394

表7-23 历年全社会用电量
Total Electricity Consumption Over Years

年份 Year	总计 Total	比上年增长 Growth Rate over Preceding Year(%)	全行业用电		
			总计 Total	农业 Agriculture	工业 Industry
1978	70905				43704
1979	89023	25.6			56404
1980	106695	19.9			66886
1981	119606	12.1			72878
1982	129011	7.9			78879
1983	147338	14.2			91251
1984	164071	11.4			93618
1985	185167	12.9			98512
1986	223048	20.5			123033
1987	253457	13.6			140978
1988	279914	10.4			148756
1989	285460	2.0			218247
1990	314858	10.3	271855	16657	233766
1991	365090	16.0	315484	17682	273333
1992	421441	15.4	363939	18601	316558
1993	482578	14.5	416063	18680	359972
1994	552044	14.4	467366	20325	400080
1995	619447	12.2	517935	21262	439498
1996	670281	8.2	551953	22039	457688
1997	718416	7.2	595479	21339	496127
1998	799300	11.3	667837	20470	560624
1999	914936	14.5	778181	21063	664623
2000	1134811	24.0	983475	25777	840125
2001	1266535	11.6	1107317	30111	943788
2002	1520751	20.1	1333570	26115	1146566
2003	1890027	24.3	1651392	22305	1416625
2004	2189528	15.8	1967731	20410	1703126
2005	2684887	22.6	2421555	19142	2110735
2006	3135530	16.8	2833457	17176	2490873
2007	3671231	17.1	3321752	19856	2934498
2008	3849407	4.9	3453560	20562	3027597
2009	4002520	4.0	3577500	21990	3101523
2010	4590431	14.7	4092098	24240	3542660
2011	5053017	10.1	4517125	27067	3886156
2012	5140915	1.7	4547780	28724	3845918
2013	5593943	8.8	4932666	33422	4149789
2014	5767787	3.1	5159482	33393	4352456

单位:万千瓦时(10000 kwh)

Production Consumption				生活用电 Living Consumption		
其中 of Which		建筑业 Construction	第三产业 Tertiary Industry	总计 Total	其中 of Which	
轻工业 Light Industry	重工业 Heavy Industry				城市 Urban	农村 Rural
				4325		
				4835		
				5355		
				6315		
				6734		
				7500		
				9313		
				12603		
				17662		
				22881		
				29510		
				33088		
103301	130465	3770	21432	43003	11926	31077
122714	150619	3179	24469	49606	13406	36200
146272	170286	3898	28780	57502	15499	42003
171383	188589	5870	37412	66515	18972	47543
186145	213935	8016	46961	84678	26002	58677
209890	229608	9855	57175	101512	31626	69886
209606	248082	13586	72226	118328	40536	77792
240220	255907	12132	78013	122937	43257	79680
262246	298378	10589	86743	131463	48670	82793
305906	358717	9745	92495	136755	50740	86015
394760	445365	12559	117573	151336	59557	91779
402840	540948	14234	133418	159218	65054	94164
483275	663292	15523	160889	187188	74294	112886
574100	842525	21672	212462	238635	95616	143019
647516	1055610	31570	244195	221797	105639	116158
775922	1334813	34520	257158	263332	135827	127505
897750	1593123	36255	289154	302073	152348	149725
1013214	1921284	42460	324937	349479	174873	174606
1016912	2010684	44590	360812	395847	198536	197311
1045023	2056500	52322	401664	425020	216319	208701
1182101	2360559	62833	462365	498333	249932	248401
1260629	2625527	74231	529671	535891	271889	264003
1242699	2603219	79121	594017	593135	301647	291489
1303187	2846603	81823	667632	661277	334887	326389
1322290	3030166	81207	692426	608304	310525	297779

表7-24 2014年主营业务收入前20位的工业企业
The Top 20 Enterprises on Annual Revenue from Principal Business in 2014

序号 No.	企业名称 Name of Enterprises	注册类型 Registered Type
1	中国石油化工股份有限公司镇海炼化分公司 Sinopec Zhenhai Refining & Chemical Co. ,Ltd.	股份有限公司 Share - holding Corporations Ltd.
2	中海石油宁波大榭石化有限公司 CNOOC Petrochemical Ningbo Daxie Co. ,Ltd.	与港澳台商合资经营 Equity Joint Ventures with HongKong,Macao &Taiwan
3	上海大众联合发展(宁波)有限公司 Shanghai Volkswagen joint development (Ningbo) Co. , Ltd.	其他有限责任公司 Other Limited Liability Corporations
4	宁波群志光电有限公司 Ningbo grouomark Photoelectric Co. , Ltd.	外资企业 Enterprises with Foreign Investment
5	浙江逸盛石化有限公司 Zhejiang Yisheng Petrochemical Co. ,Ltd.	与港澳台商合资经营 Equity Joint Ventures with HongKong,Macao &Taiwan
6	宁波卷烟厂 Ningbo Cigarette Factory	国有企业 State - owned Enterprises
7	万华化学(宁波)有限公司 Wanhua Chemical (Ningbo) Co. , Ltd	其他有限责任公司 Other Limited Liability Corporations
8	宁波钢铁有限公司 Ningbo Steel Co. ,Ltd.	其他有限责任公司 Other Limited Liability Corporations
9	宁波乐金甬兴化工有限公司 Ningbo LG Yongxing Chemical Industry Co. ,Ltd.	中外合资经营 Chinese - foreign Equity Joint Ventures Enterprises
10	宁波申洲针织有限公司 Ningbo Shenzhou Weaving Co. ,Ltd.	港澳台商独资 HongKong,Macao & Taiwan Funded Sole
11	宁波奥克斯空调有限公司 Ningbo Aux Air - condition Co. ,Ltd.	其他有限责任公司 Other Limited Liability Corporations
12	浙江国华浙能发电有限公司 Zhejiang Guohua Zheneng Power Generation Co. ,Ltd.	其他有限责任公司 Other Limited Liability Corporations
13	宁波宝新不锈钢有限公司 Ningbo Baoxin Stainless Steel Co. ,Ltd.	中外合资经营 Chinese - foreign Equity Joint Ventures Enterprises
14	浙江吉利汽车有限公司 Zhejiang Geely Automobile Co. , Ltd	私营有限责任公司 Private limited liability company
15	宁波市江北大创铜线有限公司 Ningbo Jiangbei Dachuang Copper Wire Co. ,Ltd.	其他有限责任公司 Other Limited Liability Corporations
16	中海浙江宁波液化天然气有限公司 CNOOC Zhejiang Ningbo LNG Co. , Ltd	其他有限责任公司 Other Limited Liability Corporations
17	宁波镇海炼化利安德化学有限公司 Ningbo ZRCC Lyondell Chemical Co. ,Ltd.	与港澳台商合作经营 Co - operative Business Operation with HongKong,Macao & Taiwan
18	宁波富德能源有限公司 Ningbo Fu Tak Energy Limited	其他有限责任公司 Other Limited Liability Corporations
19	宁波金田铜业(集团)股份有限公司 Ningbo Jintian Copper Group Co,. Ltd.	股份有限公司 Share - holding Corporations Ltd.
20	宁波群友光电有限公司 Ningbo group Friends of the photoelectric Vo. ,Ltd.	外资企业 Enterprises with Foreign Investment

主要统计指标解释

【工业总产值】 是以货币形式表现的,工业企业在一定时期内生产的工业最终产品或提供工业性劳务活动的总价值量。它是反映一定时期内工业生产总规模和总水平的指标。

工业总产值包括:本期生产的成品价值、对外加工费收入和在制品半成品期末期初差额价值三部分。

【工业销售产值】 是以货币形式表现的,工业企业在一定时期内销售的本企业生产的工业产品或提供工业性劳务活动的价值总量。它是反映一定时期内工业企业产品销售总规模和总水平的重要指标。

【工业增加值】 是指工业企业在报告期内以货币形式表现的工业生产活动的最终成果,是企业全部生产活动的总成果扣除了在生产过程中消耗或转换的物质产品和劳务价值后的余额,是企业生产过程中新增加的价值。

【固定资产原价】 固定资产原值指企业在建造、购置、安装、改建、扩建、技术改造某项固定资产时所支出的全部货币总额。它一般包括买价、包装费、运杂费和安装费等。

【流动资产】 流动资产是指可以在一年或者超过一年的一个生产周期内变现或者耗用的资产,包括现金及各种存款、短期投资、应收及预付货款、存货等。

【主营业务收入】 指企业在销售商品(不一定是本企业生产)、提供劳务及让渡资产使用权等日常活动中所产生的收入

【主营业务成本】 指企业在销售商品、提供劳务及让渡资产使用权等日常活动而发生的实际成本。

【主营业务税金及附加】 指企业日常活动应负担的税金及附加,包括营业税、消费税、城市维护建设税、资源税、土地增值税和教育费附加等。

【利润总额】 指企业在生产经营过程中各种收入扣除各种耗费后的盈余,反映企业在报告期内实现的亏盈总额,包括营业利润、补贴收入、投资净收益和营业外收支净额。

【利税总额】 指企业利润总额、主营业务税金及附加和本年应交增值税之和。

【资产总计】 指企业拥有或控制的能以货币计量的经济资源,包括各种财产、债权和其他权利。资产按其流动性(即资产的变现能力和支付能力)划分为:流动资产、长期投资、固定资产、无形资产、递延资产和其他资产。

【负债合计】 指企业所承担的能以货币计量,将以资产或劳务偿付的债务,偿还形式包括货币、资产或提供劳务。负债一般按偿还期长短分为流动负债和长期负债。

【所有者权益】 指企业投资人对企业净资产的所有权。企业净资产等于企业全部资产减去全部负债后的余额,其中包括投资者对企业的最初投入,以及资本公积金、盈余公积金和未分配利润,对股份制企业即为股东权益。

【实收资本】 指投资者按照企业章程,或合同、协议的约定,实际投入企业的资本。企业实收资本按照投资主体划分为国家资本、集体资本、法人资本、个人资本、港澳台资本和外商资本六种。根据"资产负债表"中的"实收资本"项填列。实收资本中如有以外币形式投入的资本,需折合成人民币形式填写。

【综合能源消费量】 指一定时期、一定地域内工业企业在工业生产活动中实际消费的各种能源的总和净值。计算综合能源消费量时,需要先将使用的各种能源折算成标准燃料后再进行计算。

Explanatory Notes on Main Statistical Indicators

【Gross Industrial Output Value】 is in a form of currency. Total value of end - products or industrial services activities industrial enterprises provide in the period. It reflects the total achievements and overall scale of industrial production during a given period.

It includes the value of the finished products in a given period, the value of industrial services rendered to other units and the changes in the value of the semi finished products and products in process between the beginning and closing of the period.

【Industrial Sales Output Value】 is in a form of currency. Is the total volume of industrial products sold in value terms of an industrial enterprise and Industrial services activities, which reflects the total achievements and overall sales scale of industrial production during a given period.

【Value Added of Industry】 refers to the final results of industrial production in money terms during the reporting period. Is the total business results of all production activities deducted consumption in the production process and converted the value of material goods and services. Is the production process to increase the value of new.

【Original Value of Fixed Assets】 refers to the original value of all fixed assets owned by industrial enterprises, calculated at the cost paid at the time of purchase, installation, reconstruction, expansion, and technical innovation and transformation of the said assets, which includes expenses on purchase, package, transportation, and installation, etc.

【Liquid Assets】 is assets that can be turned into cash or consumed in more than one year or in a year, including cash and deposits, short - term investments, accounts receivable and prepaid inventories.

【Main Business Income】 refers to the enterprises in selling products (not necessarily in this enterprises'production), providing services and transferring assets, daily activities such as the right to the revenue that generated.

【Main Business Cost】 refers to the actual incurred costs the enterprises sell products, provide services, transfer assets, and other daily activities.

【Main Business Taxes and Surcharges】 refers to taxes and surcharges in the enterprises'daily production activities, including sales tax, consumption tax, urban maintenance and construction tax, resource tax, land tax and education surcharge, etc.

【Total Profits】 refers to the Surplus an enterprise products in the process of production and business activities after deducting all cost, reflecting the company's profit and loss during the reporting period, including operating profit, subsidy income, net investment income and the net non - operating income and expenditure.

【Total Profits and Taxes】 refer to total corporate profits taxes, business taxes and surcharges, and the sum of VAT of this year.

【Total Assets】 refer to all assets which are owned or controlled by enterprises, including circulating assets, long - term investment, fixed assets, intangible assets and deferred assets, other long - term assets, and defertaxes, etc. The summation of above items is equal to total assets shown in the balance sheets of the enterprises. (1) Circulating assets (working capital) refer to assets which can be cashed in or spent or consumed in an operating cycle of one year or over one year, including cash, all kinds of deposits, short term investment, receivables, advance payment, stock, etc. (2) Fixed assets refer to the net value of fixed assets, clearance of fixed assets, project under construction, fixed assets losses in suspense. These are corporations'fund holdings. (3) Intangible assets refer to the assets without material form used by enterprises over a long time, such as patents, non - patent technologies, trade marks, copyright, land use right, business reputation, etc

【Total Liabilities】 refer to the debts that enterprises are responsible for repayment, including liquid liabilities, long term liabilities and deferred taxes, etc. Total liabilities correspond to the summation item of liabilities shown in the balance sheets of the enterprises. Liabilities include short term loans and long - term loans.

【Creditors'Equity】 refers to equity investment in an enterprise net assets of the enterprise ownership. Net assets equal total assets minus total liabilities of business the balance, including the investor's initial investment in the enterprise, and capital reserve, surplus reserve and undistributed profits of the joint - stock company is the shareholders'equity.

【Paid - in capital】 refers to the investors in accordance with corporate charter, or contract, to the agreement, the actual capital invested enterprises. Business investment in paid - in capital in accordance with the main division of the state capital, collective capital, corporate capital, personal capital, Hong Kong, Macao, Taiwan capital and foreign capital six. Filled according to the "paid - up capital" items in the "balance sheet". Paid - up capital in any foreign currency in the form of capital investment required to fill out the form converted into RMB.

【**Comprehensive Energy Consumption**】 in a certain period, certain areas of industrial enterprises in the industrial production activities in the actual consumption of energy is the sum of net. Calculation of comprehensive energy consumption, need to be used in a variety of energy conversion to standard fuel after calculation.

NINGBO 2015 Statistical YearBook

8 CHAPTER

第八篇

固定资产投资和建筑业

INVESTMENT IN FIXED ASSETS AND CONSTRUCTION

固定资产投资和建筑业
Investment Fixed Assets and Construction

主要统计指标
Major Statistics Indicators

2014 年固定资产投资额	Value of Investment Fixed Assets	3989.46	亿元	100 million yuan
比上年增长	Increase Over Last Year	16.6	%	
2014 年房地产开发投资额	Value of Investment in Real Estate Development	1328.14	亿元	100 million yuan
比上年增长	Increase Over Last Year	18.3	%	
2014 年房屋竣工面积	Floor Space of Building Completed	12710855	平方米	sq. m
比上年增长	Increase Over Last Year	46.5	%	
2014 年商品房销售面积	Floor Space of Commercial Building Sold	7264365	平方米	sq. m
比上年增长	Increase Over Last Year	-0.5	%	
2014 年商品房实际销售额	Sales Volume of Commercial Buildings	7805375	万元	10000 yuan
比上年增长	Increase Over Last Year	-3.7	%	
2014 年商品房待售面积	Floor Space of Sale Building	6772365	平方米	sq. m
比上年增长	Increase Over Last Year	37.8	%	
2014 年建筑业总产值	Gross Output Value of Construction	37131235	万元	10000 yuan
比上年增长	Increase Over Last Year	18.5	%	

表8-1 历年固定资产投资情况 Invesment in Fixed Assets Over the Years

单位:亿元(100 million yuan)

年份 Year	总计 Total	其中 of Which 限额以上项目投资 Above Designated Size	工业投资 Industrial Investment	基础设施投资 Infrastructure Investment	房地产开发投资 Real Estate Development
1978	5.02				
1979	5.79				
1980	6.50				
1981	6.39				
1982	8.57				
1983	7.69				
1984	10.95				
1985	18.08				
1986	22.01				
1987	29.46				
1988	35.81				
1989	32.79				
1990	39.28				2.49
1991	51.42				3.00
1992	76.25				7.36
1993	129.27				25.44
1994	184.60				50.46
1995	264.19				71.59
1996	309.97				65.90
1997	300.57				51.92
1998	309.81				43.87
1999	318.93				46.54
2000	360.75				59.71
2001	470.28				87.08
2002	601.27				125.97
2003	740.92	556.66			184.26
2004	1026.64	782.38			244.26
2005	1268.55	1009.05			259.50
2006	1413.00	1099.42			313.58
2007	1486.54	1153.65			332.89
2008	1610.86	1303.11			307.75
2009	1860.45	1485.93	709.45	620.32	374.51
2010	2034.99	1477.72	619.01	610.87	557.27
2011	2385.50	1630.56	668.36	697.25	754.94
2012	2901.42	2017.07	817.24	845.71	884.35
2013	3422.95	2299.81	1061.90	846.70	1123.14
2014	3989.46	2661.32	1263.22	971.03	1328.14

注:自2003年以后总计数为限额以上固定资产投资口径(即限额以上项目投资与房地产开发投资之和)

Note: The norm of the total count of fixed asset investment excessing the quota since 2003. That is the sum of real estate development investments and projects investments excessing the quota.

表 8-2 各县(市)固定资产投资完成情况(2014)
Investment in Fixed Assets by Region

指标	Indicators	全市 Total
固定资产投资完成额(按经营地)	**Total(By Place of Business)**	**39894626**
固定资产投资完成额(按建设地)	**Total(By Place of Building)**	**39894626**
限额以上项目投资	**Investment in Fixed Assets Above Designed Size**	**26613236**
按行业分	Group by Sector	
农林牧渔业	Framing, Forestry, Animal Husbandry and Fishery	451542
采矿业	Mining and Quarrying	]18282
制造业	Manufacuring	11336348
电力、燃气及水的生产和供应业	Electric Power, Gas and Water Production and Supply	1277615
建筑业	Construction	14445
批发和零售业	Wholesale and Retail Trade	455890
交通运输、仓储和邮政业	Transportation, Storage and Post	3030527
住宿和餐饮业	Hotel and Catering Services	265899
信息传输、软件和信息技术服务业		110429
金融业	Financial Industries	124695
房地产业	Real Estate Industries	3122965
租赁和商务服务业	Leasing and Business Service Industries	560491
科学研究和技术服务业		63386
水利、环境和公共设施管理业	Water Conservancy, Environment and Public Facility Management	4275672
居民服务、修理和其他服务业		59135
教育	Education	605504
卫生和社会工作		307500
文化、体育和娱乐业	Culture, Sports and Entertainment	358852
公共管理、社会保障和社会组织		174059
房地产开发投资完成额(按经营地)	**Real Estate Development(By Place of Business)**	**13281390**
#住宅	Residential Buildings	7732540
房地产开发投资完成额(按建设地)	**Real Estate Development(By Place of Building)**	**13281390**
#住宅	Residential Buildings	7732540
城镇项目投资	**Investment in Fixed Assets in Town**	**16893982**
农村非农户投资	**Investment about Rural non Farm Households**	**9719254**

注:本表按2011年修订的国民经济行业标准统计。

Note: Statistics in this table are classified as the national economic category that was modified in 2011.

单位:万元(10000 yuan)

市区 Urban Disctict	#鄞州 Yinzhou	余姚 Yuyao	慈溪 Cixi	奉化 Fenghua	象山 Xiangshan	宁海 Ninghai
22518377	**5883933**	**5155915**	**6356722**	**1813268**	**1848034**	**2202310**
22452497	**5933325**	**5156152**	**6360715**	**1821652**	**1852034**	**2251576**
13967163	**3429571**	**3752850**	**4579316**	**1274901**	**1323911**	**1715095**
27196	3115	62959	182833	64725	62032	51797
16933	9853				799	550
5707754	1646360	1845989	2462256	369838	419008	531503
703996	76961	263376	25269	71648	83849	129477
11175	7165	1000		1770	500	
229570	28247	65606	79981	9459	55691	15583
2077553	430937	234013	319473	173232	91122	135134
95560	44327	75518		5606	55184	34031
78024			9030			23375
98446	6232		21011			5238
1583066	562571	499374	498471	204712	53362	283980
313902	4157	39120	128118	68812	3313	7226
47628	3726	484	9010	4153	5	2106
2226380	443879	496948	550081	229372	360528	412363
12335	1		34568	712	4520	7000
315553	97292	96270	117587	27214	15954	32926
148653	38283	28671	45044	10705	45566	28861
176677	11373	15369	92512	20530	43901	9863
96762	15092	28153	4072	12413	28577	4082
8551214	**2454362**	**1403065**	**1777406**	**538367**	**524123**	**487215**
4723888	1519677	775297	1230861	376104	377440	248950
8485334	**2503754**	**1403302**	**1781399**	**546751**	**528123**	**536481**
4685346	1552799	775534	1234033	376104	380440	281083
9883616	**1130917**	**1505587**	**3064875**	**807536**	**559021**	**1073347**
4083547	**2298654**	**2247263**	**1514441**	**467365**	**764890**	**641748**

表8－3 部分年份分产业固定资产投资完成额
Fixed Assets Investment by Industry in Partial Years

单位：万元(10000 yuan)

指标	Indicators	2010	2011	2012	2013	2014
总计	**Total**	**21932830**	**23855072**	**29014258**	**34229529**	**39894626**
第一产业	Primary Industry	113543	183918	270188	211682	451542
第二产业	Secondary Industry	6975776	6683611	8198682	10662308	12646690
第三产业	Tertiary Industry	14843511	16987543	20545388	23355539	26796394
限额以上项目投资	**Investment in Fixed Assets Above Designed Size**	**14777197**	**16305624**	**20170744**	**22998128**	**26613236**
第一产业	Primary Industry	104237	183918	270188	211682	451542
第二产业	Secondary Industry	6312915	6683611	8198682	10662308	12646690
第三产业	Tertiary Industry	8360045	9438095	11701874	12124138	13515004
城镇限额以下投资	**Investment in Fixed Assets Below Designed Size in Town**	**168730**				
第一产业	Primary Industry	294				
第二产业	Secondary Industry	103551				
第三产业	Tertiary Industry	64885				
农村非农户限额以下投资	**Investment in Fixed Assets about Non－peasant Householdsa & Below Designed Size in Rural Area**	**667306**				
第一产业	Primary Industry	9012				
第二产业	Secondary Industry	559310				
第三产业	Tertiary Industry	98984				
房地产开发	**Real Estate Development**	**5572683**	**7549448**	**8843514**	**11231401**	**13281390**
#住宅建设	Residential Buildings	3231195	4168184	5156454	6423263	7732540
农村私人固定资产投资	**Private Investment in Rural Areas**	**746914**				

表8-4 部分年份城镇以上新增固定资产及房屋建筑面积 Newly Increase Fixed Assets and Floor Space of Buildings Above City and Town Level in Partial Years

单位:万元,万平方米(10000 yuan,10000 sq. m)

年份	本年新增固定资产额 Newly Increase Fixed Assets in This Year	房屋施工面积 Floor Space of Buliding Under Construction	#住宅 Residential Buildings	房屋竣工面积 Floor Space of Buildings Completed	#住宅 Residential Buildings
1990	179769	308.76	137.73	180.48	77.30
1991	289108	362.09	175.07	182.28	88.11
1992	253780	518.29	254.60	209.38	91.38
1993	516881	906.08	501.36	383.28	224.91
1994	908056	1205.39	615.30	528.40	285.92
1995	1007217	1386.64	760.99	515.02	312.26
1996	1433274	1395.46	681.71	579.60	332.59
1997	1758309	1264.97	543.00	442.76	232.08
1998	1685871	1156.62	467.16	506.87	232.26
1999	1915400	1050.10	519.91	499.65	233.31
2000	2464806	1208.39	681.38	446.70	227.64
2001	2776661	1626.01	886.08	622.64	341.45
2002	2382537	2342.77	1132.48	745.33	365.88
2003	3292041	3401.43	1744.41	971.64	550.62
2004	3603854	4062.61	2225.05	996.97	546.09
2005	5708349	4600.43	2225.51	1562.32	680.51
2006	7321849	4542.09	2186.55	1427.87	671.66
2007	7166189	5715.13	2190.54	1452.22	535.06
2008	7523565	6505.64	2447.55	1746.09	712.79
2009	11797353	6741.74	2352.59	1669.41	500.54
2010	9781355	7679.59	2741.93	1486.97	470.94
2011	12296942	9792.22	3532.76	2232.56	672.49
2012	10643686	10925.24	4037.87	2025.64	615.75
2013	18423979	12227.39	4422.44	2558.33	666.48
2014	20319735	11798.76	4694.56	2780.58	880.96

表 8-5 城镇以上固定资产投资完成情况(2014)
Investment in Fixed Assets of City and Town Level and Above

指标	Indicators	计划总投资 Total Investment of Project	累计完成投资 Accumulative Finish Total Investment
总计	**Total**	**57933561**	**38867982**
按登记类型	**By Registered Type**		
内资	Domestic - investment Enterprises	47981593	32141634
国有	State - owned	30992949	20797522
港澳台投资	Hongkong, Macao and Taiwan Funded	4192664	3144629
外资	Foreign Funded Enterprises	5752004	3580106
按隶属关系	**By Subordination**		
中央	Central	1470489	1203773
地方	Local	56463072	37664209
按建筑性质	**By type of Construction**		
#新建	New Construction	30315352	20050012
扩建	Expansion	19361138	12025081
改建	Reconstruction	3359013	2508586
按国民经济行业分组	**By Sector**		
农林牧渔业	Framing, Forestry, Animal Husbandry and Fishery	969521	546953
采矿业	Mining and Quarrying	75000	7080
制造业	Manufacuring	17435345	11664248
电力、燃气及水的生产和供应业	Electric Power, Gas and Water Production and Supply	2549882	2077865
建筑业	Construction	14436	14741
批发和零售业	Wholesale and Retail Trade	637291	506573
交通运输、仓储和邮政业	Transportation, Storage and Post	12181207	7886606
住宿和餐饮业	Hotel and Catering Services	380542	302326
信息传输、软件和信息技术服务业		179988	154592
金融业	Financial Industries	538172	339675
房地产业	Real Estate Industries	8238998	4954135
租赁和商务服务业	Leasing and Business Service Industries	817057	704933
科学研究和技术服务业		235148	160709
水利、环境和公共设施管理业	Water Conservancy, Environment and Public Facility Management	10545225	7459240
居民服务、修理和其他服务业		98390	76504
教育	Education	1032383	710676
卫生和社会工作		756432	405975
文化、体育和娱乐业	Culture, Sports and Entertainment	904324	613683
公共管理、社会保障和社会组织		344220	281468

注:本表按 2011 年修订的国民经济行业标准统计。

Note: Statistics in this table are classified as the national economic category that was modified in 2011.

单位:万元(10000 yuan)

本年完成投资 Investment Completed of the Year	按构成分 by Composition					本年新增固定资产 Newly Increased Fixed Assets of the Year	本年房屋施工面积(平方米) Floor Space Under Construction (sq. m)	本年房屋竣工面积(平方米) Floor Space Completed (sq. m)
	建筑工程 Construction	安装工程 Installation	设备工器具购置 Purchase of Equipment and Instruments	其他费用 Others	#土地购置费 Purchase of Land			
16893982	**9174203**	**522949**	**3847245**	**3349585**	**1887758**	**13627948**	**43765947**	**15094967**
13980289	7858314	410314	2528573	3183088	1790826	9476449	36103372	11361764
8361097	5188919	185385	719330	2267463	1236143	5024100	16581220	4150575
1561799	586136	73693	783166	118804	64271	1697048	3566905	1894972
1350281	729690	38942	535506	46143	31311	2454451	4095170	1838231
345343	101595	37542	178997	27209	6868	809536	416879	224307
16548639	9072608	485407	3668248	3322376	1880890	12818412	43349068	14870660
7617628	4855217	187903	862526	1711982	1067626	5286391	23542317	6918713
5290560	2941440	138959	990565	1219596	617597	4706469	15329625	5852403
1139200	807350	7760	67774	256316	134614	809353	1108579	291969
279032	243784		24831	10417	6829	262789	12916	11600
7080		1180	5900					
6036581	2399222	306780	2777626	552953	310654	5950564	17078216	7813201
824894	337314	80820	353893	52867	2558	1214847	538893	328214
9103	9008			95	95	6833	23754	
213873	147411	4680	6836	54946	49216	229467	1312630	640239
2364141	1264228	97494	278328	724091	369088	1330314	1649684	341040
88812	70570	5187	2769	10286	5318	102584	464628	236548
85141	19563	8978	42306	14294	13577	77790	133497	48197
113180	87692	131	18328	7029	1100	23974	556037	4400
1869086	1350380	1634	17269	499803	307465	1531493	15328789	3390530
495628	232556	1189	215085	46798	35565	399039	864659	303394
53429	35970	579	10403	6477	4343	89291	396654	180473
3385963	2253232	2748	14265	1115718	598757	1618989	1135034	270613
48272	15792	29	29553	2898		24931	70381	25500
404330	288530	1073	4988	109739	73191	364341	1674113	770793
212358	158358	5948	10612	37440	17858	135946	1051959	373206
280813	158518	4040	29803	88452	79606	166833	847815	175299
122266	102075	459	4450	15282	12538	97923	626288	181720

表8-6 各县(市)城镇以上固定资产投资主要指标(2014)
Main Indicators of Investment in Fixed Assets of City and Town Level and Above by Region

指标	Indicators	全市 Total
计划总投资	**Total Investment of Plan**	**57933561**
本年完成投资	**Finished Investment of This Year**	**16893982**
按经济注册类型分	**By Registration Status**	
国有经济	State – Owned Units	8361097
集体经济	Collective – owned Units	151792
其他有限责任公司	Share – holding Corporation Units	2205280
股份有限公司	Other Limited Liability Corporations	597044
港澳台投资经济	HongKong, Macao and Taiwan Funded	1561799
外商投资经济	Foreign Funded	1350281
按隶属关系分	**By Administrative Relationship**	
中央	Central	345343
省	Province	267369
省辖市	Municipalities	2225585
县(市)、区	Counties and Districts	5414187
其他	Others	8641498
按建设性质分	**By Type of Construction**	
新建	New Construction	7617628
扩建	Expansion	5290560
改建	Reconstruction	1139200
按构成分	**By Use of Funds**	
建筑工程	Construction	9174203
安装工程	Installation	522949
设备工器具购置	Purchase of Equipment and Instruments	3847245
其他费用	Others	3349585
按国民经济行业分	**By Sector**	
农林牧渔业	Framing, Forestry, Animal Husbandry and Fishery	279032
采矿业	Mining and Quarrying	7080
制造业	Manufacuring	6036581
电力、燃气及水的生产和供应业	Electric Power, Gas and Water Production and Supply	824894

注:①本表按2011年修订的国民经济行业标准统计。②从2012年开始国家预算内资金改为国家预算资金,以下表同。

①Statistics in this table are classified as the national economic category that was modified in 2011. ②The state on budget funds have been change into state budget funds since 2012, same as the following tables.

单位:万元(10000 yuan)

市区 Urban District	#鄞州 Yinzhou	余姚 Yuyao	慈溪 Cixi	奉化 Fenghua	象山 Xiangshan	宁海 Ninghai
35965730	**4148531**	**3239038**	**10082849**	**2787281**	**1785802**	**4072861**
9883616	**1130917**	**1505587**	**3064875**	**807536**	**559021**	**1073347**
5104073	625298	791078	551803	538495	383523	992125
122001	96560	11070	14205	492		4024
1008956	178925	46301	1025423	17001	38141	69458
443626	41653	108152	36879	8387		
1246134	4501	168476	125186	22003		
612156	23470	44193	685716	5948	2268	
334092	2408				11251	
267369						
2045169	258912		66487	113929		
2506484	388535	781573	382582	322537	391312	1029699
4730502	481062	724014	2615806	371070	156458	43648
4481458	405838	386261	1801168	528372	383209	37160
2933553	352231	388257	750770	132839	72617	1012524
694615	257200	282427	37774	9060	91661	23663
4358010	551562	1052280	1993842	507997	460256	801818
471952	3563	20551	16588	4104	7213	2541
2575047	80349	232795	868375	126867	23969	20192
2478607	495443	199961	186070	168568	67583	248796
24081		29033	165304	9763	32132	18719
7080						
3357158	311730	519937	1769313	283361	38651	68161
573359	16700	96337	12059	48391	1821	92927

表 8－6 续表 Continued

指标	Indicators	全市 Total
建筑业	Construction	9103
批发和零售业	Wholesale and Retail Trade	213873
交通运输、仓储和邮政业	Transportation, Storage and Post	2364141
住宿和餐饮业	Hotel and Catering Services	88812
信息传输、软件和信息技术服务业		85141
金融业	Financial Industries	113180
房地产业	Real Estate Industries	1869086
租赁和商务服务业	Leasing and Business Service Industries	495628
科学研究和技术服务业		53429
水利、环境和公共设施管理业	Water Conservancy, Environment and Public Facility Management	3385963
居民服务、修理和其他服务业		48272
教育	Education	404330
卫生和社会工作		212358
文化、体育和娱乐业	Culture, Sports and Entertainment	280813
公共管理、社会保障和社会组织		122266
本年新增固定资产	**Newly Increased Fixed Assets in This Year**	**13627948**
按资金来源分	**By Source of Funds**	
#国家预算资金	State Budget	1418949
国内贷款	Domestic Loans	3069131
利用外资	Foreign Investment	432958
自筹资金	Fund Raising	11816154
房屋建筑面积(平方米)	**Floor Space of Buildings (sq. m)**	
施工面积	Floor Space of Buildings Under Construction	43765947
#住宅	Residential Buildings	7438027
竣工面积	Floor Space of Buildings Completed	15094967
#住宅	Residential Buildings	1687501
本年竣工房屋价值(万元)	Value of Building Completed (10000 yuan)	5443300
#住宅	Residential Buildings	629179

单位:万元(10000 yuan)

市区 Urban District	#鄞州 Yinzhou	余姚 Yuyao	慈溪 Cixi	奉化 Fenghua	象山 Xiangshan	宁海 Ninghai
6833	6221			1770	500	
128708	8001	9109	21658	8759	45636	3
1898813	285748	141096	55058	75204	60488	133482
24158	1	14727		1553	42479	5895
77126						8015
86931			21011			5238
1004644	178218	274692	246585	90862		252303
309745			110538	68812	3313	3220
41619	2408	484	9010	205	5	2106
1765385	247742	356196	441286	165994	250505	406597
6177			31873	712	2510	7000
226766	35567	33115	84914	16926	10474	32135
117915	31911	15002	7735	8805	34313	28588
146789	6670	9202	85038	18919	15100	5765
80329		6657	3493	7500	21094	3193
7904162	**627119**	**1345831**	**2743293**	**452980**	**411626**	**770056**
927105	64515	39817	276486	29270	65938	80333
2625525	489615	2800	91279	69848	95985	183694
421230	11391	8494		3234		
5830128	807288	1253936	2800352	778988	386346	766404
21458630	4824189	3464634	10523160	3890638	1088039	3340846
4830535	1223373	749270	780097	338117	47937	692071
7460876	1378338	2204199	3124781	1317504	258130	729477
1383764	278514	137399	73093	40933	47937	4375
2367233	508992	434909	2067079	236768	61324	275987
509281	153451	58030	29285	14231	9587	8765

表8－7 全市房地产企业开发投资情况(2014)
Develop and Investment of Enterprises for Real Estate Development

指标	Indicators	总计 Total	按控股情况分 国有 State－owned	集体 Colloective－owned
计划总投资	**Total Investment of Plan**	**51860821**	**8145509**	**462112**
本年完成投资	**Investment Made of the Year**	**13281390**	**2135759**	**75566**
土地购置费	Purchase of Land	3903698	571387	
配套工程投资	Ancillary Works			
按构成分	**By Composition**			
建筑工程	Construction	7149493	1161174	69976
安装工程	Installation	858934	76757	2575
设备工器具购置	Purchase of Equipment and Instruments	166574	14180	307
其他费用	Others	5106389	883648	2708
按工程用途分	**By Purpose**			
住宅	Residential Buildings	7732540	1140290	32180
办公楼	Office Buildings	1014591	193101	9826
商业营业用房	Buildings for Commercial Business	1843337	214330	16684
其他	Others	2690922	588038	16876
本年新增固定资产	Newly Increased Fixed Assets in the Year	6691787	1595942	167242
待开发土地面积(平方米)	Land Space Needed Development (sq. m)	3275179	751598	202897
本年购置土地面积(平方米)	Land Space Purchased in the Year (sq. m)	2320808	634072	
本年土地成交价款	Actual Land Price of the Year	771783	75553	

单位:平方米,万元(sq. m,10000 yuan)

By Holding Status			按隶属关系分 By Administrative Relationship				
私人 Private	港澳台商 Hongkong, Macao&Taiwan Funded	外商 Foreign Funds	一级 Firstl Class	二级 Secend Class	三级 Third Class	四级 Fourth Class	其他 Others
32429583	**5170580**	**3458363**	**3444540**	**3158870**	**17711125**	**1717023**	**25829263**
8307873	**1428182**	**888226**	**781769**	**719593**	**4317699**	**430198**	**7032131**
2771966	170734	272217	342300	214578	952079	84521	2310220
4064187	1095598	494518	292950	397806	2584542	271304	3602891
620082	54781	53925	34439	54371	320837	56695	392592
103684	20626	27221	6399	5349	54246	5718	94862
3519920	257177	312562	447981	262067	1358074	96481	2941786
4907647	858573	557275	505362	420323	2769721	320577	3716557
663285	93604	19682	52686	30708	233759	14461	682977
1125720	194342	196366	35980	93279	442343	43176	1228559
1611221	281663	114903	187741	175283	871876	51984	1404038
4125774	175032	455768	501903	712136	3329044	238560	1910144
1664721	460424	107013	57575	49897	1239824	117616	1810267
1520128		56452		25871	475613	153031	1666293
579757		63232		11713	183767	57512	518791

表 8-8 全市房地产企业房屋施工及竣工情况(2014) Buildings Construction and The Completed of Enterprises for Real Estate Development

指标	Indicators	总计 Total	按控股情况分 国有 State-owned	集体 Colloective-owned
房屋施工面积	**Floor Space of Buildings Under Consrtuction**	**74221626**	**12673173**	**892600**
1. 住宅	Residential Buildings	39507551	7058789	322586
2. 办公楼	Office Buildings	5990839	1279279	121762
3. 商业营业用房	Buildings for Commercial Business	10471623	967705	221471
4. 其他	Others	18251613	3367400	226781
本年新开工房屋施工面积	**Floor Space of Newly Started of The Year**	**14682100**	**2497197**	
1. 住宅	Residential Buildings	7957427	1283778	
2. 办公楼	Office Buildings	991683	245463	
3. 商业营业用房	Buildings for Commercial Business	2004611	130696	
4. 其他	Others	3728379	837260	
房屋竣工面积	**Floor Space of Buildings Completed**	**12710855**	**3384229**	**348664**
#不可销售面积	Floor Space for Connot	2695096	741923	52560
1. 住宅	Residential Buildings	7122105	1981567	224973
2. 办公楼	Office Buildings	1212732	441175	5021
3. 商业营业用房	Buildings for Commercial Business	1384198	186549	31922
4. 其他	Others	2991820	774938	86748
商品住宅竣工套数(套)	**Completed Residencial House (flat)**	**54066**	**17756**	**1925**
竣工房屋价值	**Value of Buildings Completed (10000 yuan)**	**5628802**	**1274926**	**137083**
1. 住宅	Residential Buildings	3264472	723814	104545
2. 办公楼	Office Buildings	547349	163520	1448
3. 商业营业用房	Buildings for Commercial Business	741774	73762	9889
4. 其他	Others	1075207	313830	21201
出租房屋面积	**Floor Space of Lease House**	**316680**	**63177**	
1. 住宅	Residential Buildings			
2. 办公楼	Office Buildings	79188	30329	
3. 商业营业用房	Buildings for Commercial Business	203501	32848	
4. 其他	Others	33991		
待售面积	**Floor Space of Vacant Building**	**6772365**	**1129554**	**167500**
1. 住宅	Residential Buildings	3430306	613945	100230
2. 办公楼	Office Buildings	786426	179512	5021
3. 商业营业用房	Buildings for Commercial Business	1442342	201584	32466
4. 其他	Others	1113291	134513	29783

单位:平方米,万元(sq. m,10000 yuan)

By Holding Status			按隶属关系分 By Administrative Relationship				
私人 Private	港澳台商 Hongkong, Macao&Taiwan Funded	外商 Foreign Funds	一级 Firstl Class	二级 Secend Class	三级 Third Class	四级 Fourth Class	其他 Others
45269284	**8417895**	**4533231**	**4196400**	**4669548**	**29560907**	**2318388**	**33476383**
24156823	4828562	2145025	2777630	2893204	16362142	1454533	16020042
3669360	450356	241266	136578	204177	2357862	62574	3229648
6750124	755878	1341608	185406	518036	3139357	218206	6410618
10692977	2383099	805332	1096786	1054131	7701546	583075	7816075
9796671	**1207789**	**522762**	**438490**	**593542**	**4106303**	**229880**	**9313885**
5198667	792939	343319	314853	305618	2283561	136075	4917320
668385	77835			39231	241208	15056	696188
1538250	119163	32388	6409	60218	377567	37366	1523051
2391369	217852	147055	117228	188475	1203967	41383	2177326
7683943	**429886**	**619696**	**1465234**	**1359874**	**6379197**	**508058**	**2998492**
1748761	61081	21848	232530	230343	1568254	54491	609478
4131033	298941	427542	1071946	869063	3182095	357120	1641881
684597		65737	9949	60271	913021		229491
1054525	4594	36041	39367	150799	673497	32584	487951
1813788	126351	90376	343972	279741	1610584	118354	639169
28389	**2568**	**2866**	**7570**	**7710**	**25943**	**2281**	**10562**
3496281	**147694**	**455120**	**451473**	**489168**	**3005764**	**218106**	**1464291**
1951522	102700	356404	341122	271788	1606398	157819	887345
336646		38804	2300	24356	415725		104968
543342	1421	52439	13620	98999	408868	25192	195095
664771	43573	7473	94431	94025	574773	35095	276883
109875	**37925**			**176455**	**59225**	**957**	**80043**
22134	26725			24003	26706		28479
60066	4884			152452	32244	957	17848
27675	6316				275		33716
4303788	**481212**	**431263**	**656375**	**851196**	**3002297**	**264356**	**1998141**
2191955	227327	263613	337849	409632	1634723	179686	868416
492051	41320	57217	325	131812	370857	1187	282245
758957	168351	99736	144132	162593	545778	34422	555417
860825	44214	10697	174069	147159	450939	49061	292063

表 8-9 全市房地产企业房屋销售情况(2014)
Building Sale Situation of Enterprises for Real Estate Development

指标	Indicators	总计 Total	按控股情况分	
			国有 State-owned	集体 Colloective-owned
商品房销售面积	**Floor Space of Building Sold**	**7264365**	**871159**	**29890**
1. 住宅	Residential Buildings	5951952	716041	19839
2. 办公楼	Office Buildings	508969	40864	5397
3. 商业营业用房	Buildings for Commercial Business	505575	72575	1030
4. 其他	Others	297869	41679	3624
现房销售面积	Floor Space of Completed Building	1646056	353115	16729
1. 住宅	Residential Buildings	1085954	236240	12583
2. 办公楼	Office Buildings	227712	30209	
3. 商业营业用房	Buildings for Commercial Business	190034	46707	678
4. 其他	Others	142356	39959	3468
期房销售面积	Floor Space of Forward Delivery Building	5618309	518044	13161
1. 住宅	Residential Buildings	4865998	479801	7256
2. 办公楼	Office Buildings	281257	10655	5397
3. 商业营业用房	Buildings for Commercial Business	315541	25868	352
4. 其他	Others	155513	1720	156
商品房销售额	**Sales Volume of Commercial Buildings**	**7805375**	**654923**	**25407**
1. 住宅	Residential Buildings	6481530	517582	17336
2. 办公楼	Office Buildings	453284	44939	5048
3. 商业营业用房	Buildings for Commercial Business	656358	74861	1596
4. 其他	Others	214203	17541	1427
现房销售额	Sales Volume of Completed Building	1603257	202203	13703
1. 住宅	Residential Buildings	1114931	129494	11321
2. 办公楼	Office Buildings	182064	29346	
3. 商业营业用房	Buildings for Commercial Business	201949	26620	1048
4. 其他	Others	104313	16743	1334
期房销售额	Sales Volume of Forward Delivery Building	6202118	452720	11704
1. 住宅	Residential Buildings	5366599	388088	6015
2. 办公楼	Office Buildings	271220	15593	5048
3. 商业营业用房	Buildings for Commercial Business	454409	48241	548
4. 其他	Others	109890	798	93

单位:平方米,万元(sq. m,10000 yuan)

By Holding Status			按隶属关系分 By Administrative Relationship					
私人 Private	港澳台商 Hongkong, Macao&Taiwan Funded	外商 Foreign Funds	一级 Firstl Class	二级 Secend Class	三级 Third Class	四级 Fourth Class	其他 Others
5010255	**569598**	**448082**	**620288**	**561116**	**2763869**	**206424**	**3112668**
4060611	518606	358064	546136	455347	2190811	165142	2594516
357783	28534	67873	9949	29746	284089	15076	170109
364178	8411	12795	28078	36450	152414	19476	269157
227683	14047	9350	36125	39573	136555	6730	78886
1018853	64600	168867	225610	169925	739576	23887	487058
681382	55691	88215	183000	102638	489059	14308	296949
127927	3369	64292		29746	161799	47	36120
121023	2521	10393	16391	15419	30403	7517	120304
88521	3019	5967	26219	22122	58315	2015	33685
3991402	504998	279215	394678	391191	2024293	182537	2625610
3379229	462915	269849	363136	352709	1701752	150834	2297567
229856	25165	3581	9949		122290	15029	133989
243155	5890	2402	11687	21031	122011	11959	148853
139162	11028	3383	9906	17451	78240	4715	45201
5547063	**680446**	**467954**	**847897**	**530972**	**2515253**	**203851**	**3707402**
4560607	619024	396562	752556	444081	1956084	167356	3161453
300968	35166	52661	14428	19414	258377	8328	152737
511171	12395	12770	59521	38778	191717	24612	341730
174317	13861	5961	21392	28699	109075	3555	51482
1149666	70730	149727	275312	187095	669345	20781	450724
813806	63507	88551	231302	135986	447301	9150	291192
97910	3112	48755		19414	131442	27	31181
157424	2882	8961	29425	20643	31041	10672	110168
80526	1229	3460	14585	11052	59561	932	18183
4397397	609716	318227	572585	343877	1845908	183070	3256678
3746801	555517	308011	521254	308095	1508783	158206	2870261
203058	32054	3906	14428		126935	8301	121556
353747	9513	3809	30096	18135	160676	13940	231562
93791	12632	2501	6807	17647	49514	2623	33299

表8-10 全市房地产企业经营情况(2014)
Main Economy Indicators of Real Estate Development

指标	Indicators	总计 Total	按控股情况分 国有 State - owned	集体 Colloective - owned
本年资金来源合计	**Total Capital Source in This Year**	**18531690**	**2450200**	**93281**
上年末结余资金	Balance at End of Previous Year	3809190	387602	5254
本年资金来源小计	Subtotal Capital of This Year	14722500	2062598	88027
1. 国内贷款	Domestic Loans	3556098	621693	9900
2. 利用外资	Foreign Investment	26680		
3. 自筹资金	Self - Financed Capital	6656941	1237072	53265
4. 其他资金来源	Others	4482781	203833	24862
本年各项应付款合计	Total Account Payable This Year	3220782	407859	42403
年末资产负债情况	**Assets and Liabilities of Year - end**			
资产总计	Total Assets	669276871	159324496	6726329
#本年固定资产折旧	Depreciation of Fixed Assets in This Year	859497	96910	6133
负债总计	Total Liabilities	494182796	116172241	5752515
所有者权益合计	Creditors´Equity	175094075	43152255	973814
实收资本合计	Total Capital Hold	122913223	13353405	1127113
损益情况	**Expenditureznd Income**			
主营业务收入	Prime Operating Revenue	75547007	8250934	897423
土地转让收入	Land Transferred	73763	73763	
商品房屋销售收入	Commercial Buildings Sold	72042117	7525088	828177
房屋出租收入	Buildings Leased	1113500	180201	1406
其他收入	Others	2317627	471882	67840
主营业务成本	Prime Operating Costs	56039773	5464033	760067
主营业务税金及附加	Sales Taxes and Extra Charges	6850421	956854	72857
主营业务利润	Prime Operating Profits	12656813	1830047	64499
销售费用	Sales Expenses	2708082	166285	19169
管理费用	Manage Expenses	4189175	434606	53366
财务费用	Finance Expenses	2639978	529445	86056
营业利润	Business Profits	2476698	857028	-95072
利润总额	Total Profits	2340104	962431	-91969
应付职工薪酬	Employee Compensation Payable	2099787	302587	23998

单位:万元(10000 yuan)

By Holding Status			按隶属关系分 By Administrative Relationship				
私人 Private	港澳台商 Hongkong, Macao&Taiwan Funded	外商 Foreign Funds	一级 Firstl Class	二级 Secend Class	三级 Third Class	四级 Fourth Class	其他 Others
11654516	**1982150**	**1391929**	**1198244**	**774590**	**5953835**	**620719**	**9984302**
2185948	440932	601857	321874	59063	1287621	167916	1972716
9468568	1541218	790072	876370	715527	4666214	452803	8011586
2079789	477014	92762	213160	163368	1255527	126430	1797613
	2775	23905					26680
4272669	560531	286275	225302	227744	1906466	212640	4084789
3116110	500898	387130	437908	324415	1504221	113733	2102504
1913976	578666	209016	102273	277597	1232594	52656	1555662
368648832	58314805	40430854	72368384	83337166	212777559	15354255	285439507
568226	54270	85138	51107	146168	346341	28654	287227
289324392	31178445	26537042	51300062	64286684	161348004	11621962	205626084
79324440	27136360	13893812	21068322	19050482	51429555	3732293	79813423
66057020	23389257	12419181	7254205	4986948	35754863	3565343	71351864
52090292	8771599	3840887	9583746	7627102	28663418	3283435	26389306
				73763			
49904474	8613082	3659903	9510272	7148381	26489716	3267647	25626101
516841	113919	145094	53577	292911	354124	9840	403048
1668977	44598	35890	19897	112047	1819578	5948	360157
39008009	7018152	2706048	5152537	5945597	22291103	2891726	19758810
4804005	612765	291656	1170279	816520	2410349	212513	2240760
8278278	1140682	843183	3260930	864985	3961966	179196	4389736
2024214	220134	173082	200547	169197	1028359	52074	1257905
2856103	308358	390686	472495	523199	1490421	130500	1572560
1536839	147140	131871	212580	775086	759793	57583	834936
627443	479280	110340	2412786	-514331	479822	-130719	229140
262420	490854	140187	2441290	-424729	666898	-111358	-231997
1319179	215416	172686	257447	154437	662299	61976	963628

表 8－11 各县(市)、区房地产企业开发投资情况(2014)
Develop and Investment of Enterprises for Real Estate Development

指标名称	Indicators	全市 Total	市区 Urban Disctict
计划总投资	**Total Investment of Plan**	**50000754**	**31704201**
本年完成投资	**Investment Made of the Year**	**12754482**	**8024306**
土地购置费	Purchase of Land	3641323	2565655
配套工程投资	Ancillary Works		
按构成分	**By Composition**		
建筑工程	Construction	6970375	4116533
安装工程	Installation	826719	437833
设备工器具购置	Purchase of Equipment and Instruments	164094	109406
其他费用	Others	4793294	3360534
按工程用途分	**By Purpose**		
住宅	Residential Buildings	7551504	4542852
办公楼	Office Buildings	900040	801790
商业营业用房	Buildings for Commercial Business	1763373	1103606
其他	Others	2539565	1576058
本年新增固定资产	Newly Increased Fixed Assets in the Year	6305463	3951790
待开发土地面积	Land Space Needed Development (sq. m)	3203077	1792167
本年购置土地面积	Land Space Purchased in the Year (sq. m)	2320808	1495029
本年土地成交价款	Actual Land Price of the Year	771783	485832
本年资金来源合计	Total Funding Sources	17890653	11746582
上年末结余资金	At the End of the Balance of Funds	3676876	2186669
本年资金来源小计	**Total Fund Source of the Year**	**14213777**	**9559913**
1. 国内贷款	1. Domestic Loans	3516978	2283171
2. 利用外资	2. Use of Foreign Capital	26680	23905
3. 自筹资金	3. Self－Financing	6436221	4402060
4. 其他资金来源	4. Other Sources	4233898	2850777
本年各项应付款合计	**The Total Payment of the Year**	**3121356**	**1613320**

注：本表房地产开发投资按建设地统计，表 8－12、8－13 同。

Note: Real Estate development investment is recorded by region in this table, as well as table 8－12. 8－13

单位:平方米,万元(sq. m,10000 yuan)

海曙区 Haishu	江东区 Jiangdong	江北区 Jiangbei	北仑区 Beilun	镇海区 Zhenhai	鄞州区 Yinzhou	余姚 Yuyao	慈溪 Cixi	奉化 Fenghua	象山 Xiangshan	宁海 Ninghai
2133741	**5259308**	**4334991**	**4533434**	**4068719**	**11374008**	**4631735**	**7103614**	**2373639**	**2169204**	**2018361**
441214	**1203858**	**1406316**	**1374297**	**1144259**	**2454362**	**1403065**	**1777406**	**538367**	**524123**	**487215**
142508	518832	672388	174214	246368	811345	233385	342683	232992	133215	133393
145067	423591	572955	959971	759714	1255235	885858	1164820	234400	306678	262086
30801	40447	36953	93112	49136	187384	161139	147001	33358	31385	16003
2310	8524	15094	23526	9354	50598	33350	14046	3283	2989	1020
263036	731296	781314	297688	326055	961145	322718	451539	267326	183071	208106
173164	637614	674487	762716	775194	1519677	775297	1230861	376104	377440	248950
134852	152033	163108	120278	58594	172925	33843	25652	9996	11151	17608
40670	123199	172630	246147	121382	399578	288464	187996	53819	50452	79036
92528	291012	396091	245156	189089	362182	305461	332897	98448	85080	141621
353028	291330	361994	1105470	999543	840425	1086367	719936	181672	215197	150501
66348	129899	282147	667532	98161	548080	174420	586702	29665	445716	174407
6874	27052	134808	869156	104589	352550	253446	147057	50346	359148	15782
4812	31586	69303	101622	53616	224893	110507	36337	39408	95337	4362
745025	1987872	1667825	1656863	1459021	4229976	1665758	2619447	654241	599169	605456
152325	299511	495839	284025	249542	705427	260522	1062861	55712	42052	69060
592700	**1688361**	**1171986**	**1372838**	**1209479**	**3524549**	**1405236**	**1556586**	**598529**	**557117**	**536396**
110994	432567	281999	337518	281085	839008	355303	360461	167245	157997	192801
		23905				2775				
382505	760219	692965	752990	630847	1182534	545597	750326	310245	250746	177247
99201	495575	173117	282330	297547	1503007	501561	445799	121039	148374	166348
53172	**148724**	**71046**	**306011**	**434149**	**600218**	**598221**	**600046**	**90576**	**124840**	**94353**

表8-12 各县(市)、区房地产企业房屋施工及竣工情况(2014) Buildings Construction and The Completed of Enterprises for Real Estate Development

指标名称	Indicators	全市 Total	市区 Urban Disctict
房屋施工面积	**Floor Space of Buildings Under Consrtuction**	**71751166**	**41728448**
1.住宅	Residential Buildings	38815346	21212837
2.办公楼	Office Buildings	5388407	4724855
3.商业营业用房	Buildings for Commercial Business	10031734	5710757
4.其他	Others	17515679	10079999
本年新开工房屋施工面积	**Floor Space of Newly Started of The Year**	**14373723**	**9616815**
1.住宅	Residential Buildings	7815663	5128067
2.办公楼	Office Buildings	961483	777882
3.商业营业用房	Buildings for Commercial Business	1954728	1386075
4.其他	Others	3641849	2324791
房屋竣工面积	**Floor Space of Buildings Completed**	**12137922**	**7238362**
#不可销售面积	Floor Space for Connot	2563533	1798811
1.住宅	Residential Buildings	6975086	4042081
2.办公楼	Office Buildings	966038	819437
3.商业营业用房	Buildings for Commercial Business	1360177	645968
4.其他	Others	2836621	1730876
商品住宅竣工套数(套)	**Completed Residencial House (flat)**	**53100**	**31554**
竣工房屋价值(万元)	**Value of Buildings Completed(10000 yuan)**	**5242488**	**3290255**
1.住宅	Residential Buildings	3129704	1938600
2.办公楼	Office Buildings	394165	328439
3.商业营业用房	Buildings for Commercial Business	724851	361642
4.其他	Others	993768	661574
出租房屋面积	**Floor Space of Lease House**	**316680**	**298983**
1.住宅	Residential Buildings		
2.办公楼	Office Buildings	79188	79188
3.商业营业用房	Buildings for Commercial Business	203501	186004
4.其他	Others	33991	33791
待售面积	**Floor Space of Vacant Building**	**6523286**	**3757188**
1.住宅	Residential Buildings	3401528	1653213
2.办公楼	Office Buildings	662128	596694
3.商业营业用房	Buildings for Commercial Business	1403364	847630
4.其他	Others	1056266	659651

单位：平方米，万元(sq. m，10000 yuan)

	海曙区 Haishu	江东区 Jiangdong	江北区 Jiangbei	北仑区 Beilun	镇海区 Zhenhai	鄞州区 Yinzhou	余姚 Yuyao	慈溪 Cixi	奉化 Fenghua	象山 Xiangshan	宁海 Ninghai
	1957099	**5425213**	**4255148**	**8524285**	**7445998**	**14120705**	**7613271**	**11488936**	**3000395**	**3750874**	**4169242**
	952907	1791114	1844789	4693091	4451048	7479888	4213077	6626442	2191183	2469147	2102660
	320499	965590	737094	757002	539578	1405092	74144	261095	19505	99454	209354
	193518	1002303	467053	1058511	796964	2192408	1395825	1739927	316831	297704	570690
	490175	1666206	1206212	2015681	1658408	3043317	1930225	2861472	472876	884569	1286538
	209063	**1192598**	**1277171**	**1694201**	**1130637**	**4113145**	**954027**	**825794**	**737770**	**884234**	**1355083**
	106832	517663	456387	1121243	541236	2384706	560176	669989	498468	592212	366751
	32675	158388	256894	9881	66898	253146	10968	14960	836	31051	125786
	17006	201144	185265	150324	295596	536740	135649	60147	48306	60924	263627
	52550	315403	378625	412753	226907	938553	247234	80698	190160	200047	598919
	777207	**556397**	**758656**	**2050994**	**1941751**	**1153357**	**2120367**	**1314472**	**339190**	**580230**	**545301**
	135331	125653	183347	572868	650381	131231	423945	116102	32763	150072	41840
	468254	233155	491348	1173001	1168273	508050	1172793	871716	206940	365124	316432
	60496	108776	79461	107767	183850	279087		65737		20929	59935
	57147	65745	6655	303226	138035	75160	526873	51839	95841	35088	4568
	191310	148721	181192	467000	451593	291060	420701	325180	36409	159089	164366
	3790	**1437**	**2885**	**9574**	**9981**	**3887**	**8855**	**5430**	**1975**	**3291**	**1995**
	325337	**225470**	**270846**	**1052632**	**856151**	**559819**	**885668**	**696915**	**63180**	**175040**	**131430**
	177824	87991	177277	633548	566353	295607	480705	495217	18353	106259	90570
	34530	46288	27363	28404	83279	108575		38804		8291	18631
	40876	28089	2259	176997	57523	55898	257091	60598	32921	11614	985
	72107	63102	63947	213683	148996	99739	147872	102296	11906	48876	21244
	28766	**193577**	**6680**	**957**	**8240**	**60763**	**15978**			**1719**	
	6140	50914	1568			20566					
	22551	136347	4792	957	8240	13117	15778			1719	
	75	6316	320			27080	200				
	299884	**531143**	**394477**	**1112157**	**701394**	**718133**	**973113**	**833523**	**317065**	**276436**	**365961**
	29930	154451	193034	617030	316889	341879	503519	565255	247083	205976	226482
	67255	168858	74809	114563	97233	73976	1712	60550		2320	852
	132774	113601	49470	191643	165143	194999	336564	108163	57638	50590	2779
	69925	94233	77164	188921	122129	107279	131318	99555	12344	17550	135848

表8－13 各县(市)、区房地产企业房屋销售情况(2014)
Building Sale Situation of Enterprises for Real Estate Development

指标名称	Indicators	宁波市 Total	市区 Urban Disctict
商品房销售面积	**Floor Space of Building Sold**	**6988444**	**4404176**
1. 住宅	Residential Buildings	5767488	3622723
2. 办公楼	Office Buildings	430739	351316
3. 商业营业用房	Buildings for Commercial Business	504786	268711
4. 其他	Others	285431	161426
现房销售面积	Floor Space of Completed Building	1551999	947844
1. 住宅	Residential Buildings	1059278	620231
2. 办公楼	Office Buildings	171797	121247
3. 商业营业用房	Buildings for Commercial Business	189693	101993
4. 其他	Others	131231	104373
期房销售面积	Floor Space of Forward Delivery Building	5436445	3456332
1. 住宅	Residential Buildings	4708210	3002492
2. 办公楼	Office Buildings	258942	230069
3. 商业营业用房	Buildings for Commercial Business	315093	166718
4. 其他	Others	154200	57053
商品房销售额	**Sales Volume of Commercial Buildings**	**7448682**	**5180378**
1. 住宅	Residential Buildings	6202997	4346270
2. 办公楼	Office Buildings	381499	329911
3. 商业营业用房	Buildings for Commercial Business	654856	378356
4. 其他	Others	209330	125841
现房销售额	Sales Volume of Completed Building	1515762	984747
1. 住宅	Residential Buildings	1083037	684045
2. 办公楼	Office Buildings	130995	99001
3. 商业营业用房	Buildings for Commercial Business	201625	115243
4. 其他	Others	100105	86458
期房销售额	**Sales Volume of Forward Delivery Building**	**5932920**	**4195631**
1. 住宅	Residential Buildings	5119960	3662225
2. 办公楼	Office Buildings	250504	230910
3. 商业营业用房	Buildings for Commercial Business	453231	263113
4. 其他	Others	109225	39383

单位:平方米,万元(sq. m,10000 yuan)

海曙区 Haishu	江东区 Jiangdong	江北区 Jiangbei	北仑区 Beilun	镇海区 Zhenhai	鄞州区 Yinzhou	余姚 Yuyao	慈溪 Cixi	奉化 Fenghua	象山 Xiangshan	宁海 Ninghai
250914	**459591**	**442018**	**856940**	**545202**	**1849511**	**810846**	**799775**	**250833**	**324446**	**398368**
112659	361070	403395	707486	402729	1635384	640391	660147	219974	315304	308949
87410	47208	13361	74008	35847	93482	17461	56658		1255	4049
24333	37340	13164	31826	73830	88218	100353	41891	23146	3983	66702
26512	13973	12098	43620	32796	32427	52641	41079	7713	3904	18668
79241	67374	78760	222749	233567	266153	209270	209135	55873	53614	76263
60694	37378	70116	134985	141843	175215	138139	136336	49434	52652	62486
8599	12369	758	39298	34338	25885		46501			4049
4714	11966	570	15319	27758	41666	58491	22553	6169	487	
5234	5661	7316	33147	29628	23387	12640	3745	270	475	9728
171673	392217	363258	634191	311635	1583358	601576	590640	194960	270832	322105
51965	323692	333279	572501	260886	1460169	502252	523811	170540	262652	246463
78811	34839	12603	34710	1509	67597	17461	10157		1255	
19619	25374	12594	16507	46072	46552	41862	19338	16977	3496	66702
21278	8312	4782	10473	3168	9040	40001	37334	7443	3429	8940
351838	**862319**	**666861**	**614967**	**446972**	**2237421**	**680193**	**681013**	**244408**	**340079**	**322611**
199432	711713	616795	487216	328540	2002574	527368	549219	216113	331197	232830
92294	56105	13786	45759	26036	95931	10593	36021		1006	3968
52712	80075	26488	24483	76370	118228	101934	61292	25913	6320	81041
7400	14426	9792	57509	16026	20688	40298	34481	2382	1556	4772
109378	88616	123003	178562	154314	330874	147993	207964	55088	56472	63498
83997	50867	114662	102613	88347	243559	99735	139216	47835	55373	56833
9892	16465	894	21909	25284	24557		28026			3968
11618	16997	1247	10477	26103	48801	40766	37600	7166	850	
3871	4287	6200	43563	14580	13957	7492	3122	87	249	2697
242460	**773703**	**543858**	**436405**	**292658**	**1906547**	**532200**	**473049**	**189320**	**283607**	**259113**
115435	660846	502133	384603	240193	1759015	427633	410003	168278	275824	175997
82402	39640	12892	23850	752	71374	10593	7995		1006	
41094	63078	25241	14006	50267	69427	61168	23692	18747	5470	81041
3529	10139	3592	13946	1446	6731	32806	31359	2295	1307	2075

表8－14 各县(市)农村非农户固定资产投资主要指标(2014)
Main Indicators of Investment in Fixed Assets of Non－peasant Households in Rural Area by Region

指标	Indicators	全市 Total
本年完成投资	**Finished Investment of This Year**	**9719254**
按国民经济行业分	**By Sector**	
农林牧渔业	Framing, Forestry, Animal Husbandry and Fishery	172510
采矿业	Mining and Quarrying	11202
制造业	Manufacuring	5299767
电力、燃气及水的生产和供应业	Electric Power, Gas and Water Production and Supply	452721
建筑业	Construction	5342
批发和零售业	Wholesale and Retail Trade	242017
交通运输、仓储和邮政业	Transportation, Storage and Post	666386
住宿和餐饮业	Hotel and Catering Services	177087
信息传输、软件和信息技术服务业	Information Transmission, Software and Information Technology Services	25288
金融业	Financial Industries	11515
房地产业	Real Estate Industries	1253879
租赁和商务服务业	Leasing and Business Service Industries	64863
科学研究和技术服务业	The Scientific Research and Techinical Services	9957
水利、环境和公共设施管理业	Water Conservancy, Environment and Public Facility Management	889709
居民服务、修理和其他服务业	Residents Service, Repair and Other Services	10863
教育	Education	201174
卫生和社会工作	Health and Social Work	95142
文化、体育和娱乐业	Culture, Sports and Entertainment	78039
公共管理、社会保障和社会组织	Public Management, Social Security and Social Organization	51793

注：本表按2011年修订的国民经济行业标准统计。

Note: Statistics in this table are classified as the national economic category that was modified in 2011.

单位:万元(10000 yuan)

市区 Urban Disctict	#鄞州 Yinzhou	余姚 Yuyao	慈溪 Cixi	奉化 Fenghua	象山 Xiangshan	宁海 Ninghai
4083547	**2298654**	**2247263**	**1514441**	**467365**	**764890**	**641748**
3115	3115	33926	17529	54962	29900	33078
9853	9853				799	550
2350596	1334630	1326052	692943	86477	380357	463342
130637	60261	167039	13210	23257	82028	36550
4342	944	1000				
100862	20246	56497	58323	700	10055	15580
178740	145189	92917	264415	98028	30634	1652
71402	44326	60791		4053	12705	28136
898			9030			15360
11515	6232					
578422	384353	224682	251886	113850	53362	31677
4157	4157	39120	17580			4006
6009	1318			3948		
460995	196137	140752	108795	63378	110023	5766
6158	1		2695		2010	
88787	61725	63155	32673	10288	5480	791
30738	6372	13669	37309	1900	11253	273
29888	4703	6167	7474	1611	28801	4098
16433	15092	21496	579	4913	7483	889

表8－15 部分年份城镇以上固定资产投资主要指标

Main Indicators of Investment in Fixed Assets of City and Town Level and Above in Partial Years

单位：万元(10000 yuan)

指标	Indicators	2010	2011	2012	2013	2014
计划总投资	**Total Investment of Plan**	**44888914**	**47604813**	**53339541**	**59425031**	**57933561**
累计完成投资	**Accumulative Finished Investment**	**28253456**	**29262704**	**33757190**	**40548529**	**38867982**
本年完成投资	**Finished Investment of This Year**	11182943	12129369	14592260	15947207	16893982
按经济注册类型分	**By Registration Status**					
国有经济	State－Owned Units	5804442	6119819	7536985	7736160	8361097
集体经济	Collective－owned Units	95167	123743	197593	191237	151792
股份有限公司	Share－holding Corporation Units	362382	1372970	2001386	2494453	2205280
其他有限责任公司	Other Limited Liability Corporations	1037261	332185	312382	457394	597044
外商投资经济	Foreign Investment	991368	593015	775985	1247695	1561799
港澳台投资经济	HongKong, Macao and Taiwan Funded	492546	1098615	776115	1081757	1350281
其他经济	Others	2399777				
按隶属关系分	**By Administrative Relationship**					
中央	Central Government		504730	570359	363148	345343
省	Province		91767	98111	84923	267369
省辖市	Municipalities		2679433	2806848	2132136	2225585
县(市)、区	Counties and Districts		3456025	4884449	5776578	5414187
其他	Others		5397414	6232493	7590422	8641498
按建设性质分	**By Type of Construction**					
新建	New Construction	5532359	6171252	7532996	7908261	7617628
扩建	Expansion	2783093	3419622	3975993	4840637	5290560
改建	Reconstruction	1005946	763358	1073554	919695	1139200
其他	Others	1861545				
按构成分	**By Use of Funds**					
建筑工程	Construction	6031102	6828481	8244176	9058625	9174203
安装工程	Installation	753456	845852	877726	984366	522949
设备工器具购置	Purchase of Equipment and Instruments	2077616	1928683	2215934	2535697	3847245
其他费用	Others	2320769	2526353	3254424	3368519	3349585
按资金来源分	**By Source of Funds**					
#国家预算资金	State Budget	593052	733398	1292692	1730012	1418949
国内贷款	Domestic Loans	2574096	2572961	2838994	2654528	3069131
利用外资	Foreign Investment	556315	556010	542222	678476	432958
自筹资金	Self－Financed Capital	6684896	7382210	8942861	10113689	11816154

表8-16 部分年份建筑业生产经营及主要财务指标
Basic Statistics and Main Financial Indicators of Construction Enterprises in Partial Years

单位:万元(10000 yuan)

指标	Indicators	2011	2012	2013	2014
企业个数(家)	**Number of Enterprises (unit)**	**844**	**922**	**976**	**986**
建筑业总产值	**Gross Output Value of Construction**	**19333581**	**25091179**	**31354555**	**37131235**
1.建筑工程	Construction	17219536	22149575	27745638	32690737
2.安装工程	Installation	1585508	2205438	2699734	3435898
3.其他	Building Repair and Maintenance	528536	736167	909183	1004600
竣工产值	Output Value of Buildings Completed	10890263	13418936	18465941	21963605
房屋建筑施工面积(万平方米)	Floor Space of Buildings Under Construction (10000 sq. m)	18161	22343	25043	27350
房屋建筑竣工面积(万平方米)	Floor Space of Buildings Completed (10000 sq. m)	5180	6058	7842	8252
年末自有机械设备总台数(台)	Number of Machinery and Equipmen (year - end) (set)	111675	113171	122951	126337
年末自有机械设备总功率(万千瓦)	Total Power of Machinery and Equipment (10000kw)	200.62	203.23	235.32	272.31
年末自有机械设备净值	Net Value of Machinery and Equipment	580421	660815	684957	698445
计算劳动生产率的年平均人数(万人)	Average Employed Persons by Calculatied Labor Productivity(10000 persons)	76.96	89.04	98.76	115.2
年末资产负债	**Asset and Liabilities at Year - end**				
流动资产	Circulating Assets	9910592	1243742	14077843	15651990
固定资产小计	Fixed Assets	1138322	1326727	1415679	1395325
固定资产原价	Original Value of Fixed Assets	15562940	1786162	1933304	2108123
本年折旧	Depreciation in This Year	916184	136199	126002	144271
资产总计	Total Assets	121273097	15082502	16867867	19208318
流动负债	Liquid Liabilities	75386632	9396904	9803478	11381904
长期负债	Long - term Liabilities				
所有者权益	Creditors´Equity	41842087	5191820	5954929	7037525
损益及分配	**Expenditure, Income and Distribution**				
工程结算收入	Revenue of Project Settlement Accounts	14577208	17996050	22766196	25322165
工程结算成本	Costs of Project Settlement Accounts	12957730	15973781	20254742	22605266
工程结算税金及附加	Taxes and Extra Charges on Project Settlement Accounts	463273	588015	739751	821267
工程结算利润	Profits of Project Settlement Accounts	1116603	1386848	1771703	1895632

表8－17 建筑业企业生产情况(2014) Basic Statistics on Production of Construction Enterprises

指标	Indicators	企业个数(家) Number of Enterprises (unit)	建筑业总产值 Gross Output Value of Construction	在外省完成的产值 Output Value of Other Province
总计	**Total**	**986**	**37131235**	**15983452**
按登记注册类型分组	**By Registered Type**			
内资企业	Domestic Funded Enterprises	983	37098235	15980105
国有企业	State－owned Enterprises	5	101260	725
集体企业	Collective－oened Enterprises	3	9371	0
股份合作企业	Share－holding Cooperative Enterprises	2	221902	104202
有限责任公司	Limited Liability Corporations	97	4054602	1164703
股份有限公司	Share－holding Corporations Ltd.	18	8573569	6500922
私营企业	Private Enterprises	858	24137532	8209553
港、澳、台商投资企业	HongKong,Macro and Taiwan Funded	2	32865	3347
外商投资企业	Enterprises with Foreign Investment	1	134	
按建筑业行业分组	**By Sector**			
房屋和土木工程建筑业	Building and Civil Engineering	620	33814209	15158083
房屋工程建筑	Building	348	25558807	11532611
土木工程建筑	Civil Engineering	272	8255402	3625472
建筑安装业	Construction Installation	144	1682581	496436
建筑装饰业	Construction Decoration	175	1169396	131633
其他建筑业	Other Construction	10	48426	21261
按控股情况分组	**By Holding Status**			
国有控股	State－holding	40	2907531	862360
集体控股	Collective－holding	19	836977	141185
私人控股	Private－holding	921	33312599	14971456
港澳台控股	Hong Kong, Macao and Taiwan Holdings			
外商控股	Foreign－holding			
按企业资质等级分组	**By Qualification Criteria**			
施工总承包	Construc General Contractor	564	34061901	15359876
特级	Special Class	6	8635099	5430042
一级	First Class	101	17622732	8314027
二级	Second Class	145	4711519	1286337
三级	Third Class	312	3092552	329471
专业承包	Special General Contractor	422	3069334	623576
一级	First Class	60	1858636	459766
二级	Second Class	110	633778	103895
三级	Third Class	252	576920	59914

单位:万元(10000 yuan)

建筑业总产值按构成分			承包工程完成产值 Gross Output Value of Contract Project			竣工产值 Output Value of Buildings Completed
1. 建筑工程 Construction	2. 安装工程 Installation	3. 其他 Others	1. 直接从建设单位承揽工程 Contract Project from Construction Unit Directly	其中 of Which 自行完成 Finish by Oneself	2. 从建设单位以外承揽工程 Contract Project Outside Construction Unit	
32690737	**3435898**	**1004600**	**36100027**	**35486696**	**1644540**	**21963605**
32661102	3435898	1001235	36067027	35453696	1644540	21963283
101260			94073	94073	7187	77652
6237	3135		9371	9371		12004
221902			221902	221902		159365
2940506	912265	201831	4151883	3845538	209063	1936598
7282452	940221	350896	8474507	8265852	307717	5658364
22108745	1580278	448508	23115291	23016959	1120572	14119300
29500		3365	32865	32865		188
134			134	134		134
31039954	2001487	772768	32980556	32664678	1149531	20050195
23683528	1335640	539639	25175253	24908002	650805	14954676
7356426	665847	233130	7805303	7756676	498726	5095519
256825	1250668	175089	1544424	1259458	423124	946207
1014377	117785	37235	1158615	1147316	22080	796601
45383	3043		46113	45605	2821	45328
2105328	634903	167300	2887196	2619443	288089	1143564
425477	399116	12384	866584	836863	114	661866
30096160	2395319	821121	32284483	31977497	1335102	20112590
30768715	2458681	834505	33373537	32851024	1210877	19984949
7896319	599448	139333	8635099	8537088	98012	5070749
15914416	1224054	484261	17224181	16820518	802215	10118200
4404473	194521	112524	4542727	4531154	180365	2665795
2553507	440658	98387	2971530	2962266	130286	2130205
1922022	977217	170095	2726489	2635671	433663	1978656
1260262	501417	96957	1584120	1543098	315538	1086777
352632	242142	39004	617191	594717	39061	481817
309128	233658	34134	525179	497857	79064	410062

表 8－17 续表 Continued

指标	Indicators	房屋建筑施工面积（平方米）Floor Space Under Construction (sq. m)	其中 of Which #本年新开工 Newly Operating Projects in this Year	#投标承包面积 Floor Space of Biding System
总计	**Total**	**273500361**	**107310475**	**204933860**
按登记注册类型分组	**By Registered Type**			
内资企业	Domestic Funded Enterprises	273500361	107310475	204933860
国有企业	State－owned Enterprises			
集体企业	Collective－oened Enterprises			
股份合作企业	Share－holding Cooperative Enterprises	2080919	1100577	2080919
有限责任公司	Limited Liability Corporations	13655140	5272018	10321023
股份有限公司	Share－holding Corporations Ltd.	74681525	21152589	63057502
私营企业	Private Enterprises	183082777	79785291	129474416
港、澳、台商投资企业	HongKong, Macro and Taiwan Funded			
外商投资企业	Enterprises with Foreign Investment			
按建筑业行业分组	**By Sector**			
房屋和土木工程建筑业	Building and Civil Engineering	270934636	105817272	203265576
房屋工程建筑	Building	259833850	101354352	194643808
土木工程建筑	Civil Engineering	11100786	4462920	8621768
建筑安装业	Construction Installation	1175920	726078	910394
建筑装饰业	Construction Decoration	174167	102485	
其他建筑业	Other Construction	20000	10000	5000
按控股情况分组	**By Holding Status**			
国有控股	State－holding	6446008	1307686	6035116
集体控股	Collective－holding	3999086	1926807	3998830
私人控股	Private－holding	262365893	103677417	194801110
港澳台控股	Hongkong, Macao&Taiwan－holding			
外商控股	Foreign－holding			
按企业资质等级分组	**By Qualification Criteria**			
施工总承包	Construc General Contractor	265884041	102370168	202690791
特级	Special Grade	81485691	19531486	70345337
一级	First Grade	138658490	58737506	110244380
二级	Second Grade	28617645	14804952	14957431
三级	Third Grade	17122215	9296224	7143643
专业承包	Special General Contractor	7616320	4940307	2243069
一级	First Grade	5027757	3294417	1274847
二级	Second Grade	1816589	1153546	546435
三级	Third Grade	771974	492344	421787

房屋建筑竣工面积（平方米）Floor Space Completed (sq. m)	竣工房屋价值（万元）Value of Completed Building (10000yuan)	年末自有机械设备总台数（台）Number of Machinery and Equipment (year – end) (set)	年末自有机械设备总功率（千瓦）Total Power of Machinery and Equipment (kw)	年末自有机械设备净值（万元）Net Value of Machinery and Equipment (10000yuan)	年末人数（人）Employed Persons at Year – end (person)	计算劳动生产率的年平均人员（人）Average Employed Persons by Calculatied Labor Productivity (person)
82517081	**14876426**	**126337**	**2723060**	**698445**	**1124216**	**1151645**
82517081	14876426	126330	2722599	698424	1123517	1150992
		363	15423	940	3382	3514
		30	530	6	333	307
958567	158463	3834	11852	1661	4042	4030
3770943	680208	12935	283234	137938	61421	106838
18782446	4333176	13865	333071	73830	235601	220262
59005125	9704579	95303	2078489	484051	818738	816041
		7	461	21	676	625
					23	28
81817755	14782690	106057	2453224	643233	1012237	1046911
77113986	13868656	78801	1495132	322074	808618	808792
4703769	914034	27256	958092	321159	203619	238119
484128	62842	11872	145615	34183	40482	43143
119714	14603	7113	69382	10567	51895	45512
		327	7868	575	1982	1704
1150368	261406	9194	201601	108288	26995	70922
1391585	245238	6382	53685	11838	14854	23569
79715864	14350167	110525	2455321	571519	1080876	1055255
77815390	14566619	102983	2374077	593207	1012193	1042921
17368889	3970495	11384	222674	76749	214288	234362
41648195	8062479	49535	1199568	270680	494949	525402
10959623	1574184	25507	488620	130122	189381	170402
7838683	959461	16557	463215	115656	113575	112755
4701691	309807	23354	348983	105238	112023	108724
3042147	207066	7526	132135	22078	66761	65907
1384167	70229	10298	72297	30472	25346	21862
275377	32512	5530	144551	52689	19916	20955

表 8－18　建筑业企业财务情况(2014)
Main Financial Indicators of Construction Enterprises

指标	Indicators	年末资产负债		
		资产合计 Total Assets	流动资产合计 Circulating Assets	固定资产合计 Fixed Assets
总计	**Total**	**19208318**	**15651990**	**1395325**
按登记注册类型分组	**By Registered Type**			
内资企业	Domestic Funded Enterprises	19146837	15595323	1392748
国有企业	State－owned Enterprises	247129	234646	3375
集体企业	Collective－oened Enterprises	23925	13004	2420
股份合作企业	Share－holding Cooperative Enterprises	37011	33975	1727
有限责任公司	Limited Liability Corporations	3318795	2796923	298041
股份有限公司	Share－holding Corporations Ltd.	4280220	3594603	124139
私营企业	Private Enterprises	11239757	8922173	963046
港、澳、台商投资企业	HongKong,Macro and Taiwan Funded	59931	55207	2486
外商投资企业	Enterprises with Foreign Investment	1550	1460	91
按建筑业行业分组	By Sector			
房屋和土木工程建筑业	Building and Civil Engineering	16774721	13602119	1183475
房屋工程建筑	Building	10692419	9246780	627423
土木工程建筑	Civil Engineering	6082302	4355339	556053
建筑安装业	Construction Installation	1487043	1251673	128516
建筑装饰业	Construction Decoration	624546	543423	50704
其他建筑业	Other Construction	37111	28461	7834
按控股情况分	**By Holding Status**			
国有控股	State－holding	2715415	2370628	214178
集体控股	Collective－holding	451264	362459	46928
私人控股	Private－holding	15930803	12826550	1121086
港澳台控股	Hong Kong, Macao and Taiwan Holdings			
外商控股	Foreign－holding			
按企业资质等级分组	**By Qualification Criteria**			
施工总承包	Construc General Contractor	16769747	13682308	1112363
特级	Special Class	4497616	3898009	124990
一级	First Class	7592768	5914807	511190
二级	Second Class	2590265	2148575	239988
三级	Third Class	2089098	1720917	236196
专业承包	Special General Contractor	2438570	1969681	282963
一级	First Class	1117193	965338	83927
二级	Second Class	557265	411071	85407
三级	Third Class	764113	593273	113629

单位:万元(10000 yuan)

Total Assets and Liabilities at Year - end			损益及分配 Expenditure, Income and Distribution		
#本年折旧 Depreciation in this year	负债合计 Current Liabilities	所有者权益 Creditors' Equity	工程结算收入 Revenue of Project Settlement Accounts	工程结算成本 Costs of Project Settlement Accounts	工程结算税金及附加 Taxes and Extra Charges on Project Settlement Accounts
144271	**12170792**	**7037525**	**25322165**	**22605266**	**821267**
143985	12111841	7034996	25291406	22573504	820226
444	213962	33167	91926	84327	2234
892	17807	6118	12197	10593	308
215	18410	18601	108885	100522	3555
20624	2376984	941812	3528788	3164176	80077
24146	3180834	1099386	4036737	3665429	126506
97664	6303845	4935912	17512873	15548458	607545
277	57883	2048	30625	31661	1036
9	1068	482	134	102	5
119041	10621740	6152981	22247315	19985709	746139
49989	6968693	3723726	16010157	14497536	543935
69052	3653047	2429256	6237158	5488174	202204
12777	1005875	481168	1801679	1550066	32342
5687	356487	268059	858542	720523	28949
3916	17592	19519	44457	33281	1823
12787	2037030	678385	2667486	2412677	47997
5169	323693	127571	626721	559557	19696
124580	9713489	6217314	21968883	19580280	752627
111217	10607764	6161984	22806457	20480376	750393
10897	3510423	987193	4766072	4381900	147803
54128	4372270	3220498	11848450	10620619	377303
19471	1496587	1093678	3617307	3236054	129727
26722	1228484	860614	2574629	2241804	95559
33054	1563028	875542	2515708	2124890	70874
8319	769246	347947	1346826	1170373	36931
7146	305012	252252	564619	460252	15989
17588	488770	275343	604263	494265	17955

表 8 – 18 续表 Continued

		损益及分配	
		工程结算利润 Profits of Project Settlement Accounts	其他业务利润 Other Profits from Business
总计	**Total**	**1895632**	**37580**
按登记注册类型分组	**By Registered Type**		
内资企业	Domestic Funded Enterprises	1897676	37580
国有企业	State – owned Enterprises	5365	202
集体企业	Collective – oened Enterprises	1296	
股份合作企业	Share – holding Cooperative Enterprises	4808	413
有限责任公司	Limited Liability Corporations	284535	28092
股份有限公司	Share – holding Corporations Ltd.	244802	1681
私营企业	Private Enterprises	1356871	7192
港、澳、台商投资企业	HongKong, Macro and Taiwan Funded	–2071	
外商投资企业	Enterprises with Foreign Investment	27	
按建筑业行业中类分组	**By Sector**		
房屋和土木工程建筑业	Building and Civil Engineering	1515467	31908
房屋工程建筑	Building	968687	15703
土木工程建筑	Civil Engineering	546780	16205
建筑安装业	Construction Installation	219272	2177
建筑装饰业	Construction Decoration	109071	1847
其他建筑业	Other Construction	9352	1611
按控股情况分	**By Holding Status**		
国有控股	State – holding	206812	5264
集体控股	Collective – holding	47468	12819
私人控股	Private – holding	1635976	19397
港澳台控股	Hong Kong, Macao and Taiwan Holdings		
外商控股	Foreign – holding		
按企业资质等级分组	**By Qualification Criteria**		
施工总承包	Construc General Contractor	1575689	31759
特级	Special Grade	236369	1280
一级	First Grade	850528	16770
二级	Second Grade	251526	13012
三级	Third Grade	237266	697
专业承包	Special General Contractor	319944	5822
一级	First Grade	139522	3210
二级	Second Grade	88379	766
三级	Third Grade	92043	1846

单位:万元(10000 yuan)

Expenditure, Incomeand Distribution				应付职工薪酬 Employee Compensation Payable
管理费用 Management Expense	财务费用 Financial Expense	营业利润 Operating Profits	利润总额 Total Profits	
618406	**201143**	**1046351**	**1065936**	**5107740**
616475	200155	1051314	1070896	5102592
3416	85	2255	2305	11416
846	-144	379	380	2066
1034	-1065	5739	6483	33461
127478	11677	169490	177674	606355
62311	55025	130394	133273	1157571
421390	134578	743056	750781	3291722
1900	988	-4960	-4957	4869
30		-3	-3	279
446169	180996	879559	891766	4618605
243064	128716	587006	592272	3515430
203105	52280	292552	299494	1103175
104351	8497	101161	103037	236139
46176	7870	44780	48061	183592
2263	34	2892	3015	5188
96205	7509	108434	114617	429951
26291	-2281	35372	36421	117379
492380	193985	902827	914938	4552081
475321	168886	923723	936107	4655125
63384	46357	114607	119035	999550
242838	89304	532246	536162	2510913
83717	23163	158138	160612	693506
85382	10062	118732	120298	451156
143085	32257	122628	129829	452615
57969	16335	55554	58073	279693
37843	6369	36724	38049	87133
47274	9553	30351	33707	85788

表 8－19 新增生产能力或效益(2014)
Newly Increase Production Capacity or Benefit

指标	单位	Indicators	Unit	本年新增 Added at this Year
裂化设备能力	处理万吨/年	Cracker	10000 tons/year	4
钢材	万吨/年	Steels	10000 tons/year	2076.4
铜冶炼	吨/年	Copper smelting	tones/year	200000
铜加工材	吨/年	Copper	tones/year	24600
水力发电	万千瓦	Hydro－electric power	10000 kw	0.05
火力发电	万千瓦	Thermal power	10000 kw	0.75
风力发电	万千瓦	Wind Power	10000 kw	9952.65
太阳能发电	万千瓦	Solar power	10000 kw	0.4
其他发电	万千瓦	Other power	10000 kw	25000
输电线路长度(11 万伏及以上)	公里	Length of Transmission Lines (110,000 Volts and Above)	kilometer	78.51
塑料树脂及共聚物	吨/年	Plastic Resin and Copolymer	tons/year	1056017
合成橡胶	吨/年	Synthetic rubber	tons/year	30800
化学纤维	吨/年	Chemical Fiber	tons/year	1087200
棉纺锭	锭	Cotton Spindles	Spindles	245000
毛纺锭	锭	Wool spindles	Spindles	5000
家用电冰箱	万台/年	Household Refrigerators	10000 units/year	140
新建公路	公里	New Highway	kilometer	130.43
一级公路	公里	First Standard Road	kilometer	1
二级公路	公里	Second Standard Road	kilometer	9.6
改建公路	公里	Road Reconstruction	kilometer	209.7
二级公路	公里	Second Standard Road	kilometer	65.05
新建独立公路桥梁	延长米	New Highway Bridge	meter	508
新建独立公路桥梁	座	New Highway Bridge	units	3
新(扩)建港口码头	年吞吐量:万吨	New (extension) port	Annual throughput: tons	2885
新(扩)建港口码头	年吞吐量:标准集装箱	New (extension) port	Annual throughput: standard containers	60003
新(扩)建港口码头	泊位:个	New (extension) port	units	5
#新(扩)建沿海港口码头	年吞吐量:万吨	New (extension) port	Annual throughput: tons	2885
新(扩)建沿海港口码头	泊位:个米	New(extension) port	units	5
新(扩)建公路客、货运站	个	New (Expanding) Existing Road Passenger and Freight Station	units	1
新(扩)建公路客、货运站	平方米	New (Expanding) Existing Road Passenger and Freight Station	square meters	1081
城市自来水供水能力	万吨/日	Tap Water Supply Capacity	10000 tons/day	8
城市污水处理能力	万吨/日	Urban Sewage Treatment Capacity	10000 tons/day	4.68

表8-20 本年完成建筑业总产值前20位企业(2014) The Top 20 Enterprises of Completed Total Output Value for Construction Industry

企业名称 Name of Enterprises	资质等级 Grade of Natural Endowments
龙元建设集团股份有限公司 Longyuan Construction Group Co. ,Ltd.	房屋建筑工程施工总承包特级 Whole Contract To Project of Building Construction by Special Grade
华丰建设股份有限公司 Ningbo Huafeng Construction Group Co. ,Ltd.	房屋建筑工程施工总承包特级 Whole Contract To Project of Building Construction by Special Grade
宏润建设集团股份有限公司 Hongrun Construction Group Co. ,Ltd.	市政工程施工总承包壹级 Whole Contract To Municipal Engineering Construction by First Grade
宁波建工集团有限公司 Ningbo Construction And Industry Group Co. ,Ltd.	房屋建筑工程施工总承包特级 Whole Contract To Project of Building Construction by Special Grade
浙江省二建建设集团有限公司 Zhejiang No. 2 Construction Group Co. ,Ltd.	房屋建筑工程施工总承包特级 Whole Contract To Project of Building Construction by Special Grade
中达建设集团股份有限公司 Zhongda Construction Group Co. ,Ltd.	房屋建筑工程施工总承包特级 Whole Contract To Project of Building Construction by Special Grade
浙江欣捷建设有限公司 Zhe Jiang Xinjie Construction Co. ,Ltd.	房屋建筑工程施工总承包壹级 Whole Contract To Project of Building Construction by First Grade
宁波市建设集团股份有限公司 Ningbo Construction Group Co. ,Ltd.	房屋建筑工程施工总承包壹级 Whole Contract To Project of Building Construction by First Grade
华锦建设股份有限公司 Huajing Construction Co. ,Ltd.	房屋建筑工程施工总承包壹级 Whole Contract To Project of Building Construction by First Grade
浙江建安实业集团股份有限公司 Zhejiang Jian'an Industry Group Ltd.	房屋建筑工程施工总承包壹级 Whole Contract To Project of Building Construction by First Grade
浙江天元建设(集团)股份有限公司 Zhejiang Tianyuan (Group) Co. , Ltd.	房屋建筑工程施工总承包壹级 Whole Contract To Project of Building Construction by First Grade
浙江新中源建设有限公司 Zhejiang New Zhongyuan Construction Co. ,Ltd.	房屋建筑工程施工总承包壹级 Whole Contract To Project of Building Construction by First Grade
大荣建设有限公司 Darong Construction Engineering Co. ,Ltd.	房屋建筑工程施工总承包壹级 Whole Contract To Project of Building Construction by First Grade
海达建设集团有限公司 Haida Construction Group Co. , Ltd.	房屋建筑工程施工总承包壹级 Whole Contract To Project of Building Construction by First Grade
华恒建设集团有限公司 Huaheng Construction Group Co. , Ltd.	房屋建筑工程施工总承包壹级 Whole Contract To Project of Building Construction by First Grade
浙江万华建设有限公司 zhejiang wanhua Construction Co. ,Ltd.	房屋建筑工程施工总承包壹级 Whole Contract To Project of Building Construction by First Grade
浙江银晨集团有限公司 zhejiang yinchen Construction Group Co. , Ltd.	房屋建筑工程施工总承包贰级 Whole Contract To Project of Building Construction by second Grade
中石化宁波工程有限公司 sinapec ningboengineering Co. , Ltd.	化工石油工程施工总承包一级 Chemical petroleum engineering total construction by First Grade
博宏恒基集团有限公司 Bohohk Group Co. ,Ltd	房屋建筑工程施工总承包壹级 Whole Contract To Project of Building Construction by First Grade
宁波市政工程建设集团有限公司 Ningbo Municipal Engineering Construction Group Co. ,Ltd.	市政工程施工总承包壹级 Whole Contract To Municipal Engineering Construction by First Grade
浙江新曙光建设有限公司 shuguang holdings Co. , Ltd.	房屋建筑工程施工总承包壹级 Whole Contract To Project of Building Construction by First Grade

表8－21　1、2级资质等级房地产开发经营企业(2014)
Enterprises for Real Estate Developing & Managing with Certificate in First, Second Grade of Natural Endowments

企业名称	Name of Enterprises	资质等级 Grade of Natural Endowments
宁波信达中建置业有限公司	Ningbo Xinda Zhongjian Real Estate Co. ,Ltd.	1
宁波宁兴房地产开发集团有限公司	Ningbo Ningxing Real Estate Developing Co. ,Ltd.	1
宁波维科置业有限公司	Ningbo Veken Real Estate Co. ,Ltd.	1
宁波中房置业股份有限公司	Ningbo Zhongfang Real Estate Co. ,Ltd.	1
宁波房地产股份有限公司	Ningbo Real Estate Co. ,Ltd.	1
宁波银亿房地产开发有限公司	Ningbo Yingyi Real Estate Developing Co. ,Ltd.	1
宁波市交通房地产有限公司	Ningbo Jiaotong Real Estate Co. ,Ltd.	1
宁波市甬佳房地产开发有限公司	Ningbo Yongjia Real Estate Developing Co. ,Ltd.	1
仑江集团有限公司	Lun Jiang Group Co. ,Ltd.	1
宁波市镇海区住房发展投资有限公司	Ningbo Zhenhai House Developing & Investment Co,. Ltd.	1
宁波中万置业有限公司	Ningbo Zhongwan Properties Co. ,Ltd.	1
宁波华泰股份有限公司	Ningbo Huatai Co. ,Ltd.	1
雅戈尔置业控股有限公司	Youngor (Ningbo) Real Estate Co. ,Ltd.	1
宁波东方建设开发有限公司	Ningbo Dongfang Construction Development Co. ,Ltd.	1
宁波奥克斯置业有限公司	Ningbo Aux Ltd.	1
得力房地产有限公司	Ningbo Deli Real Estate Co. ,Ltd.	1
华丰置业有限公司	Huafeng Properties Co. ,Ltd.	1
宁波市五环房地产开发有限公司	Ningbo Wuhuan Estate Co. ,Ltd.	1
余姚市房地产开发经营有限公司	Yuyao Real Estate Developing Co. ,Ltd.	1
新中宇集团有限公司	Xin zhongyu Group Co. ,Ltd.	1
宁波舜大房地产开发有限公司	Ningbo Shunda Real Estate Developing Co. ,Ltd.	1
恒元置业有限公司	Hengyuan Properties Co. ,Ltd.	1
浙江兴润置业投资有限公司	Zhejiang Xingrun Real Estate Co. ,Ltd.	1
宁波金达利房地产开发集团有限公司	Kinderly Real Estate Developing Co. ,Ltd.	2
宁波联合建设开发有限公司	Ningbo Lianhe Construction Developing Co. ,Ltd.	2
宁波新园置业有限公司	Ningbo xinyuan Real Estate Co. ,Ltd.	2
宁波市宁丰三盛投资发展有限公司	Ningbo Ningfengsansheng Developing & Investment Co,. Ltd.	2
宁波教育实业集团育才建设开发有限公司	Ningbo Education Industrial Group Yucai Construction Development Co. ,Ltd	2
宁波开投置业有限公司	Ningbo Kaituo Properties Co. ,Ltd.	2
宁波新恒德置业有限公司	Ningbo Xinhengde Ltd.	2
宁波好阳光集团有限公司	Ningbo Good Sunshine Group Co. ,Ltd.	2
宁波东部新城开发投资有限公司	Ningbo Dongbuxincheng Developing & Investment Co,. Ltd.	2
宁波新都置业有限公司	Ningbo Xindu Properties Co. ,Ltd.	2
浙江山水房地产开发有限公司	Zhejiang landscape Real Estate Development Co. ,Ltd.	2
宁波市拓展房地产开发有限公司	Ningbo Tuozhan Real Estate Developing Co. ,Ltd.	2
宁波大榭房地产有限公司	Ningbo Daxie Estate Co. ,Ltd.	2
宁波市北仑华信置业有限公司	Ningbo Beilun Huaxin Properties Ltd.	2
宁波新隆房地产股份有限公司	Ningbo Xinlong Real Estate Co. ,Ltd.	2
宁波申洲置业有限公司	Ningbo Shenzhou Properties Ltd.	2
宁波经济技术开发区房地产总公司	Ningbo Economic and Technological Development Zone Real Estate Corporation	2
宁波市镇海茗园房地产开发有限公司	Ningbo Zhenhai Mingyuan Real Estate Co. ,Ltd.	2

表 8－21 续表 Continued

企业名称	Name of Enterprises	资质等级 Grade of Natural Endowments
宁波市镇海华鑫房地产开发有限公司	Ningbo Zhenhai Huaxin Real Estate Developing Co. ,Ltd.	2
宁波沧海新城房地产开发有限公司	Ningbo Canghai Xincheng Real Estate Developing Co. ,Ltd.	2
宁波富豪房地产开发有限公司	Ningbo Fuhao Real Estate Developing Co. ,Ltd.	2
浙江华茂置业发展有限公司	Zhejiang Huanmao Real Estate Development Co. ,Ltd.	2
宁波康园房地产开发有限公司	Ningbo Kangyuan Real Estate Development Co. ,Ltd.	2
宁波万科房地产开发有限公司	Ningbo Wanke Real Estate Development Co. ,Ltd.	2
宁波华垠房地产开发有限公司	Ningbo Huayin Real Estate Development Co. ,Ltd.	2
宁波和协拓展置业有限公司	Ningbo Hexie Real Estate Development Co. ,Ltd.	2
宁波布利杰置业发展有限责任公司	Ningbo Bulijie Real Estate Co. ,Ltd.	2
宁波广博建设开发有限公司	Ningbo Guangbo Real Estate Development Co. ,Ltd.	2
沧海控股集团有限公司	Ningbo Sea Holding Group Co. ,Ltd.	2
宁波市奥丽赛置业有限公司	Ningbo Aolisai Real Estate Co. ,Ltd.	2
宁波金沃房地产开发有限公司	Ningbo Jinwo Real Estate Development Co. ,Ltd.	2
宁波华龙投资建设开发有限公司	Ningbo Hualong Investment Construction and Development Co. ,Ltd.	2
宁波鸿泰置业有限公司	Ningbo Hongtai Real Estate Co. ,Ltd.	2
象山县地产房产开发总公司	Xiangshan Real Estate Developing Corporation	2
象山县城投置业有限公司	Xiangshan Real Estate Co. ,Ltd	2
象山华丰房地产有限责任公司	Xiangshan Huafeng Real Estate Co. ,Ltd.	2
象山房地产开发有限公司	Xiangshan Real Estate Developing Co. ,Ltd.	2
象山县万象房屋开发有限公司	Xiangshan Wanxiang Real Estate Developing Ltd.	2
象山辉峰房地产开发有限公司	Xiangshan Huifeng Real Estate Developing Co. ,Ltd.	2
宁波巨鹰房地产开发有限公司	Ningbo Juying Real Estate Developing Co. ,Ltd.	2
宁波华翔房地产有限公司	Ningbo Huaxiang Real Estate Co. ,Ltd.	2
宁海县和兴房地产开发有限公司	Ninghai Hexing Real Estate Developing Ltd.	2
宁波兴普房产有限公司	Ningbo Xingpu Real Estate Co. ,Ltd.	2
宁波前程房地产有限公司	Ningbo Future Real Estate Co. ,Ltd.	2
浙江万里房地产开发有限公司	Zhejiang Wanli Real Estate Developing Ltd.	2
宁波舜龙房地产开发有限公司	Ningbo Sunlong Real Estate Development Co. ,Ltd.	2
宁波万基房地产开发有限公司	Ningbo Wanji Real Estate Developing Ltd.	2
浙江舜泉置业有限公司	Zhejiang Shunquan Real Estate Co. ,Ltd.	2
余姚市赛格特经济技术开发有限公司	Yuyao Saigete Economic & Technology Developing Co. ,Ltd.	2
宁波大丰房地产开发有限责任公司	Ningbo Dafeng Real Estate Co. ,Ltd.	2
宁波杭州湾裘皮有限公司	Ningbo Hangzhou Qiupi Real Estate Co. ,Ltd.	2
余姚市东方房产有限公司	Yuyao Dongfang Real Estate Co. ,Ltd.	2
慈溪市大通房地产开发有限公司	Cixi Datong Real Estate Developing Co. ,Ltd.	2
宁波美华实业有限公司	Ningbo Meihua Industrial Co. ,Ltd.	2
慈溪市飞龙房地产开发有限公司	Cixi Feilong Real Estate Developing Co. ,Ltd.	2
宁波香格房地产开发有限公司	Ningbo Xiangge Real Estate Co. ,Ltd.	2
宁波金峰房地产开发有限公司	Ningbo Jinfeng Real Estate Development Co. ,Ltd.	2
宁波滕头房地产开发有限公司	Ningbo Tengtou Real Estate Development Co. ,Ltd.	2
奉化市城市建设投资有限公司	Fenghua City Constuction Co. ,Ltd.	2

主要统计指标解释

【全社会固定资产投资】 固定资产投资是社会固定资产再生产的主要手段。通过建造和购置固定资产的活动,国民经济不断采用先进技术装备,建立新兴部门,进一步调整经济结构和生产力的地区分布,增强经济实力,为改善人民物质文化生活创造物质条件。这对我国的社会主义现代化建设具有重要意义。

固定资产投资额是以货币表现的建造和购置固定资产活动的工作量,它是反映固定资产投资规模、速度、比例关系和使用方向的综合性指标。全社会固定资产投资按经济类型可分为国有、集体、个体、联营、股份制、外商、港澳台商、其他等。按照管理渠道,全社会固定资产投资总额分为基本建设、更新改造、房地产开发投资和其他固定资产投资四个部分。

【房地产开发投资】 指房地产开发公司、商品房建设公司及其他房地产开发法人单位和附属于其他法人单位实际从事房地产开发或经营的活动单位统一开发的包括统代建、拆迁还建的住宅、厂房、仓库、饭店、宾馆、度假村、写字楼、办公楼等房屋建筑物和配套的服务设施,土地开发工程(如道路、给水、排水、供电、供热、通讯、平整场地等基础设施工程)的投资;不包括单纯的土地交易活动。

【农村非农户投资】 农村非农户建造和购置固定资产投资计划固定资本形成总额在500万元以上的项目,农村非农户包括以下二大类:

第一类为企业单位,分成(1)集体企业,包括集体直接经营及集体所有租赁给个人的企业;(2)股份合作企业;(3)联营企业;(4)有限责任公司(5)股份有限公司;(6)私营企业(7)与港澳台商合资、合作企业;(8)中外合资、合作企业;(9)其他企业。

联营和合资企业按其是否由农村集体与个人相对控股或绝对控股,或由农村集体、个人实际管理来确定是否纳入农村固定资产投资统计范围,其投资额按实际发生额全额统计;个体工商户外雇从业人员8人以上(含8人)的按企业统计。

第二类为乡镇行政事业单位及社会群众团体。

【新增固定资产】指通过投资活动所形成的新的固定资产价值。包括已经建成投入生产或交付使用的工程价值和达到固定资产标准的设备、工具、器具的价值及有关应摊入的费用。它是以价值形式表示的固定资产投资成果的综合性指标,可以综合反映不同时期、不同部门、不同地区的固定资产投资成果。

【新增生产能力(或工程效益)】指通过固定资产投资活动而增加的设计能力或工程效益,它是用实物形态表示的固定资产投资的成果。新增生产能力的计算,是以能独立发挥生产能力或工程效益的单项工程(或项目)为对象。当单项工程(或项目)建成,经有关部门鉴定合格,正式移交投入生产,即可计算新增生产能力。

新增生产能力或工程效益有以下几种表现形式:

⑴以建设项目或单项工程建成后的年产能力表示,如煤炭开采、石油开采等。

⑵以建设项目或单项工程建成后处理原料的能力表示,如选矿工程的年处理矿石能力、洗煤厂年洗原煤能力等。

⑶以新增的主要设备数量或容量表示,如棉纺锭锭数、发电机组容量等。

⑷以建筑物容积、容量、面积或长度表示,如水库容量、铁路公路里程等。

新增生产能力的数量一般按设计能力计算。设计能力是指设计文件中规定的在正常情况下能够达到的生产能力,而不论投产后的实际产量如何。以设备数量、建筑物容积、面积、长度等表示的新增生产能力或工程效益,则按建成的实际数量计算。

【建筑业统计单位】 指从事房屋、构筑物建造和设备安装活动的法人企业。建筑业法人企业应同时具备的条件是:①依法成立,有自己的名称、组织机构和场所,能够承担民事责任;②独立拥有和使用资产,承担负债,有权与其他单位签订合同;③独立核算盈亏,能够编制资产负债表。

【建筑业总产值(即自行完成施工产值)】 指建筑业企业或附属施工单位自行完成的按工程进度计算的建筑安装生产总值。施工产值包括:

①建筑工程产值:指列入建筑工程预算内的各种工程价值。

②设备安装工程产值:指设备安装工程价值。

③房屋、构筑物修理产值:指房屋、构筑物修理所完成的价值,但不包括被修理房屋、构筑物本身的价值和生产设备的修理价值。

④非标准设备制造产值:指加工制造没有定型的、非标准的生产设备的加工费和原材料价值,不论是现场还是附属加工厂为本单位承建工程制造的非标准设备的价值,都应计算产值。

【房屋建筑施工面积】 指报告期内施工的全部房屋建筑面积。包括本期新开工的面积、上期跨入本期继续施工的房屋面积、上期停缓建在本期恢复施工的房屋面积、本期竣工的房屋面积及本期施工后又停缓建的房屋面积。

【房屋建筑竣工面积】 指在报告期内房屋建筑按照设计要求已全部完工,达到住人和使用条件,经验收鉴定合格,正式移交使用单位的建筑面积。

【自有机械设备年末总台数】 指归本企业(或单位)所有,属于本企业固定资产的生产性机械设备年末总台数。包括施工机械、生产设备、运输设备以及其他设备。

【自有机械设备年末总功率】 指本企业(或单位)自有施工机械、生产设备、运输设备以及其他设备等列为在册固定资产的生产性机械设备年末总功率,按设定能力或查定能力计算。包括机械本身的动力和为该机械服务的单独动力设备,如电动机等。计算单位用千瓦,动力换算可按 1 马力 =0.735 千瓦折合成千瓦数。电焊机、变压器、锅炉不计算动力。

【工程结算收入】 指企业(或单位)按工程的分部分项自行完成的建筑产品价值并已与甲方在报告期内办理结算手续的工程价款收入,以及向甲方收取的除工程价款以外的按规定列作营业收入的各种款项,如临时设施费、劳动保险费、施工机械调迁费等以及向甲方收取的各种索赔款。

【工程结算利润】 指已结算工程实现的利润。如为亏损以" - "号表示。其计算公式为:

工程结算利润 = 工程结算收入 - 工程结算成本 - 工程结算税金及附加

Explanatory Notes on Main Statistical Indicators

[Total Investment in Fixed Assets in the Whole Country] Investment in fixed assets is the essential means for social reproduction of fixed assets. By means of construction and purchase of fixed assets, more advanced technologies and equipment are adopted in the national economy, and new sectors are established, which promote the adjustment of economic structure and the regional distribution of productive forces and enhance the economic strengths so as to provide the material conditions for improving people's livelihood. This is significant for speeding up the drive of socialist modernization in China.

Amount of investment in fixed assets refers to the volume of activities in construction and purchases of fixed assets in monetary terms. It is a comprehensive indicator which shows the size, pace, proportional relations and use orientation of the investment in fixed assets. Total investment in fixed assets in the whole country includes, by registration type of ownership, the investment by the state – owned units, collective units, individuals, joint ownership units, share – holding units, as well as investment by businessmen from foreign countries and from Hong Kong, Macao and Taiwan, and by other units. According to China's current management system, the investment in fixed assets in the whole country is classified into the following four parts: investment in capital construction, investment in innovation, investment in real estates development and other investment in fixed assets.

[Investment in Real Estate Development] It includes the investment by the real estate development companies, commercial buildings construction companies and other real estate development units of various types of ownership in the construction of house buildings, such as residential buildings, factory buildings, warehouses, hotels, guesthouses, holiday villages, office buildings, and the complementary service facilities and land development projects, such as roads, water supply, water drainage, power supply, heating, telecommunications, land leveling and other projects of infrastructure. It excludes the activities in simple land transactions.

[Individual Investment in Rural Areas] The individual investment in the rural areas includes the investment in house construction and purchase of productive fixed assets by the individuals in the rural areas.

[non – agricultural investment in rural areas] refers to the project which the estimated total investment amount of its fixed assets built or bought by the non – agriculture units in rural areas is over 5 million yuan. The non – agricultural units include two kinds as below:

I. enterprises. 1. Collective Co. (including companies both directly managed by collective leadership and rent to the private), 2. Stock – hoiding cooperation, 3. Joint Ownership Enterprises, 4. Limited liability Corporations, 5. Share – holding corporations Ltd., 6. Private enterprises, 7. Joint ventures or Cooperative Operation with Hong kong, Macao and Taiwan, 8. Foreign joint ventures or Cooperative Operation Enterprises, 9. other Enterprises

whether the associated companies and the joint ventures should be considered as the rural fixed assets depends on whether they are actually possessed or managed by rural communities or privates. Their investment amounts refer to the capital which had been actually invested into the enterprises. Private businesses which employ 8 or more workers should be considered as enterprises in statistics

II. public undertakings and public communities in rural areas.

[Newly Increased Fixed Assets] refer to the newly increased value of fixed assets through investment, including the value of projects completed and put into production, the value of equipment, tools, and vessels considered as fixed assets, as well as the relevant expenses as investment in fixed assets. This is a comprehensive indicator of investment in fixed assets, reflecting the achievements of investment in fixed assets in different periods, different sect ors, and different regions.

[Newly Increased Production Capacity] refers to the increase of designed capacity and project efficiency through investment in fixed assets, which reflects the accomplishment of investment in fixed assets in kind. The calculation of newly increased production capacity is based on individual project which operates independently and efficiently. When an individual project is completed and checked and accepted and put into production, it is counted as newly increased production capacity.

The newly increased production capacity and project efficiency are usually expressed in one of the following forms:

(1) annual production capacity, such as extraction of coal and petroleum;

(2) raw material processing capacity, such as ore dressing capacity of ore dressing projects, the dressing capacity of a coal washery;

(3) number or capacity of major equipment increased, such as the number of cotton spindles increased and the capacity of generating sets increased;

(4) physical measures of construction, such as volume, capacity, area, and length, for instance, the capacity of reservoirs, the length of railways or highways.

Newly increased production capacity in terms of quantity is calculated in designed capacity in general, which refers to the production capacity of a project under normal conditions designed in construction documents regardless of the actual output.

[Statistical units in construction industries] refers to the legal enterprises which build architectures or install equipments. The legal enterprises should meet all the demands as follows, 1. being formed legally with own name, organizational structure and working place. Can fully bear civil responsibilities. 2. possessing and using its own assets independently, which means it should be able to incur liabilities and has right to make contracts with other enterprises. 3. should be an independent accounting unit which can draw balance sheet.

[Gross Output Value of Construction (Output Value of Projects Under Construction)] refers to total of construction products, expressed in money terms, completed by construction and installation enterprises during a given period of time. It includes:

(1) Output value of construction projects, that is the value of projects covered by the project budgets;

(2) Output value of installation projects, that is the value of the installation of equipment, (excluding the value of the equipment to be installed);

(3) Output value of repair of buildings and structures, that is the value created through the repairs of buildings or structures, but does not include the value of buildings or structures being repaired and the value of the repair of production equipment;

(4) Output value of manufactured non - standard equipment, that is the value of no-standard production equipment (including raw materials and manufacturing cost) made for the construction project, and the equipment manufactured by subsidiary workshops.

[Floor Space under Construction] refers to total floor space of all buildings under construction during the reference period, including floor space of newly started buildings during the reference period, floor space of construction extended from the previous period to the current period, floor space of construction suspended during the previous period and resumed in the current period, floor space of construction completed in the current period, and floor space of construction started and then suspended in the current period.

[Floor Space of Buildings Completed] refers to the floor space of buildings completed in the reference period, which have come up to the designed standards and have been put into use.

[Total Number of Machinery and Equipment Owned by the Construction Enterprises] refers to the number of machines and equipment owned by the enterprises (or units, and listed as the fixed assets of the enterprises (or units) by the end of the year, including machinery and equipment for construction, production and transportation.

[Total Power of Machinery and Equipment Owned by the Construction Enterprises] refer to the total power of machinery and equipment owned by the enterprises (or units), and listed as the fixed assets of the enterprises (or units) by the end of the year, including machinery and equipment for construction, production and transportation. The power of the machinery is calculated on basis of the designed or verified capacity, covering the power of the machinery/equipment and the separate power equipment serving the machinery/equipment (such as electric motors), but excluding welders, transformers and boilers. The unit use for the calculation of power is kilowatt, with horsepower converted to kilowatt by 1horsepower = 0.735 kilowatt.

[Income from Settlement of Projects] refers to the income received by the construction enterprise/unit from the completed portion of the project through settlement procedures with the contracted during the reference period, and other charges to the contracted as operational costs, such as facility fee, labor insurance premium, moving cost of construction unit, as well as various types of claims to the contracted.

[Profit from Settlement of Projects] refers to profit realized through settled projects. It is calculated with the following formula:
Profit from Settlement of Projects = Income from Settlement of projects – Settled Cost – Settled Taxes and Other Cost.

NINGBO

2015

Statistical YearBook

9

CHAPTER

第九篇

港口、交通、运输、邮电

PORT, TRANSPORTATION, POST AND TELECOMMUNICATION SERVICE

港口、交通、运输、邮电
Port, Transportations, Post and Telecommunications

主要统计指标
Major Statistics Indicators

2014 年全社会客运量	Total Passenger Traffic	16508	万人	10000 persons
比上年增长	Increase Over Last Year	-33.4	%	
2014 年全社会货运量	Total Freight Traffic	40407	万吨	10000 tons
比上年增长	Increase Over Last Year	14.1	%	
2014 年港口货物吞吐量	Cargo Handled at Ports	52646	万吨	10000 tons
比上年增长	Increase Over Last Year	6.2	%	
2014 年集装箱吞吐量	Container Handled at Ports	1870	万标箱	10000 TEU
比上年增长	Increase Over Last Year	11.5	%	
2014 移动电话用户	Number of Mobile Telephone Subscribers	1267	万户	10000 subcribers
比上年增长	Increase Over Last Year	3.2	%	
2014 年固定电话用户	Number of Local Telephone Subscribers	270	万户	10000 subcribers
比上年增长	Increase Over Last Year	-9.4	%	

表9-1 历年港口、交通、邮电基本情况
Basic Statistics on Port,Transportation and Telecommunications Over the Years

年份 Year	港口货物吞吐量（万吨） Cargo at Throughput Ports (10000 tons)	集装箱吞吐量（万标箱） Container Throughput (10000 TEU)	货运量（万吨） Freight Traffic (10000 tons)	客运量（万人） Passenger Traffic (10000 persons)	固定电话用户（万户） Number of Local Telephone Subscribers (10000 subscribers)
1978	214		1385	2966	1.07
1979	236		1430	3369	1.19
1980	326		1562	4156	1.36
1981	349		1496	4654	1.53
1982	371		1617	5192	1.71
1983	483		1641	5652	1.86
1984	597		1810	6026	2.22
1985	1040		2015	6527	2.60
1986	1797		3204	7373	2.91
1987	1940		3745	7473	3.55
1988	2002		5408	7277	4.64
1989	2209		4570	7686	5.37
1990	2554	2.2	4763	7378	6.19
1991	3390	3.6	5070	8757	8.05
1992	4367	5.3	6492	9773	12.22
1993	5321	7.9	7583	11224	18.59
1994	5850	12.5	8711	17776	27.86
1995	6853	16.0	9577	19705	41.78
1996	7638	20.2	10460	21152	53.33
1997	8220	25.7	10547	21719	67.75
1998	8707	35.3	10317	21736	83.74
1999	9660	60.1	10344	22211	104.13
2000	11547	90.2	10819	22736	130.15
2001	12852	121.3	11283	23225	163.21
2002	15398	185.9	12429	23752	203.58
2003	18543	277.2	13919	24938	242.00
2004	22586	400.5	16026	27291	296.72
2005	26881	520.8	17664	28412	339.41
2006	30969	706.8	22238	29146	345.08
2007	34519	935.0	24363	30693	334.98
2008	36185	1084.6	27508	32250	338.24
2009	38385	1042.3	29028	33791	301.41
2010	41217	1300.4	30553	33911	317.39
2011	43339	1451.2	31228	28745	312.45
2012	45303	1567.1	32616	28053	308.00
2013	49592	1677.4	35409	24793	298.00
2014	52646	1870.0	40407	16508	270.00

表9－2 港口吞吐情况(2014)
Basic Statistics On Cargo at Ports Throughput

单位:万吨(10000 tons)

指标	Indicators	吞吐量 Capacity 总计 Total	吞吐量 Capacity 外贸 Foreign Trade	其中 of Which 出口量 Export 合计 Total	其中 of Which 出口量 Export 外贸 Foreign Trade	其中 of Which 进口量 Import 合计 Total	其中 of Which 进口量 Import 外贸 Foreign Trade
货物吞吐量	**Cargo at Throughput Ports**	**52646**	**29723**	**20634**	**10599**	**32012**	**19124**
#转口货物	Cargo of Transfer	12494	6141	6247	3	6247	6137
货物分类	**Type of Cargo**						
煤炭及制品	Coal And Its Products	7413	1153	1045		6368	1153
石油及制品	Petroleum And Its Products	7982	5318	1849	177	6133	5141
金属矿石	Metal Ores	10220	5874	4334		5886	5874
钢铁	Steel and Iron	992	80	112	20	879	61
矿建材料	Mineral Building Materials	1882		578		1304	
水泥	Cement	1013		226		787	
木材	Timber	22	10			22	10
非金属矿石	Nonmetal Ores	480	2	10	2	471	
化肥及农药	Chemical Fertilizers and Pesticides	20	17	17	17	3	
盐	Salt	135	86			135	86
粮食	Grain	201	149	38		163	149
机械设备	Machinery Equipment	4	1	2	1	2	
化工原料及制品	Industrial Chemicals And Its Products	1388	803	147	14	1241	789
轻工、医药	Products of Leight Industry and Medicine	58	22	3		55	22
农林牧渔业产品	Products of Farming, Forestry, Animal Husbandry And Fishery	12	9	2		10	9
其他	Others	20817	16198	12272	10368	8544	5830
旅客吞吐量(万人次)	**Number of Passenger In－And Out (10000 person. times)**	**161.50**					

表9－3 港口国际集装箱吞吐量(2014) International Container Throughput at Ports

航线	Shipping Lines	箱数(箱) Number of Container	重量(吨) Weigh(ton)	
			合计 Total	货重 Weigh of Cargo
总计	**Total**	**18700360.75**	**193558715**	**154856022**
国际航线合计	International Lines	15623682.25	148782005	116596464
非洲合计	Africa	714903.75	7619878	6131492
亚洲合计	Asia	6768642.00	70552343	56559160
欧洲合计	Europe	3177491.75	29034370	22548005
北美洲合计	North America	3353488.50	27877414	21064227
南美洲合计	South America	894885.25	7292922	5403815
大洋洲及太平洋岛屿合计	Oceania	466638.25	3469174	2467178
世界其他	Others	247632.75	2935904	2422587
内支线合计	Total of Domestic Sub－Line	863639.00	13057334	11257867
天津	Tianjin	8680.00	153812	135979
大连	Dalian	10402.00	80332	58883
上海	Shanghai	1559.00	35821	32466
江苏	Jiangsu			
浙江	Zhejiang			
福建	Fujian			
山东	Shandong			
中国其他	Others	7175.50	111624	96464
国内航线合计	Total of Domestic Lines	2213039.50	31719376	27001691

表9-4 历年客运量
Passenger Traffic Over the Years

单位:万人(10000 persons)

年份 Year	合计 Total	其中 of Which			
		铁路 Railway	公路 Highway	水路 Waterway	航空 Civil Aviation
1978	2966	105	2311	550	
1979	3369	122	2692	555	
1980	4156	317	3241	598	
1981	4654	351	3714	598	
1982	5192	366	4277	549	
1983	5652	411	4737	504	
1984	6026	480	5073	473	
1985	6527	502	5575	450	
1986	7373	482	6472	418	1.2
1987	7473	497	6536	438	2
1988	7277	536	6339	399	3.1
1989	7686	527	6790	366	3.2
1990	7378	462	6611	299	6
1991	8757	445	8006	295	11
1992	9773	414	9076	268	14
1993	11224	435	10523	245	21
1994	17776	486	16993	265	32
1995	19705	506	18870	283	45
1996	21152	405	20432	262	53
1997	21719	342	21101	222	55
1998	21736	300	21199	182	55
1999	22211	278	21734	146	53
2000	22736	288	22255	133	59.7
2001	23225	349	22700	115	61
2002	23752	393	23160	135	64
2003	24938	438	24320	115	65
2004	27291	567	26510	119	95
2005	28412	607	27570	113	122
2006	29146	745	28120	121	160
2007	30693	842	29541	130	180
2008	32250	1770	30130	152	198
2009	33791	1700	31545	142	403
2010	33911	1012	32340	107	452
2011	28745	2186	25960	97	501
2012	28053	1119	26285	123	527
2013	24793	1273	22850	124	546
2014	16508	3556	12144	171	636

注:2011年,客运量为营业性客运量。

Note:In 2011,passenger volume is a business volume of passenger.

表9-5 历年货运量
Freight Traffic Over the Years

单位:万吨(10000 tons)

年份 Year	合计 Total	其中 of Which				
		铁路 Railway	公路 Highway	水路 Waterway	航空(吨) Civil Aviation(ton)	管道 Pipeline
1978	1385	45	625	715		
1979	1430	67	681	682		
1980	1562	167	709	686		
1981	1496	170	714	612		
1982	1617	186	788	643		
1983	1641	217	810	614		
1984	1810	234	883	693		
1985	2015	284	955	776		
1986	3204	310	1910	984	237	
1987	3745	337	2576	832	371	
1988	5408	380	4196	832	567	
1989	4570	398	3443	729	500	
1990	4763	355	3800	608	800	
1991	5070	302	4143	625	1600	
1992	6492	429	5328	710	2200	25
1993	7583	428	6255	868	3262	32
1994	8711	455	7113	1112	4000	31
1995	9577	527	7843	1173	4900	34
1996	10460	573	8509	1233	5200	44
1997	10547	551	8642	1314	5400	41
1998	9952	569	8195	1143	6900	44
1999	10344	609	8154	1534	9000	46
2000	10819	682	8219	1829	11000	88
2001	11283	725	8300	2156	10000	101
2002	12429	980	8630	2716	12500	102
2003	13919	1158	9070	3568	13812	122
2004	16026	1210	9890	4734	18725	190
2005	17664	1207	10480	5619	23450	356
2006	22238	1238	11725	7349	23505	1924
2007	24363	1274	12889	8706	23608	1492
2008	27508	2171	13550	9993	24549	1792
2009	29028	2377	15594	11050	68700	1774
2010	30553	2060	16220	12265	81200	2109
2011	34385	2960	15280	13771	90000	2366
2012	32616	1924	16570	14113	90800	2443
2013	35409	2168	17790	15441	94900	2641
2014	40407	2364	21918	16113	114000	

表9-6 历年全社会旅客周转量和货物周转量
Total Turnover Volume of Passengers and Turnover Volume of Freight Traffic Over the Years

单位:万人公里,万吨公里(10000 tons - km,10000 persons - km)

年份 Year	旅客周转量 Turnover Volume of Passengers			货物周转量 Turnover Volume of Freight Traffic			
	总计 Total	其中 of Which		总计 Total	其中 of Which		
		公路 Highway	水路 Waterway		公路 Highway	水路 Waterway	管道 Pipeline
1985	147863	135273	12590	132890	34369	98521	
1986	176321	163351	12970	219594	86541	133053	
1987	182877	168280	14597	294320	130907	163413	
1988	191911	176853	15058	271187	89321	181865	
1989	193779	180061	13718	319319	135845	183474	
1990	202868	190057	12811	308099	134299	173800	
1991	229727	215573	14154	438528	187032	251496	
1992	270125	258068	12057	608363	242989	365157	217
1993	324919	314471	10448	777570	262057	515229	284
1994	623257	610761	12496	1243892	448457	795435	
1995	699514	685120	14394	1450892	495929	954674	289
1996	735912	721653	14259	1742582	523495	1218722	365
1997	755941	740381	15560	1853782	533382	1320018	382
1998	752757	741848	10909	1887113	491380	1395325	408
1999	771393	764287	7106	2311376	481555	1829381	440
2000	800193	794858	5335	2367484	482518	1884241	723
2001	822326	818704	3622	2727939	492170	2231435	4335
2002	870546	867830	2716	3342614	521700	2844927	5517
2003	921901	919900	2001	4559749	553005	4002654	4090
2004	992957	990870	2087	5545297	608310	4932308	4679
2005	1042307	1040410	1897	7478890	644800	6806210	27880
2006	1060134	1058100	2034	10361127	719114	8696860	945153
2007	1213443	1211162	2281	11298162	812007	9775967	710188
2008	1235559	1232691	2868	12470705	856713	10745112	868880
2009	1245586	1242710	2876	13216223	1351300	10999544	865379
2010	1362007	1360600	1407	15753422	2465250	13288172	997675
2011	1383064	1382100	963	20903442	2815110	16884961	1203371
2012	1431814	1430930	884	20710458	3025860	17684598	1232617
2013	1242765	1242030	735	22307108	3254460	19052648	1351735
2014	780393	779567	826	20615264	3355532	17259732	

表9－7 公路运输工具拥有量(2014)
Number of Means of Transportation Through Highway

指标	单位	Indicators	Unit	营业性 Business 合计 Total	营业性 Business 个体 Individual
总计	**辆**	**Total**	**unit**	**85918**	**41406**
汽车	辆	Automobile	unit	85918	41406
载客汽车	辆	Buses And Cars	unit	3669	
	客位		seat	111401	
#大型	辆	Large－Sized	unit	1602	
	客位		seat	73500	
中型	辆	Middle－Sized	unit	1907	
	客位		seat	36823	
载货汽车	辆	Trucks	unit	101148	41841
	吨位		ton	827769	119166
①普通载货汽车	辆	Ordinary Trucks	unit	60062	40785
	吨位		ton	209807	106382
#大型	辆	Large－Space	unit	14454	6555
	吨位		ton	155716	66238
重型	辆	Heavy	unit	10408	3705
	吨位		ton	131714	44588
中型	辆	Middle	unit	1233	545
	吨位		ton	4385	1941
②专用载货汽车	辆	Trucks for Special Purpose	unit	3623	247
	吨位		ton	61670	3056
#集装箱车	辆	Container Trucks	unit	14710	6
	TEU		TEU	1660	

表9-8 水路运输工具拥有量(2014)
Number of Means of Transportation Through Waterway

指标	单位	Indicators	Unit	总计 Total	其中 of Which 内河 Freshwater	沿海 Coastal	远洋 Ocean
总计	艘	**Total**	**unit**	**641**	**62**	**574**	**6**
机动船	艘	**Motor Vessels**	**unit**	**636**	**62**	**569**	**5**
净载重量	吨位	Dead Weight	ton	5549861	8569	5207463	333829
载客量	客位	Passenger Capacity	seat	4186	3136	1050	
标准箱位	TEU	Standard Container Space	TEU	6895		6495	
功率	千瓦	Power	kw	1120949	7521	1068378	45050
机动船按类别分		**Group by Type on Motor Vessels**					
客船	艘	Passenger Ships	unit	43	34	9	
载客量	客位	Passenger Capacity	seat	2207	1636	571	
功率	千瓦	Power	kw	7011	3280	3731	
客货船	艘	Passenger - cargo Vessels	unit	9	3	6	
净载重量	吨位	Dead Weight	ton		434		
载客量	客位	Passenger Capacity	seat	1979	1500	479	
功率	千瓦	Power	kw	2574	506	2068	
货船	艘	Cargo Ships	unit	584	25	554	5
净载重量	吨位	Dead Weight	ton	5549861	8569	5207463	333829
标准箱位	TEU	Standard Container Space	TEU	3522		6495	
功率	千瓦	Power	kw	1111364	3735	1062579	45050
#①油船	艘	Tanker	unit	119		119	
净载重量	吨位	Dead Weight	ton	416827		416827	
功率	千瓦	Power	kw	136928		136928	
②集装箱船	艘	Container Ships	unit	9		9	
净载重量	吨位	Dead Weight	ton	93072		93072	
标准箱位	TEU	Standard Container Space	TEU	6495		6495	
功率	千瓦	Power	kw	49323		49323	
拖船	艘	Tugboats	unit				
功率	千瓦	Power	kw				
驳船	艘	Barges	unit	5		5	
净载重量	吨位	Dead Weight	ton	8872		8872	

表9-9 部分年份运输线路里程长度
Length of Transportation Routes in Partial Years

单位:公里(km)

指标	Indicators	2010	2011	2012	2013	2014
公路总里程	**Overal Length For Highway**	**9884**	**10439**	**10661**	**10892**	**11045**
按技术等级分:	**Divided by Grade**					
①等级公路	Highway Grade	9272	9881	10102	10350	10507
高速公路	Express Way	370	416	463	496	496
一级公路	Highway Grade 1	769	945	960	1059	1126
二级公路	Highway Grade 2	876	784	813	775	777
三级公路	Highway Grade 3	1492	1551	1550	1533	1576
四级公路	Highway Grade 4	5764	6026	6173	6355	6425
准四级公路	Near Highway Grade 4		159	143	132	108
②等外公路	Highway Without Grade	612	559	559	542	539
按路面等级分	**Divided by Road Surface**					
高级路面	High Grade Road Surface	8985	9736	10003	10298	10523
次高级路面	Sub - High Grade Road Surface	453	395	380	361	296
中级路面	Medium Grade Road Surface	446	309	278	233	227
低级路面	Lower Grade Road Surface					
按行政等级分	**Divided by Adminitrative Level**					
国道	State Way	453	497	497	497	497
省道	Province Way	718	724	771	804	804
县道	County Way	2671	2819	2844	2885	2939
乡道	Township Way	2137	2186	2188	2189	2196
专用道	Special Use Way	84	56	56	56	56
村道公路里程	Village Way	3821	4158	4306	4462	4554
内河通航里程	**Length of Navigable Inland Waterways**	**927**	**927**	**927**	**927**	**927**

表9－10 历年电信业主要指标
Main Indicators of Telecommunications Services Over the Years

年份 Year	固定电话用户 （万户） Number of Local Telephone Subscribers （10000 subcribers）	#农话 Rural Telephone Subscribers	移动电话 （万户） Number of Subscribers of Mobile Telephone （10000 subscribers）	国际互联网用户 （户） User of International Computer Network （user）
1978	1.07	0.49		
1979	1.19	0.53		
1980	1.36	0.58		
1981	1.53	0.64		
1982	1.71	0.70		
1983	1.86	0.76		
1984	2.22	0.89		
1985	2.60	1.05		
1986	2.91	1.14		
1987	3.55	1.35		
1988	4.64	1.68		
1989	5.37	1.92		
1990	6.19	2.15		
1991	8.05	2.88		
1992	12.22	4.92	0.14	
1993	18.59	7.49	0.80	
1994	27.86	11.60	1.92	
1995	41.78	17.80	4.71	
1996	53.33	23.10	9.05	
1997	67.75	31.14	16.44	
1998	83.74	41.40	25.72	4248
1999	104.13	54.39	56.75	37334
2000	130.15	72.69	117.92	70928
2001	163.21	90.13	195.65	93208
2002	203.58	91.52	256.86	104293
2003	242.00	107.20	379.31	835674
2004	296.72	94.79	421.00	1040127
2005	339.41		467.10	1705300
2006	345.08		514.70	908123
2007	334.98		757.70	1737851
2008	338.24		821.58	1027689
2009	301.41		866.87	1360000
2010	317.39		845.50	1720000
2011	312.45		1029.46	1900000
2012	308.00		1088.00	2360500
2013	298.00		1228.00	2500000
2014	270.00		1267.00	2810000

注：2006年起，国际互联网用户统计口径有变化。

Note：From 2006，international Internet user's statistical method will change .

表9-11 部分年份邮政业务情况
Basic Statistics on Post Services in Partial Years

指标	单位	Indicators	unit	2011	2012	2013	2014
邮政局、所数	处	Number of Post Offices	unit	279	280	280	271
#在农村的	处	Rural Area	unit	193	193	194	190
邮路总长度(单程)	公里	Lengh of Postal Routes	km	5019	5071	9604	10051
农村投递路线	公里	Rural Delivery Routwes	km	27977	27062	27233	27426
邮政业务总量	万元	Business volume of Post Services	10000 yuan	88746	76125	87977	82629
函件	万件	Number of Letters	10000 pcs	12520.80	11842.25	10451.32	9354.12
#国际函件	万件	International Letters	10000 pcs	43.20	131.91	265.36	526.01
国内函件	万件	Domestic Letters	10000 pcs	12477.60	4915.03	10185.96	8828.11
集邮业务	万枚	Philately	10000 pcs	2281.00	2260.46	2700.32	1998.00
报纸期发份数	万份	Newspaper Issued	10000 copies	91.33	91.84	135.06	111.98
杂志期发份数	万份	Magazine Issued	10000 copies	62.09	57.59	65.58	70.22
订销报纸累计份数	万份	Number of Newspaper Circulation	10000 copies	25881.00	28653.80	33991.76	36182.05
订销杂志累计份数	万份	Number of Magazine Circulation	10000 copies	656.00	702.80	1224.47	1183.97

表9－12 各县(市)邮政业务基本情况(2014)
Basic Statistics on Post Services by Region

指标	单位	Indicators	unit	全市 Total	市区 Urban Districts	余姚 Yuyao	慈溪 Cixi
邮政局、所数	处	Number of Post Offices	unit	271	125	42	34
#在农村的	处	Rural Area	unit	190	80	28	27
邮路总长度(单程)	公里	Lengh of Postal Routes	km	10051	7962	499	632
农村投递路线	公里	Rural Delivery Routwes	km	27426	9944	5117	5769
邮政业务总量	万元	Business volume of Post Services	10000 yuan	82629	41071	10685	17321
函件	万件	Number of Letters	10000 pcs	9354.12	5637.85	461.28	2004.84
国际函件	万件	International Letters	10000 pcs	526.01	425.20	42.66	56.48
国内函件	万件	Domestic Letters	10000 pcs	8828.11	5212.65	418.62	1948.36
集邮业务	万枚	Philately	10000 pcs	1998.00	1609.00	94.00	102.00
报纸期发份数	万份	Newspaper Issued	10000 copies	111.98	56.48	13.16	19.96
杂志期发份数	万份	Magazine Issued	10000 copies	70.22	44.26	5.39	7.30
订销报纸累计份数	万份	Number of Newspaper Circulation	10000 copies	36182.05	16942.19	5383.40	6974.57
订销杂志累计份数	万份	Number of Magazine Circulation	10000 copies	1183.97	757.89	85.02	117.93

表9－12 续表 Continued

指标	单位	Indicators	unit	奉化 Fenghua	象山 Xiangshan	宁海 Ninghai
邮政局、所数	处	Number of Post Offices	unit	28	24	18
#在农村的	处	Rural Area	unit	19	21	15
邮路总长度(单程)	公里	Lengh of Postal Routes	km	371	305	282
农村投递路线	公里	Rural Delivery Routwes	km	2690	1789	2117
邮政业务总量	万元	Business volume of Post Services	10000 yuan	5438	3209	4905
函件	万件	Number of Letters	10000 pcs	647.81	263.63	338.71
国际函件	万件	International Letters	10000 pcs	1.50	0.03	0.14
国内函件	万件	Domestic Letters	10000 pcs	646.31	263.60	338.57
集邮业务	万枚	Philately	10000 pcs	50.00	48.00	95.00
报纸期发份数	万份	Newspaper Issued	10000 copies	7.08	6.76	8.54
杂志期发份数	万份	Magazine Issued	10000 copies	4.06	5.88	3.33
订销报纸累计份数	万份	Number of Newspaper Circulation	10000 copies	2403.40	2068.15	2410.34
订销杂志累计份数	万份	Number of Magazine Circulation	10000 copies	57.68	89.48	75.97

主要统计指标解释

【公路里程】 指在一定时期内实际达到《公路工程技术标 JTJ01 - 88》规定的等级公路,并经公路主管部门正式验收交付使用的公路里程数。其计算单位为:公里。它包括大中城市的郊区公路以及通过小城镇街道部分的公路里程,也包括桥梁、渡口的长度,但不包括大中城市的街道、厂矿、林区生产用道和农业生产用道的里程。两条或多条公路共同经由同一路段,只计算一次,不得重复计算里程长度。公路里程是反映公路建设发展规模的重要指标,也是计算运输网密度等指标的基础资料。

【货(客)运量】 指在一定时期内,各种运输工具实际运送的货物(旅客)数量。是反映运输业为国民经济和人民生活服务的数量指标,也是制定和检查运输生产计划,研究运输发展规模和速度的重要指标。货运按吨计算,客运按人计算。货物不论运输距离长短,货物类别,均按实际重量统计;旅客不论行程远近或票价多少,均按一人一次作为客运量统计。半价票、小孩票也按一人统计。

【货物(旅客)周转量】 指在一定时期内,由各种运输工具运送的货物(旅客)数量与其相应运输距离的乘积之总和,是反映运输业生产总成果的重要指标,也是编制和检查运输生产计划,计算运输效率、劳动生产率以及核算运输单位成本的主要基础资料。通常以吨公里和人公里为计算单位。计算货物周转量通常按发出站与到达站之间的最短距离,也就是计费距离计算。

【港口货物吞吐量】 指由水运进出港区范围,并经过装卸的货物数量,包括邮件及办理托运手续的行李、包裹以及补给运输船舶的燃、物料和淡水。其计量单位为吨。货物吞吐量的货种分类及其主要流向流量,反映了港口在国内外物资交流和对外贸易运输中的地位和作用。吞吐量可以分为进口、出口,又可以分为国内贸易和对外贸易。

【邮电业务总量】 指以货币表现的邮电部门用于传递信息和提供其他邮电服务的总数量。它综合反映了一定时期邮电工作的总成果,是研究邮电业务量构成和发展趋势的重要指标。根据邮电管理体制不同,分为中央国营业务总量和地方国营业务总量。它用各种邮电分类业务量,如函件件数、电报份数、长话张数、市内电话和农村电话的年均户数、订销报刊累计份数等,分别乘以相应的平均单价(不变价),加总后再加上出租电路和设备的收入、代用户维护电话交换机和线路等设备的收入、其他业务收入求得。

Explanatory Notes on Main Statistical Indicators

【Length of Highways】 refers to the length of highways which are built in conformity with the grades specified by the highway engineering standard formulated by the Ministry of Communications, and have been formally checked and accepted by the departments of highways and put into use. The length of highways includes that of the suburb highways at large and medium-sized cities, highways passing through streets at small cities and towns, and also the length of bridges and ferries. It does not include the length of streets in big and medium-sized cities and highways built for the production purpose at factories, mines, forest areas and agricultural areas, If two or more highways go the same section of the way, the length of the section is only calculated for once and no duplication is allowed. The length of highways is an important indicator to show the development of the highway construction and to provide essential information to calculate the transport network density.

【Freight(Passenger) Traffic】 refers to the volume of freight (passenger) transported with various means. Freight transport is calculated in to ns and passenger traffic is calculated in the number of persons. Despite the type of freight and traveling distance, the freight transport is calculated by the principle that one person can be counted only once in one travel. The passenger who travel with a half price ticket or a child ticket is also calculated as one person. The freight (passenger) traffic provides a quantitative measure to show how the transport industry serves the national economy and people, and is also an important indicator for planning the transport industry and for studying the development scale and speed of the transport industry.

【Freight Ton – kilometers(Passenger – kilometers)】 refers to the sum of the products of the volume of transported cargo(passengers) multiplying by the transport distance, usually using ton-kilometer and passenger-kilometer as units for measurement. Normally, the shortest distance between the departure station and the destination station(i. e. , the payable distance) is the basis to calculate the freight ton – kilometers. This is an important indicator to show the total results of the transport industry, to prepare and examine the transport plan and to measure the efficiency, the labor productivity and the unit cost of transport.

【Volume of Freight Handled】 refers to the volume of cargo passing in and out the harbor area of the major coastal ports and having been loaded and unloaded. The volume includes that of the coastal matters, registered luggage and fuels, materials and fresh water as supplies of the ships. The volume of freight dandled maybe classified as import, export, or as domestic trade and foreign trade. The volume of freight handled by type of cargo and by main flow direction reflects he position and function of the ports in the inflow of Chinese and foreign commodities and in the transportation of foreign trade.

【Business Volume of Post and Telecommunications】 refers to the total amount of the information delivered and other post and telecommunications services provided by the post and telecommunications departments for the customers. It is derived by first multiplying the business volume of different types, such as number of letters, telegrams, long distance calls, city and rural telephone subscribers and accumulated number of newspapers and journals subscribed and sold, etc. by their respective average unit price (fixed price) and then adding these products together: plus the income from maintenance of telephone exchanges and lines, and the income from other business operations. The business volume of post and telecommunications indicates the total achievements made by the post and telecommunications department during a given period of time in a comprehensive way, and is an important indicator to study the composition and development of the post and telecommunications business.

10 CHAPTER

第十篇

国内贸易、餐饮业

DOMESTIC TRADE AND CATERING TRADE

国内贸易、餐饮
Domestic Trade and Catering Trade

主要统计指标
Major Statistics Indicators

				总计 Total	比上年增长(%) Increase Over Last Year(%)
2014年社会消费品零售总额	万元	Total Retail Sales of Consumer Goods	10000 yuan	29920297	13.5
#批发零售贸易业	万元	Wholesale and Retail Sale	10000 yuan	27301207	13.5
住宿及餐饮业	万元	Hoteling and Catering Trade	10000 yuan	2619090	13.5
限额以上批发业主要指标		Main Indicators of Wholesales Trade Above Designated Size			
企业数	个	Number of Enterprises	unit	2579	14.1
从业人员数	人	Number of Employees	person	89740	17.6
销售总额	万元	Total Sales Value	10000 yuan	113834787	35.8
资产总计	万元	Total Assets	10000 yuan	37876176	15.2
利润总额	万元	Total Profits	10000 yuan	1097144	20.1
限额以上零售业主要指标		Main Indicators of Retail Trade Above Designated Size			
企业数	个	Number of Enterprises	unit	732	8.3
从业人员数	人	Number of Employees	person	68696	4.4
销售总额	万元	Total Sales Value	10000 yuan	12620672	8.0
资产总计	万元	Total Assets	10000 yuan	6161209	8.0
利润总额	万元	Total Profits	10000 yuan	104725	-41.7
2014年住宿餐饮业从业人员数	人	Number of Employees in Catering Trade and Hoteling	person	41626	-8.1
2014年个体工商户数	户	Number of Individual Industry and Commerce	Households	401053	8.5
2014年私营企业数	个	Number of Private Enterprises	unit	203627	17.1

表10-1 历年社会消费品零售总额
Total Retail Sales of Consumer Goods Over the Years

单位:万元(10000 yuan)

年份 Year	全市 Total	其中 of Which	
		市区 Urban District	县(市)合计 Total County
1978	70663	26175	44488
1979	87628	32386	55242
1980	111793	40368	71425
1981	130182	47157	83025
1982	139809	50056	89753
1983	156913	55343	101570
1984	187876	66573	121303
1985	253306	99210	154096
1986	304587	117850	186737
1987	354706	133444	221262
1988	490453	191994	298459
1989	528158	215768	312390
1990	549750	232255	317495
1991	633841	273167	360674
1992	794007	335769	458238
1993	1182147	522124	660023
1994	1634110	666060	968050
1995	2268195	919410	1348785
1996	2591764	1011445	1580319
1997	2885811	1154527	1731284
1998	3133608	1211018	1922590
1999	3457632	1321484	2136148
2000	3892920	1459537	2433383
2001	4141801		
2002	4628655		
2003	5215347		
2004	6667809		
2005	7621595	3625494	3996101
2006	8879552	4209769	4669783
2007	10450094	4922829	5527266
2008	12532605	5869060	6663545
2009	14344121	7633573	6710548
2010	17045103	6962526	10082577
2011	20188617	10891450	9297167
2012	23292590	12458556	10834033
2013	26357078	14077290	12279788
2014	29920297	16197618	13722679

表 10-2 部分年份分行业社会消费品零售总额 Total Retail Sales of Consumer Goods by Sector in Partial Years

单位:万元(10000 yuan)

年份 Year	社会消费品零售总额 Total Retail Sales of Consumer Goods	# 市的零售额 City	按行业分 Grouped by Sector		
			批发和零售贸易业 Wholesale and Retail Sale Trades	住宿及餐饮业 Hoteling and Catering Trade	其他 Others
1990	549750				
1991	633841				
1992	794007				
1993	1182147				
1994	1634110				
1995	2268195	1320420	1628556	125442	514198
1996	2591764	1555917	1929652	159592	502520
1997	2885811	1703928	2104330	199683	581798
1998	3133608	1792796	2356047	187135	590426
1999	3457632	2018154	2599967	276889	580776
2000	3892920	2247696	2965818	378127	548975
2001	4141801	2401013	3124797	442042	574962
2002	4628655	2737749	3442080	570221	616354
2003	5215347	3084765	4434412	672047	108888
2004	6667809	3947129	5845803	771788	50218
2005	7621595	4696200	6667717	917878	36000
2006	8879552	5470496	7862357	1012258	4937
2007	10450094	6428170	9289383	1158312	2400
2008	12532605	7839658	11124980	1405045	2580
2009	14344121	9207400	12776963	1564398	2760
2010	17045103	12737090	15461677	1583426	
2011	20188617	13674900	18343579	1845038	
2012	23292590	19549110	21159838	2132752	
2013	26357078	22135123	24048524	2308553	
2014	29920297	24689817	27301207	2619090	

注:①2004年以前,住宿及餐饮业统计数据仅包含餐饮业。②2005-2008年零售额数据根据第二次经济普查结果做出调整。③2010年零售额的计算方法根据报表制度有所调整。

Note:①Hoteing and catering trade statistics only include the catering trade, before 2004. ②2005-2008 Retail sales data of the year 2005-2008 according had been adjusted to the results of the second economic census. ③Calculation of retail sales in 2010 had been adjusted according to the reporting system.

表 10-3 零售业零售业态(2014) Status of Retail Sale

指标	Indicators	法人单位数(个) Number of Corporation (unit)	销售合计(万元) Total Sale (10000 yuan)	其中 of Witch	
				批发 Wholesale	零售 Retail
零售企业合计	**Total Retail Sale Enterprise**	**725**	**12620672**	**1585298**	**11035373**
按经营方式分:	**Grouped by Management Method**				
独立店	Sole Shop	618	8917038	796952	8120086
连锁商店总店	Chain General Shop	29	1596485	377635	1218850
连锁商店分店	Chain Shop	24	1350518	262232	1088286
其他	Others	54	756630	148479	608151
按零售业态分:	**Grouped by Retail Sale Line**				
百货商店	Department Store	37	1066751	134995	931756
超级市场	Super Market	38	1569837	404790	1165083
专业(专卖)店	Special (Special Sale) Shop	594	9304641	919500	8385141
其他	Others	56	679442	126013	553393

表 10－4 部分年份批发零售贸易及住宿餐饮业总额
Total Sales of Wholesale, Retail Sale and Hotel Catering Trade in Partial Years

单位：万元(10000 yuan)

指标	Indicators	2010	2011	2012	2013	2014
批发零售贸易业合计	**Wholesale and Retail Trade**					
销售总额	**Total Sale Value**	**75065955**	**93937682**	**106107789**	**122063824**	**160611147**
批发额	Wholesale	59901950	76303606	85747965	98908263	134256996
零售额	Retail Sale	15164006	17634076	20359824	23155560	26354151
1. 限额以上	Above Designated Size					
批发额	WholeSale	48594953	64989031	70289363	83074297	114098642
零售额	Retail Sale	8536179	10545544	10969875	14243145	12961779
2. 限额以下	Under Designated Size					
批发额	Wholesale	11306997	11314575	15458602	15833967	20158354
零售额	Retail Sale	6627827	7088532	9389949	8912416	13392372
住宿餐饮业合计	**Hotel and Catering Service**					
营业总收入	**Total Service Income**	**1998337**	**2516281**	**3089844**	**3613778**	**3814520**
#零售额	Retail Sale	1583426	1723695	1956446	2206169	2479968
1. 限额以上	Above Designated Size					
营业总收入	Total Service Income	882009	1068003	1109732	1152603	1030732
#零售额	Retail Sale	608977	757017	806779	836445	744928
2. 限额以下	Under Designated Size					
营业总收入	Total Service Income	1116328	1448278	1980112	2461175	2783788
#零售额	Retail Sale	974449	966678	1149668	1369724	1735040

注：销售额及营业额均仅含产业单位数据。

Note: Total sales and turnover include data of industrial units.

表 10－5 限额以上批发贸易业单位数和从业人员数(2014)
Number of Units and Employees of Wholesale Trade Above Designated Size

单位:个、人(unit,person)

指标	Indicators	法人企业数 Number of Corporations	从业人数 Number of Employees
批发业合计	**Wholesale Trade**	**2579**	**89740**
#国有及国有控股	State－owned and State－holding	82	6784
按注册类型分	**Grouped by Registration Type**		
内资企业	Domestic Funded Enterprises	2482	83602
国有企业	State－Owned Enterprises	3	1456
集体企业	Collective－Owned Enterprises	3	271
股份合作企业	Share Cooperative Enterprises	1	15
联营企业	Joint－owned Enterprises		
有限责任公司	Limited Liability Corporations	408	22066
股份有限公司	Share－holding Corporations Ltd.	29	2866
私营企业	Private Enterprises	2036	56921
港、澳、台商投资企业	Hongkong,Macao and Taiwan Funded	45	3662
外商投资企业	Foreign Funded	52	2476
按行业分	**Grouped by Sector**		
农畜产品批发	Agricultural and Livestock Products	15	739
食品、饮料及烟草制品批发	Food,Beverages and Tobaccos	118	9668
#烟草制品批发	Tobacco	1	1424
纺织、服装及日用品批发	Textile,Garments and Daily Consumer Articles	575	36932
#服装批发	Garments	188	9566
家用电器批发	Household Appliances	112	19381
文化、体育用品及器材批发	Culture,Sports Appliances and Equipments	120	4304
医药及医疗器材批发	Medicines and Medical Appliance	48	3148
矿产品、建材及化工产品批发	Mineral Products,Building Materials,Chemical Products	1223	20605
#石油及制品批发	Petroleum and Related Products	143	3731
金属及金属矿批发	Metal and Metallic Ore	500	6819
机械设备、五金交电及电子产品批发	Machine Equipments,Hardware,Electric Appliances,Electronic Equipment	408	13040
#汽车、摩托车及零配件批发	Motor Vehicles,Motorcycles and Parts	66	2111
其他批发	Others	72	1304

表 10 - 6 限额以上零售贸易业单位数和从业人员数(2014)
Number of Units and Employees of Retail Trade Above Designated Size

单位:个、人(unit,person)

指标	Indicators	法人企业数 Number of Corporations	从业人数 Number of Employees
零售业总计	**Total**	**732**	**68696**
#国有及国有控股	State - owned and State - holding	67	6027
按注册类型分	**Grouped by Registration Type**		
内资企业	Domestic Funded Enterprises	692	55621
国有企业	State - Owned Enterprises	10	680
集体企业	Collective - Owned Enterprises	8	103
股份合作企业	Share Cooperative Enterprises	3	44
联营企业	Joint - owned Enterprises	2	28
有限责任公司	Limited Liability Corporations	167	14338
股份有限公司	Share - holding Corporations Ltd.	16	8386
私营企业	Private Enterprises	479	31935
港、澳、台商投资企业	Hongkong, Macao and Taiwan Funded	22	4041
外商投资企业	Foreign Funded	18	9034
按行业分	**Grouped by Sector**		
综合零售	Comprehensive Retail	74	26094
百货零售	General Merchandise	35	5217
超级市场零售	Super Market	32	20138
食品、饮料及烟草制品专门零售	Food, Beverages and Tobaccos	28	1426
纺织、服装及日用品专门零售	Textile, Garments and Articles for Daily Use	59	6857
#服装零售	Garments	32	5226
文化、体育用品及器材专门零售	Culture, Sports Appliances and Equipments	36	1930
#图书零售	Books	12	975
医药及医疗器材专门零售	Medicines and Medical Appliance	32	3689
汽车、摩托车、燃料及零配件专门零售	Automobile, Motorcycles, Fuels and Parts	377	21665
#汽车零售	Motor Vehicles	273	18389
家用电器及电子产品专门零售	Household Appliances and Electronic Products	80	4326
#家用电器零售	Household Appliances	38	2592
通信设备零售	Communication Equipment	15	895
五金、家具及室内装修材料专门零售	Hardware, Furniture and Decoration Materials	16	1799
无店铺及其他零售	Non - shop and Others	29	910

表10－7 限额以上批发贸易业购进、销售、库存总额(2014)
Total Purchases, Sale and Inventory of Wholesale Trade Above Designated Size

指标	Indicators	购进总额 Total Purchases	进口 Imports
批发业	**Wholesale Trade**	**104283146**	**9906522**
#国有及国有控股	State－owned and State－holding	18604648	806464
按注册类型分	**Grouped by Registration Type**		
内资企业	Domestic Funded Enterprises	97810801	9082393
国有企业	State－Owned Enterprises	1081292	
集体企业	Collective－Owned Enterprises	320525	18307
股份合作企业	Share Cooperative Enterprises	4513	
联营企业	Joint－owned Enterprises		
有限责任公司	Limited Liability Corporations	38527849	3171057
股份有限公司	Share－holding Corporations Ltd.	6107866	755546
私营企业	Private Enterprises	51764461	5137483
港、澳、台商投资企业	Hongkong, Macao and Taiwan Funded	2597577	322565
外商投资企业	Foreign Funded	3874767	501565
按行业分	**Grouped by Sector**		
农畜产品批发	Wholesale of Agricultural and Livestock Products	150315	12474
食品、饮料及烟草制品批发	Wholesale of Food, Beverages and Tobaccos	4234550	23012
#烟草制品批发	Tobacco	1052240	
纺织、服装及日用品批发	Wholesale of Textile, Garments and Daily Consumer Articles	13271859	1214064
#服装批发	Garments	4367289	552284
家用电器批发	Household Appliances	4391017	225794
文化、体育用品及器材批发	Wholesale of Culture, Sports Appliances and Equipments	1952295	99365
医药及医疗器材批发	Wholesale of Medicines and Medical Appliance	1018691	169904
矿产品、建材及化工产品批发	Mineral Products, Building Materials and Chemical Products	73805999	7734272
#石油及制品批发	Petroleum and Related Products	7920922	85000
金属及金属矿批发	Metal and Metallic Ore	29221376	3610168
机械设备、五金交电及电子产品批发	Machine Equipments, Hardware, Electric Appliances, Electronic Equipment	8634709	339003
#汽车、摩托车及零配件批发	Motor Vehicles, Motorcycles and Parts	2675342	23288
其他批发	Others	1214728	314430

单位:万元(10000 yuan)

销售总额 Total Sales	其中 of Which			年末库存总额 Inventory (year – end)
	批发 Wholesale	出口 Exports	零售 Retail Sale	
113834787	**112293687**	**17060116**	**1541100**	**3463870**
21744150	21183701	855726	560449	514570
105865319	104424273	16388405	1441046	3172501
1485620	1485620			36600
339749	339372	258877	377	10407
4818	4818			
40887274	40440145	5048284	447129	1221614
8605096	8235005	1004042	370091	221756
54538425	53914976	10077203	623449	1682122
3016507	2957077	283743	59430	159501
4952961	4912338	387968	40623	131868
152120	146160	680	5961	37031
5203449	5003924	201490	199525	258965
1454996	1454996			36415
15090548	14827656	7454341	262892	395290
4868702	4751668	2481000	117035	125318
5225737	5094284	1735496	131452	126658
2126287	2109289	938081	16998	73624
1140494	925191	38189	215303	144000
79614762	78907997	4384790	706765	2098360
9658441	9151736	32016	506704	156852
31625852	31590426	2316469	35426	952175
9106269	8976221	3746329	130048	391503
2816208	2736850	293633	79358	40010
1400858	1397250	296216	3608	65097

表 10－8 限额以上零售贸易业购进、销售、库存总额(2014)
Total Purchases, Sale and Inventory of Retail Trade Above Designated Size

指标	Indicators	购进总额 Total Purchases	进口 Imports
零售业合计	**Retail Trade**	**11269737**	**527981**
#国有及国有控股	State－owned and State－holding	2071243	42047
按注册类型分	**Grouped by Registration Type**		
内资企业	Domestic Funded Enterprises	8920313	340571
国有企业	State－Owned Enterprises	55657	
集体企业	Collective－Owned Enterprises	34742	
股份合作企业	Share Cooperative Enterprises	11476	
联营企业	Joint－owned Enterprises	9805	
有限责任公司	Limited Liability Corporations	2592177	107544
股份有限公司	Share－holding Corporations Ltd.	1114278	656
私营企业	Private Enterprises	5077588	232371
港、澳、台商投资企业	Hongkong, Macao and Taiwan Funded	866366	66417
外商投资企业	Foreign Funded	1483058	120993
按行业分	**Grouped by Sector**		
综合零售	General Retail	2233429	7277
百货零售	General Merchandise	902804	7277
超级市场零售	Super Market	1285698	
食品、饮料及烟草制品专门零售	Retail of Food, Beverages and Tobaccos	116253	16
纺织、服装及日用品专门零售	Retail of Textile, Garments and Daily Use Articles	599937	1777
#服装零售	Garments	398565	1777
文化、体育用品及器材专门零售	Retail of Culture, Sports Appliances and Equipments	172587	
#图书零售	Books	61707	
医药及医疗器材专门零售	Retail of Medicines and Medical Appliance	812466	
汽车、摩托车、燃料及零配件专门零售	Retail of Motor Vehicles, Motorcycles, Fuels and Parts	6506339	518906
#汽车零售	Motor Vehicles	5149808	518906
家用电器及电子产品专门零售	Retail of Household Appliances and Electronic Products	506056	5
#家用电器零售	Household Appliances	342066	
通信设备零售	Communication Equipment	68548	5
五金、家具及室内装修材料专门零售	Retail of Hardware, Furniture and Decoration Materials	227179	
无店铺及其他零售	Non－shop and Other Retail	95491	

单位:万元(10000 yuan)

销售总额 Total Sales	其中:of Which 批发 Wholesale	出口 Exports	零售 Retail Sale	年末库存总额 Inventory (year – end)
12620672	**1585298**	**3589**	**11035373**	**1286345**
2202392	483796		1718596	101043
9866589	908995	3589	8957594	1095874
61071	46		61025	12784
36581	533		36049	2304
12343			12343	5408
10548			10548	494
2824270	91822	1408	2732448	312785
1375842	332567		1043275	111312
5517841	478431	2181	5039410	650705
1144173	215599		928574	104772
1609909	460704		1149205	85699
2639187	548649		2090538	220568
1042408	135166		907242	67182
1550602	404619		1145983	151270
133462	23064		110398	12904
979478	149041	767	830438	208746
680630	123361		557269	150081
228847	4065		224782	62530
68835	46		68788	20004
869458	115916		753542	83730
6894174	587858	1408	6306315	588448
5468750	285635		5183115	561668
540158	59607	1413	480550	58000
364745	21221		343525	32996
74282	15361	1413	58921	7936
229011	89299		139712	25678
106898	7799		99099	25741

表10－9 限额以上批发贸易业主要财务指标(2014)
Main Financial Indicators of Wholesale Trade Above Designated Size

指标	Indicators	年末资产负债 流动资产合计 Current Funds	#存货 Inventories	固定资产原价 Original Value of Fixed Assets
批发业合计	Wholesale Trade	33466875.2	3193611.4	1533972.0
#国有控股	State – holding	4467577.8	558337.2	364833.1
按注册类型分	Grouped by Registration Type			
内资企业	Domestic Funded Enterprises	30016141.9	2953038.8	1430562.0
国有企业	State – Owned Enterprises	585854.3	31282.1	105151.7
集体企业	Collective – Owned Enterprises	121980.3	10417.8	13577.6
股份合作企业	Share Cooperative Enterprises	720.0		195.9
联营企业	Joint – owned Enterprises			
有限责任公司	Limited Liability Corporations	11408057.0	1204079.5	414806.0
股份有限公司	Share – holding Corporations Ltd.	1599856.5	187213.1	147713.3
私营企业	Private Enterprises	16298830.3	1519975.9	748894.8
港、澳、台商投资企业	Hongkong, Macao and Taiwan Funded	1460854.3	180649.9	64032.8
外商投资企业	Foreign Funded	1989879.0	59922.7	39377.2
按行业分	Grouped by Sector			
农畜产品批发	Agricultural and Livestock Products	97884.3	43865.7	27172.8
食品、饮料及烟草制品批发	Food, Beverages and Tobaccos	1790239.2	236656.1	204559.8
#烟草制品批发	Tobacco	584118.6	31124.2	103906.4
纺织、服装及日用品批发	Textile, Garments and Daily Consumer Articles	6004093.3	346204.6	255812.6
#服装批发	Garments	2714865.6	133948.5	104594.1
家用电器批发	Household Appliances	871958.2	70176.5	16844.6
文化、体育用品及器材批发	Culture, Sports Appliances and Equipments	736534.6	69329.1	39579.4
医药及医疗器材批发	Medicines and Medical Appliance	505921.3	86687.4	62547.1
矿产品、建材及化工产品批发	Mineral Products, Building Materials, Chemical Products	20572985.4	2001767.1	713226.5
#石油及制品批发	Petroleum and Related Products	1862788.4	174142.9	201698.1
金属及金属矿批发	Metal and Metallic Ore	8953516.2	928275.8	242070.7
机械设备、五金交电及电子产品批发	Machine Equipments, Hardware, Electric Appliances, Electronic Equipment	3332561.8	345746.8	174140.1
#汽车、摩托车及零配件批发	Motor Vehicles, Motorcycles and Parts	492048	39147	15810
其他批发	Others	302014.3	53008.9	49014.2

单位:万元(10000 yuan)

Total Assets and Liabilities at the Year - end				损益与分配 Profit, Loss and Distribution	
本年折旧 Depreciation in this year	资产合计 Total Asset	负债合计 Total Liabilities	所有者权益 Creditors' Equity	主营业务收入 Major Business Revenue	主营业务成本 Major Business Costs
104081.6	**37876176.9**	**31776753.5**	**6099489.8**	**104461743.4**	**100674700.5**
16989.1	5068340.3	3497291.0	1571049.3	18921433.9	18083706.6
98705.7	33736220.5	28723209.8	5013077.1	97305351.0	94052809.3
4946.1	668355.2	18972.7	649382.5	1269759.7	930940.3
175.4	136871.7	104518.2	32353.5	337203.3	325254.1
30.7	790.9	284.7	506.2	4818.3	4512.5
24868.9	12645409.0	10736147.9	1909261.1	36832042.9	35593955.4
7601.7	1952644.9	1700539.3	252105.6	7945190.0	7792625.0
61082.5	18331116.4	16162458.9	2168723.9	50912000.1	49401248.4
3352.8	1582135.4	1195037.4	387098.0	2754406.7	2435514.9
2023.1	2557821.0	1858506.3	699314.7	4401985.7	4186376.3
673.0	123718.6	91422.4	32296.2	146604.7	141576.8
10868.0	2078218.6	1167635.9	910582.7	4213966.6	3371016.5
4903.1	666045.4	18569.3	647476.1	1243585.9	905777.0
20379.7	7042722.3	6204516.8	838205.5	14510075.1	13571241.7
7209.3	3522389.6	3114285.3	408104.3	4630042.3	4370096.6
1917.6	893532.2	803130.4	90401.8	1864315.8	1560034.5
3089.2	812693.6	640127.4	172566.2	2092523.5	1981675.8
5900.2	604163.2	415599.0	188564.2	1005538.7	887699.4
45842.2	22739917.4	19593051.5	3146932.3	72592891.6	71305105.6
12512.7	2277878.5	1812774.9	465103.6	8496835.1	8313901.5
13568.0	9886901.2	8431832.3	1455068.9	29525296.1	29055405.0
14091.2	3917282.1	3247480.7	669801.4	8559514.1	8130548.5
1435	510335	446862	63474	2464160	2374360
2795.4	422621.4	298638.5	123982.9	969155.9	924277.6

表 10－9 续表 Continued

指标	Indicators	损益与分配 主营业务税金及附加 Tax and Extra Charge	管理费用 Management Cost
批发业合计	**Wholesale Trade**	**166170.7**	**837726.4**
#国有控股	State－holding	102110.7	125554.1
按注册类型分	**Grouped by Registration Type**		
内资企业	Domestic Funded Enterprises	157321.4	745238.1
国有企业	State－Owned Enterprises	76286.1	41559.7
集体企业	Collective－Owne Enterprises	241.1	3308.6
股份合作企业	Share Cooperative Enterprises	6.2	76.4
联营企业	Joint－owned Enterprises		
有限责任公司	Limited Liability Corporations	41489.5	230785.2
股份有限公司	Share－holding Corporations Ltd.	3726.0	32375.0
私营企业	Private Enterprises	35548.9	437122.3
港、澳、台商投资企业	Hongkong, Macao and Taiwan Funded	5564.1	70669.7
外商投资企业	Foreign Funded	3285.2	21818.6
按行业分	**Grouped by Sector**		
农畜产品批发	Agricultural and Livestock Products	125.9	4623.0
食品、饮料及烟草制品批发	Food, Beverages and Tobaccos	87349.0	142951.1
#烟草制品批发	Tobacco	76265.9	41538.9
纺织、服装及日用品批发	Textile, Garments and Daily Consumer Articles	16522.3	227630.9
#服装批发	Garments	5816.3	80780.0
家用电器批发	Household Appliances	4898.9	28155.1
文化、体育用品及器材批发	Culture, Sports Appliances and Equipments	1446.1	31497.0
医药及医疗器材批发	Medicines and Medical Appliance	2908.5	29067.7
矿产品、建材及化工产品批发	Mineral Products, Building Materials, Chemical Products	50810.7	262519.7
#石油及制品批发	Petroleum and Related Products	17353.9	35980.3
金属及金属矿批发	Metal and Metallic Ore	14793.0	91472.7
机械设备、五金交电及电子产品批发	Machine Equipments, Hardware, Electric Appliances, Electronic Equipment	5400.5	122477.2
#汽车、摩托车及零配件批发	Motor Vehicles, Motorcycles and Parts	625	12766
其他批发	Others	1478.3	13135.1

单位:万元(10000 yuan)

Profit, Loss and Distribution			工资福利与税金 Wages, Welfare and Tax in this Year	
财务费用 Financial Expenses	营业利润 Business Profits	利润总额 Total Profits	本年应付职工薪酬总额 Total Employee Compensation Payable	本年应交增值税总额 Total Value - added Taxes Payable
448390.9	**920902.9**	**1097143.7**	**747364**	**510844**
9940.9	493959.0	558558.8	119709	221552
400103.7	725720.3	879041.8	693534	463473
-17847.2	226058.8	231403.0	38860	57346
994.3	930.5	1443.9	2824	11
11.0	13.0	8.2	216	52
115746.2	386888.2	456594.1	216549	234807
11018.0	33200.8	48187.0	43918	17055
290181.4	78621.6	141312.5	391148	154017
7610.9	80538.7	83114.5	33549	38295
40676.3	114643.9	134987.4	20281	9076
2108.4	-4705.4	1511.9	4329	524
-4398.1	334575.2	352739.7	90831	119369
-17850.5	225642.9	231009.0	38548	57150
102546.5	97334.6	114796.7	254191	67455
70076.4	28508.5	49732.5	68764	13535
3500.0	11504.5	2589.9	96220	37049
6365.7	15059.6	17712.7	28469	2895
8109.7	30919.6	36458.6	23491	20267
275251.9	354168.5	453064.9	240985	266966
16968.9	76085.8	93251.7	56439	104870
137641.5	152478.0	190368.9	93778	52820
47175.8	81083.7	106611.5	97430	24090
3364	15185	19838	13579	1656
10468.6	10373.2	12078.6	5410	8930

表 10-10 限额以上零售贸易业主要财务指标(2014) Main Financial Indicators of Retail Trade Above Designated Size

指标	Indicators	年末资产负债		
		流动资产合计 Current Funds	#存货 Inventories	固定资产原价 Original Value of Fixed Assets
零售业总计	**Total**	**4084735.1**	**1063452.8**	**1198704.2**
#国有控股	State - holding	544833.4	79640.9	108029.6
按注册类型分	**Grouped by Registration Type**			
内资企业	Domestic Funded Enterprises	3600364.4	904264.4	831003.6
国有企业	State - Owned Enterprises	81257.4	7312.1	11107.6
集体企业	Collective - Owned Enterprises	5334.2	2738.8	1995.4
股份合作企业	Share Cooperative Enterprises	3866.5	1101.6	1212.1
联营企业	Joint - owned Enterprises	922.8	311.4	559.9
有限责任公司	Limited Liability Corporations	1061841.8	244408.7	237795.3
股份有限公司	Share - holding Corporations Ltd.	612207.3	67460.6	159001.9
私营企业	Private Enterprises	1833209.9	580823.7	419013.3
港、澳、台商投资企业	Hongkong, Macao and Taiwan Funded	305572.4	86367.8	138145.0
外商投资企业	Foreign Funded	178798.3	72820.6	229555.6
按行业分	**Grouped by Sector**			
综合零售	Comprehensive Retail	1096807.3	117045.1	622511.1
#百货零售	General Merchandise	599964.8	32356.6	293218.2
超级市场零售	Super Market	485888.1	82550.0	328244.0
食品、饮料及烟草制品专门零售	Food, Beverages and Tobaccos	51051.2	13365.3	14176.5
纺织、服装及日用品专门零售	Textile, Garments and Articles for Daily Use	452729.6	190266.7	24484.5
文化、体育用品及器材专门零售	Culture, Sports Appliances and Equipments	172600.5	52553.2	28579.8
医药及医疗器材专门零售	Medicines and Medical Appliance	279661.5	74698.5	24451.0
汽车、摩托车、燃料及零配件专门零售	Automobile, Motorcycles, Fuels and Parts	1715040.7	533753.0	388098.8
#汽车零售	Motor Vehicles	1581862.0	518066.8	350439.4
家用电器及电子产品专门零售	Household Appliances and Electronic Products	189174.1	47444.2	18179.8
五金、家具及室内装修材料专门零售	Hardware, Furniture and Decoration Materials	25481.0	10867.9	60550.5
无店铺及其他零售	Non - shop and Others	102189.2	23458.9	17672.2
按经营方式分组	**Grouped by Management Method**			
#独立商店	Sole Shop	3117972.7	844959.5	711454.2
连锁商店总店	Chain General Shop	547365.1	99094.3	307465.2
连锁商店分店	Chain Shop	208892.4	56345.6	18260.2
按零售业态分组	**Grouped by Retail Sale Line**			
#百货商店	Department Store	602996.0	36260.6	292630.2
超级市场	Super Market	491110	82128	329240
专业店	Special Shop	1584222.4	439818.2	280423.3
专卖店	Special Sale Shop	1142162.0	386854.8	222597.7
便利店	Convenience Shop	21248.9	3457.8	3169.9

单位:万元(10000 yuan)

Total Assets and Liabilities at the Year - end				损益与分配 Profit, Loss and Distribution	
本年折旧 Depreciation in this year	资产合计 Total Asset	负债合计 Total Liabilities	所有者权益 Creditors' Equity	主营业务收入 Major Business Revenue	主营业务成本 Major Business Costs
82352.2	**6161208.6**	**4477588.9**	**1683619.7**	**10365575.4**	**9325233.9**
5471.3	937975.4	456830.2	481145.2	1282326.1	1153543.4
57907.9	5055451.7	3730876.5	1324575.2	8692446.8	7883995.5
1111.6	100723.5	82840.2	17883.3	56332.2	45691.7
126.6	7216.4	2825.3	4391.1	31842.3	30161.2
115.1	4484.3	3934.8	549.5	10827.5	10143.1
47.7	2018.9	175.0	1843.9	9858.3	9024.1
19322.4	1503791.3	1069569.6	434221.7	2482369.1	2234435.8
6111.6	1039770.8	521691.8	518079.0	1197147.2	1076579.2
31055.3	2394958.9	2048566.9	346392.0	4877380.6	4455142.2
9868.4	673128.0	392803.3	280324.7	969658.8	809821.1
14575.9	432628.9	353909.1	78719.8	703469.8	631417.3
34967.0	2115250.7	1368392.0	746858.7	2268282.4	1959293.3
12713.2	1262064.4	721536.6	540527.8	877489.6	728164.8
22105.8	841615.9	634051.1	207564.8	1351032.4	1196724.1
1058.6	63956.9	47648.9	16308.0	115758.1	101486.5
2530.9	756494.1	478536.4	277957.7	792335.8	555797.9
2196.0	204372.0	143407.1	60964.9	216997.7	181416.1
1259.8	313635.1	237161.0	76474.1	739259.8	683019.2
35308.7	2288746.6	1845148.5	443598.1	5458610.1	5153141.2
33081.1	2082600.4	1741991.8	340608.6	4891383.6	4627362.5
1527.1	209234.9	171074.8	38160.1	462319.9	408388.2
2809.1	90558.8	89061.9	1496.9	221953.3	208915.4
695.0	118959.5	97158.3	21801.2	90058.3	73776.1
52177.0	4646061.9	3353833.9	1292228.0	7896112.9	7202017.4
19393.6	880426.1	611648.0	268778.1	1336399.7	1177949.2
2433.8	250467.2	209241.5	41225.7	476758.8	369735.8
12670.0	1254595.1	728344.7	526250.4	897861.0	745947.4
22280	859320	639597	219723	1367906	1211387
22596.5	1993594.2	1523460.0	470134.2	4351219.3	3993763.1
20483.2	1519928.8	1209503.2	310425.6	3142945.5	2865720.6
273.6	26096.8	23082.6	3014.2	46157.2	39396.1

表 10－10 续表 Continued

指标	Indicators	损益与分配 主营业务税金及附加 Tax and Extra Charge	管理费用 Management Cost
零售业总计	**Total**	**34470.9**	**326426.3**
#国有控股	State－holding	5443.6	28780.3
按注册类型分	**Grouped by Registration Type**		
内资企业	Domestic Funded Enterprises	26945.2	259450.4
国有企业	State－Owned Enterprises	98.3	3684.7
集体企业	Collective－Owned Enterprises	66.1	509.1
股份合作企业	Share Cooperative Enterprises	19.3	309.8
联营企业	Joint－owned Enterprises	25.0	171.0
有限责任公司	Limited Liability Corporations	11019.7	77205.5
股份有限公司	Share－holding Corporations Ltd.	3816.1	28842.1
私营企业	Private Enterprises	11874.3	148416.5
港、澳、台商投资企业	Hongkong, Macao and Taiwan Funded	4700.7	48213.3
外商投资企业	Foreign Funded	2825.0	18762.6
按行业分	**Grouped by Sector**		
综合零售	Comprehensive Retail	15647.0	103802.7
#百货零售	General Merchandise	10387.9	61286.9
超级市场零售	Super Market	5074.1	39695.0
食品、饮料及烟草制品专门零售	Food, Beverages and Tobaccos	271.2	4476.3
纺织、服装及日用品专门零售	Textile, Garments and Articles for Daily Use	4583.3	43343.4
文化、体育用品及器材专门零售	Culture, Sports Appliances and Equipments	2400.0	10393.3
医药及医疗器材专门零售	Medicines and Medical Appliance	1100.5	16554.9
汽车、摩托车、燃料及零配件专门零售	Automobile, Motorcycles, Fuels and Parts	7740.9	117587.0
#汽车零售	Motor Vehicles	6675.9	110580.9
家用电器及电子产品专门零售	Household Appliances and Electronic Products	1731.3	14782.4
五金、家具及室内装修材料专门零售	Hardware, Furniture and Decoration Materials	764.5	10163.4
无店铺及其他零售	Non－shop and Others	232.2	5322.9
按经营方式分组	**Grouped by Management Method**		
#独立商店	Sole Shop	24591.9	220583.6
连锁商店总店	Chain Genera Shop	5406.4	57204.8
连锁商店分店	Chain Shop	2186.0	17201.1
按零售业态分组	**Grouped by Retail Sale Line**		
#百货商店	Department Store	10681.7	63034.6
超级市场	Super Market	5111	42443
专业店	Special Shop	9772.7	101852.4
专卖店	Special Sale Shop	6930.2	92453.2
便利店	Convenience Shop	141.3	2288.6

单位:万元(10000 yuan)

Profit, Loss and Distribution			工资福利与税金 Wages, Welfare and Tax in this Year	
财务费用 Financial Expenses	营业利润 Business Profits	利润总额 Total Profits	本年应付职工薪酬总额 Total Employee Compensation Payable	本年应交增值税总额 Total Value - added Taxes Payable
92980.1	**70016.6**	**104725.2**	**399978**	**118015**
2790.7	56289.3	72835.3	39485	12805
78177.4	55133.7	87698.6	314260	92537
-120.3	1179.4	2412.4	6226	255
78.0	339.9	320.3	567	277
80.8	-12.9	-22.8	228	102
0.5	485.6	479.2	122	118
18846.2	22346.2	45884.3	91718	28808
5230.3	38196.2	40153.5	43796	10898
54033.0	-10596.0	-4714.6	171219	51965
9769.1	39049.7	39661.2	46889	17677
5033.6	-24166.8	-22634.6	38829	7801
12208.1	25088.1	33646.9	137711	27090
10590.0	37602.1	40650.2	43274	12172
1535.6	-11610.1	-7211.6	91599	14377
736.9	2229.4	2858.2	6353	1474
9261.9	49844.2	52294.4	64863	28609
392.8	4270.4	6784.3	14116	2561
5747.7	12105.2	11630.0	19483	7677
58829.9	-17708.1	3535.7	124198	40358
56857.0	-40079.7	-17693.4	115619	33243
2616.6	-1258.2	-1320.7	22839	8201
2995.5	-8383.9	-8389.0	6717	836
190.7	3829.5	3685.4	3700	1208
81654.8	63688.8	89764.8	240554	80291
5255.1	69.5	4534.8	92820	15198
651.4	12156.6	15366.3	36637	16296
11030.4	35650.5	38928.0	44418	12245
1237	-11887	-7513	92186	14511
35703.3	44037.4	52343.6	131101	45388
34887.5	1064.2	18717.7	102401	38216
139.1	-1367.3	-112.9	4555	670

表 10－11 限额以上批发零售贸易业主要商品分类销售额(2014) Sales of Wholesale and Retail Trade Above Designated Size by Category of Commodities

单位:万元(10000 yuan)

类别	Category	合计	批发 Wholesale	零售 Retail
食品、饮料、烟酒类	Food, Beverage, Tabacco and Liquor	4630050	3337766	1292284
#粮油类	Grain and Oil	2702370	1671554	1030815
饮料类	Beverage	294381	150485	143896
烟酒类	Tabacco and Liquor	1633300	1515727	117573
服装鞋帽、针、纺织品类	Garments, Shoes, Hats Knitwear and Textile	5759398	4606148	1153250
#服装类	Garments	3598799	2716621	882178
鞋帽类	Shoes, Hats	452675	309062	143613
针、纺织品类	Knitwear and Textile	1707924	1580465	127459
化妆品类	Cosmetics	171120	79749	91371
金银珠宝类	Jewelry	471415	181607	289809
日用品类	Articles for Daily Use	3173270	2854657	318613
五金、电料类	Hardware and Electrical Appliances	1182703	1142096	40608
体育、娱乐用品类	Recreation and Sports Articles	141342	126278	15064
书报杂志类	Books and Newspapers	65299	2916	62383
电子出版物及音像制品类	Electronic Publications and Audio－video Products	2052		2052
家用电器和音像器材类	Household Appliances and Audio－video Equipments	2105365	1593882	511483
中西药品类	Medicines	1465197	643730	821467
文化办公用品类	Culture and Office Articles	1416515	1244784	171731
家具类	Furnitures	281774	135754	146020
通讯器材类	Telecommunication Appliances	654165	478291	175874
煤炭及制品类	Coal and Coal Products	5505232	5501236	3996
木材及制品类	Timber and Timber Products	298445	292539	5906
石油及制品类	Petroleum and Products	11457690	9811093	1646597
化工材料及制品类	Chemical Materials and Products	15888826	15888826	
金属材料类	Metal Materials	23088486	23088486	
建筑及装潢材料类	Materials for Construction and Decoration	614727	527624	87102
机电产品及设备类	Mechanical and Electrical Equipments	1962148	1956419	5729
汽车类	Automobile	5711648	668861	5042786
种子饲料类	Seeds and Forage	70446	70446	
棉麻土畜类	Cotton and Flax Products	73709	73709	

表 10－12 住宿餐饮业单位数和从业人员数(2014)
Number of Units and Employees of Catering Trade and Hotel

单位:个、人(unit,person)

指标	Indicators	法人企业数 Number of Corporations	从业人数 Number of Employees
总计	**Total**	**426**	**41626**
住宿业	**Hotel**	**188**	**23158**
#国有及国有控股	State－owned and State－holding	23	3017
按登记注册类型分组	Grouped by Registration Type		
内资企业	Domestic Funded Enterprises	175	20117
国有企业	State－Owned Enterprises	7	580
集体企业	Collective－Owned Enterprises	3	375
股份合作企业	Share Cooperative Enterprises		
有限责任公司	Limited Liability Corporations	38	6809
股份有限公司	Share－holding Corporations Ltd.	7	1691
私营企业	Private Enterprises	120	10662
港、澳、台商投资企业	Hongkong,Macao and Taiwan Funded	7	2098
外商投资企业	Foreign Funded	6	943
按行业分	Grouped by Sector		
旅游饭店	Tour Hotel	123	18450
一般旅馆	Common Hotel	62	4546
餐饮业	**Catering Trade**	**238**	**18468**
#国有及国有控股	State－owned and State－holding	4	550
按登记注册类型分组	Grouped by Registration Type		
内资企业	Domestic Funded Enterprises	233	17997
国有企业	State－Owned Enterprises	2	77
集体企业	Collective－Owned Enterprises		
股份合作企业	Share Cooperative Enterprises		
有限责任公司	Limited Liability Corporations	25	3485
股份有限公司	Share－holding Corporations Ltd.	2	226
私营企业	Private Enterprises	202	14152
港、澳、台商投资企业	Hongkong,Macao and Taiwan Funded	5	471
外商投资企业	Foreign Funded		
按行业分	Grouped by Sector		
正餐服务业	Dinner Services	219	16730
快餐服务业	Snack Services	8	904
饮料及冷饮服务业	Beverage Services	1	229
其他餐饮服务业	Others	10	605

表 10－13 星级住宿业和限额以上餐饮业经营情况(2014)
Main Operation Indicators of Catering Trade and Star－rated Hotel

指标	Indicators	营业额 Business Revenue	其中	
			客房收入 Room Rate Revenue	餐费收入 Catering Revenue
总计	**Total**	**775477**	**210856**	**492165**
住宿业	**Hotel**	**437462**	**170128**	**208769**
#国有及国有控股	State－owned and State－holding	48937	15931	27910
按登记注册类型分组	Grouped by Registration Type			
内资企业	Domestic Funded Enterprises	358532	144412	161192
国有企业	State－Owned Enterprises	8266	3414	3832
集体企业	Collective－Owned Enterprises	4996	1560	3160
股份合作企业	Share Cooperative Enterprises			
有限责任公司	Limited Liability Corporations	126893	42492	58165
股份有限公司	Share－holdingCorporations Ltd.	31551	10561	12081
私营企业	Private Enterprises	186826	86386	83955
港、澳、台商投资企业	Hongkong, Macao and Taiwan Funded	65387	19449	41448
外商投资企业	Foreign Funded	13543	6267	6129
按行业分	Grouped by Sector			
旅游饭店	Tour Hotel	362701	125938	186160
一般旅馆	Common Hotel	72213	42286	22306
餐饮业	**Catering Trade**	**338015**	**40729**	**283396**
#国有及国有控股	State－owned and State－holding	9631	2462	6897
按登记注册类型分组	Grouped by Registration Type			
内资企业	Domestic Funded Enterprises	329421	38371	278222
国有企业	State－Owned Enterprises	902	182	719
集体企业	Collective－Owned Enterprises			
股份合作企业	Share Cooperative Enterprises			
有限责任公司	Limited Liability Corporations	66302	12119	50101
股份有限公司	Share－holding Corporations Ltd.	3801	677	2977
私营企业	Private Enterprises	257744	25368	223778
港、澳、台商投资企业	Hongkong, Macao and Taiwan Funded	8594	2357	5174
外商投资企业	Foreign Funded			
按行业分	Grouped by Sector			
正餐服务业	Dinner Services	300270	40729	246240
快餐服务业	Snack Services	16497		16114
饮料及冷饮服务业	Beverage Services	2985		2985
其他餐饮服务业	Others	18263		18057

单位:万元

of Which		年末餐饮营业面积（平方米）Business Area of Catering in the Year-end (sq. m)	年末拥有床位数（个）Hold Beds in the Year-end (bed)	年末拥有餐位数（位）Hold Seat of Catering in the Year-end (unit)
商品销售收入 Commodity Sales Revenue	其他收入 Others			
10221	**62234**	**39686**	**63971**	**192610**
6792	**51773**	**33393**	**54528**	**82479**
944	4151	2908	4974	10014
6359	46569	30447	50453	73216
4	1016	928	1710	2520
41	236	325	518	1510
2006	24230	6228	10036	23531
3162	5748	1943	2945	5375
1146	15339	21023	35244	40280
418	4072	1898	2662	5393
16	1132	1048	1413	3870
5931	44672	19407	30821	68413
807	6814	13644	23151	13838
3429	**10461**	**6293**	**9443**	**110131**
	271	321	480	818
3285	9543	6036	9056	108333
		51	82	400
1727	2354	1363	1962	16111
	147	123	202	1205
1558	7041	4480	6785	90215
144	919	257	387	1798
3259	10042	6293	9443	99854
	383			6366
				500
170	36			3411

表 10－14 部分年份限额以上批发零售贸易业主要财务指标
Main Financial Indicators of Wholesale and Retail Trade Above Designated Size of Partial Years

单位:亿元(100 million yuan)

指标	Indicators	2010	2011	2012	2013	2014
主营业务收入	Prime Operating Revenue	5170.16	6758.04	7279.60	8697.30	11482.7
主营业务成本	Operating Costs	4891.90	6429.19	6941.90	8306.90	10999.9
主营业务税金及附加	Tax and Extra Charge	10.80	12.03	12.90	15.90	20.1
其他业务利润	Profits from Other Business	17.71	19.23	17.70	18.70	11.8
管理费用	Management Cost	59.26	72.27	80.30	94.10	116.4
财务费用	Financial Expenses	21.64	34.66	40.10	38.30	54.1
利润总额	Total Profits	69.47	82.92	62.10	109.40	120.2
资产总计	Total Assets	1879.26	2449.18	2804.40	3857.40	4403.7.
#流动资产	Current Assets	1617.44	2140.55	2433.70	3363.00	3755.2
#存货	Inventory	274.32	342.24	338.10	382.70	425.7
负债合计	Total Liabilities	1497.65	1987.55	2299.20	3156.70	3625.4
所有者权益合计	Total Owner's Equities	381.61	461.63	505.20	700.70	778.3
应付职工薪酬	Employee Compensation Payable		63.79	76.60	92.10	115

表 10－15 部分年份星级住宿业及限额以上餐饮业主要财务指标
Main Financial Indicators of Catering Trade Above Designated Size and Star－rated Hotel in Partial Years

单位:亿元(100 million yuan)

指标	Indicators	2010	2011	2012	2013	2014
主营业务收入	Prime Operating Revenue	73.7	83.1	86.7	75.4	76.5
主营业务成本	Operating Costs	30.1	35.0	35.7	30.7	30.2
销售费用	Business Expenses	21.5	23.7	27.3	26.8	25.6
主营业务税金及附加	Tax and Associate Charge	4.1	4.6	4.7	4.2	4.2
管理费用	Management Cost	16.8	18.8	19.9	19.7	19.6
#税金	Taxes	0.8	0.7	0.7	0.6	0.7
财务费用	Financial Expenses	3.5	4.8	5.2	4.8	4.6
利润总额	Total Profits	-0.5	-2.0	-3.8	-7.2	-6.9
资产总计	Total Assets	149.3	182.1	186.9	187.1	182.6
#流动资产	Current Assets	54.7	72.3	76.7	72.6	65.6
负债合计	Total Liabilities	112.5	142.9	151.7	160.6	171.2
所有者权益合计	Total Owner's Equities	36.9	39.1	35.2	26.5	11.3
应付职工薪酬	Employee Compensation Payable		16.2	18.8	20.4	19.3

表 10-16 亿元以上商品交易市场成交情况(2014)
Basic Statistics of Commodity Exchange Market with Total Sale Over 100 million Yuan

单位:万元(10000 yuan)

指标	Indicators	摊位个数(个) Number of Stalls (unit)	总成交额 Transaction Volume
总计	**Total**	**71023**	**30806054**
食品、饮料、烟酒类	Food, Beverage, Tabacco and Liquor	35806	5609999
食品类	Foodstuff	34876	5319130
#粮油类	Grain and Oil	981	506853
肉禽蛋类	Meat. Poultry and Egg	3037	560417
水产品类	Aquatic Product	21560	2243883
蔬菜类	Garden Stuff	7449	1392406
干鲜果品类	Dry Fruit and Fresh Fruit	1849	615571
饮料类	Beverage	251	117333
烟酒类	Tabacco and Liquor	679	173536
服装鞋帽、针、纺织品类	Garments, Shoes, Hats Knitwear and Textile	8518	1544140
服装类	Garments	5584	839921
鞋帽类	Shoes, Hats	1002	349046
针、纺织品类	Knitwear and Textile	1932	355173
化妆品类	Cosmetics	162	30569
日用品类	Articles for Daily Use	2676	381472
五金、电料类	Hardware and Electrical Appliances	2467	438723
体育、娱乐用品类	Recreation and Sports Articles	89	3083
书报杂志类	Books and Newspapers	5	18
电子出版物及音像制品类	Electronic Publications and Audio - video Products		
家用电器和音像器材类	Household Appliances and Audio - video Equipments	243	38304
中西药品类	Medicines		
文化办公用品类	Culture and Office Articles	1448	195025
家具类	Furnitures	2044	310899
通讯器材类	Telecommunication Appliances		
煤炭及制品类	Coal and Products	55	1666802
木材及制品类	Timber and Timber Products	795	172261
石油及制品类	Petroleum and Products	65	1886705
化工材料及制品类	Chemical Materials and Products	3310	7958561
金属材料类	Metal Materials	4232	7325411
建筑及装潢材料类	Materials for Construction and Decoration	3942	1362026
机电产品及设备类	Mechanical and Electrical Equipments	145	64241
汽车类	Automobile	826	605386
种子饲料类	Seed and Feedstuff	145	34942
棉麻类	Cotton and Flax Products		
其他类	Others	2481	1037987

表 10-17 个体工商业情况(2014)
Basic Statistics of Individual Industry and Commerce

指标	Indicators	全市期末实有 Total at the End of this Year	其中 of Which	
			本期开业 Openning for this Term	城镇 Districts
户数(户)	**Number of Households(unit)**	**401053**	**70977**	**192748**
农、林、牧、渔业	Farming. Forestry. Animal Husbandry and Fishery	4316	1060	1288
采矿业	Mining and Quarrying Industry	40	1	9
制造业	Manufacturing Industry	83495	12119	20707
电力、燃气及水的生产和供应业	Electric Power,Gas and Water Production and Supply	26	1	8
建筑业	Construction	2072	346	1024
交通运输业、仓储和邮政业	Transportation and Warehousing	30508	5874	15138
信息传输、计算机服务和软件业	Information Transmission,Computer Service and Software Industries	397	106	253
批发和零售业	Wholesale and Retail Trade	216300	36258	116370
住宿和餐饮业	Hotel and Catering Trade	23315	6712	13385
房地产业	Real Estate Industries	1130	198	865
租赁和商务服务业	Leasing and Business Service Industries	4835	1025	3294
居民服务和其它服务业	Resident Service and Other Service Industries	30466	6402	18045
卫生、社会保障和社会福利业	Health Care,Social Security and Social Welfare	464	53	315
文化、体育和娱乐业	Culture,Sports and Entertainment	2272	579	1190
其它行业	Others	1		
从业人员(人)	Emplyment Personnel(person)	871391	158636	417018
农、林、牧、渔业	Farming. Forestry. Animal Husbandry and Fishery	13787	3676	4256
采矿业	Mining and Quarrying Industry	158	5	34
制造业	Manufacturing Industry	270552	41502	89564
电力、燃气及水的生产和供应业	Electric Power,Gas and Water Production and Supply	48	1	13
建筑业	Construction	7438	1546	3820
交通运输业、仓储和邮政业	Transportation and Warehousing	38735	7057	18284
信息传输、计算机服务和软件业	Information Transmission,Computer Service and Software Industries	644	174	434

注:本表数据来自于宁波市工商行政管理局。

Note:Data in this table are obtained from Ningbo Administration for Industry & Commerce.

表 10－17 续表 Continued

指标	Indicators	全市期末实有 Total at The End of This Year	其中 of Which 本期开业 Openning for This Term	其中 of Which 城镇 Districts
批发和零售业	Wholesale and Retail Trade	385213	64012	201243
住宿和餐饮业	Hotel and Catering Trade	67207	19868	42928
房地产业	Real Estate Industries	2125	393	1662
租赁和商务服务业	Leasing and Business Service Industries	9454	2062	6587
居民服务和其它服务业	Resident Service and Other Service Industries	65097	15635	41271
卫生、社会保障和社会福利业	Health Care, Social Security and Social Welfare	994	121	685
文化、体育和娱乐业	Culture, Sports and Entertainment	7088	1907	4298
其它行业	Others	2		
注册资金(万元)	Registered Capital (10000 Yuan)	2521162	587349	1287753
农、林、牧、渔业	Farming. Forestry. Animal Husbandry and Fishery	178130	49292	55348
采矿业	Mining and Quarrying Industry	2561	500	853
制造业	Manufacturing Industry	722072	121345	201936
电力、燃气及水的生产和供应业	Electric Power, Gas and Water Production and Supply	226	1	41
建筑业	Construction	25857	4712	11279
交通运输业、仓储和邮政业	Transportation and Warehousing	162003	31982	79112
信息传输、计算机服务和软件业	Information Transmission, Computer Service and Software Industries	1747	493	1102
批发和零售业	Wholesale and Retail Trade	960729	246081	616359
住宿和餐饮业	Hotel and Catering Trade	228899	69557	159925
房地产业	Real Estate Industries	4521	877	3695
租赁和商务服务业	Leasing and Business Service Industries	37016	9135	24863
居民服务和其它服务业	Resident Service and Other Service Industries	149489	44584	99153
卫生、社会保障和社会福利业	Health Care, Social Security and Social Welfare	11064	1360	7418
文化、体育和娱乐业	Culture, Sports and Entertainment			

表 10－18　私营企业基本情况(2014)
Basic Statistics on Private Enterprises

指标	Indicators	全市期末实有 Total at the End of this Year	其中 of Which	
			本期开业 Openning for this Term	城镇 Districts
户数(户)	**Number of Households(unit)**	**203627**	**38052**	**124276**
农、林、牧、渔业	Farming. Forestry. Animal Husbandry and Fishery	3179	764	927
采矿业	Mining and Quarrying Industry	96	9	34
制造业	Manufacturing Industry	79591	8793	31161
电力、燃气及水的生产和供应业	Electric Power, Gas and Water Production and Supply	150	21	62
建筑业	Construction	8594	1893	6200
交通运输业、仓储和邮政业	Transportation and Warehousing	5258	1046	3825
信息传输、计算机服务和软件业	Information Transmission, Computer Service and Software Industries	4352	1309	3711
批发和零售业	Wholesale and Retail Trade	62650	13872	47829
住宿和餐饮业	Hotel and Catering Trade	2378	421	1738
房地产业	Real Estate Industries	3046	466	2074
租赁和商务服务业	Leasing and Business Service Industries	17729	5160	14534
居民服务和其它服务业	Resident Service and Other Service Industries	3784	805	2836
卫生、社会保障和社会福利业	Health Care, Social Security and Social Welfare	215	35	141
文化、体育和娱乐业	Culture, Sports and Entertainment	2081	717	1639
其它行业	Others	5		2
从业人员(人)	Emplyment Personnel(person)	2131592	376726	1250422
农、林、牧、渔业	Farming. Forestry. Animal Husbandry and Fishery	24602	6076	6585
采矿业	Mining and Quarrying Industry	971	82	382
制造业	Manufacturing Industry	1108796	90323	507371
电力、燃气及水的生产和供应业	Electric Power, Gas and Water Production and Supply	1305	283	468
建筑业	Construction	74141	20985	49346
交通运输业、仓储和邮政业	Transportation and Warehousing	42853	10064	30500
信息传输、计算机服务和软件业	Information Transmission, Computer Service and Software Industries	36954	13812	29939

注:本表数据来自于宁波市工商行政管理局。
Note: Data in this table are obtained from Ningbo Administration for Industry & Commerce.

表 10 - 18 续表 Continued

指标	Indicators	全市期末实有 Total at the End of this Year	其中 of Which	
			本期开业 Openning for this Term	城镇 Districts
批发和零售业	Wholesale and Retail Trade	486835	130408	362964
住宿和餐饮业	Hotel and Catering Trade	20338	3844	14612
房地产业	Real Estate Industries	24890	4630	15876
租赁和商务服务业	Leasing and Business Service Industries	161703	52424	130055
居民服务和其它服务业	Resident Service and Other Service Industries	29151	7533	21236
卫生、社会保障和社会福利业	Health Care, Social Security and Social Welfare	1756	377	1164
文化、体育和娱乐业	Culture, Sports and Entertainment	17056	6645	12642
其它行业	Others	16		16
注册资金(万元)	Registered Capital (10000 Yuan)	80070241	22134923	59961877
农、林、牧、渔业	Farming, Forestrym, Animal Husbandry and Fishery	576745	144201	245763
采矿业	Mining and Quarrying Industry	29598	4428	12027
制造业	Manufacturing Industry	13888122	1244189	6277440
电力、燃气及水的生产和供应业	Electric Power, Gas and Water Production and Supply	104356	13816	61558
建筑业	Construction	4448893	626972	3497071
交通运输业、仓储和邮政业	Transportation and Warehousing	2108831	427053	1804714
信息传输、计算机服务和软件业	Information Transmission, Computer Service and Software Industries	893576	372165	813441
批发和零售业	Wholesale and Retail Trade	11482372	2395038	9782208
住宿和餐饮业	Hotel and Catering Trade	302572	32304	217861
房地产业	Real Estate Industries	5753139	305702	4325865
租赁和商务服务业	Leasing and Business Service Industries	35727329	15342284	29230594
居民服务和其它服务业	Resident Service and Other Service Industries	344525	68727	279313
卫生、社会保障和社会福利业	Health Care, Social Security and Social Welfare	84352	47060	80491
文化、体育和娱乐业	Culture, Sports and Entertainment	363634	151965	325757
其它行业	Others	12010		12010

表 10－19 限额以上服务业企业主要经济指标
Main Economic Indicators of Service enterprises Above Designated Size

指标	Indicators	企业数 Number of Enterprises	#亏损企业 Loss－making Enterprises	从业人员数 Number of Employees	资产总计 Total Asset
总计	**Total**	**6810**	**2186**	**737596**	**340926486**
#国有控股企业	State－holding Enterprises	592	139	164161	242443351
按注册类型分	Grouped by Registration Type				
内资企业	Domestic Funded Enterprises	6523	2098	675066	265579489
国有企业	State－Owned Enterprises	136	22	31482	21898140
集体企业	Collective－Owned Enterprises	54	11	3516	1357337
股份合作企业	Share Cooperative Enterprises	22	6	4619	8485663
联营企业	Limited Liability Corporations	7		684	39835
有限责任公司	Share－holding Corporations Ltd.	1201	363	179938	51478820
股份有限公司	Private Enterprises	186	57	68195	146684067
私营企业	Private enterprises	4875	1633	381884	35410372
其他企业	Other enterprises	42	6	4748	225256
港澳台商投资企业	Hongkong, Macao and Taiwan Funded	148	49	37070	8573168
外商投资企业	Foreign－invested enterprises	139	39	25460	66773829
按行业分	Grouped by Sector				
批发和零售业	Wholesale and retail trade	3306	1101	160132	44037386
交通运输、仓储和邮政业	Transport, storage and postal service	1109	302	104488	16542807
住宿和餐饮业	Accommodation and catering industry	423	229	42364	1825960
信息传输、计算机服务和软件业	Information transmission, computer services and software industry	197	65	19275	2856007
金融业	Financial sector	180	58	67378	252610499
房地产业	Real Estate industry	181	57	45859	638465
租赁和商务服务业	Rental and business services sector	686	204	239681	18719766
科学研究、技术服务与地质勘查业	Scientific research, technical services and geological prospecting industry	330	46	25676	1241583
水利、环境和公共设施管理业	Irrigation works, environment and public facilities management	74	28	8102	1302741
居民服务和其他服务业	Resident and other services	148	43	8740	213681
教育	Education	55	9	4343	85367
卫生和社会福利业	Hygiene and social welfare	37	14	4721	261941
文化、体育与娱乐业	Civilization, sports and entertainment industry	84	30	6837	590284
公共管理、社会保障与社会组织	Public management, , The social security and social organization				

注：房地产业不包括房地产开发经营，限上服务企业包含了批发和零售业、住宿和餐饮业。

Note: Real Estate excludes Real estate development and management, Wholesale, retail, accommodation and catering are included above designated size.

单位：个、万元(unit,10000 yuan)

负债合计 Total Liabilities	所有者权益合计 Crediters´ Equity	营业收入 Business Revernue	营业成本 Business Costs	营业税金及附加 Tax and Extra Charge	三项费用 Three Costs	应付职工薪酬 Employee Compensation Payable	营业利润 Business Profits	利润总额 Total Profits
305263668	**35663593**	**153329752**	**138789482**	**1096181**	**9557201**	**5820550**	**4726280**	**5185614**
222561184	19882167	42134912	35482947	711448	3058988	2090542	3133982	3377470
240591011	24989254	138170405	126675663	956088	7950235	5129989	3249368	3642680
20299055	1599084	3648306	2628124	142052	358560	350774	533750	541752
1175912	181425	487441	415675	4316	49279	29532	18575	19992
7670947	813661	530718	255036	13486	138802	96107	123703	122263
28782	11053	36501	28732	954	5132	8222	1683	1701
38490192	12988628	46483676	43373330	158206	2347138	1385653	1092944	1342103
143513925	3170142	22264155	19069298	462392	1718079	993481	1093909	1141114
29307107	6104041	64596281	60829469	173574	3294665	2228380	375279	463939
105092	120165	123327	75998	1108	38581	37839	9525	9817
3614227	4958940	4959396	3951674	26581	644105	305871	480728	501970
61058430	5715399	10199951	8162145	113512	962861	384689	996185	1040965
36254342	7783110	115268399	110504441	203539	4081539	1147342	990920	1201869
7878284	8664524	10093652	8814323	36510	791601	866203	650670	740196
1712469	113491	777926	303044	42303	497945	192504	-61772	-69564
626292	2229715	1715228	809241	27376	451356	199608	422215	449214
244049378	8561121	19265160	13848477	653395	2426168	1305430	2293175	2327135
447685	190780	352457	195711	19330	132692	193282	5951	7850
12333492	6386984	4067622	3265427	80654	645944	1422748	230455	295541
506128	735455	938148	515679	16291	246908	257323	162761	175852
974945	327796	233031	160537	4705	69484	51874	-3488	5949
117978	95703	192879	141660	2999	42057	39625	6795	9534
41604	43763	88309	47198	3749	24693	32615	12748	13305
127069	134871	129744	62841	470	63453	40011	3119	3736
194003	396281	207197	120904	4860	83362	71985	12732	24997

表10－20　批发业销售收入前20位企业(2014)
The Top 20 Enterprises of Wholesales Trade at Sales Revenue

排名 No.	企业名称	Name of Corporation	所在区域	Location
1	浙江前程石化股份有限公司	Zhejiang Future Petrochemical Co. ,Ltd.	高新	Gaoxin
2	浙江浙能富兴燃料有限公司	Zhejiang Energy Fuxing Fuel Co. ,Ltd	北仑	Beilun
3	浙江吉利汽车销售有限公司	Zhejiang Geely Automobile Sales Co. , Ltd	北仑	Beilun
4	淮北矿业集团大榭煤炭运销有限公	Huaibei Coal Mining Group Daxie coal distribution Co. ,Ltd	北仑	Beilun
5	中基宁波集团股份有限公司	China－Base Ningbo Foreign Trade Co. ,Ltd.	鄞州	Yinzhou
6	宁波恒逸贸易有限公司	Ningbo Hengyi Trading Co. ,Ltd.	北仑	Beilun
7	宁波神化化学品经营有限责任公司	Ningbo Sunhu Chem Products Co. ,Ltd.	江东	Jiangdong
8	远大物产集团有限公司	Grand Group Corporation	北仑	Beilun
9	万华化学(宁波)能源贸易有限公司	Wanhua Chemical (Ningbo) Energy Trading Co. , Ltd.	北仑	Beilun
10	新兴发展(宁波)金属资源有限公司	Emerging Development (Ningbo) Metal Resources Co. ,Ltd.	北仑	Beilun
11	中国石化销售有限公司浙江宁波石油分公司	China Petrochemical Sales Co. , Ltd. Ningbo, Zhejiang Petroleum Company	高新	Gaoxin
12	浙江省烟草公司宁波市公司	Ningbo branch of Zhejiang Tobacco	江东	Jiangdong
13	宁波君安物产有限公司	Ningbo Junan Resources Co. ,Ltd.	江东	Jiangdong
14	远大石化有限公司	Ningbo Yuanda Petrochemical Co. ,Ltd.	高新	Gaoxin
15	宁波山煤华泰贸易有限公司	Ningbo Mountain Coal Huatai trade Co. , Ltd	北仑	Beilun
16	宁波美的联合物资供应有限公司	Ningbo United States joint Supplies Co. , Ltd	北仑	Beilun
17	中航国际钢铁贸易有限公司	Pict AVIC international steel trade Co. ,Ltd.	北仑	Beilun
18	中海油大榭贸易有限公司	CNOOC Daxie Trade Co. , Ltd.	北仑	Beilun
19	宁波杉杉物产有限公司	Ningbo Shanshan Resources Co. ,Ltd.	鄞州	Yinzhou
20	中国石化化工销售有限公司宁波经营部	Sinopec Chemical Sales Co. ,Ltd. Operating the Department of Ningbo	海曙	Haishu

表 10－21 零售业销售收入前 20 位企业(2014) The Top 20 Enterprises of Retail Trade at Sales Revenue

排名 No.	企业名称	Name of Corporation	所在区域	Location
1	中石化碧辟(浙江)石油有限公司宁波分公司	BP Sinopec (Zhejiang) Petroleum Co. ,Ltd. Ningbo Branch	海曙	Haishu
2	宁波医药股份有限公司	Ningbo Pharmaceutical Co. ,Ltd.	海曙	Haishu
3	三江购物俱乐部股份有限公司	Ningbo Sanjiang Shopping Mall Co. ,Ltd.	海曙	Haishu
4	宁波太平鸟风尚男装有限公司	Ningbo Peace Bird fashion clothing Co. ,Ltd.	高新	Gaoxin
5	浙江华联商厦有限公司	Zhejiang Hualian Trade Co. ,Ltd.	余姚	Yuyao
6	宁波欧尚超市有限公司	Ningbo Auchan Supermarket Co. ,Ltd.	海曙	Haishu
7	浙江大生医药有限公司	Zhejiang Tai Sang Medicine Co. ,Ltd.	北仑	Beilun
8	宁波太平鸟时尚服饰股份有限公司	Ningbo Peace Bird fashion clothing Co. ,Ltd.	海曙	Haishu
9	宁波丰颐汽车销售有限公司	Ningbo FengYi Automobile Sales Co. ,Ltd.	鄞州	Yinzhou
10	宁波捷骏汽车销售服务有限公司	Ningbo Junjie Auto Sales & Service Co. ,Ltd.	江东	Jiangdong
11	宁波市北仑加贝购物俱乐部(普通合伙)	Ningbo beilun Jiabei Shopping Mall	北仑	Beilun
12	宁波润达汽车销售服务有限公司	Ningbo Runda Auto Sale & Service Co. ,Ltd.	江北	Jiangbei
13	宁波宝恒汽车销售服务有限公司	Ningbo Baoheng Auto Sale & Service Co. ,Ltd.	鄞州	Yinzhou
14	宁波中基汽车销售服务有限公司	Ningbo Zhongji Car Sales Services Co. ,Ltd.	鄞州	Yinzhou
15	宁波新江厦连锁超市有限公司	Ningbo New Jiangxia Supermarket Chains Co. ,Ltd.	鄞州	Yinzhou
16	银泰百货宁波海曙有限公司	Intime Department Store Co. ,Ltd. Ningbo Haishu	海曙	Haishu
17	宁波浙国美电器有限公司	Ningbo, Zhejiang Gome Co. , Ltd	海曙	Haishu
18	宁波甬宁苏宁云商商贸有限公司	Ningbo Yong Ning Suning cloud provider Trading Co. , Ltd	海曙	Haishu
19	宁波天华汽车销售服务有限公司	Ningbo Tianhua Automobile Sales Co. ,Ltd.	镇海	Zhenhai
20	宁波利星汽车服务有限公司	Ningbo Li Star Automobile Service Co. , Ltd.	江北	Jiangbei

表 10－22　星级住宿业营业收入前 20 位企业(2014)
The Top 20 Enterprises of Hotelat Business Revenue

排名 No.	企业名称	Name of Corporation	所在区域	Location
1	香格里拉大酒店(宁波)有限公司	Shangri－La Hotel (Ningbo) Co. ,Ltd.	江东	Jiangdon
2	宁波华侨饭店有限公司	Ningbo Howard Johnson Hotel Co. ,Ltd.	海曙	Haishu
3	宁波雅戈尔达蓬山旅游投资开发有限公司	Ningbo Youngor up Toyama Tourism Investment Development Co. , Ltd.	慈溪	Cixi
4	宁波南苑集团股份有限公司	Ningbo Nanyuan Group Co. ,Ltd.	海曙	Haishu
5	宁波东港波特曼大酒店有限公司	Portman Plaza Hotel Ningbo	江东	Jiangdon
6	宁波太平洋大酒店有限公司	Ningbo Pacific Hotel Co. ,Ltd.	余姚	Yuyao
7	慈溪市杭州湾大酒店有限公司	Cixi Golden Harbour Tourism Co. ,Ltd.	慈溪	Cixi
8	宁波市凯洲实业有限公司	Ningbo Kai Zhou Industrial Co. ,Ltd.	海曙	Haishu
9	宁波开元大酒店有限公司	Ningbo Kaiyuan Grand Hotel Co. ,Ltd.	江东	Jiangdon
10	宁波万达置业有限公司万达索菲特大饭店	Sofitel Wanda Ningbo Wanda Hotel Properties Co. ,Ltd.	鄞州	Yinzhou
11	余姚宾馆有限责任公司	Yuyao Hotel Co. ,Ltd.	余姚	Yuyao
12	宁波新晶都酒店有限公司	Holiyacht Crystal Hotel	江东	Jiangdon
13	宁波九龙湖开元华城度假村有限公司	Ningbo Kaiyuan Huacity Jiulong Lake Co. ,Ltd.	镇海	Zhenhai
14	余姚中塑石浦大酒店有限公司	Yuyao Zhongsu Shipu Hotel	余姚	Yuyao
15	宁波市鄞州天港禧悦酒店管理有限公司	Ningbo Yinzhou Tiangangxiyue Inn Management Co. ,Ltd.	鄞州	Yinzhou
16	宁波南苑商务旅店连锁股份有限公司	Ningbo Nanyuan Business Hotel Chain Co. ,Ltd.	鄞州	Yinzhou
17	浙江三碧酒店股份有限公司	Zhejiang 3－B Hotel	江北	Jiangbei
18	余姚辰茂河姆渡酒店有限公司	Yuyao Excemon Hemudu Hotel	余姚	Yuyao
19	宁波伯豪酒店管理有限公司	Ningbo Bo Hao Hotel Management Co,. Ltd	鄞州	Yinzhou
20	宁波和丰花园酒店有限公司	Ningbo Hefeng Garden Hotel Co. , Ltd.	江东	Jiangdon

表10－23 餐饮业营业收入前20位企业(2014)
The Top 20 Enterprises of Catering Trade at Business Revenue

排名 No.	企业名称	Name of Corporation	所在区域	Location
1	宁波南苑环球酒店管理有限公司	Nanyuan International Hotel Management Co. ,Ltd.	鄞州	Yinzhou
2	宁波市来必堡餐饮管理有限公司	Ningbo Laibi Fort Restaurant Management Co. ,Ltd.	海曙	Haishu
3	宁海金海开元名都大酒店有限公司	Ninghai Jinhai Hotel Management Co. ,Ltd.	宁海	Ninghai
4	宁波外婆家餐饮有限公司	My Grandmother's Home in Ningbo Catering Co. ,Ltd.	海曙	Haishu
5	宁波杭州湾新区世纪金源大饭店有限公司	Ningbo Hangzhou Bay Empark Hotel	慈溪	Cixi
6	宁波海底捞餐饮管理有限公司	Ningbo Haidilao Restaurant Management Co. ,Ltd.	海曙	Haishu
7	宁波东方明珠娱乐有限公司	Ningbo Oriental Pearl Amusement Co. ,Ltd.	江东	Jiangdong
8	余姚阳明温泉山庄实业有限公司	Yuyao Yangming Hot Spring Resort	余姚	Yuyao
9	宁波石浦酒店管理发展有限公司	Ningbo Shipu Restaurant Management Development Co. ,Ltd.	鄞州	Yinzhou
10	宁波汤岛涮餐饮管理有限公司	Ningbo Tang Island Shabu Restaurant Management Co. , Ltd	海曙	Haishu
11	余姚四明湖开元度假村有限公司	Yuyao Siminghu Century Resort Co. ,Ltd	余姚	Yuyao
12	宁波四季永逸大饭店有限公司	Luotuo Forever Peace Hotel	镇海	Zhenhai
13	宁海世贸中心大酒店有限公司	Ninghai World Trade Center Hotel Co. , Ltd	宁海	Ninghai
14	宁波市江东天港禧悦酒店管理有限公司	Ningbo Jiangdong Sky Harbor Jubilee Paradise Hotel Management Co. ,Ltd.	江东	Jiangdong
15	余姚雍和宫大酒店有限公司	Yuyao Yonghogong Restaurant Co. ,Ltd.	余姚	Yuyao
16	宁波恒元大酒店有限公司	Ningbo Hengyuan Hotel Co. ,Ltd.	慈溪	Cixi
17	宁波银苑大酒店有限公司	Ningbo Yinyuan Restaurant Co. ,Ltd.	鄞州	Yinzhou
18	浙江竹林人家餐饮有限公司	Zhejiang Bamboo Country Food Co. ,Ltd.	海曙	Haishu
19	浙江向阳渔港集团股份有限公司	Zhejiang Xiangyang Port Group Co. ,Ltd.	江东	Jiangdong
20	慈溪市杭州湾环球酒店有限公司	Cixi Hangzhou Bay International Hotel Co. , Ltd.	慈溪	Cixi

表10－24　年成交额前20位的交易市场(2014)
The Top 20 Commodity Exchange Market with Transaction Volume

排名 No.	企业名称	Name of Corporation	所在区域	Location
1	余姚市中国塑料城	China Plastic Exchange Market (Yuyao)	余姚市	Yuyao
2	宁波镇海大宗生产资料交易中心	Ningbo Zhenhai Mass Production Trading Center	镇海区	Zhenhai
3	浙江长三角石油化工发展有限公司(石油化工交易中心)	Zhejiang Changsanjiao Petroleum Chemical Industry Co. ,Ltd.	慈溪市	Cixi
4	宁波镇海液体化工产品交易市场	Ningbo Zhenhai Liquid Chemical Products Market	镇海区	Zhenhai
5	宁波市镇海煤炭交易市场有限公司	Ningbo Zhenhai Coal Exchange Co. ,Ltd.	镇海区	Zhenhai
6	宁波华东物资城	East China Material Market of Ningbo	江东区	Jiangdong
7	宁波市镇海厚恒物资城	Ningbo Zhenhai Houheng Material City	镇海区	Zhenhai
8	余姚市模板市场	Yuyao MasterPlate Market	余姚市	Yuyao
9	慈溪市农副产品批发市场	Cixi holesale Market of Farm & Sideline Products	慈溪市	Cixi
10	宁波江北华东物资城浙甬市场开发有限公司	Ningbo Jiangbei East China Material City Zhejiang Ningbo arket development Co. Ltd.	江北区	Jiangbei
11	宁波轻纺城	Ningbo Light Textile Market	鄞州区	Yinzhou
12	余姚市农副产品批发市场	Yuyao holesale Market of Farm & Sideline Products	余姚市	Yuyao
13	慈溪市工业品批发市场	Cixi holesale Market of Industrial Products	慈溪市	Cixi
14	浙江象山水产城实业有限公司	Zhejiang iangshan Aquatic Product City Industrial Co. ,Ltd.	象山县	Xiangshan
15	宁波鄞州新时代钢材市场	Ningbo Yinzhou New Times Steel Market	鄞州区	Yinzhou
16	慈溪市周巷副食品批发市场	Cixi Zhouxiang Wholesale Market of Subsidiary Food	慈溪市	Cixi
17	宁波华东物资城王家弄市场	Wangjia ong Market of East China Material Market	鄞州区	Yinzhou
18	宁波万国商城	Ningbo Wanguo Commodity Market	鄞州区	Yinzhou
19	宁波市路林综合市场股份有限公司	Ningbo Lin Road Comprehensive Market Co. , Ltd.	江北区	Jiangbei
20	慈溪市胜山服装布料市场	Cixi Shenshan Garment and Cloth Market	慈溪市	Cixi

主要统计指标解释

【社会消费品零售额】 指各种经济类型的批发零售贸易业、餐饮业、制造业和其他行业对城乡居民和社会集团的消费品零售额。这个指标反映通过各种商品流通渠道向居民和社会集团供应的生活消费品来满足他们生活需要，是研究人民生活，社会消费品购买力、货币流通等问题的重要指标。社会消费品零售额包括：(1)售给城乡居民作为生活用的商品和修建房屋用的建筑材料；(2)售给社会集团的各种办公用品和公用消费品(3)售给 机关、团体、学校、部队、企业、事业单位的职工食堂和旅店(招待所)附设专门供本店旅客食用，不对外营业的食堂的各种食品、燃料；企业、单位和国营农场直接售给本单位职工和职工食堂的自已生产的产品；(4)售给部队干部、战士生活用的粮食、副食品、衣着品、日用品、燃料；(5)售给来华的外国人、华侨、港澳(台)同胞的消费品；(6)居民自费购买的中、西药品、中药材及医疗用品；(7)报社、出版社直接售给居民和社会集团的报纸、图书、杂志、集邮公司出售的新、旧纪念邮票、特种邮票、首日封、集邮册、集邮工具等；(8)旧货寄售商店自购、自销部分的商品；(9)煤气公司、液化石油气站售给居民和社会集团的煤气灶具和罐装液化石油气；(10)农民售给非农业居民和社会集团的商品。不包括售给国民经济各部门企业、事业单位(包括国有经济的农场)生产经营用的各种原材料、燃料、设备、工具等和售给批发零售贸易业、餐饮业作为转卖用的商品、旧货寄售商店受托寄售卖出的商品、服务业的营业收入、邮局出售邮票的收入、自来水、电力、煤气生产(供应)单位的产品供应收入，也不包括农民之间的商品销售。

【限额以上批发企业】 指年销售额在2000万元及以上，并且年末从业人员在20人及以上的批发贸易企业。

【限额以上零售企业】 指年销售额在500万元及以上，并且年末从业人员在60人及以上的零售企业。

【限额以上餐饮企业】 指年销售额在200万元及以上，并且年末从业人员在40人及以上的餐饮企业。

【批发零售贸易业商品购、销、存总额】 指以各种经济类型的批发、零售贸易业(不包括个体)为总体的商品购、销、存。

【商品购进总额】 指从本企业(单位)以外的单位和个人购进(包括从国外直接进口)作为转卖或加工后转卖的商品。这个指标反映批发零售贸易业从国内、国外市场上购进商品的总量。商品购进总额包括：(1)从工农业生产者购进的商品；(2)从出版社、报社的出版发行部门购进的图书、杂志和报纸；(3)从各种经济类型的批发零售贸易企业(单位)购进的商品；(4)从其他单位购进的商品，如从机关、团体、企业单位购进的剩余物资，从餐饮业、服务业购进的商品，从海关、市场管理部门购进的缉私和没收的商品，从居民收购的废旧商品等；(5)从国(境)外直接进口的商品。不包括企业(单位)为自身经营用，和未通过买卖行为而收入的商品以及销售退回、商品升溢等。

【商品销售总额】 指对本企业(单位)以外的单位和个人出售(包括对国(境)外直接出口)的商品。这个指标反映批发零售贸易业在国内市场上销售商品以及出口商品的总量。商品销售总额包括：(1)售给城乡居民和社会集团消费用的商品；(2)售给工业、农业、建筑业、运输邮电业、批发零售贸易业、餐饮业、服务业等作为生产、经营使用的商品；(3)售给批发零售贸易业作为转卖或加工后转卖的商品；(4)对国(境)外直接出口的商品。不包括：出售本企业(单位)自用的废旧包装用品，未通过买卖行为付出的商品，经本单位介绍，由买卖双方直接结算，本单位只收取手续费的业务，购货退出的商品以及商品损耗和损失等。

Explanatory Notes on Main Statistical Indicators

[Total Retail Sales of Consumer Goods] refer to the sum of retail sales of consumer goods by the establishments in wholesale trade, retail sale trade, catering trade, manufacturing industry and other industries of different types of ownership, to urban and rural residents and social groups. This indicator is used to show the supply of consumer goods through various channels to households and institutions to meet their demands, and is therefore very important for the study of the issues on people's livelihood, on the purchasing power of consumer goods and on the circulation of money. The retail sales of consumer goods include: (1) commodities sold to urban and rural residents for residential use and building materials sold to them for the construction or repair of houses; (2) food and fuels sold to canteens of institutions, enterprises, schools, military units and to canteens of hotels and hostels that only serve their guests, and commodities produced by enterprises, institutions or state farms and sold directly to their employees or their canteens; (3) grain and non – staple food, clothing, daily articles and fuels sold to military personnel; (4) consumer goods sold to foreigners, overseas Chinese, and Chinese compatriots from Taiwan, Hong Kong and Macao during their stay in the mainland of China; (5) Chinese an d western medicines, herbs and medical facilities purchased by residents; (6) newspapers, books and magazines directly sold to residents and social groups by publishers, new and old commemorative stamps, special stamps, first day covers, stamp albums and other stamp collection articles sold by stamp companies; (7) consumer goods purchased and then sold by second – hand shops; (8) stoves and other heating facilities and liquified gas sold by gas companies to households and institutions; (9) commodities sold by farmers to non – agricultural residents and social groups. Excluded under this heading are: raw materials, fuels, equipment, tools sold to enterprises, institutions and state farms for production purpose; commodities sold to trade establishments for re – selling; commissioned sales at second – hand shops; operational income of urban public utilities; stamps sold at post offices; income of water, power, gas production and supply establishments from the supply of their products; and sales of commodities among farmers.

[Enterprises of Over – norm Wholesale Volume] refers to wholesale trade enterprises that register an annual sales volume of over 20 million yuan RMB and a total year-end staff of more than 20.

[Enterprises of Over – norm Retail Sales Volume] refers to those that register an annual sales volume of over 5 million yuan RMB and a total year – end staff of more than 60.

[Catering Enterprises of Over – norm Sales Volume] refers to those that register an annual sales volume of over 2 million yuan RMB and a total year – end staff of more than 40.

[Purchase, Sales and Stock of Commodities by Wholesale and Retail Trade] refer to the purchase, sales and stock of commodities by wholesale and retail establishments of different ownership (excluding individual sellers).

[Total Purchases of Commodities] refer to the purchases of commodities by the establishments from other establishments or individuals (including direct import from abroad) for the purpose of re – selling, either with or without further processing of the commodities purchased. This indicator is used to show the total value of purchases of commodities by wholesale and retail establishments from domestic and overseas markets. The total purchases include: (1) agricultural and industrial products purchased from producers; (2) books, magazines and newspapers purchased from distribution departments of the publishers; (3) commodities purchased from wholesale and retail establishments; (4) commodities purchased from other units, such as surplus materials purchased from government agencies, enterprises or institutions, commodities purchased from catering and service establishments, confiscated goods purchased from customs authorities or market management agencies, second – hand goods and wastes purchased from residents; and (5) commodities directly imported from abroad. Excluded are commodities purchased by establishments (units) for use in their own business operation, commodities obtained without buying or selling procedures, rejected commodities, etc.

[Total Sales of Commodities] refer to selling of commodities by the establishments to other establishments and individuals (including direct export) . This indicator is used to show the total value of sales of commodities at domestic markets and export. The total sales include: (1) commodities sold to urban and rural residents and social groups for their consumption; (2) commodities so ld to establishments in industry, agriculture, construction, transportation, post and telecommunications, wholesale and retail trades, catering trade and public utility for their production and operation; (3) commodities sold to wholesale an d retail establishments for re – selling, with or without further processing; and (4) commodities for direct export to other countries. Excluded are selling of waste packaging materials used by the establishments (units) themselves, commodities transferred without buying or selling procedures, commission income from brokerage in transactions whose settlement is directly handled by buyers and sellers , rejected commodities in the purchase, loss in commodities, etc.

NINGBO 2015 Statistical YearBook

11 CHAPTER

第十一篇

对外经济、旅游

FOREIGN TRADE AND TOURISM

对外经济、旅游
Foreign Trade and Tourism

主要统计指标
Major Statistics Indicators

2014 年自营进出口总额	Total Direct Import and Export	10470406	万美元	USD 10000
比上年增长	Increase Over Last Year	4.4	%	
2014 年自营出口总额	Total Exports	7310904	万美元	USD 10000
比上年增长	Increase Over Last Year	11.3	%	
2014 年自营进口总额	Total Imports	3155319	万美元	USD 10000
比上年增长	Increase Over Last Year	9.1	%	
2014 年新签合同数	Number of Projects of Signed Contracts	468	个	unit
比上年增长	Increase Over Last Year	5.9	%	
2014 年实际利用外资金额	Value of Foreign Captial Actually Used	402514	万美元	USD 10000
比上年增长	Increase Over Last Year	22.9	%	
2014 年接待境外旅游者人数	Number of Received Oversea Tourists	1396802	人	person
比上年增长	Increase Over Last Year	9.7	%	
2014 年旅游创汇收入	Foreign Exchange Earnings	77832	万美元	USD 10000
比上年增长	Increase Over Last Year	-2.2	%	
2014 年国内旅游总收入	Earning From Domestic Tourism	1020.3	亿元	100 million yuan
比上年增长	Increase Over Last Year	12.8	%	

表 11－1 历年对外经济贸易基本情况
Basic Statistics on Foreign Economy and Trade Over the Years

单位:万美元(USD 10000)

年份 Year	外商直接投资情况 Foreign Direct Investments			自营进出口 Direct Import and Export		口岸进出口 Import and Export of Port	
	新批项目数(个) Number of Projects(unit)	合同利用外资 Foreign Capital Signed Agreements	实际利用外资 Foreign Capital Actually Used	进出口 Total	#出口 Exports	进出口 Total	#出口 Exports
1980	1	5	5				
1981							
1982						14917	10963
1983						17683	12173
1984	8	850	21			26336	16102
1985	11	682	359	1029	389	45474	23521
1986	7	447	500	2079	540	54690	34432
1987	13	4341	429	2061	791	52493	29999
1988	62	4002	689	14766	11458	78717	39155
1989	64	6295	1758	22024	18005	110175	53615
1990	89	5624	2197	29840	27962	125527	63253
1991	184	17460	2680	57339	47532	219638	87101
1992	636	156725	11497	99072	78389	260387	101699
1993	1015	107152	34455	169434	110824	328871	120138
1994	680	77149	35812	251462	174992	375919	168340
1995	496	114630	39909	385335	226825	521501	232789
1996	322	87838	50162	418573	233003	586140	252248
1997	260	45849	55408	460896	293332	663807	311848
1998	281	51198	50329	421237	296386	610109	339904
1999	364	65660	52035	500898	347721	774194	411200
2000	550	95151	62186	754065	516781	1372547	703357
2001	806	195519	87446	889202	624500	1613794	869768
2002	1017	320024	124696	1227343	816304	2145755	1232723
2003	1209	344382	172727	1880962	1207398	3394193	1888206
2004	1081	413633	210322	2611222	1668967	5157576	2664100
2005	873	421015	231079	3349427	2223256	6749471	3614462
2006	1034	442746	243018	4221188	2877052	8649306	4958297
2007	854	450107	250518	5649909	3825509	11176033	6744103
2008	528	412339	253789	6784036	4632638	14018503	8371436
2009	403	342362	220541	6081252	3865068	11692277	7317493
2010	495	404608	232336	8290424	5196745	16134445	10052342
2011	411	501463	280929	9818682	6083159	20044269	12375307
2012	437	531276	285252	9657269	6144526	19757789	12419370
2013	442	582029	327483	10032895	6571020	21190173	13397419
2014	468	702083	402514	10470406	7310904	21860834	14495673

注:2003 年起,利用外资统计口径有变动。

Note: From 2003, the Statstistical Standard which will utilize the foreign capitals have changed.

表 11－2 按企业性质分的进出口总值(2014)
Total Value of Imports and Exports by Registered Type of Enterprises

单位:万美元(USD 10000)

企业性质	Grouped by Registered Type	进出口 Imports and Exports		其中 of Which 出口 Exports		进口 Imports	
		贸易额 Value	增长率(%) Rate of Increase	贸易额 Value	增长率(%) Rate of Increase	贸易额 Value	增长率(%) Rate of Increase
合计	**Total**	**10465045**	**4.3**	**7309726**	**11.3**	**3155319**	**－8.9**
国营企业	State－Owned Enterprises	838580	6.3	501277	2.1	337304	13.2
三资企业	Foreign Funded Enterprises	3650612	－4.7	2195076	0.5	1455536	－5.3
#外合作企业	Cooperative Operation Enterprises	39603	7.7	20930	0.3	18673	17.3
外合资企业	Joint Venture Enterprises	1484763	－2.1	945826	－0.2	538937	－5.3
外商独资企业	Foreign－funded Sole Enterprises	2126246	－6.6	1228320	1.0	897926	－15.3
集体企业	Collective Owned Enterprises	373598	－11.4	273366	2.1	100232	－35.0
私营企业	Private Enterprises	5587882	12.2	4327889	19.7	1259993	－7.5
个体工商户	Individual Enterprises	12997	23.7	10826	24.0	2171	22.1

注:本表至 11－5 表数据来自宁波海关。

Note: Data from Tables 11－2 to 11－5 are obtained from Ningbo Customs.

表 11－3 按贸易方式分的进出口总值(2014)
Total Value of Imports and Exports by Trade Property

单位:万美元(USD 10000)

企业性质	Grouped by Registered Type	进出口 Imports and Exports		其中 of Which 出口 Exports		进口 Imports	
		贸易额 Value	增长率(%) Rate of Increase	贸易额 Value	增长率(%) Rate of Increase	贸易额 Value	增长率(%) Rate of Increase
总额	**Total**	**10465045**	**4.3**	**7309726**	**11.3**	**3155319**	**－8.9**
一般贸易	General Trade	8287243	6.1	6071527	14.2	2215716	－11.0
进料加工贸易	Processing by Supplied Material	1542857	－0.4	996324	1.1	546533	－3.0
来料加工装配贸易	Processing by Import Material	160254	－12.7	106139	－8.6	54115	－19.6
外商投资企业作为投资进口的设备、物品	Imports of Foreign－invested Enterprises As Investment in Equipment&Goods	14801	－61.7			14801	－61.7
保税监管场所进出境货物	Import & Export in Supervision Areas of Protective Tariff Zone	290810	4.7	83831	－17.3	206979	17.4
海关特殊监管区域物流货物	Goods of Special Customs Supervision Logistics	158158	5.5	47381	53.7	110777	－7.0
海关特殊监管区域进口设备	Imported Equipment of Special Customs Supervision Zones	1782	66.4			1782	66.4
物流中心进出境货物	Import & Export Goods in Logistics Center	2468	－45.1	804	－35.2	1664	－48.8
其他	Others	6670	－64.9	3719	－74.4	2951	－34.1

表 11－4 分洲别及主要国家(地区)的进出口总值(2014)
Total Value of Exports and Imports by Continent and Country

单位:万美元(USD 10000)

地区 Region	进出口 Imports and Exports		其中 of Which 出口 Exports		进口 Imports	
	贸易额 Value	增长率(%) Rate of Increase	贸易额 Value	增长率(%) Rate of Increase	贸易额 Value	增长率(%) Rate of Increase
合计 Total	**10465045**	**4.3**	**7309726**	**11.3**	**3155319**	**-8.9**
亚洲 Asia	4171777	1.1	2248251	10.0	1923526	-7.6
#东盟 The Aaaociation of Southeast Asian Nations	867890	5.1	528208	18.6	339682	-10.7
中国香港 Hongkong, China	255850	-3.5	244583	-2.3	11267	-24.0
日本 Japan	664483	-5.4	356977	-2.6	307506	-8.4
韩国 Republic of Korea	428479	-0.9	187510	3.6	240968	-4.2
中国台湾 Taiwan, China	733884	-9.2	93202	5.2	640682	-11.0
非洲 Africa	467895	5.9	398092	10.9	69804	-16.0
欧洲 Europe	2595280	8.6	2233614	13.1	361666	-12.8
#欧盟 European Free Trade Association	2238232	10.8	1925761	15.6	312471	-11.6
南美洲 South America	789313	0.4	590787	3.3	198527	-7.4
北美洲 North America	1912119	7.4	1615994	14.9	296124	-20.7
#美国 USA	1705003	8.8	1475899	15.7	229104	-21.7
大洋洲 Oceania	528604	4.5	222988	5.7	305616	3.7

表11－5　部分年份按各大洲分的进出口分类表
Total of Exports and Imports by Continent in Partial Years

单位:万美元(USD 10000)

指标	Indicators	2010	2011	2012	2013	2014
进出口总额	**Total Value**	**8290424**	**9818682**	**9657269**	**10032895**	**10465045**
亚洲	Asia	3351962	4032006	4028317	4114668	4171777
非洲	Africa	299694	383281	383516	442000	467895
欧洲	Europe	2211169	2521035	2295008	2403962	2595280
#欧盟	European Union	1881681	2086243	1911695	2020533	2238232
南美洲	South America	716580	877477	863475	786217	789313
北美洲	North America	1362281	1620770	1681639	1780733	1912119
大洋洲	Oceania	348612	384033	405258	505259	528604
出口	**Export**	**5196745**	**6083159**	**6144526**	**6571020**	**7309726**
亚洲	Asia	1561718	1860362	1889581	2033716	2248251
非洲	Africa	239464	298086	315709	358853	398092
欧洲	Europe	1755764	2009977	1851381	1988768	2233614
#欧盟	European Union	1560351	1721005	1561309	1666829	1925761
南美洲	South America	419562	534138	565966	572066	590787
北美洲	North America	1034205	1192375	1320751	1406621	1615994
大洋洲	Oceania	186032	188220	201138	210997	222988
进口	**Import**	**3093679**	**3735523**	**3512743**	**3461875**	**3155319**
亚洲	Asia	1790244	2171644	2138736	2080952	1923526
非洲	Africa	60230	85195	67807	83147	69804
欧洲	Europe	455404	511058	443627	415194	361666
#欧盟	European Union	321330	365238	350386	353704	312471
南美洲	South America	297019	343339	297509	214151	198527
北美洲	North America	328076	428396	360887	374112	296124
大洋洲	Oceania	162580	195813	204120	294262	305616

表 11-6 按投资方式分的利用外资基本情况(2014) Utilization of Foreign Capital by Investment Way

单位:万美元(USD 10000)

指标	Indicators	项目数(个) Projects (unit)	合同利用外资 Foreign Capital Contracted	实际利用外资 Foreign Capital Actually Used
总计	**Total**	**468**	**702083**	**402514**
对外借款	**Foreign Loans**			
外国政府贷款	Foreign Government Loans			
国际金融组织贷款	Loans from International Financial Organization			
外国银行商业贷款	Commercial Loans from Foreign Banks			
其他	Others			
外商直接投资	**Foreign Direct Investment**	**468**	**702083**	**402514**
合资经营	Joint Venture Enterprises	152	142190	82884
合作经营	Cooperative Operation Enterprises			151
独资企业	Foreign - funded Sole Enterprises	314	527773	292373
外商投资股份制	Share - system Enterprises	2	32120	27106
外商其他投资	**Other Foreign Investment**			

注:本表至 11-9 表数据来自宁波市对外贸易经济合作局。

Note: Data from Tables 11-6 to 11-9 are obtained from Ningbo Municipal Bureau of Foreign Trade & Economic Cooperation.

表 11-7 部分年份按投资方式分的利用外资基本情况 Utilization of Foreign Capital by Investment Way in Partial Years

单位:万美元 (USD 10000)

指标	Indicators	2010	2011	2012	2013	2014
合同利用外资	**Foreign Capital Contracted**	**404608**	**501463**	**531276**	**582029**	**702083**
对外借款	Foreign Loans					
外商直接投资	Foreign Direct Investment	404608	501463	531276	582029	702083
合资经营	Joint Venture Enterprises	87743	129624	79038	101402	142190
合作经营	Cooperative Operation Enterprises	3674	2573	345	63	
独资企业	Foreign - funded Sole Enterprises	308159	367406	443435	476770	527773
实际利用外资	**Actual Used Foreign Capital**	**232336**	**280929**	**285252**	**327483**	**402514**
对外借款	Foreign Loans					
外商直接投资	Foreign Direct Investment	232336	280929	285252	327483	402514
合资经营	Joint Venture Enterprises	80959	61695	70949	72235	82884
合作经营	Cooperative Operation Enterprises	29	664	560	103	151
独资企业	Foreign - funded Sole Enterprises	150768	215230	208879	250433	292373

表11－8 部分年份按行业分外商直接投资情况
Foreign Direct Investments by Sectors in Partial Years

指标	Indicators
总计	**Total**
农、林、牧、渔业	Farming, Forestry, Animal Housbandry and Fishery
#农业	Farming
制造业	Manufacturing
#纺织业	Textile Industry
纺织服装、鞋、帽制造业	Textile Clothing. Shoes. Cap Manufacturing
文教体育用品制造业	Cultural. Educational and Sports Goods Manufacturing
化学原料及化学制品制造业	Raw Chemical Materials and Chemical Products
塑料制品业	Plastic Products
金属制品业	Metal Products
通用设备制造业	General Equipment Manufacturing
专用设备制造业	Special Equipment Manufacturing
交通运输设备制造业	Transport Equipment Manufacturing
电气机械及器材制造业	Electric Equipment and Machinery Manufacturing
通信设备、计算机及其他电子设备制造业	Communication Equipment. Computer and Other Electronic Equipment Manufacturing
仪器仪表及文化、办公用机械制造业	Instruments. Meters. Cultural and Office Machinery
电力、燃气及水的生产和供应业	Electricity, Gas and Water Production and Supply
建筑业	Construction
交通运输、仓储和邮政业	Transport, Storage and Post
批发和零售贸易业	Wholesale and Retail Sale Trade
餐饮业	Catering Service
房地产业	Real Estate Management
居民服务和其他服务业	Resident Services and Other Services Industries
其他行业	Other Sectors

单位:万美元(USD 1000)

新批项目数(个) Number of Newly Projects(unit)			合同利用外资 Foreign Capital Signed Agreements			实际利用外资 Foreign Investment Actually Used		
2012	2013	2014	2012	2013	2014	2012	2013	2014
437	**442**	**468**	**531276**	**582029**	**702083**	**285252**	**327483**	**402514**
4	4	2	127	3642	1405	171	1077	402
4	4	2	73	2638	1405	171	77	402
208	161	161	315277	249095	367030	127785	136456	182323
1	2	1	-1606	11947	2504	2046	1974	1205
7	2	5	7968	2967	23666	7149	1920	29845
1	1	2	2783	2221	5312	1145	678	3336
8	3	3	30511	26050	29265	25140	29253	18602
16	19	7	17063	33221	18240	6160	3206	9999
17	7	8	21207	11682	20044	5886	5823	3376
31	26	15	50142	18763	92522	12595	10858	13219
15	18	19	6833	23631	30467	3915	17931	15688
32	27	15	39833	28880	28297	12218	9256	7197
31	26	24	47935	37636	40532	5221	10071	19472
19	19	14	40094	26890	15497	10654	21826	39487
6	1	3	8977	7446	3202	4579	7509	2236
4	1	3	3353	1932	4156	1786	283	5294
5	2		13294	3102	-3288	1993	4427	293
3	4	3	4077	15095	9942	2759	29353	4664
144	177	15	70049	92571	136691	52233	31710	70492
4	3	4	-51	355	334	31	12	100
8	16	6	82198	164978	41936	68947	94204	111272
1		1	4		16			
1			4					

表11－9 部分年份按国别(地区)分的外商直接投资情况
Foreign Direct Investment by Country and Territory in Partial Years

国别、地区	Country, Region	新批项目数(个) New Projects(unit)		
		2012	2013	2014
总计	**Total**	**437**	**442**	**468**
香港	Hongkong, China	151	197	189
台湾省	Taiwan, China	44	20	41
日本	Japan	17	10	14
韩国	Korea Rep	12	20	15
印度尼西亚	Indonesia	2	1	5
新加坡	Singapore	13	14	12
文莱	Brunei	1	1	
马来西亚	Malaysia	5	3	3
泰国	Thailand			1
阿拉伯联合酋长国	United Arab Emirates	1	2	
毛里求斯	Mauritius	1	1	1
英国	United Kingdom	6	5	8
德国	Germany	15	9	10
法国	France	6	10	5
意大利	Italy	7	7	9
荷兰	Netherlands	7	3	3
比利时	Belgium	1		1
西班牙	Spain	2	5	6
瑞典	Sweden	6	3	1
瑞士	Switzerland	1	1	
俄罗斯	Russia	2	3	2
巴哈马	The Bahamas			
巴西	Brazil	1	2	2
开曼群岛	Cayman Islands	3	2	1
乌拉圭	Uruguay			
英属维尔京群岛	British Virgin Islands	19	15	11
加拿大	Canada	9	11	11
美国	United States	35	46	48
澳大利亚	Australia	14	4	9
库克群岛	The Cook Islands			
新西兰	New Zealand	6	2	3
萨摩亚	Samoa	7	8	6

单位:万美元（USD 10000）

合同利用外资 Foreign Investment Contracted			实际利用外资 Actual Utilization of Foreign Capital		
2012	2013	2014	2012	2013	2014
531276	**582029**	**702083**	**285252**	**327483**	**402514**
317369	466585	396965	187026	225647	279124
37923	5551	40148	1719	489	4689
6089	14385	64502	5166	8147	3156
4195	8464	2521	2090	5076	577
109	2479	63	15	160	
20440	8871	48742	8148	8135	27740
-359	914		225	39	
171	224	-693	94	177	393
15		16		15	
5	1034	500	9	526	280
-427	2700	4000	341	280	
5965	5524	3914	745	360	370
3682	419	6950	878	1981	2544
10006	4591	4746	1420	1293	7886
1343	1417	3988	173	288	22
205	258	932	2966	1	7
78	-64	2420	41	118	
187	31	194	152	47	66
145	28	542	224	30	59
2487	11	449	2140	271	
8	41	16			
80	29	65	249	616	18
7729	-27604	-26578	5984	8480	2484
	5				
36884	23203	20430	22165	18724	15136
4174	4095	499	723	850	444
5599	16633	15620	4219	1975	3883
7730	1308	3600	928	433	393
3509	13	4200	114	158	300
27024	9103	3841	10532	18433	5716

表 11－10 部分年份旅游业简况
Basic Statistic on Tourism in Partial Years

指标		Indicators	Unit	2012	2013	2014
旅行社合计	（家）	International Travel Agencies	(unit)	364	302	297
#出境旅行社	（家）	Outbound Travel Agencies	(unit)	18	18	19
国内入境旅行社	（家）	Domestic Inbound Travel Agencies	(unit)	267	284	278
旅游星级饭店	（家）	Star－rated Hotel	(unit)	170	160	148
国内旅游总人数	（万人次）	Number of Domestic Tourists	(10000 person－times)	5748	6226	6875
旅游总收入	（亿元）	Income of Tourism	(100 million yuan)	862.8	953.5	1068.1
#旅游创汇	（万美元）	Foreign Exchange Earnings	(USD 10000)	73428	79656	77832
国内旅游总收入	（亿元）	Domestic Tourism Receipts	(100 million yuan)	816.4	904.2	1020.3

注：本表至 11－12 表数据来自宁波市旅游局。
Note：Dara from Tables 11－10 to 11－12 are obtained from Ningbo Municipal Bureau of Tourism.

表 11－11 部分年份国际旅游情况
Basic Statistic on International Tourism in Partial Years

指标	单位	Indicators	Unit	2012	2013	2014
接待过夜境外旅游者人数	**（人）**	**Number of Oversea Tourists Staying Overnight**	**(person)**	**1162088**	**1273439**	**1396802**
外国人		Foreigner		631033	666231	778251
台湾同胞		Compatriots from Taiwan, China		282622	337725	347403
香港同胞		Compatriots from Hongkong, China		186801	196144	198239
澳门同胞		Compatriots from Macao, China		61632	73339	72909
接待过夜境外旅游者人天数	**（人天）**	**Person－days of Oversea Tourists Staying Overnight**	**(person－day)**	**3275117**	**3546179**	**3616930**
外国人		**Foreigner**		1883598	1909898	1998193
台湾同胞		**Compatriots from Taiwan, China**		705084	860814	885493
香港同胞		**Compatriots from Hongkong, China**		515853	547397	527548
澳门同胞		**Compatriots from Macao, China**		170582	228070	205696

表 11-12 部分年份接待外国旅游者人数(按国别分) Number of Foreign Tourists by Country in Partial Years

单位:人(person)

国家(地区)	Country	2010	2011	2012	2013	2014
总计	**Total**	**538932**	**608899**	**631033**	**659392**	**778251**
亚洲	Asia	252894	264007	270656	262926	332142
#日本	Japna	96111	99371	80214	76916	79128
韩国	Korea Rep	56309	55243	56171	53939	78129
印度尼西亚	Indonesia	12161	11589	10555	9830	9247
马来西亚	Malaysia	14066	15383	14496	13269	11592
新加坡	Singapore	17817	18965	18751	17762	20954
泰国	Thailand	9250	12000	14210	15225	14668
印度	India	12579	15516	18003	18851	20046
欧洲	Europe	135517	164423	163241	194765	194239
#英国	United Kingdom	20245	27227	29019	35659	37531
法国	France	18481	21243	23166	26497	28116
德国	Germany	19574	26126	23524	29282	33140
意大利	Italy	14237	16236	14691	18323	18223
俄罗斯	Russia	16705	19771	7698	16243	14075
美洲	America	92254	113920	125750	132026	132581
#美国	United States	62230	80571	73084	79415	77863
加拿大	Canada	15870	19460	22416	24881	28922
大洋洲	Oceania	32746	37696	41096	37113	34393
#澳大利亚	Australia	18311	23033	24515	22704	22918
非洲	Africa	10372	11835	18431	21332	26000
其他	Others	15180	17018	11881	11230	58354

表 11－13　宁波市前十名出口企业(2014)
The Top 10 Enterprises For Export in Ningbo

序号 No	企业名称	Name of Corporation	所在区域	Location
1	宁波申洲针织有限公司	Ningbo Shenzhou Shitong Weaving Group Co. ,Ltd.	北仑区	Beilun
2	宁波群志光电有限公司	Ningbo Qunzhi Photoelectric Co. ,Ltd.	北仑区	Beilun
3	浙江造船有限公司	Zhejiang Shipbuilding Co. ,Ltd.	奉化	Fenghua
4	宁波市慈溪进出口股份有限公司	Ningbo Cixi Import & Export Co. ,Ltd.	慈溪	Cixi
5	万华化学(宁波)能源贸易有限公司	Wanhua Chemical (Ningbo) Energy Trading Co. ,Ltd.	北仑区	Beilun
6	中基宁波集团股份有限公司	China－Base Ningbo Group Co. ,Ltd.	鄞州区	Yinzhou
7	宁波全胜达商贸有限公司	Ningbo Jinshengda Trading Co. ,Ltd.	北仑区	Beilun
8	宁波宝禾通商贸有限公司	Ningbo Baohetong Trading Co. ,Ltd.	北仑区	Beilun
9	浙江新景进出口有限公司	Zhejiang Xinjing Import & Export Co. ,Ltd.	北仑区	Beilun
10	宁波金盛禾商贸有限公司	Ningbo Jinshenghe Trading Co. ,Ltd.	北仑区	Beilun

表 11－14　宁波市前十名进口企业(2014)
The Top 10 Enterprises For Import in Ningbo

序号 No	企业名称	Name of Corporation	所在区域	Location
1	宁波群志光电有限公司	Ningbo Qunzhi Photoelectric Co. ,Ltd.	北仑区	Beilun
2	浙江逸盛石化有限公司	Zhejiang Yisheng Pertochemical Co. ,Ltd.	北仑区	Beilun
3	中基宁波集团股份有限公司	China－Base Ningbo Group Co. ,Ltd.	鄞州区	Yinzhou
4	宁波钢铁有限公司	Ningbo Steel Company Limited	北仑区	Beilun
5	宁波金田铜业(集团)股份有限公司	Ningbo Jintian Copper Group Co. ,Ltd.	江北区	Jiangbei
6	台化塑胶(宁波)有限公司	Formosa Plastics (Ningbo) Co. ,Ltd.	北仑区	Beilun
7	台塑聚丙烯(宁波)有限公司	Formosa Polypropylene (Ningbo) Co. ,Ltd.	北仑区	Beilun
8	宁波萍钢贸易有限公司	Ningbo Steel Company Limited	北仑区	Beilun
9	宁波舜宇光电信息有限公司	Ningbo Shunhong Universal Photoelectric Information Co. ,Ltd.	余姚	Yuyao
10	中信金属宁波能源有限公司	CITIC Ningbo Energy Metals Co. ,Ltd.	北仑区	Beilun

主要统计指标解释

【进出口总额】 海关进出口总额是指实际进出我国国境的货物总金额。包括对外贸易实际进出口货物,来料加工装配进出口货物,国家间、联合国及国际组织无偿援助物资和赠送品,华侨、港澳台同胞和外籍华人捐赠品,租赁期满归承租人所有的租赁货物,进料加工进出口货物,边境地方贸易及边境地区小额贸易进出口货物(边民互市贸易除外),中外合资经营企业、中外合作经营企业、外商独资经营企业进出口货物和公用物品,到、离岸价格在规定限额以上的进出口货样和广告品(无商业价值、无使用价值和免费提供出口的除外),从保税仓库提取在中国境内销售的进口货物以及其他进出口货物。进出口总额用以观察一个国家在对外贸易方面的总规模。我国规定出口货物按离岸价格计算,进口货物按到岸价格计算。

【利用外资】 指我国各级政府、部门、企业和其他经济组织通过对外借款、吸收外商直接投资以及用其他方式筹措的境外现汇、设备、技术等。

【外商直接投资】 是指外国企业和经济组织或个人(包括华侨、港澳台胞以及 我国在境外注册的企业)按我国有关政策、法规,用现汇、实物、技术等在我国境内开办外 商独资企业、与我国境内的企业或经济组织共同举办中外合资经营企业、合作经营企业或作 合作开发资源的投资(包括外商投资收益的再投资)以及经政府有关部门批准的项目投资总 额内,企业从境外借入的资金。

【外商其他投资】 指除对外借款和外商直接投资以外的各种利用外资的形式。包括企业在境内外股票市场公开发行的以外币计价的股票(目前主要是在香港证券市场发行的 H 股和在境内证券市场发行的 B 股)发行价总额,国际租赁进口设备的应付款,补充贸易中外商提供的进口设备、技术、物料的价款,加工装配贸易中外商提供的进口设备、物料的价款。

【旅游人数】 包括入境国际旅游者人数、出境居民人数和国内旅游者人数。

(1)入境国际旅游者人数:指来中国参观、访问、旅行、探亲、访友、休养、考察、参加会议和从事经济、科技、文化、教育、宗教等活动的外国人、港澳和台湾同胞的人数。不包括外国在我国的常驻机构,如使领馆、通讯社、企业办事处的工作人员;来我国常住的外国专家、留学生以及在岸逗留不过夜人员。

(2)出境居民人数:指大陆居民因公务活动或私人事务短期出境的人数。公务活动出境居民人数包括在国际交通工具上的中国服务员工,因私出境居民人数不包括在国际交通工具上的中国服务员工。

(3)国内旅游者人数:指我国大陆居民和在我国常住 1 年以上的外国人、港澳台同胞离开常住地在境内其他地方的旅游设施内至少停留一夜,最长不超过 6 个月的人数。

【国际旅游(外汇)收入】 指入境旅游的外国人、华侨、港澳台同胞在中国大陆旅游过程中发生的一切旅游支出,对国家来说就是国际旅游(外汇)收入。

Explanatory Notes on Main Statistical Indicators

[Total Imports and Exports] refer to the value of commodities imported into and exported from the boundary of China. They include the actual imports and exports through foreign trade, imported and exported goods under the processing and assembling trades and materials, supplies and gifts as aid given gratis between government and by the United Nations and other international organizations, and contributions denoted by overseas Chinese, compatriots in Hong Kong, Macao and Taiwan and Chinese with foreign citizenship, leasing commodities owned by tenants at the expiration of leasing period, the imported and exported commodities processed with imported materials, commodities trading, imported and exported small value trading goods in border areas (excluding mutual change goods), the imported and exported commodities and articles for public use of the Sino – foreign joint ventures, Sino – foreign cooperative enterprises and ventures exclusively with foreign own investment. They also included import and export of samples and advertising goods for those CIF or FOB value are beyond the permitted ceiling (excluding goods of no trading or no use value and free commodities for export), imported goods sold in China from bonded warehouse and other imported and exported goods. The indicator of total imports and exports at customs can be used to observe the total size of external trade in a country. In accordance with the stipulation of the Chinese government, imports are calculated at CIF, while exports are calculated at FOB.

FOB refer to Free on Board. CIF refer to Cost Insurance and Freight.

[Utilization of Foreign Capital] refers to remittance, equipment and technology financed from abroad, by loans, foreign direct investment and other forms undertaken by the Chinese governments at all levels, by various departments, enterprises and other economic units.

[Direct Investment by Foreign Entrepreneurs] refers to the investments inside China by foreign enterprises and economic organizations or individuals (including overseas Chinese, compatriots from Hong Kong and Macao, and Chinese enterprises registered abroad), following the relevant policies and laws of China, for the establishment of ventures exclusively with foreign own investment, Sino – foreign joint ventures and cooperative enterprises or for cooperative exploration of resources with enterprises or economic organizations in China. It includes the re – investment of the foreign entrepreneurs with the profits gained from the investment and the funds that enterprises borrow from abroad in the total investment of projects which are approved by the relevant department of the government.

[Other Overseas Investments] refer to all kinds of investments except the foreign loan and the FDI. They include: the total value (in foreign currency) of the stocks of one enterprises distributed publicly both at home and abroad(now mainly refer to H. shares at HK bond market, and B. shares at China mainland bond market); the rent charges of the foreign equipments; the total value of Technology, raw material and foreign equipment provided by foreign investors in supplemental trades, and value of foreign raw material, equipment in the trade of assemble machining.

[tourists number] is a sum of overseas tourists, local residents going abroad and domestic tourists.

overseas tourists number. Which refers to the number of foreigners and residents from Hongkong, Macao and Taiwan who come to China to go sightseeing, travel, visit relatives and friends, spend holidays, inspect, attend conferences and to do activities in economics, science, education, religious etc. Personnel as below are not taken into calculation, office workers in Chinese standing bodies at abroad, such as in embassies, news agencies, oversea offices of companies. Foreign experts and students living in China and foreigners who enter China only for voyage transferring are also not calculated.

number of local residents going abroad. Which refers to the number of mainland China residents who go abroad either for official business or for private affairs. Number of Chinese workers who serve in the international transportation vehicles are included in those who xit for official business, but not in those for private affairs.

domestic tourists. Which refers to the number of people who leave their living places to stay in the tourism facilities for at least one night but no more than 6 months, including mainland China residents, foreigners, residents from HK, Macao and TW who lived in China for more than one year.

[Foreign Exchange Earnings from International Tourism] refer to the total expenditures of the foreigners, overseas Chinese, compatriots from HongKong, Macao and Taiwan in the process of their tourism in the mainland of China. Their expenditures mentioned above are foreign exchange earnings to China.

NINGBO

2015

Statistical YearBook

12

CHAPTER

第十二篇

文化、教育、卫生 体育、科学技术

CULTURE,EDUCATION, PUBLIC HEALTH AND SPORTS, SCIENCE & TECHNOLOGY

文化、教育、卫生、体育、科学技术
Culture, Education, Public Health, Sports and Science & Technology

主要统计指标
Major Statistics Indicators

2014 年群艺馆、文化馆	Number of Mass Art Center and Cultural Center	12	个	unit
2014 年公共图书馆	Number of Public Libraries	12	个	unit
2014 年电影观众人次	Number of Spectator	3267	万人次	10000 person – times
2014 年各类学校数	Number of Various School	2082	所	unit
2014 年各类学校招生人数	Number of New Students Enrollment of Various Schools	261197	人	person
2014 年各类学校在校学生数	Number of Students Enrollment of Various Schools	1317239	人	person
2014 年各类学校毕业人数	Number of Graduates by Various Schools	249401	人	person
2014 年专任教师数	Number of Full – time Teacher	79231	人	person
2014 年高等学校在校生人数	Number of Students Enrollmentin Institutions of Higher Education	150854	人	person
2014 年医疗机构床位数	Number of Beds in Health Institutions	30852	张	bed
2014 年卫生技术人员数	Number of Medical Technical Personnel	54109	人	person
2014 年医生数	Number of Doctors	20984	人	person
2014 年参赛获奖数	Number of Obtain Awards by Athletic Competition	1044	枚	unit
2014 年有线电视用户数	Number of User Terminal for Cable TV Station	249.3	万户	10000 users

表 12-1 部分年份文化事业单位、机构、人员及活动情况
Basic Statistics on Cultural Institutions and Personnel in Partial Years

指标	单位	Indicators	Unit	2010	2011	2012	2013	2014
艺术表演团体	**个**	**Art Performance Troupes**	**unit**	**6**	**5**	**5**	**4**	**4**
机构人员数	人	Persons of Institutions	persons	403	410	518	484	497
国内演出场次	场次	Internal Performances	times	1214	970	1180	1016	1232
国内观众人次	千人	Internal Spectator	1000 persons times	3433	1207	1111	1013	1180
艺术表演场所	**所**	**Art Performance Places**	**unit**	**6**	**7**	**6**	**5**	**3**
机构人员数	人	Persons of Institutions	persons	91	82	77	76	42
演出场次	场次	Performances	times	1822	1430	2300	5535	616
观众人次	千人	Spectator	1000 persons times	408	316	689	624	173
公共图书馆	**个**	**Public Libraries**	**unit**	**12**	**13**	**12**	**12**	**12**
机构人员数	人	Persons of Institutions	persons	294	343	345	361	384
总藏量	万册	Total Collections	10000 volumes	610	734	733	668	722
古籍	千册	Ancient Books	1000 volumes	17	113	166	141	141
图书	万册	Books	10000 volumes	351	483	448	601	649
群艺馆.文化馆	**个**	**Mass Art Center and Cultural Center**	**unit**	**12**	**12**	**12**	**12**	**12**
机构人员数	人	**Persons of Institutions**	**persons**	262	318	311	303	309
文化站	**个**	**Cultural Center**	**unit**	**147**	**148**	**149**	**147**	**147**
机构人员数	人	Persons of Institutions	persons	331	447	449	503	560
文物单位		**Historical Relic Protection Units**						
文物保护管理机构	个	Historical Relic Protection Institutions	unit	13	13	13	12	12
国家级文保单位	个	Historical Relic Protection Units of State Level	unit	22	22			31
博物馆.纪念馆	个	Museums, Memorial Hall	unit	15	7	6	18	18
文物商店	个	Historical Relic	unit	1	1	1	1	1
电影放映单位		**Film Projecting Units**						
放映管理机构	个	Projecting Management Institutions	unit	9	11	11	11	12
电影院	个	Movie House	unit	16	15	33	49	57
放映队	个	Projecting Teams	unit	176	167	117	71	72
电影放映场次	万场	Projecting Performance	10000 times	10.3C	14.60	2.89	43.28	43.20
电影观众人次	万人次	Spectator	10000 persons times	1900.00	1490.00	860.70	946.79	3267.00

注：本表至 12-4 表数据来自宁波市文化广电新闻出版局。
Note: Data from Tables 12-1 to 12-4 are obtained from Ningbo Bureau of Culture Radio & TV, Press and Publication.

表 12-2 各县(市)文化事业单位、机构、人员及活动情况(2014)
Basic Statistics of Cultural Institutions and Personnel by Region

指标	单位	Indicators	Unit	全市 Total
艺术表演团体	个	**Art Performance Troupes**	**unit**	**4**
机构人员数	人	Persons of Institutions	persons	497
国内演出场次	场次	Internal Performances	times	1232
国内观众人次	千人	Internal Spectator	1000 persons times	1180
艺术表演场所	所	**Art Performance Places**	**unit**	**3**
机构人员数	人	Persons of Institutions	persons	42
演出场次	场次	Performances	times	616
观众人次	千人	Spectator	1000 persons times	173
公共图书馆	个	**Public Libraries**	**unit**	**12**
机构人员数	人	Persons of Institutions	persons	384
总藏量	万册	Total Collections	10000 volumes	722
古籍	千册	Ancient Books	1000 volumes	141
图书	万册	Books	10000 volumes	649
群艺馆. 文化馆	个	**Mass Art Center and Cultural Center**	**unit**	**12**
机构人员数	人	Persons of Institutions	persons	309
文化站	个	**Cultural Center**	**unit**	**147**
机构人员数	人	Persons of Institutions	persons	560
文物单位		**Historical Relic Protection Units**		
文物保护管理机构	个	Historical Relic Protection Institutions	unit	12
国家级文保单位	个	Historical Relic Protection Units of State Level	unit	31
博物馆. 纪念馆	个	Museums, Memorial Hall	unit	18
文物商店	个	Historical Relic	unit	1
电影放映单位		**Film Projecting Units**		
放映管理机构	个	Projecting Management Institutions	unit	12
电影院	个	Movie House	unit	57
放映队	个	Projecting Teams	unit	72
电影放映场次	万场	Projecting Performance	10000 times	43.20
电影观众人次	万人次	Spectator	10000 persons times	3267.00

市区 Urban District	#鄞州 Yinzhou	余姚市 Yuyao	慈溪市 Cixi	奉化市 Fenghua	象山县 Xiangshan	宁海县 Ninghai
2	**1**	**1**				**1**
324	30	110				63
712	143	320				200
624	112	256				300
2						**1**
41						3
521						95
126						48
7	**1**	**1**	**1**	**1**	**1**	**1**
231	23	27	56	14	29	27
496	132	58	67	22	42	38
78		36	8	0.03		20
456	126	50	53	22	37	32
7	**1**	**1**	**1**	**1**	**1**	**1**
181	26	30	26	34	19	19
61	**23**	**21**	**18**	**11**	**18**	**18**
293	139	58	97	20	41	51
7	1	1	1	1	1	1
18	5	4	4	1	3	1
6		3	8		1	
1						
7	1	1	1	1	1	1
28	10	9	9	4	3	4
17	7	14	12	11	3	15
24.30	4.30	6.30	5.70	2.20	2.00	2.70
2086.00	344.00	381.00	320.00	150.00	90.00	240.00

表 12-3 各县(市)广播电视基本情况(2014) Basic Statisits on Broadcasting and Television by Region

指标	单位	Indicators	Unit	全市 Total
广播电视机构		**Broadcasting and Television Institutions**		
电台	座	Broadcasting Station	set	9
电视台	座	Broadcasting and Relaying Stations	set	9
广播电视站	个	TV and Transfer Stations	set	111
全年播出公共节目时间		**Full - year Broadcasting & TV Hours**		
广播播音时间	小时	Broadcasting Hours	hour	92435
#制作节目播出时间	小时	Time of Self - Producting Programs	hour	71460
电视播出时间	小时	Hours Through TV Broadcasting	hour	90983
#制作节目播出时间	小时	Time of Self - Producting Programs	hour	27431
公共电视套数	**套**	**TV Channel**	**set**	**13**
公共广播套数	**套**	**Public Broadcasting Band**	**set**	**13**
发送功率		**Transfer Power**		
中波功率	千瓦	Middle - Wave Power	kw	41
调频功率	千瓦	Frequency Modulation Power	kw	85.1
电视功率	千瓦	TV Power	kw	33.60
有线电视用户数	**万户**	**Number of User Terminal of Cable TV Station**	**10000 users**	**249.3**

表 12-4 部分年份广播电视基本情况 Basic Statisits on Broadcasting and Television in Partial Years

指标	单位	Indicators	Unit	2012	2013	2014
广播电视机构		**Broadcasting and Television Institutions**				
电台	座	Broadcasting Station	set	1	9	9
电视台	座	Broadcasting and Relaying Stations	set	10	9	9
广播电视站	个	TV and Transfer Stations	set	111	111	111
全年播出公共节目时间		**Full - year Broadcasting & TV Hours**				
广播播音时间	小时	Broadcasting Hours	hour	95936	91005	92435
#制作节目播出时间	小时	Time of Self - Producting Programs	hour	76905	74351	71460
电视播出时间	小时	Hours Through TV Broadcasting	hour	91210	90281	90983
#制作节目播出时间	小时	Time of Self - Producting Programs	hour	31949	28739	27431
公共电视套数	**套**	**TV Channel**	**set**	**14**	**13**	**13**
公共广播套数	**套**	**Public Broadcasting Band**	**set**	**14**	**13**	**13**
有线电视用户数	**万户**	**Number of User Terminal of Cable TV Station**	**10000 users**	**227.873**	**244.85**	**249.31**

市区 Urban District	#鄞州 Yinzhou	余姚 Yuyao	慈溪 Cixi	奉化 Fenghua	象山 Xiangshan	宁海 Ninghai
4	1	1	1	1	1	1
4	1	1	1	1	1	1
43	20	19	19	9	13	8
57899	5859	8120	6387	6401	6205	7423
45469	4917	7149	4647	4302	3800	6092
56422	5121	5840	8760	6570	6821	6570
12558	1301	2000	5777	2600	1930	2566
8	**1**	**1**	**1**	**1**	**1**	**1**
8	**1**	**1**	**1**	**1**	**1**	**1**
41						
74.0	0.6	3.1	0.2	5.0	0.6	2.2
26.80	2.00	2.60	3.00	0.30	0.60	0.30
118.6	**45.6**	**30.2**	**42.3**	**16.0**	**20.1**	**22.1**

表 12－5 部分年份学生入、升学率
Percentage for Enrollment and Graduation of Students

单位：%

指标	Indicators	2010	2011	2012	2013	2014
小学学龄儿童入学率	Enrollment Rate for Children of School Age	100.00	100.00	100.00	100.00	100.00
小学毕业升学率	Graduation Rate for Pupils	100.00	100.00	100.00	99.99	100.00
初中毕业升学率	Graduation Rate for Students of Secondary School6	99.09	99.09	99.02		99.09
升入普通高中	Rate of Enrolling Senior School	49.49	49.88	50.13	51.19	50.92
升入职业高中	Rate of Enrolling Vacational Senior School	49.49	49.21	48.96	47.83	48.17
升入中专技校	Rate of Entrolling Technical Secondary School					
高等教育毛入学率	Gross Enrollment Rate of Higher Education	50.00	55.00			

表12－6　各县(市)各类学校数(2014)
Number of Various Schools by Region

项目	Item	全市 Total	市区 Urban District
各类学校数	**Number of Various School**		
(一)全日制学校	**Number of Full－time School**	**2080**	**836**
高等学校	Regular Institutions of Higher Education	14	14
#大专	Junior Colleges	6	6
初中	Regular Secondary Schools	209	85
高中	Senior Secondary Schools	83	39
职业中学	Vocational Secondary Schools	52	21
普通小学	Primary Schools	457	179
特殊教育学校	Special Education Schools	11	6
幼儿园	Kindergarten	1254	492
(二)成人学校数	**Number of School for Adult Education**	**2**	
成人高校数	Number of Higher Education for Adult	2	
成人中学	Secondary Education for Adult		

注：本表至12－8表数据来自宁波市教育局。高等学校中包省属学校。

Note：Data from Tables 12－6 to 12－8 are obtained from Ningbo Municipal Bureau of Education. Regular institutions of higher education including the provincial school.

单位:所(unit)

#鄞州 Yinzhou	余姚市 Yuyao	慈溪市 Cixi	奉化市 Fenghua	象山县 Xiangshan	宁海县 Ninghai
303	**306**	**409**	**156**	**148**	**225**
31	31	36	17	22	18
13	10	16	5	6	7
9	9	6	5	5	6
73	87	88	26	23	54
1	1	1	1	1	1
176	168	262	102	91	139

表 12－7　各县(市)各类学校学生情况(2014)
Basic Statistics on Student of Various Schools by Region

项目	Item	全市 Total	市区 Urban District
各类学校招生人数	**New Students Enrollment of Various Schools**	**261197**	**153210**
研究生	Postgraduates	1418	1418
普通高校	Institutions of Higher Education	41209	41209
#大专	Junior Colleges	18584	18584
初中	Regular Secondary Schools	64200	27073
高中	Senior Secondary Schools	28013	13165
职业中学	Secondary Vacational Schools	22984	11277
普通小学	Primary Schools	79464	35221
特殊教育学校	Special Education Schools	134	72
成人高校	Higher Education for Adult	23775	23775
各类学校在校学生数	**Students Enrollment of Various Schools**	**1317239**	**700780**
研究生	Postgraduates	4195	4195
普通高校	Institutions of Higher Education	146659	146659
#大专	Junior Colleges	54798	54798
初中	Regular Secondary Schools	189840	82804
高中	Senior Secondary Schools	90298	39467
职业中学	Secondary Vacational Schools	69268	31378
普通小学	Primary Schools	482556	211611
特殊教育学校	Special Education Schools	955	496
成人高校	Higher Education for Adult	55048	55048
成人中学	Secondary Education for Adult		
幼儿园在园人数	Persons of Kindergarten	278420	129122
各类学校毕业人数	**Graduates by Various Schools**	**249401**	**140843**
研究生	Postgraduates	1139	1139
普通高校	Institutions of Higher Education	37711	37711
#大专	Junior Colleges		
初中	Regular Secondary Schools	53832	24557
高中	Senior Secondary Schools	35627	13984
职业中学	Secondary Vacational Schools	25962	10662
普通小学	Primary Schools	73946	31644
特殊教育学校	Special Education Schools	97	59
成人高校	Higher Education for Adult	21087	21087
成人中学	Secondary Education for Adult		

单位:人(person)

#鄞州 Yinzhou	余姚市 Yuyao	慈溪市 Cixi	奉化市 Fenghua	象山县 Xiangshan	宁海县 Ninghai
29697	**27187**	**31569**	**14029**	**15048**	**20154**
9676	9922	10586	4855	5168	6596
4015	3333	4819	1898	1993	2805
3876	2916	3129	1687	1408	2567
12121	10993	13016	5579	6469	8186
9	23	19	10	10	
185655	**148835**	**200746**	**74076**	**83273**	**109529**
28729	27753	31261	13581	14984	19457
12606	11896	17630	6289	6758	8258
12427	9465	10853	5902	4858	6812
82051	67570	87551	32833	35322	47669
129	137	135	45	82	60
49713	32014	53316	15426	21269	27273
29057	**26732**	**36215**	**13518**	**14399**	**17694**
7980	7108	8536	3995	4055	5581
4791	4878	8279	2577	2794	3115
4209	3764	5470	1926	2143	1997
12077	10969	13912	5018	5402	7001
	13	18	2	5	

表 12－8 各县(市)各类学校教职工情况(2014)
Basic Statistics on Teachers and Staff of Various Schools by Region

项目	Item	全市 Total	市区 Urban District
各类学校教职工人数	**Number of Teachers and Staff of Various Schools**	**105719**	**55294**
高等学校	Regular Institutions of Higher Education	11460	11460
#大专	Junior Colleges		
普通中学	Regular Secondary Schools	29649	13191
职业中学	Secondary Vacational Schools	6264	2732
普通小学	Primary Schools	24510	10558
特殊教育学校	Special Education Schools	289	179
成人高校	Higher Education for Adult	662	662
成人中学	Secondary Education for Adult		
幼儿园	Kindergarten	32885	16512
各类学校专任教师人数	**Number of Full－time Teachers of Various Schools**	**79231**	**40901**
普通高校	Institutions of Higher Education	7808	7808
#大专	Junior Colleges		
初中	Regular Secondary Schools	14817	6598
高中	Senior Secondary Schools	8492	3836
职业中学	Secondary Vacational Schools	5647	2445
普通小学	Primary Schools	24916	11165
特殊教育学校	Special Education Schools	254	150
成人高校	Higher Education for Adult	475	475
#电大	Radio and TV Universities	347	347
成人中学	Secondary Education for Adult		
幼儿园	Kindergarten	16822	8424
各类学校兼任教师人数	**Number of Part－time Teachers of Various Schools**	**1031**	
普通中学	Regular Secondary Schools	73	
职业中学	Secondary Vacational Schools	523	
普通小学	Primary Schools		
成人高校	Higher Education for Adult	435	
成人中学	Secondary Education for Adult		

单位:人(person)

#鄞州 Yinzhou	余姚市 Yuyao	慈溪市 Cixi	奉化市 Fenghua	象山县 Xiangshan	宁海县 Ninghai
15228	**12545**	**17219**	**5710**	**7003**	**7948**
3752	4284	5140	2051	2910	2073
1164	837	1114	531	505	545
4183	3919	4805	1509	1289	2430
34	31	32	13	16	18
6095	3474	6128	1606	2283	2882
11904	**8947**	**13346**	**4674**	**5248**	**6115**
2178	1988	2732	1093	1191	1215
1298	1021	1644	593	669	729
1099	769	1025	453	443	512
4078	3280	4822	1626	1730	2293
31	30	28	13	15	18
3220	1859	3095	896	1200	1348

表 12 - 9 历年教职工数和在校学生数
Number of Teachers and Staff and Students Enrollment Over the Years

单位:万人(10000 persons)

年份 Year	在校教职工 Teachers and Staff	#教师 Teachers	在校学生 Students Enrollment 大学生 Higher Education	中学生 Secondary Schools	小学生 Primary Schools
1978	4.15	3.55	0.10	27.16	59.11
1979	4.01	3.53	0.21	23.04	57.85
1980	4.28	3.48	0.25	20.99	56.39
1981	4.13	3.23	0.20	19.36	52.02
1982	3.31	2.75	0.15	18.77	46.67
1983	3.72	3.06	0.16	19.48	41.71
1984	3.73	3.00	0.21	21.42	38.50
1985	3.94	3.16	0.27	23.47	36.43
1986	4.09	3.28	0.34	24.35	36.90
1987	4.21	3.34	0.39	23.48	36.41
1988	4.32	3.47	0.45	20.34	38.69
1989	4.45	3.56	0.49	18.75	41.84
1990	4.24	3.34	0.49	19.65	42.70
1991	4.34	3.39	0.48	22.01	41.62
1992	4.37	3.47	0.53	24.39	40.16
1993	4.59	3.61	0.66	25.03	40.40
1994	4.75	3.76	0.83	26.76	41.92
1995	5.00	4.01	0.98	28.93	41.29
1996	5.12	4.17	1.04	30.07	41.80
1997	5.27	4.32	1.15	29.93	43.14
1998	5.44	4.40	1.25	29.00	43.91
1999	6.16	4.81	1.68	25.12	43.36
2000	6.59	5.17	2.59	27.98	42.40
2001	6.86	5.12	4.34	29.60	42.24
2002	7.05	5.27	6.21	30.86	44.55
2003	7.46	5.61	7.99	30.99	45.26
2004	7.85	5.92	9.60	32.09	47.61
2005	8.59	6.46	11.12	40.25	47.60
2006	8.68	6.55	12.13	40.95	47.38
2007	9.09	6.84	12.76	41.12	47.15
2008	9.27	7.04	13.04	41.70	46.80
2009	9.13	7.42	13.75	41.42	45.03
2010	9.61	7.29	14.08	40.61	46.19
2011	9.82	7.70	14.14	39.13	47.61
2012	9.95	7.63	14.54	37.55	47.88
2013	10.37	7.82	14.90	36.43	48.70
2014	10.57	7.92	15.09	34.94	48.26

注:在校教职工包括幼儿园。

Note:The number of teachers and staff include kinder - gardens

表 12-10 部分年份教育事业基本情况
Basic Statistics on Education in Partial Years

单位：人(person)

指标	Indicators	2009	2010	2011	2012	2013	2014
学校数(所)	**Number of Schools(unit)**						
高等学校	Institutions of Higher Education	15	14	14	14	14	14
中等专业学校	Specialized Secondary Schools						
普通中学	Regular Secondary Schools	306	301	299	299	297	292
职业中学	Vocational Secondary Schools	57	56	57	55	55	52
小学	Primary Schools	536	513	490	476	465	457
专任教师	**Number of Full-time Teachers**						
高等学校	Institutions of Higher Education	6933	7146	9086	7374	7524	7808
中等专业学校	Specialized Secondary Schools						
普通中学	Regular Secondary Schools	22718	22961	22897	23021	23203	23309
职业中学	Vocational Secondary Schools	4734	4955	5283	5519	5714	5647
小学	Primary Schools	21184	21577	22265	23139	24025	24916
招生数	**New Student Enrollment**						
高等学校	Institutions of Higher Education	42644	42806	43735	44001	42946	42627
中等专业学校	Specialized Secondary Schools						
普通中学	Regular Secondary Schools	110570	107982	99456	98660	95960	92213
职业中学	Vocational Secondary Schools	30058	27781	28469	25569	25707	22984
小学	Primary Schools	74952	84725	87239	85933	84926	79464
在校学生数	**Student Enrollment**						
高等学校	Institutions of Higher Education	137495	140818	144424	145358	148954	150854
中等专业学校	Specialized Secondary Schools						
普通中学	Regular Secondary Schools	332945	325407	308563	295203	285912	280138
职业中学	Vocational Secondary Schools	81293	80724	82783	80294	78345	69268
小学	Primary Schools	450322	461931	476085	478816	486971	482556
毕业生数	**Number of Graduates**						
高等学校	Institutions of Higher Education	37118	37733	38022	38226	37269	38850
中等专业学校	Specialized Secondary Schools						
普通中学	Regular Secondary Schools	110130	105199	104584	99238	94869	89459
职业中学	Vocational Secondary Schools	26406	24835	24270	26908	26502	25962
小学	Primary Schools	79440	76536	69412	73173	70889	73946

表12－11 部分年份平均每一专任教师负担的学生数
The Ratio of Student Enrollment and Full－time Teachers in Partial Years

单位：人(person)

年份 Year	高等学校 Institutions of Higher Education	中等专业学校 Specialized Scendary Schools	普通中学 Regular Secondary Schools	职业中学 Vocational Secondary Schools	小学 Primary Schools
1994	8.9	15.9	19.9	16.1	25.7
1995	9.1	18.0	20.0	16.2	24.6
1996	9.7	23.5	19.7	14.6	24.2
1997	10.7	21.7	18.3	16.6	24.2
1998	11.3	22.4	17.4	17.2	24.7
1999	12.8	22.3	16.9	16.6	24.5
2000	11.3	24.1	17.7	16.2	23.9
2001	15.7	30.5	17.8	16.5	23.7
2002	17.6	26.1	17.8	17.5	24.4
2003	18.9	24.1	17.0	27.9	24.5
2004	17.0	20.4	16.6	26.5	24.7
2005	18.5	15.9	16.0	29.6	23.9
2006	18.7	9.4	16.0	28.0	23.5
2007	19.2	7.0	15.6	27.1	22.9
2008	19.1	6.2	15.4	23.4	22.4
2009	19.8		14.7	17.2	21.3
2010	19.7		14.2	16.3	21.4
2011	15.6		13.5	15.7	21.4
2012	19.7		12.8	14.6	20.7
2013	19.8		12.3	13.7	20.3
2014	19.3		12.0	12.3	19.4

表12－12 部分年份平均每万人口在校学生数
Student Enrollment Per 10000 Populations in Partial Years

单位：人(person)

年份 Year	大学生 University and College Students	中专学生 Specialized Scendary Schools Students	中学学生 Regular Secondary Schools Students	职业中学生 Vocational Secondary Schools Students	小学生 Primary Schools Schools
1994	15.8	30.5	458.0	53.4	801.1
1995	18.5	37.3	488.8	60.5	784.2
1996	19.7	47.5	511.7	57.6	791.4
1997	21.7	43.7	493.1	69.8	811.4
1998	23.3	47.7	463.0	79.7	821.9
1999	31.3	50.8	467.9	82.2	807.6
2000	48.0	46.5	518.4	81.6	785.6
2001	80.1	41.8	545.9	83.3	779.1
2002	113.9	35.3	566.5	93.5	817.8
2003	145.9	34.4	565.8	119.0	826.4
2004	174.3	32.3	582.5	134.6	864.2
2005	199.3	26.1	582.3	143.4	858.2
2006	215.2	17.8	595.6	137.6	848.1
2007	226.0	13.4	594.2	134.2	835.2
2008	229.6	11.1	604.6	129.4	823.8
2009	240.8		583.1	142.4	788.6
2010	245.3		566.8	140.6	804.6
2011	245.7		536.4	143.9	827.6
2012	251.9		650.7	139.1	829.8
2013	257.3		493.9	135.3	841.2
2014	259.2		481.4	119.0	829.2

表 12－13 历年卫生事业主要指标 Basic Statistics on Health Care Over the Years

年份 Year	卫生机构数（个）Number of Health Institutions (unit)	#医院 Hospitals	卫生机构床位（张）Number of Beds in Health Institutions (bed)	#医院 Hospitals	卫生技术人员（万人）Number of Medical technical (10000 persons)	#医生 Doctors
1978	949	400	5989	5549	0.93	0.36
1979	1013	398	6618	5871	0.99	0.36
1980	1032	397	6948	6368	1.06	0.38
1981	1077	394	7537	7015	1.13	0.44
1982	1100	400	8130	7230	1.19	0.48
1983	1107	396	8372	7525	1.24	0.50
1984	1117	396	8823	7954	1.28	0.53
1985	1123	311	9067	8250	1.30	0.54
1986	1181	320	9436	8605	1.34	0.56
1987	1199	327	9922	9057	1.41	0.60
1988	1259	330	10447	9629	1.46	0.73
1989	1293	331	11073	10067	1.53	0.74
1990	1301	344	11449	10522	1.58	0.75
1991	1313	345	11731	10816	1.66	0.76
1992	1270	303	12175	11259	1.69	0.78
1993	1262	300	12529	11633	1.70	0.80
1994	1257	345	12976	12090	1.76	0.84
1995	1257	345	13193	12316	1.74	0.87
1996	1123	297	13012	12299	1.78	0.88
1997	1678	296	13654	8849	1.83	0.92
1998	1407	296	13689	9481	1.86	0.91
1999	961	54	13795	9364	1.89	0.93
2000	929	56	14535	9968	1.92	0.95
2001	921	57	14393	10246	1.96	0.97
2002	1263	58	14653	10292	2.01	0.99
2003	1297	55	15279	10654	2.15	1.06
2004	1555	58	17053	12119	2.51	1.14
2005	1667	265	18458	17856	2.91	1.32
2006	1854	268	19711	19339	3.25	1.46
2007	2270	255	21000	20306	3.53	1.54
2008	2276	257	22155	21523	3.69	1.51
2009	2359	243	23475	22299	4.00	1.62
2010	2377	230	26097	24762	4.31	1.72
2011	4221	106	27127	23046	4.67	1.84
2012	4035	108	28290	24296	4.92	1.91
2013	4032	109	29356	25753	5.15	1.99
2014	4077	123	30852	27538	5.41	2.10

表 12-14 各县(市)卫生事业单位机构情况(2014)
Basic Statistics on Health Care Institutions by Region

指标	Indicators	全市 Total
卫生事业机构数	**Number of Health Care Intitiutions**	**4077**
1、医院合计	Total Hospitals	123
综合医院	Comprehensive Hospitals	62
中医医院	Hospitals of Chinese Medicine	12
中西医结合医院	Combined Chinese and Western Medicine Hospital	3
专科医院	Specialized Hospitals	45
口腔医院	Oral and Dental Hospitals	7
眼科医院	Ophthalmology Hospitals	3
心血管病医院	Cardiovascular Hospital	1
妇产(科)医院	Obstetrics and Gynecology Hospitals	5
儿童医院	The Children's Hospital	2
精神病医院	Mental Hospitals	6
皮肤病医院	Dermatology Hospital	2
骨科医院	Orthopedist Hospitals	4
康复医院	Healing Hospitals	5
美容医院	Cosmetic Surgery Clinic	1
其他专科医院	Others Specialized Hospitals	9
护理院	Nursing Home	1
2、社区卫生服务中心(站)	Community Sanitation Service Sites	567
社区卫生服务中心	Community Health Center	57
社区卫生服务站	Community Health Service Station	510
3、卫生院	Local Hospitals	110
乡镇卫生院	Town and Township Local Hospitals	110
中心卫生院	Center Locale Hospitals	32
乡卫生院	Towhship Locale Hospitals	78
4、村卫生室	Village Health Room	2083
5、门诊部	Clinics	125
6、诊所. 卫生所. 医务室	Special Clinics	993
7、急救中心(站)	First - aid Centre(Stations)	8
8、采供血机构	Blood Collecting and Supplying Organization	1
9、妇幼保健院(所、站)	Maternity and Child Care Centers or Stations	11
10、专科疾病防治院(所、站)	Specialized Prevention and Treatment Centers or Stations	3
11、疾病预防控制中心	Center for Disease Control and Prevention	13
12、卫生监督所(中心)	Health Supervision Centers(Center)	13
13、计划生育技术服务机构	Family Planning Technical Service Institutions	7
14、医学科学研究机构	Research Institution of Medicine	3
15、医学在职培训机构	Medical Institution of On - the - job Training	5
16、临床检验中心(所、站)	Clinical Laboratory (Station)	4
17、统计信息中心	Statistical Information Center	1
18、其他卫生机构	Others Health Care Institutions	7

注:本表至 12-17 表数据来之宁波市卫生局。

Note: Data from Tables 12 - 14 to 12 - 17 are obtained from Ningbo Municipal Bureau of Health.

单位:个(unit)

市区 Urban District	#鄞州 Yinzhou	余姚 Yuyao	慈溪 Cixi	奉化 Fenghua	象山 Xiangshan	宁海 Ninghai
1626	**579**	**540**	**712**	**473**	**264**	**462**
76	13	8	17	9	8	5
37	8	5	12	2	4	2
6	1	1	1	1	2	1
3	1					
30	3	1	4	6	2	2
6	1			1		
2			1			
				1		
3			2			
2						
2		1	1	1	1	
1				1		
1				1		2
3	1			1	1	
1						
9	1					
		1				
361	87	98	37	41		30
41	7	7	6	2		1
320	80	91	31	39		29
18	16	14	16	22	17	23
18	16	14	16	22	17	23
5	5	5	5	4	7	6
13	11	9	11	18	10	17
541	302	276	513	286	187	280
79	17	14	28	2	1	1
506	137	124	93	108	46	116
4	1	1	1	1		1
1						
6	1	1	1	1	1	1
2	1		1			
8	1	1	1	1	1	1
8	1	1	1	1	1	1
4	1	1	1			1
3						
1		1	1		1	1
4	1					
1						
3			1	1	1	1

表 12－15 各县(市)卫生事业人员、床位情况(2014)
Number of Health Care Personnel and Beds by Region

指标	Indicators	全市 Total
从业人员总计(人)	**Total Employment(person)**	**64657**
卫生技术人员	Medical Technical Personnel	54109
医生数	Number of Doctors	20984
执业医师	Medical Practitioner	18300
执业助理医师	Assistant Medical Practitioner	2684
注册护士	Register Nurse	20864
药师(士)	Pharmacists	3510
技师(士)	Laboratory Technicians	2898
检验师	Laboratory Examiner	2216
其他	Others	5853
见习医师	Trainee Doctors	2417
其他技术人员	Other Technical Personnel	1960
管理人员	Manager	2143
工勤技能人员	Logistics Workers	4755
每千人拥有卫生技术人员	Number of Medical Technical Personnel Per 1000 Persons	9.27
每千人拥有医生	Number of Doctors Per 1000 Persons	3.59
每千人拥有注册护士	Number of R. N. Per 1000 Persons	3.57
卫生事业床位数(张)	**Number of Beds (bed)**	**30852**
医院床位	Beds of Hospitals	27538
社区卫生服务中心床位	Beds of Health Service Center of Communities	573
卫生院床位	Beds of Local Hospitals	2114
妇幼保健院(所、站)床位	Beds of Maternity and Child Care Centers	557
专科疾病防治院(所、站)床位	Beds of Specialized Prevention Stations	50
每千人拥有总床位	Total Beds of Per 1000 Persons	5.28
每千人拥有医院卫生院床位	Beds of Hospitals and Local Hospitals Per 1000 Persons	5.18

市区 Urban District	#鄞州 Yinzhou	余姚 Yuyao	慈溪 Cixi	奉化 Fenghua	象山 Xiangshan	宁海 Ninghai
36442	**8852**	**6741**	**9470**	**3944**	**3463**	**4597**
30970	7493	5589	7808	3099	2970	3673
11733	3021	2124	3126	1315	1211	1475
10736	2618	1758	2491	1116	1021	1178
997	403	366	635	199	190	297
12135	2639	2214	2925	1134	1137	1319
1963	541	364	531	200	231	221
1691	393	285	419	134	156	213
1297	313	214	320	104	128	153
3448	899	602	807	316	235	445
1313	300	303	388	170	96	147
1047	256	146	327	189	93	158
1489	275	161	268	68	87	70
2617	749	536	658	342	134	468
13.49	8.79	6.68	7.47	6.41	5.41	5.86
5.11	3.55	2.54	2.99	2.72	2.21	2.35
5.28	3.10	2.65	2.80	2.34	2.07	2.11
18268	**3560**	**2776**	**3783**	**2246**	**1899**	**1880**
17569	3136	2371	2937	2035	1621	1005
357	88	100	116			
336	336	305	424	161	258	630
6			256	50		245
			50			
7.96	4.18	3.32	3.62	4.64	3.46	3.00
7.95	4.18	3.32	3.32	4.54	3.43	2.61

表 12－16　各级医院工作情况(2014)
Medical Treatment of Various Hospitals

指标	Indicators	门诊人次合计 (万人次) Out－Patients (10000 person－times)
全市总计	**Total**	**8576**
1、医院合计	Total Hospitals	3953
综合医院	Comprehensive Hospitals	2780
省辖市属医院	Urban Hospitals Administered by Province	581
#市第一医院	The No. 1 Hospital of Ningbo	175
市第二医院	The No. 2 Hospital of Ningbo	148
宁大附院	The No. 3 Hospital of Ningbo	105
市李惠利医院	Li Huili Hospital of Ningbo	136
市华慈医院	Hua Ci Hospital of Ningbo	17
中医医院	Hospitals of Chinese Medicine	618
#市中医院	Hospital of Chinese Medicine of Ningbo	109
中西医结合医院	Combined Chinese and Western Medicine Hospital	19
专科医院	Specialized Hospitals	535
口腔医院	Oral and Dental Hospitals	43
眼科医院	Ophthalmology Hospitals	53
心血管病医院	Cardiovascular Hospital	11
妇产(科)医院	Obstetrics and Gynecology Hospitals	200
#市妇儿医院	Hospital for Maternity and Child of Ningbo	194
儿童医院	The Children's Hospital	12
精神病医院	Mental Hospitals	91
#市康宁医院	Kangning Hospital of Ningbo	17
皮肤病医院	Dermatology Hospital	11
骨科医院	Orthopedist Hospitals	87
康复医院	Healing Hospitals	10
美容医院	Cosmetic Surgery Clinic	
其他专科医院	Others Specialized Hospitals	17
护理院	Nursing Home	1
2、社区卫生服务中心(站)	Health Service Center of Communities	1542
3、卫生院	Pict Local Hospitals	1669
5、门诊部	Policlinic	183
4、村卫生室	Village Health Room	669
6、诊所、卫生所、医务室	Clinic	347
7、妇幼保健院(所、站)	Maternity and Child Care Centers or Stations	178
8、专科疾病防治院(所、站)	Specialized Prevention and Treatment Centers or Stations	26

本年入院人数（万人）Inpatients in this Year (10000 persons)	平均住院日（天）Average Day In－patients (day)	本年出院人数（万人）Discharged Patient in this Year (10000 persons)	期末实有病床数（张）Factual Beds at the Year－end (bed)	平均开放病床数（张）Average Openning Bed (bed)	病床使用率（%）Occupancy of Hospital Beds (%)
97.0	**9.8**	**96.9**	**30852**	**30120**	**85.1**
89.5	9.8	89.5	27538	26858	88.7
68.9	9.0	68.8	19550	19116	89.0
22.1	9.1	22.1	5814	5746	96.6
5.8	9.4	5.8	1570	1558	96.1
6.9	9.6	6.9	1939	1928	94.2
3.6	9.4	3.6	965	927	99.2
5.8	8.2	5.8	1340	1333	98.6
6.9	10.8	6.9	2223	2220	91.0
1.6	13.8	1.6	600	598	98.6
0.2	8.6	0.2	160	160	22.1
13.6	13.5	13.6	5505	5262	88.9
			60	37	
1.0	4.8	1.0	170	170	79.0
0.6	9.5	0.5	150	150	93.6
5.2	7.7	5.2	1345	1208	91.2
5.2	7.6	5.2	1255	1126	95.1
0.3	6.3	0.3	45	45	106.7
1.4	56.1	1.4	1824	1814	100.4
0.5	41.6	0.5	520	519	110.8
			40	40	
4.2	9.7	4.2	1235	1196	92.5
0.3	35.1	0.3	348	327	72.0
			12		
0.6	5.0	0.6	276	274	32.5
0.05	51.8	0.04	100	100	73.4
0.7	14.1	0.7	573	568	47.3
3.8	9.7	3.8	2114	2095	48.9
			20		
2.9	6.1	2.9	557	550	88.2
	66.7		50	50	58.5

表 12－17 居民病伤死亡原因(2014)
Main 10 Diseases of Death in Urban Residents

死亡人数(人)

指标	Indicators	合计 Total
宁波市总计	**Total in Ningbo**	**36779**
十种死因合计	Main 10 Causes of Death	34617
1、恶性肿瘤	Malignant Tumour	11961
2、脑血管病	Cerebral Vascular Disease	6616
3、呼吸系病	Respiratory Disease	5299
4、心脏病	Cardiopathy	3980
5、损伤和中毒	Trauma and Toxicosis	3315
6、内分泌等疾病	Internal System Disease	1028
7、消化系统疾病	Digestive Disease	941
8、神经系统疾病	Nervous system diseases	678
9、传染病	Infectious Disease(Respiratory Tuberculosis not Included)	425
10、泌尿系疾病	Urologic Diseases	374
市区总计	**Total in Urban Destricts**	**13282**
十种死因合计	Main 10 Causes of Death	12453
1、恶性肿瘤	Malignant Tumour	4624
2、脑血管病	Cerebral Vascular Disease	2175
3、呼吸系病	Respiratory Disease	1905
4、心脏病	Heart Disease	1277
5、损伤和中毒	Injury and Poisoning	1163
6、内分泌等疾病	Internal System Disease	454
7、消化系统疾病	Digestive Disease	327
8、神经系统疾病	Nervous system diseases	243
9、传染病	Infectious Disease(Respiratory Tuberculosis not Included)	143
10、泌尿系疾病	Urologic Diseases	142

Number of Death (person)		死因构成 (%) Composition of Death(%)	死亡专率(/10万) Death Rate (per 0.1 million persons)		
男 Male	女 Female		合计 Total	男 Male	女 Female
20712	**16067**	**100.00**	**631.98**	**714.61**	**550.00**
19739	14878	94.12	594.83	681.04	509.30
8055	3906	32.52	205.53	277.92	133.71
3399	3217	17.99	113.68	117.27	110.12
2765	2534	14.41	91.05	95.40	86.74
1983	1997	10.82	68.39	68.42	68.36
1764	1551	9.01	56.96	60.86	53.09
451	577	2.80	17.66	15.56	19.75
513	428	2.56	16.17	17.70	14.65
316	362	1.84	11.65	10.90	12.39
274	151	1.16	7.30	9.45	5.17
219	155	1.02	6.43	7.56	5.31
7361	**5921**	**100.00**	**580.97**	**653.12**	**510.83**
6998	5455	93.76	544.71	620.91	470.62
3040	1584	34.81	202.26	269.73	136.66
1091	1084	16.38	95.14	96.80	93.52
977	928	14.34	83.33	86.69	80.06
658	619	9.61	55.86	58.38	53.40
582	581	8.76	50.87	51.64	50.12
192	262	3.42	19.86	17.04	22.60
173	154	2.46	14.30	15.35	13.29
112	131	1.83	10.63	9.94	11.30
91	52	1.08	6.26	8.07	4.49
82	60	1.07	6.21	7.28	5.18

表 12－18　部分年份全市体育工作情况
Basic Statistics on Physical Culture Schools and Sports in Partial Years

指标	单位	Indicators	Uuit	2011	2012	2013	2014
各类体校情况		**Various Physical Culture and Sports School**					
体育运动学校数	个	Physical Education and Sports School	unit	1	1	1	1
在校学生数	人	Student Enrollment	person	720	810	750	750
专职教练员	人	Full－time Coaches	person	60	47	62	62
业余体校个数	个	Sparetime Sports Schools	unit	5	5	6	6
#重点业余体校	个	Emphatic Sparetime Sports School	unit	5	5	5	5
业余体校在校学生数	人	Student Enrollment in Sparetime Sports Schools	person	840	910	1020	850
业余体校送入优秀运动队	人	Number of Persons from Sparetime Sports School Enrolling Excelent Sports Team	person	36	39	42	80
业余体校考入高等院校	人	Number of Persons Admitted to Institutions Higher Education from Sparetime Sports School	person	50	50	52	30
传统项目布局情况		**Distribution on Traditional Events**					
分布学校数	个	Number of Distributing Schools	unit	131	136	146	145
#中学	个	Secondary Schools	unit	37	21	46	10
小学	个	Primary Schools	unit	94	125	100	135
市区新增健身设施	套	New built Health－care Facilities in Urban Districts	set				
参加活动学生人数	人	Number of Participants in Student	person	19200	9620	20050	22000
参加田径学生	人	Track and Field	person	8000	4500	9000	8200
参加游泳学生	人	Swimming	person	2000	1100	1000	3100
参加射击学生	人	Shoot	person	1000	220	200	500
参加蓝球学生	人	Basketball	person	2000	600	2000	2200
参加排球学生	人	Volleyball	person	1600	400	1500	1200
参加足球学生	人	Football	person	1600	1200	2000	3500
参加乒乓排球学生	人	Pingpong	person	2000	800	2350	1600
参加羽毛球学生	人	Badminton	person	1000	800	2000	1700
游泳池情况(体育系统)		**Swimming Pool Managed by Physical Department**					
游泳池个数	个	Number of Swimming Pools	unit	11	6	17	12
#室内游泳池	个	Indoor	unit	10	4	12	10
游泳池活动场次	场次	Number of Running Swimming Pool	times	13000	11000	1530	13500
#室内游泳池	场次	Indoor	times	10500	9500	497	10500
参赛获奖数	**枚**	**Number of Obtain Awards by Athletic Competition**	**unit**	**963**	**593**	**992**	**1044**
#省级及以上金牌	枚	Gold Medals Won in Province Level Competitions	unit	383	173	389	384
#省级及以上银牌	枚	Silver Medals Won in Province Level Competitions	unit	315	180	318	350
#省级及以上铜牌	枚	Bronze Medals Won in Province Level Competitions	unit	265	240	285	310

表 12－19 部分年份科技活动情况 Scientific and Technological Activities in Partial Years

指标	Indicators	2010	2011	2012	2013	2014
研究与试验发展经费支出（亿元）	Expenditure on R&D (100 million yuan)	85.70	114.29	134.46	157.33	175.63
#规上工业（亿元）	Industrial Enterprises above Designated Size (100 million yuan)	78.25	97.50	122.20	141.96	160.00
研究与试验发展经费支出占地区生产总值的比重（%）	of GDP(%)	1.66	1.89	2.04	2.20	2.31

表 12－20 部分年份工业企业科技活动情况 Scientific and Technological Activities of Industrial Enterprises in Partial Years

指标	Indicators	2011	2012	2013	2014
企业数（个）	Number of Enterprises (unit)	6627	6762	7140	7383
#有 R&D 活动（个）	Number of Enterprises Having R&D Activities(unit)	2389	2993	3205	3322
#有科技机构（个）	Number of R&D Institutions(unit)	1665	1913	2013	1947
年末从业人员（人）	Number of Employees at the End of the Year(person)	1486967	1465624	1471175	1489082
R&D 人员合计（人）	Total R&D Personnel(person)	57026	69815	79807	83473
R&D 人员折合全时当量合计（人年）	Full－time Equivalent of R&D Personnel (man－years)	47555	54934	63972	67070
R&D 项目数（项）	R&D Projects(item)	8776	10853	12476	13139
R&D 经费内部支出（万元）	Intramural Expenditure R&D Projects (million yuan)	975034	1222028	1419568	1600005
R&D 经费外部支出（万元）	External Expenditure on R&D Projects (million yuan)	29992	45070	47930	43049
新产品开发项目数（项）	Number of New Products(unit)	9904	12359	13648	14473
新产品开发经费支出（万元）	Expenditure on New Products Development (million yuan)	1213976	1493212	1671386	1770151
专利申请数（件）	Patent Applications(piece)	16972	24804	24972	21828
#发明专利（件）	Inventions (piece)	2083	3637	3997	4037
有效发明专利数（件）	Inventions In Force(piece)	4173	4434	4865	6536
引进技术经费支出（万元）	Expenditure for Acquisition of Technology (million yuan)	11342	26343	15772	14376
消化吸收经费支出（万元）	Expenditure for Assimilation of Technology (million yuan)	5900	2629	2058	3010
购买国内技术经费支出（万元）	Expenditure for Purchase of Domestic Technology (million yuan)	19960	31381	26419	37683
技术改造经费支出（万元）	Expenditure for Technical Renovation(million yuan)	494741	463787	451818	647095

表 12－21　规模以上工业企业科技活动情况（2014）
Scientific and Technological Activities of Industrial Enterprises Above Designated Size

指标	Indicators	企业个数（个）Number of Enterprises (unit)	有 R&D 的企业数（个）Number of Enterprises Having R&D Activities (unit)
总计	**Total**	**7383**	**3322**
按企业规模分	**Grouped by Enterprises Size**		
大型企业	Large－Sized	115	85
中型企业	Medium－Sized	965	624
按登记注册类型分	**Grouped by Registered Type**		
内资企业	Domestic Funded Enterprises	5496	2437
国有企业	State－owned Enterprises	17	3
集体企业	Collective－owned Enterpriese	11	3
股份合作企业	Share Cooperative Enterprises	24	10
有限责任公司	Limited Liability Corporations	610	289
股份有限公司	Share－holding Corporations Ltd.	126	86
私营企业	Private Enterprises	4704	2046
其他企业	Other Enterprises	4	
港、澳、台商投资企业	Hong Kong, Macao & Taiwan Funded	1002	507
合资经营企业	Joint venture Enterprises	494	271
合作经营企业	Cooperative Enterprise	17	9
港、澳、台商独资经营企业	Hong Kong, Macao and Taiwan－funded Enterprises	473	220
港、澳、台商投资股份有限公司	Hong Kong, Macao and Taiwan Investment Ltd.	17	7
其他港澳台投资企业	Other Hong Kong, Macao and Taiwan Funded Enterprises	1	
外商投资企业	Foreign Funded Enterprises	885	378
中外合资经营企业	Sino－foreign Joint Venture Enterprises	444	218
中外合作经营企业	Sino－foreign Contractual Joint Ventures	17	9
外资企业	Foreign－funded Enterprises	415	145
外商投资股份有限公司	Foreign Investment Joint Stock company	8	5
其他外商投资企业	Other Foreign Funded Enterprises	1	1
按隶属关系分	Grouped By Administrative Relationship		
中央企业	Central Enterprises	14	5
地方企业	Local Enterprises	7369	3317

企业办科技机构(个) Number of R&D Institutions (unit)	企业办机构仪器设备原价(万元) Original Value of Machine and Equipment for Operated(Million)	R&D 人员(人) R&D Personnel (person)	R&D 人员折合全时当量合计(人年) Full-time Equivalent of R&D Personnel (man-years)	R&D 经费内部支出(万元) Intramural Expenditure R&D Projects (million yuan)	新产品开发经费支出(万元) Expenditure on New Products Development (million yuan)	发明专利申请数(项) Invention Patent Number of Applications	有效发明专利数(项) Effective Invention Number of patents
1947	**1013355**	**83473**	**67070**	**1600005**	**1770151**	**4037**	**6536**
67	364024	15323	12703	365274	425535	557	868
465	316195	29850	24856	584842	640569	1198	2102
1407	537546	54207	42602	1009349	1078686	2776	4396
		79	28	1166	250	17	
1	30	13	8	275	355		
4	790	144	100	1721	1944	2	6
180	107904	10445	8422	228790	244357	494	777
65	145895	5465	4773	124773	135887	285	505
1157	282928	38061	29271	652624	695892	1978	3108
312	250141	18165	15300	381303	427126	698	1327
172	150851	9579	7873	204161	213829	394	760
8	2097	354	312	9859	11206	4	10
124	90287	7430	6344	147926	176819	268	451
7	6882	802	770	19357	25272	32	106
1	25						
228	225668	11101	9168	209353	264338	563	813
135	180333	7343	6108	145812	186879	382	550
4	3879	122	107	1972	3360		2
87	40197	3453	2792	58441	69140	160	240
1	940	64	43	1166	2997	11	11
1	319	119	119	1962	1962	10	10
4	4310	427	371	9001	6883	35	96
1943	1009045	83046	66700	1591005	1763268	4002	6440

表12-22 规模以上工业企业R&D人员情况(2014)
R&D Personnel of Industrial Enterprises Above Designated Size

指标	Indicators
总计	**Total**
按企业规模分	**Grouped by Enterprises Size**
大型	Large - Sized
中型	Medium - Sized
小型	Small - Sized
微型	Micro - Sized
按登记注册类型分	**Grouped by Registered Type**
国有企业	State - owned Enterprises
集体企业	Collective - owned Enterpriese
股份合作企业	Share Cooperative Enterprises
有限责任公司	Limited Liability Corporations
股份有限公司	Share - holding Corporations Ltd.
私营企业	Private Enterprises
港、澳、台商投资企业	Hong Kong, Macao & Taiwan Funded
外商投资企业	Foreign Funded Enterprises
按国民经济行业大类分	**Grouped by Sector**
农副食品加工业	Farm and Sideline Products Processing
食品制造业	Food Manufacturing
酒、饮料和精制茶制造业	Wine, Beverages and Refined Tea Manufacturing
纺织业	Textile Industry
纺织服装、服饰业	Clothing, Apparel Industry
皮革、毛皮、羽毛及其制品和制鞋业	Leather, Fur, Feather and Its Products and Footwear Industry
木材加工和木、竹、藤、棕、草制品业	Timber Processing, Bamboo, Rattan, Cane Palm, and Straw Products
家具制造业	Furniture Manufacturing
造纸和纸制品业	Paper - making and Paper Products Manufacturing
印刷和记录媒介复制业	Printing and Record Duplicating
文教、工美、体育和娱乐用品制造业	Culture, Art Sports and Recreation Supplies Manufacturing
石油加工、炼焦和核燃料加工业	Petroleum Processing, Coking & Nuclear Fuel Processing
化学原料和化学制品制造业	Raw Chemical Materials and Chemical Products
医药制造业	Medicines Manufacturing
化学纤维制造业	Chemical Fiber Manufacturing

R&D 人员合计 Total	#1. 参加项目人员 Personnel Engaged All S&T Projects	2. 管理和服务人员 S&T Management and Service	#女性 Female	#研究人员 Researchers	#1. 全时人员 Full – time	2. 非全时人员 Part – time
83473	**80315**	**3158**	**18142**	**14456**	**58658**	**24815**
15323	14861	462	3643	2635	12598	2725
29850	28681	1169	6971	4673	21052	8798
38209	36686	1523	7516	7103	24976	13233
91	87	4	12	45	32	59
79	73	6	14	31	33	46
13	13		1	3	4	9
144	140	4	16	23	75	69
10445	10103	342	2449	1830	7376	3069
5465	5187	278	1091	906	3932	1533
38061	36625	1436	7765	6352	26101	11960
18165	17603	562	4457	2946	13343	4822
11101	10571	530	2349	2365	7794	3307
471	453	18	153	132	291	180
386	342	44	141	114	108	278
73	69	4	14	16	37	36
2984	2885	99	1564	457	1961	1023
1414	1389	25	899	147	713	701
107	104	3	40	11	75	32
107	101	6	27	28	88	19
504	491	13	113	87	292	212
1162	1156	6	291	134	465	697
480	463	17	185	105	240	240
3134	3029	105	735	480	2303	831
51	48	3	14	4	49	2
3199	3050	149	707	592	2375	824
727	686	41	261	125	572	155
610	598	12	73	65	327	283

表 12－22 续表 1 Continued

指标	Indicators
橡胶和塑料制品业	Rubber and Plastic Products Industry
非金属矿物制品业	Nonmetal Mineral Products
黑色金属冶炼和压延加工业	Smelting and Pressing of Ferrous Metals
有色金属冶炼和压延加工业	Smelting and Pressing of Nonferrous Metals
金属制品业	Metal Products Manufacturing
通用设备制造业	General Purpose Equipment Manufacturing
专用设备制造业	Special Purpose Equipment Manufacturing
汽车制造业	Automobile Manufacturing
铁路、船舶、航空航天和其他运输设备制造业	Railroad, Marine, Aviation and Other Transport Equipment Manufacturing
电气机械和器材制造业	Electric Equipment and Machinery Manufacturing
计算机、通信和其他电子设备制造业	Computer, Communications and Othe Electronic Equipment Manufacturing
仪器仪表制造业	Instrument Manufacturing
其他制造业	Other Manufacturing
废弃资源综合利用业	Waste Comprehensive Utilization of Resources Industry
金属制品、机械和设备修理业	Metal Products, Machinery and Equipment Repair Industry
电力、热力生产和供应业	Production and Supply Electric Power and Thermal Power
水的生产和供应业	Production and Supply Tap Water
按地区分	**Grouped by Districts**
海曙区	Haishu
江东区	Jiangdong
江北区	Jiangbei
北仑区	Beilun
镇海区	Zhenhai
鄞州区	Yinzhou
象山县	Xiangshan
宁海县	Ninghai
高新区	Gaoxin
余姚市	Yuyao
慈溪市	Cixi
奉化市	Fenghua

单位:人(Person)

R&D 人员合计 Total	#1. 参加项目人员 Personnel Engaged All S&T Projects	2. 管理和服务人员 S&T Management and Service	#女性 Female	#研究人员 Researchers	#1. 全时人员 Full - time	2. 非全时人员 Part - time
3121	3026	95	593	569	1933	1188
797	779	18	178	191	495	302
1434	1374	60	190	410	605	829
1950	1912	38	340	293	1503	447
3684	3568	116	610	562	2690	994
10245	9865	380	1807	1918	7188	3057
5897	5680	217	876	1166	4320	1577
9313	8806	507	1533	1520	7004	2309
941	912	29	206	170	658	283
18935	18178	757	3933	2970	13676	5259
7454	7161	293	1743	1300	5689	1765
3734	3654	80	822	715	2809	925
330	316	14	69	67	151	179
13	13		3	4	2	11
56	51	5	12	28	23	33
136	132	4	5	66	11	125
24	24		5	10	5	19
1208	1156	52	623	134	551	657
370	357	13	88	77	246	124
4112	3973	139	885	736	2592	1520
10034	9689	345	2135	1996	7740	2294
5306	5065	241	1299	887	3530	1776
17872	17390	482	4107	2738	13272	4600
2974	2709	265	509	689	1611	1363
6889	6695	194	1487	1021	4732	2157
2304	2131	173	560	427	1859	445
10860	10764	96	2091	2134	7776	3084
17397	16433	964	3509	2837	11912	5485
4147	3953	194	849	780	2837	1310

表 12－22 续表 2 Continued

指标	Indicators
总计	**Total**
按企业规模分	**Grouped by Enterprises Size**
大型	Large – Sized
中型	Medium – Sized
小型	Small – Sized
微型	Micro – Sized
按登记注册类型分	**Grouped by Registered Type**
国有企业	State – owned Enterprises
集体企业	Collective – owned Enterpriese
股份合作企业	Share Cooperative Enterprises
有限责任公司	Limited Liability Corporations
股份有限公司	Share – holding Corporations Ltd.
私营企业	Private Enterprises
港、澳、台商投资企业	Hong Kong, Macao & Taiwan Funded
外商投资企业	Foreign Funded Enterprises
按国民经济行业大类分	**Grouped by Sector**
农副食品加工业	Farm and Sideline Products Processing
食品制造业	Food Manufacturing
酒、饮料和精制茶制造业	Wine, Beverages and Refined Tea Manufacturing
纺织业	Textile Industry
纺织服装、服饰业	Clothing, Apparel Industry
皮革、毛皮、羽毛及其制品和制鞋业	Leather, Fur, Feather and Its Products and Footwear Industry
木材加工和木、竹、藤、棕、草制品业	Timber Processing, Bamboo, Rattan, Cane Palm, and Straw Products
家具制造业	Furniture Manufacturing
造纸和纸制品业	Paper – making and Paper Products Manufacturing
印刷和记录媒介复制业	Printing and Record Duplicating
文教、工美、体育和娱乐用品制造业	Culture, Art, Sports and Recreation Supplies Manufacturing
石油加工、炼焦和核燃料加工业	Petroleum Processing, Coking & Nuclear Fuel Processing
化学原料和化学制品制造业	Raw Chemical Materials and Chemical Products
医药制造业	Medicines Manufacturing
化学纤维制造业	Chemical Fiber Manufacturing

单位：人(Person)

R&D 人员折合全时当量合计(人年) Full－time Equivalent	#研究人员 Researchers	#1. 基础研究人员 Basic Research	2. 应用研究人员 Applied Research	3. 试验发展人员 Experimental Development
67070	**11603**		**239**	**66831**
12703	2211		144	12558
24856	3923		85	24772
29465	5455		10	29455
47	15			47
28	10			28
8	2			8
100	16			100
8422	1490		7	8416
4773	783			4773
29271	4866		87	29183
15300	2493		145	15155
9168	1943			9168
364	100			364
300	96			300
61	14			61
2343	370			2343
939	85			939
92	8.3			92
96.1	26.9			96.1
402.3	71.2			402.3
913.1	110.6			913.1
328.9	61.9			328.9
2284.1	369.2		0.8	2283.3
51	4			51
2403.3	450.6			2403.3
590.9	101.7			590.9
499.4	52.4			499.4

表 12－22 续表 3 Continued

指标	Indicators
橡胶和塑料制品业	Rubber and Plastic Products Industry
非金属矿物制品业	Nonmetal Mineral Products
黑色金属冶炼和压延加工业	Smelting and Pressing of Ferrous Metals
有色金属冶炼和压延加工业	Smelting and Pressing of Nonferrous Metals
金属制品业	Metal Products Manufacturing
通用设备制造业	General Purpose Equipment Manufacturing
专用设备制造业	Special Purpose Equipment Manufacturing
汽车制造业	Automobile Manufacturing
铁路、船舶、航空航天和其他运输设备制造业	Railroad, Marine, Aviation and Other Transport Equipment Manufacturing
电气机械和器材制造业	Electric Equipment and Machinery Manufacturing
计算机、通信和其他电子设备制造业	Computer, Communications and Other Electronic Equipment Manufacturing
仪器仪表制造业	Instrument Manufacturing
其他制造业	Other Manufacturing
废弃资源综合利用业	Waste Comprehensive Utilization of Resources Industry
金属制品、机械和设备修理业	Metal Products, Machinery and Equipment Repair Industry
电力、热力生产和供应业	Production and Supply Electric Power and Thermal Power
水的生产和供应业	Production and Supply Tap Water
按地区分	**Grouped by Districts**
海曙区	Haishu
江东区	Jiangdong
江北区	Jiangbei
北仑区	Beilun
镇海区	Zhenhai
鄞州区	Yinzhou
象山县	Xiangshan
宁海县	Ninghai
高新区	Gaoxin
余姚市	Yuyao
慈溪市	Cixi
奉化市	Fenghua

单位：人(Person)

R&D 人员折合全时当量合计（人年）Full - time Equivalent	#研究人员 Researchers	#1. 基础研究人员 Basic Research	2. 应用研究人员 Applied Research	3. 试验发展人员 Experimental Development
2280.3	387.9		27.4	2252.8
652.4	159.8			652.4
1174	335.7			1174
1563.1	249.6			1563.1
2728	401.6			2728
8485.6	1608.1		144.4	8341.2
4765.9	962			4765.9
7975.4	1221.5			7975.4
801.4	135.9			801.4
15231	2369.4		61.9	15169.1
6206	1108.9		4.4	6201.6
3149.5	631.6			3149.5
256.9	53.5			256.9
10.4	2.9			10.4
17.3	8.6			17.3
83.2	34.1			83.2
21.7	9			21.7
938.6	111.1			938.6
291.9	64.9			291.9
3574.8	650.3			3574.8
8615	1779.4			8615
4089.2	646.6		91.2	3998
14767.7	2263.7			14767.7
2140.4	500			2140.4
4874.8	717.3			4874.8
2002.2	364.8			2002.2
8693.4	1721			8693.4
13805.7	2207.1			13805.7
3276.5	577		147.8	3128.7

表 12-23 规模以上工业企业 R&D 经费情况(2014)
R&D Fund of Industrial Enterprises Above Designated Size

指标	Indicators	R&D 经费内部支出合计 Internal Expenditures	(一)按活动 #1. 基础研究支出 for Basic Research
总计	**Total**	**1600005**	
按企业规模分	**Grouped by Enterprises Size**		
大型	Large - Sized	365274	
中型	Medium - Sized	584842	
小型	Small - Sized	648199	
微型	Micro - Sized	1691	
按登记注册类型分	**Grouped by Registered Type**		
国有企业	State - owned Enterprises	1166	
集体企业	Collective - owned Enterpriese	275	
股份合作企业	Share Cooperative Enterprises	1721	
有限责任公司	Limited LiabilityCorporations	228790	
股份有限公司	Share - holding Corporations Ltd.	124773	
私营企业	Private Enterprises	652624	
港、澳、台商投资企业	Hong Kong, Macao & Taiwan Funded	381303	
外商投资企业	Foreign Funded Enterprises	209353	
按国民经济行业大类分	**Grouped by Sector**		
农副食品加工业	Farm and Sideline Products Processing	12789	
食品制造业	Food Manufacturing	10051	
酒、饮料和精制茶制造业	Wine, Beverages and Refined Tea Manufacturing	1500	
纺织业	Textile Industry	51347	
纺织服装、服饰业	Clothing, Apparel Industry	28156	
皮革、毛皮、羽毛及其制品和制鞋业	Leather, Fur, Feather and Its Products and Footwear Industry	968.4	
木材加工和木、竹、藤、棕、草制品业	Timber Processing, Bamboo, Rattan, Cane Palm, and Straw Products	2023.2	
家具制造业	Furniture Manufacturing	780.2	
造纸和纸制品业	Paper - making and Paper Products Manufacturing	25208	
印刷和记录媒介复制业	Printing and Record Duplicating	7138.6	
文教、工美、体育和娱乐用品制造业	Culture, Art, Sports and Recreation Supplies Manufacturing	45094.2	
石油加工、炼焦和核燃料加工业	Petroleum Processing, Coking & Nuclear Fuel Processing	1410.4	
化学原料和化学制品制造业	Raw Chemical Materials and Chemical Products	103074.4	
医药制造业	Medicines Manufacturing	14239.9	
化学纤维制造业	Chemical Fibe Manufacturing	13921.8	

类型分组(Grouped by Activity Type)		(二)按支出用途分组(Grouped by Objects of Expenditure)				
2. 应用研究支出 for Applied Research	3. 试验发展支出 for Test Development	1. 经常费支出 Regular fee Expenditure	#人员劳务费 Staff Labour Costs	2. 资产性支出 Asset Expenditures	#①土建工程支出 Civil Engineering Expenditures	②仪器设备 Instruments and Equipment
4239	**1595766**	**1482393**	**554876**	**117612**	**2118**	**115495**
2368	362906	336500	111526	28774	413	28360
1568	583274	546122	206414	38719	1070	37649
303	647896	598181	236311	50019	633	49386
	1691	1590	626	100	1	99
	1166	1166	126			
	275	275	93			
	1721	1632	830	89		89
188	228603	211202	71761	17589	312	17277
	124773	110567	38944	14206	667	13539
1678	650946	603282	227714	49342	541	48801
2373	378930	358986	132748	22317	317	22000
	209353	195283	82659	14070	281	13789
	12789	9805	2728	2985	11	2974
	10051	9272	2228	780	12	767
	1500	1234	450	266		266
	51347	50342	17301	1006	35	970
	28156	26898	9874	1258	4	1253
	968.4	950.9	496	17.5		17.5
	2023.2	1945.6	652.4	77.6	0.1	77.5
	7180.2	6909.1	3166.7	271.1	9	262.1
	25208	24723.8	5195.4	484.2	0.8	483.4
	7138.6	6627	3126.4	511.6	10.1	501.5
4.8	45089.4	41825.9	17144.9	3268.3	19.8	3248.5
	1410.4	1376.1	341.2	34.3		34.3
	103074.4	98869	22419.6	4205.4	58.8	4146.6
	14239.9	13092.5	5815.6	1147.4	31.1	1116.3
	13921.8	11962.4	3349.1	1959.4	2.6	1956.8

表 12－23 续表 1 Continued

指标	Indicators	R&D 经费内部支出合计 Internal Expenditures	(一)按活动 #1. 基础研究支出 for Basic Research
橡胶和塑料制品业	Rubber and Plastic Products Industry	52691.7	
非金属矿物制品业	Nonmetal Mineral Products	14783.9	
黑色金属冶炼和压延加工业	Smelting and Pressing of Ferrous Metals	32431.2	
有色金属冶炼和压延加工业	Smelting and Pressing of Nonferrous Metals	55240.7	
金属制品业	Metal Products Manufacturing	52901.9	
通用设备制造业	General Purpose Equipment Manufacturing	183979.1	
专用设备制造业	Special Purpose Equipment Manufacturing	106790.1	
汽车制造业	Automobile]Manufacturing	193819.9	
铁路、船舶、航空航天和其他运输设备制造业	Railroad, Marine, Aviation and Other Transport Equipment Manufacturing	22876.8	
电气机械和器材制造业	Electric Equipment and Machinery Manufacturing	347082.9	
计算机、通信和其他电子设备制造业	Computer, Communications and Other Electronic Equipment Manufacturing	145893.9	
仪器仪表制造业	Instrument Manufacturing	57984.9	
其他制造业	Other Manufacturing	6019.6	
废弃资源综合利用业	Waste Comprehensive Utilization of Resources Industry	445.2	
金属制品、机械和设备修理业	Metal Products,Machinery and Equipment Repair Industry	163.1	
电力、热力生产和供应业	Production and Supply Electric Power and Thermal Power	2505.6	
水的生产和供应业	Production and Supply Tap Water	292.6	
按地区分	**Grouped by Districts**		
海曙区	Haishu	18056.6	
江东区	Jiangdong	5292.5	
江北区	Jiangbei	81230.7	
北仑区	Beilun	225675.6	
镇海区	Zhenhai	106266.4	
鄞州区	Yinzhou	391629.1	
象山县	Xiangshan	61997.6	
宁海县	Ninghai	103183.3	
高新区	Gaoxin	52237	
余姚市	Yuyao	203588.2	
慈溪市	Cixi	280891.2	
奉化市	Fenghua	69957.1	

单位:万元(10000 yuan)

类型分组(Grouped by Activity Type)		(二)按支出用途分组(Grouped by Objects of Expenditure)				
2. 应用研究支出 for Applied Research	3. 试验发展支出 for Test Development	1. 经常费支出 Regular fee Expenditure	#人员劳务费 Staff Labour Costs	2. 资产性支出 Asset Expenditures	#①土建工程支出 Civil Engineering Expenditures	②仪器设备 Instruments and Equipment
573.5	52118.2	47038.3	17468.6	5653.4	125.1	5528.3
	14783.9	13491	5074.9	1292.9	36.1	1256.8
	32431.2	29291	9430.6	3140.2	30.4	3109.8
	55240.7	52289.6	14311.3	2951.1	19.6	2931.5
	52901.9	49478.8	21609	3423.1	87.9	3335.2
2368.2	181610.9	169907.1	71647.8	14072	186.6	13885.4
	106790.1	99732.4	40096.5	7057.7	181.4	6876.3
	193819.9	174411.5	72067.1	19408.4	175.1	19233.3
	22876.8	21899.4	5140.6	977.4	4.3	973.1
1131.1	345951.8	318892.6	118328	28190.3	952.1	27238.2
161.5	145732.4	136175	55625.2	9718.9	101.2	9617.7
	57984.9	54796.7	26270.1	3188.2	6.8	3181.4
	6019.6	5800.8	2358.7	218.8	16.1	202.7
	445.2	410.2	123.2	35		35
	163.1	163.1	103.6			
	2505.6	2490.8	723.7	14.8		14.8
	292.6	292.6	209.5			
	18056.6	17146.8	7487.8	909.8	4.1	905.7
	5292.5	5067.9	2656.2	224.6		224.6
	81230.7	77331	32796.4	3899.7	29.5	3870.2
	225675.6	215226.9	75821.2	10448.7	134.5	10314.2
1755.6	104510.8	99513.7	37506.6	6752.7	50.7	6702
	391629.1	361883.7	134281	29745.4	112.5	29632.9
	61997.6	55490.9	18387.7	6506.7	60.9	6445.8
	103183.3	96073.6	35088.9	7109.7	58.4	7051.3
	52237	46820.7	17321.8	5416.3	50.1	5366.2
	203588.2	184971.9	70869.1	18616.3	1058.1	17558.2
	280891.2	261226.1	98949.7	19665.1	456.4	19208.7
2483.5	67473.6	61640	23709.3	8317.1	102.4	8214.7

表 12－23 续表 2 Continued

指标	Indicators	(三)按资金来源分组 1. 政府资金 Government Funds	2. 企业资金 Enterprise Funds
总计	**Total**	**20069**	**1563537**
按企业规模分	**Grouped by Enterprises Size**		
大型	Large－Sized	4378	360263
中型	Medium－Sized	6722	571860
小型	Small－Sized	8969	629722
微型	Micro－Sized		1691
按登记注册类型分	**Grouped by Registered Type**		
国有企业	State－owned Enterprises		1166
集体企业	Collective－owned Enterpriese		234
股份合作企业	Share Cooperative Enterprises		1721
有限责任公司	Limited Liability Corporations	2524	224511
股份有限公司	Share－holding Corporations Ltd.	2802	121671
私营企业	Private Enterprises	5393	637396
港、澳、台商投资企业	Hong Kong, Macao & Taiwan Funded	5216	373435
外商投资企业	Foreign Funded Enterprises	4135	203402
按国民经济行业大类分	**Grouped by Sector**		
农副食品加工业	Farm and Sideline Products Processing	956	11816
食品制造业	Food Manufacturing	127	9921
酒、饮料和精制茶制造业	Wine, Beverages and Refined Tea Manufacturing	21	1479
纺织业	Textile Industry	146	50804
纺织服装、服饰业	Clothing, Apparel Industry	215	27358
皮革、毛皮、羽毛及其制品和制鞋业	Leather, Fur, Feather and Its Products and Footwear Industry		800.4
木材加工和木、竹、藤、棕、草制品业	Timber Processing, Bamboo, Rattan, Can Palm, and Straw Products	30	1893.2
家具制造业	Furniture Manufacturing	1	6472.1
造纸和纸制品业	Paper－making and Paper Products Manufacturing	12	25157.3
印刷和记录媒介复制业	Printing and Record Duplicating	322	6816.6
文教、工美、体育和娱乐用品制造业	Culture, Art, Sports and Recreation Supplies Manufacturing	241.1	44054.2
石油加工、炼焦和核燃料加工业	Petroleum Processing, Coking & Nuclear Fuel Processing		1410.4
化学原料和化学制品制造业	Raw Chemical Materials and Chemical Products	1626	100303.1
医药制造业	Medicines Manufacturing	670.9	13526.4
化学纤维制造业	Chemical Fiber Manufacturing		13449.9

单位:万元(10000 yuan)

(Grouped by Sources of Fund)		R&D 经费外部支出 External Expenditures			
3. 境外资金 fOffshore Funds	4. 其他资金 for Test Development		对境内研究机构支出 Research Institutions in Spending	对境内高等学校支出 Within the College Expenses	对境外支出 On Foreign Spending
1229	**15171**	**43049**	**16509**	**5835**	**7364**
	632	14807	4114	643	4446
202	6058	14309	6950	2184	1812
1027	8481	13672	5410	3009	881
		261	35		226
		25	2	23	
	42				
		3			
	1755	5189	2717	1629	112
	300	3394	1713	818	473
824	9011	9149	3838	1739	179
183	2470	16072	3795	1136	3891
223	1593	9217	4444	490	2709
	17	191	22	169	
	3	105	40	8	
	397	5409	32	21	124
	582	253	244	9	
	168				
	100				
59.4	647.7	150.4	48	91.4	
	38.7	20		20	
		352.9			352.9
172.3	626.6	556.4	375.7	123.4	27.3
	1145.3	1717.7	187.9	1261.2	23.3
	42.6	1620.8	988.6	372.5	
	471.9	5	5		

表 12 - 23 续表 3 Continued

指标	Indicators	（三）按资金来源分组 1. 政府资金 Government Funds	2. 企业资金 Enterprise Funds
橡胶和塑料制品业	Rubber and Plastic Products Industry	291.1	50326.1
非金属矿物制品业	Nonmetal Mineral Products	485.4	13984.4
黑色金属冶炼和压延加工业	Smelting and Pressing of Ferrous Metals	60.6	32276.8
有色金属冶炼和压延加工业	Smelting and Pressing of Nonferrous Metals	853	53668.1
金属制品业	Metal Products Manufacturing	673.6	51447.7
通用设备制造业	General Purpose Equipment Manufacturing	2964.3	180011
专用设备制造业	Special Purpose Equipment Manufacturing	1059.1	104422.4
汽车制造业	Automobile Manufacturing	1237.3	190997.9
铁路、船舶、航空航天和其他运输设备制造业	Railroad, Marine, Aviation and Other Transport Equipment Manufacturing	217	22431.1
电气机械和器材制造业	Electric Equipment and Machinery Manufacturing	3277.1	342602.3
计算机、通信和其他电子设备制造业	Computer, Communications and Other Electronic Equipment Manufacturing	3263.8	140530.1
仪器仪表制造业	Instrument Manufacturing	1293.4	56223.5
其他制造业	Other Manufacturing	24.6	5947.4
废弃资源综合利用业	Waste Comprehensive Utilization of Resources Industry		445.2
金属制品、机械和设备修理业	Metal Products, Machinery and Equipment Repair Industry		163.1
电力、热力生产和供应业	Production and Supply Electric Power and Thermal Power		2505.6
水的生产和供应业	Production and Supply Tap Water		292.6
按地区分	**Grouped by Districts**		
海曙区	Haishu	47.7	17975.4
江东区	Jiangdong	22.6	5269.9
江北区	Jiangbei	1985.9	77943.6
北仑区	Beilun	2836.5	222200.1
镇海区	Zhenhai	1565.2	103888.2
鄞州区	Yinzhou	4860.3	382594.4
象山县	Xiangshan	884.4	60737.9
宁海县	Ninghai	569.4	101949.2
高新区	Gaoxin	715.4	50662.9
余姚市	Yuyao	2580.7	197427.6
慈溪市	Cixi	1443.4	275528.1
奉化市	Fenghua	2557.6	67359.2

单位:万元(10000 yuan)

(Grouped by Sources of Fund)		R&D 经费外部支出 External Expenditures			
3. 境外资金 fOffshore Funds	4. 其他资金 for Test Development		对境内研究机构支出 Research Institutions in Spending	对境内高等学校支出 Within the College Expenses	对境外支出 On Foreign Spending
	2074.5	1417	102.9	218	72.7
	314.1	344.3	171.1	137.7	
	93.8	340.3	83.5	104.4	
	719.6	101.5	59.8	39.5	
260.5	520.1	643.7	345	145	8
	1003.8	5590.9	2866.7	697.6	783.6
20.7	1287.9	1997.6	448.4	363.1	380.8
465.6	1119.1	9087.2	3965.7	173.6	4485.6
	228.7	846.3	837.7	3.7	
110.7	1092.8	6400.9	2629.6	1484.4	15.2
96.2	2003.8	5010.4	2862.9	272.7	858.5
43.7	424.3	688.9	114.6	91.6	232.2
	47.6	17.4	0.4		
		23.3		23.3	
		158.4	77.7	5.2	
	33.5	47	2		
		153.8	140.7	13.1	
96.2	1205	438.2	268.9	50.3	111.2
	639	6962.5	4165.9	436.7	1431.9
29.8	783.2	7204.9	626	1127.6	31.3
144.2	4030.2	9033.1	3485	988.2	3495.6
	375.3	323.9	251.6	72.3	
	664.7	993.5	435.7	348.8	118.9
	858.7	970.5	307.3	110.3	225.8
194.5	3385.4	11343.7	3452.6	1027	1635.7
764.4	3155.3	4131.5	2526.1	1221	188.7
	40.3	1446.3	847.4	439.3	125.3

表 12－24 部分年份科协系统活动情况
Basic Statistics on Science and Technology Associations in Partial Years

指标	Indicators	2011	2012	2013	2014
基本情况	**Basic Situation**				
科协机构数(个)	Insitutions of Science and Technology(unit)	90	91	92	93
直属单位	Organizations Attached to the Institutions	6	6	6	6
科技馆(科普活动中心)	S&T Museum(Activity Center of Popular Science)	8	8	4	4
活动情况	**Activity Situation**				
举办学术交流活动(次)	Number of Academic Exchange Activities	293	450	400	684
科普讲座次数(次)	Number of S&T Popularization Lectures(times)	1317	5252	11320	5673
宣讲活动受众人数(人)	Propaganda Lecture the Audience			1064499	665202
播放科技广播、影视节目(次)	Radio and Television Programs about S&T			67320	40695
编著科技图书(种)	Number of Editor S&T Books	50	104	45	93
举办青少年科技竞赛(次)	Number of Teenagers´S&T Competition	136	114	136	171
开展"讲、比"活动企业数(个)	Enterprise Number of S&T Competition Acitivities	149	275	149	295

注：本表和 12－21 表数据来自宁波市科协。

Note：a) Data in Tables 12－19 and 12－21 are obtained from Ningbo Associations for Science and Technology.

①S&T is a short form that means Scientific and Technological. The other table are the same.

表 12－25 部分年份市级以上科技成果鉴定、获奖、专利授权情况
Basic Statistics on Verification, Award－Winning and Patent Right of Above Municipal Level in Partial Years

单位：个(unit)

指标	Indicators	2010	2011	2012	2013	2014
科技成果登记	Scientific and Technological Enrollment of Results		428	457	510	536
科学技术奖	Science and Technology Awards	120	106	107	115	108
国家级	State Level	4	1	1	3	1
省级	Province Level	24	26	26	32	28
市级	Municipal Level	92	79	80	80	79
授权专利数	Number of Patent Applications Approved	25971	37342	59175	58406	43286
#发明	Inventions	1209	1625	2065	2246	2832
实用新型	Utility Models	11230	12966	21407	28367	21627
外观设计	Designs	13532	22751	35703	27793	18827

注：本表和 12－22 表数据来自宁波市科技局。

Note：Data in Tables 12－20 and 12－22 are obtained from Ningbo Municipal Bureau of Science and Technology.

表12－26 科协系统情况(2014)
Basic Statistics on Science and Technology Associations

指标	单位	Indicators	Unit	市科协 S&T Associations of Ningbo Municipal	县(市)区科协 S&T Associations by Region	市级学(协)会 S&T Associations for Municipal Level
科协组织和机构		**Basic Situation**				
科协机构数	个	Institutions of Science and Technology	unit	1	11	81
直属单位	个	Organizations Attached to the Institutions	unit	3	3	
团体会员(学会、协会、研究会)	个	Group members (Academy, the Association, the Research Council)	unit	81	216	3674
企事业科协	个	Enterprise and Non－profit Organizations Institutions of S&T	unit	9	127	
科学普及活动		**Activity for Popular Science**				
举办科普讲座	次	Number of S&T Popularization Lectures	times	114	639	4920
播放科技广播、影视节目	次	Radio and Television Programs about S&T	times	3865	36830	
宣讲活动受众人数	人	Propaganda Lecture the Audience	person	85800	234582	344820
举办实用技术培训	次	Number of Practical Technology Training	times	900	1929	
青少年科技教育		**Teenagers S&T Education**				
举办青少年科技竞赛	次	Number of Teenagers´S&T Competition	times	10	161	
举办青少年科技夏(冬)令营	次	Number of Teenagers´S&T Summer (Winter) Camp	times	4	19	
举办青少年科技培训	人次	Number of Teenagers´S&T Training	person－time	6	232	
科普基础设施建设		**Infrastructure of Popular Science**				
科技馆(科普活动中心)	个	S&T Museum (Activity Center of Popular Science)	unit	1	3	
科普教育(示范)基地	个	S&T Education (Model) Base	unit	36	97	
科普画廊(活动站、中心室)	个	Gallery of Popular Science	unit		2913	
学术交流		**Academic Activities**				
举办学术交流活动	次	Number of Academic Exchange Activities	unit	34	37	613
编著科技图书	种	Number of Editor S&T Books	kind	3	43	47
接待或派往境外科技团组(人数)	个(人次)	Receive or Sent Foreign S&T Group	unit (person－time)	121	325	528
科技活动和社会服务		**S&T Activities and Social services**				
开展"讲、比"活动企业数	个	Enterprise Number of S&T Competition Acitivities	unit	130	165	
院士工作站	个	Academician Workstation	unit	83	52	
表彰奖励科技工作者	人	Award of Scientific and Technical Workers	person		269	186
反映科技工作者建议	条	Number of S&T Workers´Proposal	piece	4	132	54
普网工程培训	人次	Universal Network Engineering Training	person－time	20200	20152	

表 12-27 各县(市)计量标准质监情况(2014)
Basic Statistics On Standard Measuring and Quality Supervising by Region

指标	单位	Indicators	Unit
计量验收情况		**Measuring Implements Test**	
已开展强制检定数	项	Measurement Implement Tested Compulsively	kind
开展强制检定种数	种	The Kind of Measurement Implement Tested Compulsively	kind
强制检定实际检出数	件	Actual Quantity Checked by Compulsively Examined Out	piece
计量仪器实际检出数	件	Actual Quantity Checked by Messurement Implement Tested	piece
质监情况		Quality Supervision	
国家监督抽查批次	批次	Batch of supervises and Check by Country	batch. time
#合格批次	批次	Regular Batch	batch. time
批次合格率	%	Ratio of Regular by Batch	%
省定期监督抽查企业数	个	Number of Enterpriese of Periodic Supervises and Check by Province	unit
省定期监督抽查批次	批次	Batch of Periodic supervises and Check by Province	batch. time
#合格批次	批次	Regular Batch	batch. time
批次合格率	%	Ratio of Regular by Batch	%
宁波市质量指数		Index of Product Quality about NingBo	

注:本表数据来自宁波市质量技术监督局。

Note: Data in this table are obtained from Administration of Quality and Technology Supervision of Ningbo Municipality.

全市 Total	市区 Urban District	#鄞州 Yinzhou	余姚市 Yuyao	慈溪市 Cixi	奉化市 Fenghua	象山县 Xiangshan	宁海县 Ninghai
38	38	19	11	13	12	10	12
80	80	27	22	23	21	16	19
1154602	738652	93317	100593	80352	78702	73027	93276
1272600	808517	125169	107963	87571	89199	82940	96410
393	96	39	75	195	7		20
350	90	38	73	165	7	38	15
89.06	93.75	97.44	97.33	84.62	100.00		75.00
1313	694	353	86	356	77	51	49
1313	694	353	86	356	77	51	49
1239	645	343	83	322	71	51	46
94.36	92.94	97.17	96.51	90.45	92.21	100.00	93.88
98.24	97.75	99.50	99.24	97.88	94.21	100.00	99.13

表 12－28 各县(市)市级以上科技成果鉴定、获奖、专利情况(2014)
Basic Statistics on Verification, Award－Winning and Patent Right of Above Municipal Level by Region

单位:个(unit)

指标	Indicators	全市 Total	市区 Urban District	#鄞州 Yinzhou	余姚 Yuyao
科技成果登记	Scientific and Technological Enrollment of Results	536	476	39	12
科学技术奖	Science and Technology Awards	108	81	25	10
国家级	State Level	1	1		
省级	Province Level	28	19	6	1
市级	Municipal Level	79	58	19	9
授权专利数	Number of Patent Applications Approved	43286	22265	12081	7093
发明	Inventions	2832	1882	697	259
实用新型	Utility Models	21627	12550	4793	1953
外观设计	Designs	18827	8878	6291	4881

表 12－28 续表 Continued

单位:个(unit)

指标	Indicators	慈溪 Cixi	奉化 Fenghua	宁海 Ninghai	象山 Xiangshan
科技成果登记	Scientific and Technological Enrollment of Results	12	9	16	11
科学技术奖	Science and Technology Awards	8		2	7
国家级	State Level				
省级	Province Level	2			3
市级	Municipal Level	6		2	4
授权专利数	Number of Patent Applications Approved	7867	1335	1939	2710
发明	Inventions	385	96	88	120
实用新型	Utility Models	4175	990	1748	994
外观设计	Designs	4881	249	103	1596

注:国家级科学技术奖包括参与完成项目。

Note: Science and Technology Awards at State Levelincluded Participating.

主要统计指标解释

【艺术表演团体】 指从事戏曲、音乐、舞蹈、杂技等专业艺术表演,有独立帐 户,实行单独核算的团体。不包括半工半艺、半农半艺和民间职业剧团。

【艺术表演观众人数(人次)】 指售票、包场演出或民族地区免费演出的艺术表演观众人次数。不包括彩排审查和内部观摩演出的观众人次数。

【电影放映单位】 指具有放映机器设备、固定或不固定的放映场所与专职或兼职的放映技术人员,经有关部门登记批准,经常为一定的观众对象放映电影的机构。包括经批准对外开放进行营业,并与电影发行放映管理机构分帐的专用放映单位和军委系统租片单位。

【普通高等学校】 指按照国家规定的设置标准和审批程序批准举办,通过国家统一招生考试,招收高中毕业生为主要培养对象,实施高等教育的全日制大学、独立设置的学院和高等专科学校、短期职业大学。

【成人高等学校】 指按照国家有关规定审批,招收通过全国成人高教统一招生 考试的具有高中毕业或同等学历的在职从业人员利用脱产、半脱产、业余或函授等多种形式 对其实施高等学历教育,培养高等教育专科或本科毕业水平的专门人才,修业年限、课程设 置和总学时数均按高等学历教育要求付诸实施的学校。包括广播电视大学、职工高等学校、农民高等学校、管理干部学院、教育学院、独立设置的函授学院等。

【小学学龄儿童入学率】 指调查范围内已入小学学习的学龄儿童占校内外学龄儿童总数(包括弱智儿童在内,但不包括盲聋哑儿童)的比重。计算公式为:

小学学龄儿童入学率 = 已入学的小学学龄儿童数 × 100%

校内外小学学龄儿童总数

【医院】 指名称为医院,设有固定床位能收容病人住院并能为病人提供医疗、护理服务的医疗机构。包括县及县以上医院、农村乡卫生院、其他医院三部分。按所属性质分为卫生部门、工业及其他部门,集体经济单位三类。其中县及县以上医院按业务性质分为 综合医院和专科医院。

【卫生技术人员】 指卫生事业机构支付工资的全部固定职工和合同制职工中现任职务为卫生技术工作的专业人员。具体包括中医师、西医师、中西医结合高级医师、护师、中 药师、西药师、检验师、其他技师、中医士、西医士、护士、助产士、中药剂士、西药剂士 、检验士、其他技士、其他中医、护理员、中药剂员、西药剂员、检验员,其他初级卫生技术人员。

【医生】 指经卫生部门审查合格,从事医疗工作的专业人员。分为中医医生和西医医生。包括卫生技术人员中的中医师、西医师、中西结合高级医师、中医士、西医士和其他中医。

【专利申请数】 指当年单位向专利管理机关提出专利申请并被受理的件数。

Explanatory Notes on Main Statistical Indicators

【Art Troupe】 refers to the troupe which is engaged in drama, opera, music, dance, acrobatics or other art performance, opens independent accounts with banks and has self - supporting accounting system; excluding the troupes which h are engaged partly in industrial or agricultural activities, partly in art performance and the professional troupes organized by the people.

【Number of Sectors at Art Performance】 refers to the number of attendants at commercial shows completely booked shows or free shows given in minority national areas, and does not include the number of spectators at rehearsals for examination and initial shows for study.

【Film Projection Units】 refer to units with film projection equipment, full or part time projectionists, permanent or nonpermanent places, approved by related administrative departments to show films regularly for certain groups of audience, including those film projection units which have been approved to give commercial shows and run business with independent accounting system as well as those film-renting units of the military system.

【Regular Institutions of Higher Learning】 refer to educational establishments set up according to the government evaluation and approval procedures, enrolling graduates from senior secondary schools and providing higher education courses and training for senior professionals. They include full - time universities, colleges, high professional schools and short - term professional universities.

【Institutions of Higher Learning for Adults】 refer to educational establishments, set up in line with relevant rules approved by the government, enrolling staff and workers with senior secondary school or equivalent education, and providing higher education courses in many forms of full - time, part - time, spare - time, or correspondence for adults. Professionals thus trained receive a qualification equivalent to graduates studying regular courses at regular universities, colleges and professional colleges. Institutions of higher learning for adults include Radio and TV universities, schools of high education for staff and workers and peasants, colleges for management cadres, pedagogical colleges, independent correspondence colleges.

【Enrollment Rate of Primary School - age Children】 refers to the proportion of school - age children enrolled at schools to the total number of school - age both in and outside schools (including retarded children, but excluding blind, deaf and mute children). The formula is:

$$\text{Enrollment Rate of Primary School - age Children} = \frac{\text{Total Primary School - age Children at Schools}}{\text{Total Primary School - age Children at and Outside Schools}} \times 100\%$$

【Hospitals】 refer to medical institutions named as "hospital" with permanent hospital beds, which are able to take in patients and provide them with medical and nursing services. Hospitals are classified into three categories : hospitals at or above the county - level, hospitals of rural townships, and other hospitals. According to their ownership, hospitals can be classified into three categories: hospitals under the public health departments, hospitals under industrial and other departments and collective - owned hospitals. Hospitals at or above county level are divided into comprehensive and specialized hospitals.

【Medical Technical Personnel】 refers to all permanent medical staff and workers employed by medical institutions, including doctors of Chinese and Western medicine, senior doctors who integrate traditional Chinese therapeutics with Western therapeutics in practice, senior nurses, pharmacists of Chinese and Western medicine, laboratory specialists, other specialists, paramedics of Chinese and Western medicine, nurses, midwives, druggists in Chinese and Western medicine, laboratory technicians, other technicians, other practitioners of Chinese medicine, nursing attendants, pharmacological workers of Chinese and Western medicine, laboratory workers, and other primary medical personnel.

【Doctors】 refer to qualified professional medical workers approved to practice by public health departments. They are classified into doctors of Chinese medicine, doctors of Western medicine, senior doctors who integrate traditional Chinese therapeutics with Western therapeutics in practice, paramedics of Chinese medicine and Western medicine, and other specialists of Chinese medicine.

【Applied Number of Patents】 refers to the number of patent applied by a unit to the patent office and then accepted in a reporting year.

NINGBO

2015

Statistical YearBook

13

CHAPTER

第十三篇

市政、环保、民政、政法及其他

CIVIL FACILITIES, ENVIRONMENT, CIVIL AFFAIRS, JUDICATURE AND OTHERS

市政、环保、民政、政法及其他
Civil Facilities, Environment, Social Welfare, Judicature and Others

主要统计指标
Major Statistics Indicators

2014 年人均日生活用水量	Per Capita Daily Consunption of Tap water for Resiential Use	259.98	升	liter
2014 年人均拥有道路面积	Per Capita Area of Paved Roads	20.89	平方米	sq. m
2014 年人均公园绿地面积	Per Capita Public Green Areas	11.45	平方米	sq. m
2014 年建成区绿化覆盖率	Coverage Rate of Green Area in Developed Area	38.55	%	
2014 年废水排放总量	Total Volume of Waste Water Discharged	61725	万吨	10000 tons
2014 年工业废气排放量	Volume of Industrial Waste Gas Emission	6366	亿标立米	100 million cu. m
2014 年环境噪声达标面积	Standardization Areas of Environment Noise	260.21	平方公里	sq. km
2014 年收养性福利单位床位数	Number of Beds in Socail Welfare – Units for Adopting	41996	张	bed
2014 年社会救济总人数	Number of Persons Receiving Relief	51282	人	person
2014 年末实有社团机构数	Factual Number of Social Organizations at The Year – end	2351	个	unit
2014 年基层工会数	Number of Trade Unions at Basic – Level	27476	个	unit
2014 年律师人数	Number of Lawyers	1898	人	person
2014 年办理公证事项	Number of Notarized Documents	82614	件	case
2014 年调解纠纷总件数	Number of Mediating Disputes	115615	件	case
2014 年交通事故数	Number of Traffic Accident	2519	件	case
2014 年档案馆数	Number of Archives	12	个	unit

表 13-1 部分年份市政公用事业基本情况
Basic Statistics on Municipal Public Utilities in Partial Years

指标	单位	Indicators	Unit	2011	2012	2013	2014
供水及供气		**Water Supply and Gas Supply**					
年供水总量	万吨	Annuall Volume of Tap Water Supply	10000 tons	68617	70122	72619	75303
#居民家庭用水量	万吨	Water Consumption for Residents Use	10000 tons	22439	23130	23354	27569
人均日生活用水量	升	Per Capita Daily Consumption of Tap Water for Residential Use	liter	240.31	239.49	229.91	259.78
用水普及率	%	Percentage of Population with Access to Tap Water	%	100.00	100.00	100.00	100.00
液化石油气供气总量	万吨	Total Volume of Liquefied Petroleum Gas	10000 tons	21.66	20.13	19.42	16.23
#家庭用量	万吨	For Residents Use	10000 tons	10.37	10.09	10.53	9.99
用液化气人口	万人	Population with Access Liquefied Petroleum Gas	10000 persons	193.81	202.46	163.94	156.59
燃气普及率	%	Percentage of Population with Access to Gas	%	100.00	100.00	100.00	100.00
市政设施		**Municipal Infra - strucutre**					
年末城市实有道路面积	万平方米	Area of Paved Roads (Year - end)	10000 sq. m	6930.45	7124.64	7276.62	7423.94
人均拥有道路面积	平方米	Per Capita Area of Paved Roads	sq. m	20.44	20.53	20.54	20.89
排水管道长度	公里	Length of Sewage Pipes	km	6574.75	6907.36	7761.90	8099.21
排水管道密度	公里/平方公里	Density of Sewage Pipes	km/sq. km	14.60	15.11	16.57	16.71
公共交通		**Public Traffic**					
年末实有公交营运车辆	标台	Number of Public Transportations Vehicles under Operation	unit	5302.50	6143.90	7149.00	7474.00
每万人拥有公共交通车辆	标台	Number of Public Transportations Vehicles Per 10000 Persons	unit	6.96	8.08	12.30	10.35
年末实有出租汽车数	辆	Operating Taxes at Year - end	unit	5551	5834	6360	6370
城市绿化		**Afforestation in Cities**					
园林绿地面积	公顷	Green Areas in Parks and Gardens	hectare	16666	17107	17640	18683
#公园绿地面积	公顷	Public Green Areas	hectare	3662	3807	3986	4069
人均公园绿地面积	平方米	Per Capita Public Green Areas	sq. m	10.80	10.97	11.25	11.45
建成区绿地率	%	Rate of Green Area in Developed Area	%	34.27	34.76	34.91	35.26
建成区绿化覆盖率	%	Coverage Rate of Green Area in Developed Area	%	37.82	38.21	38.23	38.55
环境卫生		**Environmental Sanitation**					
污水处理率	%	Percentage of Sewage Disposed	%	84.16	85.75	88.42	89.95
城市生活垃圾无害化处理率	%	Innocuous Disposal Rate of Living Garbage	%	100.00	100.00	100.00	100.00

注:2009 年开始,排水管道密度为建成区排水管道密度。

Note: Densitly of sewage pipes from 2009 refered to builting area.

表 13 - 2 各县(市)城市市政、公用事业情况(2014)
Basic Statistics on Civil Facilities and Public Utilities by Region

指标	单位	Indicators	Unit
城市面积		**City Areas**	
建成区面积	平方公里	Developed Areas	sq. km
城市建设用地面积	平方公里	land Areas of the Urban Construction	sq. km
居住用地面积	平方公里	For Residential Building Uses	sq. km
公共管理与公共设施面积	平方公里	For Public Management and Utilities Uses	sq. km
工业用地面积	平方公里	For Industry Uses	sq. km
供水及供气		**Water Supply and Gas Supply**	
年供水总量	万吨	Annuall Volume of Tap Water Supply	10000 tons
#居民家庭用水量	万吨	Water Consumption for Residents Use	10000 tons
人均日生活用水量	升	Per Capita Daily Consumption of Tap Water for Residential Use	liter
用水普及率	%	Percentage of Population with Access to Tap Water	%
液化石油气供气总量	吨	Total Volume of Liquefied Petroleum Gas	ton
#家庭用量	吨	For Residents Use	ton
用液化气人口	万人	Population with Access Liquefied Petroleum Gas	10000 persons
燃气普及率	%	Percentage of Population with Access to Gas	%
市政设施		**Municipal Infra - strucutre**	
年末城市实有道路面积	万平方米	Area of Paved Roads(Year - end)	10000 sq. m
人均拥有道路面积	平方米	Per Capita Area of Paved Roads	sq. m
排水管道长度	公里	Length of Sewage Pipes	km
建成区排水管道密度	公里/平方公里	Density of Drainpipes	km/sq. km
公共交通		**Public Traffic**	
年末实有公交营运车辆	标台	Number of Public Transportations Vehicles under Operation	unit
每万人拥有公共交通车辆	标台	Number of Public Transportations Vehicles Per 10000 Persons	unit
年末实有出租汽车数	辆	Operating Taxes at Year - end	unit
城市绿化		**Afforestation in Cities**	
园林绿地面积	公顷	Green Areas in Parks and Gardens	hectare
#公园绿地面积	公顷	Public Green Areas	hectare
人均公园绿地面积	平方米	Per Capita Public Green Areas	sq. m
建成区绿化覆盖面积	公顷	Coverage Area of Green Area in Developed Area	hectare
建成区绿地率	%	Rate of Green Area in Developed Area	%
建成区绿化覆盖率	%	Coverage Rate of Green Area in Developed Area	%
环境卫生		**Environmental Sanitation**	
污水处理率	%	Percentage of Sewage Disposed	%
城市生活垃圾无害化处理率	%	Innocuous Disposal Rate of Living Garbage	%

注:本表数据来自宁波市城乡建委。

Note:Data in this table are obtained from Ningbo Municipal Construction Committee.

全市 Total	市区 Urban District	余姚市 Yuyao	慈溪市 Cixi	奉化市 Fenghua	象山县 Xiangshan	宁海 Ninghai
484.75	308.56	49.24	44.50	18.75	28.61	35.09
569.90	366.29	47.04	42.45	38.47	36.35	39.30
148.76	80.97	14.00	20.09	12.36	10.01	11.33
32.34	19.07	3.09	2.77	1.28	4.35	1.78
195.84	137.05	12.90	9.00	12.50	10.20	14.19
75303	50111	4941	9997	3110	4006	3138
27569	18521	2141	2976	1317	1195	1419
259.78	339.97	148.84	173.25	148.26	186.70	245.65
100.00	100.00	100.00	100.00	100.00	100.00	100.00
162309.16	98346.03	4931.69	29910.00	6483.16	13975.76	8662.52
99944.04	47005.59	3629.00	27980.00	5318.00	9469.85	6541.40
156.59	30.00	27.00	40.00	25.00	20.59	14.00
100.00	100.00	100.00	100.00	100.00	100.00	100.00
7424	2951	1072	1717	435	741	509
20.89	15.84	23.87	33.14	13.06	36.00	27.38
8099	4670	771	1299	207	565	588
16.71	15.13	15.66	29.19	11.02	19.74	16.75
7474	5516	622	717	207	206	206
10.35	15.80	7.00	6.90	4.10	2.90	3.50
6370	4627	450	605	200	210	278
18683	11390	2104	1912	976	978	1323
4069	1983	481	673	401	285	245
11.45	10.64	10.71	13.00	12.05	13.86	13.19
18685	11811	2087	1745	764	864	1414
35.26	35.04	37.75	35.33	37.45	29.18	37.42
38.55	38.28	42.38	39.22	40.76	30.20	40.30
89.95	92.35	86.30	86.00	85.18	79.94	88.15
100.00	100.00	100.00	100.00	100.00	100.00	100.00

表 13－3 各县(市)环境保护基本情况(2014)
Basic Statistics on Environment Protection, Enviroment Sanitation by Region

指标	单位	Indicators	Unit
废水排放总量	**万吨**	**Volume of Waste Water Discharged**	**10000 tons**
工业废水排放总量	万吨	Industrial Waste Water Discharged	10000 tons
生活污水排放量	万吨	Discharged Amount of Living Sewage	10000 tons
化学需氧量(COD)排放量	**吨**	**Discharged Amount of Chemical oxygen demand (COD)**	**tons**
工业废水中化学需氧排放量	吨	Discharged Amount of COD in Industrial Waste Water	tons
工业用水总量	万吨	Water Consumption for Industrial Use	10000 tons
工业重复用水率	%	Rate of Water Utilized Repeatedly in Industry	%
废水治理设施数	套	Number of Administration Facility of Waste Water	unit
工业废气排放量	**亿标立米**	**Industrial Waste Gas Emission**	**100 million cu. m**
工业二氧化硫排放量	吨	Industrial Sulphur Dioxide Emission	ton
工业氮氧化物(NOx)排放量	吨	Industrial Nitrogen Oxide (NOx) Emissions	ton
工业烟尘排放量	吨	Soot Emission	ton
一般工业固体废物产生量	**万吨**	**Volume of Industrial Solid Wastes Produced**	**10000 tons**
一般工业固体废物综合利用量	万吨	Volume of General Industrial Solid Waste Utilized	10000 tons
一般工业固体废物处理量	万吨	Volume of General Industial Solid Waste Treated	10000 tons
一般工业固体废物倾倒丢弃量	吨	Volume of General Industrial Solid Wastes Dumped Discarded	ton
工业固体废物综合利用率	%	Rate of Industrial Solid Waste Utilized	%
工业固体废物处置利用率	%	Rate of Industrial Solid Waste Treated and Utilized	%
工业污染处理本年施工项目数	个	Number of Projects Treating Industrial Pollution	unit
建设项目"三同时"环保投资额	万元	Investment Amount of Construction Project " Three Simultaneous " of Environment Protection	10000 yuan
环境噪声达标面积	平方公里	Standardization Areas of Environment Noise	sq. km

注:本表数据来自宁波市环境保护局。工业"三废"统计范围为重点调查工业企业与非重点调查单位测算之和。

Note:a) Data in this table are obtained from Ningbo Environment Protection Bureau. b) Statistical Information of Waste Water, Waste Gas and Waste Residue Collected is calculated data that investigate industrial enterprise especially and non－investigate unit especially

全市 Total	市区 Urban Districts	#鄞州 Yinzhou	余姚 Yuyao	慈溪 Cixi	奉化 Fenghua	象山 Xiangshan	宁海 Ninghai
61724.81	**38720.14**	**10247.81**	**5702.87**	**8180.78**	**2966.48**	**3181.83**	**2972.71**
16545.63	10678.03	1202.08	1381.34	1588.65	899.42	1373.73	624.47
45179.17	28042.10	9045.72	4321.53	6592.14	2067.06	1808.10	2348.25
61338.00	**24361.89**	**8874.02**	**10670.75**	**11609.24**	**4676.36**	**4797.55**	**5222.21**
20152.56	10977.20	1929.43	3409.00	2201.84	1135.50	1716.81	712.21
528088.95	497987.53	4393.58	2631.14	4175.83	1675.95	9884.40	11734.10
82.70	71.28	53.15	12.13	35.53	20.78	79.11	88.18
969	499	110	74	153	107	74	62
6365.57	**4352.31**	**81.09**	**236.38**	**124.83**	**28.30**	**733.10**	**890.65**
118102	79723	3213	3895	8175	2353	9064	14892
162113	98679	1975	5356	2943	435	18587	36113
30577	20066	663	2904	2022	384	2884	2316
1196.32	**877.15**	**17.64**	**12.84**	**20.49**	**4.50**	**123.08**	**158.26**
1114.20	819.30	15.74	12.54	10.24	3.48	112.44	156.20
56.80	32.38	2.28	0.30	10.26	1.21	10.59	2.06
90.76	82.00	86.44	89.33	47.12	65.64	91.17	98.56
97.81	98.66	99.61	100.00	100.00	92.65	99.97	100.00
56	28	1	2	24		1	1
366667.90	233540.20	11316.70	19733.30	47922.30	19348.20	28607.90	17516.00
260.21	151.82	17.93	24.35	31.05	9.09	23.90	20.00

表13-4 各县(市)社会团体机构情况(2014)
Basic Statistics on Social Organizations and Unions by Region

指标	Indicators	全市 Total
上年准予登记社团机构数	Number of Social Organizations Authorized in Last Year	2227
年末实有社团机构数	Factual Number of Social Organizations at the Year - end	2351
年末实有民办非企业数	Factual Number of Civilian - run Non - enterprises at the Year - end	3464

注:本表至13-8表数据来自宁波市民政局。

Note:Data from Tables 13 -4 to 13 -8 are obtained from Ningbo Municipal Bureau of Civil Affairs.

表13-5 各县(市)社会福利、优抚、救济工作情况(2014)
Basic Statistics on Social Welfare,Subsidy and Commiseration by Region

指标	单位	Indicators	Unit
收养人数	**人**	**Number of Adopted Persons**	**person**
优待情况		Favoured Treatment	
安置军转干部、士兵	人	Setting Military Cadres or Soldiers Transferred to Civilian Work	person
优待军属户数	户	Service men's Families	household
优待总金额	万元	Total Amount of Give Special Treatment	10000 yuan
抚恤、补助情况		**Special Pensions,Allowances and Relief**	
年末享受定补人数	人	Number of Persons Receiving Periodical Subsidies at the Year - end	person
#在乡复员军人	人	Rural Demobilized Soldiers	person
#在乡退伍军人	人	Rural Veteransn	person
伤残人员	人	Number of Wounded or Disabled Health	person
年末定期抚恤人数	人	Number of Persons Receiving Periodical Commiseration	person
#烈士家属	人	Members of Revolutionary Martyr's Family	person

单位:个(unit)

市区 Urban District	#鄞州 Yinzhou	余姚 Yuyao	慈溪 Cixi	奉化 Fenghua	象山 Xiangshan	宁海 Ninghai
1229	180	199	290	170	170	169
1301	208	215	301	176	176	182
1620	399	365	707	217	215	340

全市 Total	市区 Urban District	#鄞州 Yinzhou	余姚 Yuyao	慈溪 Cixi	奉化 Fenghua	象山 Xiangshan	宁海 Ninghai
394	**74**	**21**	**67**	**89**	**45**	**61**	**58**
2594	924	421	406	507	256	207	294
4464	1178	526	843	907	506	428	602
6749.50	2364.10	861.50	1250.40	1058.10	740.70	545.10	791.10
37275	14583	7080	7195	5083	3970	1941	4503
2654	904	438	362	654	256	266	212
30983	11428	6113	6563	4280	3231	1505	3976
2288	907	231	337	419	227	173	225
723	288	71	110	134	64	52	75
349	125	47	69	48	24	33	50

表 13－6 民政部门收养性福利优抚事业情况(2014)
Basic Statistics on Adopting, Welfare & Special Pensions by Civil Administration Department

指标	单位	Indicators	Unit	全市 Total	其中 of Which #市区 Urban District	光荣院 Homes for Disabled Veterans
收养性福利单位数	个	**Number of Adopting Socail Welfare Units**	**unit**	**22**	**16**	**2**
全部职工人数	人	**Total Numeber Staff and Workers**	**person**	**530**	**407**	**17**
#女性	人	Female	person	351	285	8
年末固定资产原值	万元	**Original Value of Fixed Assets at the Year－end**	**10000 yuan**	**31050**	**25243**	**89**
各院病床数	张	**Number of Beds in Each Hospital**	**bed**	**5039**	**3822**	**66**
年末在院人数	人	**In－patients at the Year－end**	**person**	**3230**	**2343**	**50**
#优抚人员	人	Adopting Persons for Enjoying Favoured Treatment	person	107	94	24
"三无"对象人员	人	Non Depending on, Non Ability to Labor and Non Income	person	613	509	
自费人员	人	Persons on Self－expense	person	2525	1733	26
#老年人	人	Old People	person	2396	1515	50
青壮年人员	人	Young People	person	434	394	
少年儿童	人	Juvenile and Child	person	400	334	

表 13－6 续表 Continued

指标	单位	Indicators	Unit	其中 of Which 社会福利院 Social Welfare Homes	儿童福利院 Welfare Homes for Children	精神病福利院 Welfare Homes for Mental Patients
收养性福利单位数	个	**Number of Adopting Socail Welfare Units**	**unit**	**18**	**1**	**1**
全部职工人数	人	**Total Numeber Staff and Workers**	**person**	**438**	**27**	**48**
#女性	人	Female	person	298	21	24
年末固定资产原值	万元	**Original Value of Fixed Assets at the Year－end**	**10000 yuan**	**22458**	**1553**	**6951**
各院病床数	张	**Number of Beds in Each Hospital**	**bed**	**4309**	**304**	**360**
年末在院人数	人	**In－patients at the Year－end**	**person**	**2537**	**283**	**360**
#优抚人员	人	Adopting Persons for Enjoying Favoured Treatment	person	23		60
"三无"对象人员	人	Non Depending on, Non Ability to Labor and Non Income	person	344	223	46
自费人员	人	Persons on Self－expense	person	2185	60	254
#老年人	人	Old People	person	2196		150
青壮年人员	人	Young People	person	229		205
少年儿童	人	Juvenile and Child	person	112	283	5

表 13 - 7 城乡居民最低生活保障情况(2014)
Basic Statistics on Receiving Lowest Cost - of - living in Urban and Rural Area

地区	Region	社会救济总人数(人) Number of Persons Receiving Relief (person)	城镇低保人数(人) Number of ①RLCU (person)	城镇低保家庭数(户) Households of RLCU ① (household)	城镇低保资金支出(万元) Expenditure for RLCU (10000 yuan)	农村低保人数(人) Number of RLCR② and Receiving Relief (person)	农村低保家庭数(户) Households of RLCR② (household)	农村救济资金支出(万元) Expenditure for RLCR② (10000 yuan)
宁波市	**Total**	**51282**	**7712**	**5718**	**4794.90**	**43570**	**29842**	**19207**
市区	Urban District	10095	5303	3927	3569.70	4792	3135	3066
#鄞州区	Yinzhou	3618	567	426	362.50	3051	1855	1905
余姚市	Yuyao	8558	698	524	407.40	7860	4704	3470
慈溪市	Cixi	8082	491	375	284.80	7591	5351	3902
奉化市	Fenghua	7649	575	420	239.80	7074	5369	2695
象山县	Xiangshan	8517	407	299	191.60	8110	5259	2851
宁海县	Ninghai	8381	238	173	101.60	8143	6024	3222

注:①RLCU 是城镇低保的缩写。

②RLCR 是农村低保的缩写

Note:①RLCU is the short form that means Receiving Lowest Cost - of - living in Urban Area.

②RLCR is the short form that means Receiving Lowest Cost - of - living in Rural Area.

表 13 - 8 社会收容遣送情况(2014)
Basic Statistics on Accepted and Relief

	遣送站情况 Repatriated Units			本年救助(人次) Relief Person in this Year (person - times)
	站数(个) Number of Units (unit)	年末职工人数(人) Number of Staff and Workers (person)	年末固定资产原值(万元) Original Value of Fixed Assets (10000 yuan)	
全市总计 Total	8	65	2269.10	9143

表 13－9 各县(市)妇联工会组织及活动情况(2014)
Basic Statistics on Women Federation and Trade Unions by Region

指标	单位	Indicators	Unit
妇联组织机构		**Women's Federation**	
市、县(市)区妇联	个	Women's Federation in Municipal, County and Urban District	unit
镇、乡(街道)妇联	个	Women's Federation in Township, Town (Subdistrict)	unit
基层妇代会	个	Basic－Level Women Congress	unit
机关事业单位妇委会	个	Women Commission of Agencies and Institutions	unit
团体会员	个	Group Member	unit
人员状况		**Cadre of Women's Federation**	
市、县(市)区级干部	人	Level of Municipal, County and Urban District	person
镇、乡(街道)级干部	人	Cadre in Township, Town(Subdistrict)	person
妇联工作情况		**Works of Women's Federation**	
双学双比及巾帼建功活动		Activity of Double Study And Double Compare, And Women Making Contribution	
参赛数	万人	Number of Participants	10000 persons
#女农民技术人员	人	Female Peasant Technician	person
先进女能手	人	Female Advanced Expert	person
巾帼建功先进个人	人	Advanced Women by Making Contribution	person
工会基本情况		**Trade Unions**	
1. 基层工会数	个	Number of Trade Unions at Basic－Level	unit
2. 工会专职干部人数	人	Number of Full－Time Cadres of Trade Unions	person
3. 建立工会单位全部职工	人	Total Staff And Workers of Establishing Trade Unions	person
#女职工	人	Female Staff And Workers	person
工会会员	人	Member of Trade Unions	person
#女会员	人	Female Member	person
4. 本年度职工提出合理化建议	件	Advanced Rationalization Proposals	case
本年度已实施合理化建议	件	Implement Rationalization Proposals	case
本年度已实施合理化建议产生的效益	万元	Economic Benefit Created by Rationalization Proposals	10000 yuan

注：本表数据来自宁波市总工会和宁波市妇联。

Note: Date in this table are obtained from Ningbo Federation of Trade Unions and Ningbo Women's Federation .

全市 Total	市区 Urban District	#鄞州 Yinzhou	余姚 Yuyao	慈溪 Cixi	奉化 Fenghua	象山 Xiangshan	宁海 Ninghai
12	7	1	1	1	1	1	1
147	61	23	21	18	11	18	18
4525	2565	1419	265	325	391	590	389
561	308	49	37	75	48	69	24
46	21	1	5	12	1	4	3
107	67	9	10	7	9	8	6
202	98	46	22	18	14	18	32
23					23		
29.54	4.64	1.04	8.60	4.00	7.80	1.50	3.00
12348	98	82	72	156	12000		22
77	10	3		7		40	20
110	34	8		31		10	35
27476	15223	4781	3612	3343	1810	2272	1652
1915	976	27	295	322	160	8	124
3649799	671642	18308	475106	487705	230311	233212	205969
1593693	877156	272263	236251	217185	94243	76906	91952
3551476	1968915	598998	451451	483184	218838	225095	203993
1570164	863302	264301	231819	215652	93034	74998	91359
263521	186931	12411	24877	31178	2278	6438	11819
154279	126255	4256	8123	12237	1289	2262	4113

表 13－10　各县(市)、区公务员及参照公务员管理的群团机关工作人员情况(2014)
Basic Statistics on Civil Servant and Employee Refer to Civil Servant in Government Organ by Region

单位:人(person)

指标	Indicators	合计 Total	其中:女 of which: Female	按行政级别分 By Administrations Level 省部级 Province Level	地厅司局级 Department/ Bureau Level	县处级 County Level	乡科级 Section Chief	科员及以下 Section and Below
全市	**Total**	**28031**	**7113**	**4**	**286**	**7261**	**16199**	**4370**
市直单位	Municipal Department	7105	1515	4	258	3684	2642	517
市区	Urban Districts	9333	2531		24	3409	5160	740
海曙区	Haishu	1092	335		4	396	606	86
江东区	Jiangdong	1018	295		4	397	562	55
江北区	Jiangbei	1263	355		6	456	709	92
镇海区	Zhenhai	1372	344		5	543	717	107
北仑区	Beilun	1848	456		2	625	1086	135
鄞州区	Yinhzou	2740	746		3	992	1480	265
县合计	**Total of County**	**11593**	**3067**		**4**	**168**	**8397**	**3024**
余姚	Yuyao	2697	718		1	38	1981	677
慈溪	Cixi	2844	784		1	36	2018	789
奉化	Fenghua	1921	511		1	34	1456	430
象山	Xiangshan	2113	544			32	1453	628
宁海	Ninghai	2018	510		1	28	1489	500

表 13－11 部分年份律师、公证工作基本情况
Basic Statistics on Lawyers and Notarization in Partial Years

指标	Indicators	2011	2012	2013	2014
律师工作情况	**Lawyers**				
律师事务所(个)	Number of Law Offices(unit)	121	128	129	140
个人律师事务所(个)	Personal Law Office(unit)	32	34	35	40
合伙制律师事务所(个)	Law Offices in Partnership(unit)	89	94	94	100
律师数(人)	Number of Lawyers (person)	1390	1495	1733	1898
#专职律师(人)	Full－time Lawyers (person)	1302	1437	1556	1684
聘请担任常年法律顾问单位(家)	Number of Units with Permanent Legal Advisors(unit)	7079	5265	5378	5681
民事案件代理(件)	Agent of Civil Cases (case)	27819	20492	21673	29548
经济案件代理(件)	Agent of Economic Cases (case)				
#索回赔数（万元)	Debt and Indemnity Claimed (10000 yuan)				46751
刑事辩护和代理(件)	Agent of Criminal Defense (case)	6003	3715	3920	4421
非诉讼法律事务(件)	Agent of Non－Litigious Legal Affairs (case)	1761	1495	1441	1997
行政案件代理(件)	Agent of Administrative Action (case)	731	611	292	489
涉外及港澳台法律事务(件)	Legal ffairs With Foreign, HongKong, Macao, Taiwan(case)	24		4	27
解答法律文书(件)	Legal Advisory Services (case)	5676	22518	21194	18774
代写法律文书(件)	Legal Document Written on Behalf of Clients(case)	4920	2688	3139	3931
公证工作情况	**Notarization**				
公证处(个)	Notary Offices (unit)	11	11	11	11
#办理涉外公证(人)	Registered Foreign Affairs (person)	31	33	29	31
公证人员人数(人)	Notarial Personnel (person)	90	91	150	150
#公证员(人)	Notaries(person)	53	56	56	55
办理公证事项(件)	Notarized Documents (case)	62851	60899	83564	82614
国内经济公证(件)	Domestic Economic Affairs(case)	10308	8567	8726	7740
国内民事公证(件)	Domestic Civil Affairs(case)	32020	27578	36467	37016
涉外及港澳台公证(件)	Documents on Foreign, HongKong, Macao, Taiwan(case)	20523	24664	38371	37858
接待来访（人次)	Reception (person－times)	75693	5896	31580	30000
处理来信（件)	Treatment (case)	230	162	102	1650

表 13－12 部分年份基层司法工作及人民调解情况
Basic Statistics on Basic－Level Judicial Work and People Mediation in Partial Years

指标	Indicators	2011	2012	2013	2014
基层法律服务	**Basic－Level Service for Legal Advice**				
司法助理员人数(人)	Number of Judicial Assistants (person)	268	397	968	931
专职司法助理员(人)	Full－Time Judicial Assistants(person)	268	291	660	578
兼职司法助理员(人)	Part－Time Judicial Assistants (person)		106	308	353
基层法律服务所(所)	**Basic－Level Service for Legal Advice (unit)**	**74**	**74**	**74**	**74**
配备工作人员(人)	Provide Staff (person)	497	463	517	510
代理讼诉事务 (件)	Agent of Litigious Affairs (case)	9380	10763	9958	10230
代理非讼诉事务 (件)	Agent of Non－Litigious Legal Affairs (case)	966	1067	990	1351
调解纠纷 (件)	Mediating Disputes (case)	320	3153	2369	3130
协办公证 (件)	Handling Document Jointly (case)				
见证 (件)	Witness (case)				
担任法律顾问 (件)	Taking Legal Advisors (case)	2550	6348	4124	4308
代写法律文书 (件)	Legal Document Written on Behalf of Clients (case)	3127	965	649	1307
解答法律咨询人次 (人次)	Legal Advisory Services(person－times)	3350	37307	60770	32020
挽回经济损失 (万元)	Economic Loss Avoided and Reclaimed (10000 yuan)	41688	47232	12324	74716
办理法律援助事务 (件)	Handling Succorab leLegal Affairs (case)	6038	545	15534	755
参与司法行政工作 (人次)	Participating Judicial Administration (person－times)	247	124		311
人民调解工作	**Peoples Mediation**				
人民调解委员会 (个)	Peoples Mediation Committees (unit)	4786	4793	4683	4540
调解人员数 (人)	Number of Mediators(person)	18379	19251	18895	18243
调解纠纷总件数 (件)	Number of Mediating Disputes (case)	127927	126447	117549	115615
调解成功件数 (件)	Number of Success (case)	126154	124658	115624	114075
婚姻、继承、瞻养抚养 (件)	Marrige,Rights of Inheritance,Supporting and Fostering (case)	7722	7010	6151	6108
房屋宅基地 (件)	Ground of Building (case)	4240	3542	2792	2011
债务 (件)	Debt (case)	2876	3670	2088	2092

注:本表数据来自宁波市司法局。

表 13－12 续表 Continued

指标	Indicators	2011	2012	2013	2014
生产经营（件）	Production & Management (case)	1046	1665	1323	1367
邻里关系（件）	Relation of Neighborhood (case)	21291	18366	15473	14595
赔偿（件）	Compensation (case)	15842	12772	15441	12858
其他调解（件）	Other Mediating (case)	73137	79152	74281	76584
调解纠纷成功率（%）	Rate of Mediating Success (%)	98.6	98.6	98.4	98.7
防止可能发生非正常死亡事件（件）	Avoiding Accident of Abnormal Deaths (case)	36	29	34	33
防止可能发生非正常死亡人次（人次）	Avoiding Accident Times of Abnormal Deaths (person－times)	55	36	34	34
安置帮教工作情况	Placement and help and Educate				
刑释人员数(当年)(人)	Number of Ex－Convict Personnel in this Year (person)	2411	2667	3223	3835
刑释人员数(五年内)(人)	Number of Ex－Convict Personnel in Current 5 Years (person)	12296	12889	13421	14437
解教人员数(当年)(人)	Number of Unchain Labor Reeducation in this Year(person)	170	118	128	
刑释人员安置数(当年)(人)	Number of Placement of Ex－convict in this Year (person)	2441	2662	3196	3712
刑释人员帮教数(当年)(人)	Number of Help&Educate of Ex－convictin this Year(person)	2523	2729	2653	3727
重新犯罪人数(当年)(人)	Number of Re－criminal in this Year (person)	113	155	140	131
重新劳教人数(当年)(人)	Number of Again Labor Reeducation in this Year (person)	10	11	2	
监狱，劳教工作	Prison and Labor Reeducation				
市属监狱（所）	Number of Prison (unit)	2	2	2	3
年内新收押罪犯(人)	Detain Criminal in this Year(person)	3497	337	4249	4380
年内刑满释放(人)	Ex－Convict Personnel in this Year(person)	2693	2755	3833	5198
市属劳教所（所）	Numbet of Labor Reeducation Unit (unit)	1	1		
年内新收容劳教人员(人)	Newly Accept Labor Reeducation Personnel in this Year(person)	383	393	17	
年内解除劳教(人)	Unchain Labor Reeducation (person)	541	387	370	
年内新收容收教人员(人)	Newly Accept Take in Reeducation Personnel in this Year(person)	29	28	31	
年内解除收教(人)	Unchain Labor Reeducation (person)	32	27	29	

Note: Data in this table are obtained from Bureau of Justice of Ningbo Municipality.

表 13－13　二级人民法院收、结案情况(2014)
Cases Accepted & Settled by People's Court

单位:件(case)

指标	Indicators	上年留案 Retained in Last Year	全年新收案 New Accepted in this Year	办结案件数 Number of Cases Closed	年末未结案件 Retained Caseat Year－end
总计	**Total**	**11235**	**15136**	**151633**	**12738**
一审案件数	Number of First Trial Cases	7970	97151	96417	8704
刑事	Criminal Case	307	13299	13301	305
民商事	Civil & Economic Case	7632	83220	82525	8327
行政	Administrative Case	31	632	591	72
二审案件数	Number of Second Trial Case	325	4835	4656	504
刑事	Criminal Case	30	787	771	46
民事	Civil Case	177	2273	2242	208
商事	Economic Case	110	1536	1414	232
行政	Administrative Case	8	239	229	18
审判监督	Number of Cases Judged and Supervised	32	150	164	18
刑事	Criminal Case	13	51	58	6
民商事	Civil & Economic Case	19	97	104	12
行政	Administrative Case		2	2	
执行	Carry out Case	2862	43693	43106	3449
刑事案件(有财产部分)	Criminal Case(With Property)	56	641	644	53
民事	Civil Case	2631	31188	30622	3197
行政	Administrative Case		1	1	
行政非审查与执行	Administration No－examine and Carry Out	44	2659	2647	56
其他案件	Others Case	131	9204	9192	143
申诉申请再审	Appeal and Applying for Review	42	724	709	57
审查行政非诉	Apply for Non－Litigation Administrative Cases	4	2895	2894	1
司法赔偿	Juridical Compensation		5	4	1
减刑	Commutation		3297	3297	
假释	Parolee		386	386	

表 13－14 人民法院及检察院补充信息(2014)
Added Information of People's Court and Procurator's Offices

指标	单位	Indicators	unit	总计 Total
人民法院		**People's Court**		
办结申诉申请再审案件	件	Appeal and Applying for Review Closed	case	709
处理群众来信	件次	Deal with Letter from People	case－times	3094
群众来访人数	人次	People Come to Appeal for Help	person－times	4142
判决被告人	人	Adjudge defendant	person	17895
判处罪犯	人	Sentence Criminals	person	17893
宣告无罪	人	Declare Innocent	person	2
五年以上有期徒刑直到无期徒刑	人	Fixed－term Imprisonment of More than 5 years until Life Imprisonment	person	955
不满五年有期徒刑	人	Fixed－term Imprisonment of Below 5 years	person	7041
缓刑	人	Probation	person	5722
免于刑事处分	人	Avoid Criminal Sanction	person	93
其他处理	人	Others	person	4082
#18－25 周岁罪犯	人	Between 18 until 25 Years Old	person	3782
#少年犯	人	Juvenile Criminal	person	800
#女性犯罪	人	Female Criminal	person	1647
一审民商案件中解决争议标的	万元	Solve Amount of Disputed Bid for Civil & Economic Case in First Instance	10000 yuan	5745167
执行案件中执结标的	万元	Carry out Amount of Money in Carry out Case	10000 yuan	1582220
办结经济犯罪	件	Closed Economic Criminal	case	1016
为国家,集体挽回经济损失	万元	Retrieve Economic Losses for State & Collective	10000 yuan	5464
办结申请公示催告和支付令的案	件	Closed Apply to Show the Demand Commonly & Indemnity	case	967
标的	万元	Total Amount of Money	10000 yuan	14872
检察机关		**Procurator's Offices**		
立案查处贪污贿赂犯罪	件	Cases Registered for Corruption and Bribery	case	182
立案查处贪污贿赂犯罪	人	Cases Registered for Corruption and Bribery	person	218
立案查处渎职侵权犯罪	件	Cases Registered for Abuse and Dereliction of Duty	case	43
立案查处渎职侵权犯罪	人	Cases Registered for Abuse and Dereliction of Duty	person	46
批捕各类犯罪嫌疑人	人	Approve to Arrest Crime Suspects	person	10098
起诉各类犯罪被告人	人	Accuse Crime Suspects	person	17575
受理群众来信来访	件	Accept Public Report, Accuse Crime and Visit	case	2479
举报	件	Reporting of the Offence	case	695
控告	件	Accuse	case	541
申诉	件	Appeal	case	1231
提出民事行政抗诉	件	Submit Civil and Administrative Counterappeal.	case	12

表 13－15　各县(市)火灾情况(2014)
Basic Statistics on Fires by Region

指标	单位	Indicators	Unit	全市 Total
火灾起因情况		**Cause of Fire**		
放火	起	Arson	case	71
电器	起	Electric Appliances	case	860
违章操作	起	Operation Against Rules	case	372
生产作业	起	Production Operations	case	117
吸烟	起	Smoking	case	43
其他原因	起	Others	case	2893
重大火灾		**Heavy Fire**		
起火	起	Fire	case	
损失	万元	Losses	10000 yuan	
死亡	人	Deaths	person	
损失情况		**Situation of Losses**		
起数	起	Number	case	7010
死亡	人	Deaths	person	17
伤人	人	Injuries	person	18
损失	万元	Losses	10000 yuan	7385.37

市区 Urban District	#鄞州 Yinzhou	余姚 Yuyao	慈溪 Cixi	奉化 Fenghua	象山 Xiangshan	宁海 Ninghai
50	22	9	1	1	10	
407	100	66	13	154	44	176
207	32	21	5	17	80	42
71	10	10	8	8	5	15
18	2	2	1	10	1	11
1933	959	493	12	8	403	44
3476	1327	1051	1007	454	588	434
5		3	6		2	1
8	4	4	2		2	2
3811.30	1449.59	1710.65	343.43	218.16	613.83	688.00

表13-16 交通事故情况(2014)
Basic Statistics on Traffic Accident

指标	Indicators	合计(Total) 事故次数(次) Number of Accident (case)	死亡人数(人) Deaths (person)	受伤人数(人) Injuries (person)	直接损失(万元) Direct Pecunlary Losses (10000 yuan)
总计	**Total**	**2519**	**605**	**2476**	**710.29**
机动车	Motor Vehicles	2118	532	2023	647.64
客运车辆	Passenger Vehicles	72	13	72	10.81
公共汽车	Buses	26	5	24	9.42
一般货运	General Cargos	373	168	285	155.21
企事业单位	Institutions and Enterprises	18	9	11	4.28
军队武警	Armed Forces				
私用轿车	Individuals	770	119	781	248.71
其他	Others	538	115	519	139.09
摩托车	Motorcycles	284	87	300	65.18
拖拉机	Tractors	37	16	31	14.94
非机动车	Non-motor-driven Vehicles	391	69	447	60.50
其他及行人	Others and Pedestrians	10	4	6	2

城市(Urban)				农村(Rural)			
事故次数(次) Number of Accident (case)	死亡人数(人) Deaths (person)	受伤人数(人) Injuries (person)	直接损失(万元) Direct Pecunlary Losses (10000 yuan)	事故次数(次) Number of Accident (case)	死亡人数(人) Deaths (person)	受伤人数(人) Injuries (person)	直接损失(万元) Direct Pecunlary Losses (10000 yuan)
1048	**169**	**1089**	**263.43**	**1471**	**436**	**1387**	**446.86**
871	145	885	234.35	1247	387	1138	413.29
41	4	42	5.15	31	9	30	5.66
15	1	16	5.58	11	4	8	3.84
119	44	99	40.52	254	124	186	114.69
7	2	5	3.25	11	7	6	1.03
369	42	389	105.33	401	77	392	143.38
206	30	203	46.64	332	85	316	92.45
105	21	121	27.16	179	66	179	38.02
9	1	10	0.72	28	15	21	14.22
175	24	202	28.98	216	45	245	31.52
2		2	0.1	8	4	4	2.05

表 13－17　全市档案人员及馆藏和编研情况(2014)
Conditions of Files Stored and Used in the Archives

指标	单位	Indicators	Unit	全市 Total	其中 of Which		
					市局馆 Municipal	市区合计 Urban District	县市合计 County
机构数	**个**	**Number of Institutions**	**unit**				
档案行政管理机构(档案馆)	个	Administrative Department of Archives	unit	12	1	6	5
现有工作人员数	人	Number of Staff and Workers	person				
档案行政管理机构(档案馆)	人	Administrative Department of Archives	person	178	40	60	78
馆藏档案		**Archives Stored**					
全宗	个	Whole Volume	unit	2678	458	883	1337
案卷	卷	Files	volume	1414925	250135	427865	736925
以件为保管单位档案	件	Archives Which Regard a Storage Unit by Files	pieces	489481	53837	275609	160035
录音、录象影片档案	盘	Records, Films on Videotape	copy	2886	656	736	1474
照片档案	张	Pictures	pieces	244566	44923	101637	98006
馆藏资料	册	Number of Material Stored	volume	125963	32950	39238	53775
档案馆总建筑面积	平方米	Floor Space of Archives	sq. m	44315	7900	22670	13745
档案库房建筑面积	平方米	Floor Space of Storerooms	sq. m	16732	3500	8384	4848
本年档案资料利用		Use of Material in This Year					
利用人次	人次	Number of Persons Using Material	times	41032	2596	13486	24950
利用档案	卷次	Number of Archives Used	volume	63954	12099	19923	31932
利用资料	册次	Number of Material Used	times	5298	2703	2132	463
利用档案	件次	Number of Archives Used	times	10596		1494	9102
本年编研档案资料内部参考	**万字**	**Compiling and Researching Material Restricted**	**10000 words**	**122**	**10**	**79**	**34**
本年编研档案资料公开出版物	**万字**	**Public Press Compiling and Researching Material**	**10000 words**	**79.6**	**8**	**70**	**1.6**

注：统计范围：市，县(市)区档案局，国家综合档案馆

Note: Statistical Limits are Archives of Each District and County

主要统计指标解释

【全年供水总量】 指公用自来水厂和自备水源的社会单位全年的供水总量,包括有效供水量及损失水量。

【城市人口用水普及率】 指城市用水的非农业人口数(不包括临时人口和流动人口)与城市非农业人口总数的比例。计算公式:

用水普及率 =(城市用水的非农业人口数 ÷ 城市非农业人口数)×100%

【公共绿地】 指供游览休息的各种公园、动物园、植物园、陵园、以及花园、游园和供旅游休息用的林荫道绿地、广场绿地。不包括一般栽植的行道树及林荫道的面积。

【废水排放总量】 包括生产废水和生活污水。生产废水指企、事业单位在生产、科研过程中向外排放的所有排放口的废水量总和。生活污水指城镇居民区和企、事业单位职工集中居住区排放的污水量。

【工业废水排放量】 指经过企业厂区所有排放口排到企业外部的工业废水量 。包括生产废水、外排的直接冷却水、超标排放的矿井地下水和与工业废水混排的厂区生活污水,不包括外排的间接冷却水(清污不分流的间按冷却水应计算在内)。

【工业废气排放量】 指企业厂区内燃料燃烧和生产工艺过程中产生的各种排人空气的含有污染物的气体的总量,以标准状态(273K,101325Pa)计。

【工业粉尘排放量】 指企业在生产工艺过程中排放的颗粒物重量。如钢铁企业的耐火材料粉尘、焦化企业的筛焦系统粉尘、烧结机的粉尘、石灰窑的粉尘、建材企业的水泥粉尘等。不包括电厂排人大气的烟尘。

工业粉尘产生量 = 工业粉尘排放量 + 工业粉尘回收量

【工业固体废物产生量】 指企业在生产过程中产生的固体状、半固体状和高浓度液体状废弃物的总量,包括危险废物、冶炼废渣、粉煤灰、炉渣、煤矸石、尾矿、放射性 废物和其他废物等;不包括矿山开采的剥离废石和掘进废石(煤矸石和呈酸性或碱性的废石 除外)。酸性或碱性废石是指采掘的废石其流经水、雨淋水的 pH 值小于 4 或 pH 值大于 10.5 者 。

【社会福利事业单位】 指集中收养社会孤老,残,幼的机构。包括由民政部门管理的社会福利院、儿童福利院、精神病人福利院和城镇集体办的福利院,以及农村集体举 办的敬老院。

Explanatory Notes on Main Statistical Indicators

【Annual Volume of Water Supply】 refers to the total volume of water supplied by the public water – works and those owned by individual enterprises and institutions during the whole year, including both the effective water supply and loss during the water supply.

【Percentage of Urban Population with Access to Tap Water】 refers to the ratio of urban non – agricultural population (excluding temporary and mobile population) with access to tap water to the total urban non – agricultural population. The formula is: Percentage of Population with Access to Tap Water = (Urban Non – agricultural Population with Access to Tap Water ÷ Urban Non – agricultural Population) 100%

【Public Green Area】 refers to green areas of various parks, zoos, botanical gardens, cemeteries, amusement parks, tree – flanked boulevards, green – land squares for tourism and relaxation. Area with trees planted along – side the streets and boulevards are excluded.

【Total Discharge of Sewage】 includes production sewage and domestic sewage. Production sewage refers to the total discharge by the enterprises and institutions in their production and scientific research. Domestic sewage refers to the discharge by urban and rural residential communities and the residential neighborhoods of the enterprise/institutions staff.

【Volume of Industrial Waste Water Discharged】 refers to the volume of industrial waste water discharged, through all outlets, to the outside of industrial enterprises, including waste water produced, direct cooling water, underground water from mines that does not meet the standard of discharge, and the domestic sewage mixed up with industrial waste water when discharged, but excluding discharged indirect – cooling water.

【Volume of Waste Gas Emission】 refers to waste gas emitted from burning of fuels and from production process in the area of the factory, and is measured by 10000 standard cubic metres each year under normal condition.

【Industrial Dust Discharged】 refers to the total weight of solid dust discharged by industrial enterprises in the production process, such as dust of refractory materials from iron plants, dust from coke – screening system or from sintering machines of coking plants, dust from lime kilns, cement dust from building material enterprises, etc. but excluding smoke and dust discharged by power plants.

【Volume of Industrial Solid Wastes Produced】 refers to the total volume of solid, semi-solid or high concentration liquid residue produced by industrial enterprises in their production process, including dangerous wastes, residues from melting, slag, powdered coal ash, gangue, chemical residues, tailings, radioactive residues and other residues, but excluding stripped or dug stones in mining (except gangue and acid or alkali stones which are stones washed or soaked by water with a pH value smaller than 4 or larger than 10.5.)

【Social Welfare Institutions】 refer to institutions taking care of old people without children, handicapped people and orphans. They include social welfare institutions run by civil affairs departments, children's welfare institutions social welfare institutions for mental patients, and collective-owned old people's homes in tualareas.

中国统计出版社最新图书简目

（仅供参考，以实际出版为准）

统计资料

中国统计年鉴　中国统计摘要　中国发展报告
中国经济普查年鉴2013　国际统计年鉴　金砖国家联合统计手册
中国-东盟国家统计手册　中国区域经济统计年鉴　中国县域统计年鉴
中国城市统计年鉴　中国农村统计年鉴　中国地区经济监测报告
中国贸易外经统计年鉴　中国对外直接投资统计公报　中国商品交易市场统计年鉴
大中型批发零售和住宿餐饮企业统计年鉴　中国零售和餐饮连锁企业统计年鉴　中国住户调查年鉴
中国价格统计年鉴　中国农产品价格调查年鉴　全国农产品成本收益资料汇编
中国环境统计年鉴　中国能源统计年鉴　国外资源、能源和环境统计资料汇编
中国工业统计年鉴　中国建筑业统计年鉴　中国房地产统计年鉴
中国城市建设统计年鉴　中国城乡建设统计年鉴　中国第三产业统计年鉴
中国证券期货统计年鉴　中国科技统计年鉴　中国高技术产业统计年鉴
工业企业科技活动资料　中国劳动统计年鉴　中国人口和就业统计年鉴
中国人才资源统计报告　中国社会统计年鉴　中国文化及相关产业统计年鉴
文化及相关产业统计概览　中国教育经费统计年鉴　中国民政统计年鉴
中国民族统计年鉴　中国工会统计年鉴　中国残疾人事业统计年鉴
中国妇女儿童状况统计资料（英）　中国乡镇街道行政区域简册

省级综合统计年鉴系列

北京 天津 河北 山西 内蒙古 辽宁 吉林 黑龙江 上海 江苏 浙江 安徽 福建 江西 山东 河南 湖北 湖南
广东 广西 海南 重庆 四川 贵州 云南 西藏 陕西 甘肃 青海 宁夏 新疆 新疆生产建设兵团

市(县)级综合统计年鉴系列

天津滨海新区 石家庄 唐山 邯郸 保定 沧州 邢台 廊坊 承德 衡水 秦皇岛 张家口 太原 大同 阳泉 长治 晋城
朔州 晋中 运城 忻州 临汾 呼和浩特 呼和浩特新城区 鄂尔多斯 包头 沈阳 大连 长春 四平 哈尔滨 齐齐哈尔
黑龙江垦区 上海浦东新区 南京 无锡 徐州 常州 苏州 南通 连云港 淮安 盐城 扬州 镇江 泰州 宿迁 江阴
丹阳 杭州 宁波 温州 嘉兴 绍兴 金华 衢州 舟山 台州 丽水 合肥 安庆 马鞍山 福州 厦门 宁德 南昌 九江
上饶 新余 抚州 济南 青岛 枣庄 滕州 郑州 洛阳 平顶山 三门峡 南阳 商丘 济源 武汉 十堰 荆州 宜昌 荆门
咸宁 长沙 广州 深圳 惠州 东莞 南宁 柳州 桂林 来宾 海口 三亚 成都 贵阳 昆明 西安 兰州 庆阳 银川
乌鲁木齐 兵团一师 兵团十师

调查年鉴系列

天津 山西 内蒙古 辽宁 吉林 上海　福建 河南 湖北 湖南 广西 重庆　四川 云南 甘肃 宁夏 新疆

“十二五”规划教材

统计学（经济管理类专业本科适用，单薇 等）　抽样调查理论与方法（冯士雍 等）
贝叶斯统计（茆诗松 等）　统计学（黄良文 等）　试验设计（茆诗松 等）
统计学：从数据到结论（吴喜之）　医学统计学（于浩）　统计学（经济、管理类专业基础教材，张小斐）
概率论与数理统计三十三讲（魏振军）　概率论与数理统计三十三：学习指导与习题解答（魏振军）
非参数统计（吴喜之 等）　统计学：经济与管理中的数据分析（李慧云 等）
卫生管理统计学（新编医学院校基础课教材，尚磊）　医院统计学（新编医学院校基础课教材，徐天和 等）
社会统计学（蒋萍 等）　现代金融投资统计分析（李腊生 等）
国民经济核算初级教程（经济类、统计类、管理类专业适用，蒋萍 等）

重点图书

图解中国经济2015　新编英汉汉英统计大词典　中华医学统计百科全书
挑大学选专业2016—考研择校指南　挑大学选专业2015—高考志愿填报指南